BRITISH POLITICS
IN THE AGE OF ANNE

BRITISH POLITICS
IN THE AGE OF ANNE

GEOFFREY HOLMES

REVISED EDITION

THE HAMBLEDON PRESS

LONDON AND RONCEVERTE

Published by The Hambledon Press 1987

102 Gloucester Avenue, London NW1 8HX (U.K.)

309 Greenbrier Avenue, Ronceverte WV 24970 (U.S.A.)

ISBN 0 907628 73 7 (Cased)
    0 907628 74 5 (Paper)

First Edition: Macmillan, London 1967

British Library Cataloguing in Publication Data

Holmes, Geoffrey, *1928-*
    British politics in the age of Anne. — 2nd ed.
    1. Great Britain — Politics and government —
    1702-1714
    I. Title
    320.941   JN2121702

Library of Congress Cataloging-in-Publication Data

Holmes, Geoffrey S., 1928-
    British politics in the age of Anne.

    Bibliography: p.
    Includes index.
    1. Great Britain — Politics and government —
    1702-1714.   I. Title.
    DA495.H59   1987   941.06'9   87-14833

Contents

TO

ELLA

Introduction to
Revised Edition*

Party and Politics

I⊤ is now twenty years since I finished writing *British Politics in the Age of Anne*. That is a long time in the bustling, hyper-professional world of late 20th-century historical writing and scholarship. Few serious historical studies can be entirely divorced from their context, least of all large-scale works of analysis and interpretation. That being so, and because one can no longer re-create the historiographical climate of the 1960s in which *British Politics* was written,[1] there is a sense in which to try to produce a 'revised edition' is to attempt the impossible. I have not allowed this consideration to oppress me unduly. There were, after all, many other aims in mind while the original work was on the anvil besides that of refuting a particular interpretation of the structure of early 18th-century politics.[2] Thus the reissuing of the book, twelve years after its going out of print, not only enables me to make numerous corrections in the text, appendices and notes, some to rectify misprints or minor factual slips, the rest to revise dates or statistics and certain other items of information in the light of fresh findings or maturer thought. More important, it affords me an opportunity, through the vehicle of a new Introduction, to consider what conclusions of substance

* I am indebted to David Hayton, Clyve Jones, Eveline Cruickshanks, Bill Speck and John Beckett for assisting me in various ways during the preparation of this edition. I am particularly grateful to Mr Jones for help with the Appendix of manuscript sources which follows this Introduction, and to Dr Hayton both for advice on that Appendix and for bringing to my attention a miscellany of errors in the original text and index which had escaped my vigilance.

1. 'The historian writing in the age of Namier, or at least under his shadow . . .' – so runs the book's very first sentence.
2. See pp. 1–6 below, and cf. pp. 405–18.

reached in 1965–6 I would wish to endorse, modify, or perhaps even abandon, twenty years on. It is an opportunity to look again at a whole interpretation in the light of all the primary evidence now available and of the abundance of secondary writing bearing on the subject which has appeared in the meantime.

Between 1966 and 1986 a great deal of fresh manuscript material dating from the late 17th and early 18th centuries has been unearthed, including some collections which I could have used with much profit had I known of their existence in the 1950s and '60s. Other relevant archives, especially continental archives, of which historians were formally aware but which up to that time had barely been touched by students of English history, have been made more accessible through microfilms and transcripts.[3] During the same period the body of secondary literature bearing on many parts of the subject has grown vastly. The history of Church and Dissent, and the relations between the clergy and the politicians; political ideology; politics and finance in the City of London; Jacobitism; the press and its role in the party struggle; the behaviour of the electorate and the struggle in the constituencies: these are just some of the dimensions which are far better understood today than they were two decades ago. Our knowledge of Scottish politics and politicians has been transformed out of all recognition. Inevitably there are facets of the Augustan political scene, highlighted by recent monographs or articles, which can be touched on only in passing in the present essay.[4] But no serious re-assessment of politics in the age of Anne could fail to take account of the social and economic backcloths to the period, since these have been illuminated in many more ways than could reasonably have been anticipated in the mid 1960s. At that time pre-industrial English society between 1660 and 1760 was still a neglected subject, attracting

3. See pp. lxiii–lxvi below for an Appendix of SUPPLEMENTARY MANUSCRIPT SOURCES FOR THE STUDY OF EARLY 18th-CENTURY BRITISH POLITICS.

4. For instance, investigations of popular disorders have revealed much about the politicization of the early 18th-century crowd, while thanks to two detailed studies of the magistracy we now know how successfully Whigs and Tories at this period managed to manipulate the commissions of the peace for partisan ends. See G. Holmes, 'The Sacheverell Riots: the Church and the Crowd in Early-Eighteenth-Century London', *Past and Present*, 72 (1976); N. Rogers, 'Popular Protest in Early Hanoverian London' [1715–16], *Past and Present*, 79 (1978); L. K. J. Glassey, *Politics and the Appointment of Justices of the Peace, 1675–1725* (Oxford, 1979); Norma Landau, *The Justices of the Peace, 1679–1760* (Berkeley and L.A., 1984). Cf. p. 25 below.

hopeful generalization more than systematic investigation. Recent historiography has changed all that. And not surprisingly in a computer-conscious age, quantification has been called for and refined statistical techniques applied to try to resolve fundamental questions which now interest political as well as socio-economic historians: questions such as literacy levels, demographic trends, or prices. For that matter, political historians themselves have resorted to similar techniques since 1970 to analyse poll-books or to determine 'who ran' the House of Commons.[5]

Paradoxically, one of the historiographical trends of the past twenty years which has done most to assist the interpretation of Queen Anne's reign is the attention paid to the reigns which immediately preceded and followed it. In addition to the publication of first-class biographies of William III and George I,[6] the history both of the court and the parties from 1689 to 1702, and again from 1714 to 1727, has by now been so closely studied that we are able to view the politics of the years in between with a longer and distinctly clearer perspective than was possible in the mid-1960s. The identification and collation of many new division lists and other parliamentary lists, especially for the years 1689–1701 and 1715–19,[7] has meant that the solidity of party allegiance in those years can be measured with some confidence. This in turn has helped scholars to make more informed judgments on the arguments about the pattern of parliamentary and court politics under William III and the early Hanoverians which have been advanced in the string of book-length

5. See W. A. Speck and W. A. Gray, 'Computer Analysis of Poll Books: An Initial Report', *Bull.I.H.R.* 43 (1970); and further studies of early 18th-century voting behaviour, utilising computer analysis, by Speck and Gray, in *Bull.I.H.R.* 48 (1975) and in *Guildhall Studies in London History*, 1 (1975), and by J. F. Quinn *et al.*, in 'Yorkshiremen go to the Polls', *Northern History*, 21 (1985). See also T. K. Moore and H. G. Horwitz, 'Who Runs the House? Aspects of Parliamentary Organization in the Later Seventeenth Century', *Journ. Mod. Hist.* 43 (1971).

Note: In all footnotes to this Introduction I use the abbreviations listed on pp. lxxiii–iv.

6. S. B. Baxter, *William III* (1966); R. Hatton, *George I: Elector and King* (1978).

7. See I. F. Burton, P. W. J. Riley & E. Rowlands, *Political Parties in the Reigns of William III and Anne: The Evidence of Division Lists* (*Bull.I.H.R.* Spec. Suppl. 7, 1968); A. N. Newman (ed.), *The Parliamentary Lists of the Early Eighteenth Century* (Leicester, 1970); D. Hayton and C. Jones (eds.), *A Register of Parliamentary Lists, 1660–1761* (Leicester, 1979); E. Cruickshanks, D. Hayton and C. Jones, 'Divisions in the House of Lords on the Transfer of the Crown and other Issues, 1689–94: Ten New Lists', *Bull.I.H.R.* 53 (1980); D. Hayton and C. Jones (eds.), *A Register of Parliamentary Lists, 1660–1761: A Supplement* (Leicester, 1982).

studies,[8] as well as interpretative essays,[9] to appear in the past two decades.

It may seem improbable that any consensual view could emerge from a literature so extensive and diverse. Nevertheless the conviction has grown, and strengthened with almost every new contribution to the debate, that there was a *basic* polarity in parliamentary politics, not simply from the Revolution Settlement of 1689 to the earliest years of Hanoverian Britain but, in a modified form, far into George II's reign; and that this polarity remained, what it had been from the beginning, that of Whig and Tory. With regard to the first thirty years or so after the Revolution no-one has made this point more crisply than David Hayton: '. . . in this period "Court and Country" ceased to represent a standing political division. *A* Country party manifested itself from time to time; *the* Country party did not have a continuous existence. Whigs and Tories co-operated – in Parliament on Country measures, at elections sometimes, on a Country platform – but they did not lose their identity. They still remained Whigs and Tories first and foremost.'[10] On the opposition politics of the period 1720–42, also, Eveline Cruickshanks has written decisively: 'There was indeed a "country platform" . . . but there was

8. D. Rubini, *Court and Country, 1688–1702* (1968); R. Sedgwick (ed.), *The History of Parliament: The House of Commons, 1715–1754* (2 vols, 1970); B. W. Hill, *The Growth of Parliamentary Parties, 1689–1742* (1976); H. Horwitz, *Parliament, Policy and Politics in the Reign of William III* (Manchester, 1977); L. J. Colley, *In Defiance of Oligarchy: The Tory Party, 1714–60* (Cambridge, 1982). See also J. M. Beattie, *The English Court in the Reign of George I* (Cambridge, 1967), chs. 5, 7; J. H. (now Sir John) Plumb, *The Growth of Political Stability in England, 1675–1725* (1967), chs. 3, 5, 6.

9. See H. Horwitz, 'The Structure of Parliamentary Politics' and E. L. Ellis, 'William III and the Politicians', both in G. Holmes (ed.), *Britain after the Glorious Revolution, 1689–1714* (1969); J. C. D. Clark, 'The Decline of Party, 1740–1760' (*E.H.R.* 93, 1978) and 'A General Theory of Party, Opposition and Government, 1688–1832' (*Hist. Journ.* 23, 1980); W. A. Speck, 'Whigs and Tories dim their glories: English political parties under the first two Georges', in J. Cannon (ed.), *The Whig Ascendancy: Colloquies on Hanoverian England* (1981); E. Cruickshanks, 'The Political Management of Sir Robert Walpole, 1720–42' in J. Black (ed.), *Britain in the Age of Walpole* (1984). D. Hayton, 'The "Country" interest and the party system, 1689–c. 1720', in C. Jones (ed.), *Party and Management in Parliament, 1660–1784* (Leicester, 1984), is of outstanding importance. See also the article by Colin Brooks, cited below p. xxxix, n. 113; and L. J. Colley and M. Goldie, 'The principles and practice of eighteenth-century party', *Hist. Journ.* 12 (1979).

10. Hayton, 'The "Country" interest', *loc. cit.* p. 65. See also H. L. Snyder, 'Party Configurations in the Early Eighteenth-Century House of Commons', *Bull.I.H.R.* 45 (1972).

no country party.'[11] These are conclusions that few, if any, students of late 17th or 18th century politics would have reached without deep misgivings in the 1950s or early 1960s.

But where do they leave the concept of an 'age of Anne' in British politics? The assumption underlying so much of what I wrote twenty years ago was that there was a period in the early 18th century, not precisely coterminous with the Queen's reign but extending very little outside it, in which both the substance of politics and the way the political system worked was sufficiently distinctive to justify study in its own right: that these were indeed the climactic years of 'the first age of Party'. This assumption, I believe, still holds, though there is a need to be rather more accommodating now about the time-span associated with it. Indisputably there was a 'watershed', locatable in the last twelve months or so of King William's reign, dividing the undulating uplands of post-Revolution politics from their high plateau.[12] It is equally clear that Queen Anne's death, in itself, made at least two very significant changes to the landscape. First, it brought to the throne in August 1714 a king who was deeply distrustful of the Tories and who, in sharp contrast with his two predecessors,[13] felt no rooted ideological or moral objection to presiding over a state in which one party enjoyed a permanent monopoly of influence and profit. Then, within weeks, it put paid to the 'managerial' system[14] which for the best part of two decades had preserved some kind of balance, if at times an uneasy one, between the ambitions and aspirations of the party leaders and the principles and prerogatives of the Crown. The prompt retirement of the duke of Shrewsbury, following hard on the heels of the fall of Lord Treasurer Oxford, marked this system's demise. In 1716 a further quintessential feature of high Augustan political topography, the statutory maximum of three years on the life of every Parliament, was also erased. Erected in 1694, it had done much to keep party heats on the boil by precipitating four of the eight General Elections held between January 1701 and January 1715. But it was bulldozed away by the

11. Cruickshanks, *loc. cit.* (n. 9 above), pp. 32–3. She adds: 'It is significant that historians who have done detailed work on the period [since 1970] . . . all agree on a Whig-Tory division, not a court-country one'. Speck (n. 9), however, has been one prominent dissentient, as was Rubini, earlier, on William III's reign (n. 8).

12. Cf. pp. 47, 63–4, 82–3, 406–8 and *passim* below; G. Holmes and W. A. Speck (eds.), *The Divided Society: Party Conflict in England, 1694–1716* (1967), pp. 3–4, 20–25.

13. See ch. 6 below.

14. See below, pp. 188–94 *et seq.*

Septennial Act, a display of *realpolitik* by the now ascendant Whigs for which the Jacobite Rebellion of 1715–16 provided the excuse but which, as many libertarians in their own party conceded, was desperately hard to justify in terms of any principle they had ever espoused.

Whereas the first eight Elections of the 18th century, down to 1715, were crammed into 14 years, placing all but the most rock-solid electoral interests in jeopardy and producing violent oscillations in party fortunes and in the composition of the House of Commons, the next eight were spread out over 43 years – ideal conditions for the consolidation of territorial and government influence and for the erosion of the electorate's independence. But even in the short term the effects of the Septennial Act signalled the fact that the special hallmarks of the politics of the age of Anne were fast disappearing. It is inconceivable that between 1701 and 1715 either party could have survived in an election year two such traumas as the recent defection of half its Cabinet ministers to the Opposition[15] or a massive financial scandal, without suffering such serious damage at the polls that the monarch would have been forced to turn, in part at least, to their opponents. And yet, both in 1718, when Whig divisions were potentially crippling, and early in 1721, when the South Sea Bubble debris still littered the arena, a revivified Tory party found itself denied by law the chance to translate its advantages into votes and power. By the time the first septennial milestone was finally reached in 1722 the opportunity had gone; and it would not present itself again as long as the old Tory party lived.[16] The 1722 Election certainly demonstrated the Tory party's capacity for survival as an organized entity; and as Linda Colley has shown,[17] Toryism retained for forty more years a degree of political relevance which went beyond mere atavistic survivalism. But equally this Election left no room for doubt in the mind of any realist that for a party

15. The defectors, over the space of 12 months, were Townshend (dismissed, April 1717); Devonshire, Walpole, Methuen, Orford (resigned March–April 1717); and Cowper (resigned April 1718).

16. Compare the situation 12 months earlier when large numbers of Whigs had been prepared to back a vote of censure on their own prime minister, and many had been hustled into changing their minds only by their leaders' desperate plea that unless Sunderland was acquitted of malpractices in the South Sea crisis 'the ministry are blown up, and must and necessarily will be succeeded by a Tory one'. Thomas Brodrick, M.P., to Lord Midleton, 16 March 1721, printed in William Coxe, *Memoirs of . . . Sir Robert Walpole* (1798), ii, 214. In all contemporary quotations in this Introduction spelling has been modernized.

17. See n. 8 above.

whose strength in the House of Lords was already shattered beyond hope of repair there could be no future prospect of breaking their opponents' supremacy without that remotest of contingencies, a total withdrawal of the Crown's favour from the Whigs. Down to George II's death in 1760 it was only in a few fleeting interludes of undue Tory euphoria that it could seriously be contemplated. 1722 thus marks the line at which the last vestiges of the politics of party, in the clear-cut form that had characterized the age of Anne, disappeared and the politics of oligarchy, which recognized and incorporated the divisions between Whigs and Tories without being dictated by them, became firmly established as the dominant pattern for the future.

Oligarchic politics as practised in the age of Walpole and the Pelhams was an intricate game, played out by a limited number of players according to certain recognized rules. But it was not a national occupation. Only very rarely and briefly – as in 1733 – did it acquire what may be called a 'social dimension'. In sharp contrast, 'the most extraordinary feature of the age of Anne [as it seemed to me in the 1960s, and still does] was the unprecedented extent to which party strife, the inescapable and all-pervading distinction between Tory and Whig, invaded and finally took possession of the very lives of the politically-conscious'.[18] In chapters 1 and 9 we see something of what this implied away from Whitehall and Westminster – the conditions which prompted William Speck and me to describe the England of those years unequivocally as the *Divided Society*.[19] Since then, however, with a growing understanding of some of the social trends of the late 17th and early 18th centuries has come an awareness of certain 'softer contours on the social terrain', easily lost sight of from a perspective where political schism and social fissures loom so large. In a paper first composed in 1979[20] I sought to trace the continuity of some of those features through from their origins in the years between the Restoration and the 1690s to the point at which they blend into the stabler social, as well as political landscape of early Georgian England. Higher living standards over a period of much improved agricultural productivity, of food prices that were in general favourable to the

18. Pp. 20–1 below.
19. Also in 1967. See above n. 12.
20. Geoffrey Holmes, 'The Achievement of Stability: the Social Context of Politics from the 1680s to the Age of Walpole', in J. Cannon (ed.), *The Whig Ascendancy* (1981).

consumer and of demographic stasis;[21] the steady development of what has been called both 'the new urban society' and 'the urban renaissance' in pre-industrial England;[22] the rapidly growing amount of both business and professional wealth being injected into provincial society, particularly in the towns: these, I have suggested, were powerful forces working in the long term, down to the mid 18th century, towards fusion rather than towards fission in the social order, and contributing to the ultimate achievement of greater political stability.[23]

The reality of the 'divided society' of the age of Anne may therefore have been rather more finely shaded in some respects, and rather more complex, than I depicted it in the late 1960s. But a reality it was, none the less. The wealth of important work produced in the meantime on aspects of early 18th-century England as different in character as the behaviour of the electorate, the activities of the press and the condition of the Church of England amply confirms that the impact of party conflict there, as so often elsewhere, was for the most part starkly divisive.

The English and Welsh electorate, which had reached well over 300,000 by the end of Anne's reign,[24] comprised a reasonably representative, if

21. In addition to the relevant sources cited in the paper just referred to (n. 20 above), massive documentation and analysis of these trends is now available in Joan Thirsk (ed.), *The Agrarian History of England and Wales*, Vol V, *1640–1750*, Parts 1 and 2 (Cambridge, 1985) and E. A. Wrigley and R. S. Schofield, *The Population History of England 1541–1871* (1981). See also J. R. Wordie, 'The Chronology of English Enclosure, 1500–1914', *Econ. H.R.* 36 (1983).

22. J. Stevenson, J. Barrett and P. Corfield, *The Rise of the New Urban Society 1660–1780* (Milton Keynes, 1977); P. N. Borsay, 'The English Urban Renaissance: the development of provincial urban culture, *c.* 1680–*c.* 1760', *Social History*, 5 (1977); P. Clark (ed.), *The Transformation of English Provincial Towns, 1600–1800* (1984), Introduction, and esp. pp. 49–61, for an up-to-date guide to the recent historiography of the pre-industrial town.

23. The thesis should not, of course, be pushed too far. For instance, it sits less happily on some towns than on others, as Joyce Ellis has shown in regard to Newcastle-on-Tyne (P. Clark [ed.], *op. cit.* pp. 190–227).

24. I have estimated that by 1722 it probably stood at between 330,000 and 340,000. The widely credited figure for *c.* 1715–22 of 250,000–260,000 fails to take account of 'turn-out', which was rarely more than 75% at any General Election, and sometimes less. See G. Holmes, *The Electorate and the National Will in the First Age of Party* (Lancaster, 1976), pp. 18–23, for the evidence on which this revision is based. It has since been strengthened by the publication of careful work on the poll books and canvass lists of the counties of Cumberland and Westmorland (R. Hopkinson, 'The Electorate of Cumberland and Westmorland in the late Seventeenth and early Eighteenth Centuries', *Northern Hist.* 15, 1979).

randomly composed, cross-section of society above the ranks of the very poor and propertyless. (The tiny Scottish electorate – well under 3000 voters – was infinitely more exclusive). The 'forty-shilling freeholders' of the shires ranged socially from the élite of the squirearchy to tens of thousands of quite humble farmers and many urban craftsmen, tradesmen and shopkeepers;[25] and the social spread of the 110,000 or so borough voters was wider still, a fact amply documented by those contemporary poll books which record occupations as well as votes. Over the past twenty years the behaviour of the late Stuart and early Georgian electorate has been subjected to intense scrutiny.[26] And the two overriding conclusions which have emerged – not least from poll-book analysis – match remarkably exactly the 'twin phenomena' Professor Speck detected in his 1970 study of *The Struggle in the Constituencies*: the existence in the age of Anne both 'of an electorate clearly divided along party lines during general elections' and of 'a substantial floating vote between elections'.[27] The former is most vividly manifest in the amount of 'plumping' which poll books regularly reveal in situations which presented the acid test of party solidarity for the early 18th-century electorate – namely, when one party could put up only one candidate in a two-member constituency against their opponents' pair. The vote was a cherished possession in the unreformed electoral system and no elector would carelessly throw one of his two away; so it is all the more striking to find as many as 85 or even 90 per cent of the single candidate's votes in such circumstances being cast solely for him and his party. Whereas a majority of voters remained consistent in their allegiance, however, an equally significant minority, in some cases as high as twenty per cent, switched sides. And along with the proclivities of new voters, such switches – then, as now – were crucial in determining the outcome of General Elections. No serious

25. J. H. Plumb, 'The Growth of the Electorate in England from 1600 to 1715', *Past and Present*, 45 (1969); D. Hirst, *The Representative of the People? Voters and Voting in England under the Early Stuarts* (Cambridge, 1975), pp. 29–34.

26. See the articles based on computer analysis of poll books cited at n. 5 above; also, W. A. Speck, *Tory and Whig: the Struggle in the Constituencies, 1701–1715* (1970); *id.*, 'The General Election of 1715', *E.H.R.* 90 (1975); R. Hopkinson, art. cit. (n. 24 above); J. Cannon, *Parliamentary Reform, 1640–1832* (Cambridge, 1973), ch. 2. For the Elections of 1715 and 1722, see R. Sedgwick (ed.), *The History of Parliament: the House of Commons, 1715–1754* (1970), i, 189–381 *passim*.

27. *Tory and Whig*, p. 22. For reasons given above, p. ix, the original edition of *British Politics in the Age of Anne* deliberately concentrated for the most part on the centre of politics. Although containing many references to individual General Elections its only sustained section on electoral politics occurs in chapter 9 (pp. 312–21 below).

student of electoral politics in this period would deny that non-political factors played some part in them: venality; a basically self-interested or deferential response to a recent change of ministry at the centre, and therefore to a change in the local patronage situation; or deferential voting of a more personal kind, reflecting a similar change of allegiance by a patron or landlord. And yet, the way the parties conducted their election campaigns nationally suggests that they believed the bulk of the floating vote was a 'conviction' vote and that it could be seduced by playing on political or religious fears or prejudices. They had much evidence to sustain their belief. After the 1710 Election, for example, few doubted that many thousands of former Whig supporters had switched sides because of their fears that the Whigs were threatening the Church of England; and in both 1708 and 1715 it was widely accepted that large numbers of former Tory supporters voted Whig because they were persuaded that a Tory Parliament would threaten the Protestant Succession.[28]

In making conversions and in fortifying the faithful both Whigs and Tories exploited the contemporary press to full effect. My 1967 view of the press as 'an increasingly formidable political engine', especially after 1695,[29] has been corroborated and amplified in many ways by the specialized work of the various scholars who, from their different angles, have subsequently

28. See below, pp. 106–7, p. 107 n.* The most forceful of a number of recent attempts to argue against the view that the Augustan electorate was highly politicized and to re-emphasise ministerial patronage and magnate influence have been by J. C. D. Clark, *English Society, 1688–1832* (Cambridge, 1985), pp. 15–26, and L. J. Colley, *In Defiance of Oligarchy*, pp. 17–20, 118–19, 120. Their arguments are in turn addressed by W. A. Speck, 'The Electorate in the First Age of Party' in C. Jones (ed.), *Britain in the First Age of Party 1680–1750: Essays presented to Geoffrey Homes* (1987), a most valuable and temperate discussion of the many controversial issues raised by studies of the electorate, which I read in typescript after this section of the Introduction had been written. For a subtler approach than those of Clark and Colley to the positing of a more 'deferential' model for the behaviour of the electorate, based on the study of two polls (1713, 1715) in a single – and in some ways untypical – county, see Norma Landau, 'Independence, Deference, and Voter Participation: The Behaviour of the Electorate in Early-Eighteenth-Century Kent', *Hist. Journ.* 22 (1979). There are, however, some serious flaws in Dr Landau's logic. For instance, few of the factors she adduces to explain the 'swing' in Kent between 1713 and 1715 can explain the often critical shift of votes in the average constituency between 1708 and 1710, because for the most part the local circumstances they presuppose did not exist in October 1710.

29. See below, p. 30; also pp. 30–3 *passim*.

explored the subject.[30] By the beginning of the 18th century pamphlets printed in London by the tens of thousands to promote a party cause at the onset of a new election campaign were already being pumped assiduously round the provinces; while in 1705, for the first time, propaganda was directed during a General Election not just at the electorate at large but at key constituencies.[31] In 1709–10 one chain of events alone, the impeachment, trial and triumph of the Anglican clergyman, Dr. Henry Sacheverell,[32] released an unprecedented flood of paper on the hapless electorate before and during the General Election of October 1710 – no fewer than 575 editions of relevant tracts, broadsheets and sermons, published between 5 November 1709 and 1 November 1710.[33] The fundamental differences between the age of Anne and the age of Walpole are reflected in the change, both of tone and target, which came over their political propaganda. By the 1720s and 1730s the approach of the polemicists had become at once far more secular and far more satirical, their polarities pro-government and pro-opposition at least as much as Whig and Tory, the issues on which they concentrated increasingly the standard preoccupations of Country versus Court, even to the point of divergence from the more complex priorities of rank-and-file parliamentary politicians.[34]

30. E.g. W. A. Speck, 'Political Propaganda in Augustan England', *Trans. R. Hist. Soc.* 5th ser., 22 (1972); J. O. Richards, *Party Propaganda under Queen Anne: The General Elections of 1702–13* (Athens, Georgia, 1972); Pat Rogers, *Grub Street: Studies in a Subculture* (1972); H. L. Snyder, 'Newsletters in England, 1689–1715: with special reference to John Dyer', in D. H. Bond and W. R. McLeod (eds.), *Newsletters to Newspapers: Eighteenth Century Journalism* (West Virginia, 1977); J. A. Downie, *Robert Harley and the Press: Propaganda and Public Opinion in the Age of Swift and Defoe* (Cambridge, 1979). Downie's essay 'The Development of the Political Press, 1688–1742' (in C. Jones [ed.], *Britain in the First Age of Party, 1680–1750)*, analyses the changing language of politics to make a telling contribution to the debate on the growth of political stability. Swift's political writings have received much attention, including a comprehensive treatment by Downie in *Jonathan Swift: Political Writer* (1984), and P. B. Hyland's 'Richard Steele, the Press and the Hanoverian Succession, 1713–1716' (Lancaster Univ. Ph.D. thesis, 1984) is a penetrating study of the influence of the most gifted Whig propagandist of the day, over a period which included two General Elections, and of the context in which he wrote.

31. Speck, 'Political Propaganda', *loc. cit.* p. 28; Richards, *op. cit.* pp. 64n., 70–1.

32. See below pp. 92–3 and *passim* (538–9).

33. F. F. Madan, *A Critical Bibliography of Dr Henry Sacheverell*, ed. W. A. Speck (Lawrence, Kansas, 1978), pp. 18–193; G. Holmes, *The Trial of Doctor Sacheverell* (1973), pp. 72–5.

34. Speck, 'Political Propaganda', *loc. cit.* pp. 26–32; M. Harris, 'Print and Politics in the Age of Walpole', in J. Black (ed.), *op. cit.* pp. 189–210; ch. 4 below for Court-Country issues. Cf. above, pp. xii–xiii.

The Church of England also reflected by the 1730s a political scene much changed since Anne's reign. In the first two decades of the 18th century no group in English society, not even the gentry, presented such a face of discord and dissension on account of their political convictions as the Anglican clergy. With the status of religious minorities, the future of the religious establishment and the very health of religion itself among the most obtrusive and emotive issues confronting the lay politicians and the electorate, the cause of bitter divisions between Tories and Whigs,[35] the place of the clergy themselves in political life remained appropriately a central one. By the 1720s, however, it was rapidly becoming peripheral. And this too was appropriate; because after the failure of the Whig ministry of Stanhope and Sunderland to repeal the Test and Corporation Acts in 1719 it was only at brief and widely spaced intervals through the rest of the century that religious squalls whipped up the waters of politics to a height that caused serious alarm.[36] Moreover, if the angry disagreements which had rent the clergy between 1700 and 1720 were muted thereafter, so also was a good deal of their former vitality.

The effects on the Established Church of its invasion by Whig-Tory enmity are considered at various points in the original text of this book.[37] What emerges less clearly from what I wrote in 1967, because it was at that time far from perfectly understood, is how far such phenomena as the struggles in Convocation, divergent and divisive attitudes to Protestant Dissent, and the use of the pulpit for party ends were symptomatic simply of a politicized clergy and how far of a malaise within the Church itself and in the religious life of England. Furthermore, how can we explain the sheer depth of the Church's political embroilment after the Revolution? Why, for instance, did an episcopate which in 1680 had been Divine Right Tory to a man lean thirty years later quite heavily towards support of the Whig party?[38] Why, in most English counties – as we can now be sure from their surviving poll books – did an average of 75–80 per cent of the parish clergy remain

---

35. See below, pp. 97–108; G. Holmes, *Religion and Party in Late Stuart England* (Hist. Assn., 1975).

36. Notably in 1733, 1735–6, 1753, 1779–80 and 1787–90. This is not to dissent from Jonathan Clark's recent contention that 'the Church must occupy a large place in any picture of eighteenth-century English society': it merits very serious attention. See J. C. D. Clark, *op. cit.* p. 277 and ch. 5, *passim*. For the Test and Corporation Acts see below, p. 105.

37. See for example pp. 28–30, 98, 99–100, 106, 398–400 below.

38. See below, pp. 434–5.

fiercely committed to the Tories in the General Elections of Anne's reign, while the remainder doggedly opposed candidates who claimed to be standing in 'the Church interest'? Such questions as these need perplex us no longer; for much has been learned in the past twenty years about the internal condition of the Church at this period and about the complex of problems which beset the Anglican clergy in the first generation after the Revolution, inducing in many of them a crisis of confidence and in some a basic crisis of faith. Disoriented by the undermining of their old role as the monarchy's chief prop; harassed for 19 years of war by the highest taxation they had ever known, a grievous aggravation of the perennial problem of clerical poverty; deeply concerned at falling church attendances, and conversely at the high profile of the dissenters following the Toleration Act; and most of all disturbed by the rationalist and increasingly sceptical attitude displayed in fashionable intellectual circles towards traditional Christianity: for all these reasons, and others,[39] Anglican divines found themselves by 1700 gravely at odds over where lay the best road ahead for them and their church. In 1701 King William reluctantly recalled Convocation, and in so doing provided a theatre in which the newly emerging 'High' and 'Low' parties in the Church could consolidate and acquire a recognised leadership. And from then until its suppression in 1717 it was the Lower House of Convocation, as Dr. Bennett has explained, to which the High Churchmen looked to frame solutions to the Church's problems, and the lay Tories in the House of Commons – duly supported from the pulpit, in print and at the polls by High Church parsons – from whom they hoped to secure the legislation that would give these solutions statutory effect.

It was essentially this strategy – of which the Occasional Conformity and Schism bills[40] were but two salient features – which locked the clergy so

39. See, *inter alia*, G. V. Bennett, *The Tory Crisis in Church and State 1688–1730: The Career of Francis Atterbury, Bishop of Rochester* (Oxford, 1975), especially chs. 1 and 3; *id.*, 'Conflict in the Church', in G. Holmes (ed.), *Britain after the Glorious Revolution, 1689–1714* (1969); G. Holmes, *The Trial of Doctor Sacheverell* (1973), ch. 2, 'The Church'; *id.*, *Augustan England: Professions, State and Society 1680–1730* (1982), ch. 4; G. F. A. Best, *Temporal Pillars: Queen Anne's Bounty, the Ecclesiastical Commissioners and the Church of England* (Cambridge, 1964), chs. 1–3; J. H. Pruett, *The Parish Clergy under the Later Stuarts: The Leicestershire Experience* (Urbana, Illinois, 1978); M. R. Watts, *The Dissenters: from the Reformation to the French Revolution* (Oxford, 1978), ch. 4; A. Brockett, *Nonconformity in Exeter, 1650–1875* (Manchester, 1962), chs. 4, 5; J. Redwood, *Reason, Ridicule and Religion: The Age of Enlightenment in England, 1660–1750* (1976); M. C. Jacob, *The Newtonians and the English Revolution* (1976).

40. See below, pp. 54–5, 100–4.

firmly, and to their ultimate detriment, into the party battles of the age of
Anne. For however much Low Church bishops and parsons, marshalled by
Archbishop Tenison, would have preferred mainly non-political remedies
for the Church of England's ills, as would leading moderates such as Bishop
Nicolson of Carlisle,[41] the relentless pressure of their opponents soon forced
them in self-defence to seek the protection of the Whigs, both in Parliament
and in the dioceses. The Sacheverell affair of 1709–10[42] was the lurid climax
of the Church's entanglement in party politics. Its anti-climax came in the
1720s in the shape of that erastian alliance between Low Churchmen and
Whigs which did much to condition the political, as well as religious climate
of Walpole's day.

The Working of Politics

Important though it was at a time when 'Namierism' was rampant[43]
simply to demonstrate the reality of a two-party division in Augustan politics
and society, the deeper concern of *British Politics in the Age of Anne* lay with
finding answers to two questions: what was politics in this period about –
what were its themes, issues, preoccupations and priorities? and how did
politics work, at the centre of affairs? For some inscrutable reason the
working of politics, within its post-Revolution framework of monarchical
government, regular parliamentary sessions and strong party loyalties, has
received less attention subsequently than its substance. Nevertheless the
dramatis personae on the centre stage have attracted their fair share of the
limelight; and it has been mainly through studies of individuals, and through
the interest shown in ministerial and Court in-fighting, in the organization
and management of both Houses of Parliament and in the influence of
parliamentary pressure-groups[44] that the fresh research of the 1970s and early
1980s has filled out my picture of the 'high' political system in operation.

41. For Nicolson's politics, see C. Jones and G. Holmes (eds.), *The London Diaries of
William Nicolson, Bishop of Carlisle, 1702–1718* (Oxford, 1985), pp. 24–51 and *passim*.
42. See above, p. xix.
43. See below, pp. 1–9.
44. On the Jacobites, see below pp. xxxv–vii. On the October Club, see H. T. Dickinson.
'The October Club', *H.L.Q.* 33 (1970); D. Szechi, *Jacobitism and Tory Politics, 1710–14*
(Edinburgh, 1984), pp. 48–184 *passim*; on the Scots, G. Holmes and C. Jones, 'Trade, the
Scots and the Parliamentary Crisis of 1713', *Parl. History*, 1 (1982); on the rival East India
interests of 1697–1702, H. Horwitz, 'The East India Trade, the Politicians and the
Constitution, 1689–1702', *Journ. Brit. Studs.* (1978), pp. 9–18.

At the centre of that picture the conscientious, tenacious, pain-wearied figure of Queen Anne herself remains obstinately in place, fortified there by Edward Gregg's authoritative biography.[45] Professor Gregg's book is more than a portrait of a Queen; it is a much-needed adjunct to all earlier accounts of the court and ministerial heartland of politics during her reign, especially strong after 1710. Whether the new evidence he utilizes justifies the more extravagant general claims he makes for Anne's political influence and achievements[46] is for readers to decide for themselves: for my own part, I prefer to abide by my more guarded, though still substantial, reappraisal of 1967.[47] Nevertheless it is remarkable how by one means or another the Queen did contrive to realize some of her most cherished hopes and ambitions, outfacing or outlasting formidable political opposition in the process. Her heart was set on the Union of England and Scotland and on a just but profitable peace with France after the bloodshed of Malplaquet, and they both came to pass. She was resolved to protect her beloved Church of England from blatant political exploitation, and she did so.[48] As Gregg reminds us, she took her own unwavering view of the succession question, determined that the House of Hanover should succeed her but equally resolute about keeping it at arm's length during her lifetime; and she died in the knowledge that on this critical issue her single-mindedness had triumphed over others' expediency.[49] One must add, too, that even in her long and exhausting struggle against 'the merciless men of both parties',

45. *Queen Anne* (1980). A predecessor, David Green's *Queen Anne* (1970), though less fully researched, is a sensitive and well-written non-professional study. The same writer's *Sarah, Duchess of Marlborough* (1967) is the best life of the termagant royal favourite whose influence and decline I discuss briefly below (pp. 210–12 and ch. 6 *passim*) and who receives scathing treatment from Gregg.

46. They are summed up in Gregg, *op. cit.* pp. 402–5.

47. See below, pp. 188, 192–210, 414–15. It is important not to place more on the ascertainable facts than they will bear. Thus the Cabinet minutes that have survived simply do not entitle us to translate the undoubted regularity of the Queen's presence at meetings into an effective 'presiding role', while those appearances *incognita* in the House of Lords which did from time to time affect the temper of debates and probably swayed some votes (see below, pp. 390–1) can hardly be said to have remotely approached 'assiduous attendance'. Cf. Gregg, *op. cit.* p. 403.

48. See, for example, G. V. Bennett, 'Robert Harley, the Godolphin Ministry and the Bishoprics Crisis of 1707', *E.H.R.* 82 (1967); Gregg, *op. cit.* ch. 9, 'The Bishoprics Crisis'.

49. Henry Snyder's important reconstruction of 'The Last Days of Queen Anne', *H.L.Q.* 34 (1971), makes use of the journal account of Sir John Evelyn, who had his information from Lord Chancellor Harcourt.

while she clearly lost some battles she did not lose the war.[50]

That Anne managed to see even these objectives achieved (and there were others), in the course of a war which cruelly underscored her own exceedingly limited grasp of state affairs, was in its way a considerable feat. It could never have been accomplished, however, unless the statesmen she was forced to depend on to direct her government and manage her ministries, notably her two prime ministers, Lord Godolphin and Robert Harley, earl of Oxford, had sympathized with some of her ideals and prejudices and found it conducive to efficient administration to implement others.[51] It is clear, for instance, that Oxford's adroit management of the House of Lords played an utterly essential part in securing parliamentary approval of the peace with France between December 1711 and the spring of 1713 and, for another year at least, in protecting the Court and the ministry from Whig exploitation of their difficulties over the Protestant Succession. His characteristically resourceful methods have been the subject of an expert study by Clyve Jones[52] which continues the rehabilitation of the Upper House that began with chapter 12 of the present book in 1967. Appropriately, if largely coincidentally, Oxford's last session in the Lords before his death – that of 1723, when he defied his physical infirmities to support the brave but unsuccessful defence of Bishop Atterbury – was to prove in retrospect the conclusive end of that House's 'golden age', which had opened in 1701.

Harley, 'the Sorcerer', continues in other ways to cast his spell over almost every historian of post-Revolution politics, although none has so far written the truly definitive biography which his mountainous legacy of papers deserves. Given half a chance he will upstage most other heroes through the sheer pervasiveness of his influence and the mystery which often shrouds his

---

50. See below, pp. 198–210.

51. E.g. the fostering of a non-political civil service, to which Godolphin and Oxford made decisive contributions. Holmes, *Augustan England* (1982), pp. 243–5 and ch. 8 *passim*.

52. C. Jones, '"The Scheme Lords, the Necessitous Lords and the Scots Lords": the Earl of Oxford's management and the "Party of the Crown" in the House of Lords, 1711–14', in *idem*. (ed.), *Party and Management in Parliament, 1660–1784* (Leicester 1984); cf. below, pp. 384–94, 400–02. Subsequently, in an essay of major importance ('The House of Lords and the Growth of Parliamentary Stability, 1701–1742', in *idem* [ed.], *Britain in the First Age of Party, 1680–1750* [1987]), the same scholar has placed the 'golden age', along with the whole problem of the management of the Upper House, in a far wider setting. For the fullest recent general assessment of the role of the Lords in early 18th-century politics, see Jones and Holmes (eds.), *London Diaries of William Nicolson*, Intro., pp. 62–105.

true intentions. In Gareth Bennett's fluent, fascinating study of Bishop Francis Atterbury, even that dynamic figure and born political animal is not infrequently nudged aside by Robert Harley. Dr. Bennett's book, being as central to the political as well as the ecclesiastical history of the age of Anne as its title suggests,[53] is admirably complementary to the present work. Harley's political aims and methods, his relations with the Queen and with the Tory party are considered in depth, and we also see the ex-Puritan portrayed in a role which I perforce found little space for, that of ecclesiastical manager and manipulator.[54] Harley's Puritan background and its imprint on his subsequent career has intrigued both the professional historians, Angus McInnes and Sheila Biddle, who in the early 1970s tried to grapple with his story at length.[55] One of the most subtle, oblique and complex politicians who have ever lived will always defy any interpretation of his career that is too simplistic. This was a point made by a number of McInnes's reviewers about a thesis which detected a magic key in Harley's 'ineradicable Country psychology' and the tensions this supposedly produced in a man compelled to take high responsibility and office against his natural inclinations. What both authors do convincingly show is that a sensitive understanding of Harley's domestic ambience (he was in many ways a very private public figure), his religious faith and his implicit trust in Providence do help to unravel some knots in his political behaviour. But, as I have written elsewhere,[56] 'I fancy that certain twists and turns of [his] career will remain mysterious, and something of the man himself will always elude us. To adapt a Harleian figure of speech, the abundant evidence has something of the quality of fine sand: the harder one squeezes it between the hands, the more it runs through the fingers.'

There could be no greater contrast, in temperament, methods, religious belief and political instinct, than that between Harley and Henry St. John, Viscount Bolingbroke, his one-time friend and ally who became his bitterest rival. The interplay between them[57] has been studied not only at book length

53. See above, n. 39.
54. For a valuable exploration of another previously neglected facet of 'the Master's' manifold activities, his exploitation of the press as an instrument of government, see Downie, *Robert Harley and the Press* (n. 30 above).
55. A. McInnes, *Robert Harley, Puritan Politician* (1970); S. Biddle, *Bolingbroke and Harley* (U.S.A., 1973; London, 1975). Neither is a biography in the true sense. They are best seen as extended essays.
56. *E.H.R.* 87 (1972), p. 127.
57. See below, pp. 262–3, 269–70 and *passim.*

by Biddle and in an essay by the present writer[58] but in the only thoroughly professional and authoritative biography of Bolingbroke ever attempted.[59] I have never doubted that the way the political system worked in the early 18th century was influenced almost as much by quirks of human personality as by the system itself. I should like to think that this conviction is stamped on every chapter in Part Two; and in view of it, it is reassuring that Professor Dickinson's assessment of Bolingbroke in the years 1701–15 accords quite closely with my own. The paradox and the fascination of the man is that in some respects nature had endowed him almost too prodigally for the highest political prizes which he coveted; yet at the same time she had betrayed him. His gifts dazzled Swift into eulogising him as 'the greatest young man I ever knew' and made him, as Secretary of State under Harley, an arbiter of the peace of Europe before his mid thirties.[60] But he was badly flawed. Inveighing against the dangers threatening the Church[61] was a bizarre role for a man who rarely went to one, and yet who aspired to lead 'the Church Party'; and neither his freethinking nor his moral aberrations could recommend him as a potential prime minister to a strait-laced Queen. More serious for him and for the Tory party was that his transcendent talents were prey to an unstable temperament. Bolingbroke lacked ballast, and palpably lacked judgment. His bolt to the Pretender's court in 1715 is not incomprehensible to students of his character and previous record.

The other major statesman with whose fortunes Harley's were entwined was his predecessor as Lord Treasurer, the earl of Godolphin. In some respects Harley had much more in common with Godolphin, a veteran of pre-Revolution politics, than with St. John, whose debut on the Westminster stage was as late as 1701; for Godolphin was, like himself, a congenital moderate and a 'manager' rather than a partisan. Yet the two relationships ran strangely parallel in course, both beginning with a fruitful period of friendship and co-operation, and both ending with an epic quarrel and ultimately in Harley's fall from office. Henry Snyder's 1967 essay on the partnership between Harley and Godolphin from 1701–8 made the point that the latter's political acumen, and especially the painstaking care he took over

---

58. G. Holmes, 'Harley, St. John and the Death of the Tory Party' (1969: reprinted with postscript in *idem*, *Politics, Religion and Society in England, 1679–1742* [1986]).

59. H. T. Dickinson, *Bolingbroke* (1970).

60. Though his dominance over the Utrecht negotiations has been exaggerated: below, n. 80.

61. As below, pp. 54–5.

parliamentary management, has been underrated; and Godolphin's stature grew still further when the leading modern expert on post-Revolution finance pronounced him an outstanding head of the Treasury.[62] However, as with his co-'duumvir' of the years 1702–10, the duke of Marlborough, no secondary work yet exists in which one can study Godolphin's political influence half as well as in Snyder's vast three-volume edition of the two men's correspondence.[63]

Of the front-line leaders of the Whigs and the High Tories who figure prominently in the pages that follow, and in particular in chapters 7 and 8, only two – Nottingham and Somers – have been the subject of major published work in the past two decades.[64] Henry Horwitz's study of Nottingham, a model of its kind, is instructive on many counts. It contains the most valuable post-Walcott analysis of a major personal connexion in the early 18th century and an assessment of the shattering first effects on it of Nottingham's great apostasy in December 1711,[65] the desertion to the Whigs

62. H. L. Snyder, 'Godolphin and Harley: A Study of their Partnership in Politics', *H.L.Q.* 30 (1967); P.G.M. Dickson, *The Financial Revolution in England . . . 1688–1756* (1967), pp. 58–64, 361. For Godolphin's management of Parliament see also H. L. Snyder, 'The Defeat of the Occasional Conformity Bill and the Tack', *Bull.I.H.R.* 41 (1968).

63. See Appendix, p. lxiii below. Books on Marlborough published since 1967 have concentrated on his military prowess. See I. F. Burton, *The Captain-General* (1968); Correlli Barnett, *Marlborough* (1974). Note, however (1) Snyder's re-examination of a vital incident in the weakening of the duumvirate's position with Queen Anne (cf. below, p. 190 n.*), 'The Duke of Marlborough's Request of his Captain-Generalship for Life', *Journ.Soc. Army Hist.Research*, 45 (1967); (2) the stress laid in some recent studies of early 18th-century politics on the sheer loathing which Marlborough, even more than Godolphin, came to inspire among most Tories after 1709, 'the Jacobite wing of the party especially because of his double-dealing with St. Germain'. E. Cruickshanks, 'Religion and Royal Succession: The Rage of Party, 1679–1760', in C. Jones (ed.), *Britain in the First Age of Party* (1987), p. 33; D. Szechi, *op. cit.* pp. 40, 107. My own references to Marlborough's relations with the Tories, even to their parliamentary attack on him in Jan. 1712 (e.g. below, pp. 142, 191, 297, 310), do not bring out this revulsion sufficiently clearly.

64. H. Horwitz, *Revolution Politicks: The Career of Daniel Finch, second Earl of Nottingham* (Cambridge, 1968); W. L. Sachse, *Lord Somers: A Political Portrait* (Manchester, 1975). Scarcity of surviving papers is a problem, but enough material does exist to justify work on the third earl of Sunderland (see unpublished Univ. of California Ph.D. dissertation by H. L. Snyder [1963]) and on Lord Chancellor Cowper. My once-promised study of Wharton of the Junto has never, alas, got much further than the accumulation of notes. He is a glorious subject.

65. Cf. below, pp. 272–5, 334–5.

over 'No peace without Spain' which many contemporaries attributed to
pique at the Queen's rejection of his claims to office but which Horwitz
regards firmly as a matter of principle.[66] It also strongly reinforces the
argument advanced below, that Nottingham's unique position in the
hierarchy of the High Tories owed more to his unsullied standing as
'defender of the Church of England' than to electoral influence or the intricate
web of family relationships in which he was placed.[67] In sharp contrast Lord
Rochester,[68] widely acknowledged as *the* leader of the Tories at the end of
William III's reign, lost much ground to Nottingham thereafter, and not least
because he was seen to be exploiting religious issues to further his political
aims and ambitions. The most interesting work done in recent years on the
largest and most feared power-group in Augustan politics, the Whig Junto,[69]
has been in article form rather than in Professor Sachse's lengthy 'political
portrait' of Lord Somers.[70] Much of it has concentrated on the year of their
peak influence in Anne's reign, 1709, which was also the year before their fall.
We see how the tensions between 'the five lords' and Godolphin, and the bad
blood between them and the Queen which had been a key element in court
and parliamentary politics since 1706, persisted even in the noon day of their
triumph. Godolphin's determination and cunning in fighting to preserve his
own primacy, despite his apparent capitulation in 1708, is also made evident,
and it is clear that the Junto's complaints about his continuing double-dealing
in 1709 were not misplaced. Of course, the Junto lords were not immune
from divisions among themselves; indeed in this very year there were some
vulnerable salients in the apparently formidable front they presented to the
Queen, her managers and the political world at large.[71] David Hayton has
highlighted these, in particular a damaging if relatively short-lived breach of
trust between Somers and Wharton in relation to the proposed repeal of the
Test in Ireland, and in the same essay has taken further my reservations about

66. *Revolution Politicks*, pp. 229–34, 269; cf. below, pp. 198, 200 & n.

67. *Ibid.* p. 267. Horwitz contends – correctly, in my view – that Nottingham's
influence was at its height in the six years or so following the death of Sir Christopher
Musgrave and the collapse of Sir Edward Seymour's health in 1704–5.

68. See below, pp. 275–7 and *passim*.

69. See below, pp. 235–45, 288–91 and ch. 10, section I *passim*.

70. For my assessment of Sachse's earnest but rather unsatisfying book see the review
in the *Times Literary Supplement*, 5 March 1976.

71. See below, pp. 237, 239.

the unanimity of the Whigs in their attitudes towards Church and Dissent.[72] It is not without irony that the party's ambivalence over the granting of full civil rights to Protestant nonconformists, which was to divide it more ostentatiously in 1719 and again in 1736, were already detectable to the close observer in 1709 – the very year that Dr. Henry Sacheverell, by trumpeting from St. Paul's pulpit the imminence of a total sell-out by the Whigs to the Puritan 'fanatics', set in train the sequence of events which led in less than a year to the Junto's rout.[73]

The Substance of Politics

I

Unscrupulous though they were, Sacheverell's words struck a responsive chord in the ears of a political nation conditioned to regard its parties in stereotype terms. Hence the *furor* they created. When I first sought out the political and religious issues and principles, as distinct from the more material considerations, which supplied the substance of conflict between the Tory and Whig parties of the age of Anne,[74] it was religious principle which appeared to me to provide 'the strongest threads of continuity' between the original parties of Charles II's reign and their post-Revolution successors. The Glorious Revolution, and still more the inaccurately-labelled 'Toleration Act' (1689),[75] inevitably led to some redefinition of the religious problem; but in reacting to it the partisans took sides from much the same basic motives that had characterized their reactions to a persecuted Dissent and an exclusive Anglican supremacy in the 1670s and 1680s. I have found no reason

72. See below, p. 105.
73. D. Hayton, 'Divisions in the Whig Junto in 1709: Some Irish Evidence', *Bull.I.H.R.* 55 (1982). Note also C. Jones, 'Godolphin, the Whig Junto and the Scots: a new Lords' Division-List from 1709' [on the disqualification of the duke of Queensberry], *Scottish Hist. Rev.* 58 (1979); H. L. Snyder, 'Queen Anne versus the Junto: The Effort to place Orford at the head of the Admiralty in 1709', *H.L.Q.* 35 (1972).
74. See below, chs. 2–3, pp. 51–115.
75. For the narrowness of this measure, which nowhere proclaimed a state of 'Toleration', see below, p. 62; G. Holmes, *Religion and Party in Late Stuart England* (1975), pp. 12–13.

subsequently to change this opinion or the view that the fervour with which the Whigs of Anne's reign undeviatingly upheld the Hanoverian Succession was fired by anti-Popery sentiments that differed little in strength from those of the Exclusionists, even if they were less hysterically expressed. That said, an account written two decades ago of the ideological heredity of the parties of Queen Anne's reign is bound to stand in some need of revision. Down to the 1960s historians *per se* had shown virtually no interest in the mainstream political ideologies of late 17th and 18th century England.[76] Even on the critical events of 1688–89, which unhinged so many of the theories and assumptions of the post-Restoration generation, very little of worth had been written outside doctoral theses since Trevelyan's brief study *The English Revolution* was published in 1938, elegantly but vacuously enshrining the last relics of Whig historiography.[77] Since 1967 not only has the political thinking of both Whigs and Tories been subjected to close scrutiny[78] but the Revolution Settlement, too, has been anatomized as never before.[79] Semantics have been pressed into service and the *O.E.D.* feverishly scanned for archaic meanings that might lurk behind well-known phrases in parliamentary motions or in the Declaration of Rights.

Little of this work has any relevance for the intrinsically new issues in post-Revolution politics, issues of foreign policy or questions arising essentially from the conduct of the wars against France or the making of the peace which had no true pre-Revolution pedigree. The content of that section of chapter 2 which is concerned with such issues has, I believe, survived the

76. the stimulating work of Caroline Robbins (see n. 126 below and *Two English Republican Tracts*, ed. Robbins [Cambridge, 1969]) was for a long time sadly undervalued, largely because it was concerned with the non-mainstream radical/republican tradition.

77. An honourable exception was Peter Laslett's redating of Locke's *Two Treatises of Government* (1960) to *c.* 1681 rather than the previously accepted 1689, a justly influential piece of scholarship.

78. Notably by J. P. Kenyon, *Revolution Principles: The Politics of Party, 1689–1720* (Cambridge, 1977) and (ed.), *Halifax's Complete Works* (1969); H. T. Dickinson, *Liberty and Property: Political Ideology in Eighteenth-Century Britain* (1977); M. A. Goldie, 'Tory Political Thought, 1689–1714' (Cambridge Univ. Ph.D. dissertation, 1977) and several articles (see e.g. n. 127 below). See also J. G. A. Pocock, *The Macchiavellian Moment* (Princeton, 1975), ch. 13 and *passim*.

79. By, among others, J. Carter (in Holmes [ed.], *Britain after the Glorious Revolution*, 1969), J. R. Jones (1972), J. R. Western (1972), H. G. Horwitz (*Bull.I.H.R.* 47, 1974), R. Frankle (*Hist. Journ.* 17, 1974), J. P. Kenyon (in N. McKendrick [ed.], *Historical Perspectives*, 1974), L. G. Schwoerer (1981), J. Miller (*Hist. Journ.* 1982) and T. P. Slaughter (*Hist. Journ.* 1981, 1983).

years largely unscathed.[80] It is on some parts of chapter 3 that a lot of recent revisionism most directly impinges. For what have been mainly in question are party responses to the Revolution itself and party attitudes, then and thereafter, to those great divisive issues of principle of the period 1679–89: sovereignty and the source and nature of political authority; allegiance and obedience; rights and prerogatives.[81] A good deal to my surprise, the views on these questions I trustingly committed to print twenty years ago prove more resilient than might have been expected. One would certainly wish today to give more credit to the resourcefulness of Anglican-Tory theorists and polemicists in aiding their party's recovery from the shock of the Revolution.[82] It has been salutary, too, to be reminded that the Whigs also had their problems in adapting principles of government forged out of opposition to Catholic or crypto-Catholic autocrats to a more limited monarchical regime after 1689, which many of them were anxious to serve. And yet the impression the unwary might glean from some modern work[83] that the Revolution Settlement was, in ideological terms, not far short of being a Tory triumph and a Whig disaster must be sternly resisted.

The active rebellion of some Tories, albeit a small minority, in 1688; James II's flight; the disposal of the crown by Parliament and the terms on which it was settled – these events could not be anything but an acute embarrassment to the Tory conscience. The intellectual agility of a few clever and eloquent individuals like Simon Harcourt, Francis Atterbury and Offspring Blackall in re-locating sovereignty, by the early years of the 18th century, in 'the Legislative Power', 'the King in Parliament', in face-lifting the theory of Non-Resistance accordingly, and in isolating the traumatic events of 1688

---

80. But among a number of amplifying studies, note especially G. C. Gibbs, 'The Revolution in Foreign Policy', in Holmes (ed.), *op. cit.*, a most valuable essay; also H. T. Dickinson, 'The Tory Party's Attitude to Foreigners', *Bull.I.H.R.* 40 (1967) and 'The Poor Palatines and the Parties', *E.H.R.* 82 (1967); and two important reassessments of the Tory peace making of 1711–13, stressing (a) Lord Oxford's determination to supervise the negotiations throughout and (b) his efforts to procure a better deal for Britain's allies than they would have got from his assertive, anti-Dutch colleague, Bolingbroke: viz. A. D. MacLachlan, 'The Road to Peace, 1710–13', in Holmes (ed.), *op. cit.*, and B. W. Hill, 'Oxford, Bolingbroke and the Peace of Utrecht', *Hist. Journ.* 16 (1973). See also Gregg, *Queen Anne*, pp. 339ff. L. J. Colley, *In Defiance of Oligarchy*, pp. 13–14, makes a spirited but thinly-substantiated defence of the Tories, before 1710, as Europeanists and supporters of the war.
81. See also pp. 58–64 below.
82. Cf. below, pp. 60–1.
83. From Kenyon's persuasive *Revolution Principles*, in particular: see, e.g., p. 146.

retrospectively as the 'exceptions' that proved the rule,[84] became an ideological convenience for the Hanoverian Tory group which took shape in the last two years of the Queen's reign.[85] But they must not be taken as a sure guide to general Tory thinking or to gut party feelings. The startling revival of Divine Right and Passive Obedience preaching and writing in Anne's reign, notably in and after the year 1708,[86] was a revival of the genuine article and not of some cosmetic new model. It can be directly linked with the upsurge of Jacobitism in the second half of Anne's reign and therefore (though this was not its sole source) with the agonizing uncertainties and equivocations which Tories unquestionably experienced as the Queen's life drew to a close.[87] As Mark Goldie rightly concludes,[88] the parliamentary dilemma of the Tories in 1713–14 was to a significant degree a reflection of their own ideological split – highlighted at the very height of their triumph during the Sacheverell affair in 1710 – between the new moderates of the 'conservative natural rights school' and the far more numerous High Church extremists of the old brew. Ironically it was in these later years of Anne, years of apparent party triumph, and not in the camouflaged circumstances of the early 1690s or of 1701–2 that the true extent of the damage which the Revolution wrought on Toryism was revealed.

Too much, perhaps, has been hung of late upon the arguments paraded by the protagonists at Sacheverell's trial. Important though these were,[89] they must not be taken out of their context, with all its inevitable special pleading. And if this is true of the Tories it is even more true of the Whigs. As I have suggested, it is very necessary to remember the inhibiting effect on the Whig prosecutors of the Queen's presence at every day of the trial. Even though she

84. Kenyon, *op. cit.* pp. 119–22, 136–8; Bennett, *Tory Crisis*, pp. 103–16; Holmes, *Trial*, pp. 180–5.

85. *The Lockhart Papers* (ed. A. Aufrere, 1817), i, 475–6; and see below, p. 94.

86. Bennett, *op. cit.* pp. 106–8; Holmes, *Trial*, pp. 33–4.

87. It now seems that in the House of Commons the dithering majority may have been somewhat larger and the committed pro-Hanover and Jacobite groupings rather smaller than I originally suggested. Cf. pp. 93–4, 336–7 below with E. Cruickshanks, 'The Tories and the Succession to the Crown in the 1714 Parliament', *Bull.I.H.R.* 46 (1973), pp. 177, 184–5, and D. Szechi, *Jacobitism and Tory Politics, 1710–14.* (Edinburgh, 1984), ch. 8 and pp. 200–2.

88. Above, n. 78.

89. Cf. below, pp. 92–3, 96.

herself had joined the rebels at Nottingham in 1688 and readily admitted that she had a parliamentary title to the throne, as well as a hereditary one, Westminster Hall in 1710 was not the occasion for a party playing for high political stakes to bare its soul too nakedly.[90] Yet for an eminent scholar to dismiss the case against Sacheverell as a 'fiasco' seems a strange aberrration. Like the claim that ideologically 'the Whigs had shot their bolt' by 1710–14, it surely overstates their discomfort.[91]

The Revolution naturally reduced the intensity and changed the context of the central pre-1688 debate about the nature of government and the rights and obligations of the subject, but it did not by any means render it irrelevant. Much has been made of late of the alleged retreat of the post-Exclusion generation of Whig leaders and spokesmen towards positions of Establishment respectability and compromise. More and more as time went by, we are told, they backed away from Lockean principles, and not least from the theory that political authority was based on a 'contract'. Of course there is more than a little substance to this argument. But as the debates of both 1689 and 1710 plainly show, John Locke's rarified, cerebral variant was only one of several ways in which the politicians of the day envisaged a form of 'compact' between those who wielded authority and those from whom they claimed obedience; indeed, there were some versions of it which even found favour with Tories.[92] In any case Locke's idea of an *original* contract had never been much more than the ornamental trimming on Exclusionist ideology; and from the main basic ingredients of that ideology – government by consent, parliamentary (as opposed to divine, hereditary) kingship, and the right to resist authority in certain circumstances – there was no retreat, either after the Revolution or after William III's death. What the Whigs *did* rather than what they *said* is the surest guide to their principles; so that their unwavering support for the Protestant Succession as laid down by Parliament in 1689 and 1701, and their secret military preparations to resist the Pretender in 1714,[93] offer more persuasive evidence than tracts or treatises

90. See below, p. 97 and n.*; Holmes, *Trial*, pp. 138–40, speeches of Jekyll, Eyre, Walpole and Hawles.

91. Cf. L. Colley and M. Goldie, 'The Principles and Practice of Eighteenth-Century Party', *Hist. Journ.* 22 (1979), p. 22; Kenyon, *op. cit.* p. 146.

92. E.g. Archbishop John Sharp of York and Francis Turner, nonjuring bishop of Ely.

93. See below, pp. 83–6, 97, 473 n. 66.

or odd extracts from their speeches.[94] That said, it would be perverse to ignore the impact of political tracts that are known to have been printed by the thousand and distributed widely; and in this respect, at least, the modern tendency to downgrade the influence of Locke's ideas, contract and all, on the post-Revolution Whigs has taken a hard knock from the ingenious researches of Ashcraft and Goldsmith.[95]

In the first edition of *British Politics in the Age of Anne* I took the then fairly orthodox view that one touchstone of Whig enthusiasm for the Hanoverian Succession, and conversely of their fear of a Franco-Jacobite *coup* via England's 'back-door' to the North, was the dominant part played by the Junto and its allies in carrying through the Union of England and Scotland. I also argued that although there was a tiny handful of occasions in Anne's reign when Whig leaders demonstrably sacrificed important party principles for the sake of party advantages or the prospect of power, their flirting with a Scottish attempt to undermine the Union in June 1713 was not one of them.[96] Much important work published since then on Anglo-Scottish relations and the making of the Union has left me unrepentant on both scores.[97] Every student of early 18th-century British politics should be thankful for the interest shown over the past twenty years in the politics of Scotland and for the manuscript harvest gathered into the Scottish Record Office which has done so much to stimulate it. However, even if its yield had been at my disposal in 1966 I could not have identified myself fully with the crushingly cynical view of the motives of the 'North Britons', at every turn, taken by Patrick Riley and William Ferguson in particular. What is more, if Riley had known his Westminster and Whitehall scene as thoroughly as that of Edinburgh, would he have stuck by his thesis that the Whig Junto, too, saw the necessity for the Union by 1705–6 purely in opportunistic terms? The

---

94. Thus it is impossible to quantify the impact of Algernon Sidney's *Discourses concerning Government* (described by Caroline Robbins [1947] as a 'textbook of revolution') in order to prove or disprove Kenyon's claim that from its publication in 1698, for over two decades, it was 'certainly much more influential than Locke's *Two Treatises*'. But one *can* quantify parliamentary motions, bills and division figures.

95. R. Ashcraft and M. M. Goldsmith, 'Locke, Revolution Principles and the Formation of Whig Ideology', *Hist. Journ.* 26 (1983).

96. See below, pp. 84–5, 113, 410.

97. For a detailed appraisal of the crisis of 1713 and the role of the Whigs in it, see G. Holmes and C. Jones, 'Trade, the Scots and the Parliamentary Crisis of 1713', *Parl. History*, 1 (1982), repr. in Holmes, *Politics, Religion and Society in England, 1679–1742* (1986), pp. 109–38.

claim that they urged it forward with little else in mind than calculations of the future parliamentary balance is hard to sustain.[98]

One of the main reasons why the Whigs by 1713 were experiencing some disillusionment with the early political effects of the Union was the very large proportion of Scottish peers and M.P.s of the Episcopalian persuasion returned at the 1710 Election. The election of the sixteen representative peers had resulted in a clean sweep for the new Harley ministry's list of candidates and a serious defeat for the Junto's main allies across the border, the Squadrone, who did not in the end venture a poll. Of the 45 Scots returned to the House of Commons in 1710 nearly two-thirds were Tories. It was not only that Episcopal Tories were, from the Whig point of view, probable supporters of a hostile administration; still worse, many were known Jacobites. Daniel Szechi has calculated that 'committed Jacobites' captured some 16 Scottish seats, four times as many as in 1708, and suspected Jacobites a further four.[99] Szechi's study of *Jacobitism and Tory Politics, 1710–14* is an outstanding piece of scholarship and any student of the age of Anne seeking enlightenment from the present work on the Succession as an issue in British politics during the Queen's last years, on the Jacobites as an independent political grouping (which Szechi convinces us they were long before the 1714 session),[100] and on the history of the Tories generally in that period,[101] would be well advised to use the two books in tandem.

It is well known that the earl of Oxford maintained contact with the Pretender, through Gaultier, Torcy and the French Court, throughout much

---

98. P. W. J. Riley, 'The Union of 1707 as an Episode in English Politics', *E.H.R.* 84 (1969). See also *idem, William III and the Scottish Politicians* (Edinburgh, 1979) and *The Union of England and Scotland* (Manchester, 1978); W. Ferguson, 'The Making of the Treaty of Union of 1707', *Scottish Hist. Rev.* 43 (1964); *idem, Scotland's Relations with England: A Survey to 1707* (Edinburgh, 1977). For a balanced, less bilious view of the events leading up to the Union, see the elegant essay by Christopher Smout, 'The Road to Union', in Holmes (ed.), *Britain after the Glorious Revolution* (1969). Space does not allow me to develop my case against Riley here. Readers must, I fear, await the chapter on 'The Uniting of Britain: Scotland and England, 1690–1727', chapter 20 of my book *The Making of a Great Power: Pre-industrial Britain, 1660–1783*, to be published as vol. 3 of Longmans' series 'Foundations of Modern Britain'.

99. Szechi, *op. cit.* pp. 67, 202.

100. Cf. below, pp. 279–80 and *passim*.

101. Its excellent treatment of the October Club, in which Jacobite M.P.s like Charles Eversfield played a front-line role has been mentioned already (above, n. 44, and cf. pp. 116–17, 251–2 and 342–4 below). It is also illuminating on the inscrutably devious manoeuvres of Harley.

of his ministry; and this has tempted some historians to suspect him of playing a double game and of insincerity in his frequent professions of loyalty to the House of Hanover.[102] I have always acquitted him of such treachery, while harbouring some doubts (as Oxford himself certainly did) about the intentions – in 1714 at least – of his rival, Bolingbroke.[103] Szechi subjects the Tory administration's relations with the Jacobites, in Britain and in France, to intense scrutiny. In doing so he not simply supports the acquittal of Oxford with overwhelming evidence but at the same time constructs a convincing thesis about the Jacobites' central political strategy in the last four years of Anne and the reasons for its failure. The Pretender's adherents at Westminster remained convinced for much of the period from early 1711 to July 1714 that his peaceful restoration after the Queen's death was a realistic possibility. Because the Oxford ministry was so frequently harassed by its own truculent backbenchers, and latterly by Cabinet feuds, the Jacobites calculated that they could trade off their debating talent and their well-marshalled votes against a firm ministerial undertaking to repeal the Act of Settlement. That their strategy failed was partly due to two serious miscalculations: their belief that Anne's own sympathies were privately with her half-brother, which emphatically they were not,[104] and their hope that a Catholic prince would ultimately see the wisdom of accepting a *politique* conversion to Protestantism to appease the bulk of the Anglican Tories, an illusion which was finally and bleakly dispelled in April 1714. The main reason for their failure, however, as Szechi skilfully demonstrates, was that the Pretender himself destroyed their freedom of parliamentary manoeuvre by ordering them to put their votes at Oxford's disposal. As I have recently remarked,[105] 'in a career noted for sleight of hand, no conjuring trick proved more valuable to Oxford than the one which in 1711 convinced James Stuart that the prime minister was wholeheartedly in his interest. Not until early in 1714 did the Pretender finally acknowledge that he had been duped and

---

102. E.g. see E. Gregg, *Queen Anne*, pp. 374–9.

103. See below, pp. 84–6, 260, 268 & n.†, 270, 279–80. Oxford's sympathies *after* his fall from power, and especially after his two-year confinement in the Tower (1715–17), are a different matter however. The sincerity of his Jacobite intrigues in George I's reign may have been more genuine, though even about this modern scholars are not agreed. Cf. G. V. Bennett, *Tory Crisis*, ch. 11, *passim*, and E. Cruickshanks, 'Religion and Royal Succession', *loc. cit.* (n. 63 above) pp. 35–6.

104. On this question see Edward Gregg's unanswerable case in 'Was Queen Anne a Jacobite?', *History*, 57 (1972).

105. *T.L.S.* 1 Feb. 1985, p. 125.

remove the whip from his frustrated parliamentary party'. By then irrecoverable opportunities had been missed and time all too quickly ran out for the Jacobites on 1 August, when Anne's death left all their plans in ruins.[106]

II

Of all the ideological luggage carried over from pre-Revolution England to the reigns of the last two Stuarts, only one set became thoroughly jumbled. The traumatic last year of James II's reign had badly shaken the Tories' belief in both the sanctity and the efficacy of the royal prerogative. This became evident initially in their attitude to the constitutional settlement of 1689.[107] But the change of ruler from a Divine Right Catholic to a Calvinist Dutchman with a title to the throne which most Tories could only regard as *de facto* made them still readier to jettison their old scruples. Hence 'one of the most curious metamorphoses in post-Revolution politics' which I observed in the age of Anne – 'the gradual reconciliation in the Tory mind of anti-prerogative attitudes with sound Anglican principles'.[108] Further than that, however, and surely one of the most striking differences between the pre- and post-Revolution parties, is the degree to which, once it ceased to enjoy a monopoly of royal favour, the Tory party succeeded in rifling much of that broader wardrobe of 'Country' clothes which had hitherto been largely

106. In Dr. Szechi's view (*op. cit.* pp. 190–1), and also in that of G. V. Bennett ('English Jacobitism, 1710–1715: Myth and Reality', *Trans. R. Hist. Soc.* 5th Ser., 32, 1982, pp. 145–6), Bolingbroke was also insincere in his own overtures to St. Germain, certainly after the Pretender's refusal to change his religion. Nevertheless, it seems clear that because of his greater recklessness and his determination to win over the parliamentary Jacobite group to his own cause he was more deeply 'dipped' than his rival. His most distinguished biographer agrees: 'while Bolingbroke, just as much as Oxford, insisted that nothing could be done until the Pretender changed his religion, he was more sympathetic to Jacobitism than Oxford ever was. H. T. Dickinson, *Bolingbroke*, p. 118 and pp. 119–35, *passim*. For the views of two other recent historians of Jacobitism on both Tory party and ministerial attitudes to the Pretender's cause prior to August 1714, see E. Cruickshanks, *Political Untouchables* (1979), p. 3; B. Lenman, *The Jacobite Risings in Britain, 1689–1746* (1980), pp. 111–14.

107. See the articles by Horwitz and Frankle, cited above, n. 79.

108. Below, p. 120. Thus in a speech in 1698 Sir Bartholomew Shower effortlessly combined protestations of his devotion to the Church with a sheaf of 'Reasons for a New Bill of Rights'. J. H. Plumb, *Growth of Political Stability*, p. 140n.

(though not exclusively) the property of the Whigs, as the erstwhile party of opposition.

At much the same time as I was developing this theme in the mid-1960s and attempting to identify the men, the mentality and the measures which perpetuated a 'Country tradition' into the age of Anne,[109] Professor Plumb was taking the point still further. He argued that the years 1694–8 'witnessed the marriage of Tory politicians to a [Harley-inspired] political programme that was critical not only of the acts of government but also of the whole constitutional position'. By 1710 the Tory party had 'acquired a recognizable *persona*, based largely on the independently-minded squire's idea of himself, a patriotic *persona*, barely distinguishable from that of a Country-Whig opposition to the Court in the 1670s'.[110] And the Tories' new habiliments were all the more striking, Plumb contended, when set against the new Whig image of a party 'closely identified with both aristocracy and government', committed to the financing of full-scale war and deeply concerned with the exploitation of patronage to preserve its power. It would be natural to deduce from this that the Country platform essentially moved house, with all its props, from one party to another – along with the Harley-Foley group of Whigs,[111] who also acted as removal contractors. Yet it would now be accepted by most scholars that a 'Country interest' made up of both Whig and Tory critics of William III's ministry would have come together in the early 1690s even without Harley;[112] while the evidence is no less convincing today than it seemed to me in 1966 that the tradition of Country opposition remained a bipartisan one during Anne's reign, as it had been under William III.

Three important studies of the past ten years all confirm that

---

109. See below, ch. 4, pp. 116–47; G. Holmes, 'The Attack on "the Influence of the Crown", 1702–16', *Bull.I.H.R.* 39 (1966), repr. *idem, Politics, Religion and Society in England, 1679–1742* (1986), pp. 35–56.

110. 'The Tory, apart from public issues', he wrote, 'stood for free and frequent elections, sharp punishment for bribery and electoral corruption, low taxation, financial rectitude, accountability to Parliament, the exclusion of all place-holders and sound land-qualification for Members.' Plumb, *op. cit.*, pp. 140, 151–2; see also pp. 140–52 *passim*.

111. See below, pp. 259–61.

112. See, *inter alia*, L. Colley and M. Goldie, 'Principles and Practice of Eighteenth-Century Party', *Hist. Journ.* 22 (1979), p. 246; J. A. Downie, 'The Commission of Public Accounts and the formation of the Country Party', *E.H.R.* 91 (1976), especially the important point on p. 35, emphasising Harley's relatively junior status in the years 1691–94.

conclusion.[113] H. T. Dickinson lucidly analyses the ideological soil which made possible those temporary alliances and nurtured those parliamentary measures which I discuss in chapter 4. Readers should not be puzzled by occasional discrepancies between the aura of altruism and unanimity of motive with which he tends to endow the Country campaigns of the period and my evident reservations on this score: it is hard for the historian of ideas not to idealize the practice of politics. Colin Brooks's contribution to the debate, thoughtful and original though it is, is still more vulnerable on that count; for in his attempt to delineate what he calls a Country 'political persuasion' in post-Revolution England[114] his explicit aim is not merely to differentiate ideas but 'to separate values, emotional ties *from behaviour*'.[115] This is indeed a delicate operation, and a chancy one, and it not infrequently results in euphoric conclusions about the 'components' of this 'persuasion' which are well adrift from the common clay reality of many of the individual politicians who supported Country measures in practice.[116] Unfortunately one cannot side-step such questions as, what became of Country high-mindedness when members were faced with evidence of flagrant malpractice by representatives of their own party in disputed election cases? Not for nothing, as Professor Speck has reminded us, was the Commons' Committee of Elections called by one backbencher 'the most corrupt council

---

113. H. T. Dickinson, *Liberty and Property*, ch. 3, esp. pp. 83–5, 102–16; D. Hayton, 'The "Country" interest and the party system, 1689–*c*. 1720', in C. Jones (ed.), *Party and Management*, pp. 37–85; C. Brooks, 'The Country Persuasion and Political Responsibility in England in the 1690s', *Parliament, Estates and Representation*, 4 (1984). His title notwithstanding, Brooks's profile of a Country member has an obvious relevance for the reigns of Anne and George I also, a relevance he emphasises by pointed references to chapter 4 below.

114. How the political scientists' notion of a 'persuasion' differs in concept from the 'Country mentality' whose characteristics I sought to ascertain (below, pp. 119–26, 129–30) is unclear to me.

115. *Loc. cit.* p. 138: my italics.

116. E.g. the first three of Dr. Brooks's six 'components', viz. an outlook that was 'profoundly provincial', a 'sense of place', and the habit of viewing the whole of England as if it were 'an estate', requiring honest and frugal administration, imply an equation of the Country M.P. with an independent country gentleman; and yet, as both I (pp. 120, 222–3, 340–1 below) and David Hayton have pointed out, any analysis of those who supported Country policies at once rules out such an easy stereotype. To take but one of many exceptions: Sir John Cropley M.P. (see Index below), as the son of a London merchant permanently resident in Red Lion Square, can hardly have been fired by strong provincial loyalty, 'sense of place' or the experience of caring for a large landed estate.

in Christendom'.[117] The chief merit of the Brooks thesis lies in underlining the positive and salubrious side of the true Country politician's aims and motives rather than the negative elements of mistrust and cynicism which every ministry, to some degree, inspired;[118] its chief defect is to ignore the skeletons in the Country cupboard or, at best, to accord them a brief and nonchalant recognition before locking them hastily away out of sight.[119]

By contrast, one of the great strengths of David Hayton's essay on 'the Country Interest' of the years 1689-1720 lies in dragging these same skeletons from their murky hiding places. He recognizes the scores of politicians, both Tory and Whig, who took up Country causes when it suited them, 'acting the patriot' either to pursue factious ends or to work off a grudge against particular ministers or to promote personal ambition. In the latter category he notes especially how often a cluster of gifted young men on the way up – the 'young sparks . . . anxious to cut a figure' in the Commons – flirted extravagantly with popular and patriotic causes, doubtless in the belief (usually justified) that this would increase their bargaining power with their own leaders or the Queen's managers.[120] While I hint at this phenomenon, Hayton exposes it brilliantly and drives home the point with impressive division-list evidence.[121] His essay is the most persuasive exercise in the re-interpretation of a major political theme of this period for well over a decade. He shows, among much else, that while the Tories provided the bulk of the numbers, the 'infantry' as he puts it, of the Country forces in the late 1690s and the first two decades of the next century, it was 'Old Whigs' (with a few exceptions, notably Davenant) who were the chief ideologists and propagandists.[122] For good measure Hayton's work illuminates the structure

---

117. See C. Jones (ed.), *op. cit.* pp. 107–21; cf. below, pp. 42–4, 145–6.

118. But see also below, pp. 118, 123, 125. Brooks misleads when he claims (*loc. cit.* p. 135) that I 'fell back in conclusion into characterizing "the investigation of government accounts and administrative abuses" as "unhealthy"'. What I in fact see as unhealthy is the way a once wholesome Country cause was in Anne's reign (e.g. in 1711–12) shamelessly exploited by party men for party ends.

119. E.g. Brooks, *loc. cit.* p. 143, para 4.

120. Hayton, *loc. cit.* (n. 113), p. 53.

121. Perhaps he errs just too far at times on the side of cynicism. His treatment of Stanhope's and King's roles in the 'Whimsical' proceedings of 1705–7 is an instance (*loc. cit.* pp. 50–1; cf. below, pp. 131–3). Similarly his suggestion of a 'Junto conspiracy' to set up the struggle for the place clause in the Regency Bill so as to put pressure on Godolphin (p. 51) seems to me inherently improbable and inconsistent with solid evidence to the contrary.

122. *Loc. cit.* pp. 55–6.

as well as the content of politics, not only supporting my contention that the true Country Whigs had become a dwindling rump by Anne's reign but demonstrating that their shrinkage was even more drastic than I had imagined, and probably began as early as 1699.[123]

If the Whigs of the age of Anne were clinging on only tenuously to their predecessors' role as a Country party (so tenuously that in 1716 only 33 Whig members out of 340 could be found to vote against the Septennial Bill and for the Old Whig principle of frequent Parliaments),[124] still less, it may be thought, did they fill the bill as a *radical* party. The distinction is not a simple one; for whereas there was an active and vocal band of Whigs before 1688 convinced that after the excesses of Charles II and his brother the health and pristine purity of the body politic could only be restored by root-and-branch reforms, after the Revolution 'radicals' and 'Country-men'[125] did share a good deal of common ground as to the practical measures that were necessary to achieve reform. This is one reason why twenty years ago I was not convinced that a separate radical tradition played any significant part in the stuff of central politics in the age of Anne. The other reason is a historiographical one. It is only in the very recent past that a few historians of post-Revolution England have begun to show serious interest in taking up the baton handed on by Caroline Robbins,[126] treating the residual radical or 'commonwealth' element among the Whigs which survived the Glorious Revolution as matter for profitable investigation.[127] Mark Goldie, in particular, has stressed the bitter disillusionment of the 'True Whigs' with the work of the Convention Parliament, and not least with the alleged

123. *Loc. cit.* pp. 47–8, 50–3; cf. below, pp. 220–3. Hayton challenges a number of my ascriptions of individual M.P.s as 'Country Whigs', and except in a few cases (e.g. Sir Richard Onslow) his evidence for doing so is impressive.

124. See above, pp. xiii–xiv.

125. The former is a historian's rather than a contemporary expression, a convenience for labelling those Whigs prepared for fundamental change in the constitutional, political and (as some believed) electoral system.

126. C. Robbins, *The Eighteenth-Century Commonwealthmen* (Cambridge, Mass., 1959). See also above, n. 76.

127. Note especially M. Goldie, 'The Roots of True Whiggism, 1689–94', *History of Political Thought*, 1 (1980); also L. G. Schwoerer, *'No Standing Armies!'* (Baltimore, 1976), ch. 8; A. B. Worden (ed.), *A Voyce from the Watch Tower: Part Five: 1660–1662* (Camden Soc. 4th ser., 21, 1978), Introduction; J. A. G. Pocock (ed.), *The Political Works of James Harrington* (Cambridge, 1977), Historical Introduction, ch. 7. More recently H. T. Dickinson has contributed a valuable essay, 'The Precursors of Political Radicalism in Augustan Britain', to C. Jones (ed.), *Britain in the First Age of Party, 1680–1750* (1987).

betrayal of the party's old principles over the formula agreed for the settlement of the crown and over the terms of the Declaration of Rights.[128] The radicals, small in number in Parliament but influential and conscious of themselves as guardians of the Whig conscience, could not forgive the 'Court Whigs' (prominent among whom were Somers and Wharton) for a compromise which we can recognize was unavoidable but which they saw as shameful apostasy; and they never again trusted either the 'New Right' of their own party or the new King. Even though the one-time republicanism of the more extreme parliamentary radicals had now been transmuted into reluctant acceptance of the institution of kingship, that was deemed tolerable only within a constitutional framework set by sovereign and regularly re-elected Parliaments, a secularized and contractual monarchy with a shackled prerogative, and an unquestioned right of resistance for the subject. Despite the deaths of veteran leaders such as Hampden, Birch and Wildman, these 'True Whigs' or Commonwealthmen recovered their dynamic in the late 1690s under the intellectual leadership of John Toland and Samuel Johnson. Though strongly supporting the parliamentary attacks on the standing army and on William's land grants, they did so from an ideological position distinct from that of the Whig dissidents in Harley's New Country party who led those campaigns, and who were now sliding into ever closer association with the Tories.[129]

It must be said that during Anne's reign, as such, apart from a few more literary and propagandist flurries[130] and occasional discreet pressure on Harley, the voice of 'True' Whiggery was strangely muted. And one revealing yardstick of this is the rapidly declining influence of Whig radicals in what had long been their chief extra-parliamentary stronghold, the City of London. There, as we now know, Whiggery during the years 1689–1714 became increasingly dominated by an establishment group of wealthy aldermen, in cahoots with the Junto, while ironically the populist image

128. For the tussle over the latter, see L. G. Schwoerer, *The Declaration of Rights, 1689* (Baltimore & London, 1981); articles by Horwitz and Frankle, cited above, n. 79.

129. See below, p. 259. The radicals' ideological position was cemented by a startling sequence of publications of neo-republican texts in the years 1697–1700: not only Harrington's *Oceana* – their bible – but Milton's *Works*, Sidney's *Discourses*, and Ludlow's *Memoirs* (edited and orchestrated by Toland).

130. E.g. Robert Molesworth's *The Principles of a Real Whig* (1711). For a useful extract see H. T. Dickinson, *Politics and Literature in the Eighteenth Century* (1974).

was slowly appropriated by the Tories.[131] Nevertheless, after the dissolution of the Junto early in George I's reign the radical whig tradition did re-surface in a modified form, through the writings of Trenchard and Gordon, among others.[132] After the early 1690s there was never anything but a tiny, dedicated, vocal minority to carry the torch (they appealed to the Whig conscience in a way not unlike the influence of the nonjurors on the right-wing conforming Tories). Moreover their *popular* base – and this needs to be stressed – was at this stage almost negligible, especially outside the capital. Yet their ideas deserve a modest place in any up-to-date account of the substance of early 18th-century Whiggery.[133]

III

There can be no doubt that a Country programme of reform, including measures welcome to genuine radicals, acquired extra bite and attracted additional support in the years after 1689 as a result of the long wars against the France of Louis XIV. Thus war swelled the ranks of the civil office-holders as well as the armed forces, thereby stimulating the enthusiasm for 'place' legislation. It also increased opportunities for peculation (for example, the abuse of army and navy contracts) and roused the anger of a tax-harried legislature against corruption and those who practised it. The astringency which war lent to the disputes between Country and Court was far surpassed, however, by the bitterness it injected into the struggle between Whigs and Tories. And this was not simply because of the issues of policy and principle it threw up directly.[134] but also because of the new economic pressures it exerted on British society and its aggravation of some already-existing pressures. Earlier we observed its baleful effects on the

131. G. S. De Krey, 'Political Radicalism in London after the Glorious Revolution', *Journ. Mod. Hist.* 55 (1983); *idem, A Fractured Society: The Politics of London in the First Age of Party, 1688–1715* (Oxford, 1985).

132. Robbins, *op. cit.*; Dickinson, *Liberty and Property*, ch. 5.

133. By the 1740s it was not only in London that the radical initiative was slipping to the Tories. See L. J. Colley, 'Eighteenth-Century Radicalism before Wilkes', *Trans. R.Hist.Soc.* 5th ser., 31 (1981).

134. See above, pp. xxx–i and n. 80.

Anglican clergy.[135] Scores of London merchants and shippers found their profits seriously diminished by enemy action and high insurance premiums; and many were only too happy to divert their capital into ventures less hazardous than the trades with Spain, the Levant or the West Indies. A joint-stock boom, a radically new system of government credit finance and the establishment of a state bank, all before 1696,[136] provided their opportunity. There was no such solace for hard-hit landowners and farmers. The general level of landed rents was already depressed in many areas even before 1689. Thereafter the wartime land tax and the difficulty of finding tenants – at least, good tenants – in a period marked by violent harvest fluctuations piled up further problems on the 'mere' gentry in stiffly-taxed arable counties. The more overburdened and embarrassed among them thus became singularly ripe for political exploitation; and it was Tory leaders and polemicists who eagerly exploited them, playing on their anxieties and on their resentment against the 'monied' profiteers of the new 'financial revolution'. For the latter, like those other wartime bugbears of the landed interest, army officers and bureaucrats, could conveniently be linked with Whiggish policies and politicians. Thus was a powerful dose of the toxic of social conflict introduced into the substance of politics, especially in the middle and later years of Anne.

'The Clash of Interests', the chapter of *British Politics in the Age of Anne* which analysed this conflict and assessed its political importance, has weathered the intervening years less well than the rest. A high tide of new research into the economy, finance and society has left its timbers somewhat battered. The City of London's financial and trading community has been closely studied since 1967, beginning in that year with the publication of Dickson's classic study of the revolution in public finance.[137] A vast amount more has been learned in the last twenty years about the problems and opportunities confronting landowners in the late 17th and early 18th

---

135. See above, p. xxi.
136. See below, pp. 152–5.
137. P. G. M. Dickson, *The Financial Revolution* (n. 62 above), chs. 1, 2, 11; D. W. Jones, 'London Merchants and the Crisis of the 1690s', in P. Clark and P. Slack (eds.), *Crisis and Order in English Towns* (1970); R. Grassby, 'English Merchant Capitalism in the Late 17th Century', *Past and Present* 46 (1970); B. W. Hill, 'The Change of Government and the "Loss of the City", 1710–1711', *Econ. H.R.* 24 (1971); G. S. De Krey, *A Fractured Society* (see n. 131 above), chs. 1, 3–6.

centuries,[138] and we understand better how 'the new taxation' worked and where and how deeply it bit.[139] Some progress has been made, too, towards a clearer comprehension of both the scale and social implications of the rise of 'the military men' and of the rapid growth of the civil service.[140] In the remainder of this Introduction, with these new maps and compasses to guide us, we shall re-trace the ground first covered in chapter 5[141] and enquire how far the arguments and conclusions of that initial survey stand in need of revision.

In 1969 William Speck was able to draw upon Dickson's authoritative work on finance as well as on Clay's doctoral research into Hertfordshire and East Anglian landowners to readdress the question 'was the conflict between the landed and the monied interests . . . a myth or a reality?' and to assess how seriously it threatened the stability of the Augustan political system.[142] He concluded, as I did, that the reality was beyond question but laid still greater stress on the gravity of its political effects down to 1713. His beautifully argued essay remains to this day an indispensable complement to chapter 5. As a corrective its principal importance lay in defining more

138. The recent literature on landownership in our period is voluminous, with the most prolific contributions coming from Sir John (H.J.) Habakkuk, J. V. Beckett, C. G. A. Clay and B. A. Holderness. Most of the relevant periodical and thesis material can be found among the footnote references in Beckett's 'The Pattern of Landownership in England and Wales, 1660–1880', *Econ. H.R.* 37 (1984). See also Beckett's *The Aristocracy in England, 1660–1914* (Oxford, 1986), ch. 2, Clay's 'Landlords and Estate Management in England', ch. 14 of Joan Thirsk (ed.), *The Agrarian History of England and Wales*, V.ii (1640–1750), the parallel chapter (15) on Wales, by D. W. Howell, and two valuable book-length studies: P. Roebuck, *Yorkshire Baronets, 1640–1760* (Oxford, 1980) and P. Jenkins, *The Making of a Ruling Class: The Glamorgan Gentry, 1640–1790* (Cambridge, 1985). Also of relevance to the 'conflict of interests' is N. Rogers, 'Money, Land and Lineage: The Big Bourgeoisie of Hanoverian London', *Social Hist.* 4 (1979).

139. See C. Brooks, 'Public Finance and Political Stability: the administration of the Land Tax, 1688–1720', *Hist. Journ.* 17 (1974); J. V. Beckett, 'Local Custom and the "New Taxation" in the 17th and 18th Centuries', *Northern Hist.* 12 (1976); *id.*, 'Land Tax or Excise: the levying of taxation in seventeeth- and eighteenth-century England', *E.H.R.* 100 (1985).

140. G. E. Aylmer, 'From office-holding to civil service: the genesis of the modern bureaucracy', *Trans.R.Hist.Soc.* 30 (1980); G. Holmes, *The Professions and Social Change in England, 1680–1730*, 1979 Raleigh Lecture (1981); *id.*, *Augustan England* (see n. 39), chs. 8, 9 and Bibl. Notes, pp. 313–18.

141. Below, pp. 148–82.

142. W. A. Speck, 'Conflict in Society', in G. Holmes (ed.), *Britain after the Glorious Revolution* (1969).

strictly than I had done the terms of both the historiographical and the contemporary debates. Whereas I had concerned myself with the political allegiances of, and attitudes towards, 'businessmen' in a wide sense[143] – including manufacturers, domestic traders, contractors and overseas merchants as well as large stock- and fund-holders, brokers, private bankers and other financiers – Speck emphasised that 'the monied interest', as such, was a term used very precisely by contemporaries: referring 'not to traders and merchants in general, but to those elements in society who were involved in the new machinery of public credit . . .'[144] On the other side of the fence, while I was at pains to stress that the war years between 1702 and 1713 were 'a grim period for those middling and small gentry whose income was derived solely, or almost exclusively, from their rents', adding that 'the distinction between them and their more fortunate [landed] brethren is . . . quite basic', Speck maintained that in contemporary eyes membership of 'the landed *interest*' and exclusive dependence on rents were synonymous.[145]

If there are occasions in chapter 5 when I use the term 'monied man' too loosely, it is now clear that there are almost as many pitfalls in a usage that is over-strict. One reason why the post-Revolution 'conflict of interests' generated so much heat yet so little light is that the older social and economic groups in early 18th-century England, such as the gentry (Whigs as well as Tories), the yeomanry, the clergy, and even members of the established professions, found it difficult to analyse with any true precision that 'new interest'[146] which had burst on the scene only since 1688, accumulating so much wealth so rapidly and encroaching in the process on traditional political preserves. When I remark that 'moneyed man' was 'a pejorative expression which . . . often meant different things to different people'[147] I under- rather than overplay the ambiguity. Swift, like other Tory propagandists, found it convenient to pretend (indeed, may have partly believed) that there was a novel and discrete breed of 'retailers of money' which was wholly the product of the financial revolution inaugurated in 1693–4; which was (of course!) Whig in politics, warmongering, and electorally invasive. But the truth was infinitely more complex.

143. See below, p. 151.
144. *Loc. cit.* p. 135.
145. *Ibid*; cf. below, p. 157.
146. Bodl.MS.Eng.Misc.e.180, f.4: Henry St. John to Lord Orrery, 9 July 1709.
147. Below, p. 151.

Just a few examples of this complexity must suffice. In the first place, there were relatively few big City investors in Bank of England, East India or South Sea stock in the years 1694–1714 who were not also heavily involved in one or more other branches of business activity; and this was almost as true of the immigrant Dutch, Flemish and Huguenot business communities as of the native English. Nor, as Dickson has shown,[148] were there more than a small number of men dealing in the market in Anne's reign who were stockbrokers or jobbers pure and simple. Such notorious operators as 'Vulture' Hopkins and William Sheppard who made fortunes out of handling transactions on the market were far outnumbered by bankers or merchants for whom the jobbing trade was a profitable sideline. Furthermore, the big government creditors and the leading stockholders and directorates of both the Bank and the New (later the United) East India Company and South Sea Company were quite heavily dominated by City tycoons who had built up their capital originally through overseas commerce, or occasionally through domestic trade or manufacture. They frequently maintained a heavy commitment to one or the other, and in some cases even to both.[149] Above all, as the work of D. W. Jones and Gary De Krey has amply demonstrated, *merchant* wealth was not only crucial to the beginnings of the financial revolution – in the shape, especially, of the spare capital of the Iberian wine merchants and the West India traders[150] – but vital to its continuance. Even that quintessential 'monied man' Sir Gilbert Heathcote[151] never ceased trading, either to the Baltic or across the Atlantic, during the wars, and he continued to do so with renewed energy after they were over. Thus the distinction Henry St. John carefully drew for the benefit of his party's backbenchers, between those men of capital helping to create national wealth through foreign or domestic trade, who were to be applauded, and those simply living off that wealth like parasites, who were to be deplored,[152] was always a largely artificial one.

148. *Financial Revolution*, ch. 20, *passim*.

149. E.g. Sir Owen Buckingham, M.P. (see below, p. 522), salter, sail manufacturer and merchant trading both to the Baltic and the West Indies.

150. Modern research has fully endorsed the verdict in 1694 of that keen contemporary observer of the economy, John Houghton: that 'trade being so obstructed at sea, few that had money were willing it should be idle', and that merchants found the new joint stocks especially attractive because capital invested in them was so readily retrievable 'whensoever they had occasion'. See Jones, 'London Merchants', *op. cit.* p. 334.

151. See below, pp. 156, 174; also an Iberian merchant.

152. See below, p. 169.

Apart from those whose business pedigrees went back long before the Revolution (notably the goldsmith-bankers), the only important groups of City financiers who could be slotted neatly into St. John's pigeon-hole for the monied interest were the small number of full-time stockjobbers and the community of Sephardi Jews settled at Hampstead and Highgate. The wealthier of the latter certainly invested hugely in Bank and loan stock and their international tentacles and alien habits of life and worship made them an object of particular suspicion. Although they played no part in parliamentary or even civic affairs, Jewish financiers were thought to have exerted behind-the-scenes influence on the Godolphin ministry of 1702–10, a faint foreshadowing of the unpopularity of the Pelhams' *eminence grise*, Samson Gideon, in the reign of George II and of the outcry over the Jew Bill of 1753.[153]

Another aspect of the monied interest which flawed the neat symmetry of the image beloved of Tory propagandists was that London's private bankers and scriveners, two of the prime representatives of those 'lender[s] of money' against whom St. John directed his fire, 'who added nothing to the common stock . . . and contributed not a mite to the public charge',[154] neither constituted a 'new interest' nor, for the most part, a Whig one. G. S. De Krey has shown us how by the first two decades of the 18th century the leadership of the Tory party in London politics, while including some merchants, was dominated by domestic traders, industrialists (notably brewers) and, above all, money-lenders: 'the Tory money-lenders were at the heart of their party after 1702'.[155] Of the thirty-odd private bankers still in business by the latter half of Anne's reign, the great majority were Tory in politics and the two biggest, Sir Richard Hoare and Sir Francis Child, were prominent in Parliament. Among the few Whigs in the banking fraternity, two – George Caswall and John Blunt – went over to Harley after the ministerial *renversement* of 1710, and only the veteran Sir Robert Clayton, who died in 1707, had dabbled much in Bank of England stock or government securities. As for the scriveners, London poll books reveal that

153. Dickson, *op. cit.* p. 263; L. S. Sutherland, 'Samson Gideon: Eighteenth-Century Jewish Financier', in *idem, Politics and Finance in the Eighteenth Century*, ed. A. Newman (1984), pp. 387–98; T. W. Perry, *Public Opinion, Propaganda and Politics . . .: a Study of the Jew Bill of 1753* (Harvard, 1962).
154. *A Letter to Sir William Wyndham*, pp. 27–8.
155. G. S. De Krey, *A Fractured Society*, p. 126.

as a livery they were overwhelmingly Tory in their inclinations.[156]

There is yet a further gap that we can now perceive between Tory myth and the reality elucidated by modern scholarship. Historians have generally been prone to exaggerate, as contemporaries did, the amount of big business capital committed to the non-corporate funded loans floated by successive governments from 1693 to 1712. 'The Funds', most typically supporting annuities for lives or for 99 years,[157] were excellent investments for those of small or medium capital; but they could not offer the advantage of liquidity, nor indeed the prospect of large capital gains, to tempt many top-flight merchants and financiers.[158] Furthermore, a significant number of fundholders were provincials. And this, not least of all, sets them apart from the biggest stockholders and directors of the great financial and commercial corporations of the day who were the true core of the monied interest. Dickson's investigation of the English financial revolution[159] revealed two aspects of this core which go far to explain the acute friction that developed between those who dominated and dealt in the major corporate stocks and the aggrieved cohorts of the landed interest. Firstly, the heart of the 'monied interest' was overwhelmingly a London phenomenon: only three of the 74 men who held £5000 or more of Bank stock before the new subscription in 1709 were domiciled outside the capital or the Home Counties. Secondly, it had a remarkably large alien component, very substantial blocks of stock in both the Bank and the New and United East India Companies being held not only by Jews but by Protestant immigrants from the Continent. What is more, many were first generation arrivals and not a few of these achieved scintillating success in the City – men such as Sir Theodore Jansen, whose meteoric rise from the late 1680s was ended only by the South Sea Bubble.[160] The anonymous squire who complained to Robert Harley in March 1702 that the result of

156. See, e.g., W. A. Speck, *Tory and Whig*, p. 118. Even more than the goldsmith-bankers, the scriveners saw in the emergence of a state bank and a whole range of marketable 'gilt-edged' securities a serious threat to their traditional role as brokers, mortgagees and moneylenders.

157. But from 1710–12 a variety of lottery prizes.

158. Dickson, *op. cit.* pp. 61, 262.

159. See also Alice C. Carter's pamphlet, *The English Public Debt in the 18th Century* (1968).

160. See below, pp. 157, 531. He is said to have come to England with £10,000 in his pocket after the Revocation of the Edict of Nantes. Carter, *op. cit.* p. 17.

161. H.M.C. *Portland MSS.* viii, 96.

recent Treasury policies had been 'to enrich Dutch, Jews, French and other foreigners, scoundrel stock-jobbers and tally-jobbers who have been sucking our vitals for many years'[161] undoubtedly had a point.

Weighing just as heavily with the Tory 'men of estates' was the fact that, apart from a small minority whose families had been naturalized since the late 16th or early 17th centuries, few of these aliens ever darkened the doors of an Anglican church. The Huguenots alone had eleven churches of their own in the capital as early as 1688, and it has been claimed – no doubt with some exaggeration – that by Anne's reign the number had increased to 30.[162] But if foreign Protestants had a relatively high profile among the new breed of public creditors the native dissenting presence was even more obtrusive. Some remarkable evidence on this has recently been assembled by De Krey. For instance, of the 89 directors of the Bank between 1694 and 1715 no fewer than 38 (43%) were Presbyterians, Independents or Baptists.[163] Indeed, the most important new dimension I would incorporate now into my 1967 picture of 'the clash of interests' is the religious dimension. Like the pro-Sacheverell mobs who roamed the streets of the capital in March 1710 crying 'Down with the Bank of England and the meeting-houses; and God damn the Presbyterians and all that support them',[164] the Anglican Tory gentry of Queen Anne's reign detected an obnoxious and sinister connection between the *arrivistes* whose luxurious coaches rolled 'between the Excheq[ue]r & the Exchange'[165] and the brazenly flourishing state of religious nonconformity in London. For a landed class that had by now severed almost all its remaining ties with a Puritan past the monied men aggravated all their other sins with the most unforgivable sin of all (in Tory eyes, at least), the stigma of religious Dissent.

To compound that sin, the same men were often *social* nonconformists into the bargain. 'It is not perhaps surprising', as Alice Carter has observed, 'that investment in stocks rather than investment in land should appeal to

162. C. E. Whiting, *Studies in English Puritanism . . . 1660–1688* (1931), pp. 359–61.
163. The proportion includes some whose membership of congregations cannot be definitely established but who were of proven dissenting sympathies. One-third of the directors of the New and United East India Companies, 1698–1715, were likewise 'in the dissenting interest'. De Krey, p. 109, Table 3.8.
164. Holmes, *Trial*, pp. 167–8.
165. Bodl. MS. Carte 117, f. 177.

Jews or Huguenots, who have so much experience of migration. The migrant above all requires to keep his wealth in as "liquid" a guise as possible.'[166] I argue below that in the eyes of country gentlemen the ultimate iniquity of the monied men at large was that for twenty to thirty years after 1688 they rarely sank their capital in large landed estates.[167] Subsequent research has, for the most part, powerfully supported the assumption that a revolution in public finance changed the attitude of London businessmen towards land purchase and even towards the governing criteria of social status. From around 1693 the traditional urge to cement the gains of a successful business career by moving its profits progressively into landed property was strongly counteracted by the great flexibility and high returns of the new paper investments.[168] The reaction lasted for fully twenty years, was checked – but no more than that – by the conclusion of peace with France and Spain in 1713–14, and was not reversed until 1720, the year of the South Sea crisis. Even thereafter it remained quite normal practice for rich City financiers and merchants to stay out of the land market, save perhaps for residential purposes, until very late in their lives or active careers.[169] To many in the landed interest it seemed monstrous that Londoners whose new riches were giving them access to political influence should evade both the heavy taxation and social responsibilities which an extensive landed estate incurred.[170]

166. Carter, *op. cit.* p. 17.

167. See below, pp. 161–3. It should be added that attitudes to the Jews were ambivalent. There was resentment at their evading the Land Tax mixed with apprehension that if they acquired estates they might acquire Church advowsons with them. The religious objection, Dr. Cruickshanks has reminded me, was to be widely voiced during the Jew Bill debates of 1753.

168. There were of course exceptions, some of them surprising: e.g. the dissenting East India merchant Sir Samuel Sambrooke, and the financier Sir James Bateman, whose family were naturalized Flemings.

169. Daniel Defoe, *A Tour through England and Wales* (Everyman edn. 1928), i, 6, 158, 168; C. G. A. Clay, 'The Price of Freehold Land in the Later 17th and 18th Centuries', *Econ. H.R.* 27 (1974), pp. 184–7; Sir J. Habakkuk, 'The Rise and Fall of English Landed Families', II, *Trans. R.Hist. Soc.* 30 (1979), pp. 213–16; R. Grassby, 'English Merchant Capitalism' (n. 137 above), pp. 93–4. Cf. the slight caveat entered by Nicholas Rogers (n. 138 above) in *Social Hist.* 4 (1979), pp. 448–9; but note that the case-histories of London aldermen, on which his qualification was based, take no account of Jews, very little of naturalized foreigners (few of whom found their way on to the bench), and not much more of native dissenters, who provided only 18 out of 64 aldermen in the period 1688–1715.

170. Cf. below, pp. 161–2, 172–6.

But what of the Tory gentry's assumption that one had only to scratch a monied man to find a Whig? Suitable caution was expressed in my original text about any wholesale conflation of the monied interest with Whiggery.[171] Yet subsequent analysis of the directorates of the Bank of England, the Million Bank and the New and United East India Companies in the period 1694–1715 has revealed, among those directors involved in City corporation affairs, only 13 Tories compared with 73 Whigs. Harley's administration tried hard to protect its own creation, the South Sea Company, from a Whig takeover; but even in its first four years of life City Whigs still contrived to capture 10 of the 18 directorships that fell to the financial and mercantile community. Among London's overseas merchants, regardless of their scale of operation, Tories were vastly outnumbered.[172] It is true that the first year of Harley's Tory ministry of 1710–14 was to show that, given enough encouragement from the Treasury, some Whig financiers and one or two of the City's merchant princes were perfectly prepared to put 'business as usual' before extremes of partisanship.[173] But this made little difference to the sense of alienation experienced by the smaller fry among the London liverymen: the mass of small tradesmen, craftsmen and artisans who felt just as resentful as any country squire or parish parson of the enormous fortunes made by the new City élite. It was their votes which enabled the Tory party in the London wards to capture control of the Common Council from the once-populist Whigs.[174]

There was, therefore, a 'conflict of interests' within the City as well as between the City and those whose incomes rested entirely on the ownership of land; and it has been enriching to the understanding of politics in the age

171. See below, pp. 166–70, *passim*. The provincial examples given there are of doubtful relevance to the debate.

172. De Krey, p. 125, Table 4.2; pp. 128–30.

173. George Caswall, John Blunt, Sir James Bateman, Sir Theodore Janssen, Sam Shepheard senr., and John Ward of Hackney were prominent examples. In April 1711 Heathcote's inveterate party in the Bank of England lost control of Bank policy to the moderates. De Krey, *passim*; John Carswell, *The South Sea Bubble* (1960), ch. 3; B. W. Hill, 'Loss of the City' (above, n. 137).

174. This capture, made in 1705, was twenty years later to lead to Walpole's controversial City Elections Act. In general see H. Horwitz, 'Party in a Civic Context: London from the Exclusion Crisis to the Fall of Walpole', in C. Jones (ed.), *Britain in the First Age of Party, 1680–1750* (1987); Horwitz (ed.), 'Minutes of a Whig Club 1714–1717', Introduction, in Horwitz, Speck and Gray, *London Politics 1713–1717* (London Record Soc. 1981), pp. 1–10; De Krey, *op. cit.* ch. 5.

of Anne to learn, as we have of late, how the parties in the heart of England, the great metropolis, not only wrangled over issues of religion, foreign and war policy and trade but 'also articulated in their rivalry the deep-seated social antagonisms that cleft the City electorate in twain'.[175] On the parliamentary and national stage, however, it was the grievances of the landed interest which attracted infinitely more publicity. The work of the past twenty years has done much to confirm the reality of the controversial rise of a 'new interest' in the City, while dispelling some of the myths which have coloured our perception of its character and political bias. It remains to enquire whether the much-trumpeted plight of the landowners retains the same credibility.

When Professor Speck and I wrote about the conflict of interests in the late 1960s the study of landownership in the late 17th and early 18th centuries was still overshadowed by the arguments of H. J. (now Sir John) Habakkuk: above all, by his pioneering essay 'English Landownership, 1680–1740' (1940). In this essay, on the evidence of two counties, Northamptonshire and Bedfordshire, he worked out a complex hypothesis both to chart and explain what he saw as a decline of the lesser gentry and of the owner-occupiers to the benefit of 'the large estate and the great lord' – a hypothesis in which the war years of 1689–1713, war finance and most of all the new land tax played a central part.[176] More recently Sir John has returned to his old stamping-grounds,[177] refining but on the whole adhering to and bolstering his earlier ideas. For political historians reassessing the animosity between landed and monied interests the most important development of a thesis which now focuses more sharply than ever on the period *c.* 1690–*c.* 1720 as one of singular difficulty for landowners, is the strong emphasis on the settlement of estates. These are seen not just as a factor protecting the larger landed patrimonies but as one of the commonest root sources of financial embarrassment in gentry families under the last two Stuarts. Many such families, it is said, went into

---

175. De Krey, p. 176.
176. *Econ. H.R.* 10 (1939–40). This was followed by further essays, 1951–65, developing his arguments about interest rates and land prices, the spread of the practice of 'strict settlement', the land market, and the disappearance of the small, independent landowner. For full titles and details see Beckett, 'Pattern of Landownership', *Econ. H.R.* 37 (1984), p. 4n.
177. 'The Rise and Fall of English Landed Families, 1600–1800', I and II, *Trans. R.Hist. Soc.* 29–30 (1979–80).

the war years after 1689 already committed to the practice of making secure provision for the future of their younger sons or for the marriage portions of their daughters by charges on their estates, charges that were often made possible only by mortgages. Habakkuk argues that the spread of this practice was rapid and was much encouraged by the easier credit available in post-Restoration England, as mortgage rates came down from 10 per cent in 1624 to 5 per cent or lower by the 1680s. For such families, therefore, the most chronic problem after 1689 was not so much static or falling rent returns or high taxation – serious though these often were – but the sheer difficulty of raising credit at a time when joint stocks and government 'Funds' often proved far more attractive investments than lending on the mortgage market.[178]

If such were indeed the circumstances it was understandable if the sufferers made whipping-boys out of the politicians who implemented 'Whig' financial policies and out of the self-interested machinations of the City, even though in fact they had fallen into an unforeseeable pit of their own digging. It must be conceded that the hypothesis – and as yet it is no more – does rest upon some plausible foundations. The rapid, if geographically uneven, spread of the settlement habit after 1660 is now generally accepted, as is the fact that most settlements were attempts to make a secure provision for the whole family; and Habakkuk himself has found in the numerous estate acts of 1689–1714 further evidence as to how far down the gentry ladder the practice had already reached.[179] By the time of the mid 18th-century wars against France, moreover, it had become part of the English landowner's gospel that periods of warfare made the Funds more attractive and mortgages more scarce and expensive,[180] and there is every reason to believe that this conviction had taken root from the experience of the Spanish Succession War and its aftermath. It would be wrong, of course, to underestimate the extreme reluctance of established landed gentlemen to dismember their estates by sales; and it is probable that the truly determined owner in difficulties could usually find a lender, at a

178. Mortgage rates were pegged by law to a maximum of 6%. See Habakkuk, 'Rise and Fall', I, 199–200, 203; cf. below p. 162.

179. See n. 196 below; L. Bonfield, *Marriage Settlements, 1601–1740* (Cambridge, 1983); C. G. A. Clay, 'Property Settlements, Financial Provision for the Family and the Sale of Land by the Greater Landowners, 1660–1790', *Journ. Brit. Studies*, 21 (1981); J. V. Beckett, *The Aristocracy in England*, pp. 59, 63 n. 73.

180. Beckett, *op. cit.* p. 83. Settled land itself could not be mortgaged: hence the need for estate acts to break settlements.

pinch, even in wartime. It is even likelier that a combination of smaller-sized families, compared with the first half of the 17th century, and far wider job opportunities in business or the professions in the forty years after 1680[181] helped in general to mitigate the charges on already-settled estates and reduced the need in future settlements to make *landed* provision for younger sons. Nevertheless no up-to-date reassessment of the contribution of social tensions to party rivalry in the age of Anne can entirely neglect this new perspective, focusing on the effects of strict settlement.[182] At the very least it should have relevance to the situation in the south-east of England, the region where the lure of the new investment openings was strongest, the rates of interest charged on loans probably highest, and the turnover of gentry properties, significantly, fastest.

What is clear is that more light and shade must now be brought into the picture of the landowners' condition nationally. The keynote of the large corpus of recent work on landownership[183] has been the stress on variety. In part this has been a reaction against a hypothesis based originally on research into two counties: both south midland shires, not far distant from London, agriculturally prosperous in normal times, and in 1688 already well implanted with established aristocratic and wealthy gentry families, dominant in their county communities. Political historians, too, must learn to temper their generalizations about the plight of landowners by introducing more and subtler variables than most of us were aware of in the 1960s: the multiplicity of individual and family circumstances, for instance – circumstances resistant to type-casting and remarkably prone to chance, even in a settlement-conscious age;[184] or the extent to which difficulties

181. G. Holmes, *Augustan England* (1983), *passim*; *idem*, *Politics, Religion and Society in England, 1679–1742* (1986), pp. 262–9, 309–50. In creating many hundreds of new career opportunities in the armed services and the bureaucracy, war was actually a boon to hard-pressed landowners rather than the villain of the piece.

182. It should be noted that other effects, which have been much debated over the years by economic historians, e.g. the limitations of settlement as an instrument for holding together great estates, are not at issue here.

183. See above, n. 138.

184. Chance could, for example, burden an estate with a string of daughters, each requiring a portion and some, quite probably, a mortgage to supply it; or with a long-lived dowager; alternatively it might relieve its problems with a fortunate inheritance or a lucrative marriage. And no amount of human prescience could normally prevent the good stewardship of several generations being destroyed by one recklessly profligate owner, or by the ultimate Act of God, a failure of male heirs (a much commoner occurrence for basic demographic reasons in the century 1650–1750 than in the centuries before and after).

experienced by many families during the French wars were carried over from earlier years, sometimes from as far back as 1642–60, sometimes from the 1680s, a decade of glut harvests, depressed rents and falling land prices. Regional differences, too, profoundly affected both the problems and the opportunities of landowners. Studies of lowland counties are no sure guide to what was happening in upland counties. Direct taxation undoubtedly caused difficulties in some parts of England; yet in others it was next to negligible. The lesser gentry of Lincolnshire or Devonshire or Cumbria, though they suffered their share of wartime casualties, proved more resilient than those of the South-East. Even the small owners, 'the yeomanry', who appear in general to have done more of the suffering while the gentry did most of the moaning, fared very much better in some counties (especially pastoral counties) than in others.[185] Also to be kept in mind are the diverse fortunes *within* the same region or county dictated by, *inter alia*, soil conditions, types of farming, or the proximity of some estates to a flourishing town and therefore a busy market. Thus even during the Spanish Succession War raising a mortgage was rarely as serious a problem for landowners not far removed from booming manufacturing towns such as Leeds and Birmingham or from expanding ports such as Liverpool and Bristol as for those in the rural heart of, say, Bedfordshire or Suffolk.[186]

There were two respects in which my original argument did take careful account of the wide diversity of the English landowners' experience in the years of the wars against Louis XIV. They are best summed up in the following passage: 'it is understandable . . . that the country gentleman of *a few hundreds a year*, living in *any region that experienced the full rigours of the land tax*, should have been readily convinced that war and its concomitants, while enriching men whom he regarded as his social inferiors, was steadily encompassing his own ruin.'[187] Modern scholarship has not seriously challenged the opinion that, all other things being more or less equal, the scale of an estate was a fairly crucial determinant of the Augustan landowner's capacity to weather the economic storms of 1689–1713. And certainly it has not quarrelled in the slightest with the view of well-

185. J. V. Beckett, 'The Decline of the Small Landowner . . .', *Agric. Hist. Rev.* 30 (1982), and 'Pattern of Landownership', *loc. cit.* pp. 17–18.

186. Clay, 'Landlords and Estate Management', in Thirsk, *op. cit.* p. 172; cf. below, p. 162.

187. Below, pp. 161–2 (original not italicized).

informed contemporaries that the incidence of the new 4 shilling Aid, first voted in 1693, was very uneven. After only two years Charles Davenant, fiscal expert and economist, observed that 'the north and west have not born their due share and proportion of the common burthen'; and it is clear that this was because assiduous lobbying by members from the heavily-represented peripheral counties,[188] including Wales, had succeeded in persuading the House of Commons to perpetuate the compassionate treatment traditionally accorded them as 'poor' and 'backward' regions. As a result, the further north or west a county was, generally speaking, the more unrealistically its real estate was assessed. In 1698, when the land tax became a fixed quota levy, county by county, instead of a pound-rate tax, this situation was accepted and perpetuated. Many Yorkshire landowners were thought to be paying no more than 10 per cent of the true value of their rentals when the tax was levied at 4 shillings in the pound.[189] Cumberland and Westmorland paid, in effect, well under 5 per cent. The willingness of post-Revolution administrations to accept local custom in the raising of the land tax, and to employ local men as assessors, collectors and commissioners – in short, their opting for a quiet life to ensure peaceful acquiescence and a predictable return – all had the effect of building into the system the anomalies that were there almost from the start.[190] The latter were then further compounded by an extraordinary diversity of practice in the actual payment of the tax; for certain landlords were remarkably successful at 'passing the buck', or at least part of the buck, to their tenants.[191]

188. Cornwall alone, it will be remembered, had 44 M.P.s.

189. Though nearer 15% in parts of the East Riding. Roebuck, *Yorkshire Baronets*, p. 173.

190. It is well known that in addition personal estate and 'paper' income (e.g. dividends) soon came to be exempted in practice (see below, p. 161). It was not the case, however, that all salaries likewise escaped. In the civil service and the royal household, for instance, only the lesser functionaries, by and large, received dispensations.

On the land tax, see especially: C. Davenant, *An Essay on Ways and Means of Supplying the War* in *The Political and Commercial Works of . . . Charles D'Avenant*, ed. Sir C. Whitworth (1771), i, 23, 28; H. Horwitz (ed.), *The Parliamentary Diary of Narcissus Luttrell, 1691–1693* (Oxford, 1972), pp. 62, 312–49 *passim*; J. V. Beckett and C. Brooks, arts. cit. at n. 139 above.

191. Roebuck, pp. 228, 322; Clay, 'Landlords and Estate Management', in Thirsk, *op. cit.* p. 225; P. J. Bowden, *ibid.* pp. 72–3. The theory was that rents would be adjusted accordingly if the tenant paid. But the bargain normally worked to the latter's disadvantage.

All the same, it would be misguided to under-estimate the effects of high taxation on literally thousands of realistically assessed estates in the South and East of England. For one thing the land tax was far from being the only fiscal drain on landed resources at this period: landowners, like others, were subject to a series of poll taxes (in the 1690s), to a prodigious rise in the number and level of indirect impositions, and of course to local rates as well. Secondly, the effects were severe simply because they were so persistent. The struggle against France led to easily the most protracted period of warfare for Britain between the later Middle Ages and 1793. But further than that: there was a much longer period than the actual 19 years of fighting when the grip of direct taxation was either wholly unrelaxed or only slightly slackened. Before the land tax was imposed in 1693 there had already been four years of heavy, if more traditional impositions on real estate. Equally significant was the uneasiness of the years of formal peace which punctuated and followed the two French wars. In consequence first of the continuing threat from Louis XIV, and latterly of both the reality and fear of Jacobite insurrection, there were only four years out of 29 between 1693–4 and 1721–2 in which the rate of the land tax came down to the 'peace-time level' of 2 shillings in the pound which was to become the norm under Walpole.[192] The contrast between the pre- and post-Revolution eras was shattering. In the twenty years prior to 1689 the English Exchequer had received only £3¼ million from landowners in direct taxation, aside from their contribution to the Hearth Tax. The yield of the land taxes under William III and Anne was £46 million.

Not surprisingly, economic historians have rarely been able to pinpoint unambiguous casual links between taxation and the decision of individual owners to put all or part of their estates on the market. It is far more realistic to see the notorious land tax in much the same light as the tightness of credit: to think of them as the two last and heaviest bales – both plainly attributable to post-Revolution foreign policy and war finance – laid on the back of many an already grossly overburdened beast. Because of these two inflictions loads of debt which could have been carried with a struggle, possibly even shrugged off in, say, the 1670s or the 1730s could prove insupportable. The basic causes of indebtedness were often far removed from the political arena: ill fortune in the lottery of birth and survival;

---

192. Viz. in 1700, and 1713–15 inclusive. For the rest, landowners suffered 18 years at the highest rate and a further 7 years at 3s. in the £.

prodigality or imprudent social emulation – a factor stressed in chapter 5,[193] relegated to minor status by some recent students of the period,[194] but not infrequently highlighted by contemporaries themselves;[195] or, as was earlier suggested, heavy obligations already entered into in order to fund the increasingly common, and complex, estate settlements of late 17th-century England. But because high taxation and scarce credit translated existing embarassments into mounting financial pressures, and because they could be generalized into emotive and politically-charged issues, they inevitably became the focus of animosity and resentment on the part of the victims.

That the pressures *were* increasing and *were* for many families serious by the age of Anne would still be accepted by most historians of landownership.[196] Even the shining ones, the great squirearchs and the nobility itself, were not necessarily spared them, as the heavy land sales in this period by such families as the Fairfaxes, the Booths, the Robarteses and the Cornwallises remind us. Yet there remains logic in the assumption that (as they themselves frequently and vociferously asserted) the bedrock of the landed interest, the small to middling country gentlemen, were less well equipped to cope with these pressures than the great proprietors. The seriousness of the position in King William's reign may well have been exaggerated. Even thereafter the 'ruin' of families and the total selling up of estates is hard to document; and it is possible that the incidence of such

193. See below, p. 162.

194. E.g. Habakkuk, 'Rise and Fall', I, pp. 198–9.

195. Cf. Daniel Defoe, writing in *The Complete English Tradesman*, i (1726), 244: 'What with excessive high living, which is of late grown so much into a disease, and the ordinary circumstances of families, we find few families of the lower gentry . . . but they are in debt, and in necessitous circumstances, and a great many of greater estates too.' An exaggerated picture, without doubt; but Defoe was too good a journalist to allow hyperbole to lose *all* touch with reality.

196. Sir John Habakkuk has cited the extraordinary increase in the number of private estate Acts which Parliament was called on to pass in the quarter-century after the Revolution, to legalize the sale of settled land for the relief of financial necessities, as one statistical indicator of these rising pressures. (See 'Rise and Fall', II, 201–2, 215, where 260 such Acts are identified in that period, compared with only 77 between 1660 and 1688. Some were in favour of substantial gentry families, but most in favour of the lesser gentry). The statistics are certainly a telling pointer to the spread of the settlement habit well down the landowning league table (see above); but they may conceivably reflect little more than that, along with the greater frequency and length of parliamentary sessions after 1689. (I am grateful to John Beckett for prompting this sceptical reflection.)

ultimate disasters, as opposed to serious injuries, was not much higher in Anne's reign than at any other time in the 17th or 18th centuries. But there can be no doubt that by the second half of the Spanish Succession War, the very time when the monied men were making their most flamboyant advance, the clamour of the Tory gentry (and the less clamorous but noticeable anxiety of some Whig landowners, too) for peace, and also for the imposition of a statutory landed qualification on members of Parliament, was reflecting a genuine feeling of crisis in their ranks.[197] The price of land, for instance, which had actually risen in many areas in the 1690s, fell away again from 1701–13: not only reducing profits from sales but, more seriously, inhibiting lenders.[198] At the same time the two worst harvests for a century (1708–9) were bringing many tenants in the grain-growing regions to their knees and making rents still more difficult to get in than they had been previously.

In conclusion: the ample attention which historians have lavished over the past two decades on the economy, financial history and society of late Stuart and early Hanoverian Britain has deeply enriched our knowledge and understanding of the wider context of the party struggles of the early 18th century. *In toto* it has certainly not relegated to the level of a phoney emotion the conviction, widespread by the middle and later years of Queen Anne, that economic and fiscal changes of such moment were in progress – indecently accelerated by partisan policies and even by extra-national interests[199] – that vital parts of the social fabric of the country were threatened with grievous strains. Not even the remaining preserves of the Church of England, many Tories had come to feel, were out of jeopardy from alien influences in society and government. That said, it is now clearer than it was twenty years ago that even while the bloody and costly Spanish Succession War was still in progress and still under the direction of a seemingly entrenched Whig ministry, the wilder fears expressed were exaggerated and the political anger to some extent misplaced. Summing up, I cannot much improve on this reassessment which I made in 1981:

The rise of a 'new interest' in the City, incorporating 'a sort of property which was not known' in 1688, was no figment of Tory imaginations. It was a blazing comet

---

197. See below, pp. 75–7, 172–4, 178–80.
198. Clay, 'Price of Freehold Land' (above, n. 169).
199. See, e.g., W. A. Speck, 'Conflict in Society', (above., n. 142), pp. 137, 144.

across the London sky, and in its garish light a few emotive incidents, such as the Bank's ill-considered deputation to the Queen in June 1710, not unnaturally took on a sinister significance. But one can also understand how Westminster politicians, dazzled at the time by the comet's light, became blind during Anne's reign to those reassuring signs which can now be distinguished. They were loth to recognize that 'the conflict of interests' was primarily a metropolitan phenomenon: a source of genuine stress in the heavily taxed South-east, but of less account to the many counties where the land tax was lightly assessed and no 'new interest' had intruded into economic life. They either did not realize, or chose not to see, that the numbers of 'monied men' pure and simple – those 'retailers of money' whom Swift denounced as a threat to the constitution – were very few; that fundholders or company directors were more catholic in function, and often more traditional in background and more assimilable socially than hostile propaganda allowed. While noting with apprehension the cautious attitude of London businessmen towards land purchase, interpreting it as a device for evading a just contribution to 'the public charge', country gentlemen rarely observed that this trend pre-dated the financial revolution and even the war, and did not anticipate that it would be reversed once a saner balance was achieved between land values and rents and profits from trade or paper investment.[200]

The Peace of Utrecht took some of the heat out of the conflict but did not resolve it. Land values revived but many London businessmen remained coy in their attitude to the land market. The land tax was halved in 1713 for three years, only to go up again for the next six. Interest rates came down and the government's immediate dependence on the City for large funded loans was reduced. But a Whig ministry came into office in 1714; the international situation was soon tense again; and the unprecedented problem of a long-term National Debt of over £40 million enabled 'the monied men' still to cast their spells. When South Sea stock began to rocket in 1720 even country gentlemen, by the hundred, succumbed (in the vast majority of cases for the first and only time) to the magic lure of a paper fortune. The bursting of the Bubble, however, proved decisive. The crisis stripped away the tinsel from the world of high finance and dulled its glitter; and at the same time it made land, albeit at 24 or 26 years' purchase, seem a profitable as well as a safe investment again.[201] Even those numerous

---

200. G. Holmes, 'The Achievement of Stability', in J. Cannon (ed.), *The Whig Ascendancy*, pp. 18–19. See also the persuasive brief reassessment of the conflict of interests in Colley, *In Defiance of Oligarchy*, pp. 14–16.
201. Clay, 'Price of Land', p. 177; Beckett, *The Aristocracy in England*, p. 82.

merchants and monied men who had previously wanted little to do with it now found land unexpectedly beguiling. What is more, because the South Sea Company was in origin a Tory creation and retained right up to the time of the Bubble a strong Tory presence among its directors and principal stockholders, the opprobrium it incurred 'killed for good the dangerous myth that all the "knavery and cousenage"[202] which the country gentlemen had been coached into attributing to the monied men was purely the monopoly of the Whig side in the City'.[203] Finally, the South Sea crisis confirmed the man of the hour, Robert Walpole, for so long the quintessential Whig, in his conviction that at all costs the country now needed a lengthy period of peace, low taxation and social consensus. In this respect, as in the many others we earlier noted, the years 1720–22 saw the final curtain rung down on the politics of the age of Anne. For some years after 1714 the familiar scenes had continued to be acted out, with similar dialogue but in a theatre whose character and requirements were steadily changing. But for the age of Walpole nothing less than a new play would suffice.

Burton-in-Lonsdale,
December 1986

202. Swift's phrase: *Examiner*, No. 13, 2 Nov. 1710.
203. Holmes, 'Achievement of Stability', *loc. cit.* p. 19.

Appendix

SUPPLEMENTARY MANUSCRIPT SOURCES FOR THE STUDY OF EARLY EIGHTEENTH-CENTURY BRITISH POLITICS

THIS appendix supplements the original List of Manuscript Sources published in the first edition and adopts the same lay-out and conventions (see below, pp. 443–8). Except for many manuscripts listed under the major national repositories, it is comprised largely, but by no means entirely, of collections or documents which have only become available, for practical purposes, in the past twenty years.* I have been fairly ruthless in excluding material whose political value for William III's reign stops short before 1701.

---

* An appreciable amount of material which I had to consult in manuscript during the writing of *British Politics in the Age of Anne* is now available, in whole or in part, in print. It includes two sources of outstanding value: Henry L. Snyder (ed.), *The Marlborough-Godolphin Correspondence* (3 vols., Oxford, 1975) and Clyve Jones and Geoffrey Holmes (eds.), *The London Diaries of William Nicolson, Bishop of Carlisle, 1702–1718* (Oxford, 1985); also, *inter alia*, H. T. Dickinson (ed.), *The Correspondence of Sir James Clavering*, Surtees Soc. Publns. vol. clxxviii, (1967); *idem* (ed.), *The Letters of Henry St. John to the Earl of Orrery, 1709–1711*, Camden Miscellany, vol. xxvi (1975), pp. 137–99; Doreen Slatter (ed.), *The Diary of Thomas Naish*, Wiltshire Arch. and Nat. Hist. Soc., Records, vol. xx (1964); Worsley MSS.1 ('Liste exacte du dernier Parlement . . .'), printed as Appx. XI of R. Sedgwick (ed.), *The History of Parliament: The House of Commons, 1715–1754* (1970), i, 162–187; P. Roberts (ed.), *The Diary of Sir David Hamilton, 1709–1714* (Oxford, 1975); W. A. Speck (ed.), *An Anonymous Parliamentary Diary, 1705–6* [from Camb. Univ. Lib. Add. MS. 7093], Camden Misc., vol. xxiii (1969), pp. 29–84. To the chagrin of students of Queen Anne's reign the three best parliamentary diaries for the House of Commons between the 1688 Revolution and the period of Walpole's administration all belong to the years before June 1702. That of Anchitell Grey [1689–94] has, of course, been in print since 1769. Henry Horwitz has edited *The Parliamentary Diary of Narcissus Luttrell, 1691–1693* from the MS. in All Souls Library (Oxford, 1972); and David Hayton is preparing for publication the diary of Sir Richard Cocks, from Bodleian Library, MS. Eng. Hist. b. 209–10.

BRITISH LIBRARY
Additional MSS.
24475   *Sir Arthur Kaye*
57861-2   *Earl Coningsby*

BODLEIAN LIBRARY
MS. Ballard
3–7, 9, 12, 21, 31,
34, 36, 45, 49   various to Dr Arthur Charlett
MS. Carte
129, 180, 210–12, 238–9, 244   Jacobite Correspondence
MS. Willis
5, 15, 18, 48 *et al.*   Browne Willis
MS. Eng. Hist. b. 209–10   *Sir Richard Cocks* (see n.* above)

PUBLIC RECORD OFFICE
C. 104/113, 116   *Lord Ossulston* (Diary)
C. 110/28 (Pitt MSS.)   *Thomas Pitt*

NATIONAL LIBRARY OF SCOTLAND†
Newhailes Papers   *Sir David Dalrymple, George Lockhart*
Wodrow Papers and Letters   Robert Wodrow, *Thomas Smith*
Yester Papers   *Marquess of Tweeddale*

SCOTTISH RECORD OFFICE, REGISTER HOUSE
Breadalbane MSS.   *Earl of Breadalbane, William Cochran*
Clerk of Penicuik MSS.   *John Pringle*, Robert Pringle
Hamilton MSS.   *4th Duke of Hamilton*
Mar and Kellie MSS.   *Earl of Mar, Sir John Erskine*
Marchmont MSS.   *Earl of Marchmont*
Ogilvy of Innerquharity MSS.   *John Pringle*
Polwarth MSS.   Lord Polwarth
Seafield MSS.   *Earl of Seafield/Findlater*

NATIONAL LIBRARY OF WALES
Ottley MSS.   *Adam Ottley (Bp), Thomas Strangeways*

---

† The papers of Scottish politicians are, in general, listed only where they have significant value for politics in the Parliaments of Great Britain after 1707.

DEUTCHES ZENTRALARCHIV, MERSEBURG, E. GERMANY

Rep XI (England) 25C–

39A *passim* — Bonet to Frederick I and Frederick William I of Prussia

QUAI D'ORSAY, PARIS (*Archives du Ministère des Affaires Etrangères*)

Correspondance Politique,

Angleterre: 230–62 — Gaultier, Torcy, D'Iberville, etc.

OTHER COLLECTIONS [R.O. signifies Record Office]

Ailesbury MSS.	Wiltshire R.O. (*Lord Bruce*)
Ashburnham Letterbooks	East Sussex R.O. (*1st Lord Ashburnham*)
Beaufort (Badminton) MSS.	Duke of Beaufort (*2nd Duke of Beaufort*)
Bishop MSS.	Shropshire R.O. (*Sir Thomas Powys*)
Blair Atholl MSS.	Duke of Atholl (*1st Duke of Atholl*)
Braye MSS.	Formerly in Leicester Museum (*Sir Thomas Cave*)
Brydges MSS.	Hereford and Worcester R.O. (William & Francis Brydges)
Buccleuch (Drumlanrig) MSS.	Duke of Buccleuch (*Duke of Queensberry*)
Chaytor MSS.	N. Yorkshire R.O. (Sir William Chaytor)
Cholmondeley of Cholmondeley MSS.	Cheshire R.O. (*Earl of Cholmondeley*)
Cullum MSS.	W. Suffolk R.O. (*Sir Dudley Cullum*)
Douglas Diary	History of Parliament (*Oley Douglas*)
Ducie MSS.	Gloucestershire R.O. (*Matthew Ducie Moreton*)
Ellesmere (Brackley) MSS.	Northants R.O. (*Earl of Bridgewater*)
Evelyn MSS.	Christ Church, Oxford (*George Evelyn, Sir John Evelyn*)
Foley MSS.	Hereford and Worcester R.O. (*Philip Foley, Thomas Foley*)
Forester MSS.	Shropshire R.O. (*Sir William Forester, George Weld*)
Fox-Strangeways MSS.	Dorset R.O. (*Sir Stephen Fox, Charles Fox*)
Glasgow (Kelburn Castle) MSS.	Earl of Glasgow (*1st Earl of Glasgow*)
Goodwood MSS.	W. Sussex R.O. (*Duke of Richmond*)
Grosvenor MSS.	Duke of Westminster (*Sir Richard Grosvenor*)

Gurdon MSS.	E. Suffolk R.O. (*Richard Berney*; Thornhagh Gurdon)
Hamilton MSS.	Duke of Hamilton (Hamilton papers post-1712)
Harley (Brampton Bryan) MSS.	Hereford and Worcester R.O. [photocopies] (*Edward Harley*)
Hope-Johnstone (Raehills) MSS.	Earl of Annandale (*Marquess of Annandale*)
Jervoise MSS.	Hampshire R.O. (*Thomas Jervoise*)
Ketton-Cremer MSS.	Norfolk R.O. (*Ashe Windham*)
King Letterbooks and Lyons MSS.	Trinity College, Dublin (Archbishop King, *Francis Annesley, Earl of Wharton*, etc.)
Lambeth Palace MSS.	Lambeth Palace (*Archbishop Tenison, Edmund Gibson* [Bp.], *William Wake* [Bp.]
Lothian MSS.	Marquess of Lothian (*Thomas Coke*)
Loudoun MSS.	Huntington Library, California (*Earl of Loudoun*)
Mellerstain MSS.	Earl of Haddington (*George Baillie*)
Methuen MSS.	Kenneth A. Spencer Research Library, Univ. of Kansas (John Methuen)
Midleton MSS.	Surrey R.O., Guildford (*Thomas Brodrick, Alan Brodrick*)
Moore MSS.	Kenneth A. Spencer Library (*Arthur Moore*)
Morice MSS.	Bank of England (Humphrey Morice)
Newby Hall MSS.	Leeds Archives Office (*Sir William Robinson*)
Petworth MSS.	W. Sussex R.O. (*Duke of Somerset*)
Phelips MSS.	Somerset R.O. (William Phelips)
Portland (Harley) MSS.	Nottingham University (*Robert Harley*)
Prideaux Diary	Norfolk R.O. (Humphrey Prideaux)
Sacheverell Trial Diary	Yale University Library, Osborn MSS. (anon.)
Sandford MSS.	Somerset R.O. (*Edward Clarke*)
Shakerley MSS.	Canon Ian Dunlop (*Peter Shakerley*)
Townshend MSS.	Marquess Townshend (*Viscount Townshend*)

Preface to First Edition

It is nearly sixteen years since I first stumbled, more by accident than design, into the political world which I have tried here to re-create. Within three months of doing so I had fallen under its spell; and no historical experience since then — not even the richly varied experience that comes the way of any teacher involved in the traditional Scottish lecture-system — has ever succeeded in exorcising that spell. So although the present book has taken only two years to write, many of the ideas on which it is based have been taking shape slowly over a much longer period of time.

It was not at first conceived as a separate volume; rather as an explanatory background to a history of domestic politics during the life of Robert Harley's ministry of 1710 to 1714, which I began to write in 1962. Before that study had progressed beyond the stage of a first draft it became obvious that I had been wildly optimistic in hoping to explain in an introduction of 20–30,000 words both what politics was about in the early eighteenth century and how the political system of that day worked. Mindful of the agonies endured by generations of students confronted with essays on this field (not to mention the sufferings of teachers called upon to make it intelligible) I was eventually persuaded that the questions with which I proposed to deal deserved either to be answered thoroughly, and where possible definitively, or not at all. *British Politics in the Age of Anne* is the result of this conclusion, and also of the indulgence and understanding of my publishers, who had originally been led to expect one book from me, not two. I fear that I shall have sadly disappointed many of my students by failing to make this 'a wee book' — one of their chief criteria of excellence in judging any historical work; the only comfort I can offer them is that it would have been even longer had not the invaluable work of W. A. Speck on the constituencies in Anne's reign (soon, I hope, to be published) enabled me to concentrate very largely here on the centre of politics.

Because this is not a narrative, but a work of analysis and interpretation which draws on a crowded period of political history to illustrate and elucidate its arguments, the reader not familiar with the broad outline of events in these years will doubtless lose his bearings from time to time. To make it easier for him to recover them I have appended to the book a chronological guide to the main developments in domestic politics between 1702 and 1714, and also to a few of the outstanding military and diplomatic landmarks, and this I hope will prove a convenient source of ready reference. Some readers may well find it helpful to consult this guide before embarking on the book itself.

Since I began to explore the reign of Anne as a raw research student in 1950 I have received generous help from many quarters. My first debt was to three great seventeenth-century scholars of an earlier generation. From Sir Keith Feiling I received initial advice and encouragement; from David Ogg, who supervised my first piece of research, shrewd and patient guidance; and from Andrew Browning, my first Professor at Glasgow, the example of his own meticulous, exacting standards of scholarship, something to aspire to if not to achieve. In more recent years I have owed much to the readiness of private owners of manuscripts to allow me to examine and make use of letters and papers in their possession. Here my greatest obligation is to the Duke of Portland, the Duke of Marlborough and the Marquess of Bath. Without access to their papers, and above all to the vast Portland Loan in the British Museum, it would have been futile to attempt a reinterpretation of politics in the early eighteenth century. The Duke of Devonshire and the Trustees of the Chatsworth Settlement, the Duke of Montrose, the Marquess of Anglesey, the Earl of Bradford, Lord Methuen and Lord Egremont have all been most helpful in allowing me to comb their archives for political correspondence and to draw freely on what I found there. I am also grateful to Earl Stanhope for permission to quote from the microfilm of the Chevening MSS., so kindly lent to me by Dr. A. N. Newman, and to the Marquess of Downshire, the Marquess of Cholmondeley, the Earl of Dartmouth, the Earl of Shrewsbury, the Earl of Yarborough, Lord Newton and Miss Olive Lloyd-Baker for permission to quote from their papers, which are available in various local record offices and libraries. Sir J. G. Carew Pole was good enough to let me have photographic copies made of papers at Antony House, and Professor P. N. S. Mansergh was equally generous in the case of the diary of Bishop Nicolson for 1709–10 which is in his possession.

Several private owners not merely bore my invasion of their homes with stoicism but made the experience doubly enjoyable for me by their hospitality. I recall with especial pleasure visits to Lord Hampton at Holt, to

Admiral Sir Reginald Plunket-Ernle-Erle-Drax and Lady Drax at Charborough Park, to Sir Richard and Lady Hamilton at Walton, to Mrs. O. R. Bagot at Levens Hall and to Mr. Thomas Cottrell-Dormer at Rousham. I should also like to express my appreciation of all the help given me by the staffs of the British Museum, the Bodleian Library, the House of Lords Record Office, Register House, and a host of county record offices and local and university libraries. If I only mention here Mr. W. J. Smith, the Berkshire County Archivist, Mr. Kenneth Smith, the Carlisle City Librarian, Mr. B. C. Jones, the Archivist of the Cumberland and Westmorland Joint Archives Committee, and Mr. F. B. Stitt of the William Salt Library and the Staffordshire Record Office, it is not because I am forgetful of the consideration I have met with elsewhere.

There are obligations of a different kind which it is an equal pleasure to record. In the course of my work I have been heavily dependent on microfilm copies of documents, and much of this photography has been paid for by the University of Glasgow. The University Court also granted me a term's leave of absence at an important stage in the book's preparation. I have been spared countless hours of labour as a result of the priceless biographical work done years ago by Professor Robert Walcott and Miss Mary Ransome on the members of Queen Anne's House of Commons. To them I am extremely grateful. I have found great profit in discussions and correspondence with a number of historians working in this field, who have freely exchanged with me ideas, information and material. Dr. H. G. Horwitz, Dr. H. L. Snyder and Mr. H. T. Dickinson have helped me in all these ways; and so, immeasurably, has Dr. W. A. Speck, whose boundless zeal for the period has also been a constant tonic to me over the past five years. In addition, Dr. Speck read the first draft of this book in typescript, as did Dr. J. J. Tumelty, and each had valuable suggestions to make which I have tried to incorporate in the final version. Dr. I. F. Burton and Professor C. D. Chandaman have both put at my disposal their specialist knowledge, the one of Queen Anne's army, the other of late-seventeenth-century finance.

Of what my wife has contributed to the making of this book — as transcriber, translator, indexer, secretary, typist, chauffeur, and not least as adviser and critic — my colleagues and friends know enough to realise that whatever words I chose here to express my debt to her would be sadly inadequate. So I will say simply 'thank you'. Its faults apart, this is her book as much as mine.

GLASGOW   G. S. H.
July 1966

Note on Dates and Quotations

In the text all dates are given in the Old Style of the Julian Calendar, though it is assumed that each new year began on 1 January and not, as in formal O.S. usage, on 25 March. In the footnotes the dating of letters normally follows the same rule, though where I cite a letter written before 25 March in any year, which in the original bears only the formal O.S. date, I use square brackets to make quite clear in what year it was actually written (e.g. 17 Jan. 1701[−2]). In references to letters written from the Continent, or to letters written by Continental envoys or agents in London, I give both their Old and New Style dates, the former first (e.g. 11/22 Dec. 1710).

In quoting from printed documents I reproduce the printed form exactly, except in a very few cases where the original punctuation, retained by the editor, obscures the sense. Passages quoted from manuscripts retain the spelling, though not all the initial capital letters, of the original; their punctuation, however, has been modernised.

List of Abbreviations

Addison Letters	*The Letters of Joseph Addison* (ed. W. Graham, 1941)
Add. MSS.	Additional Manuscripts, British Museum
Bodl.	Bodleian Library, Oxford
Bolingbroke Corr.	*Letters and Correspondence . . . of Henry St. John, Lord Viscount Bolingbroke* (ed. G. Parke, 1798)
Boyer	A. Boyer, *History of the Life and Reign of Queen Anne* (1722)
Boyer, *Annals*	A. Boyer, *History of the Reign of Queen Anne digested into Annals* (1702–13)
B.M.	British Museum
Bull. I.H.R.	*Bulletin of the Institute of Historical Research*
Burnet	G. Burnet, *A History of My Own Time* (Oxford, 1833)
C.J.	*House of Commons' Journals*
Cowper Diary	*The Private Diary of William, First Earl Cowper* (ed. E. C. Hawtrey, 1833)
Coxe	W. Coxe, *Memoirs of the Duke of Marlborough* (Bohn edn., 1847–8)
C.U.L.	Cambridge University Library
Econ. H.R.	*Economic History Review*
E.H.R.	*English Historical Review*
Hervey L.B.	*The Letter Books of John Hervey, First Earl of Bristol* (1894)
H.L.	Huntington Library, California
H.L.Q.	*Huntington Library Quarterly*
H.M.C.	Historical Manuscripts Commission

L.J.	*House of Lords' Journals*
Luttrell	N. Luttrell, *A Brief Historical Relation of State Affairs from September 1678 to April 1714* (1857)
Norris Papers	*The Norris Papers* (ed. T. Heywood, Chetham Society, 1846)
N.U.L.	Nottingham University Library
Oldmixon	J. Oldmixon, *The History of England during the Reigns of King William and Queen Mary, Queen Anne, King George I* (1735)
Parl. Hist.	W. Cobbett, *The Parliamentary History of England* (1806)
Priv. Corr.	*The Private Correspondence of Sarah, Duchess of Marlborough* (1838)
P.R.O.	Public Record Office
S.H.	Staatsarchiv Hannover
Swift Corr.	*The Correspondence of Jonathan Swift* (ed. F. Elrington Ball, 1910–14)
Verney Letters	*Verney Letters of the Eighteenth Century* (ed. Lady Verney, 1930)
Vernon Corr.	*Letters Illustrative of the Reign of William III ... Addressed to the Duke of Shrewsbury by James Vernon, Esq.* (ed. G. P. R. James, 1841)
Wentworth Papers	*The Wentworth Papers 1705–1739* (ed. J. J. Cartwright, 1883)
W.S.L.	The William Salt Library, Stafford

Introduction

Introduction

THE historian writing in the age of Namier, or at least under his shadow, finds it difficult even to begin to describe and analyse the political life of Queen Anne's Britain without venturing into controversial territory. And yet before 1941 such an analysis would probably have been deemed unnecessary. Until then the long-established premise that the politics of Queen Anne's reign received its dynamic from the contest for supremacy between two parties, which were the direct and natural heirs of the Whig and Tory parties of Charles II's reign, had scarcely been challenged. It is true that major work on the period produced during the 1920's and the early 1930's* had questioned some of the airier suppositions and more sweeping assertions of the 'Whig school' of nineteenth-century historians. Sir Keith Feiling, in particular, had taught us that the ideal of 'government by party' was vigorously resisted and only fleetingly realised between 1688 and 1714; and he had also shown how the differences within the two parties, and above all within the Tory party, were often as politically significant as the divisions between them. Indeed, the broad distinctions made between 'moderate' and 'High' Tories, and later between 'Hanoverian' and 'Jacobite' Tories, were so generally accepted by 1930 that even the late Dr. Trevelyan had progressed far enough from his first rigid Whig-Tory interpretation of the period† to be able to write that 'the political history of the Queen's reign cannot be understood *merely* in the terms of controversy between the two historic parties'.‡

* Notably W. T. Morgan's *English Political Parties and Leaders in the Reign of Queen Anne* (1920); Keith Feiling's *History of the Tory Party* (1924); G. M. Trevelyan's *England under Queen Anne* (1930–4); and W. S. Churchill's *Marlborough: His Life and Times* (1933–4).

† G. M. Trevelyan, *England under the Stuarts* (1st edn. 1904). See also his Romanes Lecture 'The Two-Party System in English Political History' (1926).

‡ *England under Queen Anne*, i (hereafter cited as *Blenheim*), 328. The italics are mine. The modified views of the 20's and 30's were crystallised by H. N. Fieldhouse in a sadly-neglected paper, published in 1938 ('Bolingbroke and the Idea of Non-Party Government', *History*, N.S. 23).

For all the reservations that had been made, however, the dichotomy between Whig and Tory still seemed the basic political fact of the age, a fact without which few of the major events of Anne's reign in domestic politics made any real sense. The Ark of the Covenant was still inviolate. Today this is no longer so. During the past twenty-five years, and especially over the course of the last decade, an important movement of historical opinion has seriously undermined this time-honoured premise. The leading revisionist has been the American scholar, Robert Walcott. Inspired by the work of Sir Lewis Namier on the 1750's and 1760's, he has claimed, both in a pioneering essay in 1941 and in a full-scale study in 1956, that the manoeuvres of the leading politicians of Anne's day are only fully intelligible if we recognise that they were carried on 'within a multi-party framework' and not within a two-party one.* To Professor Walcott the really vital ingredients in the so-called party politics of the early eighteenth century were organised connexions, grouped round a series of power-seeking political chieftains, together with a 'government interest' which regularly enlisted under the standard of the administration of the day, and a 'country' group of politicians who were correspondingly predisposed to oppose the Court, no matter who held office. Such ingredients, we are told, were of far greater relevance to the working of politics, except on relatively rare occasions, than the rough-and-ready division of men into Whig and Tory. At the same time the political individuality of Queen Anne herself, whose historical stature had mildly increased rather than diminished as a result of the intensive studies of the 20's and early 30's,† has suffered further relegation, this time to the point of virtual anonymity. Anne, Dr. Walcott concedes at one point, 'was not a nonentity'; yet his work has the inevitable effect of suggesting, by its very neglect of her political rôle in all but a few occasional crises, that a nonentity was virtually what she was.‡

Above all, he believes, the political mechanics of the period hinged on the movements and machinations of the seven organised groups which he identifies after 1700: groups whose members, while mostly bearing a party tag, owed allegiance first and foremost to a particular leader or group of leaders, and were cemented together more by electoral, family, and personal

---

* R. Walcott, *English Politics in the Early Eighteenth Century* [hereafter cited as *English Politics*] (Oxford, 1956), p. 160, and *passim*. See also Walcott's essay, 'English Party Politics, 1688–1714', in *Essays in Modern English History in Honor of W. C. Abbott* (Harvard, 1941), pp. 84–5.

† Professor Morgan's work was of particular interest in this respect.

‡ *English Politics*, p. 96, and *passim*.

relationships than by party loyalty. So much stress does he lay on the size and importance of these 'connexions' that in a formidable series of appendices he lists their adherents in detail — a total of 212 for the last Parliament of William III (slightly more than two-fifths of the total membership of the House of Commons) and 224 for the first Parliament of Anne.* In allocating politicians to their respective groups, a task which he undertakes with remarkable self-confidence in view of the apparent limitations of his evidence,† he is frequently compelled to stretch to their utmost limits the often tenuous electoral connections and the even slenderer genealogical threads which provide his main criteria of selection and association.‡ Nevertheless he is satisfied that Queen Anne's governments, in seeking to establish or maintain a majority in successive Houses of Commons, were influenced far less than used to be thought by the necessity of allying with either the Whig or Tory 'parties', or even with a coalition of the two, and far more by the prospects of securing co-operation from various permutations or combinations of these seven key parliamentary groups.§

Other scholars, besides Walcott, have inevitably felt the magnetic pull of Namier's concept of mid-eighteenth-century politics while working in the very different field of later Stuart Britain. J. H. Plumb, in his printed work of the 1950's, is the most obvious and the most distinguished example. He paints with a far subtler brush than Walcott. He rejects outright certain details of the latter's picture and considers some of its broader lines to be overdrawn. Yet the political world of the young Walpole, which Professor Plumb himself so strikingly depicts, is far removed in many essentials from the world revealed on the canvases of Feiling and Trevelyan, and farther

---

* *English Politics*, pp. 200–15, 218–29.

† For this evidence, which for reasons of space was understandably not supplied in his book, Walcott invited scholars to consult the voluminous notes which he had compiled on the members of Anne's Parliaments and which he deposited on microfilm with the History of Parliament Trust. Detailed examination of these notes leaves one with two overriding impressions: admiration and gratitude for the invaluable groundwork which Walcott's industry provides for any student working in this field, mixed with surprise, verging at times on incredulity, at many of the conclusions he himself draws from the material he has so laboriously gathered.

‡ Walcott briefly summarises the criteria he uses in *English Politics*, pp. 34–5. It is true that he also makes use of the voting records of M.P.s, as revealed by 12 division-lists relating to the period 1689–1715. But while such lists are helpful in separating Whig from Tory groups they can scarcely help Walcott at all in deciding, for instance, which High Tories to allocate to the 'Hyde-Seymour' connexion in Anne's reign and which to the 'Nottingham-Finch' connexion.

§ *Ibid.* pp. 158–60.

still from the traditional picture enshrined in the works of such nineteenth-century giants as Macaulay, Stanhope and Lecky. While acknowledging the existence of a 'broad dichotomy' in the political life of Augustan England, and stressing that on one side of the dividing-line, the Whig side, men were capable of coherent action, he believes that little consistent meaning can be attached to what he calls the party labels of the day, at least at the centre of political life. For there the factional struggles and the ambitions and eccentricities of individual politicians 'created a bewildering world of intrigue where party attitudes could suddenly acquire importance and then cease to have meaning just as quickly. They were picked up [he adds] or laid aside according to the politician's need as he fought for power or clung to office'.*

Entirely new dimensions have thus been revealed during the past quarter of a century in a scene which had all too often theretofore been presented as an over-simplified plane. The work of Professor Kenyon on the reign of William III† has contributed as notably to this transformation as that of Walcott and Plumb, and the net result has been considerably to enrich our knowledge of the whole post-Revolution period. Unfortunately, as far as the reign of Anne is concerned, the work of the 40's and 50's has also produced its own distortions, some of them so acute that they have become every bit as misleading as the old orthodoxies, and perhaps more so. The tinsel and glitter of new ideas are never easy to resist; but it has been alarming none the less to find two eminent scholars, working primarily on the period after 1714, recently disregarding the warning notes sounded by a number of Dr. Walcott's reviewers‡ and embodying his conclusions, in a way that can only be described as uncritical, into their prologues to Hanoverian politics.§

---

* See J. H. Plumb's reviews of Walcott, *op. cit.*, in *E.H.R.* lxxii (1957) and *Spectator* 196 (Jan.-June 1956), p. 322; *Sir Robert Walpole: The Making of a Statesman* (1956), pp. 63, 65 n.; also *ibid.*, chapters 1–2 *passim*.

† J. P. Kenyon, *Robert Spencer, Earl of Sunderland, 1641–1702* (1958), pp. 224 *et seq.*

‡ Apart from J. H. Plumb (*E.H.R.*, *loc. cit.*), Mark Thomson (*History*, N.S. 42 [1957]) and the reviewer in the *Times Literary Supplement* (55 [1956] p. 147) were particularly guarded.

§ See Dorothy Marshall, *Eighteenth Century England* (1962), pp. 59–63; A. S. Foord, *His Majesty's Opposition, 1714–1830* (1964), pp. 19–28. Dr. Marshall moves the more cautiously, but even she is betrayed into such remarkable statements as that 'In most cases the leaders of such groups [as the Whig Junto] had a vague [*sic*] predilection to a whig or tory position . . .' (How Wharton would have enjoyed reading that!). Professor Foord is less circumspect. 'Those labels' [i.e. Whig and Tory], he writes, 'were often adopted by, or foisted upon, men who had little in common and few or no real ties. In 1714 and for many years thereafter, the basic political unit was the group or connexion, often called a party,

What started out as a stimulating hypothesis in 1941 is already, it seems, well on the way to becoming accepted textbook dogma — not merely the 'revised version' but the 'new authorised version'.

The irony is that while this transformation has been under way the opening-up of precious new sources of material, and the improved accessibility of other sources, has led in the past fifteen years or so to a more intensive study of post-Revolution politics than ever before. Much of this work, undertaken largely by a new generation of scholars under the initial inspiration of Dr. Plumb, S. H. F. Johnston and the late David Ogg, is as yet unpublished; but few whose research has been concerned with the years after 1702 have found it possible to accept the revised version of the political life of that period, at least in the extreme form in which Dr. Walcott presents it.* For let us be quite clear what it is we have been asked to accept. J. H. Plumb has shown us the contest of Whig and Tory as but one part of a complex of rivalries and relationships: often a highly important element in politics, particularly in the localities, but never quintessential.† By the arch-revisionist, however, we have been offered as the true foundation of the structure of early-eighteenth-century politics something radically different from anything which previous scholars had envisaged. In place of the firm

formed under the leadership of a successful politician' (*op. cit.* p. 20). It may be noted that Sir Ivor Jennings, *Party Politics*, ii: *The Growth of Parties* (1961), pp. 22–31, also appears to endorse the Walcott interpretation completely.

* There has already been a foretaste of this reaction in printed articles by J. G. Sperling, W. A. Speck, Angus McInnes and H. Horwitz. (See Sperling's 'The Division of 25 May 1711 on an Amendment to the South Sea Bill: a Note on the Reality of Parties in the Age of Anne', *Hist. Journal*, iv [1961]; Speck's 'The Choice of a Speaker in 1705', *Bull. I.H.R.* xxxvii [1964]; McInnes's 'The Political Ideas of Robert Harley', *History*, N.S. 50 [1965]; and Horwitz's 'Parties, Connections, and Parliamentary Politics, 1689–1714', *Journal of British Studies*, Nov. 1966.)

Equally significant have been the unpublished doctoral dissertations of B. W. Hill ('The Career of Robert Harley, earl of Oxford, from 1702 to 1714', Cambridge, 1961), E. L. Ellis ('The Whig Junto', Oxford, 1962), H. Horwitz ('The Political Career of Daniel Finch, second Earl of Nottingham, 1647–1730', Oxford, 1963), and of W. A. Speck ('The House of Commons, 1702–14: A Study in Political Organization', Oxford, 1965).

† Since this was written Professor Plumb has delivered his Ford Lectures at Oxford in Michaelmas Term, 1965, on the subject of *The Growth of Political Stability in England, 1675–1725*. In these lectures, and especially in that entitled 'The Rage of Party', he gives much more weight to the rôle of Whig-Tory divisions in post-Revolution politics than in his earlier published works. The great suspicion which, as his students well know, he has always felt about the Walcott thesis, but which was understandably guarded in print a decade ago, is now uninhibited, and the thesis is substantially rejected.

rock of party principle and rivalry on which the historians of an earlier generation so confidently built we are invited to substitute the shifting sands of clan warfare and the quest of individuals and party groups alike for office and power. To this quest, we are assured, considerations of principle or even of policy had only limited relevance. Dr. Walcott's very latest word on the subject, written as recently as 1962,* still leaves his original thesis virtually intact though making a few cautious concessions to traditionalism.†

It will be as well to make it clear from the start that the present book, like the more detailed study of the last four years of Anne which the author has undertaken, is written in a very different conviction. It is hoped, by the end of this volume, to leave the reader in no reasonable doubt that whatever the complexities of the body politic in the early years of the eighteenth century, its life-blood was the existence and conflict of two major parties. When we look back over the years since 1941, the years in which the study of Augustan politics has been subject to the Namier influence, it would seem that two main factors have conspired to obscure this fundamental truth about party. One has been an understandable but excessive preoccupation with new methods of investigation; or rather, with 'method' for its own sake. There can be no question, of course, of the enormous value of the techniques of historical investigation which Sir Lewis Namier perfected. These techniques, with their concentration on the electoral background and political record of every member of Parliament, however humble, and on the accumulation at this level of all the discoverable biographical and genealogical data which might conceivably be relevant, are an indispensable aid to the study of politics in the age of Anne; just as they can help to illuminate any period of modern British history. No serious student of political history can afford to ignore them; though he may be forgiven for wondering, from time to time, whether the immense addition to his labours which they involve is altogether commensurate with the value of the yield. Long years of panning some of the muddier streams of the genealogical reference-books and the local and family histories can leave the optimistic prospector with what must sometimes seem a very small residue of the gold-dust of truly enlightening historical discovery for which he is always hoping. Yet this is work that must be done. The crucial point is that it does not absolve us in any way from the responsibility of observing other phenomena as well. Biographical evidence has to become the historian's servant and not his master; it has, after all, no in-

* 'The Idea of Party in the Writing of Later Stuart History' (*Journal of British Studies*, No. 2, May 1962).

† For a fuller discussion of this paper see pp. 38 *et seq.* below.

herent superiority over other types of evidence, and it carries the dangerous liability that by focussing attention exclusively on the trees it can easily persuade us that it is they and not the wood which really matter.

A second explanation, one may suggest, of much of the confusion and controversy which still surround the interpretation of post-Revolution politics is that scholars have tried too hard to find formulae that would apply equally to William's reign and to Anne's. If, in trying to explain both what politics was concerned with and how it was carried on at this stage of Britain's political development, I have confined the scope of my analysis deliberately to the reign of Anne, this has not been simply for artificial reasons or even for reasons of convenience. It seemed not merely sensible to recognise but essential to emphasise that the pattern of politics after 1701 was not the same in many respects as that which persisted during the 1690's. William III's reign, in politics as in the development of the constitution and as in the field of public finance, was a transitional period, an age of experiment. Not even Macaulay ever supposed that its political life could be interpreted in simple two-party terms;* although it is nevertheless the opinion of one leading authority of the past decade that

Despite every attempt to exorcise these terms, 'whig' and 'tory', they remain indispensable to an understanding of the 1690's. Politics were based on groups, which determined positive affiliations, but the labels 'whig' or 'tory', attached to a man or his group, defined their attitude towards the Revolution and certain other fundamentals (e.g. religious comprehension) on which compromise was virtually impossible. They thus possessed a powerful negative effect, determining which Commons groups a man could not join, which measures he could not support.†

By the time of Anne's succession, however, the new political habits and attitudes which post-Revolution conditions had produced had solidified; the structure of politics had consolidated; and the historian's vision, as he studies it, is correspondingly clearer. Looking at the blurred, kaleidoscopic image of the years 1689–1701 he can scarcely be blamed for rejecting as unrealistic a plain two-party framework of politics, and for believing that pre-Revolution party distinctions had no more than a spasmodic, or at most a negative, relevance to the real business of politics in the 1690's.‡ But the

* See, e.g., *History of England*, iv (1855), pp. 298–9.

† J. P. Kenyon, *Sunderland*, p. 248 n.

‡ Even this belief may perhaps be shaken in time as more detailed work on William III's Parliaments, by Dr. Rubini, Dr. Horwitz and others, yields its results. Certainly it would be a gross over-simplification to suggest that political confusion suddenly gave way to political clarity in March 1702. As I shall hope to indicate later, the basic distinction

sharper, firmer contours of the years between 1702 and 1714 surely evoke
a very different response. To this writer, at least, it has seemed that the
existence in the Augustan state of two great parties, transcending and dwarf-
ing all lesser political groupings, together with the fact that the vast majority
of Englishmen who played any active part in politics in these years were *in
some measure* identified with one or other of them and involved in their
conflict — that they were, in short, either Whigs or Tories — must be the
basis, the starting-point, of all further enquiry. The more one soaks oneself,
year after year, in the political correspondence, the parliamentary speeches,
the memoirs, the diaries, the pamphlet literature of this most politically-
conscious of periods, the more convinced one must become that the division
of men into Whig and Tory was no mere incidental or peripheral matter to
the Harleys and the St. Johns, the Whartons and the Halifaxes, the Nottinghams and the Rochesters of Queen Anne's Britain — any more than it was
a matter of secondary consideration to Queen Anne herself. To the great
ones, as to the humblest High Church justice of the peace in some remote
county, or to the dissenting common-councilman in some decayed parliamentary borough, it was an utterly basic fact: the most dominating, inescapable fact of political life at all levels from the very beginning of the reign
to the very end.

This is not to say that the fact needs no qualification, for of course it does.
Although it was the basic fact of political life, it was far from being the only
fact of importance. One should not, for instance, approach the study of
Anne's reign without being fully aware of the presence of a no-man's-land
between or outside the two camps, where a very small minority of politicians
contrived to maintain an existence independent of party ties, and equally
aware of the fact that over this no-man's-land the spirit of Queen Anne
herself — a far-from-negligible figure in the pattern of politics — uneasily
brooded. We shall also need to accept as a truism that within each camp the
party men spoke at times not with one voice but with many; that there was
nothing monolithic about either of the parties (though in fact their resemblance to modern political parties was neither so slight nor so coincidental as
has sometimes been suggested). We shall find, furthermore, that there were
certain occasions between 1702 and 1714, though they were relatively few
and brief, when at the centre of politics the distinction between Whig and

between Whig and Tory was more important after 1694 (the year of the Triennial Act
and of William's reluctant alliance with the Whig Junto) than it had been since 1690; and
it was still more important in the last year of William's life than it was between 1694 and
the end of 1700.

Tory was of less relevance than the even older distinction between "Court" and "Country": that is to say between Government, whatever its political complexion, and Opposition that was temporarily bipartisan or multi-partisan. And above all we must accept that to talk of a two-party *system* in the early eighteenth century is a rather ludicrous over-simplification of the unique relationship which existed in Anne's reign between the parties on the one hand and the Crown and the administration on the other.

And yet, when all the qualifications have been made, we shall still find ourselves face to face time and again with one ineluctable truth: that without "the detested names of Whig and Tory",* and without the basic conflict of attitude, policy or principle which these names embodied, relatively few political situations of any importance in our period either possess or convey much real meaning.

---

* The Duke to the Duchess of Marlborough, 9/20 Oct. 1704, printed in Wm. Coxe *Memoirs of the Duke of Marlborough* (Bohn edn., 1847–8), i, 235.

PART ONE

The Character of Politics

CHAPTER ONE

Tory and Whig

THE first step towards comprehending the character of the political world of Queen Anne's day is, one might think, a very simple and a very natural one. It is to study the vocabulary which contemporaries used to describe the political attitudes and questions of their own age. Why it should have become fashionable of late to ignore this terminology is not at all clear. Perhaps an instinctive distrust of the obvious is one of the occupational hazards involved in applying new methods of enquiry to any period. If so, the scholar working in the field of the early eighteenth century needs more than most to be on his guard against it, for in the language of early-eighteenth-century politics are to be found some of the most valuable clues to its character.

Admittedly, due allowance has to be made for the looseness with which many contemporaries often employed their terms. The mental reservations which correspondents would inevitably make when using certain words or phrases may have been implicit to them and familiar to their friends; but the fact that they were mental and not verbal can be misleading to the unwary twentieth-century reader.* Yet it is surely much more dangerous, and also rather arrogant of us, to assume that the practising politicians and political observers of Anne's day did not normally understand what their own politics was about, and that they used a vocabulary to describe it that was out of date, irrelevant or at best inadequate. On the contrary, by quoting them liberally it is easier by far to convey the authentic atmosphere of the years 1702–14 than by attempting to superimpose on the period an alien terminology. In the interests of illumination it may quite often be necessary to augment or explain contemporary terms with others of a more modern denomination.†

---

* So too can the occasionally mistaken use of labels, the application of a familiar term to a political situation or grouping that was in fact new, unfamiliar, and as yet imperfectly comprehended.

† In this study I have tried to preserve and emphasise the distinction by reserving double quotation-marks solely for Augustan terms and phrases, including contemporary quotations, and by employing single quotes elsewhere.

But the object of this grafting process (as it has seemed to this writer, at least) should be to supplement rather than to substitute, and to do so, as far as possible, in terms that would not have been wholly unintelligible to the men of Augustan Britain. The second condition is not without its point, as Dr. Walcott demonstrates when he describes the gradual changes in the character of Queen Anne's administration between 1702 and 1710 as 'the process by which the Godolphin ministry changed from a Court-Churchill-Harley-Rochester-Nottingham Coalition into a Court-Churchill-New-castle-Junto combination'.[1]* For here is language that may have some value as a means of communicating ideas to modern students but which would, one suspects, have been so much gibberish in the ears of Rochester, Harley, the Junto and the Churchills themselves.

How, then, did these men and their fellows describe and discuss the political world which they inhabited? Possibly the most striking thing to emerge from their written testimony is the remarkably few allusions they made to those 'connexions' which have been seen as the real stuff of early-eighteenth-century politics. That such groups existed in Parliament was certainly recognised. There were "those . . . that must follow their leaders", Robert Monckton conceded;[2] "men of my own knowledge", as Sir John Percival discerned in 1714, who had "all along govern'd themselves by the lights of other men, and justify'd the Ministry's proceedings on noe other acco$^{t.}$ than because some great friends of their owne were then of that side".[3] Nor were contemporaries naïve enough to imagine that these men were entirely dis-interested when they attached themselves to one or other of the great political patrons; for in power, as one commentator observed in 1715, "ceux ci recommandent et tachent d'avancer ceux qui s'attachent personellement à eux, leurs parents et leurs dépendants . . ."[4] Yet individually, with one or two notable exceptions, these political clans are but rarely mentioned by name. This is not so in the case of the Junto and its followers, whose singular rôle within the Whig party was widely accepted and understood. They were frequently distinguished by phrases like "the Juncto Lords & their ad-herents", and less frequently by such variants as "the Junctonians" or even (in acknowledgement of the primacy of their most eminent figure, Lord Somers) as "the Summerian Whigs".[5] Contemporary references to the Harleyites, especially in the years from 1704 to 1709 when "Robin" Harley and his "mirmidons"[6] followed a course that was often clearly dis-tinguishable from that of other Tories, are also fairly numerous.† But years

---

* Figures in the text refer to the Notes on pp. 459–518.

† Thus we read of "Mr. Harley & all his gang" and "Mr. Harleys squadron" (P.R.O.

of meticulous combing of the political correspondence of Anne's day will only throw up a few isolated allusions to "the Ld Rochesters friends",[7] to "Sir Edw. Seymour and his gang",[8] to the Earl of Nottingham's "own party or family",[9] or to "the united Power of the Marlborough and Godolphin familyes".[10] Mention of "his Grace [of Newcastle] and his creatures",[11] of "all my Ld. Anglesea's Interest",[12] and of "the Speaker [Hanmer] and his squadron",[13] is also rare enough to attract particular notice when it does occur. This great dearth of contemporary reference to specific connexions deserves to be stressed; for it is clearly not what we might reasonably expect if the combined membership of such groups really accounted (as we have recently been assured it did)* for almost half of the typical House of Commons of the early eighteenth century.

The deficiency may be explained in part, perhaps, by the fact that the Englishman of Queen Anne's reign often found it simpler and more natural to use generic terms, or broader, more blanket-like expressions, to embrace associations of politicians of which these individual groups may have been a part, but which also included many independents of similar views. For example, when Mrs. Burnet wrote of "the worst sort of Tories" in 1704, the Duke of Shrewsbury and James Vernon of "the angry party" and "the angry corner" of the House of Commons in 1707, or Lord Cowper of "the old Torys" in 1710,[14] we can scarcely doubt that the followers of Lords Rochester and Nottingham were prominent in their thoughts; but it is also fairly certain that in each case the authors had others in mind as well, independent noblemen like Buckingham and Jersey in 1704 and 1710, country gentlemen like Hanmer, Grahme and Ralph Freeman in 1707. And the very fact that political attitudes and opinions rather than kinship and clientage were implicitly assumed to be the common denominator in all these collections of Tories is in itself indicative of the priorities of contemporary politicians and the perspectives of contemporary observers. Similarly, when the differences over policy between "High" and "moderate" Tories became acute in 1704–5 the terms in which they are described by contemporaries leave us in no doubt that they amounted to something much more complex than a split between the Rochester, Seymour and Nottingham factions and those Tories who looked to Harley or Godolphin for a lead. Harley's own evidence in July 1704, for instance, that "the angry people heer [among the Tories] find the ground begin to fal from under them, &

30/24/21/148, 150); "Mr. Harley and his friends" (*Addison Letters*, p. 91); "Harley and his party" (Burnet, v, 348), and so forth.

* See p. 3 above.

that those who used to follow them wil not run mad with them"[15] implies that a considerable body of independent Tories were involved: that there were moderates within the party who on issues of genuine Tory principle had often taken their cue from the great men on 'the right', but who as soon as the latter promoted ultra-partisan, destructive measures, parted company with the High Tory connexions and drifted towards the centre.*

Of all the comprehensive terms used in the years 1702–14 to embrace major political groupings the most telling must surely be that ubiquitous phrase "our friends". It was a phrase that was standard currency on both sides when men were talking or writing about members of their own party; and time and again the context makes it plain that what they meant by it was not just 'the members of our connexion' but, at very least, 'fellow-Whigs of our own persuasion' or 'fellow-Tories who share our views'. When Lord Halifax, for example, lamented to the Duke of Newcastle after the fall of the Whigs in 1710 that "Our friends are quite gone off the stage"[16] the recent fate of Cowper and Devonshire, Boyle and Smith was as much his concern as the departure from office of his Junto colleagues, Somers and Orford, or of his brother, Sir James Montagu. In the hour of tribulation, if not always in the hour of triumph, party was more important than clan.[17]

While the letters, the diaries and the memoirs of the time have relatively little to say about this connexion or that, this group or that, they bristle with the words "party" and "parties". However their writers may have interpreted these terms they use them perpetually; and in nine cases out of ten it is perfectly plain that these are used with two parties, and two parties only, in mind. Thus Harley would "take it for granted that no one party in the House can carry it for themselves without the Queen's servants joyne with them", or would "with grief" observe "that the leaders (or zealots rather) of both parties are frequent even now, in their reflections on the Queen's ministers . . .";[18] Marlborough would write longingly to Godolphin of the time "when the Queens service will permit mee to be . . . out of the power of the partys, for I am very sure I can please neither . . .";[19] while Anne hereself would pray for liberation from "the mercyless men of both partys",

---

* I make no apology for using here and elsewhere those 'apologetic epicycles' to which Dr. Walcott takes exception, and which he seems to imagine were never applied to this period until invented for our confusion by 'historians such as Feiling' (*English Politics*, pp. 156–7). In fact there is ample justification in contemporary usage for employing terms like 'wings', 'sections', 'centre' or 'coalition'; especially as they usually involve the basic distinctions between the "warm" and "moderate" men in both parties, distinctions about which, as we shall see (e.g. p. 19 and pp. 252–3 below), the politicians of Anne's reign were absolutely clear.

and would protest: "All I desire is, my liberty in encouraging and employing all those that concur faithfully in my service, whether they are called Whigs or Tories, not to be tied to one, nor the other".[20]

Like the Queen, men commonly looked no further than the traditional names of Whig and Tory to describe the two parties which bulked so large in their political vocabulary. One could fill a sizeable volume with examples, and still have some to spare. But euphemisms too were many and various: sometimes resorted to deliberately or out of affectation (by Swift, for instance),[21] more often indulged in out of sheer fashion or habit. Thus the Tories, generally the more sensitive of the two about calling a spade a spade and never loth to parade their religious before their secular principles, had firmly appropriated the term "the Church Party" by the end of William's reign:* and thereafter they frequently preferred this and similar appellations like "the High Church Party", "the Church of England Party", "the Churchmen", or simply "the Church".[22] Such in Anne's reign were the universally-recognised labels which euphemistic licence bestowed on a body of politicians which by 1710 included freethinkers like St. John, as well as occasional conformists like Samuel Shepheard, and Edward Harley and his Foley cousins, but which ironically excluded more than half the bishops.† It was predictable, perhaps, that after the bitter disputes in Convocation in 1701 and 1702 the term "Low-Church Party" should be increasingly applied first to the Whig clergy[23] and then (though mainly by their opponents)[24] to the Whigs as a whole. There was a type of Whig whom the cap clearly fitted: a type epitomised by Ralph Bell, M.P. for Thirsk, who went "to church in the morning, and, (to humour his father) to the meeting in the afternoon".[25] Yet there were scores of Whigs inside Parliament and many thousands outside—good, sound, middle-of-the-road members of the Established Church — who were just as obviously maligned by such a label, and who had cause to resent it when it stuck. Far more grateful to the Whigs themselves was Lord Wharton's special contribution to the usage of his day, "the honest interest",[26] just as the Tories virtually took out a patent on those

---

* There seems to have been a subtle transition in Tory usage in the years 1701–2 from such half-way expressions as "the Church (or Country) party" and "the Tories or Church party" to the unqualified "Church Partie". See, e.g., Add. MSS. 22851, f. 121; P.R.O. 30/24/20/57: Shaftesbury to Benjamin Furley, 27 Feb.; Longleat MSS. Thynne Papers, xiii, f. 285: Lord Weymouth to Hon. James Thynne, 20 Mar. 1702. Cf. Boyer, p. 14.

† That these labels could be equally misleading at local level is evident from Gervase Scroop's contemptuous attack on Tories in Shropshire "that cloak themselves with a pretence of defending the Church" as "men that never go to Church, but for the most part atheists and libertines". Monson MSS. 7/13/124: 1 July 1710.

other well-worn phrases "the gentlemen" and "the gentlemen of England".
Finally there were the less polite synonyms for Whig and Tory, the terms of
abuse or cant: on the one hand "the fanatick party", or "the Presbeterian
faction", "the low Church vermin", the "Anti-Churchmen" and "the
republican clan";[27] on the other hand "the Jack party",* "the French
party", "the Sacheverellites" and "the rigids".[28]

The terminology of Augustan politics allowed for a certain flexibility in
classifying individuals as opposed to parties. And yet few commentators and
observers were not conscious of the need first and foremost to place politicians
into one or other of the two basic categories of Whig and Tory, whatever
subsequent embellishments they might add. Nothing could be more striking
in this respect than the pains which contemporaries almost invariably took
to sum up the progress and results of the General Elections of 1702–13 in
strictly party terms — terms that were not only concrete but often meticu-
lously precise. Writing from London on 20 May 1708 a correspondent of
the Duke of Montrose observed that "The Elections here goe well, the
Whigs reckon about 30 votes more than they had last parlmt."; but a more
thorough Whig analysis later in the month revealed "122 new members, in
wch the computors say we have gain'd 28 upon the Torys".[29] No early-
eighteenth-century "computor" was more thorough or better informed in
his assessment of the constituencies than Charles Spencer, Earl of Sunderland, the youngest of the lords of the Junto. He followed the course of this
1708 Election — the most successful the Whigs enjoyed in the whole of
Anne's reign — with the zest and precision of a modern psephologist.
Against a list of members of the House of Commons in the 1707–8 session
he noted all the changes in representation as the results reached him, marking
Whig losses with an 'L', gains with a 'g', and leaving unannotated the changes
in membership which involved no change in party allegiance. For some
reason, with 69 seats in England and Wales still to be filled, he left his
calculations unfinished: perhaps he was well satisfied that with 31 net gains
already recorded the Whigs were certain of the most comfortable working
majority in his own memory.[30]

Two years later, however, it was the Tories who were scanning their
newspapers eagerly for the latest batch of results; and less than three weeks
after the great electoral struggle of 1710 had begun the newly-elected
member for the city of Hereford, who prided himself on being "pretty

---

* A popular abbreviation for the Jacobites, but sometimes applied, needless to say, to
the Tories as a whole (e.g. Temple Newsam MSS. Corr. Box 9, f. 83: Wm. Evan to
[Lord Irwin], 3 Sept. 1701; Add. MSS. 33273, f. 29).

exact", noted that "my calculation is 178 Tories, 61 Whigs & 14 doubtfull, as I take them from the Gazettes".[31] The local score was kept in just the same way. As early as 1701 Thomas Morice was promising the Warwickshire Tory, Sir John Mordaunt, "that from Cornwall you will have 37 or 38 out of the 44" members,[32] and Bishop Nicolson's confident forecast in August 1710 "that the county of Cumberland would (as at present) send up five Whigs for one Tory"[33] was exactly fulfilled three months later. "This time 3 years [ago]", a Kent clergyman exulted in 1713, "ther were ten Whigs elected in this county & but 8 Church-men: now we have 13 Churchmen & but 5 Whigs".*

In addition to his party label, however, a man would occasionally carry a recognised qualification of that label. Everyone at the centre of politics, for example, knew the difference between Lord Dartmouth, who was "looked upon as a tory" but "known to be no zealous party man", or his friend William Benson, whose addiction to Toryism was always "very moderate", and the Earl of Nottingham, who was "party sense in person without respect to the reasons of things";[34] just as there were few Whigs in the House of Commons between 1702 and 1713 who would not mentally have placed Henry Boyle, a man "without any party violence" in a category apart from that "true Whig", Edmund Dunch, or that "virulent party-man", Matthew Aylmer.[35] There were the lukewarm and the hot partisans in both camps, and anyone with any pretensions to political judgement was aware who was which. When the lords of the Junto, preparing to celebrate their final triumph in November 1708 after a protracted pursuit of power, let it be known that "none but staunched men are to be employed",[36] there was little need for them to be more specific. They knew, and almost every Whig at Westminster must have known, who had earned the badge of courage in the parliamentary tussles of the past three years.

At intervals in Anne's reign, during periods of temporary confusion when party distinctions had become a trifle blurred, as in the winter of 1707–8,†

---

* Bodl. MS. Ballard 15, f. 107: John Johnson to Dr. Charlett, 5 Sept. 1713 (he included the Cinque Ports of Kent in his calculation). The violent swing to the Whigs in Cornwall between 1713 and 1715 was even more staggering to the local "computors": a Tory supremacy of 40 members to 4 in the last Parliament of Anne was transformed by the return of "therty three Whigs certaine to eleven Torys" in the first Parliament of George I. See H.M.C. *Portland MSS.* v, 330–1; B.M. Loan 29/311/4 (a marked list of Cornish members sent by Lord Lansdowne to Oxford, 11 Sept. 1713); National Library of Wales, Brogyntyn MSS.: [Sir] W. Pendarves to [Mrs. Godolphin], 1 Feb. 1715.

† Readers of Dr. Walcott's book may think it surprising that he selects the notoriously confused parliamentary session of 1707–8 (*English Politics*, pp. 125–54) for a 'case study

the spring of 1711, or the summer of 1713, there were always those who tried to convey the realities of the situation more accurately by discussing it in other terms than the standard ones of Whig and Tory. Sometimes they would fall back on the still older designations of "Court" and "Country", or settle for an *ad hoc* line of demarcation between those "for or against the government".[37] But new alignments of politicians could rarely be described for long in this or any other way without adding to the confusion, and this explains why, even when the parties were patently divided (as were the Whigs in 1707–8 and the Tories in 1713–14) most commentators were extremely reluctant to drop the names Whig and Tory from their vocabulary. Thus despite the deep rifts within the Tory party by the autumn of 1713, with dissension over trade, over foreign policy and even over the succession, the dissidents continued to be sharply distinguished from the Whigs in virtually every contemporary account; and this though the pamphleteers were studiously producing "new distinction between the Tories themselves, as Hanover Tory and Pretender's Tory, English Tory and French Tory, for trade or against it".[38] Equally striking is the promptitude with which, once these interludes of cross-voting were over, politicians and observers alike reverted to the orthodox terminology which was applicable to the political norm. Three days after the House of Commons had completed its enquiry into the conduct of the war in Spain on 24 February 1708, with a division in which both errant Whigs and Harley's moderate Tories came back to their respective folds, Joseph Addison welcomed the return to normality with the undisguised relief of the mariner finding himself in well-charted waters after navigating through shoals. "We look upon the Debate of last Tuesday . . .", he told Lord Manchester, "as that which has fixt all men in their proper parties."[39]

*　　*　　*

The political vocabulary of the early eighteenth century, then, was based quite manifestly on the assumption that the essence of politics between 1702 and 1714 was the contention of two great national parties for supremacy. Nor is it really necessary to penetrate the tangled thicket of Court rivalries or attempt any microscopic scrutiny of the battle-scarred parliamentary arena of these years to begin to appreciate why this assumption was so universally made. For the most extraordinary feature of the age of Anne was the unprecedented extent to which party strife, the inescapable and all-

of the party system at work' that purports to be typical of early-eighteenth-century politics.

pervading distinction between Tory and Whig, invaded and finally took possession of the very lives of the politically-conscious. In spheres far removed from the confines of the Court and "the Parliament-House", or for that matter of the parliamentary boroughs, a man's party allegiance became a fact of considerable, and often of supreme, importance.

For one thing party coloured the social life of the upper and middle classes to a remarkable degree. In London, especially, the talk of the coffee-houses and the not invariably polite society of the clubs and the fashionable dinner tables all reflected the political schism within the nation. As the reign went on it became increasingly rare for the leading partisans of the Whigs and Tories to meet each other socially, unless they happened to be relatives or to have strong local interests in common. St. John protested warmly to a political opponent in 1710 that "though measures are to be kept with party, yet friendship may be preserved too".[40] But in the next four years these brave words proved very hard for him or anyone at the heart of the battle to live up to. Even the Low Church bishops, to judge from the diaries of two of their doughtiest champions,* rarely carried brotherly love so far as to dine with or call on their High Church fellows after 1710, except on purely formal occasions.[41] For some of their lay brethren social contact with those of contrary political opinions became almost unthinkable. The Earl of Sunderland, engaged to dine with his Junto friend Lord Halifax in 1713, declined to cross the threshold when he found the coach of the Tory Lord Treasurer, Oxford, standing at the door.[42] Social habits contracted in town, moreover, were not easily abandoned in the country. Welbeck would offer its princely hospitality to a Spencer, a Somers, a Townshend or a Cavendish during the summer months,[43] but hardly to a Hyde, a Seymour or a Bromley.

For the aristocratic Whigs and for the few chosen ones they took under their patronage the most exclusive social centre in London was the Kit-Cat Club, where the toasts were "to the immortal memory of King William"[44] and to the healths of various ladies who combined the twin virtues of raving beauty and Whiggish fervour. Later in Anne's reign a group of Tory leaders and men of letters founded their own dining-club to rival the Kit-Cat, the Society of Brothers, its ostensible aims cultural and convivial, its underlying purpose frankly political: "A number of valuable people will be kept in the same mind", St. John promised his friend, Lord Orrery, "and others will be made converts to their opinions".[45] A club of similar name, but whose

---

* Those of William Wake, Bishop of Lincoln (Christ Church, Wake MSS. 1770) and William Nicolson, Bishop of Carlisle, formerly a moderate Tory (Tullie House, Carlisle).

raison d'être was far less lofty, indeed almost purely alcoholic, was the Board of Brothers, established in July 1709 under the auspices of the Duke of Beaufort and the Earls of Denbigh and Scarsdale. But its membership was rigidly Tory, and the "brothers" were expected to observe certain basic Tory virtues even in their cups. "By a vote of the Board *nemine contradicente*", it was minuted in December 1709, "that it be in the power of the President to silence any brother who shall in his liquor or any otherwise talke anything that shall ridecule the Holly scripture or religion". And when their party found itself in power again in the winter of 1710–11 the members of the Board were able to achieve a sense of responsibility appropriate to the occasion by ordering "That all bumpers be excluded the board except one to Church & Queen to avoid excess & reproach".[46]

The real hub of social life for most upper- and middle-class Londoners, however, was not the club but the coffee-house. The number of such houses in London and Westminster by 1714 was probably in the region of 650.[47] They were notorious breeding-grounds of political gossip and rumour: "the whisper of the day", Addison once wrote, would be published "by eight o'clock in the morning at *Garraway's*, by twelve at *Will's*, and before two at the *Smyrna*;"[48] and many of the more fashionable houses developed into informal political forums.[49] More significant is the fact that in some of these establishments there was strict political segregation. "All the news I can tell", Peter Wentworth told his brother after the latter had been appointed a peace plenipotentiary, "is that at the Whig Coffee houses you are cursed, and in all the Tory houses blest & cry'd up to the skys"; and the cousin of Sir John Pakington, a highflying Tory M.P., thought himself lucky to "come off with a whole skin" when he rashly "stepped into a Whig coffee-house" on the eve of a General Election.[50]

The Tories patronised Ozinda's Chocolate House in St. James's Street and the Smyrna in Pall Mall; while in the famous Cocoa Tree on the south side of Pall Mall a Whig was a still rarer bird.[51] The St. James's Coffee House was the favourite haunt of the Whigs. Lord Mohun, one of the Junto's loyallest if least reputable henchmen, was "always . . . in an evening to be heard of" there, and it was there, too, that Wentworth overheard Whig M.P.s feverishly assessing their election prospects in August 1710.[52] But the St. James's was not without its rivals in catering for the honest interest. It was in "Button's coffee house near Covent Garden, where the chief of the Whiggish party generally resorted" that the Reverend Thomas Carte claimed to have seen copies displayed of the famous exchange of letters between Queen Anne and Godolphin on the admission of Shrewsbury to the ministry in April 1710.[53] Those Whigs with a taste for gambling might, however, prefer White's, and Whig army officers found their natural habitat at Old Man's in the Tilt Yard. This last establishment, stoned by a Tory mob during Sacheverell's trial, was kept by that staunchest of Whig hostesses, Jenny Man, of whom the *Flying-Post* wrote in November 1712:

> Alas! alas! for *Jenny Man*,
> 'Cause she don't love the Warming-Pan,
> High Church will all her Actions scan
>   Since she was an Inch long, Sirs:
> She is no Friend to Right Divine
> Therefore she must not sell French Wine,
> But Tea and Coffee, very fine,
> And sure that is no Wrong, Sirs.[54]

Not least among Whig rendezvous stood Pontack's in Lombard Street. A celebrated "French Eating-House" rather than a coffee-house purely and simply, Pontack's attracted many of the leading City businessmen and served as a useful place of liaison between them and the party hierarchs.[55]

Augustan London lived its politics whole-heartedly. The upper crust even contrived to do so in sickness as well as in health. A fashionable doctor could lose a lot of patients if he espoused a party cause too warmly; certainly the eminent Dr. Oliphant's London practice suffered severely from the loss of Whig patients when, as M.P. for Ayr Burghs after 1710, he went over to the Tories along with his patron, Argyll.[56] Such a society offered to the non-political minority but little refuge. Even an evening spent at Drury Lane or the Haymarket would often stir party blood as much as a morning at the St. James's or the Cocoa Tree, for no medium of social activity was more thoroughly involved in the antagonisms of Tory and Whig than the contemporary theatre.

By a strange chance most of the successful dramatists of the day — from Congreve, Addison, Rowe and Vanbrugh to D'Urfey, Thomas Baker, Charles Gildon and Mrs. Centlivre — happened to be Whigs. Indeed apart from George Granville, who dabbled in opera as well as Cornish elections, and Colley Cibber, who trimmed his sails to the prevailing wind after the Whig rout in 1710, the Tories could offer little competition.[57] Patronage of the stage by the Whig leaders was also very generous: four contemporary dramatists, among them Rowe and Congreve, dedicated plays to Halifax, and two others honoured Somers and Wharton, while the Kit-Cat Club contributed handsomely to the building of the new Haymarket theatre, opened in April 1705.* With a virtual monopoly of talent and powerful backing, Whig writers did not hesitate to project their political opinions not only into serious plays, but even into the comedy of manners which became so popular in the early eighteenth century; and up to 1710, at least, they had a good deal of scope. Nicholas Rowe's *Tamerlane*, first performed in 1701 and a firm favourite for the next nine years, depicted the Whig ideal of a constitutional monarch, and John Dennis's *Liberty Asserted*, which was performed the record number of 11 times in its first year (1704), was even more specific in giving dramatic expression to "Revolution principles". Indeed Addison's *Cato* seems to have been one of the few plays of real note produced in Anne's reign which satisfied both sides.

> ... the contention is which party shall applaud it most [explained a leading Whig to his friend] ... At Court I met Mr. Harcourt (the Lord Chancellor's son) and asked him how he liked our play. Your play! my Lord, 'Tis ours, says he; or at least you will allow Cato to belong to us, by reason Mr. Booth [who played the title rôle] is one of us. Very good, quoth I, take him i' God's name; you purchased him at the rate of 54 guineas which Lord Bolingbroke collected among you young gentlemen at the play the other night. At that rate, my Lord, says he, if your friends will give him 60, you may bring him over. Upon which I observed that ... they might make the best of their player since we had our poet; and bribe him if you can.[58]

That Tory customers were kept satisfied later in the reign was mainly due to the government's control over licences, and indirectly over the management of Drury Lane, a control which in the hands of Vice-Chamberlain Coke and Secretary Bolingbroke did at least succeed in redressing the balance to the extent of keeping the more inflammatory pieces off the London stage.[59] To quell the Whigs in this particular field, however, was beyond the power of any administration. A satirical opera by Porrel, for instance, which was put on for six weeks in 1711 to a subscription audience at a crown a ticket, was regarded as an exclusive party entertainment. "Mr. Walpole and Mr. Mackertney were managers, received the tickets at the door and suffered no Tory to mix with them in this extraordinary pleasure".[60]

If the Whig-Tory conflict deeply coloured London society it left its mark no less indelibly on the provinces. Even among the lower orders of society, the unrepresented masses, there is little suggestion of a uniform

---

* A section of the auditorium was subsequently reserved for the exclusive use of the Kit-Catters, free of charge. There were only 4 Tories among the original 29 subscribers, who each promised 100 guineas in four equal instalments. N.U.L. Portland (Holles) MSS. Pw2/571: paper endorsed "The Names of the Subscribers to the building of a New Theatre in the Haymarket".

apathy. Swift's manservant was surprised to find "the rabble here . . . much more inquisitive in politicks than in Ireland"; and what was true of London was true of most large provincial towns, with the parliamentary cities and boroughs naturally more distracted by party rivalries than those without representation. Here, and in some counties too, elections brought flashes of colour, excitement, and sometimes violence into workaday lives — "not a chambermaid, prentice or schoolboy . . . but what is warmly engaged on one side or the other".[61] The higher up the social pyramid a man was, however, the more he could expect to feel the intruding power of party, and the upper strata of county society were as thoroughly permeated as any sector of the nation's life by the strife of Tory and Whig. The key institutions and offices in every shire — the Lord Lieutenancy, the deputy lieutenancies, the militia officers and officials, the Commissioners and Receiver of the Land Tax and other collectorships, the commission of the peace — became so many focal points of local rivalries in which party allegiance after 1701 played an increasingly important part. Voters everywhere and at all times sought official protection, through the local leaders of their own party, "from so many commissioners, both in the peace & militia, who [could] crush them at pleasure";[62] and the local magnates, when in a position to oblige them, took good care to do much more than restore the balance of power. Thus no fewer than 29 Whig magistrates were removed from the Devonshire bench in the first two years of Anne's reign,[63] and it can hardly have been for ignorance of the law that Lord Somers, William III's Lord Chancellor until 1700, was struck off the list of J.P.s for Worcestershire before the General Election of 1702.[64]

Obviously these local prizes did far more than confer social prestige; they were all of them vital ingredients in the building up of what contemporaries called "interest" — that magical word in the language of the day, in which was comprehended not only large rent-rolls or conveniently-placed estates but all the diverse elements which enabled the Tory landowners in one area, the Whigs in another, to secure local supremacy. And local supremacy was cherished not merely because it carried with it prestige in the county, and the ability to get local jobs for one's own friends, relations and clients, but above all because of the electoral power it conferred and the consequent opportunity to influence national issues.* In this fiercely competitive county society not only local Land Tax officials but even Post Office officials became, in many areas, pawns in the national party game. It was no coincidence

---

* There is a masterly development of this aspect of the background to contemporary politics in J. H. Plumb, *Sir Robert Walpole : The Making of a Statesman*, pp. 42–50.

that Receiverships, for instance, were quite frequently procured for men who had been prominent election managers for their party — men like William Burslem in Staffordshire, John Prinn and Thomas Webb in Gloucestershire and James Caswall in Herefordshire — or that the Earl of Sunderland, while Secretary of State, should have contrived to extend the authority of the Whig Receiver for Northamptonshire over Rutland, the territory of the High Tory leader, Lord Nottingham.[65] As for the post, it was at the best of times a risky medium of communication for politicians (a fact which explains the early-eighteenth-century penchant for writing in code);[66] but before and during elections letters might well be tampered with or deliberately delayed as a matter of course, so that it became a matter of great advantage to both party interests to get the local postmasters under their own control.[67]

When party rivalries in the shires were not being absorbed by the electoral struggle they readily found other channels. A new commission of the peace gave the local pillars of one party the coveted opportunity to lord it over their opponents at the Quarter Sessions;[68] and Whig and Tory pride was always much at stake in the county race meetings, like those at Quainton, Brackley, York and Lincoln, as well as in the great spring and autumnal gatherings at Newmarket. That staunch Tory gentleman, Sir Thomas Cave, positively congratulated himself at having been forced to miss the season's sport at Brackley in October 1712: "I must confess", he admitted to his father-in-law (who was less fortunate), "my spiritts would have bin upon the frett to see King Tom.* runn away with the prize, and well may the Whigs have the best Horses since they have all the money . . ."[69]

There was a third world, very different from the world of the shire or of London society but of rapidly-growing importance, which the party war invaded in the early eighteenth century. This was the world of business and finance, one in which the Whigs inherited from William III's reign a great natural advantage but which they could never wholly monopolise. The desperate need of governments in most years between 1689 and 1713 for loans to support the wars against Louis XIV made this a fertile field for men of capital on the make; and the competing business groups which struggled for the plums inevitably sought the backing of the politicians of one side or another or became directly involved in politics themselves. The great duel between the Tory-supported Old East India Company and the Whig-dominated New Company in the years 1698–1702 established a pattern of party rivalry in the City which persisted to the end of Anne's reign. We find

* i.e. Lord Wharton.

it repeated in the several Tory attempts to undermine public confidence in the Bank of England, which was the most hated symbol of the preponderance of Whig business interests; in the ready welcome given by the Tories to men of capital who were "disobliged" by the Whig ruling clique of the United East India Company after 1708;[70] in the bid of the Tory "moneyed men" to capture the directorates both of the Bank and of the East India Company in 1711; or in the eagerness with which Tory merchants, goldsmiths and financiers — men like Sir James Bateman, Samuel Clarke, George Caswall and Sir Theodore Janssen — invested in the South Sea Company when it came into being under the auspices of the Harley ministry.*

The armed forces were no more immune from the effects of political division in the nation than were the social and business worlds. The struggle for promotion in the higher ranks of both army and navy frequently hinged on the possession of influential friends in power, and it was no minor consideration whether the politics of any aspirant coincided with those of the party in the ascendant at Court, or, if he were an army man, whether they were acceptable to the Captain-General. The violent political storm which blew up over the disposal of Lord Essex's regiment in January 1710, when for the first time Queen Anne made a lucrative military appointment contrary to Marlborough's advice, underlined the enormous patronage which the duke had enjoyed since 1702;[71] and there seems little doubt that in the years 1704–10, when Marlborough and Godolphin were never free from some measure of dependence on the Whigs in Parliament, Whig officers carried off the bulk of the most coveted prizes in the army. Galway, Peterborough and Stanhope, for instance, the leading generals in the Peninsula between 1704 and 1710, were all Whigs, even if Peterborough was a distinctly unorthodox one.[72] The 21 officers commissioned major-general or lieutenant-general between 1 May 1707 and 1 January 1709 included a dozen Whig stalwarts, among them Cadogan, Palmes, Meredith, Mordaunt, Temple and Farrington, but only one Tory (Webb) currently a member of the House of Commons, and indeed only five Tories in all.† By 1710 not merely political but parliamentary voting considerations were clearly dictating Whig recommendations for army promotion.[73]

* These points are developed at length in Chapter 5.

† The other 4 Tories promoted were Northumberland, North and Grey, Barrymore and George Hamilton. The last two became M.P.s later in the reign. By contrast, in addition to the six mentioned above, three other sitting Whig members, Stanhope, Shannon and Emmanuel Howe, received major-general's or lieutenant-general's commissions in this period. See Charles Dalton, *English Army Lists and Commission Registers, 1661–1714,* vols. v, vi, 1702–14 (1902, 1904).

After the summer of 1710, however, the prospects of Whig military men were strikingly affected by the change in party fortunes at home. Before the end of the year three Whig generals had been suspended and forced to sell out for drinking damnation to the new ministry.[74] In addition "it was thought necessary [as Boyer remarked], in order to strengthen the hands of the new Ministry and the Church Party, to do justice to some military gentlemen who seem'd to have been neglected under the last Ministry".[75] The command in Portugal was given to Lord Portmore, who was credited with Tory views though he claimed to have "never affected to be a party man";[76] Charles Ross, an ex-Jacobite who was now a Scottish member of Parliament, was made General of Dragoons over the heads of ten more senior Lieutenant-Generals;[77] while Marlborough's own hands in the field of military patronage were deliberately tied by the institution in February 1711 of the new Committee of the Council at the War Office.[78] The new pattern was maintained for the rest of the reign. The expedition to Quebec in 1711 was put in the hands of Abigail Masham's Tory brother, Jack Hill; Marlborough himself was replaced by Ormonde at the end of that year; and in 1714, when the war was over, Ormonde and Bolingbroke began to weed out recalcitrant Whigs from key posts in the army in anticipation of the possibility of a disputed succession, going down in the process to regimental level, and in the case of the Guards to company level.[79]

More obvious to the ordinary Briton, since it impinged so much more on his own life, was the way in which the spirit of party permeated the churches in the age of Anne. In Scotland to be an Episcopalian was to be, almost *ipso facto*, a Tory and not infrequently a Jacobite. The ministers of the Kirk, on the other hand, found their most natural champions among the Scottish Whigs and the associated followers of the "Squadrone",* and after the Union among the English Whigs and Low Church clergy.[80] In England it would not be strictly true to say that party seriously divided the Anglican Church on a theological plane: a genuine theological controversy, such as that produced by William Whiston's Arian doctrines in 1711, could even unite Whig and Tory divines. But there often appeared to be a serious cleavage within the Church, as in sermon, pamphlet and debate the protagonists of the "High" and "Low" schools of thought sought quasi-theological justification for positions that were in essence more political than religious.† "A

---

* See pp. 242–5 below.

† The history of the Anglican Church in Anne's reign is best approached through the many notable biographical contributions of the past two decades, of which the most illuminating to the layman, as far as the Church's general character is concerned, are

good sermon", especially one preached on an official occasion, tended to be judged primarily by its political content; so that when the Tory peers complained forcibly in the House of Lords in 1712 of the address preached by Trimnell of Norwich (a Junto client) on the anniversary of Charles I's execution, "the Bishop of Sarum thanked God he was there and professt he never heard a better".[81] "That wch. they call religion", protested one Anglican clergyman in 1710, "seems to me to look no farther than the affairs of this world ... Our disputes are not for the sake of truth, but zeal for parties".[82]

The most serious and the most conspicuous effect which the conflict of Tory and Whig had upon the Church of England was to divide it on a personal level. There were times when it made a bear-garden of the Convocation of Canterbury, where the rancorous disputes between the bishops, marshalled by Tenison, and the Lower House, led by the fiery Atterbury, were more productive of violent antipathies than of constructive religious work. But equally distressing were the personal conflicts in many dioceses, where Whig and Tory loyalties drove a wedge of political animosity between Low Church bishops and their predominantly High Church cathedral and parish clergy. In the diocese of Worcester William Lloyd's vigorous campaigning (despite his 80-odd years) on behalf of Whig candidates in the county elections, and his attempts to harry his clerical flock into following his lead, were the cause of much bad blood. "The good Bp.", remarked a local baronet in 1702, "charges his Clergy in his visitation every where, upon theyr canonicall obedience, not to give theyr votes for Sr J[ohn] Pak[ington]",[83] and there was satisfaction in many a Worcestershire vicarage later that year when the House of Commons denounced Lloyd's intervention in the election as "malicious, unchristian and arbitrary" and he was deprived by the Queen, at their request, of his post of Lord Almoner.[84] At Carlisle the feud between Bishop Nicolson and his dean and chapter ran so high in the middle years of the reign that in the end Nicolson sought the help of Lord Somers and his Whig friends in 1708 to settle the matter by act of Parliament.[85] And just as Nicolson's *bête noire* was Atterbury, Burnet's was Thomas Naish, sub-dean of Salisbury, "the perfect incendiary" of his diocese and a perpetual obstacle to the bishop's electioneering in Wiltshire between 1701 and 1705. The political disagreement between the two men reached such a pitch after the 1705 Election that Burnet brought a lawsuit against Naish, had him deprived of the rectory of St. Edmunds,

N. Sykes's masterly *William Wake, Archbishop of Canterbury* (2 vols. Cambridge, 1957) and G. V. Bennett's admirable study of *White Kennett, 1660–1728* (1957).

relieved him of his seal of office as Surrogate and suspended him for three years. And although the suspension was later relaxed, the financial hardship involved in this vendetta would probably have broken Naish's spirit had not some of the leading Wiltshire Tories, from Lord Weymouth and the two knights of the shire downward, rallied to his aid with "many good gifts".[86]

Even more than the dissensions in the religious world, however, it was the influence of the Press which brought home most forcibly to the ordinary, literate subject of Queen Anne the depth and breadth of the fissure which ran through the political nation. Since the lapsing of the Licensing Act in 1695 had removed any effective censorship the Press had developed into an ancreasingly formidable political engine; and by the early years of Anne's reign its energies had already been firmly harnessed in the service of Whig and Tory. The production of party propaganda or government propaganda employed the talents not only of some of the commanding figures of English literature — Swift, Addison, Steele and Defoe — but of most of the rank and file of what came to be known, half-affectionately, half-contemptuously as "Grub Street". Many of the practitioners were common party hacks, mere "scribblers" in the contemporary phrase; but others were journalists of real if varied abilities, whose names became household words far more than those of many a member of Parliament. Of such a calibre were the ex-Huguenot exile, Abel Boyer; Oldmixon and Dyer, who epitomised the most violent extremes of party prejudice; Roper of the *Post Boy*, Tutchin of the *Observator*, and Ridpath of the *Flying-Post*.

Of the privately-sponsored newspapers, of which there were already 18 in London alone by 1709 as well as several in the provinces, a majority were politically committed. The *Post Boy*, throughout the reign as a whole, was probably the most widely read of the Tory prints. With an average sale of some 3000–4000 copies per issue between 1704 and 1712, and with many other copies (in accordance with contemporary practice) regularly given away, it would not be surprising if many numbers of the *Post Boy* passed through the hands of upward of 50,000 readers.[87] Outside the London area, however, its circulation cannot have approached that of John Dyer's manuscript Newsletter, the political bible of the Tory squire and parson, with its flagrant party bias and its Jacobitical undertones;* nor by 1710–11 could it

---

* A large squad of clerks was regularly employed in transcribing Dyer's intemperate prose thrice-weekly for the enlightenment of "the Church interest", not only in every part of England but even in outposts abroad. "Let me know by your next whether Dyer's Letter be of any use to you . . .", Charles Davenant wrote to his son Henry, English minister at Frankfort, "& whether he has been punctual in sending. If you doe not like it I will

compete with the *Examiner*, a new weekly political journal of rare quality*
for the more sophisticated Tory readers. The *Rehearsal* (from 1704 to 1709)
and the *Supplement* were two other papers which consistently expressed the
Tory point of view. Yet up to 1710, at least, the Whigs held a decided
advantage in the newspaper war. The *Observator* gave them firm support;
and the *Post Man* (which had at least as heavy a circulation as the *Post Boy*),
the *British Mercury* and the *Evening Post* were as favourable as their overwhelming emphasis on foreign news permitted. Buckley's *Daily Courant*,
originally non-committal, made some valuable contributions to the party
cause later in the reign, thanks to the author's access to inside information
from the Continent and from allied representatives in London.[88] As for
George Ridpath's *Flying-Post*, it was a tower of strength to the Whigs
throughout, and most of all in the closing years of the reign when its editor
was fearless in attacking the Tory peace and upholding the Hanoverian
cause. When he was being hounded by the ministry in 1712 a donation of
"two guineas for Ridpath" became an accepted "touch stone" of Whiggery
in the coffee-houses and the clubs.[89]

Nothing betrayed the political sympathies of newspapers more plainly
than their coverage of General Elections. This became steadily more
ambitious as the reign went on, progressing from the mere printing of polls,
mostly without comment, in 1702 to quite detailed reports of many individual contests in 1710 and 1713. Comparison of some of these reports
indicates that the editors of Anne's day had little to learn about journalistic
bias. The *Rehearsal*, for instance, contrasted the "body of all the chief gentry
and most reputable yeomanry of the county" attending "the noble Tackers"
into Ipswich for the Suffolk election in May 1705 with the "scoundrel
medly" which accompanied the Whig candidates; "excepting Sir Thomas
Felton and two more, I do not think there were three Gentlemen to head
that herd".[90] Readers of the *Post Man* would have been justifiably puzzled
by this intelligence, for only a few weeks before a Suffolk correspondent had
told them how these same Whig candidates had met the Duke of Grafton,
the Lord Lieutenant and leader of the Whig interest in the county, a mile

stop it after the current quarter . . . 'twill be 5 *l.* p. annum savd". (B.M. Lansdowne
MSS. 773, f. 29: 21 Apr. 1704. The subscription for domestic readers was £4 p.a.).
Specimens of the handiwork of this "sawcy scribler" (Add. MSS. 28893, f. 137) will be
found in 'A Collection from Dyer's Letters concerning the elections of the present
Parliament' (London, 1705). There is a complete run for 1709 and 1710 in B.M. Loan
29/320–1, and four large volumes covering the period Jan. 1702–Nov. 1711 are preserved
in the Marquess of Bath's archive at Longleat.

* Written by Swift from 2 Nov. 1710 to 7 June 1711.

from Ipswich "with 13 ... coaches full of Gentlemen, 500 Freeholders, and Captain Boll with 24 ship standards or Ensigns", and that "the horse ... placed in order and march'd two and two ... reach'd above a mile".[91] As well as finding in their newspapers election reports duly slanted to their tastes, the electors in London, Westminster, Southwark, Surrey and Middlesex also looked to them for campaign literature and even for instructions from the local party managers.[92]

The commitment of the press to the party battle was not, of course, confined to the newspapers and weekly journals. Every political crisis of the period, whether that over the Spanish succession in 1701, Occasional Conformity from 1702 to 1704, Sacheverell's impeachment in 1710, the making of peace in 1711–12 or the Hanoverian succession in 1713–14, produced its own storm of pamphlets. For weeks before every General Election pamphlets and broadsheets alike descended "thick as hail".[93] In 1710 the printing presses poured out material of this kind so freely that Swift complained to Dean Stearne that it could "very well employ a man every day from morning till night to read them". He himself solved the problem by not reading any,[94] but his self-abnegation was untypical. By the eve of the Election the demand for Tory publications had become so overwhelming that it was observed "that the hawkers would not cry the Whig-ones at last".[95] Indeed it is abundantly clear from many kinds of contemporary evidence that the appetite of the literate public for this type of polemical literature was avid. The printers ran off 10,000 copies of one successful pamphlet before the 1713 Election; Defoe's *The True-Born Englishman*, its author claimed, sold 80,000; while *Faults on Both Sides* had "a prodigious run" in 1710.[96] Most significant of all was the attitude of the authorities towards those who traded on this popular craving. "We are fain to send messengers among your printers and booksellers", wrote one exasperated Under-Secretary in October 1711, "to stop a little this madness & folly of the press", and the imposition of a stamp duty of a penny a sheet in 1712 underlined official concern at the enormous potential power of the pen in a divided society.*

In fact, although Whig and Tory politicians both owed much to their respective "Grub Street" armies the debt was reciprocal. Journalism may have been a profession with many occupational hazards in the age of Anne:

---

* Chetwynd Diplomatic MSS. D.649/8: George Tilson to Jn. Chetwynd, 16 Oct. 1711. The duty imposed in 1712 would have been still more swingeing had not the Commons in committee reduced the government's original proposal by half. They also rejected its plan to extend the duty to written news-sheets like Dyer's. Folger Library, L.C. 3460–1: Newsletters to Sir R. Newdigate, 1, 3 May 1712.

it brought Defoe to the pillory, and earned Abel Roper a sound thrashing in the lobby of the House of Commons from an infuriated Whig M.P.; while Tutchin's taunts once so infuriated Marlborough that he threatened to "find some friend that will break his and the printer's bones".[97] But thanks to the sustained political excitement generated by the conflict of parties it became, for the successful writer at least, a more lucrative profession than ever before.[98]

* * *

Most of the evidence so far surveyed would appear to lend heavy support to a basically traditionalist interpretation of British politics in Anne's reign. And yet, impressive as its cumulative effect is, it does not by itself carry complete conviction. For we have still to meet the critics of the conventional view on their own chosen ground, that of Parliament. It has been shown that the men of the early eighteenth century continually *assumed* that the character of politics in their day was moulded chiefly by the struggle for supremacy between two parties which were recognisable entities, each of far more importance than its component parts. Contemporary life, at a wide variety of levels, was so permeated by the rivalry between Whig and Tory that it is hard to see how this assumption could have been avoided. But whether it could be squared with the facts of the parliamentary situation is a question which cannot be adequately judged without testing the assumption against the most searching of all the criteria that can be applied to it — namely the evidence contained in the surviving division-lists of the period.

Even making due allowance for the inevitable limitations of this evidence, the results of such tests could hardly be more conclusive. The vocabulary of contemporary politicians and the obvious saturation of so many fields of national life by the spirit of party offer cold comfort to those who try to interpret politics in the age of Anne and politics in the age of Newcastle in similar terms. But the division-lists destroy the validity of such attempts completely. They do so, as recent detailed work on the Commons' lists has demonstrated, for the simple reason that they hoist the revisionists with their own petard.*

The multi-party interpretation of the politics of Queen Anne's reign rests in the end on the hypothesis that parliamentary divisions regularly cut across conventional two-party lines, and that the politician who divided

---

* This analysis has been undertaken by W. A. Speck of Newcastle University in the course of his work for an Oxford D.Phil. dissertation on 'The House of Commons, 1702–14: a Study in Political Organization'. I owe much to his generosity in making his findings available to me before the completion of his thesis in Sept. 1965.

consistently on the Whig or Tory side on "party matters" (that is, questions in which party principle, some aspect of party policy, or simply party advantage were involved) was the exception rather than the rule. Dr. Walcott puts it this way: 'The "Tory" side in any one division *inevitably* included many who at other times voted "Whig" and vice versa'.[99] Analysis of 9 of the 10 Commons' division-lists for the years 1702–14 which are known to be still in existence,* and the correlation of the results with 3 general parliamentary lists of the period which classify members of the House of Commons under party heads, including one for 1714 with invaluable information on voting behaviour,† reveals just how unfounded such an assumption is. It shows that of the 1064 English and Welsh M.P.s whose names appear on these 12 lists only a small fraction, roughly one eighth, are *ever* found 'cross-voting' or voting 'against the party line', either on the very representative selection of questions with which the 9 specific divisions were concerned or on the still wider range of issues embraced by the general list for 1714; and this proportion, we must remember, included the genuine government members‡ as well as the errant party men. On the other hand the Tories can

* The 10th, the division on the repeal of the place clause of the Act of Settlement in Feb. 1706, was a Court/Country issue as opposed to a Whig/Tory one. The other 9 divisions were concerned respectively with the Abjuration oath (Feb. 1703), the "tack" of the Occasional Conformity bill (Nov. 1704), the election of a Speaker (Oct. 1705), the Naturalization bill (Mar. 1709), the impeachment of Sacheverell (1710), the South Sea bill (May 1711), "No Peace without Spain" (Dec. 1711), the Treaty of Commerce with France (June 1713), and the condemnation of Richard Steele (Mar. 1714). The limitations of some of these lists as precise evidence are discussed by Speck, *loc. cit.*, and also by R. Walcott, 'Division Lists of the House of Commons, 1689–1715' (*Bull. I.H.R.* xiv, 25–36), who indicates the location of 6 out of the 9. The list for Oct. 1705 is printed *ibid.* xxxvii, 38–46; that for Dec. 1711, *ibid.* xxxiii, 233–4; and that for May 1711 in *Hist. Journal*, iv (1961), 193.

5 new division-lists relating either to the Commons or to the Lords, 1702–14, have been unearthed in the past few years, and it seems very likely that more will soon come to light. It is known, for instance, that lists were circulated both after the Commons' division on the Hanoverian arrears on 12 May 1714 and after the Lords' division on the Land Grants bill in May 1712 (B.M. Loan 29/66/3: Lord Harley to Abigail Harley, 13 May 1714; Trumbull Add. MSS. 134: T. Bateman to Trumbull, 26 May 1712).

† Viz. a list of members returned at the General Election of 1710, marked "Whig", "Tory" and "Doubtful", in B.M. Stowe MSS. 223, ff. 453–6; a list of members of the exclusively Tory October Club [1711], printed in A. Boyer's *Political State of Great Britain*, March 1712; and a "Liste Exacte du Dernier Parlement" [i.e. that of 1713–14], divided into Whigs, Tories, "Whigs who often voted Tory" and "Tories who often voted Whig" (the last two categories, except for a few "Court Whigs", being made up almost entirely of so-called "Hanoverian Tories"): in Worsley MSS. 1.

‡ See pp. 355–7 below.

show 495 members who never deviated on any of these issues from the ortho-dox party position. This is an impressive tally, though it is only fair to say that it would be slightly reduced were there any authentic lists of members who voted against the tacking of the Occasional Conformity bill to the Land Tax bill in 1704 to match those which enumerate "the tackers" themselves.* The Whigs' record is more impressive still. Although there are considerably fewer Whigs than Tories among the grand total, no less than 439 of them appear on the Whig side in every division for which they register a vote or are firmly classified as Whigs in every general list which has survived. In the end we are left with a mere 130 members out of the whole 1064 who appear, even superficially, as political hybrids.[100]

So much can be deduced simply from a correlation of the lists themselves, without bringing to bear on them extraneous information which can make possible a rather more precise identification of the politics of some of the individuals involved, as well as allowing some insight into the motives which activated the cross-voters. When this more searching scrutiny is made it reveals no significant change in the general pattern of voting behaviour; but it does illuminate certain aspects of it more clearly. It suggests most forcibly, for example, that the deviations of the Tories, who make up much the greater part of those who voted inconsistently, reflect in most cases not so much erratic personal behaviour, or the vagaries of specific connexions, as the uneasy state of the Tory conscience on such fundamental questions as the peace settlement and the succession. Thus of the 130 members who are known to have cast votes variously on the Whig and Tory side between 1703 and 1714 no fewer than 95 were Tories who defaulted in the three controversial divisions of 7 December 1711, 18 June 1713 and 18 March 1714, all of which involved these issues directly or indirectly.† Even then the scale of the defections, on two of these occasions at least, was very small — less than 5% of the Tory strength in the House in December 1711 and between 8 and 9% in March 1714. And on three other questions of principle where no serious difference of opinion in the party existed — on the ex-tension of the time allowed for taking the abjuration oath,‡ on the bill for a General Naturalization of Foreign Protestants§ and on Sacheverell's

---

* See pp. 102–3 below.

† Among the English and Welsh members 11 Tories defaulted in the division on "No Peace without Spain", 76 in that on the Commerce bill and 21 in the Richard Steele division, but several names occur in two or more of these lists. In addition 3 Scottish Tories voted with the Whigs against the Bill of Commerce and the condemnation of Steele.

‡ See pp. 90–1 below.　　　　　§ See pp. 69, 105–6 below.

impeachment — desertions on the Tory side, very significantly, were virtually non-existent. As for the Whigs, the more closely the lists are analysed the more remarkable is the impression of consistency and cohesion which emerges. The division-lists alone reveal only 10 Whigs in all who voted against their party, and one of those was Sir Robert Raymond, Harley's Solicitor-General from 1710 to 1714, who was a Whig of the most apologetic variety.[101] In addition the Worsley list of Queen Anne's last Parliament names 8 other Whigs who cast an occasional Tory vote in the course of the 1714 session, and 5 of these appear on strict examination to have been under some degree of obligation to the Court, enough to make it inexpedient for them to oppose the government on any and every occasion.[102] These figures speak so eloquently for themselves that they require no further comment.

For the House of Lords the surviving lists are fewer than for the Commons and, since over half of them relate to cognate issues, slightly less satisfactory as an overall guide to political conduct. For Anne's reign itself only four actual division-lists can as yet be deployed. Two of these have long been in print in the *Parliamentary History*: those for 14 December 1703, naming the peers who voted for and against giving a Second Reading to the Occasional Conformity bill, and 20 March 1710, listing those who voted Dr. Sacheverell guilty and not guilty of high crimes and misdemeanours.[103] The remaining two are recently-discovered manuscript lists: one a record of the division of the House on 16 January 1703 over the "penalties amendment" to the first Occasional Conformity bill, the vital amendment by which the bill stood or fell; the other a "list of peers who voted in Duke Hamilton's case" on 20 December 1711.[104] However, the deficiency can partly be made up by making use of three additional lists, all of which supply valuable information about the political behaviour of the members of the House of Lords in the early eighteenth century. The first, relating to the division on the impeachment of Lord Somers, the Whig leader, on 17 June 1701, was printed in a contemporary pamphlet and is authenticated by a manuscript version among the papers of Robert Harley.[105] The other two are detailed and obviously reliable estimates, one by Lord Treasurer Oxford, the other by the Earl of Nottingham, of how the Lords would divide on particular issues of vital importance late in Anne's reign. The first issue was the Treaty of Commerce with France (the bill giving effect to which never, in fact, reached the Upper House because, to the government's amazement, it was thrown out by the Commons at the Third Reading in June 1713), and the second was the Schism bill of June 1714.[106]

Of the six questions to which the Lords' lists refer, three (Occasional

Conformity, the Sacheverell case and the Schism bill) involved clear-cut issues of Whig and Tory principle, while a fourth (Somers's impeachment) roused party loyalties to a marked degree.* The Treaty of Commerce was an issue on which the Tories were genuinely divided in opinion (though the peers were far less so than the commoners, who had their elections to consider in a few weeks' time) but on which the Whigs were almost unanimous. Finally there was the Hamilton division, in which the House determined that the recent award of a new title in the peerage of Great Britain to a Scottish representative peer, the Tory Duke of Hamilton, did not give him the right to a hereditary seat in Parliament. Although expected to be a "cause . . . debated without party"[107] it proved in the event to be a test of extreme partisanship, especially on the Whig side; since the Junto, in opposing Hamilton's claim to sit and vote as Duke of Brandon, sought to make an issue of party advantage out of a constitutional and legal case, while the Tory ministers appealed to their own supporters not to weaken Tory strength in the House of Lords by denying Hamilton his hereditary seat there at a critical period for the government and the party.[108] The result was that party considerations influenced more votes than would otherwise have been the case, though fewer, perhaps, than the party leaders hoped for.

There is, therefore, just sufficient reliable and relevant evidence in these various documents to make possible a thorough analysis of the voting habits of the Lords, comparable to that already undertaken for the Commons. The results of this survey are given in detail elsewhere.† Here it need only be said that, in spite of the constant presence in the Upper House of a very large body of peers who had ties with the Court of one sort or another,‡ and in spite also of the fact that two of the secular questions involved were allowed at the time to have produced some freakish voting, the lists reveal a pattern of behaviour on major issues which is not strikingly dissimilar to that shown in the Commons, though it is somewhat less pronounced. Out of 209 lay and spiritual peers whose names appear in two or more of the lists 144 neither deviated nor were expected to deviate from the path of party orthodoxy. Leaving aside the Hamilton division, which as we have seen was a very special case and in which no fewer than 17 peers register their only wayward vote, the proportion of cross-voters or prospective cross-voters is a mere 23% of the whole; and of this small minority the Tories account for two-thirds.

* See pp. 63–4 below.
† See Appendix A: 'Party Allegiance in the House of Lords, 1701–14', pp. 421–35 below.
‡ See Appendix B: 'The Queen's Servants in the House of Lords, Feb. 1714', pp. 436–9 below.

One other point emerges quite clearly from a comparison of the Lords' lists. As a test of political consistency on religious issues they could hardly be more conclusive in demonstrating that there was a firm Whig and Tory position on such questions throughout the reign of Anne, and that, with the exception of a few pure courtiers and of the Scots, the vast majority of peers adhered (or were expected to adhere) to this position in key divisions.

Most of the detailed information we have, then, on how individuals voted in Queen Anne's Parliaments seems to endorse all the more firmly a basically orthodox view of the party politics of the age, as modified by Feiling's brilliant study of the Tory party, which taught us more than forty years ago that both the composition and the principles of that party made it less disciplined and more liable to division than the Whigs. If the argument were to end here it could safely be said that the revisionists would be left with little or no ground to stand on.

In a recent paper, however,[109] Dr. Walcott has somewhat relaxed the rigidity of his earlier position by conceding that great questions of religious principle did occasionally arise in the later Stuart period which produced an orientation along broadly two-party lines. 'On issues that stirred men in the late seventeenth and eighteenth centuries [he writes] — Exclusion, the Protestant Succession, the Safety of the Church — there was clearly a "Whig" and a "Tory" side ... However, within the walls of Parliament as it concerned itself with the day-to-day work of government in the intervals between controversy over the great issues (most of them religious) the apparent division into two national parties dissolves into the multi-party structure normally associated with the reign of George III.' Naturally it is not so easy to appeal to the division-lists against this latest verdict, for, as one would expect, most lists have survived for the very reason that they were concerned with major issues which had aroused considerable public interest and excitement. Those that are in print were usually published and circulated in order to provide useful electoral ammunition and in the knowledge that their very rarity and importance would guarantee them a close scrutiny from voters all over the country.* Equally detailed information on the 'bread-and-

---

* There can be no question that they did arouse great interest and that they did influence votes. The Sacheverell lists which were circulated in 1710 are a case in point. The prospects of James Grahme in Westmorland were improved, and those of Sir Humphrey Briggs and Francis Wyndham at Bridgnorth and Gloucester seriously damaged, by the publicity given to their votes for and against the Doctor respectively. (H.M.C. *Bagot MSS.* p. 342; Monson MSS. 7/13/123: G. Scroop to Sir Jn. Newton, 26 June; Add. MSS. 28893, ff. 394, 398–9). See Luttrell, v, 561 for the case of the Whig beaten to death in 1705 for displaying a list of the "Tackers" to the electors of Queenborough.

butter' divisions which took place regularly in every Parliament simply does not exist. And yet even in those lists we do have there is enough evidence to raise very marked queries against the latest modification of the Walcott thesis.

There are, for example, 5 Commons' lists for the years 1705–14, and 2 Lords' lists for 1701–11 which have no obvious or direct relevance to religious issues. They relate to the acquittal of Somers in 1701, the choice of a Speaker in 1705, the South Sea bill, the peace preliminaries and the Hamilton case in 1711, the Commerce bill in 1713, and the censure of Richard Steele in 1714 for his anti-government writings in *The Crisis* and *The Englishman*. Only on 2 of these 7 occasions, on 20 December 1711 and on 18 June 1713, do we find a really appreciable number of Tories on the Whig side of the fence. In the Hamilton division Tory peers supplied more than a quarter of the opposition vote (17 out of 57) and in the Commerce division in the Commons Tory rebels, with 81 votes, made up roughly two-fifths of the number which so narrowly defeated the bill. But both occasions were exceptional. In the Hamilton vote, as we have seen, many of the more independent peers on both sides considered themselves released from normal party obligations ("as to this affair of ours", remarked Lord Mar soon afterwards, "there is nothing so like a Whige as a Torie and nothing so like a Torie as a Whige");[110] and according to the most authentic version we have of the Commerce bill division,[111] no fewer than 42, or more than half, of the Tories who rebelled against the Court were straying from the party fold virtually *for the first time* since this Parliament had assembled, two and a half years before, in November 1710.[112] In none of the other 5 divisions under review did the Tories account for more than a seventh of the total vote on the Whig side.[113]

What is more, when one looks more searchingly at the identity and the political and family background of the dissidents on all these occasions there is very little evidence that the pull of connexion was a major factor in their behaviour, as we should surely expect it to have been if a 'multi-party' structure in Parliament really was the political norm. The peace rebels of December 1711 were a completely heterogeneous bunch[114] as were the Tory peers who voted against the Duke of Hamilton. Of the 4 Tories who voted with the Whigs on the amendment to the South Sea bill in May 1711[115] not one was a Nottinghamite, although Lord Nottingham himself was in fact the only prominent Tory figure who was opposed to the bill.[116] Admittedly there were some followers of the Earls of Abingdon and Anglesey among the opponents of the Treaty of Commerce in 1713, but it is unlikely that they accounted for more than a fifth of all the Tory deserters on that occasion. Only in the Speaker's election of 1705, when 13 of the 27 Tories who voted for John Smith were known adherents of Robert Harley, could it be claimed that connexion played a notable part in breaking up normal two-party alignments; and even here it was not the main factor, for Smith was the *government* candidate for the Chair, and at the time of the vote Harley and seven of his friends were members of the government and committed to support it on this question.

Thus even the Tory record in these 7 divisions affords no convincing support for the theory that party denominations counted for little — and that loyalty to smaller groups or connexions counted for much — whenever non-religious issues were under debate. As for the Whig record, it goes far to demolish this theory altogether. As far as we can judge it (in only 4 of the 7 cases are we provided with the 'Tory' side in the division), it was a truly remarkable record. Only 4 Whig peers could be found to vote against Somers's acquittal in 1701, and (more surprisingly) only 9[117] declined to support the Junto in their factious attack on Hamilton in 1711, despite the fact that no Whig principle was in any way at stake. In the Commons in 1713 the 185 supporters of the Court's Commerce bill included a mere 8 Whigs, most of them in office. But the most astonishing and revealing fact of all is that among the 205 members who supported the High Tory William Bromley for Speaker in 1705 there is not a single identifiable Whig.

Both in 1705 and in 1708 the election to the Speaker's Chair was the cause of intense political excitement; and the story of these two elections, even though the second of them was not in the end taken to a division, is highly significant. Except for a period of uncertainty in October 1704, when it seemed that Harley might be forced to resign the Chair after becoming Secretary for the Northern Department, these were the only two occasions in Anne's reign when the identity of the new Speaker was not a foregone conclusion some weeks before the opening of Parliament.[118] In other words they offer us our best opportunity to observe the Whig and Tory leaders striving for a position of vantage commanding the "ordinary business" of the House. As everyone recognised, Mr. Speaker was a key figure in regulating the great bulk of parliamentary business; he, if anyone, could influence the course of those day-to-day matters which, we are now told, were impervious to Whig-Tory divisions. Yet all party men, we find, were keenly aware of the importance of controlling or influencing him. "To get *their Man*" into the Chair (as one observer so significantly put it)[119] was the pipe-dream, if not always the rational hope of ordinary members, as well as leaders, on both sides before every new Parliament. The possibility of a split between Court Tories and High Tories in October 1704, with the one side backing Harcourt and the other Bromley in case Harley stood down, had suggested to the Whigs, even at that time, that they might squeeze in a candidate of their own on a minority vote; or at least use their support of Harcourt to put the government heavily in their debt.[120] After their gains in the next General Election, however, they were in a position to bid outright for the Chair. Hence voting in October 1705 for this supposedly impartial arbiter was rigidly along party lines, with the Whigs to a man supporting a Whig candidate, and virtually every Tory backbencher together with a surprising number of Tory placemen* ignoring the pleas of the Court and backing his High Church rival.[121]

Equally instructive, however, is the fact that the success in 1705 of John Smith, a former Lord of the Treasury in the Junto administration of the 1690's and more recently a stern opponent of the Occasional Conformity bills in the Commons,[122] was not by itself sufficient to satisfy the Whig leaders — at least not for long. Neither the circumstances of his election nor his subsequent conduct in the Chair were entirely to their liking. He had stood as a Court candidate with Whig support, rather than as the party nominee endorsed by the Court;[123] and this distinction was emphasised later in the Parliament of 1705–8 when the Speaker was drawn more and more into the orbit of Lord Treasurer Godolphin and out of the control of the Whig hierarchy. Therefore in 1708, after Smith had been made Chancellor of the Exchequer and the Whigs had increased their House of Commons majority at a fresh General Election, the Junto lords were determined to have no repetition of this situation. They refused for many weeks to support the nomination of Sir Richard Onslow for the Chair of the new House on the ground that, though a zealous enough Whig and "one they formerly liked",[124] he was being put up like Smith before him as the *Court* candidate; and they insisted instead on running their own man, Sir Peter King, as a *party* nominee — "upon a Whig bottom", as the Earl of Sunderland put it.[125] Indeed they attached so much importance to this stand, and secured so much support among the Whig commoners, that but for Godolphin's last-minute capitulation to the Junto, involving the admission of Somers and Wharton to the Cabinet in November, William Bromley (who was once again the Tory candidate for the Speakership, counting on the support of all sections of his party) might well have succeeded in 1708 where he had failed in 1705.

* 17 in all. See W. A. Speck, 'The Choice of a Speaker in 1705', *Bull. I.H.R.* xxxvii (1964), 24–5.

The pattern of these two elections for Speaker, with the parties jostling for a position from which they could go far to govern the everyday business of the Commons, was by no means peculiar. That of 1705 was normally repeated whenever a contest took place over the chairmanship of one of the major working committees of the House. For instance, in November 1708 the Whigs voted William Farrer, the member for Bedford, into the chair of the Grand Committee of Supply, ejecting the long-serving Tory chairman, John Conyers, a favourite of Godolphin's who had given valuable service to the ministry since 1702.[126] They had had their eye on this vital tactical station three years earlier, but had not been quite strong enough then to prevent the Court "fixing Mr. Conyers in his throne".[127] Now, however, the Lord Treasurer was forced to bow reluctantly to the *force majeure* of party; and this meant that all the key committees had now passed into Whig hands, for in 1705 the Whigs had succeeded, after a very close struggle, in capturing the chair of the Committee of Privileges and Elections, carrying the day for Spencer Compton against Sir Gilbert Dolben.* By contrast with these straightforward party tussles in November 1705 and November 1708, it was the slightly more complex pattern of the 1708 Speaker's election which was almost repeated in reverse in 1710. Then the Tory backbenchers threatened to run their own man, Thomas Medlicott, for the Committee of Elections against a government-nominated Tory who they suspected would be too lenient towards their opponents.[128]

Control over this particular committee was especially coveted by party leaders, for the decision of controverted election cases occupied more of the time spent on public business in an average session than any other activity of the House of Commons apart from finance. Moreover the consideration of such cases grew steadily more partisan with each succeeding Parliament down to the session of 1709–10. "If the Lord should be extreme to mark what was done amiss by us in the matter of elections here, Mr. Speaker", Sir Edward Seymour is supposed to have said, with mock gravity, "the Lord have mercy upon us all."[129] Even office-holders were liable to follow the dictates of their party loyalties rather than the advice of their ministerial chiefs in voting on disputed elections. In February 1706 Godolphin com-

---

* In this contest on 7 Nov. 1705 Dolben was "set up by those who opposed the present Speaker [Smith]" a fortnight earlier, and was supported (as Bromley had been in the Speaker's election) by many Tory placemen, who ignored Godolphin's plea "not to mistake their interest" in this highly-important vote. B.M. Loan 29/64/8: [Godolphin] to Harley, "Wednesday at 2" [7 Nov.]; Lonsdale MSS.: J[ames] L[owther] to [Sir John Lowther], 8 Nov. (part in code); Blenheim MSS. A. 1–25: Harley to Marlborough, 9 Nov.

plained bitterly to Harley about "the loss of the Leicester election, and that all the Court Torys were for a Tacker . . . a very weak and foolish behaviour of those who are in office, to say no more"; but his representations could not prevent another spectacular desertion of placemen (among them some Harleyites) only a fortnight later over the Bewdley case.[130] A new peak of partisanship was reached in the winter of 1708–9 when the Whigs, relishing their first clear-cut majority since the Parliament of 1695–8, did not even bother to set up a Committee of Elections. Instead they decided all cases at the bar of the House, where there was no more than a pretence of an unbiased hearing of the evidence and where a speedy dispatch of their opponents was virtually assured.[131] After one setback due to over-confidence* the party majority secured a number of blatant decisions in favour of Whig candidates, culminating in one so grossly unjust in the case of the borough of Abingdon, where Sir Simon Harcourt was unseated,[132] that even the Bishop of Salisbury's highly selective conscience was pricked by the proceedings.† A group of Whigs in the House of Commons, including one or two who had suffered themselves from partiality in the past, did have the decency to oppose or dissociate themselves from such measures. But the number of these "squeamish gentlemen", most of them county members such as John Thornhagh, Peter Gott, Sir John Guise and Sir Harry Peachey, was too small to check the inexorable flow of the Whig tide;[133] and Tories like Sir Henry Bunbury, kept in the House until the early hours of the morning in the certain knowledge that however long they debated they would never "convince people that thirty are more than three", talked at one time of leaving the Commons in a body as a protest against these constitutional atrocities.[134]

Yet the situation did not change materially after 1710 when the Whigs lost their supremacy in the Commons. There was, admittedly, a reversion to committee procedure for the consideration of the bulk of election petitions; and on the first day the new House of Commons transacted business in November 1710 a debate which began with mutual recriminations on the

---

* In the Westminster election case (see pp. 305–6 below).

† Burnet, v, 396. Nevertheless there was a certain rough justice about Harcourt's fate, for in 1702, when one of his own friends was defending a seat won by the most dubious means, he had had no compunction himself about administering the law of the jungle to the unfortunate Whig petitioner, Sir John Guise: "not . . . in a drunken committee after dinner, but in the morning, at the barr of the House and in the face of the sun". *Memoirs of the Family of Guise* (Camden Soc., 1917), intro. p. 97; cf. Add. MSS. 33225, f. 17: Dr. Hare to Hy. Watkins, 28 Jan. 1709.

conduct of recent Parliaments in this field ended, according to one member, with

strong professions and resolutions of doing exact justice in the matter of elections without considering friend or enemy, and [promises] to forgive and overlook all past faults which might call for revenge; and that they would now in that matter consult the honour and justice of the house . . .[135]

But high-toned Tory promises of fair dealing[136] were very soon forgotten by the more vengeful and irresponsible young members, who had no patience with the restraint counselled by older and wiser heads in the party.[137] A few Whig members survived petitions — notably those returned for Lymington and Rye — but their opponents were soon glorying in "a train of victories in the house of Commons, in matter of elections", and even attempting to withhold writs to make it impossible for opponents whose elections had been declared void to get themselves rechosen in the current session.[138] After the 1713 Election a Dutch agent gloomily predicted that more than 50 out of roughly 160 Whigs just returned would be, as he put it, "chassés de la Chambre"; and while this proved to be an excessively pessimistic view it is a fact that by May 1714 a former member for Tewkesbury, now a spectator rather than a protagonist, was accusing the Committee of Elections of being "more partiall than ever I knew 'em".[139] Even Scottish elections after 1710 began to be judged more as "party causes" than on their merits; so that Mungo Graham, despite a seemingly cast-iron case and the refusal of most Scots members to vote according to "the art of Parliament", lost his seat for Clackmannanshire in February 1711 because many Tories "went up to the gallerys and skulkt their rather than vote as conscience dictated".[140]

No division-lists were ever published recording how M.P.s cast their votes in disputed election cases. Yet constituents and party managers had their own ways and means of discovering how this member or that had voted on these issues — or indeed on any other issue which involved party fortunes or party principles. And a politician could expect to be judged not merely on his reaction in a few crises of major import, like those over Occasional Conformity, the Regency bill or Sacheverell's impeachment, but on the consistency of his record throughout a whole session or more. When young Lord Pelham recommended Edmund Dunch to Boroughbridge in 1713 it was in the comforting knowledge that he had "always voted in Parliament with Mr. Jessop", who was the member for neighbouring Aldborough and a model of Whig orthodoxy. After the 1701 session of Parliament Sir John Kaye, who had sat as a Tory for Yorkshire, was bluntly told by Sir William

Lowther "that [if] he voted as he was inform'd he did last sessions . . . he must expect none of his interest if he stood againe". On the other hand Mrs. Burnet praised the Whig candidate for Hampshire, Thomas Jervoise, as "a worthy gentleman . . . who has hardly ever voted wrong in any Parliament", and approved Sir Richard Cocks's plans to contest Gloucestershire since she thought he had "voted well last year".[141]

There are two other categories of evidence which bear very much on the day-to-day parliamentary behaviour of individuals in both Houses of Queen Anne's Parliaments. Neither has ever been analysed before — a curious fact, for they both repay the closest study, and especially before any sweeping generalisation is made about what went on 'within the walls of Parliament . . . in the intervals between controversy over the great issues'. One is contained in the *Commons, Journals,* which supply the names of the two tellers on each side in every division recorded in the full House between 1702 and 1714. Collectively these names furnish a rich store-house of information, particularly when it is remembered that often (though not always) when a man was appointed a teller it meant that he had already made his position clear in the preceding debate. The other evidence is contained in the Proxy Book of the peers for the years 1685–1733, preserved among the manuscripts of the House of Lords.[142] Whenever a peer was to be absent he could, if he wished (and he usually did), leave his proxy with a relative, friend or party colleague who could then vote on his behalf if proxies were called for in the House.* The entrusting of a fellow-peer with one's proxy was an unusually searching test of a man's political attitudes and consistency, especially if he intended to be away for a prolonged period when he had no idea what motions or bills would come before the Lords in his absence.

Both these categories of evidence are, in their different ways, equally impressive as monuments to party loyalty and as corroboration of the basically two-party structure of parliamentary politics. From a study of the tellers, correlated with the appropriate division figures in the *Journals,* it can be deduced that as a general rule there were only three types of parliamentary business, other than purely private legislation, which could lead to men telling against what we know (or can reasonably assume) to have been the bulk of their party and which could sometimes produce substantial cross-voting. The first, predictably enough, was business which involved Court/ Country loyalties, such as place bills and bills against bribery and corruption

---

* Proxy votes were not allowed when the Lords were in committee on a bill. See, e.g., Nicolson's MS. Diary, 4 Dec. 1702.

in elections.* The second was financial business at the Report stage of Ways and Means, when constituency interests were at stake in the voting of new taxes and duties.† The third was legislation involving trade and trading interests, of which the East India Company bill and the two Africa Company bills of 1712 are just three examples.[143] The only notable exceptions to the general rule are found in two or three sessions like those of 1707–8 and 1714 when the two parties were really badly split for a while, either over tactics or over broad principles. As for the peers, the occasions when they left a proxy with a noble lord who was not of their own party were remarkably few; and most of those concerned were a handful of peers whose affiliations with the Court were as strong as or stronger than those with a party. Out of a total of 111 entries in the Proxy Book between 1704 and 1707, for example, there are a mere 5 instances of a Whig peer leaving his proxy with a Tory or vice versa. Three of these cases involved Court Whig Household officers — Somerset, Kent and St. Albans — entrusting their proxies to Lord Treasurer Godolphin at a time when Whig support of the Court in the House of Lords was so constant as to make such a step quite unexceptionable. There was also the case of Lord Delawarr, a courtier with tepid Tory sympathies but a good sense of self-preservation,‡ who switched his proxy in the winter of 1705–6 from Byron to Bridgewater. And finally there was Christopher Vane, Lord Barnard, who blotted a good Tory record in the early years of the reign by defecting in the winter of 1706–7.§ Otherwise, from lay and spiritual peers alike, the Book tells a tale of blameless consistency throughout these three years.

* * *

We can now see why the political vocabulary of the early eighteenth century was so plainly based on the assumption that the essence of politics was the conflict between Tory and Whig. The assumption was made because the facts of political life in Parliament and in the constituencies, like the facts of social, religious, business and professional life into which party politics had intruded, made it utterly inescapable. There were those, from

---

* These issues are discussed in Chap. 4, *passim.*

† Thus Cheshire members would oppose a new leather tax, Worcestershire members a new salt duty, Northumberland and Durham members a new imposition on coal, even when these were imposed by a ministry they normally supported. Lord Coningsby told the Duke of Ormonde in Feb. 1705 that a new linen bill had got through its Committee stage in the House "in spite of Lancashire". H.M.C. *Ormonde MSS.* N.S. viii, 137: 6 Feb.

‡ See pp. 385–6 below.

§ Not unpredictably, since he had been recognized as a Whig in William III's reign.

the Queen downwards, who found these facts unpalatable, even deplorable. Yet to ignore them for long was to close one's eyes wilfully to realities.

This had not always been so in William III's reign, and certainly not in the first half of his reign. For years after the Revolution the very existence of parties had been condemned or frowned on, not only by the Crown and some of its leading servants but by almost every political theorist and writer on the constitution.[144] Their view of party as a divisive and destructive element in the body politic, preventing the nation from realising its basic urge for unity and stability, was understandable in the political confusion which prevailed for all but the middle years of the 1690's. The pre-Revolution groupings, Tory and Whig alike, found great difficulty in adapting themselves to post-Revolution conditions, and it was relatively easy then to point to the illogicalities and artificialities of the old rivalries.* By 1702, however, under the influence of triennial elections, of the domestic and foreign crises which followed the deaths of the Duke of Gloucester and the King of Spain in 1700, and of the passions stirred by the impeachment of the Whig chiefs in 1701 and by a fresh wave of animosity between Church and dissent,† this period of uncertainty had been brought to an end. The line separating Tory from Whig had once more become firm and sharp: so sharp that in April 1702 we find Ralph Hare reminding the young Walpole that to allow the Tories to gain more ground in Norfolk elections would be "letting in persons that will not give *one vote* with you".[145] Thereafter the terminology of politics did no more and no less than reflect political actuality.

It is true that Queen Anne's Britain never wholly lost its guilt-complex about party. One finds it in predictable places such as the Queen's speeches to Parliament, with their regular appeals for "an union of minds and affections" and "calming men's minds at home", their warnings against the dire effects of "intestine divisions" and their note of plaintive hope that "there will be no contention among you but who shall most promote the public welfare";[146] and also in the most unlikely places — in the writings of Swift, for instance, the most unashamed and unscrupulous of partisans in practice. Even amid the excitement and fever of the Sacheverell affair in 1710 it was possible for hardened practising politicians in the House of Commons to pay lip-service to the notion that party divisions were noxious, for one of the charges in the fourth article of impeachment framed against the chaplain of St. Saviour's was that "as a public incendiary, he persuades her majesty's subjects to keep

---

* The transitional character of politics in the 1690's, and more especially its confused ideological background, is discussed in Chap. 2, pp. 59–61.

† See pp. 63–4, 65–6, 82–3, 98–101 below.

up a distinction of faction and parties".[147] The charge was the more ironical in that the resurrection of the old party battle-cries and the baring of old scars during the prosecution of Dr. Sacheverell created a climate in which the adherents of both parties saw their politics in blacks and whites more sharply contradistinguished than at any time since the Exclusion crisis of Charles II's reign. And basic distinctions were given still clearer emphasis later in the same year by an orgy of loyal addresses from the Tory gentry in the shires, most of them echoing reactionary political theories, and by devastating Tory propaganda on the old theme of "the Church in Danger". In this almost frenetic atmosphere there took place not only the ministerial revolution which brought Robert Harley to power, but also a General Election which for sheer bitterness and fury was never equalled in the eighteenth century. And as one of the successful candidates at this Election observed, "When the Parliament was assembled, in November 1710, it soon appear'd that ... the former litle subdivisions of the two grand parties were united and made two opposites, viz. Whigs and Tories".[148]

In such circumstances the partiality for the idea of "mixed ministries", coalitions representing various spectra of opinion in both parties, which both William III and Anne and a number of their leading ministers had often betrayed since 1689,* naturally seemed to most politicians misguided and irrelevant. After 1710 the area for compromise and common action between the two parties was even smaller than it had been since 1702, smaller in fact than at any time since 1685. So it is hardly surprising that an undeviating Tory like the Earl of Jersey should have bridled up at evidence of "trimming" by Harley's new administration, "proceedings ... which plainly shew that the Art of government must be put in practice, which Art I utterly abhor";[149] or that the independent High Tories who drew up the Commons' Representation to the Queen in June 1711 should have told her quite baldly that "schemes of balancing parties in her administration" were "wild and unwarrantable".[150] Nor was it only the extremists of the October Club, "blinded by the lust of party-rule",[151] who thought so. It had seemed to a City Tory of very temperate views before that session began that "things do best that are all of a piece";[152] while for Speaker Bromley in 1711 political sanity meant simply "putting the power into the hands of our freinds"; if that were done, he sincerely believed, the future would take care of itself.[153] Even some of the most loyal Harleyites could not now approve of any new marks of official favour being conferred on men who professed and called themselves Whigs, whether or not such men acknowledged some dependence

* See pp. 198–200; pp. 367 et seq.

on the Court or on Harley personally. "You may depend upon it", warned George Granville, "that nothing can be more prejudicial to you than the appointment of Lord Radnor as lord lieutenant of Cornwall, for however that family may be under your direction here [in London], there is that general aversion to it there that they will give everything for lost if such a step be taken".[154]

The logic behind this attitude was simple enough. To nine Tories out of ten it was unthinkable (at least in public) that any Whig could ever become a loyal supporter of the monarchy and the Church of England. "Nothing has surprised me more of late", confessed a Tory peer in May 1711, "than the news of Ld. Somers's and Lord Coopers being to be of the Councell, which if true* I shall conclude the lamb will lye down with the leopard . . ."[155] That the leopard could change his spots was a possibility so remote that it probably never occurred to him for a moment, any more than it occurred to the old Jacobite Earl of Ailesbury, who once told Lord Strafford, "the wasshing of a blackamoor white or a Whig is equally practicable".[156] To those of the true Tory faith there was no hope of making saints of "the divells called Whiggs".[157] Such sentiments, needless to say, were fully reciprocated on the Whig side. No man could be as hearty as he was for the Revolution, the Toleration and the Protestant Succession, claimed one Whig in 1711, "but he must be as different from a Tory, as a Hugonot from a Papist".[158] To the party leaders on the Whig side, as on the Tory, coalition could never be more than a distasteful temporary expedient: "Ld H[alifa]x discoursing about present State of Affairs", Cowper noted in his diary, "and our making the Court Tories to act as one Party with the Whigs . . . said, we were mixing Oyl & Vinegar (very truly)".[159]

It was in this simple faith that the average politician engaged in the party-war in the age of Anne. Except at infrequent intervals between 1702 and 1714 the barriers between the two sides seemed insurmountable. A party man might on occasion desert his party in favour of the Court, as did the Tory Edward Brereton in November 1704 or the Whig Richard Hampden in the autumn of 1712, but the taunts or reproaches of his brethren often made him the more anxious thereafter to proclaim his true allegiance. By December 1712 Hampden was swearing to his friends at White's that "he was a Whig still, but he was for peace", just as Brereton, within a few months of abstaining from voting on "the Tack", was furiously protesting to his High Tory patron at Denbigh, "I had rather be called a pickpocket than a Whig".[160] Even among the professional servants of every administration

* The rumour was, in fact, quite untrue.

there were no more than a handful who disclaimed completely all party ties. Leech-like placemen such as Thomas Coke and James Brydges* professed to regard themselves as Tories by principle.[161] Of Sir John Leake, who served both the Godolphin and Harley ministries as an Admiralty Commissioner without an evident qualm, it was said "'tis known if he's of any party he's a Whig".[162] Speaking for the more or less genuine non-partisan with a professional career to make, John Cope, the future commander of the royal forces in Scotland in the '45, feelingly summed up the uncomfortable position of his own small band, caught in the perpetual cross-fire of the two warring political armies: "partys, my Lord", he told Lord Raby, "make this Town both disagreeable & dangerous for a man in employment to live in".[163]

That this conflict of parties dominated British politics in the age of Anne can stand in need of no further proof. Why it came to do so, however, is another question; and it is one that can hardly be answered until we have established what the party war of 1702–14 was concerned with. What were Whigs and Tories fighting about in Anne's reign? This must be our next consideration.

* For whom see p. 356 below.

CHAPTER TWO

The Substance of Conflict:
Old Issues and New

"YOUR Majesty may be told", wrote Lord Cowper to his new sovereign in 1714, "and it has been often said, that the only difference [between the parties] is about places".[1] Certainly the Britain of Queen Anne's day was never lacking in those who were ready to assert that this was so, either from sheer cynicism or because the whole idea of party offended against their idealistic concept of how politics and government should be carried on. In some the disillusioning experience of William III's reign had bred a cynical distrust of politicians' motives which persisted well into the reign of his successor; so that even so scholarly a critic as Marlborough's chaplain-general, Dr. Francis Hare,[2] could remain oddly insensitive to the changing climate and sharpening lines of party division which made the political world of 1708 a very different place from that of 1698. Hare's recollections of the '90's, when "as occasion served . . . the Whigs acted to the height of the Tory part, and the Tories that of Whigs", left him stubbornly convinced that "whatever these names may once have meant . . . nothing but being in or out of court is at the bottom of them".[3] On the other hand, to a young idealist like Sir John Percival, the future Earl of Egmont, present observation could be as discouraging as past experience was to others. For his friend George Berkeley, the philosopher, Percival painted the political scene as he saw it in the spring of 1710 in a most dismal light.

It must needs greive to the heart all good men who love their country, and have nothing to get by changes at court, to see the divisions now amongst us. For my share I look upon the differences between Whig and Tory to proceed only from a desire of the one to keep in & the other to get into imployment. This, their ambition, avarice and personal picque being but ill inducement for to obtain followers, one party pretends we are in danger of anarchy or Presbytery, and the other of tyranny and Popery; all which is only to beguile the multitude and support their interests . . . [but] no wonder if well meaning men rank themselves on each side according as the different partys can make impression on them, and so become zealous tools to the aims of the cunning few.⁴

A west-country clergyman, Maurice Wheeler, viewing the 1710 Election campaign from Gloucester, would not have quarrelled with Percival's conclusions: "Passive obedience and resistance are the distinguishing notions", he told Bishop Wake, "but nothing on either side is meant, but places & preferm[en]ts".⁵

Opinions such as these, coming as they do from essentially detached observers, may not surprise us. But to hear the same harsh notes echoed from the very heart of early-eighteenth-century politics seems more remarkable. Hare, Percival and Wheeler were none of them caught up personally in the political whirlwind of 1710, which first breached, then swept away the defences of the reigning Whig administration. But one man who was was Henry St. John, soon to be Viscount Bolingbroke; and the very fact of his intimate involvement makes his later analysis of his own motives, and of those of the other Tories who shared the spoils of victory with him, all the more striking at first sight. With every appearance of disarming frankness he confessed "that we came to court in the same dispositions as all parties have done; that the principal spring of our actions was to have the government of the state in our hands; that our principal views were the conservation of this power, great employments to ourselves, and great opportunities of rewarding those who had helped to raise us, and of hurting those who stood in opposition to us".⁶ This cameo of 1710 fits neatly and consistently into the later impressionistic sketches of the whole field of post-Revolution politics which Bolingbroke limned, with his journalist's pen, long after Anne's death; and the thinly-veiled, if not entirely naked, struggle for power between parties becomes an intelligible phenomenon if we once concede that the issues over which Whigs and Tories wrangled between 1689 and 1714 were as anachronistic and as artificial as this latter-day Bolingbroke insisted they were. In his *Dissertation upon Parties*, published in 1733, this theme receives its classic exposition. The author does not deny that in the years before the Revolution there had been an acute and rational division between Tory and Whig on grounds of principle. But because the crisis of 1688 forced many of the leaders on each side to act together in a national emergency, he sees the Revolution itself as "a fire, which purged off the dross of both parties"; so that thereafter "they appeared to be the same metal, and answered the same standard".⁷ Bolingbroke's conclusion is without qualification. "The real essences of whig and tory were thus destroyed";

but "men who saw the same ensigns flying, were not wise enough to perceive, or not honest enough to own, that the same cause was no longer concerned, but listed themselves on either side, as their prejudices ... or other motives ... directed them afterwards".[8]*

It is not an unduly difficult task, therefore, to marshal contemporary evidence which, by itself, creates a thoroughly unattractive impression of the character of Augustan politics: evidence which suggests that it was no less seamy and materialistic and much more hypocritical than that of politics in the mid-Hanoverian period. If such damning testimony could be convincingly substantiated we would have to accept that although the men of Queen Anne's day spoke, acted and voted — as we have seen they did — as if the substance of politics was a conflict between two great parties, these parties could claim no direct descent from the original Whig and Tory parties of Charles II's reign. We would further have to concede that the lines of their conflict were far from corresponding with deep divisions in the nation over questions of principle and public policy, if indeed such divisions existed at all. Moreover, what purported to be a combat waged for many years in deadly earnest would on this evidence be revealed, in large measure at least, as an ingenious and gigantic charade; played out on the one side by unscrupulous men — the power-politicians of both parties — who consciously exploited old enmities and obsolete battle-cries in the interest of their own advancement, and on the other side by a large number of well-meaning but deluded men who were so many pawns in the game being dictated by their leaders, and who were gulled into refighting again and again sham battles whose real issue had long since been decided.

Such an interpretation offers us one answer — at root a startlingly simple answer — to the problem of what British politics in the age of Anne was about. But Lord Cowper, in common with the overwhelming majority of those who were active participants in the struggles of 1702–14, was in no doubt that it was the wrong answer. In his view those who claimed that the

---

* It is interesting to mark the similarity between Bolingbroke's basic thesis and that advanced by his one-time friend and leader, Robert Harley, in a pamphlet drafted 25 years before. Comparing the situation in the later years of Charles II with that in 1708 Harley asserted that "The nation was then divided into those who were jealous for their libertys & property on the one hand, & others who were alarmd with the fear of a designe to overthrow the church & monarchy. And tho' now the foundation[s] of those Partys are abolishd; yet is the fury & rage stil kept up by wicked arts." See B.M. Loan 29/10/1: various drafts in Harley's hand, 24 Aug. 1708, headed "Plaine English to all who are Honest, or would be so if they knew how".

division of the political nation into parties was little more than a convenient excuse for the scramble for offices betrayed "either a superficial judgment, or a desire to hinder the true causes from being discerned".[9] And it would be hard to deny that most of the witnesses who can be called to support the claim are palpably suspect on one or other of these counts. Hare, for instance, had imbibed his patron, Marlborough's, instinctive distrust of party without any of Marlborough's practical experience of working with the party leaders and assessing their motives. Percival had been in England only a few months when he so sweepingly condemned these same men in 1710; and although he had long outgrown the undergraduate flippancy which had prompted him to inform his cousin, Thomas Knatchbull, in 1702 that "The words Whig & Tory are now out of date, but there stil runs a distinction between us of powder'd Wigs & no powder'd Wigs",[10] he had scarcely had time to develop his powers of political observation. When he came over from Ireland again in 1714 he sang a very different tune.[11]

As for the other kind of political testimony which Cowper warned against, testimony which set out deliberately to mislead, that of Bolingbroke could hardly furnish a more striking example. His *Dissertation upon Parties*, for instance, was not a historical treatise but a political tract aimed primarily at discrediting the Walpolean Whigs.* The cynical reflections in his *Letter to Wyndham* on the self-interest of the Tory ministers who came to power in 1710 were those of a man bitterly disillusioned by failure, exile and the recriminations of the party he had served. They were penned seven years after the event by a Bolingbroke already far removed from the optimistic, vital young politician who had become Secretary of State after the fall of the Whigs. Indeed the opinions of Bolingbroke the exile and propagandist are nowhere more effectively condemned than in the letters and speeches of Bolingbroke the zealous young minister and partisan of 1710–14. In the final crisis of the reign in 1714, for example, he was as much caught up in the great issues of the moment as in the struggle for power. In May of that year he lamented that "as long as the succession remained in danger, nothing else was, it seemed, to be regarded". For months past, he conceded, the threat to the Protestant succession had been "the subject of many private debates, and very fatally, in my opinion to the Church cause of some public debate too".[12] Speaking in the House of Lords a fortnight later on the First Reading of the Schism bill, an ultra-Tory measure aimed against nonconformist schools and teachers, he recommended it to the House as "a Bill of

---

* Similarly Harley's "Plaine English" in 1708 was written with a view to discrediting the duumvirate of Marlborough and Godolphin in the eyes of both parties.

the last importance, since it concerns the security of the Church of England, which is the best and firmest support of the monarchy . . ."[13]

The coincidence at the very end of our period of these two major sources of political dissension, the succession question and the question of toleration, is not without its dramatic significance. The succession had been the central issue in the Exclusion crisis of 1679–81, the years in which the Whig and Tory parties had been born if not conceived. By 1712 it had become once again, for Edmund Gibson as for many other Whigs and Tories, "the circumstance that sits heaviest upon the hearts of all thinking and serious men"; "and for my part [Gibson added], if I could see a good understanding between our Ministry and the house of Hanover, I should be in much less pain as to *who is in*, or *who is out*".[14] Similarly the advocacy of toleration for Protestant dissent had been one of the main factors which had ensured for the Exclusionist Whigs the support of the nonconformists in 1679, and which had alienated from them, and driven into the Tory camp, many High Anglican gentry who had but little enthusiasm for a Catholic successor. Here, too, by 1714 the wheel appeared to have come full circle.

But while both parties could have laid some claim in 1714 to a heredity stretching back to 1679 by lines that had never been altogether broken, it was equally certain that neither could have established a lineage that was in every respect direct and clear. Attempting to trace the descent of either party through all its vicissitudes of three and a half decades was no task for the uninitiated. One can only sympathise with the perplexity of the Huguenot historian, Paul de Rapin-Thoyras, when he tried in 1716 to analyse the conflicting principles and ideas of the British political parties in his 'Dissertation concerning the Whigs and the Tories': "these two Names", he complained, "are very obscure and equivocal Terms . . . the names Whig and Tory inspire certain confused Ideas which few people are able rightly to distintangle".[15] The confusion was no mere figment of Rapin's imagination. It undoubtedly existed; and for much of it, as we shall shortly see, the Glorious Revolution was responsible. "How often he must be in the wrong", observed St. John the politician in 1711, "who takes his measures of Whig and Tory now, from what was the constitution of them at that time";[16] and this was indisputable. For though the Revolution did not *destroy* "the proper and real distinctions of the two parties", as Bolingbroke the pamphleteer subsequently alleged, it did blur the sharply contrasting colours of these distinctions, so that the threads of party development in the years that followed, and especially in the 1690's, came to be woven into a political tapestry far more subtle and intricate in its design than that of

Charles II's later years. Yet the Revolution was not the only complicating
factor. At least equal confusion was produced by the incessant propaganda
which was an integral part of the political warfare of the reigns of both
William III and Anne. Because it was to their political advantage to do so,
the partisans of both sides in their public writings and utterances often
grossly exaggerated those genuine distinctions of principle between them
which survived the Revolution or which emerged thereafter. Determined
that the sins of a small minority of their opponents should be visited on the
vast majority the propagandists produced a habitual distortion of the images
of Whig and Tory, a distortion which the limited vision of the inexperienced,
the superficial, or the merely biased observer could never fully correct.

Invective and misrepresentation were the stock-in-trade of both parties
in the age of Anne, and not only of their pamphleteers and journalists. The
same young Tory blood who complained that his opponents "bamboozle the
world with noises of liberty & property & tell you that all who oppose them
are for the prince of Wales" would not have demurred at hearing the Whigs
as a whole dismissed by a Church of England peer (and a very moderate one
at that) as "Presbiterian Ratts", and he would assuredly have applauded the
careful priming of the election mobs at Chester and Ipswich with such
emotive slogans as "No more Rump Parliaments", "No Forty Eight", "No
Presbyterian Rebellion" and "Save the Queen's White Neck".[17] When the
Whig general James Stanhope stood for Cockermouth in 1710 he was
mercilessly libelled by a local scribe as "a person of republican principles, one
that wd. not allow her present Ma——ty any hereditary title, that wd. be
for clipping & pareing the prerogative of the Cr——n, and for the erecting
new Schemes of Government in order to ruin & undermine our present
happy constitution . . ."[18] The experienced practising politician of the day
knew well enough how to separate the few grains of wheat in the Grub
Street harvest from the vast quantity of chaff. If he were as temperate and
honest as Cowper he might even admit that the chaff predominated.[19] From
the less sophisticated onlooker, however, and certainly from the vast
majority of England's 250,000 electors, such scrupulous discrimination was
not to be expected. "'Tis the dirt each side throw at one another, and that in
such plenty as some will stick", explained Francis Hare; "and the faults of
a few on both sides, when the prejudices against each other are carried to
such heights, make it very hard for either to wipe it off".[20]

The truth of this was never more apparent than during the General
Election of 1710, when the conviction, nurtured by eight months of hostile
propaganda, that the Whigs intended the eventual subversion of the con-

stitution in Church and State at length became rooted in "the body of the Gentlemen & People".* But both parties suffered in their turn from their unfortunate association with extreme minorities, which lent a suspicion of credibility to the caricatures of the propagandists. Just how far misunderstanding could go as a result is underlined by a letter which Harley received, shortly after his return to power in 1710, from John Hooke, Justice of the Grand Sessions for Carnarvon, Merioneth and Anglesey:

I cannot list myself [he wrote] under either of the two common denominations, Whig or Tory. If to be for a Commonwealth, against all reveald religion, . . . to be for an absolute unlimited toleration, for putting all powr. into the hands of men who are easie of religion, be part of the character of the Whig, I cannot be a Whig. If to be for the Pretender, for arbitrary powr, for repealing the toleration, for persecuting good loyall Protestants who agree with the Church in fundamentals . . . enter into the character of a Tory, I cannot be a Tory.[21]

Just as the Tories could never shrug off the embarrassing presence of their Jacobite wing, even at times when the succession issue itself appeared to be dormant, so the Whigs acquired a largely undeserved reputation for anticlericalism and irreligion, and even for the encouragement of private immorality, because a relatively small atheistic or Erastian element found a more congenial political home with a party disposed to favour dissent than with a party uncompromisingly identified with the Church establishment.†

Oddly enough, however, the ceaseless campaign of smear and countersmear which accompanied the party struggle between 1702 and 1714, though making it harder in some ways to identify the motives behind the conflict, does in one way, at least, illuminate this problem. For without a

---

* Such was the considered view of James Brydges, of all politicians normally the least concerned with fundamentals of party principle. *H.L.Q.* iii (1939–40), 237: to Drummond, 24 Aug. 1710.

† See Burnet, vi, 222. In many of the Tory addresses to the Queen in the spring and summer of 1710 there was a remarkable and obviously quite deliberate emphasis, directly or by implication, on the supposed increase of vice and profanity under the recent Whig régime. A choice example was the Pembrokeshire address referring to the "prodigious growth of atheism and blasphemy, vice and immorality", which by a nice irony was presented to Anne by that bibulous west-country squire, Sir John Pakington, whose debauchery was once denounced by Bishop Lloyd from the pulpit and of whom Peter King said he "had all the vices of the males of his family without the vertues of the females" (Tullie House, Nicolson's MS. Diary, 22 Nov. 1702; Add. MSS. 29579, f. 394; cf. Pakington MSS.: Robert Priest to [Lady Pakington], 30 June 1710). Wallingford and Glamorgan also gave particular prominence in their addresses to the alleged profanities and moral turpitude of the Whigs. See *A Collection of Addresses . . . presented . . . since the Impeachment of the Reverend Dr. Henry Sacheverell* (London, 1711), i, 29, 46; ii, 9.

genuine conviction on both sides that certain principles of policy were fundamental to the public welfare and essential to their own popular appeal, neither Whigs nor Tories, we can be sure, would have devoted so much energy to accusing each other of attacking or abandoning these principles. Whig efforts to fasten the stigma of Jacobitism on their opponents may tell us little of value about the Tories; but they do make it clear that a Protestant, parliamentary succession was as vital to the Whigs during Anne's reign as it had been ever since 1679, and that they regarded their own unquestionable enthusiasm for the House of Hanover as one of their chief political assets. Similarly Tory anxiety to brand the Whigs as Presbyterians or even as infidels, wholly misleading though it may be about the victims of their propaganda, does highlight the determination of its authors to safeguard the influence of the Anglican Church from further erosion, and helps us to understand why the cry of "the Church in danger" was as effective a political weapon in the hands of the Tories as was "the Succession in danger" in those of the Whigs. The smokescreens of innuendo and misrepresentation which were so assiduously laid down by the partisans of Anne's day are admittedly not always easy to penetrate; often, indeed, they make it harder to distinguish the material issues of early-eighteenth-century politics from the merely diversionary; but at least they leave us in no doubt that issues as such were believed to carry both meaning and weight.

If the substance of political conflict in the age of Anne is to be analysed with any confidence, therefore, we must first try to isolate and then to scrutinise the more prominent of those concrete issues which divided the partisans in the years between 1702 and 1714. And this in its turn requires some understanding of the evolving traditions of the two great parties from the later years of Charles II down to the end of the seventeenth century.

*   *   *

It was the traditional issues, the issues which had given party its original meaning and justification before 1688, which most perplexed the contemporary spectator when he tried to gauge their relevance to the obvious dichotomy of political society in the early eighteenth century. Three principles in particular had distinguished the Tory from the Whig before the Revolution. One was a belief in the divine hereditary right of Kings and in non-resistance, as opposed to a theory of monarchy which was based on consent and which assumed a right of resistance to the monarch if he ceased to command this consent. These antithetical ideas had crystallised into articles of party faith as a result of the Exclusion struggle of 1679–81, when all Whigs had been prepared to reject hereditary right and some had been ready to resort to resistance* in order to ensure a Protestant succession after Charles II's death, and when John Locke had first evolved his theory of "contract" to justify such resistance if and when it became necessary. A second integral part of the ideology of pre-revolution Toryism, a natural corollary of the concepts of divine right and passive obedience, was the exaltation of the royal prerogative, in contrast to the Whig view that the ultimate sovereignty of "the people", as represented in Parliament, was the only true guarantee of the liberty and rights of property of the subject. Thirdly, all but an enlightened minority of the Tories[22] had insisted on an unqualified obedience to the Anglican State Church, of which the King was the Supreme Governor, rejecting the Whig plea that freedom of worship, at least, if not full civil rights, should be restored to Protestant dissenters.

Although at the height of the Exclusion storm, weltering in a sea of polemical writings that were for the most part improvised and superficial, relatively few of the partisans may have grasped the full significance of these opposing theoretical positions,[23] the rival ideologies not only outlived the crisis of 1679–81 but became more clearly defined thereafter; and on the Whig side they were a vital factor in ensuring the survival of the party between 1681 and 1687, when much of its original leadership and organisation were broken up. That they should have remained unaffected and unchanged by the Revolution of 1688, however, or by the revolutionary settlement of 1689, to both of which the great bulk of the Tories as well as all the Whigs were committed, was impossible. For the events of 1688–9 virtually killed one of the major issues which had divided Whig from Tory since the 1670's — that of the prerogative — and temporarily anaesthetised several others.

After the Revolution the royal prerogative was still a subject of political controversy, and remained so at least as long as William III lived. But the King's loss in 1689 of his suspending and dispensing powers and of his right to maintain a standing army in peace-time without parliamentary consent, together with his voluntary acceptance of an independent judiciary, (all changes for which the experience of James II's reign had made the Tories scarcely less anxious than the Whigs) ensured that the prerogative would never again represent a serious threat to national liberties. In consequence

---

* It is a fair supposition that had they realised that the dissolution of the Oxford Parliament in 1681 was the end of the road for Exclusion and not just the prelude to a new Election and a new Exclusion bill the many Whigs who attended that Parliament in arms would not have dispersed as tamely as they did.

it lost its central place in political thinking and all real validity as a clear-cut issue between the parties, though periodically it continued to excite the "Country members", both Whig and Tory, in the House of Commons. James II's misrule and the settlement of 1689 were not the sole reasons for this transformation. Three particularly unpalatable facts about their new monarch — that he was a foreigner, a Calvinist, and that he had no direct hereditary claim to the throne — made him unpopular with many Tories almost from the start; and his decision to employ their opponents in increasing numbers after 1693 completed their disenchantment. Tories now became more anxious to curb than to cherish the King's prerogative, and the lack of compunction which the bulk of the High Tories showed in associating themselves with the anti-prerogative platform of Harley's "New Country Party" in the late 1690's, by contrast with the insistence of Whig ministers that "we must not make the King a Doge of Venice",[24] is the surest sign of the magnitude of the change which, in this field at least, had taken place since the Revolution.

Three other political issues, all closely related, which had been sharply controversial before the Revolution lost their cutting-edge in the 1690's. The legitimacy of resistance to the monarch in extreme circumstances, the idea that regal authority was based on a compact between governor and governed, and above all the crucial problem of hereditary right — all these questions seemed to many to have been settled so nearly conclusively in favour of the Whigs by the end of 1689 that thereafter they appeared likely to agitate only the doctrinal fringe of either party. How could the Tories continue to extol passive obedience after Compton and Danby had signed the invitation to William of Orange, and some of the party's staunchest adherents had taken up arms against their anointed King? What reasonable man could deny that the offer of the crown to William and Mary in February 1689, immediately after the formal reading in their presence of the Declaration of Right, was the clearest practical application of the idea of contract-monarchy? And what of the parliamentary entail of the crown in the Bill of Rights on the heirs of William himself by a possible future marriage, in the seemingly-likely event of either Queen Mary or the next designated successor, Princess Anne, dying without surviving children?;[25] surely this in itself was enough to sound the death-knell of hereditary right? Confident that such questions involved the Tory conscience in an inescapable dilemma, there were many Whigs ready to assume by the early 1690's that the secular principles of Toryism had suffered irreparable damage.

It is true that there were also sceptics who thought otherwise. There were those who uneasily remembered the remarkable shifts to which the Tories had been prepared to resort in the Convention Parliament to evade the full theoretical consequences of the act of revolution, and more particularly to salvage something from the wreck of the principle of hereditary right.* And they were not much comforted by the reflection that none of the leading Tories who accepted high office in the early years of the Revolution monarchy, among them Danby, Nottingham and Sir Edward Seymour, had been required to do violence to their consciences by swearing allegiance to William as their "rightful and lawful King", as the Whigs themselves would have wished,[26] or even by abjuring the exiled James.† Apart from the ill-concealed intrigues of known Jacobites and non-jurors there was much private trafficking with the Court at St. Germain, especially in the early 1690's; and although in 1696, in horrified reaction to the discovery of the Fenwick assassination plot, many Tories were induced to subscribe to a voluntary Association to defend William, in which they actually recognised him as their King *de jure*, the genuine scruples which an important section of the party still held on this score were emphasised by the fact that roughly 100 members of the House of Commons refused to sign. Yet although these stubborn outcrops of Tory tradition remained a feature of the political landscape to the end of the century, they were increasingly masked by new growth which promised in time to conceal them entirely. The very ease with which the "New Country" squadron of Harley, with its ex-Whig associations, became grafted on to the Tory opposition in the middle and later years of the 1690's‡ was proof enough of how far such issues as divine right, non-resistance and contract had temporarily receded into the background. Furthermore, with every year that Princess Anne's one surviving child, the young Duke of Gloucester, grew to boyhood, and the Protestant succession appeared more and more secure in the collateral heirs of Queen Mary, the practical relevance of such issues to the future appeared to be further reduced.

The other basic matter of principle in dispute between the parties before 1688 — the argument over the position of the dissenters in the community

* Their most ingenious expedient was Danby's "abdication" fiction, designed (with the aid of the warming-pan theory) to have enabled Mary to be crowned alone as Queen as the direct hereditary successor (see Andrew Browning, *Thomas Osborne, Earl of Danby* [Glasgow, 1951], i, 421). Tory members did succeed in keeping any formal mention of a "contract" out of the Declaration of Rights. See above pp. xxxi-iv, *passim*

† Bills designed to enforce an oath of abjuration on all office-holders were thrice blocked or defeated in the early 1690's.

‡ See p. 259 below.

and their relationship to the Established Church — was also though not equally affected by the Revolution. Neither the religious problem itself nor the attitude of Whigs and Tories towards it could have remained the same after the passing of the Toleration Act in 1689. James II's Indulgence policies had forced the High Anglican church leaders to woo the nonconforming Protestants in 1688 with offers of a legal toleration more tempting than any relief that James could offer them. In the Toleration bill, drafted by the Earl of Nottingham, the Tories made good their promises. The concessions were grudgingly made, however. No penal statutes were repealed, although all Trinitarians outside the bosom of the State Church who were prepared to make a declaration against transubstantiation and swear allegiance to the new sovereigns were relieved from the actual penalties the acts imposed. At the same time attempts in both Houses of the Convention Parliament to restore the civil rights of the dissenters, both in the municipalities and in the government service, were thwarted by Anglican peers and country gentlemen. For the next decade, therefore, the position was briefly this: the Tories, though no longer able to stand forth as champions of the *only* legally-recognised Church in England, were resolved that they would go on upholding as firmly as possible the considerable privileges still remaining to the ecclesiastical establishment; while the Whigs, having seen their religious aims in some measure achieved after the Revolution, were naturally anxious to consolidate the gains already made. As long as William lived, and continued to show his personal determination to tolerate diverse religious views, there was little chance that the Tories would try to undermine the 1689 settlement in Parliament; indeed, the narrow limits of the purely legal toleration were unofficially extended between 1689 and 1702,* and but for the failure of the Whig leaders up to 1698 to remodel the episcopate to their liking this process might well have gone much further.[27] But clearly the compromise effected by the Revolution was an uneasy one. The failure in the Convention of the last parliamentary attempt to achieve a genuine comprehension of Protestant nonconformity within the Church of England, and growing Tory resentment at the official countenance shown to individual dissenters, made it certain that the religious problem would never remain far below the surface of party politics. As soon as the right stimuli were applied and the right conditions existed it was likely to erupt once more into prominence.

Taking a general view, however, of the whole field of issues over which the parties had been ranged in opposition between 1679 and 1687, it seems beyond question that a good deal of confusion persisted for the greater part

* Mainly through the lax enforcement of the Test and Corporation Acts.

of William's reign. With the Tories taking up unfamiliar and at times glaringly inconsistent positions on so many traditional fronts, with the Whigs equivocal in their attitude towards the prerogative,[28] and with both parties so often divided among themselves, it was little wonder that there were times in the 1690's when men found it far easier to interpret their politics in the old terms of "Court" and "Country". Nor was it surprising that those who dreaded the continued existence of parties and saw in it "a propensity to ruin more than natural" were quick to decry the political terminology inherited from the Exclusion period as anachronistic, and insistent that "to govern by a party" was the worst course a sovereign could possibly pursue.[29]

But by March 1702, when Queen Anne came to the throne, a marked change was already discernible; and by the end of 1702 the change had become emphatic and impossible to ignore. One reason for this transformation was that even before 1702 the Tories had recovered their lost dynamic and the Whigs their lost unity as a result of a series of factors which, though not in themselves ideological, had the effect of focusing new attention on party issues. In the localities, for instance, the antagonisms left over from Charles II's reign and in some cases from the Civil War had been but little mellowed by the Revolution. But they grew progressively more bitter and more inseparable from party allegiance after the passing of the Triennial Act in 1694. This act opened the way to a quite remarkable incidence of General Elections in England (four in the last eight years of William's reign, ten in the twenty years between 1695 and 1715), and led to a sharper definition of the lines of party division at the centre of politics in response to the pressure of feeling in the localities.* In addition, the infusion of new blood into the Tories from the New Country opposition, and the electoral and parliamentary triumphs they enjoyed in the three years from December 1697 to January 1701, had a revitalising effect upon them. And when their ambition overreached itself between April and June 1701, and the party tried unsuccessfully to destroy three of its most hated opponents, Somers, Halifax and Orford, by impeaching them for their part (passive though it was) in the transaction of the partition treaties of 1698–1700, the malice of the Tories produced its own powerful antidote. The impeachments brought about a closing of Whig ranks as nothing else had done since 1689, and Henry Whistler proved a true prophet when he wrote to his friend, Governor Pitt, in distant Madras: "this matter hath made a feud that I fear will not

---

* Lord Oxford, looking back on the political scene in April 1714, significantly put the point from which party animosities had been progressively "gathering strength" at roughly 1694. See Add. MSS. 40621, f. 193.

dye".[30] Thus both parties in the closing months of William III's life were
well prepared for a reinjection of political ideas and a reappraisal of their
policies to match their fresh cohesion and renewed sense of purpose and the
newly-whetted edge of their hostility.

In one respect, at least, this process was already well advanced. A most
important feature of politics in the 1690's had been the gradual emergence
of new issues dividing Whig from Tory at the very time when certain of the
traditional issues appeared to be losing their relevance. One ideological
source, especially, a source largely untapped before the Revolution, was
already supplying the partisans with revivifying draughts of controversial
matter long before William's death. It drew its essence and its strength from
an entirely new relationship between Britain and the Continent of Europe.
The rise and conflict of political parties before 1688 had had little opportunity to influence the course of Stuart foreign policy, which both under
Charles II and James II had been characterised by irresponsibility, isolationism (especially after 1674), and relatively low European prestige. The contrast after 1688 could scarcely have been more complete; and the intimate
involvement of the country in Continental affairs, which was one of the most
momentous effects of William III's accession, led before long, as it was
bound to do, to the growing intrusion of foreign policy issues into party
politics. Annual sessions of Parliament, the unparalleled financial demands
of the Augsburg war, and the relaxation of press censorship in 1695, encouraging for the first time since the Restoration the growth of an informed
public opinion on external affairs, all contributed to this development.
Hazily at first, but from the mid-1690's rather more clearly, two opposing
concepts of Britain's rôle in Europe took shape, the one outward-looking,
the other essentially insular; and with these basic concepts the Whig and
Tory ethos gradually became identified.

By 1702 it was the Tories who had emerged as the more isolationist and
the more xenophobic of the two parties. It was they who had opposed most
strongly the undertaking of any fresh Continental commitments by England
after the Peace of Ryswick. Tory votes in the House of Commons, albeit
clothed in "Country" garb, had been mainly responsible for forcing William
to reduce his standing army far below the limits of safety. It was Tory
members, too, who had led the outcry against the two partition treaties of
1698–1700.[31] Having convinced themselves by 1698 that the recent war
had been fought as much to further the interests of the Dutch as to line the
pockets of their political opponents at home, the Tory country gentlemen

remained sharply suspicious of the presence of pro-Dutch motives behind the King's foreign policy in the next three years; and their suspicion made them almost wilfully blind, until the eleventh hour, to the very real threat from Louis XIV's France, which overhung their own island no less than the United Provinces.

During the first year or two of peace, admittedly, such views had not been confined entirely to the Tories. Many independent Whigs had failed to see the danger involved in cutting down the army in 1698 to a derisory 8000 men; and even Whig ministers, sensitive to the reaction of public opinion against a long and exhausting war, had shown little enthusiasm for the first Partition Treaty when William condescended to inform them of its terms. Yet the Whigs as a whole accepted the idea of the interdependence of Britain and Europe more readily than their opponents. They also believed that the brotherhood of European Protestants still meant something in an age when the Popish ex-King of England and Scotland was still being sheltered, if not now actively assisted, by the most formidable military power in the world. And having supported the war more enthusiastically than the vast majority of the Tories before 1697, the Whigs were the more inclined afterwards to take a sympathetic view of William III's balance-of-power policies.

It was the parliamentary events of 1701, however, which finally impressed on the public images of the two parties the distinctive stamp they were to carry down to 1714. During that session, which followed hard after Louis XIV's recognition of his grandson, Anjou, as the new ruler of Spain, a Tory majority in the House of Commons persisted with its virulent attacks not only on the Whig ex-ministers who had been in office when the partition treaties were concluded, but also on the policies those treaties had represented; and this at a time when Louis, by a series of provocative acts, was making it brutally plain that he intended to exploit the new Franco-Spanish connection to the utmost. "Our present Parliament", Robert Molesworth justly complained in May 1701, "pleases no party that I can hear of, but the French king".[32] In the end it required Louis' reckless proclamation of James Edward Stuart as James III of England,* followed by the shock of a sudden dissolution and of a General Election in which the Whigs made great play with their opponents' disloyalty,[33] to bring many Tories to a sense of reality. In sharp contrast Whig opinion, voiced not only by the party's spokesmen in both Houses of Parliament but equally forcibly outside Parliament by the authors of the Kentish Petition, the Legion Memorial and a shoal of loyal addresses, had clearly recognised from the start of the 1701 session that

---

* Ex-King James II died in France in September 1701.

England, in her own interest, must accept her European responsibilities.

Thus in March 1702, along with the crown, and the war which (as she later said)[34] she "found ... prepared" for her, Queen Anne inherited two parties whose basic attitudes towards Europe, towards their European allies, and towards the broad principles of foreign policy had already taken shape in very different moulds. In the course of the next twelve years those attitudes varied only in degrees of emphasis. Thus the incoming Tory ministers of 1710, according to Bolingbroke, "looked on the political principles, which had generally prevailed in our government from the revolution ... to be destructive of our true interest, to have mingled us too much in the affairs of the continent, to tend to the impoverishing our people ...".[35] The strains to which the Grand Alliance had been subjected between 1701 and 1710 had only confirmed the Tories the more strongly in this frame of mind. Indeed the perpetual inability of Britain, as its paymaster, to ensure that the other confederates fulfilled their agreed "quotas", both of men and money, had convinced the gentlemen of England even before 1710 that the Spanish Succession War was being fought, at their expense, for the aggrandisement and no longer merely for the security of the allies.[36] "To give six millions with so little fruit", wailed a Tory official after another indecisive campaign in 1711; "Ld. have mercy upon us; what bubbles do our Allys make of us!"[37]

It is possible to exaggerate the xenophobia of the Tories. The post-war relationship with the Continent envisaged by St. John and many of his colleagues in the Tory administration of 1710–14 represented an obvious advance on the myopic isolationism which "Old Tories" of the Rochester school had openly advocated between 1698 and 1701, and which subsequently found favour round the tables of the October Club in 1711.[38] Indeed, one of the several drafts which Lord Treasurer Oxford prepared for the Queen's Speech at the opening of the 1714 session of Parliament, with its emphasis on the fostering of trade and on the necessity of holding a watching-brief, at least, over the power equilibrium in Europe seems almost to foreshadow the principles of Walpolean Whiggery in the 1730's, though it was still a far cry from the uninhibited Europeanism flaunted by many contemporary Whigs:

I have set before me for my rule the example of those of my predecessors who have been most renownd for their wisdome ... They made it their practice & their maxime to hold the ballance between the cont[en]d[in]g powers of Europe, to be the peace makers, & by managing of it so that where Brittaine cast in the weight, that gave the preference. This made us really formidable abroad, & brought riches [at] home, & is what God & nature by our situation has pointed out to be our true interest;

and it is that rule wch never has been departed from but when faction had turnd mens heads from the love of their country to persue imagenary schemes of Governmt or their private lucre. And [as] this is my steady rule as to forreigne affairs, so I doubt not but my Prot[estant] successors wil think it their glory to persue the same, for it is this nation's interest to aggrandise itself by trade, and when a war is necessary . . . to carry it on by sea.[39]

But while Oxford and Bolingbroke were able to rationalise the underlying principles of Tory foreign policy, as well as their objections to the Whig approach to Europe, the attitude of the average Tory squire continued throughout Anne's reign to be dictated largely by more emotional considerations. In so far as reason shaped his views at all it was mainly through the conviction — not unjustified, it must be said — that it was his purse which would always have to take the strain of any far-reaching system of foreign alliances or ambitious Continental commitments. But in the main his opinions were governed by three factors. The first was an instinctive prejudice against the foreigner and above all against the Dutch ("if you would discover a concealed Tory, Jacobite or Papist", recommended Shaftesbury's grandson in 1706, "speak but of the Dutch and you will find him out by his passionate railing").* The second was the sheer ignorance born of that unabashed insularity which Addison so tellingly satirised in his imaginary conversation with a provincial country gentleman in 1716:

finding him such a critic upon foreigners, I asked him, if he had ever travelled; He told me, he did not know what travelling was good for, but to teach a man to ride the great horse, to jabber French, and to talk against passive obedience: to which he added, that he scarce ever knew a Traveller in his life who had not forsook his principles, and lost his hunting seat.[40]

The third was his belief that Whiggery itself and all it stood for was an alien growth, which would wither without the nurture it received from foreign sources: "I scarce ever knew a foreigner settl'd in England [wrote Atterbury] . . . but became a Whig in a little time after his mixing with us".[41]

Proceedings in both Houses of Parliament, and especially in the House of Commons, in the years 1702–14, periodically mirror the fundamentally different standpoint from which the party men on each side viewed the Continental scene. Two debates which took place in the very first session

---

* P.R.O. 30/24/22/2: 3rd Earl of Shaftesbury to Mons. Van Twedde, 17 Jan. 1705–6. His confidence becomes understandable when we find the Tory peer, North and Grey, recommending the retention of Dunkirk at the peace, not to overawe the French, but because it would be "the terror of the Dutch & the envy of the rest of our allies". Bodl. MS. North c.8, f. 193: to Weymouth (draft), [July?] 1712.

of the Queen's first Parliament, on 4 and 7 January 1703, struck chords that were frequently to be repeated, with variations, throughout the reign. In the winter of 1702 the government was under strong pressure from the Dutch, backed by Marlborough, to increase the British force allotted by treaty to the Low Countries theatre. At first the High Tories in the Cabinet, led by Rochester and Nottingham, tried to dissuade their fellow ministers from bringing the matter before Parliament at all.[42] But eventually Nottingham, at least, seems to have relented; and in response to a royal message recommending the augmentation the Commons agreed in January 1703 to foot the bill which such an increase would entail. They did so, however, only after the Tories had insisted on including in their address a recommendation that, as a strict condition of making the reinforcement, the government should "insist upon it with the States General, that there be an immediate stop of all posts, and of all letters, bills, . . . trade and commerce with France and Spain".[43] The Whigs forced two divisions in an endeavour either to water down the provision or have it removed entirely, but on each occasion were fairly heavily outnumbered.[44] It needed no more than two or three campaigns to persuade most Tory members that this new war was no different from the last, in that the Dutch and the Imperialists were prepared (so they imagined) to suck England dry to defend their own territories and interests while shamelessly defaulting on their treaty obligations. Such Tories were pacified for a while by the triumph of Blenheim — "being more for their 4s. in a pound than ever yet they saw"[45] — and shortly after the opening of the following session Secretary Hedges was able to report to Marlborough from the House of Commons that "there is no mention made of the condition for prohibiting trade in the article for the troops of augmentations . . . a very good point gained at this juncture".[46] None the less Harley still found "many very honest gentlemen" who were "very uneasy possess'd wth a notion that we performe our parts, & the States suffer the common cause to languish & our efforts to be fruitless for want of supplying their proportions last year at sea"; and in the session of 1705–6, before the brilliant victories of Ramillies and Turin, Tory complaints about the disproportionate burden which England was having to bear were bitter and widespread.[47] By the time a fresh reinforcement of the British army in Flanders was proposed at the end of 1708, however, the Whigs had a working majority in the Commons, and a Tory member wrote in disgust: "We yesterday in the Com^tee gave, & today confirm'd in the House, £220,000 for 7000 foot and 3000 horse as an augmentation, without so much as being told that any of our allyes would augment their forces".[48]

A very different parliamentary issue rather later in the reign brought out even more strongly both the insularity and the extreme distrust of foreigners and foreign influences which was characteristic of so many Tories. This was the naturalization of foreign Protestants. The Tory case against Wortley Montagu's General Naturalization bill in 1709,* expressed both in Parliament, by Henry Campion,[49] and in at least one forcefully-argued pamphlet published while the bill was in preparation, was redolent with such sentiments. The pamphleteer, for example, warned against "the conflux of aliens, as would probably be the effect of such a law . . .; for these would owe allegiance to their respective princes, and retain a fondness for their native countries; and therefore, whensoever a war should break out, might prove so many spies and enemies". He also claimed "that the design of inviting multitudes of aliens to settle here might prove in time a further mischief; for they would not only be capable of voting at elections, but also of being chosen members of parliament; have admission into places of trust and authority, which in process of time might endanger our ancient polity and government, and, by frequent intermarriages, go a great way to blot out and extinguish the English race".[50] To most Whigs, eagerly welcoming the injection of foreign capital and enterprise into the English economy which Protestant refugees had already provided, and looking to Prussia as a model of what a planned immigration programme could achieve, such arguments were incomprehensible. They were, as Wortley Montagu justifiably alleged in the House, "grounded on the false supposition that foreigners would ever continue and be looked upon as such, which was sufficiently confuted by past and daily experience".[51] Nor was Whig confidence in the benefits of a liberal immigration policy unduly shaken by the unfortunate social effects of the invitation to the Protestant refugees from the Palatinate in 1709, a gesture to which leading party figures gave generous financial as well as moral support.[52] Their opponents, on the other hand, exploited popular prejudice against the Palatines to the full. Tories vehemently protested against foreigners being allowed "to send over the scum of their countries to make ourselves, who already abound in Poor, yet poorer", and they later used the Palatines' case as the stick with which to belabour the Naturalization Act in 1711 and destroy it in 1712.[53]

Dislike of the Dutch, always the most pervasive and usually the most rancorous emotion in an essentially negative Tory outlook on Europe, reached a new intensity in the Parliament of 1710–13. It had been en-

---

* See also pp. 105–6 below, and Caroline Robbins, 'A Note on General Naturalization under the Later Stuarts', *Journal of Modern History*, xxxiv (1962).

couraged since 1709 by the commercial and colonial concessions made to the Dutch in Townshend's Barrier Treaty — the lavish rewards which the Whigs had felt obliged to promise their ally to keep her in the war — and by the more recent attempt of the States-General, through its minister in London, Vryberg, to deter the Queen from dismissing her Whig ministers.* Both events had infuriated Tory opinion, and the four London members who took their seats in November 1710 were specifically pledged to their constituents to work for "a good understanding with our Protestant neighbours, without complimenting away our Commerce, or inviting them to intermeddle in the affairs of our Government".[54] But the climax was reached in the second session of this Parliament. This coincided with the efforts of the ministers of the States in London and their plenipotentiaries at Utrecht to obstruct the peace settlement on which Britain and France had privately agreed in 1711. "It is high time", thundered St. John, "to put a stop to this foreign influence on British Councils; and we must either emancipate ourselves now, or be for ever slaves".[55] In February 1712 Tory resentment spilled over into a series of censure votes unbridled in their hostility, in which moderate Court Tories and backbench extremists seem to have joined with equal enthusiasm. They began on 4–5 February by forcing through a series of resolutions condemning the failure of the Dutch to fulfil their treaty and quota obligations either at sea, in Spain or in Flanders; then in the course of three heated debates between the 13th and 16th they proceeded to castigate the commercial clauses of the Barrier Treaty and to condemn Townshend and his ministerial colleagues as "enemies to the Queen and Kingdom"; and finally they appointed a committee under the august chairmanship of Sir Thomas Hanmer to draw up a full representation, "a pepperer", as Swift called it,[56] in which the iniquities of all the allies since 1702, and especially those of the Dutch, were remorselessly catalogued.[57] The Whigs did their best to exonerate the States as well as to justify their own earlier pro-Dutch policies.[58] But they were swept aside by some of the most crushing majorities of even this most Tory of Parliaments.[59]

The Whig defence of the Dutch in the Commons in 1712 epitomised the whole attitude of the party towards the Grand Alliance, which most Whigs had regarded from the very start as a constructive and essential instrument of European settlement and domestic security rather than as a disagreeable military necessity; and hence as something to be welcomed and fostered rather than grudgingly tolerated. "God be thanked the Dutch seem resolved to joyne heartily with us against the French"; "curse be on those who now

* For Vryberg's memorial, presented to Anne on 30 June 1710, see p. 196 below.

do all they can to blow the coals between England and Holland"; such were two typical Whig reactions towards the chief confederate in the early years of the war.[60] Though privately disconcerted at times by the shortcomings of the allies,[61] the public instinct of the Whig leaders was to overlook or excuse them and to repair the damage caused.[62] For them it was not even enough that the alliance should hang together as long as the war lasted. By March 1709 the Whigs in both Houses of Parliament were already exhorting the Queen, in a joint address, "to take care, at the conclusion of the war, to continue and establish a good and firm friendship among the allies". More than that, they were also pressing that the allies "be engaged to become guarantees" for the future security of the Protestant Succession in Britain. This was a distinctively Whig scheme, which had been urged by the Junto at least as early as 1706[63] and which was to be embodied in the treaty with the States-General in 1709, and it was one that never failed to rankle with their opponents. Nothing stirred feelings more violently during the Barrier Treaty debates in February 1712 than the Whig insistence that only the help of Dutch troops could make the throne safe for Hanover in peace-time, with British public opinion hostile to the idea of a standing army. "We ought never to admit forreigners to be judges of our laws", answered Sir William Wyndham. "A standing army was what he hoped we should never see in England, but to allow of tweenty or 30,000 forreigners to come over was of more pernicious consequence . . .".[64]

The two sharply divergent views of Britain's natural relationship with Europe which gradually took shape in the 1690's, crystallised in the crisis of 1701, and by the closing years of Anne's reign had begun to seem virtually irreconcilable,* are the backcloth to two further areas of political conflict between the parties which developed after 1701. One of these was opened up at the very end of William's reign, to be contested throughout almost the whole of Anne's; the other became an issue of prime importance in the years 1708–9 and remained so until 1713. The first involved the strategy of the war, the second the making of the peace.

Given the very different premises from which most Whigs and most Tories approached the Spanish Succession war it was hardly to be expected that the politicians would agree about the conduct any more than about the diplomacy of the war. By the end of 1702 a distinctive strategical concept and an

---

* Because the Oxford ministry can only be judged on the inadequate evidence of just over one year of peace it must remain a matter for speculation how far the Tory country gentleman could have been 'educated' to accept even the very limited degree of commitment to Europe envisaged in the Speech from the Throne in March 1714.

ambitious, uncompromising attitude towards the extent of Britain's contribution to the struggle against Louis XIV had already begun to mark out the Whigs as the natural supporters of Marlborough's plans to break French military predominance. At the same time the great bulk of High Tories at Westminster were revealed either as suspicious critics or as unqualified opponents of a 'Williamist' war strategy. Two principal objections formed the basis of the orthodox Tory attitude, objections which were summed up years later by Swift in *The Conduct of the Allies*. He protested on the one hand "That, against all manner of prudence or common reason, we engaged in this war as principals, when we ought to have acted only as auxiliaries"; and, on the other hand, "That we spent all our vigour in pursuing that part of the war [i.e. on land] which could least answer the end we proposed by beginning it, and made no effort at all where we could most have weakened the common enemy, and at the same time enriched ourselves".

It was this second objection, especially, which was at the heart of the acrimonious wrangling over strategy which split Godolphin's Cabinet in the first two years of the reign and which both then and later caused periodic debates in both Houses of Parliament. The standard High Tory view stemmed from a conviction which had become rooted in the party before 1697 of the futility of large-scale Continental campaigns, particularly in the Spanish Netherlands and the north-eastern frontier area of France with their network of fortified towns; but associated with it in the minds of many Tory squires was a keen distrust, inherited from the Country opposition, of a large army of redcoats. Rochester gave expression to these beliefs and prejudices in 1702 when he complained how "in these latter days, by an unaccountable providence" the most costly efforts had been made to defeat the enemy on land, "in that part where, by the strength of his numerous garrisons, he must be, for many years at least, invulnerable", and added

Well may other Princes, and States, whose situation requires it . . . find it for their interest, for the preservation of their credit and reputation amongst their neighbours, to keep constantly in pay great numbers of land forces; in which they are still vying one with another, and boasting who can raise his thousands, and who his ten thousands: but they will be found but young statesmen for our Government, who can think it adviseable that the strength of this island should be measured by proportions so unsuitable to its true glory, and greatness . . . [65]

This distaste for land operations was not by any means confined to the extreme isolationist wing of the party. One of the friends and connections of the Harleys, Salwey Winnington, wrily remarked in the autumn of 1702 that the recent "campagne of hop pullers" in his native Worcestershire had been "as unprofitable to mee as the campagnes in Flanders have been to England".[66] But whereas some of the moderate Tories who took their cue either from Harley or Godolphin were soon convinced by Marlborough's early campaigns that a more inspired general than William III, given enough men and money, could break the exhausting stalemate which the pessimists predicted in the Low Countries, the bulk of the party succumbed only briefly, in 1704 and again in 1706–7, to the spell of the Churchill genius.

The Earl of Rochester's quarrel with the Court at the beginning of the reign, which began in the stormy Cabinet and Privy Council meetings of 1 and 2 May 1702* and ended in his resignation from the ministry in February 1703, derived much of its significance from the fact that Rochester was for many years the most insistent and eloquent voice of the powerful "wooden walls" school of thought in the Tory party. He and his like believed that the only effective way for England to make her contribution to the defeat of France, and at the same time directly further the economic objectives which figured prominently among her war aims in 1702, was to use her naval supremacy to implement a strategy based on maritime and colonial operations. However, although the idea of a strictly limited naval war could always evoke a sympathetic response from the back benches and the country manor-houses,[67] among men who had little notion of the practical difficulties involved in maintaining a large fleet permanently in Caribbean or South American waters, few experienced Tory politicians, even in 1702, were prepared to go all the way with Rochester. Jersey, Anne's first Lord Chamberlain, may have been one exception.[68] But Bromley waxed enthusiastic in the autumn of 1702 over Marlborough's opening campaign; and although in the early weeks of the new Parliament Sir Edward Seymour put so many rubs in the way of Godolphin's plans for an adequate supply for the land forces that the Treasurer protested he could "meet him nowhere but to scold", before the end of December both he and his henchman, Musgrave, had been persuaded by Lord Nottingham to acquiesce conditionally in the proposal to raise the Queen's forces in Flanders from 40,000 to 50,000.[69]

---

* At these meetings, called to approve the formal declaration of war on France, Rochester vehemently argued the case (warmly debated since March, if not earlier) for England's participation only as an auxiliary and not as a principal. But he was overborne by Marlborough, who had the backing of the moderate Tory Pembroke, and of the 3 Whigs still in the Cabinet. Norris MSS. 920 NOR. 1/155: Thos. Johnson to Norris, 7 Mar.; Wratislaw to Vienna, 1/12 May (cited Klopp, *Der Fall des Hauses Stuart*, x (1888), 43); Boyer, p. 14.

The Earl of Nottingham, Secretary of State from 1702 to 1704, whose views (unlike those of many of his colleagues) were carefully thought out and clearly defined, favoured a mixed strategy, with the emphasis on what we should now call 'combined operations': a holding-action to be fought in the Netherlands, while "a fleet, and an army accompanying it" sought out the enemy's more vulnerable points in the Mediterranean theatre, the West Indies, and later in the Iberian Peninsula.[70] Yet even Nottingham's views on the conduct of the war were in sharp contrast to those of Marlborough, Godolphin and the Whigs. Only fleetingly, after the indecisive campaign of 1703, did a section of the Whigs lose faith in an offensive war in the Low Countries.[71] But Nottingham always looked on the navy as the decisive if not the only weapon and his opposition to an over-ambitious commitment to the Flemish theatre, based on the unhappy experience of William III, was unrelenting: "good gamesters", he told Normanby,[72] "will change their cards at least, if they can't their fortune".[73]

The departure of most of the leading High Tories from the Cabinet, a process that was completed by the spring of 1704, was followed by the four most successful years of the war for Marlborough's army. Even the voices of the Rochesterites were muted between 1704 and 1708, especially after the failure of their petty and pathetic attempt to set up the Tory admiral Rooke as a rival popular champion against the Captain-General. But though Rochester was now prepared to concede the case for *some* large-scale operations on land he argued with Nottingham that the main effort should be made in Spain and not in Flanders. Nottingham had been advocating a vigorous Peninsula campaign since 1703, and after the disaster at Almanza in 1707, which to him was the culmination of a process whereby Spain "had bin in a man[n]er deliverd up to the enemy by a shameful neglect",[74] the transfer of troops to Iberia from the Low Countries became a favourite notion of the Tory opposition. During the great debate in the Lords on 19th December 1707 its leaders proposed, to Marlborough's fury, that the Netherlands army should be denuded of 20,000 troops to ensure the recovery of Spain;[75] and as late as January 1711 General Webb could still harrow many Whigs in the House of Commons by arguing

that every body was sensible that in all this war, the war in Spain had been starved, and that in Flanders very sufficiently provyded for; and that in his opinion . . . it would be necessary to send the very best of the troops they had for that service, and that if 20 batallions of the best troops in Flanders were sent it would soon be seen what a change of affairs they would make; and . . . he wish't that these who had been knock't in the head their this last year unnecessarily had been sent to Spain.[76]

Moreover, once the Tories were in the saddle again, and Marlborough's prestige at home began to wane, the 'blue-water' theorists came into play once more. During discussion of the Land Tax bill in December 1710 one zealot even proposed in all seriousness that the whole of the anticipated yield of £2 million from the tax should be appropriated to the support of the navy. Although only a diehard minority would still have gone as far as this, and the Court had no difficulty in getting the proposal rejected out of hand,[77] there was an evident determination in this new House of Commons that money voted for the navy should not be diverted, as in the past, for the support of the land forces.[78] Still more significant is the whole episode of the Quebec expedition in 1711, for which five seasoned battalions were withdrawn from Marlborough's army.[79] The enthusiastic support which St. John was able to marshal behind this project — which had already been considered and shelved by the Whigs in favour of Continental priorities[80] — and the inability of Harley, despite his primacy in the new ministry, to prevent the scheme going through, illustrate the hold which a maritime and colonial strategy continued to exercise over the Tory mind. Not even the abject failure of the Quebec attempt disillusioned its supporters. And although peace was soon to render the strategy debate temporarily academic, the "wooden walls" argument remained so useful a political weapon that in 1714 Lord Oxford, with one eye on his declining prestige, carefully wrote passages into the Queen's Speech congratulating her subjects on their deliverance "from a consuming land war" and assuring them that Britain could only remain formidable in future "by the right application of our naval force".[81]

Long before the Spanish Succession war was over, the disagreement between the parties over how it should be waged had been pushed into the second rank of political issues by more acute divisions of opinion over how and when it should be brought to an end. It is doubtful whether any other matter so continuously aggravated relations between Whig and Tory from 1708 to 1712 as the making of peace. It produced controversy on three distinct grounds: on the urgency of the country's need for peace in the first place; on what terms should be accepted as the essential requirements of a "good peace"; and on what methods could justifiably be used to open the way for a settlement and bring it to a conclusion.

By the winter of 1709–10 Tories the length and breadth of Britain were agreed on nothing more completely than on the necessity of ending the war at the first favourable opportunity; and when Parliament was dissolved the following September they were able naturally to assume the mantle of the "peace party" before an electorate whose enthusiasm for the war had been largely exhausted in the previous two years. Although it was the autumn of 1709 before Tory peace propaganda became intense, it was being disseminated, to Marlborough's disgust, at least as early as the spring of 1708.[82] Louis XIV's attempt to invade Scotland at this time with a combined Franco-Jacobite force ensured that for a while at least the seed would fall on infertile ground. But the Tories were compensated for this discouragement by the fact that Harley and his friends, with whom the Queen was known to be still in sympathy, had noticeably cooled in their attitude towards the war since their departure from office in February 1708. Harley no doubt realised that as long as the war lasted he could never be certain of breaking Marlborough's hold on the Queen. But it is also evident that a summer spent mostly in Herefordshire, free from the insistent demands of office, had made him more conscious of the first signs of a genuine war-weariness in the country at large, signs which would have been less easy to detect in London: "now everything is run out of breath", he told his friend Harcourt, "the mines are worked out, we have a necessity created of a long war, and that is now to be made an argument for most extravagant burdens . . .".*

Most Tory leaders, all the same, were prepared to concede privately in the winter of 1708–9 that peace, however desirable, was not yet practicable.[83] As Nottingham saw it "the circumstances of our enemies are not yet such as that we may from thence hope for a good one and (bad as our condition is) this is a good reason for continuing the war".[84] So the news that the *grand monarque* was suing desperately for terms the following spring came as manna to the Tories, and their disappointment was thus the more bitter when the Hague negotiations broke down in May 1709 after Godolphin and the Whigs had pitched their demands too high. Anger with the French soon gave way to mounting criticism of the Churchills and the Junto,[85] some of whose supporters made a positive merit, both then and later, of their intransigence.[86] From England, where Harley plotted to force a renewal of negotiations by obstructing supply in the next session, and where Country

---

* H.M.C. *Bath MSS*. i, 192: 16 Oct. 1708; cf. N.U.L. Portland (Holles) MSS. Pw2/95: [Harley] to Newcastle (copy), 22 Oct. The whole question of Harley's attitude to the war between 1706 and 1708 deserves detailed study. A remarkable letter he wrote to Mrs. Masham in Oct. 1708 (Longleat MSS. Portland Papers, x, f. 55: 16 Oct. [code]) confirms indications from other sources that he had been critical of the government's failure to make peace after Ramillies. But that this was because he felt the situation was then ripe for the exaction of the best possible terms rather than because, in 1706–7, he doubted the country's capacity to maintain its war effort is clear from a memorandum in his hand (? for a Cabinet meeting), endorsed "Heads, Windsor, Sept: 13: 1707" (B.M. Loan 29/9/48).

Tory members like Charles Bertie thought "Tournay & its citadell ... a dear bargain for six millions a year, & the Dutch to reap the benefitt thereof",[87] dissension actually spread to the army in the field. "All those amongst us here who are reckoned high Whigs", wrote Colonel Cranstoun from before the walls of Tournai, "or in with the Junto as you call them, seem pleased at continuing the war and reason on all occasions to persuade the world that all the offers and advances made by France were a trick to impose upon us, though ... I doubt that if we do more than take Tournay this campaign there will be many in St. Stephen's Chapel next winter of opinion we were in the wrong to push things so far and refuse offers that appeared both so reasonable and sincere".[88] The effect of the battle of Malplaquet on 31 August, a pyrrhic victory acclaimed by the Whigs but derided by their opponents,* was to aggravate these divisions in camp and country still further; and Cranstoun's hints of a parliamentary enquiry into the collapse of the Hague negotiations might well have proved prophetic[89] had not the Sacheverell affair dominated all else in the session of 1709–10.

When Robert Harley returned to office as the Queen's first minister in August 1710 it was widely understood, despite his professed intention to carry on the war vigorously, that the making of peace would be foremost among the priorities of his ministry. He and his colleagues assumed, and rightly so, that "the sence of the nation" was for it.[90] However, the precise terms on which peace ought to be made had not yet become a clear-cut party issue. By December of the following year, when the Tory administration, after concluding preliminaries with France, was at last ready to gamble on getting a parliamentary endorsement of its policies, such an issue had clearly been precipitated out of the central problem of the disposal of the Spanish crown and of sovereignty over the Spanish New World possessions. This was a development which few would have forecast with any confidence a year earlier, and no one could have envisaged at all before the battle of Almanza in 1707.[91] Even in the winter following Almanza the leaders of both parties had joined in giving formal parliamentary approval to the commitment of the allies not to conclude peace with Louis XIV as long as a Bourbon ruled in Madrid. Indeed the only dissident voice in the House of Lords in December 1707, when Somers put his famous motion on "No Peace without Spain"

---

* Contrast Townshend's paean, "the greatest action that has been done this war, when it is fairly considered in all its circumstances", and Walpole's equal enthusiasm, tempered only by anxiety about casualties, with the biting reaction of Mansel and Harley. N.U.L. Portland (Bentinck) MSS. PwA. 1404; Charborough Park MSS: Walpole to Erle, 6 Sept.; H.M.C. *Portland MSS.* iv, 527; *ibid.* ii, 208.

before the peers, was raised, not by a Tory, but by an independent Whig, Lord Scarborough.[92] St. John's *cri de coeur* in November 1708, "for God's sake let us be once out of Spain", reflects his own clear-sighted realism rather than the prevalent attitude of his party even at this stage.[93] As late as the autumn of 1710, in fact, a certain euphoria still persisted among many Tories with regard to Spain, stimulated by the news of Stanhope's victory at Saragossa in the summer. "Money is sent to supply Mr. Stanhope amply by two several ways", Harley assured the Lord Privy Seal in September; and the purposeful reference in the Queen's Speech on 27 November to the war in the Peninsula is further evidence that neither he nor other members of the new Cabinet had yet despaired of removing Philip of Anjou from the Spanish throne before peace was concluded.*

What the new ministers did not then know was that Madrid had already been evacuated for the last time. Once they had had time to assimilate this news Harley and Shrewsbury, at least, were ready to recognise that "No Peace without Spain" was a chimera; indeed they indicated as much to the French (with whom they had been tentatively negotiating since August) on 12 December, just before the news of Stanhope's surrender at Brihuega arrived to confirm their opinion.[94] The shock of Brihuega went far to quench the ardour of the Peninsula school both in the ministry at large and on the Tory benches.[95] If there were any Tories who remained mentally unprepared for the diplomatic consequences of this final setback to British hopes in Spain they received a decisive jolt in April 1711 from the death of the Emperor Joseph I. The succession to the Imperial crown of the Archduke Charles meant that his candidacy for the Spanish throne now became politically undesirable as well as militarily unattainable. So that when both Houses of Parliament were called on to pronounce a new verdict on the principle of "No Peace without Spain" on 7 December 1711, only 2 Tory peers† and 11 commoners were to be found openly voting for it. The Whig

---

* B.M. Loan 29/238, f. 373: Harley to Newcastle, 14 Sept.; *C.J.* xvi, 403. I find it hard to accept the late Dr. Trevelyan's view, based on the evidence of the Jersey-Gaultier negotiations, that '*From the moment of its formation*, the new English Ministry had been strongly inclined to abandon Spain to Philip' (*England under Queen Anne*, iii, 87). In this connection see the minutes of the meeting of the Lords of the Committee, 31 Oct. 1710, W.S.L. Dartmouth MSS.: Cabinet minutes; B.M. Loan 29/171/4: Harley to Stratford, 16 Sept.; *Journal to Stella*, 25 Dec.

† Nottingham was one, Pembroke (the ex-Lord President of the Council and Lord Lieut. of Ireland) the other. Nottingham's attitude is well known; Pembroke's seems to have escaped notice. S.H. Cal. Br. 24 Eng. 107, f. 42: Kreienberg, 4/15 Dec. 1711; B.M. Loan 29/10/16: paper in Oxford's hand endorsed "List — Dece: 10: 1711".

view, meanwhile, had not budged an inch officially since Sir Gilbert Heathcote had told Lord Treasurer Godolphin in 1709, "I call any thing a rotten peace ... unless we have Spain, for without it we can have no safety".[96] Apart from a small "juntilla" of dissident peers who had deserted to Harley in 1710 and a handful of M.P.s whose offices made them unwilling to offend the ministry, the Whigs clung to this principle as an article of party faith until almost the end of the 1712 session — not least because the Elector of Hanover persisted in the same attitude. How convinced the Whig leaders were by their own arguments it is difficult to say. St. John was fully persuaded that "those who oppose the Queen's measures know, as well as we who pursue them, that ... the end which they pretend to aim at is chimerical";[97] Wharton, Stanhope and Cowper, to name only three, were clearly sceptical;[98] yet they and almost all their fellow-Whigs in both Houses, including some "who owed the best of their bread to pensions from the Court",[99] faithfully voted in December 1711 for keeping Spain and Spanish America out of Bourbon hands. What is more, there seems little doubt that most of the rank and file did so because, like William Jessop, the member for Aldborough, they saw the abandonment of Spain as sure proof "that many who have put on the face of true Englishmen, and whom we have taken for such, are rotten at the heart".[100]

By 1712 one further aspect of the Tory peace was dividing the parties. The methods by which it was being carried through were genuinely and deeply distasteful to the Whigs. The Grand Alliance powers were under a specific obligation by the treaty of 1701 to make peace jointly or not at all. The whole course of the negotiations carried through by the Harley ministry between August 1710 and September 1711 was based on separate treating with France and calculated deceit of the allies. How many Tories would have been shocked by this had they known it was going on we cannot know. Harley and St. John could salve their own consciences with the nice distinction between "a separate treaty", which they rejected, and "separate treating".[101] Yet St. John's untypical evasiveness when charged with this second offence in the Commons in December 1711[102] suggests that he sensed some uneasiness on his own side of the House at the prospect of underhand bargaining with the enemy. For Tories still sensitive on this point Swift's *Conduct of the Allies* proved the perfect anodyne. At the time of the Commons' debate on 7 December it had been on the market little more than a week.[103] But before the end of January the *Conduct* had been through 6 editions and sold 11,000 copies ("a prodigious run", its author delightedly commented, "... considering 'tis a dear twelvepenny book"), and the

Commons, in Walpole's mocking phrase, had been "taught a new lesson".[104] Something of its effect can be gauged from the impassive reaction of the Tories in May 1712 to the insistent rumour that the Duke of Ormonde, Marlborough's successor, had been instructed to desist from active co-operation with the allies in the field while the peace talks at Utrecht were in progress. The Whigs were scandalised, but a Whig motion asking the Queen to countermand the "restraining orders" was crushed in the Lower House by 203 votes to 73.[105] "It would be a hard matter", Cowper told the Lords in their last major debate of this session, "to justify and reconcile, either with our laws or the laws of honour and justice, the conduct of some persons in treating clandestinely with the common enemy, without the participation of the allies".[106] But having just been promised peace with advantage, the Tories (or at least the overwhelming majority of them)* no longer cared about peace with honour. And neither by this time did the vast majority of the Queen's subjects.

Britain in June 1712 had been for more than ten years engaged in the greatest war in its history, "such a war [Bolingbroke afterwards wrote] as I heartily wish our children's children may never see".[107] The issues which this war had raised had nearly all, sooner or later, become party issues. Admittedly there were always a few academic observers ready to protest that such matters were not, after all, the pure milk of party conflict. Philip Yorke, then an earnest young law student, thought the great peace debates of December 1711 a "flagrant instance of the uncontroullable power of faction amongst us". It disturbed him

> to see two sets of men, some of whm. on both sides were allow'd to understand their countrey's interest, & pursue it too when it did not stand in the way of Party designs — to see these I say divide exactly to a man, according to their severall denominations, upon a generall question that is of the last consequence not only to this nation but to all Europe, and does not come under the particular consideration either of Whigg or Tory.[108]

But this rather priggish appeal for purism and patriotism did not prevent the future Earl of Hardwicke, stout young Whig that he was, from supporting the Whig case on the peace at virtually every point by logical argument.[109] And indeed it counted for little in practice that most of the questions of foreign policy, of war and of peace which were debated and decided in the

---

* There were a few exceptions, of whom Nottingham was the most prominent. "The world's grown mad", he told his wife, "& any Peace, any way, will be approv'd of". Finch-Hatton MSS.: 29 May 1712.

age of Anne were new or relatively new questions, and sometimes transient questions, with little obvious relevance to the fundamental principles in which the traditions of both parties were rooted; for the fact was that they were intensely real and important to the partisans of the day. Most of all were they full of meaning for the younger generation of politicians, represented by men like Walpole, St. John and Stanhope, all of whom began their parliamentary careers in 1701–2 — men to whom Exclusion and the Popish Plot were then little more than echoes from the past. To most of this generation the fact that these issues had no part in the pre-Revolution heritage of Whig and Tory was beside the point. What mattered in the heat of party battle was that they seemed eminently worth fighting over. And though St. John found it convenient to forget this later, we can hardly do so ourselves without misunderstanding a great deal of what politics between 1702 and 1714 was about.

CHAPTER THREE

The Substance of Conflict:
Principles and Power

ALTHOUGH the party men of Anne's day owed to King William's foreign policy a new ideological inheritance, one which sustained them in grappling with issues which their Exclusionist predecessors had scarcely envisaged, they were unable to escape from that older inheritance bequeathed to them by Whig and Tory tradition. Most of them indeed had no wish to escape from it; for this was their birthright, their natural legacy of fundamental party principle. It is true that to many politicians of the 1690's, incapable even then of evading its implications entirely, it was a legacy that sometimes seemed an encumbrance, of doubtful relevance to the confused, transitional post-Revolution world. But to those of 1702–14 it offered something infinitely more positive. It offered inspiration, challenge, frequently danger; but it never represented less than an intense political reality.

The reasons for this remarkable change must be sought primarily in the closing months of the old reign and in the opening months of the new. For this period saw the firm re-establishment of much of the traditional pattern of party rivalry, as well as the sharper delineation of that new pattern, created round essentially post-Revolution issues, which was our main concern in the previous chapter. Most of the old party distinctions, blurred or pushed temporarily into the background for some years after 1688, took on an entirely fresh significance in the light of a whole sequence of developments between July 1700 and the end of 1702.

For one thing, three events forced the Tories to take a fresh and searching look at their attitudes to divine hereditary right and the Protestant succession: the death of the Duke of Gloucester (1700), leaving only an ailing king and a semi-invalid, and now childless, princess with any legal right to the thrones of England and Scotland; the passage through Parliament of the Act of Settlement (1701) in an attempt to remedy this situation; and the enforcement of an Abjuration oath* on all public office-holders and the members

* After Louis XIV's recognition of the Pretender as James III of England.

of both houses (1702). To the Whigs all three events offered an ideal opportunity to restate and re-emphasise their own position on these same elemental questions.

The Whig position on the succession was crystal clear and unvarying. From June 1701, when the Electress Sophia of Hanover "and the heirs of her body being Protestants" were given a statutory title to the English throne after Anne's death, down to August 1714, when Sophia's eldest son was peacefully proclaimed King George I of Great Britain at St. James's Palace gate, the complete unanimity of the Whig party on this issue became the most effective linch-pin of its solidarity in periods of stress. The parliamentary cohesion it recovered at the time of the impeachments of 1701 was never more complete in the next thirteen years than when Parliament was concerned, in one way or another, with safeguarding the Hanoverian succession. No Whig was inhibited here by any feeling for the sacramental character of monarchy or by any doubts about Parliament's right to act as the final arbiter of all claims to regality. If the Earl of Wharton could tell even Queen Anne to her face that she had come to the throne in 1702 by virtue of the Bill of Rights,[1] neither he nor any Whig was likely to doubt that the Act of Settlement had established the Hanoverian claim to succeed her beyond any further debate.

Unfortunately for the prospects of Hanover, as the Whigs soon realised, the act of 1701 could designate a Protestant successor but could not necessarily ensure his peaceful accession. Here much clearly depended in the first place on the outcome of the war. The Spanish Succession war was always for the Whigs a war of religion, as well as a trade war and a war for the preservation of the Balance of Power. Their enthusiasm for the struggle against Louis XIV and their zeal for the Hanoverian cause were inseparable.* When the House of Lords was debating how best that cause could be promoted in November 1705 Lord Wharton expressed his party's sense of priorities with his customary lack of humbug and circumlocution. "The only way to do this thoroughly is to bring down the power of France — that tyrant abroad who would be a tyrant on us. The next thing is to secure the succession."[2] This second object inspired a number of attempts between 1705 and 1714 to create new parliamentary safeguards for the legal rights of the House of Brunswick-Lüneburg. With all of them (save one that was a pure

---

* Thus Somers wrote in 1706 of "my zeal for the protestant succession & for prosecuting the war against the French King who is the declared enemy to it & which is most effectually to be secured by the reducing of his power'. Add. MSS. 34521, f. 41.

sham*) the Whigs were closely associated, and in most of them they were the prime movers.

The two major legislative achievements of the reign which had these ends in view, the Regency Act of 1706 and the Act of Union of 1707, were essentially Whig achievements, even though they were carried through with the blessing of the Marlborough-Godolphin-Harley triumvirate which dominated the ministry at this stage. The Regency bill, which provided for a caretaker government (the Lords Justices) and for an automatic summons of Parliament to bridge the critical time-gap between the Queen's death and the arrival of the Hanoverian heir, was the brain-child of the Junto. Conceived, it would seem, mainly by Somers, and proposed and piloted through the House of Lords by Wharton,[3] at a time when both they and their chief associates were still out of office, it was designed (as Cowper later claimed) "to put it [the succession] in such a method as was not to be resisted but by open force of arms and a public declaration for the Pretender".[4] It had almost unanimous support from the Whig peers,[5] and the difficulties the bill met with in the Commons from the attempt of a determined group of Country Whigs to tack a place clause to it were patiently overcome by the Junto lords and a handful of their aristocratic friends.† Appropriately it was Halifax of the Junto who was sent over to Hanover at the end of the 1705–6 session to present a copy of the act to the Elector. Among the letters he took with him was one from Lord Somers, not only explaining why the Whigs had thought it necessary "to move for those solid provisions which were evidently wanting",[6] but promising fresh efforts to continue the good work. "We hope it will be further carried on", he added, "by the . . . Treaty between the Commrs. of England & Scotland for a Union of the two Kingdoms, which seems to be the only way now left open for obtaining a declaration of the same succession in Scotland which is already effected in England . . .".[7]

Of the Union, as of the Regency Act, the Whigs were the principal architects. Since Anne's accession her two chief advisers, Marlborough and Godolphin, had both accepted that a parliamentary union of the two kingdoms was the only long-term solution to the problem of their steadily deteriorating relations. But they had done so with no special enthusiasm, and the first attempt in the new reign to bring such a union about, in the winter

---

* See pp. 113–14 below.

† See pp. 132–4 below; also G. S. Holmes, 'The Attack on "The Influence of the Crown", 1702–16', *Bull. I.H.R.* xxxix (1966), for a full account of the struggle over the place clause of the Regency bill.

of 1702–3, had collapsed largely through the tepid if not downright hostile attitude of the High Tories to any treaty which involved an English guarantee of the Presbyterian Church of Scotland.[8] Without Whig initiative, wholehearted Whig co-operation, and in the final instance Whig votes it is virtually certain that the act of 1707 would never have been passed. After the salutary shock administered by the Queen's reluctant assent to the Scottish Act of Security in 1704, which threatened a separate and pro-Stuart settlement of the Crown in Scotland after her death, it was on Junto initiative and through shrewdly-applied Whig pressure on Godolphin that the Aliens bill was introduced to convince the Scots that it was in their interest to re-open negotiations.[9] When the new English team of negotiators was nominated in April 1706 Robert Walpole wrote to his brother Horace that "tis altogether constituted of Whig lords and commoners".[10] In his enthusiasm he overlooked the presence of a few ministerial Tories: Godolphin himself, for instance, Pembroke, the Lord President, and Hedges, the Secretary for the Southern Department; also Robert Harley and his friends Harcourt and Poulet. But certainly the English commission of 31 was dominated by Whigs and above all by the lords of the Junto, all five of whom were members and all of whom attended sedulously except for Halifax, who was in Hanover at the time;[11] and though Harley might complain that their private back-stage contacts with their Scottish friends were an attempt to make "useless members" out of him and his Tory associates,[12] the fact remains that their methods paid dividends. Somers's statesmanship, especially, was stamped indelibly on the final treaty, and his brother-in-law, Jekyll, ranked its negotiation along with Ramillies and Turin as "one of the great victories" of 1706.[13]

Just as the Whigs had some help from the Harleyite and Court Tories in 1705–7, so in the final period of acute anxiety about the Protestant succession in 1713–14 they found allies in Parliament among the Hanoverian or "Whimsical" Tories. But the main burden of the campaign against the Jacobite cause was taken once again upon their willing shoulders, and this at a time when virtually the whole party was politically proscribed. It was masterly tactics by the Junto, for instance, which forced the Court to accept Wharton's motion in the Lords on 30 June 1713 for an address pressing for the Pretender's removal from Lorraine or from any other country on friendly terms with Britain.[14] This vote, and a similar one moved by Stanhope in the Tory-dominated Commons, had no direct effect; but in the months that followed the Whigs were able to turn the government's reluctance to implement them into a valuable political weapon for keeping public opinion apprehensive about the succession. In the following spring it was private Whig pressure on Baron Schütz which produced what one party zealot thought "the best news that has been in England since the Change of the M[inistr]y"; for it encouraged the Hanoverian envoy to make his bold application to Lord Chancellor Harcourt for a writ of summons to enable the Electoral Prince to take his seat in the House of Lords as Duke of Cambridge.[15] There it was hoped he would hold a watching brief in the interests of his grandmother and father. Again the plan misfired;[16] and the full-dress attempt on 5 April 1714 to get the Lords to vote the Protestant succession in danger under the Oxford ministry also failed, though so narrowly that even in victory the government was thought by some to have suffered "a mortall wound".[17] As propaganda, at least, both moves were undeniably effective, and meanwhile the Whigs pursued somewhat less spectacular objectives with more success. In March, with the help of the dissident High Tory peers, Nottingham and Anglesey, they killed a strange bill proposed by Oxford which would have made it high treason to bring foreign troops into the kingdom; and the defeat of this measure kept open a legal door through which the Dutch could fulfil the terms of the revised Barrier Treaty of January 1713 and send forces, if invited, in the event of a Jacobite insurrection on the Queen's death.[18] It was in their campaign for the offer of a reward for the Pretender's capture, however, that the Whigs brought off their greatest *coup*.

The most promising base for such a move had again seemed to lie in the Upper House; for though the Whigs in the Commons could always deploy "a great deal of good argument and reason [as one of their members put it] ... Yet numbers overswayed" them all too often.[19] The party thus appeared to have suffered a severe setback when a motion calling for a proclamation which would invite Prince James Edward's apprehension "dead or alive" was lost in the House of Lords in April 1714 by 10 votes. But in June came a second opportunity. After Wharton had laid evidence before Lord Chief Justice Parker concerning the activities of the Pretender's recruiting agents in London, Oxford was forced in self-defence to wring his own proclamation out of the Cabinet, promising £5000 out of the Queen's personal income as a reward to anyone seizing the person of the Pretender if he landed in Britain. To this the Commons, at the instance of the Marquess of Hertford,[20] responded by promising a further £100,000 out of public funds (to the fury of many Tory ministers) and by an assurance "that this House will heartily concur with Her Majesty in all other measures for extinguishing the hopes of the Pretender, and all his open and secret abettors".[21]

That the House of Commons should have been induced to make such a declaration a fortnight before the prorogation of Anne's last Parliament and a mere five weeks before the Queen's death was a remarkable tribute to the determination of a heavily-outnumbered party, deprived of official countenance, to assert its most cherished principle without fear or favour. But no less was it a measure of the predicament of the Tories. For on the succession question itself, and on all the issues of principle associated with it, they were as thoroughly divided by 1714 as the Whigs were unanimous. From top to bottom the party was cleft into three distracted groups — a Jacobite wing, a Hanoverian wing, and a centre group much larger than either perching irresolutely and precariously on the fence. It has always seemed so plausible to regard these fissures of 1713–14 as inevitable and nemesic, and to trace them back to the violent shock which the Revolution had dealt to the fabric of fundamental Tory principles, that one may easily overlook the fact that nothing as disastrous as this had been easily predictable eleven years earlier.

By the end of 1702, after a painful struggle of conscience, most Tories appeared to have finally turned their backs on the past and to have come to terms with the future. In the crisis precipitated by the Duke of Gloucester's death and William's fading health the statutory provision in the summer of 1701 for a Protestant, German successor to Anne had been accepted by the overwhelming majority of Tories in Parliament, once the pill had been sweetened by the imposition of stern restrictions on the freedom of action of the Hanoverians if and when they came to the throne.[22] A Liverpudlian in London the following September found "few persons yet in mourning for K. J——s his death", and "the Jacs. . . . in great confusion" about whether to own the Pretender as their King.[23] Subsequently the replacement of a Calvinist Dutchman as sovereign by a native and Anglican Stuart princess had made it easier for all but the most obdurate among the practising politicians to take the oaths to the Queen and even to subscribe to the new oath abjuring the Pretender. The bill embodying the Abjuration oath had encountered Tory resistance in the House of Commons earlier in 1702, led by Nottingham's brother Heneage Finch; but the Commons this session had proved, in young Horace Walpole's words, "no whetstone for jacobiticall teeth",[24] and even before William's death it was clear that, with war brewing, most Tory squires were already "better prepared for the oath than for taxes".[25] Less than three weeks after Anne's accession all but one of the 431 M.P.s in town had sworn it, and only four Tory peers of any note — Scarsdale, Plymouth, Nottingham and Weymouth — still held out. The latter, moreover, was already wavering. "Though I have not absolutely resolved to take this new oath", he told his brother, "yet . . . I am much nearer doing it than I ever thought I should bee, and may possibly submit to doe it, the case beeing so much altered by the death of Kg. Wm . . ."[26] Take it he did; and to those who shied more fiercely at the obstacle Archbishop Sharp had bracing counsel to offer:

I do not know what objections yor. Lordp may have against taking that oath [he told Nottingham], other than what you intimated . . . viz. that it looks like swearing against God's Providence and Governmt. of the World. If this be yor. Lordps objection I must confesse I think there is no force in it . . . In truth according to my notion of things who ever can take the oath of Allegiance to the present Queen may safely take the oath of Abjuration . . .*

The Tories would indeed appear to have come a long way since 1687 if a moderately "High" Anglican prelate, soon to become Anne's principal adviser on Church affairs, could write in 1702: "I am of opinion that [princes] hold their crowns by the same legall right that yor. Lordp holds yor. estate, and that they may forfeite their rights as well as you may do yors. And that the Legislature is judge in one case as well as the other".†

And yet the victory for new Toryism was more ostensible than real. In the country at large there was more resistance to the Abjuration oath than there was at Westminster, a fact borne out by the frequent reluctance of Tory returning officers to tender it to voters in close-contested elections. Moreover many who did accept it did so, like John Lade, a future member of Parliament for Southwark, in a spirit that was frankly cynical, justifying themselves on the purely practical ground that "the Jacks . . . should never be able to do any thing if they . . . did not take all the oaths that could be imposed".[27] Even the Archbishop of York's conscientious advice to Nottingham, it is significant to note, included an escape-clause: "for I think you are left as much at liberty after you have taken this oath", he wrote; "nay it is as much yor. duty to own for yor. King whomsoever God in his Providence sets upon this throne, . . . tho it should prove the very person

---

* Finch MSS. G.S., bundle 22: 31 Mar. 1702. It took Nottingham 3 months to change his original opinion of the oath, that "the safest side in conscience is to refuse it". Lloyd-Baker MSS. Box 4, bundle Q. 55: Nottingham to Sharp, 10 Jan. 1702 (microfilm in the Borthwick Institute, York).

† Sharp to Nottingham, 31 Mar., *loc. cit.* Sharp, it is true, had not always inclined to the "High" party among the clergy. In later years Tenison of Canterbury could not always resist reminding his brother archbishop of their younger days, "when I was thought a much higher Ch. man at St. Martins than you at St. Giles's. To wch. the ABp of York (said his Grace of Cant.) would never make me any answer, but would shake me by the hand, and laugh very heartily". B.M. Lansdowne MSS. 1024, f. 372.

you have abjured, provided you contributed nothing to it".[28] The relative ease with which the Act of Settlement had passed through a Tory House of Commons in 1701 had also been in some respects misleading. A minority of moderate Tories, especially those who looked to Speaker Harley for leadership, worked up some enthusiasm for the measure. But of the motives and attitude of the majority Lord Cowper's diagnosis,[29] making due allowance for an element of bias even in that most fair-minded of Whigs, was probably not much mistaken:

the true reason why such a Bill passed in such a Parliament was: That the King having ... earnestly recommended that Bill to Parliament in his speech from the throne, the Tories, for fear of losing the King's favour, did not endeavour to reject it, but set themselves to clog it ... and to show their contempt and aversion whenever it came on, except when it was necessary to be present in order to load it,* and by calling Sir J[ohn] B[olles] to the chair of the Committee for that Bill, who was then thought to be distracted, and was soon after confined for being so.†

They hoped (Cowper explains) that some of the amendments made in the Commons would be unacceptable to the Whig peers and that the Lords would therefore reject the bill, and many Tories were plainly disconcerted when the Upper House decided to accept it "with all its faults".[30]

It is important to understand why so many Tories acted in this way, for in the explanation lies the clue to much that happened in party politics

---

* I.e. with restrictive clauses.

† This is exactly confirmed by Bonet's contemporary account: "Quand ils [les Tories] n'ont pû le fair tomber sous quelque pretexte populaire ils l'ont traité d'une maniere peu serieuse, et ils ont mis à la tête du Comité qui devoit presider sur ce sujet un personnage peu estimé, afin de se moquer de ceux qui disoient que ce Bill étoit une pierre de touche pour connoitre les Jacobites" (Add. MSS. 30000E, f. 183: 13/24 May 1701).

Sir John Bolles (M.P. for Lincoln, 1690–1702) was a volatile and exotic country Tory whose eccentricities had made him a figure of notoriety by 1701. In fact his "mad prank" at Lincoln assizes in 1699, when he insisted on sharing the bench with Mr. Justice Gold and had to be forcibly removed after threatening to bring the judge on his knees before the Bar of the House of Commons, had already given good cause for his sanity to be doubted (*Vernon Corr.* ii, 337–8; Luttrell, iv, 545). His parliamentary career reached a spectacular climax in the summer of 1701, for quite apart from his duties in the chair of the committee on the Settlement bill, some of the younger Tories, to their unconcealed delight, were able to use him as their secret weapon to force the reconstitution of the Commission of Public Accounts (see pp. 137–41 below) against the advice of Harley and the Court. He "went off like a bomb", one Tory told Thomas Coke, "to the amazement of Robin [Harley] and Ranelagh. He told them of millions unaccounted for, and of bargains made to cover 'em". (H.M.C. *Cowper MSS.* ii, 428: [Anthony Hammond?] to Coke, 7 June 1701).

between 1702 and 1714. It was not because they were committed Jacobites, for the great bulk of them were not. A Jacobite hard core did, of course, remain in the Tory party after 1701. Naturally it was less evident inside Parliament than outside it, where it was sustained by the writings of Charles Leslie and the non-jurors which kept alive the flickering flames of Divine Right theory. But there were Jacobites at Westminster too: men like Sir John Pakington, Viscount Bulkeley, Thomas Legh, Lewis Pryse, Thomas Strangeways and old Sir William Whitlock, whose inclinations to the exiled Stuarts were common knowledge in private though for the most part discreetly veiled in public. They and their kind were "the Non-juring Jurors" at whom Stanhope was later to scoff during the Sacheverell trial.[31] More serious, however, for the future well-being of the party was the far larger number of Tories in both Houses who were staunch enough Anglicans to be repelled by the idea of a Popish successor but whose deepest instincts remained those of their royalist antecedents. It was their still-unresolved mental dilemma which lay behind the equivocations of most Tory members during the passage of the Settlement bill. It was largely because Anne's accession gave these men an ideal excuse to defer a final crisis of conscience that they welcomed her with such undisguised relief: "never was greater joy exspressed than for the Queen's coming to the throne", one of them ex-claimed, out of a full heart, "nor lesse sorrowe for him that is gone".[32] Yet amid their transports at the dawn of the golden age they remained sullen and grudging in their commitment to Hanover; and they preferred, ostrich-like, to behave from then on as though the Queen were imperishable rather than face up squarely to the implications of the fact that she was only too mortal.

During the first half of the new reign it was this disoriented majority which was the despair of those who had hoped after 1701 to see the Tory party break loose completely from its pre-Revolution moorings. For without ever renouncing Hanover most Tories contrived over a number of major issues between 1702 and 1707 to suggest that they were prepared to do nothing positive to make its prospects more secure. Even before the Queen's first Parliament met, Sir Edward Seymour and some of his friends were thought to be hatching a scheme whereby Parliament would be moved to advise the assumption of joint sovereignty by Anne and her husband, Prince George — a patent device for evading the Act of Settlement. If the plan was ever seriously entertained (and there seems to be no firm evidence that it was),[33] it was never put into effect. But a practical test-case for demon-strating Tory sincerity did come up in the session of 1702–3. The Tories promoted a bill in the Commons to extend by a further year the time allowed for taking the Abjuration oath, and the Whigs in the House of Lords, seeing this not unnaturally as the thin end of the wedge, sent it back with drastic amendments, including a clause making it treason to "endeavour to deprive or hinder" the Hanoverians from inheriting the Crown. It would have been judicious for the Tories in the Lower House to accept the *fait accompli*; but instead they forced a division on an amendment forbidding the reinstatement of anyone who had forfeited office by refusing the oath. The result brought satisfaction to no one but the Whigs. For apart from failing by one vote to defeat the clause,[34] the dissidents were subsequently to see their names printed as an electoral blacklist of those whose loyalty to Hanover was suspect.[35]

Equally symptomatic of the party's uneasy state of mind, and still more unfortunate in tarnishing the Tory image in the eyes of the Electoral Court, was its persistent obstruction of the Regency bill in 1705–6. The efforts of the High Tory peers in November 1705 to "clog" the bill, while avoiding direct or open opposition to it, were obvious enough in their intent.[36] But they were no more than a foretaste of the tactics later adopted by non-ministerial Tories in the Commons. There, apart from supporting the place clause, they deployed almost every conceivable argument against the care-taker provisions of the bill. They objected to a regency on constitutional grounds: it would "lessen the crown in the esteem of the people", claimed Whitlock. They objected to the powers of the seven regents as far too extensive: by passing the bill, John Manley slyly observed, they would be creating "7 Kings" with power to repeal the Act of Settlement itself. They objected to the uncertainty as to who would fill these key posts when the day of crisis dawned; and the impetuous Charles Caesar got himself sent to the Tower for reminding his audience that one great man of the moment ("name the person", shouted Thomas Foley, though no one doubted it was Marlborough) was known to have corresponded with St. Germain in the last reign. The Tories even obstructed the proposal to provide for an immediate, automatic summons of Parliament at the Queen's death, Sir William Drake demanding a delay of twenty days to accommodate the Cornish and northern members. "The scars of the Rump", Manley lamented, "are upon all gentlemen's families to this day". It was all very well for the opposition to dismiss as ridiculous the charge of Coningsby and other Whigs that they were out by their tactics "to destroy the succession". But this was precisely the impression such unqualified and destructive criticism inevitably left.[37]

The resistance made to the Act of Union in Parliament in 1707, in which once more the High Tories were not supported by the Harleyites and others still associated with the ministry, could in one sense be more readily justified than opposition to the Regency bill. Not that there could be much excuse for the antics of the wild fringe who applauded Sir John Pakington in his scurrilous attacks on the whole conduct of the negotiations.[38] But the more responsible of the Union's critics expressed, and some perhaps genuinely felt, fears that the Anglican Church would suffer the taint of Presbyterianism if England and Scotland had a common Parliament as well as a common Queen. This was unquestionably true of some of the Nottinghamites, who led the resistance, and of independents like Ferrers, who in the debates in the Lords was "violent agt. the admission of Cameronians & Covenanters into our parlts."[39] Yet once again the attitude of the Tories — even their sniping at the purely economic and financial clauses of the treaty[40] — had the effect of reinforcing the impression of a party that was suspect on the score of the succession, a party that still hankered after Divine Right monarchy.

It was not, however, until Dr. Henry Sacheverell, an incendiary High Anglican clergyman, was impeached before the House of Lords early in 1710 for a sermon preached to the City dignitaries at St. Paul's that leading Tory politicians were forced into a direct and public re-examination of their basic principles. Most Tories privately agreed that Sacheverell had gone too far in his strident attack on the Revolution and on the "false brethren" in the Church of England who had forsaken the creed of their fathers; but few were prepared to condemn him severely, and during the debates in the Lords arguments were voiced which echoed those of twenty years before in the Convention Parliament. The peers heard the old Duke of Leeds* declare "he knew of no other but hereditary right"; they heard Haversham, one-time Whig but now blood-brother of Bromley, Nottingham and Rochester, challenge the view that the Queen sat on the throne principally by grace of Parliament;[41] they even heard the more moderate Bishop Hooper put the view "that the Original Compact are two very dangerous words, not to be mentioned without a great deal of caution", and express the fear that if the Revolution were made an object of political veneration "the Crown would roll like a ball, and never be fixed".[42] Indeed, enough was said in the Upper House on one day of the trial, 16 March, to cast more than a little doubt on Francis Hare's conviction that whatever Tories might do "to keep up party or to make their court" they would never willingly sacrifice the gains of the Revolution.[43]

---

* Formerly Earl of Danby and Marquess of Carmarthen, Charles II's Lord Treasurer and William III's Lord President.

In the struggle of principle between Whig and Tory in the age of Anne the significance of the Sacheverell debates and trial can easily be underestimated. These events were far more than convenient opportunities for the politicians to parade stale political theories. The managers for the Commons, the counsel for the Doctor, the leading spokesmen in both Houses, were not simply retreading old ground or glancing back over their shoulders at the Revolution. By implication, as Dr. Trevelyan has emphasised, they were also looking forward to the Hanoverian succession. And for the first time since 1706, except for a few anxious days in March 1708 before the French invasion fleet was intercepted, this contingency began to look less than secure to many Whigs. Both the Sacheverell affair itself and the near-hysterical reaction it produced in Tory circles during the following spring and summer, when loyal addresses choked with traditional party slogans showered on the Court from all parts of England, provided the true Jacobites with a remarkable stimulus.[44] "The notorious Jacks print their idol in all manner of postures", observed Cardonnel's under-secretary at the War Office, "and in time I believe they will cannonize him".[45] Of more immediate concern to the Whigs was the effect such a mood was bound to have on the coming General Election. As many Whigs had feared, the recognisably Jacobite element proved to be far more numerous in the new House of Commons elected in October 1710 than in any previous House since 1702.[46] Even before the Election Herefordshire was buzzing with Jacobite activity, encouraged by one of its county members, John Prise, while a group of Welsh M.P.s and ex-members had met at Aberystwyth and "drank to the Pretender's health and return upon their knees".[47] But after the triumph at the polls in 1710 the Jacobites were encouraged to nail their colours more provocatively to the mast. In 1711 Richard Cresswell, M.P. for Bridgnorth, toasted the Pretender openly at Bath, boasting that the majority of his Tory colleagues in the House would do likewise with but little more encouragement.[48] In the following year Lord Scarsdale, an active government supporter in the House of Lords, entertained known Jacobites and even Papists at his Derbyshire house, and one of the Pretender's most notorious young adherents, Charles Aldworth, was returned to Parliament as a member for (of all places) the royal borough of Windsor. It was little wonder that when Anne's last Parliament opened in March 1714 leading Whigs like Jekyll and King used the debate on the Address to draw public attention to the open contempt which many Tories now showed for the Abjuration oath.[49]

After the Sacheverell ferment and the electoral landslide of 1710 nothing did more to accentuate the drift to Jacobitism in the Tory party than the breach between the Oxford ministry and the Elector of Hanover in the winter of 1711–12 over the peace negotiations with France. Subsequently relations between Hanover and official Toryism, never very cordial, became glacial if still formally correct; and the conscientious doubts of a growing number of Tories were thus reinforced by the harsh practical consideration that their own supremacy, reestablished in 1710, seemed unlikely to survive the coming of a Hanoverian to the throne. But the reaction was not all in one direction. The months from December 1711 to June 1713 also produced the nucleus of a distinct Hanoverian group in the party, made up of those who reacted with alarm to the alienation of the Elector and to the sinister implications of the secret peace negotiations with France, especially when it became known that the latter had been initiated by the Jacobite Earl of Jersey.[50] From the summer of 1713, as we have seen, the Whigs made certain that the fate of the Protestant succession would be the dominant issue in politics for the remainder of the reign, and the psychological pressure on their opponents was immensely increased.[51] By the time Anne's last Parliament met at least half the Tory members in the Commons had in practical if not theoretical terms faced squarely up to the cruel dilemma in which party principle and considerations of political advantage had together placed them. There were by then scores of committed "Hanover Tories", the more determined in their renunciation of the Pretender because it was now virtually certain that he would never agree to even a nominal change of religion. The number of committed Jacobites in the House was even larger.

The unrepentant Jacobite like George Lockhart thought the Hanoverian Tories "odd animals" indeed. "They pretended", he wrote, "to reconcile the doctrine of nonresistance and passive obedience, with the principles on which the Revolution was founded and by which the deposing of kings was justifyd; they maintain'd that the succession to the crown was indefeasible and hereditary, and that the settlement thereof on the family of Hanover was no infringement . . . These are plain paradoxes, and nothing but downright infatuation cou'd move men of sense and figure in the world to act and think so inconsistently".[52] And yet in the end it was not so much the obstinate conviction of the Hanoverian Tories, clinging to their chosen path in defiance of party advantage,[53] that ensured the fatal paralysis of the Tory ministry in the last critical months and weeks of Anne's life; it was more the sheer dithering of that half of the party which in 1714, no less than in 1701–2, still hesitated to make any decision that was utterly irrevocable.

The revival of the succession question, and its development as one of the dominant themes of politics in our period, was not the only respect in which old party distinctions were given new emphasis and definition by the events of 1701–2. The very fact of Queen Anne's accession, if it enabled many Tories to postpone for some years their ultimate crisis of conscience on the question of hereditary right, also made it possible for them to rally under two at least of their other traditional banners. In March 1702, for the first time for 15 years, the Tory party felt itself to be fully identified once more with Church and Crown, the two pillars on which its original foundations rested.

Little more than nine months before, paradoxically, their advocacy of the restrictive clauses of the Act of Settlement had seemingly disposed of the Tories' last claims to be the natural defenders of the prerogative: "Before we get through this bill", one Tory member had boasted, "such care will be taken that we need not fear to have our liberties encroached upon, let our successor be who he will".[54] Yet the advent of a Stuart princess and an instinctive Tory as Queen Regnant was sufficient to reinvest the party with something of its old ethos as the party of the Crown. Ten years after the Act of Settlement was passed the Duke of Leeds, no longer politically active but still able to command respectful attention from Tories who had not even been born when he was Charles II's Lord Treasurer, could "think it the duty of every good subject to assist her Maj[tie] to preserve those few jewells which are left to the Crowne from being pulled out of it . . .";[55] and whenever it suited them to do so the Tories were ready enough after 1702 to resist what they took to be encroachments, by Parliament or anyone else, on those fields of discretionary authority legally remaining to the sovereign. Likewise the Whig leaders took every convenient opportunity to reassure those supporters who had accused them of subservience to the Crown during William's reign.* The right of the Crown to make peace and war without parliamentary consent was one issue of principle which was consequently aired. In office or out of it the Whigs remained consistent in assuming that Parliament had both a duty and a right to offer counsel to the Queen on foreign policy.† By contrast, in defending the peace preliminaries in December 1711 Tory spokesmen like Poulet, North and Grey, and Charles

* E.g. during the final day's debate on the Scottish Privy Council bill in the Lords in February 1708 Somers "took occasion [quite gratuitously] to say he hoped never to see any thing like a standing army in England". P.R.O. 30/24/21/148/2: Cropley to Shaftesbury [7 Feb.]. It was a long time before the Junto lords lived down their support of William III after Ryswick on the question of a standing army.

† See pp. 71, 78–9 above for the Whig-inspired motions leading to the addresses of March 1709 and 7 Dec. 1711. There were a number of similar votes during the 1714 session, such as that in March recommending strong diplomatic representation to relieve the Catalans from Spanish persecution.

Eversfield upheld the Crown's unfettered power to conduct foreign policy and insisted that Parliament could only give advice in this field when it was asked for.[56] But this was not a principle for which the Tories had always shown equal fervour when in opposition,[57] and there was never in fact any real question of the royal prerogative being resuscitated during Anne's reign as a valid and clear-cut issue between Whig and Tory. The contrast with 1679 or with 1689 is forcibly brought home to us when we find an Ashley-Cooper, no less, confessing in 1712 that "for my own part I am so contented with the present balance of power in our nation, and with the authority and prerogative of the Crown, such as the Tories have reduced it, that I can say from the bottom of my heart I am as an Englishman the most truly monarchical in my principle".[58]

And yet in a general sense it was true that the Tories of 1702–14 assumed their old royalist mantle. Except when their enthusiasm for Anne wore a little threadbare in the period of Whiggish predominance in the middle years of the reign, they could always in these years conjure up something of their traditional veneration for the person of the sovereign; they could even rediscover much of their old feeling for the sanctity of monarchy as an institution. The cynic might argue that this was only because the Tories recognised that the Crown, in the person of Queen Anne, had become a party political asset once more that could be exploited in debate and above all in elections. Unquestionably it was so exploited, at times quite shamelessly, while at the same time the skeletons of republicanism and regicide in the Whig cupboard were noisily rattled. Handbills given out at Guildford in support of the Tory candidates for Surrey in 1710 described them, for instance, as "true to the Queen and Church against all Managers of Oliver's Party and Principles, that once murder'd their King and thousands of the Nation, to reign over us".[59] But, as the Sacheverell trial clearly showed, the Tory attitude towards monarchy was more emotional than it was logical or unscrupulously calculated. That there was no longer a consistent philosophy behind it is evident from the equivocation which marked almost every Tory speech save Harcourt's which dealt during the trial with the question of passive obedience and non-resistance.[60] Yet by their very sophistry and illogicality these speeches testified that Toryism was still after more than twenty years afflicted with a guilt-complex about the Revolution, and that no Tory "of the highest sort" could contemplate such a possibility again with equanimity.[61]

Here the contrast with the Whigs was as sharp as ever. With the stark exception of the younger Sunderland, of whose "repeated provocations"

Anne bitterly complained,[62] Whig ministers always treated the Queen with courtesy and respect; ironically Somers and Cowper when in office showed her more personal consideration than had Nottingham and Rochester; but the Whig theory of monarchy remained patently unchanged. The aldermen of the City of London refused to print a sermon by Dean Atterbury at the mayoral election of October 1708 because they "pretended his doctrine came up to passive obedience".[63] At Sacheverell's trial Walpole confessed that he was "very sensible of the difficulty and nicety that attended the speaking to that point";* but the consideration did not lead him to tone down his view that to assert the doctrine of unqualified passive obedience was "to sap and undermine the very foundations of the Government".[64] No one who genuinely believed in the Englishman's rights of liberty and property, thought Molesworth, could ever countenance such a doctrine: "for liberty & property do not consist in the rulers not depriving me of either thro' his own lenity & good nature, but in its not being in his power to do either tho he shoud have a mind to it".[65] Moreover in the last months of Anne's reign, when the Whig Junto and their friends enlisted the support of generals like Cadogan, Argyll and Stanhope, and laid secret plans for an armed insurrection in case of a Stuart succession on the Queen's death, they showed once again that, despite a natural dread of a new civil war, they accepted not merely the theory but the practical consequences of the old Whig doctrine of resistance.[66]

In William III's reign, as we earlier saw, the strongest threads of continuity between the original parties of Charles II's reign and the post-Revolution Whigs and Tories were those of religious principle. The Whigs had continued to regard themselves as guardians of the Toleration; the Tories had remained jealously watchful for any further erosion of the privileged position still left to the Establishment by the act of 1689. Any combination of circumstances which would serve to project the issues of toleration and "the Church in danger" into the foreground of politics once more was all that was needed to bring these opinions into violent conflict in and out of Parliament. The years 1701 and 1702 saw just such a sequence of events.

* Any clear-sighted Whig could recognise that trumpeting the principle of resistance 20 years after the Revolution and in the reign of a Queen who was held in great affection was not likely to endear his party to an electorate largely reared on the sermons of High Church clergymen. On this dilemma see Lord Coningsby's 'History of Parties presented to King George the first' in B.M. Lansdowne MSS. 885, f. 82.

The first in point of time was the summoning of Convocation on 6 February 1701. The Tory ministers whom William had appointed in 1700, notably Lord Rochester, had insisted on its recall (twelve years having elapsed since its last meeting) as a condition of taking office;[67] and there seems little doubt that in doing so they were prepared to unleash the organised force of High Anglicanism, which was certain to dominate the Lower House of the Canterbury assembly, not only against the "moderate" bishops, but if necessary against Parliament itself. The acrimonious session of 1701, stirring religious passions, fostering clerical factions, and exacerbating relations between the Williamite episcopate and the leading highflying clergy, established the pattern for the Convocation controversies of the next thirteen years. And no less significant for the future was the attitude of Tory politicians towards Convocation from this first session onward. Recognising in its Lower House a weapon that could be wielded with equal effect against Whigs, latitudinarian Anglicans and dissenters, they cosseted Convocation, fawned on it, and at times even seemed to claim for it a constitutional parity with Parliament. When, in the debate on the Address in the Commons at the beginning of Anne's first Parliament, thanks were moved to the Queen for the care for the Church expressed from the Throne, this "gave Sr. Edw. Seymour occasion to take notice of the Bishops usage of the Lower House of Convocation (whom he thought the most proper committee for religion), but could never be sufferd to sit to bring things to bear for fear of having some of their [the bishops'] own books and heretical doctrines . . . exposed".[68] A month later one of the Oxford members assured the Master of University College that "the lower house of Convocation will upon all occasions find the House of Commons stand their friends . . .";[69] and in the assaults made in the Commons on Protestant nonconformity in the early years of Anne's reign the Tory vanguard was always careful to give the impression of fighting shoulder-to-shoulder with its clerical friends in their own ancient assembly.[70] Most Whigs, in contrast, regarded Convocation itself as an unnecessary source of discord, and its artificial elevation by High Tory politicians as dangerous nonsense. Lord Shaftesbury, even in 1710, could never forget "who they were, that a few hours after the King's death moved in the House of Lords to have the Convocation upon a foot of equall session with the Parliament".[71] Certainly no Whig could for a moment approve what one clergyman of Anne's day was to call "that Tory scheme (in the national politie) of setting up the Church in a superiority or indepen[den]cy of the State".[72]

The central factor in re-emphasising the religious divisions between the political parties was not, however, the revival of Convocation, important though this was. It was rather the accidental fact of William's death, and the intoxicating effect of the accession of a Church of England queen upon the Church of England party. When the Duke of Devonshire complained in July 1702 about the removal of a well-to-do Derbyshire Whig from the county commission of the peace, Lord Scarsdale dismissed the victim's case with devastating candour: "... he is a constant frequenter of conventicles, and caused a meeting-house to be built for that purpose at Alfreton; which of itself is exception enough to be made to a Queen who has so fully declared herself for the Church of England".[73] For those Tories who had heard Anne affirm from the Throne in May that "My own principles must always keep me entirely firm to the interests and religion of the Church of England, and will incline me to countenance those who have the truest zeal to support it", the fact that she had just previously promised "to preserve and maintain the Act of Toleration, and set the minds of all my people at quiet" seemed of small account in comparison. And certainly the minds of the dissenters were far from quiet in the summer and autumn of 1702. "The fanaticks could not be more dejected in Bucks than they seem at present every where else", wrote one of the members for Oxford University in answer to a clerical friend; "... some talk of persecution, they foresee its approches, & their liberty of conscience they expect will be taken from them. The abuse of it I hope will, & a stop put to that abominable hypocrisie, that inexcusable immorality of Occasional Conformity. I believe no one intends any thing farther, & if this can be obtained it will probably cure most of the evils we now labour under".* It was unfortunate for the peace of mind of the non-conformists that the emotional reaction of honest Tory hearts to the accession of a High Anglican ruler should have coincided so nearly with other circumstances which focused attention on this particular question of Occasional Conformity; for this now became the most bitterly contested of all the battlegrounds of the political parties in the years between 1702 and 1705.

It had grown increasingly common since the Revolution for dissenters whose scruples were not too nice to take communion in an Anglican church just often enough to qualify themselves for municipal and national office,

---

* Bodl. MS. Ballard 38, f. 137: Bromley to Charlett, 22 Oct. 1702. The highflying parson, Humphrey Whyle, described Occasional Conformity in identical terms to those used by his Warwickshire neighbour, Bromley: "... that abominable hypocrisie that has been so long & so injuriously (both to Church & State) ... practis'd". Walton MSS. ii, 83: to Mordaunt, 27 Nov. 1703.

meeting the demands of the Corporation and Test Acts,[74] and otherwise to
repair every Sunday to their own conventicles. There had been a Tory
outcry against this as early as 1697, when a dissenting Lord Mayor of
London, Sir Humphrey Edwin, rashly advertised his contempt for the law
by attending his meeting-house in the mayoral coach, with the sword and
insignia of the City borne before him.* Yet despite threatening gestures
from Seymour, Pakington and Howe in 1701[75] the idea of stamping the
practice out by new penal legislation did not take firm root until the following summer. It has been generally accepted that the real crusade against the
Occasional Conformists was launched by Henry Sacheverell at Oxford in
June 1702 in a typically explosive sermon preached in the University church
of St. Mary's. The Doctor served notice on the Church of England that its
very foundations were being undermined by "these crafty, faithless and
insidious persons, who can creep to our altars, and partake of our sacraments"
simply to acquire a passport to office. The remedy he prescribed was not "to
strike sail with a party that is such an open and avow'd enemy to our communion" but "to hang out the bloody flag and banner of defiance". What this
sanguinary course of action involved his hearers can have had only the
haziest notion. And in fact it is quite possible that the influence of the Oxford
sermon, even when in print,[76] in paving the way for the first Occasional
Conformity bill has been exaggerated. Had Sacheverell's words really been
on everyone's lips in the autumn of 1702 it is hard to believe that one of
Robert Harley's covey of Foley relations — a good Presbyterian by up-
bringing and still strongly sympathetic towards dissent — would have put
the Doctor's name forward for the post of Speaker's chaplain on the strength
of a letter of recommendation from Sir John Pakington, while admitting
at the same time that "I am a stranger to him farther than this letter".[77] The
real shock to the Tories in Anne's first House of Commons, one that touched
them on the raw politically as well as offending their religious susceptibilities,
was the election for the borough of Wilton in July 1702, investigated by the
Committee of Elections on 16 November.†

This small Wiltshire woollen town, a hotbed of dissent for years, had an

---

* Even Defoe, let alone the Tories, accused Edwin of "playing Bo-peep with God
Almighty". P. M. Scholes, 'Parliament and the Protestant Dissenters, 1702–19' (London
M.A. thesis, 1962), p. 21.

† Luttrell, v, 237. The investigation took place two days after the First Reading of the
Occasional Conformity bill, but the petition which had led to it had been presented on
24 Oct. and the more glaring aspects of the case were probably common knowledge at
Westminster before the bill was drafted.

unrestricted corporation franchise; and it transpired in evidence that the Whig mayor of Wilton having been forced to return a Tory the previous November, had vowed that "before another election he would make so many new burgesses, there should be no occasion for the old to attend", and what was more that "he would make none burgesses that were not Dissenters from the Dam's Teat". He was as good as his word, and by 25 June he had elected nineteen new members of the corporation, all stout non-conformists, who proceeded to do their duty by the Whig candidates in the borough the following month.[78] "This alarm'd the zeal of a Church-of-England Parliament", recorded the highflying vicar of Daventry; "and tho' I do not say it was the ground and occasion of bringing in the Occasional Bill, yet, no doubt, it was a great motive to quicken their preparation of it".[79] Certainly it must have reinforced the determination of Nottingham, the chief instigator of the bill through his friend William Bromley,[80] to bring municipal officers as well as government officials within its scope.

The parliamentary struggle over Occasional Conformity lasted from November 1702, when the original bill was brought into the Commons, until December 1704, when the third bill was rejected by the Lords.* It was never purely a struggle over principle, though it was principle which most of the protagonists naturally preferred to dwell on in their speeches.† "Making Members", one far-from-partisan Whig told a friend, "is the chief desire of most for the bill. I agree with you they are the least concerned about religion".[81] This was too harsh a judgement. But the punitive fines to be levied by the first bill on those who attended a nonconformist place of worship while holding municipal office were undoubtedly aimed at depriving the Whigs of the electoral asset of the dissenting vote in corporation boroughs. Still more complex motives came into the reckoning in 1704 when the course of the final bill was crucially affected by strong constitutional cross-currents which made party reactions less predictable. But the two division lists which survive as an exact guide to parliamentary sentiment about the first two measures, as well as the voting figures for other divisions in 1702–3, such accounts of debates as we possess[82] and the comments of contemporary

---

* The text of the original bill with the Lords' amendments is printed in *Parl. Hist.* vi, 61–68; for the less severe provisions of the 1703 and 1704 measures see H.M.C. *House of Lords MSS.* N.S. v, 297–300; vi, 229.

† An exception was Sir John Pakington, who forecast in the Commons in 1703 that eventually "by the benefit of this Occasional Conformity, the Dissenters will come to be the majority of this House" (Boyer, *Annals*, ii, 175). He, at least, was not loath to admit what everyone well knew, that party interest as well as principle was very much at stake on both sides.

correspondents all point to the same conclusion: that up to 1704 reactions to this measure were strongly governed by party loyalties, if not always by party professions of religious principle, with the powerful High Tory majority in the House of Commons checkmated by the far slenderer but cleverly marshalled Whig majority in the Lords.

Even before 1704, it is true, the attitude of the Court influenced some votes. In December 1702, when the Queen was strongly in favour of the bill and Marlborough and Godolphin not positively hostile, the Whig peers did not venture to attack it frontally; for they were well aware that some of the moderates in their own party among the office-holders and pensioners would not support them in the Lords. They concentrated instead on block-ing the measure by inserting amendments which they knew the Tory commoners would never accept, notably one which drastically modified the savage penalties imposed in the original bill. Even this was only adhered to by the Lords, after the expected dispute had developed between the two Houses, by a margin of two votes; and in the crucial division on 16 January 1703 a few Court Whig peers voted against their party and a hand-ful of others abstained.* Eleven months later, when the enthusiasm of some Tory M.P.s for a second bill had noticeably cooled,[83] when the Queen was rather less ardent,[84] and when the duumvirs were thoroughly averse to controversial legislation which endangered supply and threatened a head-on collision between Lords and Commons, some Tory peers were persuaded to abstain from voting by the Court. Yet even at this stage it is striking that only two Tories† actually voted against the Second Reading of the bill in the House of Lords and only five Whigs‡ for it.[85] Only in the session of 1704–5, when the High Church zealots in the Commons were imprudent enough to try and force the third Occasional bill past the obstacle of the Upper House by "tacking" it to the Land Tax bill — an expedient that was both factious and constitutionally dubious§ — did the front of Tory

* Nicolson's MS. diary, 7 Dec. 1702, 16 Jan. 1703. See also p. 36 above and n. 104 below, and Appendix A. Cf. H.M.C. *House of Lords MSS.* N.S. v, 158–9 for the voting on the other amendments on 16 Jan., refuting Burnet's account (v, 53–4).

† Lords Ferrers and Berkeley of Stratton. For the somewhat eccentric reasons given by one of them — possibly Ferrers — see Gloucestershire R.O. Newton MSS. D. 1844. Z.3.

‡ Schomberg, Bedford, Lindsey, Kent and Bridgewater — four of them courtiers likely to be responsive to the Queen's attitude, and the fifth, Bedford, a temporary deserter in the early years of Anne from his family's principles.

§ In Dec. 1702 the Lords had denounced by a resolution the practice of tacking "foreign" clauses to a money bill, and by 1704 it was clear that they would stand by this vote "let the consequence be what it will". *L. J.* xvii, 185; B.M. Lansdowne MSS. 773, f. 12.

unanimity crack wide open. Speaker (now also Mr. Secretary) Harley and his friends, and even Archbishop Sharp, joined Marlborough and Godolphin in soliciting moderate and Court Tory votes against what Harcourt called the "madness" of the infamous "Tack", which was crushed in the Commons after a seven-hour debate by 251 to 134.[86] "So there's an end against old Occasional this session", observed General Cholmondeley.[87] But he underestimated the consequences of this latest High Tory defeat. The subsequent Commons majority for the bill itself fell to 48 compared with 83 in the previous session, and though the High Tory peers yielded less ground (Godolphin himself still incongruously voted for a Second Reading),[88] the drop in their vote from 59 to 54, 18 short of the number needed for victory,[89] made any revival of the bill in the near future pointless.

Right through the long-drawn-out conflict of 1702–4 the Tory supporters of the Occasional Conformity bills always maintained that they represented no infringement of the Toleration Act. Even in the preamble to the first and most vicious bill the persecution of men for their conscientious beliefs was expressly condemned.[90] Their Whig opponents equally consistently held these measures to be an offence against the spirit of 1689 if not against the letter of the law. The two parties took much the same stand in 1714 when the Schism bill went through the Commons and eventually, on 15 June, passed the Lords also by 79 votes to 71. The moving spirit behind this new measure was Bolingbroke,[91] that most occasional of communicants, of whom the Reverend Jonathan Swift blithely wrote, after finding him absent from home in November 1711, "he was gone to his devotions and to receive the sacrament; several rakes did the same; it was not for piety but employments, according to act of parliament".[92] As the young Henry St. John he had also seconded Bromley over eleven years earlier in sponsoring the first two bills against the Occasional Conformists; and when in 1717 he came to analyse his motives in retrospect he was not hypocritical enough to claim that altruistic motives alone had inspired him on either occasion. "These [Occasional Conformity and Schism] bills", he conceded, "were thought necessary for our party interest". Yet he also insisted that they were "deemed neither unreasonable nor unjust" by the Tories, among whom, he said, "I verily think that the persecution of the dissenters entered into no man's head".[93] Whether Bolingbroke was qualified to speak for those High Church squires whose prejudices he exploited, as well as for secular-minded Tories of his own stamp, is open to doubt, however. The Whigs, at least, felt no confidence in their benign intentions. In fact by 1714 there were genuine and widespread fears that if the Schism bill passed and the Tories remained in office the Toleration Act itself would soon be under direct fire.[94]

In support of this conviction the Whigs could point to a material change in the situation since 1705. Now that the war was over it was no longer possible for them to appeal for moderate Tory support on the ground that urgent national interest made it impolitic to alienate the dissenters. They themselves had been forced by pressure of circumstances in 1711 to accept the necessity of some legal sanctions against Occasional Conformists, though not so severe as those proposed earlier in the reign.* Moreover, once the Sacheverell affair had raised Tory anxieties about "the Church in danger" to a higher pitch than ever in 1710, and the country gentlemen had been treated throughout that summer to "a course . . . of inflaming sermons" from the parish clergy,[95] it was scarcely to be expected that the efforts of the Church party to repel this supposed danger would be confined to a watered-down Occasional Conformity Act. From the tone of the Tory addresses to the Queen in the months that followed the Doctor's trial it seemed "very plain" to the Whig member for Cumberland "that when they are uppermost the Toleration will either be taken quite away or made ineffectual".[96] For it was not only Sacheverell now who denied quite openly that "a Toleration" existed in law, or who maintained that no "true churchman" should be prepared to see the act of 1689 allow the nonconformists anything beyond "some ease to scrupulous consciences in the exercise of their religion". Mr. Secretary St. John took up a position scarcely less extreme the following winter when he insisted that dissenters were "not tolerated" but "barely indulged".[97] To most Tories this now involved not merely stamping out Occasional Conformity but denying the dissenters their private educational facilities, which with his characteristic brand of invective Sacheverell had denounced as "seminaries wherein atheism, deism, tritheism, socinianism, with all the hellish principles of fanaticism, regicide and anarchy are openly professed and taught, to corrupt and debauch the youth of the nation". When the Whigs found not only the invaluable dissenting academies but even private nonconformist tutors proscribed in the Schism bill of 1714, and hardly a Tory voice raised against the measure in either House,[98] they could be forgiven for imagining that the way was being prepared for an early return to an exclusive and repressive State Church. "What the effects of it will be, God only knows", wrote one member of this Parliament, himself a non-Anglican; "but we must waite with patience, looking up to divine providence for relief".[99]

---

* For the circumstances see p. 113 below.

By contrast, the Whigs' own belief in liberty of conscience, and in religious toleration in so far as it was consistent with the security of the nation and the Protestant succession, was never open to question. True, only an enlightened minority, epitomised by James <u>Stanhope</u>, was prepared to see a measure of relief for Roman Catholics.[100] What is more, the Whigs were still divided, as they had been in 1689, on the wisdom of scrapping the sacramental test for government officials. After their success at the 1708 Election there were many prophecies that they would try to repeal the Test Act in the 1708-9 session; indeed, Lord Weymouth was so certain of it that he dispatched an urgent message to Bishop Hooper, bidding that worthy prelate brave the snow between Wells and London in order to save his Church and country.[101] But by the middle of January 1709 it had become clear that whatever plans the Whigs had formed for this purpose, if any, had been shelved, and even Wharton's much-publicised intention of abolishing the test in Ireland during his two viceregal visits in 1709–10 came to nothing.[102] It seems by no means unlikely, however, that had the Whigs enjoyed power longer in the middle of the reign they would have attempted to remove the civil disabilities of the Protestant nonconformists;* they were certainly fiercely opposed to any move to disfranchise them or debar them from the House of Commons: "I hope the time has not yet come, to whatsoever height some matters are carried", Walpole said in Parliament in 1714, "when property can be invaded in this way, but that people out of this House of whatsoever persuasions, if Protestants, will have the same liberties of choice as we our-selves have of speech within".[103] And at every reasonable opportunity — by their stout defence of dissenting interests in the parliamentary battles of 1702–4 and 1714, by their championing of Quaker relief clauses after 1710, and above all by their promotion of the General Naturalization bill in 1709 — the Whigs showed themselves consistent advocates of complete freedom of worship and education and of full political rights for all Protestants in Britain, including foreigners.

The Naturalization Act of 1709, even though it was demolished by the Tories three years later, was in some ways the most impressive of all the monuments to the creed of early-eighteenth-century Whiggery. It enabled all foreign immigrants who so wished to become naturalized subjects of the Queen provided they took the statutory oaths and received the sacrament in a

---

* In Dec. 1709 they were said to be "pretty confident" of securing a repeal of the Test Act in the near future (Trumbull MSS. Alphab. liii: Ralph Bridges to Trumbull, 7 Dec.), but the Sacheverell affair subsequently absorbed all their energies in this last session be-fore their fall.

church of *any* Protestant denomination. To most Whigs any form of discrimination against foreign Protestants, such as Campion's demand in 1709 that naturalization should be made conditional on the immigrant becoming an Anglican communicant, smacked of economic insanity as well as religious intolerance.[104] But as one of the bill's advocates ruefully commented, all its supporters "were reproached for their coldness and indifference in the concerns of the church".[105] This indeed was the political cross which the Whigs always had to bear as the price of their convictions.

Generally speaking the charge of hostility or even indifference to the Church of England perpetually levelled at them by their opponents was greatly exaggerated. Yet there was both a sceptical and an anti-clerical element among the Augustan Whigs — in Sunderland's circle, for example — whose views lent some substance to Tory accusations. Much of the rancour this element displayed was directed not so much against the Church as an institution as against those highflying clergy who scourged the party from their pulpits and libelled it in print. It was because the Junto Whigs agreed so readily with Marlborough that such clerics, if not brought to book, would "preach us all out of the kingdom" that they were lured into the fatal snare of Sacheverell's impeachment;[106] and once they had gone so far it was inevitable that the occasion should allow the prejudices of the party's erastian and anticlerical wing an exceptionally thorough airing, however much some moderate Whigs deplored the fact.[107] "A parson I never loved", admitted Lady Cowper's firebrand of a sister, "but now I've so great an abhorence to them, that were itt not for a few bishops I shou'd think the imps of Lucifer had putt on that habit to distroy us."[108] It was one thing to confine such sentiments to the relative privacy of correspondence; it was much more serious when they were publicly voiced. The Duke of Argyll, intemperate as always, launched into a ferocious attack in the House of Lords in March 1710, claiming "that the clergy, in all ages, have delivered up the rights and liberties of the people, and preached up the King's power in order to govern him; and therefore they ought not to be suffered to meddle with politics". And even a sophisticated political animal like Walpole declared that he thought it "high time to put a stop to that growing evil" when "the trumpet was sounded in Sion, when the pulpit took up the cudgels . . . and the people were taught for their souls and consciences sake to swallow those pernicious doctrines".[199]

Such outbursts were unquestionably damaging to the Whigs. In 1710, especially, they helped to convince even moderate clergy that "all the pulpits in England [would be] put under padlock" and to persuade large numbers of 'floating' voters that the Godolphin-Junto alliance boded ill for the

Church.* But they must be seen in due proportion. For one thing they came from men goaded beyond all patience by a particularly virulent type of political propaganda which they could scarcely ignore yet could not easily counter. Secondly, their very immoderacy tends to obscure the fact that Whig bishops, though more restrained in expression, took much the same view as many Whig laymen of the "poison" being disseminated by many of their clergy.[110] Thirdly, it deserves to be emphasised that the overwhelming mass of Whig members of Parliament were Anglicans. The number of dissenting M.P.s in Anne's reign was grossly exaggerated by Tory propagandists;† and while the proportion of nonconformists was naturally higher among the Whig electorate, at least in boroughs with trading and industrial interests, even in the constituencies it was very far from representing a predominant element in the Whig vote. Honesty compelled one Tory clergyman to admit that in his part of the country, Kent, the Whigs had "too many churchmen on their side".[111] And when that staunch Shropshire Whig, Sir John Bridgeman, sent his son up to New College in 1712 he thought to inform Dr. Aubrey that "the clergyman that has had the education of him has taken indefatigable pains with him, and has grounded him in right and regular principles, for I have nothing more at heart than to have my son brought up virtuously, and to be kept close to the doctrine and discipline of the Church of England . . ."[112]

Finally, far from being indifferent to the health of the Established Church,

---

* Wake MSS. Arch. W. Epist. 23, f. 202: Rev. Maurice Wheeler to Wake, 20 Feb. 1710; Bodl. MS. Ballard 15, f. 96.

How far either Tory politicians or the electorate and the mob really believed in the slogan of "the Church in danger" in 1710 is discussed by Mary Ransome, 'Church and Dissent in the Election of 1710', *E.H.R.* lvi (1941), 88–9. I believe she is a little too suspicious of the genuineness of these fears. James Craggs, that wily old political fox, had fewer doubts. "The people's notion is that the dispute lies entirely between Church & Conventicle", he wrote to General Stanhope. "I never saw so prevalent a fury." (Chevening MSS.: 13 Oct. 1710; also *ibid.*: Craggs to Stanhope, 3 Nov.). On 1 July Gervase Scroop wrote from Sidbury in Shropshire: "It is impossible to imagine what an influence the crying of the Church in danger has among the vulgar in this country, and when any of the high Church begs a vote for themselves or party the question they ask the freeholder is, if he be not for the Church. Then if he answers yes, then be for us they cry, that we may hinder our churches from being pulled down by Presbyterians and dissenters." Monson MSS. T/13/124: to Sir J. Newton.

† P. M. Scholes, *loc. cit.* pp. 166–70, identifies only 23, 'not all proven', sitting in the Commons at various times between 1702 and 1714. A few other names can be added to her list — those of Thomas Lamplugh, Sir Thomas Roberts and Philip Papillon, for instance — but the total cannot have been much over 30.

as they saw it, there were many Whigs in Parliament who were ready and anxious to promote it. Such a one was Colonel Maynard Colchester, who sat for Gloucestershire from 1701 to 1708, and who in 1699 had been one of five gentlemen responsible for founding the Society for Promoting Christian Knowledge.[113] Another was Sir Richard Onslow, who when offering his services to the electors of Surrey was able to secure even from a Tory bishop a testimonial to his "great services to our Establisht. Church, and the Universityes in Parliament".[114] A favourite Whig prescription for the ills of the Church was the enhancement of episcopal authority. It was to this end that during their short period of power they eagerly championed the Carlisle Cathedral bill in 1708, a test-case designed to confirm the bishops' rights of discipline and jurisdiction over their cathedral clergy.* It is often forgotten, too, that in the previous year, at the time the Union was under consideration in Parliament, a House of Commons with a Whig majority passed without a single amendment Archbishop Tenison's bill for the security of the doctrine, liturgy and rites of the Church "notwthstanding the contrary endeavours of dissenters of all denominations".[115]

The history of the Walpole regime in the 20's and 30's was to demonstrate that, given time and a lowering of both the religious and political temperatures, the eighteenth-century Whigs could identify themselves smoothly enough with the interests of a respectable Church Establishment. But political life was still too highly charged with religious passion and prejudice, still too overshadowed by the memories left by past conflicts and the fears engendered by present ones, to make such an identification possible in the Britain of Queen Anne.

*   *   *

At least two major conclusions about the character of British politics in the years from 1702 to 1714 emerge from the wide range of evidence surveyed both in the previous and the present chapter. It seems beyond question that politics was concerned for much of the time with issues of great moment on which public opinion was genuinely and often very seriously divided; and that these were mostly new issues which had crystallised, or older issues which had become recharged with life, during the last year of William III's reign and the first few months of Anne's. Time and again we have noticed — and the fact cannot be too forcibly stressed — that together the years 1701 and 1702 represent a watershed of incalculable significance

---

* See Chap. 1, p. 29 above, and n. 85; also *Court and Society from Elizabeth to Anne* (ed. from Kimbolton MSS., 1864), ii, 284: Addison to Manchester, 20 Feb.

in post-Revolution politics. Beyond that watershed the issues which gave to party conflict in the next twelve years so much of its real substance generally involved either the traditional principles of Tory and Whig or their distinctive post-Revolution attitudes. Although the divisions of national opinion rarely corresponded precisely on any single point with the line bisecting the political world into Tories and Whigs, there was an acknowledged and logical Whig position on every one of these issues; and there was also a basic, instinctive Tory position on all but the most vital question of all, that of the succession, though on almost all the major issues dividing the parties in the early eighteenth century, both old and new, unanimity for the Tories was generally harder to achieve than it was for their opponents. As far as the vast majority of active partisans were concerned, however, it is the Lord Cowper of the 'Impartial History' and not the Bolingbroke of the *Dissertation upon Parties* who must surely have the last word. "Two set parties of men", Cowper assured George I, ". . . can only be kept up by some diversity of opinion upon fundamentals, at least points of consequence; and experience shows that many who have no design on preferment either for themselves or friends, but live retired on their estates, are yet as hot or hotter than any in these distinctions."[116]

But what of the party leaders? In their case there is a final problem to consider. How far did the principles they professed and the policies they advocated, often so eloquently, stand up in practice to the conflicting pressures of office and power, pressures that bore so much more strongly on them than on the country members, the backwoods peers and the gentlemen "retired on their estates"? In other words, were the foremost politicians of the day concerned with power primarily as an end in itself or mainly as a means to achieve cherished objectives in domestic and foreign policy? It would be unrealistic to expect a simple, categorical answer to these questions. We have to be satisfied here with a series of impressions rather than firm conclusions; and because most of the Whig leaders spent the greater part of Anne's reign out of office, striving to recover the power which they had lost in 1700 and which slipped from them again in 1710, it is on their behaviour that these impressions must chiefly be based. This at least assures any hypothesis of a rigorous test; for it was the Junto lords who acquired in their own day the reputation of being the most ruthless and unscrupulous of all the party magnates, adept at "prostituting their principles to their profit".[117]

Although the Whigs did appreciably more than the High Tories to further essential government business, and especially war supply, in the first two parliamentary sessions of the reign[118] they received no reward whatever for their support in the ministerial changes of 1703–4. However, by November 1704 they seemed, in Wharton's immortal words, to "have Lord Treasurer's head in a bag", for the Court was in the direst difficulties. In the Commons there hung over it like a Damoclean sword the threat of the "Tack" — a certain death-sentence if it became a reality since the Lords were bound to throw out the Land Tax bill if clauses prohibiting occasional conformity were annexed to it. In the House of Lords itself, having rejected the policies urged by the Whig peers towards Scotland in the previous session and advised the Queen during the recess to give her assent to the Act of Security, the government faced the prospect of defending an indefensible position against both parties.[119] It knew that if the expected attack on its Scottish policy were pressed to a vote of censure the majority against it would be overwhelming and Godolphin, at least, would have little alternative but to resign.[120] In both Houses Whig votes could have decided the fate of a ministry in which the Whigs had only a negligible voice: but only at the cost of a constitutional crisis and the total dislocation of war supplies in the first case and the probability of a complete breach with Scotland in the second. The Whig party leaders have rarely received full credit for the restraint they showed at this juncture. There was not a whisper of suspicion that any Whig might vote with the tackers (nothing could be more significant than the way Harley, in canvassing votes for the government in the House of Commons, took Whig support implicitly for granted);[121] while in the Upper House at the beginning of December the Junto lords did no more than show their teeth before proceeding to reprieve Godolphin and at the same time, by initiating the Aliens bill, take a vital step towards bringing about the Union and ensuring a Protestant succession in Scotland.[122] And when the Tory chiefs, thwarted in the Lords, switched their attack on the government's handling of Scottish affairs to the Commons they found the Whigs equally determined not to play with fire. "Ther were 209 against the censure, and 151 for it", reported a Scots observer. "The Whigs and the No-Tackers joined against it; for if it had carried there would have been an address to the Queen to know who of the English Ministers had advised the Act [of Security]".[123]

Three years later, in the winter of 1707–8, the Junto Whigs still had only one of their five leaders in office, and they had begun to doubt whether their services in Parliament would ever be adequately rewarded by Marlborough and Godolphin. Their patience temporarily exhausted, they began to harry the ministry unmercifully in both Houses, actually making common cause with the Tory zealots on occasion so as to leave the duumvirs in no doubt that they could "trim" no longer. Even some of their fellow-Whigs, including four lords of the Cabinet,* and Boyle, Smith and Walpole in the Commons, regarded their actions as factious and would not support them against Godolphin. One of these "Treasurer's Whigs", Robert Molesworth, condemned them scathingly for denying the party creed. "The gentlemen who call themselves Whiggs", he wrote to Lord Shaftesbury, "I mean that were adepts of the Kitcat & Junto have changed their principles so often upon the score of dominion that I doubt not yr Ldp will see when you come to town, how little a free nation ought to rely upon them".[124] But the charge was unjust, in the current situation at least. The Junto Whigs were scrupulously careful not to endanger the next campaign against the French by their tactics. The Land Tax and Malt Tax bills were allowed to move swiftly through the Commons and by 20 December, less than six weeks after the effective beginning of the session, supplies amounting to nearly £5½ million had already been granted.[125] The Junto's henchmen pointedly refrained from associating with the opposition which almost wrecked the government's Recruiting bill in January 1708. And while it is true that "the Whig lords" made use of the government's recent military misfortunes in Spain in a way that was purely factious,[126] the two main points on which they concentrated their offensive in this session — the continuance of the Scottish Privy Council and the shortcomings of the Admiralty — were legitimate targets which certainly involved no denial of party principles.

Criticism of naval administration, in particular, was more than justified. By 1707 the Admiralty was desperately in need of new men at the helm. Although Walpole, as a leading member of the Prince's Council,† defended it in Parliament during this winter against the Junto, he had previously contemplated resignation in protest against the Admiralty's inadequacies; and it is striking that the high-toned Shaftesbury actually complimented Secretary Sunderland on opposing his kith and kin in the Cabinet over this key issue.[127] The Junto chiefs undoubtedly hoped to see their own man, Orford, eventually at the head of the Board. But they must be given credit for their readiness to accept any interim settlement which would free the navy from "the most scandalous management" of Prince George of Denmark and George Churchill.[128] The sincerity of their motives is underlined by their reaction in the course of 1709 to the failure of a new Lord High Admiral, Pembroke, to effect any substantial improvement.[129] By this time Somers and Wharton had forced their way into the Cabinet, yet "if the business of the Admiralty

---

* Somerset, Newcastle, Cowper and Devonshire.

† The rough equivalent of the Admiralty Board in the years 1702–8, when the Prince Consort was Lord High Admiral.

be not set right", Halifax told Arthur Mainwaring, "it will be impossible for 5 [Somers] to continue in his employment"; "and I thought the reason he gave for this was right [Mainwaring commented]; that he, having been at the head of all the complaints upon that subject, could not with any decency . . . continue in an employment whilst that which he found fault with continued in the same state which he had complained of; for that would look as if all were well when he had got an office".[130] Not surprisingly, it was part of Orford's terms for assuming the responsibilities of First Lord of the Admiralty in November 1709 that he should be given *carte blanche* to make a clean sweep of all officers and officials he considered inefficient.[131]

The principles of the leading Whigs were put to their sternest test between July and September 1710 when Robert Harley, striving to construct a new ministry pledged to a policy of "moderation" at home and delivered from the control of those "mercyless men of both partys" whom the Queen so disliked, tried to persuade Cowper, Boyle, Newcastle, and for a while even Somers* to stay in the Cabinet. Independent Country Whigs like James Lowther were full of apprehension for a time that their leaders might betray them;[132] but although Newcastle, after a period of indecision, eventually succumbed,[133] with the rest the deciding factor was Harley's refusal to guarantee that the existing Parliament would sit out its full statutory life. The Duke of Roxburgh had judged back in May that this would "be the test of all";[134] and so it proved. The prospect of having to work with a Tory majority in a new House of Commons, of being dependent for support on men who could be expected to try to undermine all the Whigs had worked for in recent years, at home and abroad, was too great a deterrent to co-operation with Harley. For men and policies were inseparable in the mind of the party man, even in the mind of moderates like Boyle and Cowper. "The changing hands in England", Walpole wrote at this time, "allways ends in the changing of measures".[135] When Wharton proffered his resignation to Anne in September 1710 he told her he could not "serve with Honour" in the company of men "who were takeing measures contrary to those he had always pursued";[136] and it is quite evident that Somers, Boyle and Cowper shared those sentiments. St. John found it "incredible to what a

* For Somers Anne belatedly developed a strong personal regard (cf. p. 200 below), and there seems to be evidence not only that he was put under some pressure by Harley, but also that for a time he wavered under it. See, e.g., the evidence of Dartmouth (note to Burnet, vi, 12), of Addison (in *Addison Letters*, p. 233) and of Cropley (in P.R.O. 30/24/21/165).

degree 353 [the Whigs] are united in opposition".[137] But perhaps it was not to be expected that one to whom Whig principles were repellent should appreciate the cementing power of those principles in adversity.

It was while in opposition in the last four years of the reign that the Whigs took the two steps which most historians have agreed in condemning as unscrupulous. The first was their pact with the Earl of Nottingham in December 1711, by which they agreed to acquiesce in the passing of a new Occasional Conformity bill in return for Nottingham's support against the peace policy of the ministry. The second was their association with the attempt of the Scottish peers in June 1713 to bring in a bill to dissolve the Union. In both cases it has seemed that the party high command, for the sake of a few vital votes, was prepared to throw overboard policies which the Whigs had championed consistently between 1702 and 1707. In 1713, however, this was not the case. Behind all the taunts and protests of contemporaries, based on inadequate or garbled information, there lies no convincing evidence that any leading Whig, except Wharton and possibly Sunderland, was seriously prepared to wreck "the Blessed Union" of 1707[138] merely to embarrass the administration. Even Wharton and Sunderland would have insisted that any dissolving bill should be accompanied by legislation providing effective safeguards to secure the Hanoverian succession in Scotland. In fact the whole conduct of the Whigs in this crisis has been widely misinterpreted.* On the other hand the party's meek acceptance of the fourth Occasional bill in 1711 was an unpleasant stain on its record. It is almost certainly true that the Junto believed the ministry to be on the point of bringing in its own far tougher bill to appease the High Church Tories in the Commons;[139] and it can also be said in extenuation that the pact with Nottingham seemed to the Whigs the only way of blocking a Peace without Spain, and that it was part of the bargain that the Tory leader should draft the bill "with all possible temper". But it was a betrayal of Whig principles, none the less, and Halifax was frank enough to admit it was too great a price to pay for an ally.[140]

At least, however, this was an action motivated by something more than pure party advantage. Indeed no action of the Whig Junto during Anne's reign, not even its disreputable alliance with the Jacobite Duke of Hamilton in the spring of 1708, carried political cynicism quite so far as the High Tory

---

* See especially the crucial account of the Lords' debate of 1 June 1713 in Dalhousie MSS. 14/352: Lord Balmerino to Harry Maule, 2 June, and Trumbull Add. MSS. 136/1: Ralph Bridges to Trumbull, 9 June. This question will be discussed at more length in my forthcoming book on the Oxford ministry.

motions of 1705 calling for the Electress Sophia to reside in England as a guarantee of the Protestant succession. The Hanover motions had no other purpose than to damage the standing of Marlborough, Godolphin and the Whig chiefs, either with the Queen, if they supported the invitation to the Electress, or with Hanover and the rank-and-file Whigs if they opposed it.* Of the sponsors of the motion in the House of Lords, Nottingham could perhaps claim the excuse of being by this time genuinely pro-Hanoverian, though this particular step was one he had always disavowed. But with Buckingham, Anglesey and Jersey, all Jacobite still in sympathy, it was a squalid manœuvre; and the same criticism must be made of its supporters in the Commons, although there Sir John Pakington and John Manley, at least, did have the integrity to dissociate themselves from it.¹⁴¹

All these incidents are a salutary reminder that as well as being concerned with real issues, involving the conflict of sincerely-held principles, politics between 1702 and 1714 was concerned, as it always has been, with power and the quest for office. And in a period when those competing for the highest prizes could also pay a high price for failure, when the loss of office by an individual and the loss of power by a party not only involved the loss of valuable emoluments and local prestige but could well be the prelude to public condemnation and proscription by vengeful opponents, it was inevitable that power should at times seem more important than principle. The more prominent the statesman, and the higher the stakes for which he played, the greater were the possible penalties of failure.

The impeachments of 1701 cast a long shadow over the politics of the next thirteen years. On the day Oxford's peace policy faced rejection by the House of Lords in December 1711 Wharton remorselessly revived the old bitter memories. "'Tis true [he mocked] I see some new faces among us; but even that Lord who sits on the Wool-Pack . . . may well remember that in the last reign four lords were impeach'd for having made a Partition-Treaty".¹⁴² Such would have been Oxford's fate, without much doubt, had he failed to survive this crisis; indeed as late as 1713 one violent young Whig (the Bishop of Salisbury's son) did not despair of his party being able after new

---

* The Queen was known to be resolutely opposed to the invitation, which otherwise the Whig leaders would have been ready enough to endorse. For the cruel Whig dilemma over the Hanover motions (eventually resolved to the ease of most, though not all, Whig consciences by the Junto's own expedient of the Regency bill [p. 84 above]) see H.M.C. *Portland MSS.* iv, 154: Godolphin to Harley [Nov. 1705, misdated 1704 by editor]; Add. MSS. 4291, f. 38; Blenheim MSS. A. 1–26: Brydges to Marlborough, 4 Dec. 1705; Norris MSS. NOR. 2/601: Johnson to Norris, 11 Dec.; *Hervey L.B.* i, 219, 265–6; *Correspondence of Lady Mary Wortley Montagu* (Bohn, 1887), i, 21.

elections to "take off the heads of these Bloody Peace-makers".[143] When the Whigs fell from power in 1710 Wharton, Sunderland and Stanhope had all had to face the possibility, though not in the end the reality, of impeachment: the first for his alleged misgovernment of Ireland, the second for his part in the invitation to the Palatines, and the third for his military conduct in Spain. Sunderland, at least, had had a fairly narrow escape.[144] Walpole paid for his refusal to come to terms with Harley in the autumn of 1710 by being thrown to the wolves in January 1712, by the loss of his seat in Parliament and by a temporary sojourn in the Tower. Harley himself had been threatened with possible attainder in 1708, and it may be that only Greg's refusal to incriminate him saved him from the "fire and faggot" demanded by the Whigs; his relations, at any rate, regarded his escape as a miracle of Providence, and he himself believed his life had been in danger.[145] Political disgrace after 1714 was to mean eight years of exile for Bolingbroke and two years' languishing in the Tower for Oxford, who declined to flee from certain persecution. In the eyes of history Oxford did not deserve such treatment. But in the party jungle of the early eighteenth century the only justice was that of an eye for an eye. None recognised this more clearly than Walpole, during his own imprisonment in 1712: "this barbarous injustice being only the effect of party malice, does not concern me at all", he wrote, "& I heartily despise what I shall one day revenge".[146] Revenge came in due course; yet it is only fair to say that had a Jacobite *coup* succeeded in 1714 those Whig leaders who had been active in the Revolution would have been lucky to escape with their lives.

In circumstances such as these it is little cause for wonder that the Junto lords and their Tory counterparts were occasionally ready to compromise their principles for the sake of power politics and party interest. What is really astonishing is that their falls from grace were so infrequent. And perhaps this very rarity, in a passionate and sometimes dangerous political society, is the most impressive tribute which the politicians of this period have left to the genuine substance of party conflict in their day.

CHAPTER FOUR

The "Country" Tradition

To the leading figures in both parties the possession of office and power, if rarely an object in itself, was never less than important. At all times they regarded it as a valuable source of profit, as an essential instrument of policy, and as a crucial entrenchment "to defend them [as Sir John Cropley once put it] for the time past & the time to come".[1] But in Queen Anne's Parliaments, as in those of her predecessor, there was always a body of politicians who were immune to the allurements of place or pension, no matter from which side these were offered. And there were many besides for whom a distrust of "the Court", either spasmodic or habitual, was a professed part of their political faith. In the terminology of the day both these political types were distinguished by a common phrase: they were known as "country members". Together they accounted for a substantial proportion of the membership of every House of Commons in this period; in some Parliaments, perhaps, for as much as a half.*

The distinction between the two types is not without its point. Many of the backbench squires who voted steadily in the years 1702–14 for measures which the Queen's ministers, irrespective of party, regarded as inimical to the interests of the Court, were never at any time in the running for office. They had neither the talent nor the political importance to attract official attention, and in consequence their "independence" was never seriously tested. Among abler members of the House of Commons an affected distaste for place did not always survive the temptation to share in its delights. Some of the most vociferous critics of administration in the early eighteenth century could not resist the sirens when at last they sang. In February 1711 the Tories of the October Club loudly proclaimed that offices were no better than shackles on members' freedom of action. Yet in June 1711, when the

---

* Because they so rarely polled their full strength, even on issues of major importance on which they were united, the country members' numbers can never be calculated with absolute precision.

Oxford ministry was doling out its favours at the end of the session, the uninhibited jostling for the spoils among some of these same Octobrists shocked
even St. John: "I never saw men so openly claim their hire, or offer
themselves to sale".² Edward Wortley Montagu, who promoted no fewer
than four Place bills in the teeth of opposition from both Whig and Tory
ministers between 1710 and 1713, nevertheless served as a Commissioner of
the Treasury from 1714 to 1715 and later as Ambassador to Constantinople;
and there is a curiously ironical ring about his bitter complaint in 1715 that
only three of the "Country Whigs" of Anne's reign had been employed by
George I.³ Previously John Aislabie, who had figured prominently in the
campaign to insert a place cause in the Regency bill in 1706, had accepted a
seat at the Admiralty Board under Harley in 1710. Even that doyen of the
High Church country gentlemen, Sir John Pakington, knight of the shire for
Worcestershire, who sat in the House of Commons for a total of nineteen
years after 1690 without a slur on his record as an independent member,
accepted a pension from the Oxford ministry in 1712.* There were others
who incurred less direct obligations to the Court. Pakington's counterparts
in Northamptonshire and Suffolk, Sir Justinian Isham and Sir Robert
Davers, never sought employment on their own account, but they thought
it quite in order to procure places for their eldest sons;⁴ and when Sir Richard
Vyvyan, the "Country Tory" M.P. for Cornwall, pressed not his own, but
his brother's claims to a place in the Stamp Commission in 1713 Lord Lansdowne's comment to the prime minister was eminently down to earth:
"You could not engage [Sir Richard] to you at a cheaper rate".†

   Yet it would be a mistake to regard these facts with too cynical an eye.
Among the county representatives, especially, the tradition of genuine
independence of the Court was of long standing,⁵ and it persisted after 1702.
The member for Yorkshire who wrote in 1710 that "some of us desire
nothing for our selves"⁶ made this claim with perfect justice; and it embraced not a few members who were as politically active as himself and a
handful who were in the very front rank. Sir Thomas Hanmer, one of the
wealthiest and ablest figures in the House of Commons during the years
1702–14, had a remarkable record of self-abnegation. He turned down at
least four offers to join the Oxford ministry between 1710 and 1713, thrice

---

* See p. 361 below.

† B.M. Loan 29/137/4: 18 July 1713. There are several parallel cases. In 1712 Sir
James Etheridge, M.P. for Great Marlow, asked Oxford to make his son Comptroller of
the Wine Licences — the first favour he had asked of any government, he claimed, in
nearly 18 years of parliamentary service. *Ibid.* 29/313/10: 29 May.

ignoring the bait of a Secretaryship of State;* and he likewise declined to serve George I in 1714, although strongly urged to do so by independent Whigs as well as Hanoverian Tories.[7] His friend Ralph Freeman, M.P. for Hertfordshire from 1697 to 1727 and a vigorous parliamentarian whom any ministry would have been happy to muzzle, also spurned the offers of the Tory administration after 1710 and refused to take office as a representative of the Hanoverian Tories after Anne's death.[8] Of Henry Fleetwood, a Tory squire who had sat for some years on his own interest for the "Duchy" borough of Preston, it was said shortly after the Queen's death: ". . . he has labourd long in the vineyard without any view but his countrys service, for which reason he has never receivd the least civility from the former ministers".[9]

The view that office tainted and that power corrupted may, therefore, have been an affectation with some; but there were also those (and they were not negligible in numbers) with whom it was a real conviction: those for whom the health of the body politic demanded that men of independent fortune in the Commons, and especially those who were free from obligations to any of the big party chieftains, should preserve their capacity to act as a permanent, purifying, criticising force in politics. When his son Robert entered Parliament after the 1705 Election Thomas Pitt told him: "I had rather see any child of mine want than have him get his bread by voting in the House of Commons".[10] Such men were the true heirs of the "Country" tradition of Charles II's reign, as well as inheriting the more recent legacy of anti-prerogative, anti-ministerial feeling which had been current at Westminster in the nineties; and their activities in the Parliaments of 1702–14 introduced into the politics of the day a stratum of political ideas which in one way or another ran horizontally across the normal vertical lines which divided the Whig and Tory parties and the principles for which they stood. But whereas we can still talk about country ideals and a country tradition in the age of Anne, we can no longer validly refer, like students of William III's reign, to a "Country party".

This is not to say that the country politicians of the early eighteenth century were not party men. Many of them were fierce partisans. And virtually all of them would have found it desperately hard to live up to Thomas Pitt's ideal of the model backbench member as one who would "avoid faction, and never enter the House prepossessed; but attend diligently to the debate, and vote according to [his] conscience".[11] But their predispositions were primarily to Whig or Tory attitudes or ideals, and not to the service of any "Country party". True 'independents', in fact, were a dying breed by

* However, for his secret pension on the Irish Civil List and its probable significance, see below, p. 361 n.‡.

1702. One of the last of the line was Thomas Johnson, whose attitude to the many "party causes" which he heard debated during his first session in St. Stephen's Chapel, in 1701–2, was "to take no side but as my reason directs me, though some gent. expected I should goe right or wrong".[12] But even Johnson was soon committed on most issues to the Whigs, though always remaining a typical country member. Sir John Mordaunt once promised the country gentlemen of Warwickshire that, "as I never yett came into Parliament with any other thing in View then to do what I reallie thought was for the true interest of the Publick, you may be assur'd I shall continue to Vote according to that Rule . . ." Yet no one doubted in Anne's reign that Sir John was a Tory, even though he would never have been considered a fire-eater.[13] One of the very necessary clues, therefore, to the character of Augustan politics is that "party", in the sense of Whig and Tory, and "Country" were never mutually exclusive. There were few stauncher Tories in the Commons between 1702 and 1714 than Freeman or Pakington, Thomas Strangeways or Sir Michael Warton. There were few more active or zealous Whigs than Wortley Montagu or Cropley, Peter King or Sir Richard Onslow: men who saw themselves in all honesty as jealous watchdogs of party principles, prepared to extort from their own leaders "as their hearts blood", as one of them graphically put it, measures that would "save the reputation of the Whigg administration".[14] Yet the "country" ideals shared by all these men, Tory and Whig alike, were capable of bridging at times the deep party gulf which normally divided them; so that at the end of the 1702–5 Parliament Peter King could even shake hands with High Church zealots like Bromley and Arthur Annesley and make a compact with them "to stand by each other next winter to oppose the iniquity of the times and promote the public welfare".[15]

Later it will be necessary for us to examine the composition of the country element in both parliamentary parties at this period.* The purpose of this chapter is first to look at the prejudices and ideals of the average country member of Anne's day, and so acquire some insight into what we might call 'the country mentality'; and then to consider some of the practical implications, for the political history of our period, of the attempts which were made to perpetuate the country tradition.

*　　*　　*

"What is a country gentleman?" With this tantalising and unfortunately unanswered question a leading Country Whig of Anne's reign ended a brief

* See Chaps. 7 and 8, pp. 221–3, 249–52.

commentary on the state of politics at the accession of George I.[16] The question he posed offers a natural point of departure for our present enquiry. Seen against a purely social and economic background the country gentleman of the age both was and remains easily identifiable as a distinct type. He represented the preponderant section of a gentry class which, in spite of almost two centuries of political and social advance and fusion with other elements of society, probably still contained a majority of families which subsisted entirely on the income from their landed estates. But the "country member" — the political rather than the social animal, with whom our Whig commentator of 1715 was chiefly concerned — was not so easily classified. For one thing, he was not necessarily synonymous with the country gentleman of the social and economic order. As we shall find when we analyse the structure of the political parties, the country members in Anne's Parliaments, though mostly independent "men of estates", included a small number of professional men and even merchants, as well as a few landowners who had City or mercantile or colonial connections.[17] Even the four successful Tory candidates for the City of London in 1710, all of them big businessmen, claimed country status in their election manifesto, protesting that "being independent of the Court, their debates, votes and resolutions will be free".[18] In party terms, too, the picture is by no means clearly defined. Even by the middle of the Queen's reign we find some Whigs still identifying the country interest, or "the Country" as they sometimes termed it, purely with "the staunch Whigs", the natural descendants of the Old Whigs of William III's reign.[19] Yet the ordinary country gentleman was more likely to be a Tory than a Whig by the first decade of the eighteenth century: so much so indeed, that the phrase "the gentlemen of England" became (as we saw earlier) a standard euphemism for the Tory party. One of the most curious metamorphoses in post-Revolution politics had been the gradual reconciliation in the Tory mind of anti-prerogative attitudes with sound Anglican principles; a change that was so far advanced by 1705 that a quite typical party backbencher felt that the success in the House of Commons of a bill designed to reduce the seductive influence of the Crown over members of Parliament was partial compensation for the failure of the Occasional Conformity bill: "for now the Chu. of Eng[d] is checkt", he told his son-in-law, "every little sugar-plum is pleasing to her children".[20]

All the same, there were certain views and certain antipathies which were shared by most country members of Parliament, irrespective of party. Such members had far less in common than Wortley Montagu would have had us believe when he wrote soon after Anne's death that "The Country Whigs and Country Tories were not very different in their notions, and nothing had hindered them from joyning but the fear that each have of the others bringing in their whole party";[21] but they had just enough in common to make Court-Country issues a necessary ingredient in the substance of Augustan politics. And although the country members did not comprise a completely homogeneous social group, it was inevitably the attitudes and opinions of the landed gentlemen which did most to mould the 'country mentality'.

This mentality had both its negative and its positive aspects. The negative was usually the more pronounced: a built-in, almost automatic, suspicion of Courts and courtiers, of the motives which activated them, and of the baneful influence which they wielded in the House of Commons. But the best type of country member usually had in common with his brethren some more positive attitudes and more constructive aspirations: he shared with them a genuine concern for "good husbandry" in government, and felt an obligation to his constituents to see to it that the Queen's administration was as frugal and as incorrupt as Parliament could make it. Occasionally, too, negative and positive instincts combined to produce a common reaction. It was both fear of encroaching "influence" and concern for the taxpayer's interests which thus inspired one of the most prevalent themes of country discontent in Queen Anne's reign, resentment at the growing influence of military men in civil society and in politics at large.

The most basic of the country members' characteristic attitudes, however, was a plain distrust of governments as such, and a considerable sense of apprehension at its ever-spreading tentacles. In the post-Revolution period a fairly primitive administrative machinery had to be adapted to the requirements of two wars of unprecedented magnitude, and one inevitable result was that the instruments and employees of the Crown appeared to the taxpaying squire to be growing annually more numerous and more influential, not least inside the chamber of the Commons' House. Thus mistrust of the Court was fed first and foremost by the sharp rise in the number of officeholders and pensioners sitting in the Lower House. The rise was not as steep as was commonly imagined: the general estimate of a 50% increase up to a total of 150 between 1701 and 1706 was certainly exaggerated. But the growth was undeniably disturbing, the more so since it took place notwithstanding certain restrictive legislation enacted during William III's reign.*
Suspicion of the government's motives, and of its corrupting influence on members, hardened with the realisation that the same men who out of office had championed measures to limit the number of government officials

* See p. 130 below.

entitled to sit in the House of Commons only too frequently opposed or obstructed similar measures once in office themselves. The High Tory leaders, especially, had had a dubious record on this score since the early 1690's. In January 1706 Stanhope complained of "many instances of Gent[lemen] changing [their] opinions" about Place bills in the past, and in 1710 the Commons was told that "There are few gentlemen here who have not, at one time or other, even since the Revolution, been sensible how necessary it is for our safety to make some provision in this matter. If every man who hath once been of that opinion should be so now, a bill for it would pass more unanimously than any that was ever offered to the House".[22]

The grounds on which the independent backbencher based his suspicion of "men in place" were not always as logical or rational as these. Often enough his distrust would show itself simply in a series of reflex actions, which could be induced by almost any evidence, however superficial, of dubious ministerial conduct. He never troubled to ask himself whether these reactions were consistent. Factious divisions on the administration benches or an unnatural degree of solidarity among ministers were equally capable of rousing his suspicions. "God Almighty open the Eyes and hearts of the Commons, that they may be able to discern and know, who are for the Interest of their Country" — such was the invocation of one embittered member after he had heard the Chancellor of the Exchequer clash openly in the House with a Cabinet minister who was playing party politics with supply: "nothing but pride reigns amongst most of these Courtiers — the number I hope will increase of Men truly concerned for the Public".[23] And yet, perversely, nothing more infuriated independent country gentlemen, and especially the active partisans on the back benches, than seeing men of their own party, who had been lions in opposition in a previous Parliament or session, lying down like lambs in office with ministerial colleagues of different party principles: "this in plain English", Sir John Pakington bluntly told the Commons in November 1703, "makes me believe this ministry has too great a resemblance of the last; that my lord S[underlan]d is risen from the dead, and now become prime minister of state. And now I am upon this subject [he went on] give me leave to tell some gentlemen here, who have been bellowing and roaring against persons for taking places in the late reign, that it is a reflection upon them to hold and continue their places in the company of those that they have been exclaiming against".*

---

* *Parl. Hist.* vi, 154. For the authenticity of this speech — "word for word as 'twas utter'd in the House of Commons" — see B.M. Lansdowne MSS. 773, f. 17: Charles to H. Davenant, 8 Feb. 1704.

Whether logical or not, this distrust of the Court current among the country members was widely accepted as a perfectly natural phenomenon. Indeed it is striking to find one of the leading champions of the Country Whig cause during the middle years of the reign expressing in all sincerity the view that suspicion of the executive by the nation's representatives in Parliament was not merely a natural but a constitutionally *healthy* state of affairs: "as to enacting mistrust between the people and those who may govern hereafter", he wrote of a renewed attempt in 1706 to curtail the influence of the Crown after the Hanoverian succession, "if it have that effect, I like it better than I did; for I have learnt from Demosthenes that the onely charm, the onely sure preservative which a free people can have against the incroachments of tyrants is an eternal mistrust and jealousy. This argument, however unfitt to be used in the house, or at a conference [i.e. between the two Houses], ought to be inculcated to all who mean to preserve themselves freemen".²⁴ One cannot doubt that the health of the constitution was a genuine matter for concern among the country *élite*. To maintain it, some thought, it was not sufficient even for members to preserve that continual watchfulness against the advances and the abuses of officialdom which Stanhope advocated; they must take frequent occasion to remind the public of their zeal: "for it is not enough to be uncorrupt", as one M.P. remarked, "unless we have the reputation of being so too".²⁵

No contemporary material illustrates more vividly the negative side of the country member's prejudices than the few surviving letters and the parliamentary diary* of Sir Arthur Kaye, a wealthy Yorkshire baronet, who was elected knight of the shire in the Tory interest in 1710 and was to retain his seat until 1726. Shortly after his first appearance at Westminster, at a time when Harley's Cabinet contained only one undoubted Whig,† and only three other members‡ who had no clear Tory affiliations, Kaye promised to use his influence to procure an office for his friend, Richard Beaumont of Lascelles Hall. Even at the start of his protracted solicitation on Beaumont's behalf, he clearly had some doubts as to whether the new ministry would satisfy the exacting standards of the independent gentleman much better than its Whig predecessor. It was to be hoped, he remarked, "that things will not be disposed of by the same standard of deserving them that has so long been the rule & step to preferments, but that gentlemen of familys & merit will now be advanced; and that the appearance of vertue which they

* Unfortunately detailed only for part of the 1710–11 session.
† Newcastle, Lord Privy Seal.
‡ Viz. Marlborough (still abroad), Queensberry, and Shrewsbury.

affect will become reall".[26] But Kaye's confidence in the trustworthiness even of Tory ministers was frail, and he was soon warning Beaumont against expecting quick results:

I receiv'd both yours and hope you will believe I would ply that business with all the interest and art I am capable of shewing, but there is a wide difference betwixt a sincere intention and a Court artfull way of keeping friends in expectancies [which] wee poor country men neither know how to practice, nor relish when wee see it.[27]

By the time of the Christmas recess pessimism was gaining ground fast. He could offer no encouragement to his Yorkshire neighbours who still believed that the Country Tories might "justly challenge a regard from a Ministry so young" as the one then in office.

I must tell you my opinion; that I much fear whether this Parl: will either answer those just expectations the people have from it; whether they will come into any effectual enquirys to lay open the late mismanagements, or give us that security to the Church wee have wanted & thought necessary, & now expected . . . If this be not done wee Country Gentlemen must expect as little regard as they have formerly mett with. But if it be, I hope wee may at some time or other serve our friends as well as our country.[28]

Parliamentary proceedings early in the New Year soon confirmed his forebodings. The government's tactics in securing the defeat of a new Place bill proved to be even more devious than those adopted by the previous Whig administration, though Kaye found some consolation in having helped to thwart its manoeuvres in the Commons and in thereby demonstrating "wt. the country gentlemens interest may do" when it maintained its unity.[29] When the hearing of the Tavistock election case brought to light evidence of bribery and corruption practised by a Whig member, Sir John Cope, and the ministry's supporters promptly blocked the attempt of some Country Tories to pursue the matter further, Kaye, as we would expect, saw the incident as a typical piece of Court whitewashing.[30] As for the anxious Beaumont, although Kaye was able to tell him later in the session that the prime minister had got to the point of asking for a memorandum of his name he was prompt to add that "in truth nothing is to be entirely depended on from that statesman, till 'tis actually done".[31]

The attitude of the independent member towards the whole business of power-politics, towards the manoeuvres of the party leaders and their struggles for supremacy, was frequently coloured by the tone of cynicism which marks the testimony of Sir Arthur Kaye. But behind the mask of cynical detachment, and occasionally in its place, it is often possible to detect a genuine and more positive concern for the public welfare, as the country member saw it: and not least, as we have noted, a concern for frugal and disinterested government. Many a backbench squire, and not only on the Tory side, had looked forward to a new era of "honest administration" and to "the ease of the subject in point of money" after the death of William III.[32] But a good few illusions were disturbed fairly early in the new reign by the Godolphin ministry's request to the Commons, on the Queen's behalf, for the continuance to Marlborough's heirs in perpetuity of the grant of £5000 a year which she had made to her Captain-General. During the first debate on the Queen's message, on 10 December 1702, one former backbench Tory who had recently taken office under Godolphin is reputed to have exclaimed "that though he had accepted of an employment at court, yet he never did it with a design that his mouth should be sewed up in that house, when any thing was offered that he thought detrimental to his country".[33] Among the disenchanted was Thomas Johnson. "You are sensible what a noise such things made in the late Reign", he told his friend, Richard Norris, "and now they begin in the first year." The fact that the Court was even prepared to put off consideration of the land tax to pursue the debate on the Marlborough grant both angered and saddened him. "I am troubled to see Men that I know made the greatest noise about their Constitution and the hardships of the people of England, and now . . . can do any thing — here is a gloomy change in Men".[34]

Naturally it was always easier to suspect the chiefs of the opposing party of jobbery or mismanagement or of sacrificing the national interest to feather their private nests. What is really notable is the number of those in the country ranks on both sides who found it hard to believe that *any* major ministerial upheaval or struggle for power at Court would bring much benefit in the long run to the long-suffering taxpayer. Johnson himself was one such. We find him greeting the temporary swing of the pendulum towards the Whig leaders in the closing months of William's reign with comparatively little enthusiasm: "for what have we got thus far by all our noise and new commissions?", he asked: "Our friends into offices . . . We are such an unhappy people — and purely occasioned by the Pride of Ambitious Men."[35] Similarly James Lowther of Whitehaven, who was soon afterwards elected to represent Cumberland in Parliament, drew surprisingly small comfort for a Whig from the overthrow of Robert Harley in February 1708 and the defeat of his plans to bring back a Tory bias to the ministry. "God send the publick business be carried on among them as it ought to be", was his first reaction. "Lett them employ who they will, there wil be enough* out [of office] to disturb the Publick."³⁶

Except for the tendency of all administrations to spend public money with a freedom which, to most backbenchers, seemed careless at best and dishonest at worst, no feature of the contemporary scene so troubled the average country gentleman of Anne's day as the growing political influence which came to be exercised during the Spanish Succession war by military men. To the country mentality this development seemed undesirable from every point of view; not merely because it appeared to open up yet more fruitful ground for cultivation by the Court, but also because to the landed men it epitomised the ever-swelling size of an army which only their taxes could support. "Though the civil officers should not be increased", one member of the Lower House complained in January 1710, "the continuance of the war must make the military officers more numerous and more powerful ... Promotions may be made every day in the old regiments, and new ones raised, and a very great share of these preferments falls to this House. The number of such members therefore ... seems likely to increase as long as the war lasts. The heavier the debt is upon the nation, the more of those who receive the public money will sit here, and impose the taxes out of which they are paid."³⁷

There were two particular aspects of this situation which roused the country politicians' ire. One was the increasing number of army officers who, in seeking and gaining seats in the House of Commons, were nudging out local squires in the process. The other was the apparent tendency of many of these officers, once elected, to prefer their parliamentary to their military service. Edward Wortley Montagu could be certain of a sympathetic response from the House when he inveighed against "Those who have no other fortune, depending on the war, than the command of a regiment, having nothing else to do but to make a proper disposition in the cloathing of it; by which means such an interest may be made in most of the corporations as no gentleman is able to resist".³⁸ Such a picture, even by 1710, may have been both unduly cynical and overdrawn. But it was undoubtedly evoked by fears and resentments common to many country members of both parties. The refusal of the Commons five years before this to agree to an amendment which would have excepted both army and navy officers from the provisions of a Place bill, and this at a time when the war was unusually popular,³⁹ had been some indication of the strength of backbench feeling. Even though he was himself the holder of a place in the Ordnance Office when he first

---

* I.e. enough power-politicians.

thought of contesting Cumberland in 1708, James Lowther never doubted that his claims on the electors' favour were superior to those of his fellow-Whig, George Fletcher, an army colonel and a Junto man who had represented the county since 1705.⁴⁰ "Country gentlemen", he told one of his prospective constituents quite simply, "are fitter to be Kts of the shire than offrs of the army"; and lest his own civil office (which he later surrendered) be thought a handicap to his pretensions, he hastened to add that "for a man that has a good clear estate & a handsome parcell of mony in his pocket there is not so much to be gott by a midling place as people imagine considering the confinement withal".⁴¹ The people of Cumberland, he thought, "ought to be appris'd of the unreasonableness of having three in six [of their parliamentary representatives] offrs of the army".* Even after his election as a county member, Lowther lost few opportunities of reiterating his favourite theme. The army officer, like other carpet-baggers who had no genuine stake in their constituencies, could not be expected (he maintained) to fight for the material interests of those he represented in the same way as the local landowner. He pointed this particular moral to his Whitehaven agent in January 1710. "Yesterday the Act was past for raising £500,000 by a lottery; part of the duty is a further tax upon windows, so that every house of 30 windows is to pay 30 shillings p. annum wch wil be very greivous to our country. The country may now see what they gett by chusing so many forreigners & officers".†

The long absences of officer-M.P.s from their regiments and commands made their offence yet more rank in the nostrils of the country member. Until the years 1711 and 1712, when sessions lasted longer than usual, the campaigning season in Germany and the Low Countries corresponded all too neatly, for the peace of mind of many independent backbenchers, with the normal period of the parliamentary recess. Understandably they often found it galling when measures which they had much at heart were jeopardised by the adverse votes of men whose salaries they were paying —

* Lonsdale MSS.: to W. Gilpin, 12 Feb. 1708. The Bishop of Carlisle could not but agree. "Would these gentlemen quarter themselves and their troops amongst us, they might be a security against those apprehensions we are under of danger from the North. But (I confess) I see no occasion we have for their proffer'd service in another capacity." Lloyd-Baker MSS. Box 4, bundle V.6: Nicolson to Archbishop Sharp, 19 May 1705 (microfilm in the Borthwick Institute, York).

† *Ibid.* to Gilpin, 19 Jan. 1709[-10]. The Cumberland county and borough representatives in this Parliament included two army officers, General Stanhope and Brigadier Stanwix (the latter, however, being a Carlisle man), and also two other "foreigners", Albemarle Bertie and Sir James Montagu.

and men, moreover, who were being paid to defeat the French and not to frustrate the just aspirations of men of property. By the third winter of the war more than a few landowners must have longingly envisaged, as Lord Fermanagh did, "a Bill . . . to make officers, as well as [*sic*] Members of Parlt. as others, to be with their men, and not be suffer'd to loyter in Engd. when the campaign is begun".[42] The young Leicestershire baronet, Sir Thomas Cave, already an archetypal country gentleman though not yet in Parliament himself, undoubtedly shared his father-in-law's sentiments on this tender point. Writing from London at this time, he regretted it was "too late at prest. to talk of itt by reason they will receive no new Bill"; but he pledged himself to do his utmost before the next Parliament met to promote a measure of this nature through the medium of one or other of his parliamentary friends.[43]

No such bill, however, appears to have been contemplated in the next or any subsequent session.[44] Instead, as we shall shortly see, the country members ambitiously attempted by major surgery to cut out the very roots of this tumour in the body politic, by eliminating all serving officers from the Commons after the Queen's death except for a handful of generals and admirals.* But the attempt failed and the grievance against absentee officers remained. It was aggravated in the eyes of country politicians on both sides by the disasters which overtook the allied armies in the Peninsula during 1707, and criticism came to a head during the attacks on the Godolphin administration's handling of the war in Spain on 29 January and 3 February 1708. "The House of Commons & the countrys near London", observed Lowther, "is very much dissatisfied with having so many offrs of the army in the House; they think they wld have done better to be at their posts in Spain, especially those that belong'd to the troops that were in the battle of Almanza. If they had bin there & kept their companys full it might have done great service." The outcry continued so strongly during the next few weeks that there were hopes that the army M.P.s would "certainly be routed sooner or later".[45] But these hopes, like so many other country aspirations in the early eighteenth century, were to founder on the sharp rocks of party, as well as ministerial, convenience; and their wreck was made the more certain because it proved so difficult to draw a clear dividing line for legislative purposes between the army officer and the landowner. Many military men — Sir Richard Temple of Stowe, Thomas Erle of Charborough, Sir Charles Hotham of Dalton and Henry Holmes of Yarmouth are just four examples — sat in the House as substantial country

* See *C.J.* xv, 110 and p. 132 below.

gentlemen in their own right. They could justly claim as good a title to sit there and to attend sessions as any other landed men, provided their military duties were not too blatantly neglected.

The picture that emerges, therefore, of the average country member of Parliament in Queen Anne's reign is that of a politician who was usually, though by no means invariably, a fairly substantial landowner, largely dependent on his rents for his income, and sharing most of the apprehensions and prejudices common to so many representatives of his social class. His distrust of governments and of Courts was for the most part a deep-rooted instinct, though his leaders might sometimes rationalise it into a constitutional precept. His satisfaction at the victory of his own party chiefs in any struggle for power at the centre of politics was often tempered by the uneasy consciousness that in some respects vital to the realisation of his own ideals, and to the promotion of his own interests, the change would make little material difference to official policy. Government, he was convinced, would still overspend and would still seek to lay fresh burdens on the landed men. Ministers, of whatever party, would always include their quota of black sheep, either of those who were grossly inefficient custodians of public money or of those who would shamelessly batten on the taxpayer for their private gain. To the country member the courtier, whatever his previous professions, was *ipso facto* an enemy to all attempts to pry too closely into governmental conduct, to limit ministerial influence over Parliament, or to stem that advancing tide of "military men" which was one of the country gentleman's special nightmares.

Finally, the 'independent' of Anne's day firmly believed that the courtier's vote was too strictly constrained. He prided himself by contrast (not always justifiably) on judging each question on its merits, and (with more justice) on not dancing to the tune called by the ministry of the day, even when that ministry was made up of men of his own party kidney. Because he had not, in his own words, been "more tractable . . . in obeying the word of command" in Parliament, James Lowther expected "but a scurvy time of it" from Lord Wharton and his Junto lieutenant, the Earl of Carlisle, when he stood for re-election in Cumberland in 1710. But he failed to allow for the realism of power-politicians who, as he himself admitted, were "in the main of the same opinion as myself".[46] They knew well enough that Lowther, like so many other Country Whigs, would always expiate a few "whimsical" votes by giving general support to his party — always provided he was tactfully handled. In the sense, therefore, that the genuine country member had usually to be coaxed rather than dragooned by his leaders into following the line approved by the party hierarchy, in or out of power, it can fairly be said that his cherished "independence" was no mere myth.

* * *

It is a rather more straightforward matter to gauge the impact of the 'country mentality' on the character of politics in the age of Anne than to delineate precisely the type of politician with whom these opinions and attitudes were associated. In the parliamentary history of the years 1702–14 country ideals and the perpetuation of the country tradition affected at least five fields of policy; and two of these involved political issues of real significance, even if one of them, as we shall see, was confused and perverted by party loyalties.

The most recurrent, the most self-evident and unquestionably the most important of the various country measures pursued during Anne's reign were Place bills or "self-denying" clauses and resolutions. Representing for the most part "a plain question between Court and Country in the House of Commons",[47] these appeared on average once in every session between 1702 and 1714, and no other parliamentary activity so regularly brought together independent backbenchers of both parties. The generally-accepted objective of this protracted campaign against "influence" (for it is as a campaign rather than a series of isolated sallies that we must regard it*) was drastically to reduce the power of the Crown to sway the decisions of Parliament through the presence of well over a hundred office-holders and pensioners in the Commons. For the idealists the aim was a more positive one: to preserve the constitution by wresting the decisions of the House of Commons out of the hands of a rapidly-growing body of courtiers, and vesting its future firmly in those of "the Gentlemen of England".[48] To members of this mind it had always seemed a basic defect of the Revolution Settlement of 1689 that "no provision was then made for ... purging the House of Commons from the dead weight of court officers and dependants".[49]

A limited amount of progress had already been made in this direction by the exclusion from the Commons of important groups of revenue officials in 1694, 1700 and 1701. But all attempts since 1692 to carry the principle of a "general self-denial" into law had failed,† until in 1701 a sweeping Place clause was inserted in the Act of Settlement providing that after the Hanoverians succeeded to the throne "no person who has an office or place

* See my article on 'The Attack on "The Influence of the Crown", 1702–16', *Bull. I.H.R.* xxxix (1966) of which the following paragraphs are a brief summary.

† Since this was written David Hayton has shown (*Parliament, Estates and Representation,* 5, 1985) that of the 4 attempts mentioned in my 1966 article only the last, that of 1699–1700, was "general" without reservation.

of profit under the King or receives a pension from the Crown shall be capable of serving as a member of the House of Commons". This triumph for the country ideal, however, was more apparent than real. Not only was it (like most other restrictive clauses in the Act) a party rather than a country victory, arising largely from the unpopularity of William III himself with the Tories;[50] it also came at a time when some of the sponsors of the original Place bills, especially on the Whig side, had already begun to realise that such sweeping general measures designed to take early effect were neither practicable nor even desirable. It was recognised that a House of Commons deprived, by such a general Place measure, of the information and assistance given by such ministers as the Chancellor of the Exchequer and the Secretary-at-War would be severely handicapped in its debates on vital questions of finance, foreign policy and war policy.* So that while the principle of *general* exclusion, as embodied in the Act of Settlement, continued to attract the diehards even on the Whig side, most country members were prepared, and some positively anxious, to give up the general principle if in so doing they could secure a measure of limitation on "influence", which would be more immediate and more realistic.†

Two lines of approach towards this objective were adopted at different times in Anne's reign: one, the "negative method" as it came to be called, was to promote a further series of minor measures excluding specific types or groups of office-holders from the Commons; the other was to exclude *all* office-holders with certain specified exceptions, which would allow the major Household officials and 'working ministers' to retain their seats. By February 1705 three attempts to progress along the first and more conservative line had come to nothing, though in part this complete lack of success was the fault of the country members themselves in rejecting out of hand the Lords' amendments to the only one of the three measures to reach the Upper House, amendments which would at least have excluded commissioners and officials of the Prize Office from the Commons.‡ The two

---

* This criterion of the value of a placeman as a source of *information* to the House later became an accepted guide-line for those involved in drafting the place legislation of Anne's reign. See, e.g., l'Hermitage's summary of speeches made by supporters of the 1710–11 bill at its Second Reading, Add. MSS. 17677DDD, f. 683.

† Only one *general* Place bill and one general Place clause were mooted in the new reign, and both were the products of party manœuvring by the Tories, rather than being launched on a genuine "country bottom". See *Bull. I.H.R.* xxxix (1966) 53–4.

‡ The amendments were made to a moderate bill sponsored by the Whig lawyer Peter King in Jan. 1705 which aimed to exclude the holders of all offices created since Charles II's death, and would have unseated about a score of members. See Luttrell, vi, 515; *C.J.* xiv, 482.

other "negative" projects, one in 1702 for disqualifying members of Prince George's Household and the other early in 1705 for excluding army and navy officers, failed in the Commons.[51] The chance of achieving the more ambitious alternative object of a limited inclusion must at this stage have seemed remote. But in January 1706 the country interest found itself unexpectedly in possession of a tactical weapon almost as powerful as the bill of Settlement had proved in 1701. The opportunity was created by the arrival in the Lower House from the House of Lords of the Regency bill, providing new machinery to secure the Hanoverian succession after Anne's death. This was a bill which both the government and the Whig leaders were desperately anxious to carry; and it was on this anxiety that a group of Country Whigs, led by two lawyers, Robert Eyres and Peter King, and also by Sir Richard Onslow and James Stanhope, decided to play. "The Regency bil", as Eyres shrewdly observed, "has such friends as wil see it pass with a reasonable instruction".[52] The "instruction" he and his friends proposed was the insertion of a clause "explaining, regulating and altering" the Place clause of the Act of Settlement. Its object was to replace the general and unenforceable exclusion of *all* placeholders from the Commons on the Queen's death, with a more discriminating but substantial exclusion which they were determined to see enforced.

So was born the notorious "Whimsical clause" which from 12 January until 19 February 1706 gave rise to the fiercest struggle between Country and Court in Anne's reign. In its final form it named a number of important officials together with ten general and flag officers, to an absolute maximum of 40, who were to be allowed to keep their seats in the Parliament which would assemble under the terms of the Regency bill as soon as the Queen died. All other placemen would be automatically disqualified at Anne's death.[53] The popularity of the clause with the rank and file of the Whig independents was never in doubt, and some 50 of them resolved to make their support for the bill as a whole conditional on acceptance of the clause by the Court. With Tory backbenchers only too ready to make common cause with these "Whimsicals", some out of enthusiasm for the measure itself, others because they hoped it would prove fatal to a bill for which they had no relish, the ministry was soon seriously alarmed. "Nothing will be so uneasy to the Queen as losing this bill", the Lord Treasurer admitted,[54] and as with so many former and subsequent Place bills the government had to fall back on the Upper House to counteract the excesses of the Lower. "I hope the H: of Lords will be encouraged to ruffle the Clause pretty handsomly . . .", wrote Godolphin to Harley.[55] The Lords did not disappoint him. They did not reject "the Clause", but they amended it out of all recognition. All that was left of any substance when it was sent back to the Commons was the disqualification of members appointed to new offices (by which they understood offices created "at any time hereafter") and the exclusion of officials of the Prize Office; though as a further concession, the provisions of the amended clause were to come into force, not on the death of Anne, but on the dissolution of the present Parliament.[56] But the country interest, well aware of its unusually strong bargaining position, was not impressed, and the Lords' amendments were rejected in the Commons on 4 February by 205 votes to 183.

The fortnight's deadlock which followed, during which the fate of the Regency bill hung in the balance, was only broken through the efforts of the Junto lords and their friends in the Upper House, who made a private appeal to the loyalty and party principles of the Country Whigs while formal conferences between the two Houses seemed to be making little progress. The House of Lords had made it clear that it was only prepared to countenance the "negative method" of restricting official influence; but by enlarging the scope of the concessions which this method made possible, and by reminding the "Whimsicals" of the damage which both the Whig and the Hanoverian cause might suffer if something like 100 by-elections were to take place immediately after the Queen's death, as "the Clause" envisaged, Halifax and Somers were able to make a few crucial conversions among the Country Whig leaders in the Commons: "Sr Ri[chard Onslow] fainted at last in the pursuit", wrote one of the stalwarts who remained unseduced by these arguments, "& Ro. Eyres, unknown to Peter King . . . who stood his ground very firmly, had treacherous[ly] made at my Ld Hallifax's this bargain & in the most audacious as well as infamous manner that ever was seen in the House gave up his cause, his friends & himself . . .".[57] On the following Monday the "Whimsical clause", defended to the last by Sir John Cropley, Sir William Ellys and other "patriots", finally perished by eight votes in a House of well over 400.[58]

However inadequate the final enactment might seem to the country zealots, it represented the most considerable step yet towards their objective of reducing "influence" in the Commons. The clause was to come into operation at the close of the current session; holders of all newly-created offices were to be excluded from the Commons; and so were a considerable number of existing office-holders.* On one concession especially the country

---

* Viz. Commissioners and Sub-Commissioners of the Prizes, Commissioners of Wine Licences, Transports and Sick and Wounded, Commissioners of the Navy in the outports, governors and deputy governors in the plantations, holders of pensions *durante bene placito*.

members built great hopes: "Here comes the best", wrote Cropley to his patron Lord Shaftesbury. "No man to take a place after his being elected a member of parliament, but accepting such a place shall make his election void . . . 'Tis a foundation for more & I will defy any sessions to pass without bills & divisions against the army & household".[59]

Not until the winter of 1709–10, however, was this prophecy fulfilled. By then disappointment over the very limited effect which the Place clause of the Regency Act appeared to have had in Parliament,[60] and alarm at the subservience to the Court shown in the intervening years by the Scots M.P.s in particular, had combined to rouse the Country forces to action. On 25 January 1710 Edward Wortley Montagu, now a prominent figure among the Country Whigs, rose to complain that office-holders in the Commons were "more numerous than ever, notwithstanding the several bills that have passed both Houses, and several others that have passed only this House",[61] and to introduce a bill whose abandonment of the "negative method" favoured by the Lords, and return to the principle underlying the Whimsical clause, illustrated the new mood of discontent among the country interest. All place-holders but about 50* were to be excluded from the Commons, and the bill was to take effect from the termination of the current Parliament. Small wonder that the government fought the bill tooth and nail, forcing a division at every possible stage in the Commons and trying, if they could not defeat the bill outright, to water it down with various amendments. But the bill passed the Commons, albeit by as few as 22 votes on the final reading,[62] and the Court was forced to fall back on the always-unpopular expedient of destroying it in the House of Lords.

The Tory victory in the General Election of 1710 made little difference to the strength of country feeling against the influence of the Crown. In each of the four sessions between November 1710 and July 1714 a fresh Place bill was introduced, the first three being virtually carbon copies of Wortley Montagu's. The bill of 1710–11, like that of January–February 1710, passed the Commons and was quickly and easily destroyed in the Lords; but that of 1712 was proposed in a very different political climate. Once again, as in the Regency crisis of 1705–6, the country interest found itself suddenly in a strong political position. The new bill, designed to cut down the number of suspected government dependants from 150 to just over 60, easily passed the Commons,[63] being given added force by a general resurgence of alarm about "the scandal of corruption", and a consequent atmosphere in which all manner of wild rumours circulated and gained

* Increased subsequently by amendments to about 60.

credence.* But the sudden strength of the Country position owed less to this than to the new situation in the House of Lords, where the Whigs were mounting their great offensive against the peace policy of the Oxford ministry. In spite of the repulse dealt them at the beginning of January, following the block creation of twelve new peers by the Queen over the Christmas recess, they still had an outside chance of gaining control there; for the Scottish peers, disgruntled by the Hamilton affair,† were for once wavering in their allegiance to the government. In the circumstances the Whig chiefs, who had only once since 1702 so much as flirted with their old country traditions,[64] felt bound to mortgage their future freedom of action by lending their support to the Place bill; for in the short term its passing would inevitably involve the government in acute embarrassment. Success seemed near when the Second Reading was carried by a majority of 21, but the tireless canvassing of Lord Oxford seduced from the bill's supporters a number of their Scottish and Tory allies, and secured at the meeting of the Grand Committee of the Lords on 29 February a majority of 5 for an amendment postponing the operation of the act till the end of the reign.[65] In this form the measure was of little interest to the Junto lords, and was carried no further in the Upper House.

For the country members in the Commons 29 February 1712 represented the high-water mark of the Place campaigns of Anne's reign. Wortley Montagu's last bill, introduced in 1713 at a time when the treaties of peace and commerce were the focus of political attention, roused notably less enthusiasm in the Commons than its predecessors, and a rather wild attempt by the Country Whigs to "tack" it to the Malt Tax bill was heavily defeated.[66] Only in the following session, and in the Upper House, was the country interest granted one last flicker of hope. The 1714 Place bill was sponsored by a group of Hanoverian Tories, led by Sir Arthur Kaye.[67] It met no open opposition in the Lower House, but to judge from the contemporary lack of interest in the measure — few political correspondents in March and April 1714 favour it with so much as a mention — success in the Lords was not for a moment anticipated. However, there was a last surprise in store for the country politicians. Against all expectation, a number of Tory peers, most of them Hanoverians, joined with the Whig peers to support the bill. It was committed, and emerged from the Committee substantially unchanged. Before the Third Reading on 17 April both sides seem to have combed the precincts of Westminster Palace for every available

* See Burnet vi, 113–14. How little most of these rumours and the strictures passed on the Harley ministry were deserved will be made clear in a later chapter.

† See pp. 338–9 below.

peer. The Court mustered 61 votes, the opposition 63; but when proxies were called for, the Court's numbered 19, the opposition's only 17. The votes were thus exactly equal, and the rules of the House directed that the motion for a Third Reading should be negatived. And so the last Place bill of Anne's reign, which would have reduced the number of placemen in the first Hanoverian House of Commons by well over half, and which could scarcely have failed to have a marked effect on the development of the eighteenth-century constitution had it reached the statute book, failed by the narrowest possible of parliamentary margins. What is more, there is evidence that but for the weakness of one bishop's bladder, necessitating the rather prolonged absence of the unfortunate cleric at the very time when the House was dividing, the measure would have passed.[68]

As well as the long sequence of attacks on "the influence of the Crown" in the House of Commons there was another highly-important practical consequence of the perpetuation of the country tradition into the age of Anne. This was the considerable weight attached by the leading country politicians on both sides, but more particularly on the Tory side, to the Commons' right both to scrutinise public spending and to investigate administrative abuses on the slightest suspicion of malpractice. It had long been a part of the country tradition to insist on economical government and to keep a jealous eye open for evidence of financial mismanagement or the misappropriation of parliamentary funds, and it remained so between 1702 and 1714. Some allusion has already been made to the uproar created on both Whig and Tory benches by the Queen's message to the Commons in 1702 about the Marlborough grant. Although encouraged to some extent by government colleagues of the general's, jealous of the special favours being heaped on the Churchills, this was an early demonstration that concern for frugal administration was not an ideal to which country members were to pay only lip-service in Anne's reign; any more than under William III, when the campaign against the King's grants of land to Dutch and other favourites had been one of the great achievements of the Country party. After Sir Charles Hedges, the Secretary for the Northern Province, had read Anne's message to the House on 10 December 1702, the Commons, we are told, "seemed for some time to be in amaze, and kept so long silent that (it was said) the Speaker [Harley] stood up, and looked round, to see if anybody would speak to it: and at length Mr. S—— having broke the ice, the debate ran very high on the occasion . . .".* An attempt was actually

* *Parl. Hist.* vi, 57. "Mr S——" may perhaps have been young Henry St. John, who clearly took a fairly prominent part in the proceedings.

made the following day to prevent the message being debated at all. This move was frustrated by 171 votes to 83 (the first of many occasions over the next few years when the Godolphin ministry had cause to be grateful to the Whig Junto for support).[69] But feeling against the Court and memories of "the exorbitant grants of the last reign" proved so strong in the end that the Commons in their address on 18 December, drawn up by a committee under St. John's chairmanship, made it clear that, to "their inexpressible grief", they could not comply with Anne's request.[70]

Yet while there was always in Anne's Parliaments a vociferous group of natural backbenchers which, given a free hand with parliamentary time, would happily have devoted a large part of every session to inquisitions into the conduct of the executive, this was a kind of activity which in the nature of things was peculiarly open to abuse for party ends. Ministers of the Crown were instinctively on the look-out for factious motives behind most of these campaigns for "purity"; and often enough they were justified in detecting them. Lord Oxford's ministerial lieutenants were briefly embarrassed in the House in the summer of 1713 after the discovery that the First Lord of the Admiralty was being paid an additional £2000 on his salary which was not charged on the navy estimates. But it did not escape notice that the men who stirred up country feeling on this occasion were two "under-strappers" of the Junto; and that there had been no protest from this quarter three years before when the Earl of Orford had profited from a similar device.[71] High Tory power-politicians had been just as ready earlier in the reign to make capital in opposition out of popular causes of this nature: "that faction . . . think by talking of accounts & deficiencys or misapplications", reported Secretary Harley in 1704, "they can discover any thing besides their own ill disposition & folly; a very few days wil beat them out of that sort of play, & the destinction wil appear who are for supporting the government & who are for weakening it".[72] But all too frequently perfectly genuine country politicians became accomplices, wittingly or unwittingly, in such manoeuvres. The very fact that in the period 1702–14 the rôle of scrutineer and inquisitor was mainly sustained by the Tories, though with limited support from time to time from the independent Whigs, in itself suggests that the borderline between "Country" fervour and party malice was far from being clearly defined.

There were many occasions when the country ideal of "good husbandry" was prostituted to exploit a party advantage. Nowhere is this so evident as in the work of the various House of Commons' Commissions of Public Accounts, bodies whose members were elected by ballot but who were paid a generous salary out of public funds.[73] These commissions flourished in Anne's reign only when the Tories were in power with a strong parliamentary majority at their backs. They sat from 1702 to 1704, but not again until after the General Election of 1710 when new commissions were authorised by Acts of Parliament in 1711, 1712 and 1713, each of them serving for a period of twelve months. In the seven ballots which took place to elect commissioners between 1702 and 1714 not a single Whig was chosen. And while the post was certainly no sinecure, often keeping the incumbent hard at work in London during the long summer months,* it is clear that its main purpose was to enable the holder to dig up damaging evidence against his political opponents by investigating the accounts of *previous* ministries.

The first Commission of Public Accounts to submit a report to Parliament after William III's death, in November 1702, had been elected shortly after the Queen's accession and just before the dissolution of William's last Parliament. Unlike its successors after 1710, it was composed only partly of genuine country types; for among its members were three ambitious young politicians, St. John, Tom Coke and James Brydges, who not merely aspired to office but were soon to acquire it. In fact the latter, by a nice irony, was destined to become a classic exemplar of official graft in virtually the very post which first came under fire from him and his associates in the winter of 1702–3, that of Paymaster-General of the Army.† Serious charges of misappropriation were brought against the Earl of Ranelagh, a courtier with no particular party affiliations, who had been Paymaster since James II's reign, and who had inevitably drawn attention to himself by a mode of life which the Bishop of Carlisle described as "scandalously expensive (to the tune of 50 or 60,000 l. per añ in gardening, Indian ware, etc)".[74] There was most probably some substance in these charges, although for a man who had reputedly had accounts totalling 120 million pounds pass through his hands since 1688 Ranelagh had covered his tracks so well that the Commissioners' labours had brought forth no more than a molehill of incriminating evidence. Some Country Whigs appear to have suspected that he was being unfairly victimised (Sir John Cropley, for instance, was a teller in his

---

* Baron Hill MSS. 6760: Henry Bertie to Lord Bulkeley, [London], 25 Aug. 1711. "Since I was last at Windsor it has been my week of being in the Chair of Accts. wch has so much taken up my time that I had hardly opportunity to write my last to Your Lordp . . ."

† The duties of this office were split in Dec. 1702 and two Paymasters were appointed, one for the Forces at Home, the other (the more lucrative employment) for the Forces Abroad. It was this latter office, first held by Sir Stephen Fox, to which Brydges succeeded in 1705.

favour in the only Commons' division which his case produced),[75] but the party did not think it worth while to divide the House when Ranelagh's expulsion from its membership was voted on 1 February 1703. Most Whigs probably assumed, and not without some reason, that had his innocence been apparent the ex-Paymaster had enough friends among the High Tories, including his electoral patron, Bishop Trelawney, and the Lord Lieutenant of Ireland, Lord Rochester,[76] to have saved him from disgrace.

If, however, the case against Ranelagh could be justified as part of a "country" crusade there was no mistaking the motives behind the charges that were produced against Halifax and Orford of the Junto, the two principal targets of the Commissioners of Public Accounts in the years 1702–4. Both lords had escaped the net of impeachment spread for them in 1701; but the Tories obviously hoped to enmesh them now by producing evidence of financial malpractices committed by the former as Auditor of the Exchequer since 1700 and by the latter as Treasurer of the Navy early in William's reign. In the session of 1702–3 the Commissioners concentrated mainly on Halifax, whose only crime was that he had either neglected or deliberately circumvented certain traditional Exchequer forms and practices, in the interests of efficiency and (as he himself pointed out) under pressure of a volume of auditing work for which the old procedures had never been designed.[77] The Tory majority in the Commons was persuaded to vote the Whig leader guilty of "a breach of trust" in January 1703[78] and the Attorney-General was authorised to begin proceedings against him at Common Law. But the legal prosecution petered out eventually in a *nolle prosequi*,[79] while the House of Lords showed its opinion of the matter by absolving Halifax completely on 5 February 1703, and so provoking a dispute with the Lower House which was only ended by Parliament's prorogation on the 28th.[80] By the time the next session opened, a newly-constituted Commission had at its disposal fresh ammunition to support an attack both against the Earl of Orford and a number of officials who had served under him. Again, however, the ammunition proved to be mostly blanks. Orford's accountancy had been careless (even Halifax, as Auditor, admitted this, much to his colleagues' disgust[81]), but he had so clearly not been guilty of any peculation that even in the House of Commons only 60 members could be persuaded to stay in town at a late stage of the session to censure his conduct. As for the Lords, they had no hesitation in exonerating both Orford and his subordinates;[82] and so certain were they now that true country backing in the Commons for the Commission of Public Accounts was fast dissolving, that they felt quite justified in refusing to accept a bill renewing the Commission for a further year; or rather they agreed to it only with radical amendments which they knew well enough the Commons would never accept.

The judgement of the Lords was amply vindicated. In spite of a certain popularity achieved by the Commission outside Parliament since 1702,[83] there was no general outcry from country members at its demise. Significantly the most vehement protest came from a High Tory leader, Nottingham, who was so intent on pillorying his opponents that he talked wildly at one point of "tacking" the next bill of accounts to the Land Tax to force it past the Lords. But the bill was not revived, and the only vote of censure which the House of Commons was persuaded to pass the following winter — criticising the accounts of some Whig ex-Commissioners of the Prize Office — was only carried (according to one of the victims) by surprise and with the connivance of the Speaker at a time when less than a fifth of the members were present. [84]

The eventual resurrection of the Commission of Accounts in 1711 came shortly after the end of several years of Whig government; so it was almost inevitable that to begin with, at least, it should again become a party and ministerial tool, "of no use [Walpole scathingly wrote] but to sully the character of those that are out of power, and to skreen the iniquities of those that are in".[85] The new Commissioners provided the Court with the evidence it needed in January and February 1712 to secure the expulsion of Walpole himself and Adam de Cardonnel from the House of Commons, and above all to pass a severe vote of censure on the Duke of Marlborough, all on the grounds of alleged corruption.[86] Later, it seems, they did grow rather more conscious of their position as inheritors of the country tradition. George Lockhart, the member for Midlothian, who was one of their number from 1711 right through to 1714, has left evidence that after the winter of 1711–12 he and his colleagues were anxious to investigate current accounts as well as those of the Godolphin ministry, but that all kinds of rubs were put in their way by Lord Treasurer Oxford and his Tory colleagues.[87] Certainly in 1713 they appear to have attracted some support from the Country Whigs, who, according to one of their leading lights, "exposed the measures of the ministry and the mismanagement of the public money" during this session.[88] But there seems no reason to disbelieve Lockhart's view that the more altruistic labours of the Commissioners were largely wasted: "in sundry reports, presented by them to the Parliament, severall matters which wou'd have been of great service and importance to the public, had they been duly improv'd, were laid open. But . . . such matters were intirely slighted, and no regard was shewn or notice taken of any thing that did not directly strike against the reputation of some considerable person of the opposite party."[89] So that although the Commons passed a bill late in the session of 1714 renewing the Commission for a further twelve months from 24 June 1714, it probably caused little surprise to the country members when the Lords, with the obvious encouragement of some government peers, threw it out at the Second Reading.[90]

Apart from the work of the Commissioners of Public Accounts there were in the early eighteenth century frequent parliamentary enquiries into administrative abuses or shortcomings of one sort or another which appealed to the watchdog spirit of the independent member. Some of these enquiries were essentially party moves; others were genuinely bipartisan. The contrast between the two is clearly seen in the turbulent session of 1707–8. On the one hand, the Commons' investigation of deficiencies in the Admiralty in December 1707 was almost entirely sustained by the Whigs. On the other hand, the much more searching probe which the Tories initiated into the conduct of the war in Spain, which began in the same month and lasted until almost the end of February 1708, attracted at first a good deal of support from Peter King and the Country Whigs.[91] This was mainly because there was a strong *prima facie* suspicion, probably unfounded[92] but none the less widely entertained, of gross misappropriation of the funds voted for the Peninsula in 1707. Even here, though, it is striking that only a tiny handful of Whigs persisted with their attack right up to the final stage of the Spanish enquiry on 24 February.* Of the remainder, some had in the meantime been half convinced by the government's explanations, or by its claims that "a false account" had been laid before the House by the Tory ex-ministers, St. John and Harley; but the majority had simply been awakened to the danger of bringing down the government and letting in the Tories by an adverse vote on what Addison described as "the most Important Day of this Session".[93] This, indeed, is one case where Wortley Montagu's complaint that country activity was often inhibited in Anne's reign by "the fear that each [side] have of the other's bringing in their whole party"[94] does have some substance.

---

* Addison noted that in the final division, in which the ministry triumphed by 230 votes to 175, "of the Country Whiggs only Peter King and two more one of wch was Mr. Nevil" voted against the Court (*Letters*, pp. 93–4). James Vernon observed that "Mr. King voted for the question but did not speak to it & Sr. Richard Onslow divided from him". Buccleuch (Boughton) MSS. vol. iv, letter 194: to Shrewsbury, 24 Feb. (I owe this reference to Dr. W. A. Speck and am grateful to the Duke of Buccleuch for permission to make the quotation).

After 1708, however, the country motive in most of the enquiries conducted by the House of Commons into administrative shortcomings was plainly subordinate to the party motive. A few questions — the heavy arrears being incurred by the Receivers of the Land Tax is a case in point — still aroused concern among backbenchers on all sides.[95] But the whole series of Tory-inspired investigations in 1711 and 1712 into the abuses supposedly perpetrated by the Godolphin administration — the enquiry into the Victualling Office,[96] the fantastic debates on "the missing thirty-five millions" and the attack on Paymaster-General Brydges in April 1711,[97] the attempt to censure the late Secretary of State, the Earl of Sunderland, in the same month for having encouraged the disastrous immigration of the "poor Palatines",[98] the hostile examination in February 1712 of Townshend's conduct of the Barrier Treaty negotiations[99] — rarely succeeded in convincing the average Whig backbencher that country principles were at stake. The majority of Country Whigs recognised these gambits for what in essence they were, declining to be hoodwinked by the fine flourishes of country sentiment, and all the talk of members having "mandates" from their constituents to lay bare mismanagement and corruption, with which they were accompanied. There were individual exceptions. The attack on James Brydges on 24 and 28 April 1711, which roused Henry St. John to a stirring, if not perhaps altogether disinterested, defence of his friend and colleague, did secure the backing of some independent Whigs, who (like the Tories) rightly suspected the Paymaster of making illegal profits out of his office.[100] There were even a few Whigs in the Commons in January 1712 willing to be persuaded by the spurious allegations of corruption framed against Marlborough and prepared to vote against the duke in the great divisions of the 24th;[101] though to judge from the division figures and equally reliable evidence, the number must have been negligible and was certainly outweighed by the number of Tories ready to acknowledge the injustice of the charge.[102] Generally speaking, in fact, it was only a handful of dyed-in-the-wool Country Whigs like Wortley Montagu who professed, let alone felt, sympathy with most of these Tory vendettas. And even that pillar of the Faith joined with his former allies, Onslow and King, in defending the reputation of the Duke of Marlborough.[103]

There can be no doubt, therefore, that the country ideal found far more authentic expression in Anne's reign in the promotion of measures to restrict the power of the Crown in the House of Commons than in the periodic campaigns waged against governmental mismanagement or corruption. The latter were rarely non-party in their inception, although once launched they might make an occasional appeal to pure country feeling in the House. A less dramatic, though for the most part more genuine, manifestation of this feeling was the concern shown by independent members, particularly the more substantial country gentlemen of both parties, for freedom of election. This was a cause which had given rise to a good deal of legislative activity in William III's reign, which flagged for a while thereafter, but which revived from the winter of 1707–8 onwards as the strain of triennial elections on the depleted resources of country gentlemen began to make itself almost universally felt. In the five previous sessions the Commons had contented themselves mainly with passing formal and rather meaningless resolutions against electoral improprieties, usually at their first sitting.[104] The first serious move in Anne's reign to replace empty words by concrete legislation was made by Ralph Freeman on 22 December 1707; and between then and the end of the reign Parliament was either presented or threatened with three bills against bribery and corruption in elections,* one bill designed to combat "other indirect practices" as well as bribery and corruption,† one bill to prevent "irregular proceedings" in city and borough elections,‡ another§ to illegalise the splitting of freeholds before county elections with a view to multiplying votes (a practice which had become disturbingly popular, especially since the General Election of 1705),[105] and finally a continuing bill extending the life of an act passed in William's reign to prevent false and double returns of members.‖ Among the sponsors and drafters of these measures are to be found, at one time or other, most of the familiar names on the country wings of both parties: Freeman, Scobell, Campion, Davers, Lawson, Cholmondeley, Kaye and Downe on the Tory side; King, Onslow and Richard Nevil on the Whig side, along with others like Jekyll and Hampden who were sometimes sympathetic towards country measures. The government of the day usually contrived to get at least one of its members formally associated with these various bills, perhaps to see that no too-obvious attack was made on the electoral preserves of the Crown; but the limited evidence available suggests that only one of this series of measures — that of 1710–11, which was very evidently a 'lawyer's bill'[106] — was not country-inspired.

Unfortunately, because they rarely attracted much public attention or interest, we know very little about the scope or the detailed provisions of any of these bills, save that designed to prevent vote-splitting by "fraudulent

* Dec. 1707–March 1708, Jan. 1709, Dec. 1710–April 1711.
† Feb. 1710.   ‡ Feb. 1712.
§ Feb.–May 1712.   ‖ June–July 1713.

conveyances" — the only one apart from the continuing bill of 1713 ever to reach the statute book. To judge from the standard complaints in the country gentleman's election correspondence at this period their initiators probably had two principal purposes in mind: to curb the power of the great electoral magnates in the counties, or at least the abuse of that power, and to counteract both the corruption of small boroughs by men of private fortune and their invasion by Crown influence (the latter being exerted through the medium of revenue officers, post office officials, and other local government employees).[107] The trouble seems to have been that neither the sponsors of general bills against "bribery and corruption" nor their supporters were ever entirely clear in their minds just how far they were prepared to go or what was the best way to achieve their ends. If a measure reached the committee stage the chances were that it would emerge as a rag-bag of miscellaneous clauses, some of them parochial in the extreme, others of no apparent relevance to the conduct of elections, while practical and constructive proposals were rejected in the process.[108] Even that rigid Country Tory, Sir Arthur Kaye, was but little distressed by the defeat of the 1711 bill at its Third Reading on 17 April, in spite of the fact that the Court had used its influence to kill it: "for tho [he admitted] there were many good things in it, yet the making gentlemen so liable to actions from any villain whose single oath was a conviction sway'd with me as well as others, & I believ'd wee were not in such hast to take it with its faults in the first session, when a better Bill might be prepared the succeeding meeting".[109] It is not surprising in the circumstances, and especially in view of the many vested interests at stake, that the majority of these measures proved abortive.*

Another perfectly genuine, if relatively minor, issue which was likely at times to provoke bipartisan opposition to the Court from the landed men was the question of conscription for military service. The need to raise 12,000 more troops for the campaign of 1704 in Flanders and for the new theatre of war in the Peninsula necessitated the passing in March of that year of the first of a series of Recruiting acts. It had a long and troublesome passage through the Commons; and even though three succeeding bills in the years 1705–7 met with little resistance, at a time when the war was going well,[110] conscription in any shape or form was never popular with backbenchers any

---

* Two never even got as far as a First Reading; one never emerged from committee; a fourth received its quietus at the Third Reading after 4½ months of uneasy life; while the only general bribery and corruption bill which did manage to pass the Commons (Freeman's original measure of 1707–8) was thrown out by the Lords. *C.J.* xv, 481–579 *passim*; *L.J.* xviii, 512.

more than it was with their constituents. "The insolence of officers in pressing land souldiers," Shrewsbury wrote in 1707, "and the inconvenience it is in the countrey to have their workmen, apprentices & servants pressed, is such that if the nation were not in good humour with our glorious successes it would not be born."[111] Before the following winter, however, the vein of military success seemed temporarily exhausted and the "good humour" of the previous three years was soured, particularly by the disaster at Almanza.[112] Not surprisingly the government's next Recruiting bill ran into very great difficulties in the Commons in January 1708 under cross-fire from Tory independents and from Peter King's Country Whigs. After coming near to destruction it eventually reached the statute book, rigorously amended; but the troubles experienced in executing the act incensed the country members afresh at the end of March — so much so that Godolphin was glad to take refuge in an early dissolution of Parliament.[113] Taking warning from these experiences the ministers prepared the way for a new "Bill of Recruits" in the 1708–9 session with a good deal of care. Leading Country Whigs were invited to preliminary ministerial meetings on the subject, a new formula for raising the required men was worked out, and eventually, with a gratifyingly united Whig vote behind it, a bill was sent up to the Lords at the end of January 1709 that was at least (Coningsby thought) "as good [as] the nature of the protest woud allowe".[114] With the end of the war in sight four years later the Oxford administration was only too anxious to remove this particular source of friction between Court and Country. At a Privy Council meeting held on 8 January 1713 a proclamation suspending the last Recruits Act was read and approved, a move that could not fail, one councillor was certain, to be "acceptable to the countrey, ever uneasy under that law of necessity".[115]

In some ways the most interesting of the lesser by-products of the country tradition in the age of Anne was the series of attempts made after 1707 to introduce voting by ballot into the House of Commons. This was planned to apply in the first instance only to the method of voting in disputed election cases (ballot-voting was actually given a trial in the Ashburton case in February 1708); but some of those who piloted the original measure clearly intended it as the first step towards a general change of voting practice in the House — several talked openly, for instance, about the advantages of electing the next Speaker by a secret vote — "and how convenient that will be to a court and monarchy", one placeman wryly observed, "time will shew".[116] There were even those who prophesied that it would "be as prejudicial to the Court as a Place-Bill".[117]

The first attempt in February 1708 was something of a fiasco. For one thing, the method of balloting proposed aroused considerable hilarity:

It consisted of several articles: first that a balloting-box* and balls should be provided; that it be carried about by the two clerks, one having the box, the other the balls; that the Speaker appoint two members to attend the box; that the member voting take a ball in his bare hand, and hold it up between his finger and thumb, before he put it into the box; that the members keep their places till the box be brought back to the table, and the balls there told over.[118]

Then, when the system was put into practice in the Ashburton experiment it proved not only long-winded (it took more than an hour to record 280 votes) but a physical endurance test; for it was one of the rules of the ballot, as James Vernon stressed, that "nobody must move in that time, *whatever the occasion may be*".[119] There were many members prepared to write off the whole idea as a failure there and then. The Court must have had a considerable shock, therefore, when a second attempt was made the following winter and nearly succeeded. Members had discovered during the summer that this measure, like the self-denying bill, was a popular one with their constituents;[120] and there were 350 members in the House on 22 November when "the endeavour to introduce balottry . . . was thrown out, but . . . by nine voices". It might, thought Addison, "have prov'd very fatal to all ministrys had it succeeded".[121] The proposal was not revived after a final, crushing defeat in the session of 1710–11;[122] but although it naturally attracted most of its support at each stage from the minority party, whichever that happened to be, there were without doubt backbenchers on both sides who genuinely saw it as a blow for the freedom of the individual member — his freedom not only from official influence and perhaps official retribution, but also from the pressure of the party leaders. Naturally both the ministerial bench and the more power-conscious elements of both parties resisted it strongly from the start, and its failure is a fair yardstick of the difficulties which confronted the genuine country measure in an age which put the highest premium on party advantage.[123] Loyalty to one's own party, and fear of the opposing one, would, at a pinch, usually take first place in the order of priorities even with most independent backbench members, as well as with the clients of the party leaders; and the scope for truly bipartisan activities was in consequence severely restricted.

The country tradition, then, died hard in the early eighteenth century. Indeed its life was still far from extinct by 1714. But there was no longer in

---

* Cropley called it "the Venetian box". P.R.O. 30/24/21/148: 20 Feb.

Anne's reign a "Country party". Too many of the big issues which had provided such a party with a platform in the 1690's had either lost their relevance altogether, like the question of a standing army, or become essentially issues dividing Whig from Tory, as with the Land Resumption bills of 1711–12;* or alternatively, as we have seen, they had been diverted into unhealthy channels, like the investigation of government accounts and administrative abuses. With the notable exception of Place bills and clauses, it would be fair to say that neither the old political issues which the Country tradition perpetuated nor the new ones which it precipitated after 1702 normally generated anything approaching the interest and excitement of the great "party matters" of the reign. And even where they did it was never easy for backbench members to judge where the claims of "country" ended and those of party began.

* The revival of the land grants issue after 1710, and its transformation then from a Court/Country to a Whig/Tory dispute is a major question with which I shall hope to deal in my book on the Oxford ministry.

CHAPTER FIVE

The Clash of Interests

ALTHOUGH the country campaigns traced in the previous chapter — the periodic protests of the landed gentry in Parliament against "influence", administrative abuses, and all other developments which seemed to them to jeopardise the "established constitution" of the realm — claimed backing from both parties, it was no coincidence that it was the Tory squires who so often furnished the bulk of their support. There were times, indeed, when measures that were ostensibly in the country tradition seemed much more an integral part of the party struggle. Many Tory backbenchers in the years 1702–14 who joined in the clamour against placemen, denounced the growth of corruption, or cried wolf at the merest rumour of irregularities in the government's handling of public money, would not have found it easy to analyse their own motives accurately. The original association of country measures with Whig principles had no significance at all for the younger Tories who came into the House of Commons during the latter half of Anne's reign. To them most of these measures seemed perfectly in harmony with their own partisan instincts and prejudices. Even Place bills, promoted against the wishes of Tory ministers, did not appear in the least incongruous or incompatible with true party interests to the average Tory independent. For by 1710 he was not merely concerned, as a good country member, to limit the influence of the Crown in the House of Commons. Place bills had become for him just one expression of a general Tory protest against the threatened subversion of the landed interest in England — a protest not simply against the growing power of officialdom, but against all other novel (and therefore pernicious) forces in the State. To vote for a self-denying bill, or to take part in one of the witch-hunts initiated by the Commissioners of Public Accounts, was to strike a blow against such forces: alien forces whose influence seemed to threaten not only the "ancient purity" of Parliaments, but the very structure of society and the dwindling resources of the men of estates.

When the Landed Qualifications bill, imposing a property test on prospective M.P.s, was introduced into the Tory-dominated House of Commons in December 1710, it was said to have three targets, "Courtiers, military men, and merchants", equally in view.* And politics in the age of Anne cannot be fully understood unless we appreciate that in the eyes of many backbench Tories of the day all three were essentially elements of the same problem: the desperate problem of how, in Sir John Pakington's memorable words, "to prevent the beggary of the nation, to prevent the moneyed and military men becoming lords of us who have the lands".[1] We have already considered the part played by principle in the party politics of the early eighteenth century. But principle has rarely if ever been the sole *raison d'être* of a political party. We would naturally expect most modern parties to represent recognisable interests in the community as well as to give expression to certain distinctive principles; and it need not therefore surprise us to find some evidence, *prima facie* evidence if nothing more, that one at least of the forerunners of all political parties in England was identified with the cause of a particular social and economic group. Certainly the Tory party of Queen Anne's reign both claimed to represent and was widely assumed to represent the diverse but none the less cohesive elements which made up the "landed interest" of contemporary parlance.

The spectre of being submerged in Parliament by a rising tide of placemen, army and navy officers and pensioners was clearly an important aspect of the prevailing Tory phobia of the age. But this in itself was not a fear confined specifically to the Tories. There were sometimes social prejudices as well as constitutional principles involved in the support of Place bills by the Country Whigs, as the mordant comments of Lowther and Wortley Montagu on the army officers (albeit fellow Whigs) who were usurping precious borough and county seats† make abundantly clear. Even that Junto stalwart, General Harry Mordaunt, who as both an army officer and a peer's son with landed property in Berkshire and Surrey[2] could speak with more detachment than most, once told the House of Commons that a man "possessed of a good estate . . . did not lie open to the temptations that might bias persons who had their fortunes to make against the interest of their country".[3] More bitter, however, than the strictures on "men in place", more vigorously sustained (especially as the Spanish Succession war dragged on year after year), and much more clearly a party war-cry was the Tory protest against the advance of the "moneyed men". It was from this quarter, more than from any other, that the typical Tory squire — rightly or wrongly

* Burnet, vi, 40. See also pp. 179–80 below.　　　　† See pp. 126–8.

— anticipated the chief threat to the political dominance of his own class and the political future of his own party. Even the dissenters and the Dutch could not arouse his deepest animosities more readily than those who, despite having little stake in the land of the country, and therefore in Tory eyes no prescriptive right to a place in the governing class, had waxed fat on the profits of war, and were using their new wealth to wrest political power from those whose birthright it was.

That these fears and resentments existed and that they were frequently voiced no one reading the political correspondence of this period could seriously doubt. But how profound their influence was on the character of politics in the age of Anne is a real problem. If it can be established quite firmly that sectional interests, and above all economic interests, played a major part in perpetuating the dichotomy within the political nation after 1701, the basic division between Whig and Tory must necessarily assume fresh dimensions and enhanced importance: it must appear as a rational and realistic division, irrespective of disputes over questions of principle and policy. Not only could we conclude that the parties themselves bore even less resemblance to the insubstantial, artificial creations of the Bolingbroke legend than we had supposed; it might not be far-fetched to regard the conflict between them in the years from 1702 to 1714 as being in one sense a 'class war', provided the phrase could be divorced from its nineteenth- and twentieth-century associations. The hypothesis is attractive and even plausible. But it can be no more than a hypothesis as long as so much rests upon mere assumption, especially as one of the most fruitful breeding-grounds of these assumptions proves to be the polemical literature of the period, which is particularly rich in variations on the theme of animosity between the squire and the City businessman. Can we assume, in the first place, that the Tory country gentleman who fulminated against the moneyed man was a genuine victim of fiscal inequalities and economic circumstances? Is he not more likely to have been a prey to unscrupulous propagandists within his own party? When so eminent a student of the Stuart economy and social order as Sir George Clark consistently emphasises the close integration of the landed and moneyed classes by the late seventeenth and early eighteenth centuries, and claims that 'this conflict of interests' so dear to contemporary pamphleteers, and to party leaders in search of a rallying-cry, 'was almost fictitious'* the political historian must review his own evidence on these

---

* *The Later Stuarts* (2nd edn. 1955), p. 36. It must be said that Sir George has never deviated from this opinion. In 1946 he wrote that by the early 18th century 'it is hard to find a class of mere landlords' (*The Wealth of England from 1496 to 1760*, p. 159), while

questions most carefully. Again, even though the prejudice that did exist among Tory landowners should prove to be not entirely irrational, are we entitled to assume that it was widespread? Was it, perhaps, confined only to an unfortunate and vociferous minority?

It is to the economic and fiscal background to politics that we must look at the outset in the hope of finding answers to all these questions, and so testing the assumptions in which the theory of a 'clash of interests' is rooted.[4] One thing at least seems beyond doubt. During the years between 1688 and 1714 the position of 'the businessman' in the national life was transformed. This term, in its modern sense at least, was not yet part of English usage.[5] But in seeking a general label which can be applied to a man of substance whose principal income was derived in any way from commerce, finance or industry, the historian of this period really needs some alternative to the contemporary "moneyed man", a pejorative expression which, as we shall later see, often meant different things to different people. The term 'businessman' meets this need, and also perhaps by its very associations helps us to appreciate something of the novelty and sophistication of the changes which came over the economy during the reigns of the last two Stuarts. Gregory King, in assessing the various ranks of the social order in 1688, inserted 2000 families of "merchants and traders by sea" in between over 16,500 landowning families of noble or gentle status and the other grades of secular society which he identifies. Had he written in 1714, however, instead of in 1688 King would surely have found it necessary to introduce fresh categories altogether, in recognition of the growing complexity of the business world over the previous quarter of a century. At the very least he would have had to devise some composite expression to embrace not merely merchants but bankers, scriveners, stockbrokers and factors — none of them strictly new phenomena, but all of them (save perhaps the last) invested since the Revolution with a quite new significance. Similarly the expansion of industry which had accompanied the two great wars against Louis XIV would have made it incumbent on any scientific social analyst in 1714 to distinguish men, like Sir Owen Buckingham and Sir Ambrose Crowley, for instance,[6] who were primarily and essentially manufacturers from those landowners who supplemented their incomes from the profits of industrial enterprises.*

in his Whidden Lectures, delivered in 1960, he observed that at the end of the Stuart period the interests of landed men and businessmen 'had become fused in the common interests of the governing class' (*Three Aspects of Stuart England*, p. 42).

* Prominent examples of the second type among M.P.s of the period 1702–14 were Sir

It was without any doubt the changes in the world of finance which made the deepest impression on the contemporary mind. Not everyone may have understood the nature of the financial revolution, obscured as it was by what Swift once called "such an unintelligible jargon of terms . . . as were never known in any other age or country in the world";[7] but there were few who did not recognise that a revolution of some kind had taken place since William III's accession. How could they have failed to do so when by 1710 a single word inserted in the Queen's Speech could cause a flutter on the Exchange,* and politicians assessed a ministry's prospects as much on the basis of the fluctuations of the stock-market and the state of credit as on a reading of the signs at Court or in Parliament. After the replacement of Godolphin by a new Treasury Commission in August not a few Whigs shared James Lowther's opinion that "these new managers wil be hard sett . . . to hold the staff long" with public credit so shaky and Bank stock having recently fallen 20 per cent. "The elections go entirely one way", Craggs observed in October, ". . . [but] my greatest fear is a general stop to credit, & then if they [the Tory ministers] were Caesars & Solomons we must, after all our great successes, truckle at last [to France]".[8]

Two developments of the early and mid-1690's did most to effect this transformation. One was a fundamental change in the methods of government finance. This change had its origins in the new strength which parliamentary control over war supplies imparted to the foundations of credit, and it was signified most clearly by the institution of the funded National Debt and by the establishment of the Bank of England in 1693–4. A crucial factor here was the decision of King William's financial advisers, notably Charles Montagu, to meet at least part of the cost of a war of unimagined proportions by raising long-term loans on the security of specific taxes. The Crown now preferred to attract investors with the guarantee, underwritten by Parliament, of a good rate of interest on annuities which they might enjoy for life, or even ensure thereafter for their dependants; whereas in the past governments had tempted them with the lure of a quick short-term profit, leaving prospective creditors to weigh this advantage against the uncertain prospect of an early redemption of their capital. The encouraging response to Montagu's pilot scheme of 1693,[9] and the fair degree

Roger Mostyn, Sir William Blackett, John Hanbury, Sir Humphrey Mackworth, Lord Castlecomer and Sir Richard Myddleton.

* This was the substitution of the word "indulgence" for "toleration" in the Queen's normal reference to the dissenters in her opening speech from the Throne. See *Wentworth Papers*, p. 158.

of success attending other attempts in William's reign to raise loans by funding devices, ensured that such measures would play a key part in financing the still more expensive war of the Spanish Succession; and indeed between 1704 and 1710 a total of seven loans, bringing in nearly £9,000,000, were floated by the offer of annuities. The second development, one which preceded as well as accompanied the change in government financial methods, was the extraordinary rise in the popularity of the joint-stock company as a field of investment during the years between 1689 and 1695. By the end of that period there is evidence of dealings in the shares of at least 93 English joint-stock companies,[10] promoting a rich variety of home and overseas enterprises. By far the greater number had been founded since the Revolution, many since 1692, and their paid-up capital of at least £4,000,000 represented over 10% of the estimated value of all the personal property in the country. Moreover, roughly three-quarters of this capital was subscribed to six major undertakings, of which a long-established one, the East India Company, and an entirely novel one, the Bank of England, were easily the most important.*

With the investing public caught up in the magnetic coils of a system whose mysteries were yet imperfectly understood, even by politicians and financiers, it was not to be expected that the next two decades would be without their anxieties for the new *rentier* class and above all for private speculators. There were several periods between 1695 and 1714 when even investors in public ventures had cause to fear for their money, the Bank of England being called on to survive dangerous runs on its cash resources in 1696, 1701, 1708 and 1714; while during the first and most disastrous of the periods of crisis, that of 1696–7, most of the smaller joint-stock companies, so hopefully constituted in the early 90's, went under for good. And yet once the capacity of the system, or at least of the more robust elements within it, to survive these shocks was demonstrated, investment in both company and government stocks continued to build up rapidly. By 1703 the share capital of the surviving English companies was already almost double what it had been in 1695, and by 1714 it was in the region of £20,000,000.

A vast increase in the total volume of investment, however, was but one aspect of the new commercial and financial revolution. Other distinctive features had already become clear by 1695, features which were to remain prominent throughout the reign of Anne. For one thing a new mechanism had developed to facilitate business dealings. Even before 1688 the bill of

* The remaining 4 were the Africa Company, the New River Company, the Hudson's Bay Company and the so-called "Million Adventure" or Million Bank.

exchange had begun to replace bullion as the standard medium of international payments.[11] After the Revolution domestic transactions, too, were greatly simplified and stimulated. Partly this was due to the circulation of the Bank of England's notes,* in addition to Exchequer bills and other negotiable securities; but the process owed most to the recognised, if not yet formalised, emergence of a 'Stock Exchange', based on the old Royal Exchange and the two big coffee-houses in 'Change Alley, Garraway's and Jonathan's. John Houghton's *Price of the Stocks* was published to meet the need for a standard guide to current market values, and by 1694 it was quoting the share prices of as many as 50 companies. Above all, by the middle of William's reign the stockbroker, or "stockjobber" as he was more often called, had become an absolutely indispensable limb of this vigorous young tree that had been grafted on to the stout old wood of London commercial life. It is quite true that the decline of credit and loss of confidence which marked the years 1696–7 temporarily stunted some of the more premature growth. The stockjobber — the principal scapegoat for the failures and heavy losses then incurred — had his activities circumscribed to some extent by Parliament.[12] Houghton's Lists quoted only 7 major securities in 1698, and for a while some newspapers ceased to carry any stock-market news. Yet if some of its shoots were blighted the tree itself remained basically unharmed, and by 1702 there was no longer much doubt that it had become a permanent part of the landscape. The rise and fall of share prices, and, above all, of Bank and East India Company stock, was to be recognised thereafter as "the pulse of the City & whereby the state of her health is discern'd".[13]

Meanwhile the habits and attitudes, as well as the techniques, of the business world had experienced a transformation. One development already under way by the mid-1690's was to be of far-reaching importance in the next two decades. This was the diversion of a vast amount of both private and corporate wealth from the risky field of overseas trade, where the normal hazards of storm and tempest had recently been dwarfed by the far likelier danger of loss by enemy action, into the more alluring channels now open at home. Here the habits formed in time of war were not easily changed when hostilities ceased, either between 1697 and 1701 or again after the spring of 1712. Even in the last winter of William III's reign, for instance, we find one member of the House of Commons bemoaning the fact that "our trading is now dead; . . . for [a] merchant finds a better return between the Excheqr & the Exchange then he make[s] by running a hazard

---

* These were not officially legal tender, but were from the first accepted without question in payment of taxes.

to the Indies".[14] And though the reiteration of a similar theme over twelve years later by the Tory sponsors of an act for reducing interest rates[15] may seem hard to square with the record levels achieved by English trade as a whole by 1712,[16] it is probably true that these levels would have been significantly higher had there been less investment in "the Funds" or in the various industrial activities to which war had given great stimulus.[17] At any rate, the fact that so many Tories believed it to be so is of considerable significance to us, since, as we shall see, it goes some way to explain why their animosity towards the "moneyed interest" in politics was sometimes more discriminating than is often imagined.

One further feature of the new financial world, and not the least striking, was the immense concentration of wealth, prestige and power in the hands of the directors and principal shareholders of a tiny number of privileged corporations. Three such corporations stand out as the colossi of the post-Revolution period: the Bank, the East India Company (which was in practice two companies rather than one for some years after the great split of 1698), and that much later creation, the South Sea Company, which was not founded until 1711. These three giants dominated the whole arena of business and finance not merely by the overwhelming size of their share capital, but because of their commanding interest in the National Debt. The Bank, since 1694 an indispensable agency for facilitating government borrowing, had by 1710 increased its original nominal capital of £1,200,000 to about £5,500,000. Its reputation and its apparently unshakeable alliance with the Queen's administration were such that in February 1709 the subscription list for its new 6% loan to the Godolphin ministry, which involved an increase in its stock of well over £2,000,000, was filled in under four hours; and the sight of hundreds of prospective investors being turned away disappointed from its offices in Grocers' Hall before one o'clock in the afternoon seemed one of the marvels of the age even to Englishmen, let alone to dazed and incredulous Continentals. As the Earl of Sunderland proudly wrote to his father-in-law the same evening: "The like I believe was never known in any country".[18] And yet even the glory of the Bank was slightly dimmed two and a half years later by the spectacular birth of the South Sea Company, with its £9,000,000 of share capital derived from the compulsory conversion of short-term government securities into company stock. By 1714 the three great corporate bodies were together credited with almost 40 per cent of the total funded debt of £40,357,011.

It was inevitable that changes of this magnitude should bring to many individual businessmen spectacular accretions of personal wealth, enriching successful stockbrokers like "Vulture" Hopkins[19] and especially the magic circle of City potentates who held governorships or directorships of the great corporations. This is not to say that huge City fortunes were almost unknown before the Revolution: far from it.[20] But there can be little doubt that the opportunities created by the new conditions of the 1690's were considerably greater and that they were much more widely exploited. It may be that deliberate 'playing' of the stock-market in the optimistic early years of the decade was less common than many contemporaries imagined,[21] though the fact that the amount of Royal African stock bought and sold in a mere five weeks during 1691 was equal to almost two-thirds of the company's nominal capital suggests the contrary.[22] It is clear at any rate that some of the bigger operators, with organised intelligence at their disposal, like the wine merchant Samuel Shepheard the elder, the goldsmith-banker Sir Francis Child, and the presiding genius of the Bank of England and the New East India Company Sir Gilbert Heathcote, made big capital gains by speculative dealings. In the first great period of the Bank's prosperity, for instance — the years from 1697 to 1700 when the price of its stock soared from 51 to 148½ — Heathcote is said to have cleared a profit of £60,000.[23] Quite apart from the rapid accumulation of personal fortunes, however, the family background of many of the most successful business tycoons of the period 1689–1714 heightened contemporary awareness of the fact that a revolutionary change was in progress. It did not escape notice, for example, that Samuel Shepheard, as the son of a fairly prosperous City merchant, was something of a deviation from type. Heathcote and Child, by contrast, were first-generation London financiers. Neither of them, it is true, came from wholly obscure social backgrounds; Child was the son of a Wiltshire clothier and Heathcote of a Chesterfield tradesman who had sufficient means to give his heir a Cambridge education; but there were many other rising stars of the business world at this time whose origins were notoriously humble. Sir Henry Furnese was a case in point. In an age of financial giants Furnese stood on a pinnacle of his own, if only for the astonishing confidence and success with which in Anne's reign he challenged single-handed the most powerful syndicates, English and international, in the field where he made the bulk of his great fortune, that of army remittances. Yet this man was the son of a Sandwich grocer who had died bankrupt, and he had come to London originally as apprentice to a hosier in Cheapside.* The father of

* Furnese gained his first remittance contract in 1703, and from Feb. 1705 to Aug. 1710 he engrossed all the valuable contracts for paying the forces in the Low Countries, Portugal and Spain. See J. G. Sperling, 'Godolphin and the Organization of Public Credit,

John Blunt, the ingenious secretary of the Sword Blade Company who became a major promoter of the South Sea scheme in 1711, and whose assets by 1721 were estimated at £184,000, was a Rochester shoe-maker; while Sir Ambrose Crowley, who enjoyed the unique distinction of being not only the owner of a large shipping fleet but the greatest ironmaster in Europe, was immortalised by Addison as Jack Anvil, "a person of no extraction" who had "begun the world with a small parcel of rusty iron".[24]

"I daily see rich coaches, fine liveries, splendid equipages, luxurious tables, numerous attendants & several other expensive waies of state", grumbled one Tory squire in 1702. "These are not supported for a small fund or a narrow bottom. A great deal goes to keep up this sort of state & bravery. And yet I am certain that some of these Gent[n] not many years agoe were scarce able to keep a pad nag & a drab coat; and now a Gent[n] of 5000 l. p. ann. is not a fitt companion for their greatness".[25] In the eyes of such critics the offence was aggravated because such an important element in the new City *élite* of Anne's day was made up of businessmen of French or Dutch extraction. Three of the most powerful backers of the South Sea Company, Sir Theodore Janssen, Matthew Decker and Sir James Bateman, were notable examples; Decker, indeed, had only been naturalised in 1702. Peter Delmé, John Devink, John Lambert, the Papillons and the Desbouveries were other prominent representatives of a cosmopolitan breed. Clearly, a far from unimportant factor influencing the attitude of many country gentlemen of the early eighteenth century towards the extraordinary financial and commercial developments of their time was the prominence with which both social upstarts and foreigners figured in them; and it is one we shall do well to remember when assessing the political implications of this attitude.

The most powerful determinant by far, however, was the stark contrast which so many landowners recognised between their own lot and that "sort of state and bravery" which the City magnates were able to maintain. The Spanish Succession war was on the whole a grim period for those middling and small gentry whose income was derived solely, or almost exclusively, from their rents.* The distinction between them and their more fortunate brethren is important; indeed it is quite basic to any consideration of the

---

1702–10' (Cambridge Ph.D. thesis, 1955), pp. 187–95 *passim*; Marjorie McHattie, 'Mercantile Interests in the House of Commons, 1710–13' (Manchester M.A. thesis, 1949), p. 55.

* It is not possible to question the existence in the early 18th century of a numerous landlord class which was entirely dependent economically on the land. Such doubts as have been expressed on this score (see e.g. p. 150 n. * above) have never been substantiated.

landed interest at this time, whether in an economic or a political context. There were, of course, country gentlemen who invested money in "the Funds", laid out tidy sums in the purchase of lottery tickets or dabbled in joint-stock enterprises. At the same time there were those who by capitalising on their political talents, or with the help of friends in high places, managed to supplement their revenues from the emoluments of public offices that might be worth anything from two or three hundred to a thousand pounds a year, and very occasionally more. And there were also the fortunate few who had mineral deposits on their estates (like the Blacketts of Northumberland, whose income was put at £10,000 a year in 1705), or who succeeded in making highly advantageous marriages. But the general rule in Augustan society, as we should expect, was that wealth attracted wealth. Most of the plums both in the place-market and the marriage-market fell to the aristocracy or to rich and well-connected county families. It was they, too, who were usually most ready and able to invest in the City or in the National Debt. With his great estates in Surrey, his own stake in the Turkey Company and his eldest son safely married to a "West India fortune", Sir Richard Onslow, for one, had no cause to fear by the end of Anne's reign for the future of his family.[26] When James Lowther became M.P. for Cumberland in 1708 he could look to a place in the Ordnance Office as well as to his coalmines near Whitehaven to swell the income from his rents; so that to find him buying South Sea stock in 1711 and then watching with his Whig friends in London for the judicious moment to sell[27] need not surprise us. It has been questioned, however, whether even among great landlords holdings of stock or of government securities were customarily very large.[28] And it is quite certain that the small country squires lacked in most cases the resources and in many cases the will to break in any way with their traditional economic habits. Their attitude might conceivably have been different had one of the experimental land banks of 1695–6 become established as a sound business proposition. As it was, the depressing contrast between their failure and the spectacular progress of the Bank of England only served to confirm many landlords in their suspicion of the City and all its works. The country gentleman of modest means, for psychological as well as economic reasons, simply could not avail himself of the varied opportunities open to his more prosperous and less inhibited neighbours.

We do need to recognise, therefore, that the so-called "landed interest" of Queen Anne's reign was an economic and social unit only in the sense that as a class it faced certain common problems. As one leading Tory, William Bromley, put it in 1707, "I believe all country gentlemen are under the like pressures and uneasiness"; the real trouble, as the same writer saw it, was that "all cannot so well bear them".[29] It was the plight of the less fortunate, of the numerous body of those "who have not other supports then Land",[30] and the vivid contrast it afforded with the affluence of the business community, which was the dry tinder of most of the political animosity in this period that was social or economic in origin. That much is clear. But just how serious was the plight of the "mere gentry" in the years between 1702 and 1714? This we must know before it becomes possible to judge how fierce or how widespread was the blaze when the tinder was ignited. At first sight the problem may seem to be little more than a variant of a well-worn theme: the phenomenon of the declining social group (or at least of the group which *feels* itself to be losing ground) in a period of acute political conflict. Under scrutiny, however, the situation in Anne's reign reveals certain entirely distinctive features which render any facile comparison with other periods, say with the early seventeenth century, largely invalid. Some of the difficulties facing landed men in the post-Revolution era were admittedly the product of long-term trends. But in the main they stemmed either from novel circumstances or from unfortunate coincidences: some of them by their very nature temporary factors, but none the less unpalatable for being so. And it was partly for this reason, perhaps, that the ill feeling which they aroused in the victims was directed more against an alien social group, the "moneyed men", than against the more fortunate members of their own class.

The most unhappy coincidence of factors confronting the landowning community was the combination of a new system of direct taxation, bearing very largely on income from rents, with the landlord's frequent inability either to raise rents or even to collect the full value of the rents on which he was being taxed. "Tenants are breaking every day", Bromley somewhat gratuitously told his old friend James Grahme, who was only too conversant with the country gentleman's dilemma, "and the quarterly payments of the taxes takes away the little money we receive".* With the possible exception of a few areas where farming was especially profitable, the period 1690–1714 seems to have been one of exceptional stability in rents. But the level of rents in itself was probably not the most serious local problem facing the ordinary squire. He was harder hit by the exceptional number of "bad years" when

* Levens MSS.: 11 Oct. 1707. Grahme soon afterwards contemplated the sale of his beautiful Tudor house at Levens in Westmorland to relieve his own embarrassments, but decided to cling on in the hope of reaping some reward from the period of Tory supremacy after Sept. 1710.

for a variety of reasons tenants' rents fell heavily in arrears. The situation varied considerably from one region to another. In 1707, for example, the Leicestershire gentry had not much to complain about except "a little slowness in tenants to pay their rents, more than formerly", whereas in Oxfordshire owners protested that with "every day" that passed rent returns were worsening.[31] But in the "seven barren years" at the end of the seventeenth century many landlords probably fared at least as badly as Sir John Mordaunt, some of whose tenants had "bein in ill serconstances a good while" by 1701 and were badly in arrears with their rents;[32] and similarly the agrarian depression of 1709–10, when harvests were appalling and farmers suffered heavy losses of livestock, can have left very few proprietors unaffected. Ironically they had fared little better from the glut of arable produce and the low grain prices of the years 1702–6. It was then, indeed, that the knight of the shire for Derbyshire received some of his most plaintive letters from friends and constituents, letters complaining that "the burden of taxes . . . lie very heavy by reason of the lowness of our markets for all commodities that relate to the farmers", and that at a time when "never was less money stirring, or commodities (except foreign) cheaper" nothing was being done "to enable the owners to pay so great a tax" as four shillings in the pound on land.[33]

The great scourge of the 'pure landlord', without doubt, was the new land tax. Both in its earliest form of 1693–7 and in its standard eighteenth-century form thereafter this was the most important single item in the government's annual revenue.* The landowner also suffered indirectly, as did every other section of the community, from the additional duties levied during the Spanish Succession war on a multitude of imports and consumer goods, and not least from the excise on malt. But the land tax, at its war-time rate of four shillings in the pound, was his own special cross, and it was not one that could be lightly or cheerfully borne. Because the tax was not, by the standards of a modern Treasury official, a particularly efficient one it would be wrong to assume that the weight of the burden it imposed was generally exaggerated by the country gentleman. For one thing it was a great deal more efficient than the old subsidy, or indeed than any similar imposition which had preceded it, save perhaps the Assessment as it had been administered in the 1640's and 1650's. Secondly, although the tax was apportioned unscientifically between one part of the country and another, so that a Cornish, Worcestershire or Yorkshire squire, for example, had little genuine

---

* In war-time, when the tax was levied at its maximum rate, a yield of a little over £2 million a year was normally anticipated from it.

cause for complaint,[34] it fell on the more prosperous and populous areas in the south, the home counties, the midlands and East Anglia with maximum severity.[35]

The most galling aspect of the land tax, however, for those who were saddled with it in its most punitive form for eleven successive years of Anne's reign was the relative ease with which those who enjoyed large incomes but owned little landed property were able to escape it. The avowed intention of its original projectors in 1693 had been to catch all incomes in their net, but any pretence which the imposition had to comprehensiveness had disappeared long before William's death.[36] The whole situation was aggravated by a significant change in the attitude of businessmen towards landed property in the late seventeenth and early eighteenth centuries, a change for which those who have preferred to emphasise the community of interest rather than the cleavage within the governing class have made too little allowance. Merchants and other members of the urban middle class who had made a substantial fortune in trade or in the law were no longer as eager as they had once been to buy large landed estates of several thousand acres and establish county families. In the past land had been coveted by the City capitalist for two reasons: as a means of acquiring social prestige and as a secure and often profitable investment. But government finance during the Augsburg war detracted a good deal from its appeal. Money sunk in land was as safe as ever. But money lent to the government seemed almost as safe; it usually promised a higher return than the 5% which land was normally reckoned to yield;[37] and it brought in income that was unlikely to be taxed directly. The successful businessman found at the same time that his social and political ambitions could be well enough served by marrying his daughter into the aristocracy or the upper strata of the landed gentry, and by buying a few hundred acres and a country mansion in the home counties for purely residential purposes. A few big London families, the Duncombes, the Childs, the Bankses, still accumulated large country estates between the Revolution and the death of Anne; but they were the exception. How many merchants with £20,000 to spare in 1709 could have been blamed for purchasing Bank of England stock at a time when the Bank was paying out no less than $28\frac{1}{4}\%$ in dividends in the space of eighteen months,[38] in preference to buying a heavily-taxed estate of £1000 or £1200 a year in Kent or Essex?

It is understandable, then, that the country gentleman of a few hundreds a year, living in any region that experienced the full rigour of the land tax, should have been readily convinced that war and its concomitants, while enriching men whom he regarded as his social inferiors, was steadily encom-

passing his own ruin. For such gentry not even the campaigns in the Peninsula, over which Tory leaders from time to time enthused, offered any
consolation: ". . . since we must never give over the war till we have con-
quered Spain", wrote a Northamptonshire squire on hearing the news of
Brihuega, "it is high time for poor country gentlemen with small estates to
conclude that all they have may not be enough to effect that, wch even Don
Quixot himself woud have thought impossible".[39] Yet war was not the sole
cause of this plight; nor even the coincidence of war with unfavourable
agricultural conditions. It was not only the tax-collector who made heavy
demands on incomes which were stationary or even shrinking. Heavy social
pressures, too, were being brought to bear on the English squire, pressures
which he found hard to resist though often enough he could ill afford to
succumb to them. In the post-Revolution period the standards of living of the
upper classes were rising appreciably. The status-symbols of the age were
the new mansion house, or at very least the building of a modern extension
to an old one, the park where nature was improved by man, and the display
of fine and expensive furniture. Even the nobility and the well-to-do gentry
frequently had to borrow extensively to fulfil their social and aesthetic
ambitions.[40] For the smaller landed proprietor the strain imposed on limited
resources by the urge to 'keep up with the Joneses' can be well imagined.
He could, and often did, mortgage his estates up to the hilt to pay his bills.
But even mortgages at reasonable rates were not so easy to come by at a time
when there were so many attractive alternatives open to the investor. The
wealthy Cumberland mineowner, James Lowther, doubtless caused a few
eyebrows to rise when he declined to invest some of his spare capital in
improvements to Whitehaven harbour, preferring instead to lend it "to
gentlemen of the country upon good security in these times that are so hard
upon country gentlemen".[41] Furthermore, those owners who were tempted
or forced to sell part of their land as a last way out of their difficulties found
that by the middle and later years of Anne's reign the market price in some
parts of the country had slumped well below the twenty years' purchase
which had been the norm throughout the seventeenth century.[42]

    The fiscal, economic and social background to British politics in the age
of Anne thus affords plentiful evidence of a real and rational clash of interests
in society. To say that this was a clash between the "moneyed" and the
"landed" interests would be to over-simplify the situation. But one can
fully appreciate why country gentlemen with no other resources than rents
at their command should have deeply resented the prosperity of upstart
bourgeois, whose surplus capital was not even ploughed back into foreign

trade, let alone invested in land, and whose incomes were substantially untaxed. It was a situation which bewildered the Duke of Shrewsbury after his return to England in 1706. "The members of the H: of C: are so good to load [with taxes] land, malt, salt, and every thing which ruins their own estates", he wrote, "whilst citizens not worth 100 l. at the begining of these warrs are now worth 200,000 l."[43] No doubt Tory pamphleteers and political newswriters exploited these anomalies cleverly and exaggerated the proportions and extent of the conflict.* But their propaganda would have lost much of its force had it been divorced from economic realities. Nor could it have succeeded, one must add, had not two further assumptions been firmly rooted in the country gentleman's mind. One was the conviction that those who paid the piper had every right to call the tune at Westminster. "I know not who are your candidates", the member for Knaresborough told one elector in a Yorkshire borough, "but hope you will take care to choose some honest gent of the County whose estates may entitle them to contribute to the Public Taxes".[44] The other was the unquestioning acceptance of the fact that landownership was synonymous with social and political responsibility, and that the gentry class was the only firm rock on which the constitution could stand. When Lord Ashburnham put up his son as a candidate at Hastings in 1701 it was on the basis of his "stake in our English hedge" that he sought to recommend him to the electors; and soon afterwards he wrote:

Whenever England comes to be settled and made happy it must be done by councils of such who love their country and value their estates beyond any thing else of any consideration whatsoever.[45]

A Lincolnshire baronet ten years later was roused to more than customary eloquence on the same theme: "for when landed gent. represent us in Parliamt. & do our business at home [and] in the country we may justly look for better times & that our tottering constitution may be once more fixed to the confusion & amazement of all its adversaries".[46] It was partly because these sentiments were shared by the overwhelming bulk of landowners, peers and commoners alike, that the clash of economic interests became so much a matter of political concern, as more and more moneyed men with little or no stake in the land bought their way into parliamentary seats and political prominence.

* * *

* In 1705, for example, John Dyer made the hackles of his readers rise by circulating a wild rumour of "17 strangers ... like to be chosen in Wiltshire, not one of them having a foot of land in that county ...". Dyer's Newsletter, 5 May 1705.

By the time Queen Anne came to the throne the class feeling which had been gaining force in England since the early 1690's had already begun to affect the character of politics. For at least one obvious reason it was inevitable that it should have done so. In William III's last Parliament, as Dr. Walcott has shown, there were already 61 businessmen, including manufacturers and local traders, sitting in the House of Commons.[47] True, this was rather less than one eighth of the total membership, and this proportion did not increase spectacularly in the next twelve years: it reached a peak of one seventh in the middle years of Anne.* But it was a segment of the House which always contained many individuals of exceptional influence outside as well as inside Parliament. It also included a large majority whose interests in the City kept them in town throughout the session, so that the businessmen made up a far higher proportion of the *active* membership of the Commons than of the total complement. With so direct a confrontation of landed and commercial interests in Parliament, therefore, it was unavoidable that their rivalry should become a leading political issue. That it should develop into an issue between Whig and Tory was equally predictable from the mid-90's onwards. The two most startling symbols of the new financial and economic power of the City, the Bank of England and the New East India Company, were both essentially Whig creations, owing their very existence largely to the patronage and encouragement of Montagu and other Whig ministers. The Land Bank experiments of 1695–6 were conducted in a highly partisan atmosphere against a background of Tory pamphleteering denouncing the Bank of England and advocating "the freeing of our lands from the servitude and tyranny of a devouring usury";[48] and their failure subsequently helped to resharpen party animosities in William's later years. So that even before 1701 the identification of each of the conflicting elements in society with a particular party, the landed men with the Tories, the monied men with the Whigs, was far more than a crude propaganda device. From 1701 onwards, with politics becoming increasingly polarised, and with a new Continental war ensuring not merely the continuance but the aggravation of existing social tensions, the identification of "party" and "interest" seemed still more realistic.

---

* I have identified roughly 80 such members among the M.P.s returned between 1708 and 1710, including 8 Scots. Marjorie McHattie ('Mercantile Interests in the House of Commons, 1710–13', Manchester M.A. thesis, 1949) found 64 men who were 'habitually and primarily engaged in trade, manufacturing or finance' among the 558 English and Scots members returned in 1710. This, however, was a Parliament dominated to an unprecedented extent by the Tories.

But having said so much it at once becomes necessary to affirm that this is an aspect of contemporary politics which remains (as it was at the time) peculiarly susceptible to exaggeration and distortion. One certainly cannot assume, for instance, that the Tory party even in the House of Commons was basically a one-class party; and to depict the Whigs in such colours would be quite ludicrous. Among the Whig members of every House in Anne's reign were many impeccable country gentlemen, landowners with no significant commercial or financial interests outside their own estates and often with no professional career to make. Leaving aside the leading "Country Whigs" whom we have already encountered, a random selection from one Parliament, that of 1710–13, in which the Whigs were heavily outnumbered, might have included Sir Edmund Denton of Hillesden and Preston Bisset, who had sat for Buckinghamshire since 1708; Norton Paulet, "a gentleman of 2000 l. per annum"[49] representing Petersfield; Matthew Ducie Moreton, knight of the shire for Gloucestershire, who had long since given up an army career to take over family estates that were extensive enough to justify the grant of a peerage in 1715; Richard Edge-cumbe and Hugh Fortescue, two wealthy pillars of the Whig cause in the south-west, the first of whom was to achieve a peerage under George II;[50] Harry Grey Nevil, the son of a well-to-do Berkshire landowner and Whig knight of the shire,* whose marriage had brought him a large estate in Northumberland; John Morley Trevor (Lewes) and Edmund Dunch (Cricklade), who had estates of £6000 and £4000 a year respectively in Sussex and Buckinghamshire;[51] and William Grimston of Gorhambury, who sat on his own interest for St. Albans, and who provides an excellent example of an already wealthy young landowner (his income from his estates was £6000 a year) who became even wealthier during Anne's reign by marrying into a handsome City fortune.[52] These members and many others like them were landowners of entirely independent means; even Dunch, who in common with other Whigs in this Parliament who were country gentlemen by inheritance (Thomas Erle, Sir William Ashburnham and Hugh Boscawen, for instance) continued to enjoy over and above his landed revenues the bonus of an official salary.

If the party's parliamentary representatives are a reliable guide, Whiggery still had a fairly strong hold during Anne's reign over the upper gentry in many parts of the country. The political and social correspondence of the day on the whole confirms this. Out of 21 Whigs ejected by Sir Edward

* Richard Nevil of Billingsbere, M.P. for Berkshire 1705–10. Grey Nevil sat for Wendover 1710–13.

Seymour from the Devonshire bench of magistrates between 1702 and 1704 six were country gentlemen with incomes of £1000 a year or more, while in Kent even the Tories admitted that "the very great majority of our richest gentlemen are Whigs".[53] In election correspondence, particularly, we encounter a plentiful stock of Whig landlords, in which knights and baronets figure prominently: men who never found their way into Parliament in Anne's reign but who were very active locally. There was Sir Francis Drake, who did manful work for his party in Devon and bestowed his patronage on the brilliant young Peter King at Beeralston, and Sir William Craven, a prominent lieutenant of the Spencers and Montagus in Northamptonshire.[54] There was also that choleric Suffolk gentleman, Sir Richard Gipps, who, not content with breathing fire and brimstone on his Tory neighbours, once sallied forth into the west country to beard Seymour himself in his den at Totnes; and who was so spendidly uninhibited by the hopeless task of contesting a Tory pocket borough that "the first thing he did in that town towards gaining an interest was to single out the parson of the parish, to prove to him that there was no God".[55] The zeal of Whig squires in promoting the party interest in constituencies was not always proportionate to the size of their rent-rolls. Ralph Thoresby tells of an unfortunate "gent: of 400 l. p. an." in Yorkshire who continued his political agitation even after the last election returns had been made in 1710, and who "was barbarously slain near Hull, for arguing for the Low Church".[56] In short, the familiar old textbook picture of the Whig party under William III and Anne as being primarily a party of aristocrats, merchants and dissenters fails to stand up to even the most superficial examination. The Whigs drew support from all sections of the community. And for all the party's heavy dependence for its parliamentary representatives on such sources as the legal profession, the army and the business classes it would scarcely have been a viable political alternative to its opponents without its many adherents among the country gentlemen.

The Tories for their part, though having a stronger claim than the Whigs to be the champions of specific interests, can certainly not be comprehended by any such generalisation as 'the party of the squirearchy and the Anglican clergy'. How, for instance, could one neatly fit into this formula a man like Thomas Halsey? He was Tory knight of the shire for Hertfordshire in eight Parliaments before his death in 1715; yet his will included legacies of £11,000 to each of his younger sons to bind them apprentice to a trade.[57] Or how does one classify an eccentric like Sir Humphrey Mackworth?: a country gentleman by birth but also the most notorious of a group of Tory landowners who dabbled freely (and in his case disastrously) in industrial and commercial ventures.* Clearly the Tory party was a good deal less homogeneous than many of its own supporters would have liked to believe. As well as embracing almost half the lay aristocracy in addition to hybrids like Halsey and Mackworth, Toryism was surprisingly prevalent among pure trading and financial interests during the period from 1702 to 1714. Bolingbroke was to claim three years after Anne's death that during her reign "the bank, the east-india company, and in general the moneyed interest, had certainly nothing to apprehend like what they feared, or affected to fear from the tories, an entire subversion of their property. Multitudes of our own party would have been wounded by such a blow."[58] The "multitudes" existed only in Bolingbroke's highly-charged imagination. Yet there was, without doubt, an important business element in the Tory party, with its strongholds in the City. The joint-stock trading companies and even the Bank of England had their quota of Tory directors as well as of Tory shareholders.[59] The directorate of the South Sea Company from 1711 to 1714 was almost solidly Tory;[60] and private banking in the capital was represented by the strongly High Church families of Child and Hoare.

The lines of communication between the City and the leadership of the Tory party were admittedly slender compared with those enjoyed by Godolphin and above all by the Junto. Yet Halifax and Sunderland were not the only peers who could boast valuable City connections. When Robert Harley was on the threshold of power in June 1710 he was fortunate in being able to make use of the High Tory Duke of Buckingham to sound out business opinion and seek financial backers for a new ministry which was certain to be confronted with a major credit crisis as the most serious of its immediate problems.[61] The contrary pressures exerted on Harley at this time as he faced the most taxing political decision of the summer — the decision whether or not he should persuade the Queen to dissolve Parliament as well as to change her administration — illustrate very well how conflicting interests could at times create stresses within parties as well as between them. For while the Tory landed interest was unanimous in clamouring for new elections to be held in the highly favourable climate which the Sacheverell

* Mackworth was the moving spirit behind the ill-fated "Mine Adventure" of Anne's reign. When he stood for Cardiganshire in 1709 he was profuse in his promises to "bring the white cloth trade from Shrewsbury into Cardiganshire and [to] build them a key at Aberystwyth". Penrice and Margam MSS. L. 651: W. Waller to Mansel, 11 Oct. In general see Mary Ransome's article on Mackworth's parliamentary career, *Birmingham Hist. Journal*, i (1948).

trial had created for the party, Joseph Addison was reporting that "Sir Francis Child, with the rest of the monied citizens on the Tories side, have declared to the Duke of Shrewsbury [Harley's principal collaborator], that they shall all be ruined if so great a blow be given to the public credit, as would inevitably follow upon a dissolution".[62] Nor could their opinions be lightly disregarded. For in June the Lord Mayor and other "honest" Tory aldermen and councillors had undertaken to sustain a new administration by means of "a voluntary loan" against any withdrawal of support by the Bank, and thereby to "put an end [to] that ridiculous notion that the Whiggs are the main support of the government".[63]

The Lord Mayor of London at this time, as in November 1709 when Sacheverell delivered his Guy Fawkes' day sermon to the City fathers, was the ultra-Tory, Sir Samuel Garrard. After the famous service at St. Paul's he had taken the Doctor home in the mayoral coach, and it was almost certainly he (despite his subsequent denials in the House of Commons) who egged on Sacheverell to print his incendiary words and so set in train a sequence of events which neither he nor anyone else at the time could possibly have foreseen. For all but a year since March 1701 Garrard had sat in Parliament for the tiny Buckinghamshire borough of Amersham, where his relatives the Drakes had an impregnable interest. Many other London merchants and men of capital in the Church party found borough seats, as Garrard did, in the home counties, in Wiltshire, and sometimes even farther afield; and ironically there were some of them who were just as guilty as their Whig counterparts of the charge regularly brought against the latter by frustrated Tory squires, that of elbowing out of the Commons "country gentlemen [who] were vexed, put to great expences and even baffled by them in their elections".[64] At least one group of Tory businessmen, however, had a genuine local interest of their own. These were the provincials sitting for the outports, in some of which Tory merchants were as politically active and influential as the Whigs. They were strong in Bristol, which was represented at various times in Anne's reign by Edward Colston, one of the city's chief benefactors who had made a great fortune from the Spanish trade, and by another prominent Tory trader, Joseph Earle. They were a force to be reckoned with in Liverpool, where their leader William Clayton was a member from 1698 to 1708 and again from 1713 to 1715; and they were equally well entrenched in Exeter, where the chamber of commerce was dominated by the Tory M.P.s, John Snell and Nicholas Wood, and north of the border, in Dundee.[65] Lastly, there was a small crossbred element among Tory merchant members — local sons who had made their pile in London but who had later returned to find borough seats in the neighbourhood of their birth, like the Heysham brothers at Lancaster, William Livingston at Aberdeen and Sir William Lewen at Poole.

Numerically, then, the Tory business members were never a negligible force in the House of Commons. In fact a study of the mercantile interests in Anne's fourth Parliament has shown that after the Whig electoral disaster in 1710 they actually outnumbered their Whig counterparts by as many as 41 to 23.[66] Such facts and figures do more than serve as a final commentary on the fallacy of the notion that the Tory party of Anne's reign was a one-class party; they are also enough in themselves to warn against a further misconception which the intrusion of a 'clash of interests' into party politics might easily induce. This is the assumption that the Tories, and more particularly the Tory leaders, had no interest in the advancement of foreign trade and no sympathy with the men who conducted it. This was untrue even of the old High Tory chiefs. Rochester and Nottingham, in pressing early in the war for more vigorous naval activity and for combined operations in the West Indies, were advocating a strategy which was designed to yield direct dividends in the shape of colonial acquisitions, new sources of overseas wealth, and the securing of trade routes.[67] Sir Edward Seymour, the leading High Churchman and one of the most princely land-owners in the Commons during the first part of the reign, not only had important commercial interests of his own (chiefly in the East India Company), but numbered several merchants among his closest friends and followers, including Thomas Coulson, his nominee at Totnes, and John Snell. Some of the younger Tories, however, and particularly those who associated with Harley, were even less a prey to indiscriminate prejudice than the leaders of the old guard. Harley himself was at immense pains to build up a powerful personal interest in the City of London in the years 1710–11;[68] and no Whig Secretary of State could have shown greater concern for commercial interests than did Henry St. John in his negotiations with the French and the Spaniards between 1711 and 1713. But then, St. John always made a clear distinction between his attitude towards "the merchant who brought riches home by the returns of foreign trade", which was enthusiastic, and his distaste for what he considered to be the parasitic element among the men of capital — the stockjobbers, the financial manipulators, the big government creditors, the war-contractors.[69]

We find this cry being echoed by other and humbler Tories. The High Church squire in 1702 whose resentment was concentrated partly on Dutch and Jewish financiers and partly on the "scoundrel stock jobbers and tally jobbers, who have been sucking our vitals for many years"[70] was fairly typical of his kind. It is true, there is need for caution here. The distinction between merchants trading with the Continent and the colonies and the rest of the "moneyed men" was not one that every Tory country gentleman clearly recognised, particularly by the later years of the Spanish Succession war when his capacity for discrimination had been blunted somewhat by the attacks of the cruder Tory propagandists against the City. The debates on the French Commerce bill in 1713, for example, brought an aggrieved comment from a Hertford member. "We are so intangled in the misterys of trade", he complained,"& I doubt in the iniquitys alsoe belonging to it . . .".[71] For most Country Tories, all the same, it was the parasitic element in society, those who seemed to have a vested interest in the indefinite prolongation of war, which remained the particular object of their animosity. It was no coincidence that the four prosperous merchants and bankers who carried the Tory colours in London at the 1710 Election sought to reassure their supporters that they were not "interested so far by their large shares in the Bank, to be careless of the growth or decay of our national trade, on which depends the life of this great City, and the strength and defence of the Kingdom".[72]

*   *   *

Having made these two quite essential reservations — that neither party was homogeneous, and that the Tories as a whole were not hostile to merchants who were primarily engaged in overseas trade — it is not misleading to say that by 1702 the Tory party was already identified with the defence of the special interests of the landed men. Nor could it be denied that in the course of our period the Whigs became increasingly associated (though not always so consciously or willingly) with those social forces which the Tory country gentlemen saw as most inimical to their material interests. Just how natural and how unavoidable these associations were can be seen most clearly in the case of the Tories.

The claim of the Tory party to be the natural political home of the squirearchy was perfectly realistic. No one in Anne's day would have questioned the assertion made by one of Bishop Wake's correspondents in 1710 that "the majority of the gentry upon a poll will be found Torys".[73] At local level, even more than in Parliament, the contrast between the social composition of the two parties was often strongly marked. Among the less affluent squires especially — those who had little chance of ever sitting in St. Stephen's Chapel, but whose opinions and activity could always materially affect the prospects of those who had such a chance — the Old Cause was in many places but thinly supported. There were several of the smaller English counties where stocking the commissions of the peace, the militia and the lieutenancies with political sympathisers was a real problem for any Whig administration. One can appreciate Wharton's horror in 1708 when Lord Carlisle was forced to suggest a Tory to complete his new muster of 5 deputy lieutenants in Westmorland; but there was little else to be done in "a county depopulated of gentry". And even in a county like Surrey the Whigs appear to have come desperately close to the bottom of the barrel in the years of their ascendancy between 1708 and 1710.[74] Finding suitable parliamentary candidates among local Whigs was no easy matter either in certain areas. In Cumberland, where it was said the inhabitants "of all ranks" were "five in six High Church", James Lowther was continually exercised after 1708 by the difficulty of finding a partner in case the Tories decided to break the gentleman's agreement between the parties and force a contest.[75] In most of the Welsh counties the Whig gentry were pitifully thin on the ground, and at Weobley in Herefordshire the Whigs were reduced in 1713 to canvassing support for "one Carpenter, a diminutive justice of the peace, of 160 l. per annum".[76] These were problems which the Tories rarely had to face in any region.[77]

As in the localities, so it was (though to a less emphatic degree) at Westminster. Whereas the gentry were one among several constituent elements of very similar importance on the Whig benches, they unquestionably provided the real substance of Tory strength in every House of Commons during Anne's reign. Even the two score Tory merchants and financiers in the 1710–13 Parliament shrank into insignificance beside the serried ranks of the independent High Church squires, well over 200 of them, returned on the flood tide of the 1710 Election. Such figures as Sir Thomas Crosse, the Westminster brewer, Sir Henry Johnson, the shipbuilder, Sir James Bateman, "whose chief dealings had been in stocks and funds",[78] Governor Pitt, with his vast Indian fortune, or John Blanch, the wealthy Gloucestershire clothier — all these seemed rather incongruous bedfellows in the party of Bromley and Pakington, of Atterbury and Sir Roger de Coverley. Their presence in Parliament slightly blurred the picture that was so beloved of Tory speech-makers and pamphleteers: that of a landed and clerical party defending the establishment in Church and State against subversion by a party of *nouveaux riches* and careerist politicians.

Yet such a picture was no mere caricature. Nor was the popular Tory view of their opponents altogether unrealistic. For one thing it seemed partly borne out by the dependence of the Whigs in the House of Commons on their impressive battery of lawyer-M.P.s. More than once in Anne's reign it was noticeable how their debating strength suffered towards the end of a session when many of the advocates and the Welsh judges had to go off on circuit.* But above all the closeness of the ties between the trading and investing classes and the Whig interest was no mere fiction created by Tory propaganda. The links between the City and the Whig magnates, for instance, were far closer and more numerous than anything the Tories could show. Halifax's contacts were especially widespread; but Newcastle and Sunderland also enjoyed a very special relationship with the moneyed men.[79] With malicious irony Erasmus Lewis wrote to Harley in October 1708 that "Lord Sunderland, Lord Coningsby and Sir James Forbes dined yesterday at Pontacks with their City friends, where they took Lille and raised six millions in a trice without the assistance of any but their own party".[80] But few Tories at this stage of the war would have been able to view such cabals light-heartedly; for the majority they were symptomatic of a relationship which to the hard-pressed squire appeared only too sinister.† There were many other ways, however, in which the mutual dependence of the Whigs and the bulk of the business community was manifested: in the single-minded determination with which tycoons like Sir Gilbert Heathcote and Sir Henry Furnese laboured to save the Godolphin-Junto coalition from destruction in the summer of 1710; in the great local as well as parliamentary opposition which the Whigs organised in their bid to defeat the Commercial Treaty with France in 1713; and not least in the prominent place taken on the Whig benches in the Commons, especially in the two Parliaments of 1705–10, by bankers, entrepreneurs, manufacturers, stockbrokers and government contractors, as well as by overseas merchants and men in local business and trade. Between 1708 and 1710 alone more than 50 such Whigs were elected, among them no fewer than 11 directors or ex-directors of the Bank of England.[81]

* * *

* See, e.g., *Addison Letters*, p. 96, and cf. B.M. Loan 29/45/J/9: Newsletter, 3/14 Mar. 1714. Their opponents, by contrast, were far from flush with legal talent. No ministry whose supporters were well-equipped with lawyers would have had to resort to Sir Nathan Wright as Lord Keeper, as the Tories did in 1700. The lack of Tory talent at Harley's disposal in 1710 is illustrated by the great difficulty he experienced in replacing Lord Chancellor Cowper, and also by the fact that the post of Solicitor-General continued to be filled right through his ministry by a Court Whig, Sir Robert Raymond.

† Harley's reaction to the news of the proposed six million loan was to enquire of his follower, Sir Simon Harcourt, "Is there any need of Parliament meeting? Put it! Put it!" H.M.C. *Bath MSS.* i, 193.

"The Bank" was the symbol and the epitome of all the new forces in the state which the Tories most disliked and feared. It had been their particular bane ever since its foundation in 1694, and by the middle years of Anne's reign they had become obsessed by the threat of its overweening power and by the stranglehold which it appeared to them to exercise over successive ministries. Almost inevitably, therefore, the Bank of England found itself developing, especially in the years between 1707 and 1711, into one of the storm centres of national politics; and to find a clear-cut political manifestation of the clash of interests in Augustan society one need look no further than the Tory endeavour in these years to curb, if not to eliminate, the influence of the Bank on government.

In the Committee of Ways and Means in February 1707 Tory members, backed by a vigorous pamphleteering campaign, fought strenuously but unavailingly to prevent the extension of the Bank's charter beyond its expiry date in 1711.[82] Their failure on this occasion rankled with most of them for the next four years, and with some Tories even longer. "What people then are these in a corner to whom the constitution must truckle?", enquired Swift in April 1711. "If the whole nation's credit cannot supply funds for the war without humble application from the entire legislature to a few retailers of mony, 'tis high time we should sue for a peace".[83] He wrote with particular feeling, since it was less than a week since his new masters had tried to organise the capture of the Bank in the annual elections of its Governor, Sub-Governor and directors, only to be humiliatingly repulsed. At the beginning of the parliamentary session of 1710–11 there had been noisy threats from the crowded Tory back benches that "the power of the House of Commons" would be used to eject the existing directors before the end of their term. But Harley knew better than to lend any official encouragement to so arbitrary an action: "if that should happen", wrote Arthur Mainwaring, "the Bank wou'd fall to forty the next day".[84] The prime minister recognised that if change was to come it must come from within. And so in 1711 each political party for the first time submitted its own list of 24 proposed directors to the shareholders. The Tories salted the mine by including a few of their opponents in their list of nominees; they resorted to feverish house-to-house canvassing, and even (though seemingly with no great enthusiasm) recruited the assistance of Sacheverell, who bought £500 of Bank stock to qualify for a vote. But they were unable to eject the Whigs from this their strongest City entrenchment.[85] Three years later the Elector Palatine's minister in London, whose sympathies and contacts were with the Tories, was still prepared to prophesy that "the Government . . .

will never be at its ease until it introduces some one devoted to itself among the monopolists of the Bank" — that awesome, mysterious body whose "dogmas are hidden and impenetrable to all those who are not members of their coterie from father to son".[86]

We can now see plainly enough that the average Tory of Anne's day made too fearsome a bogy of the Bank. He was too ready to accept the common Whig assumption that "they that have the money must have the management"; whereas, on the whole, events bore out the truth of Defoe's maxim that "they that have the management will have the money".[87] Certainly the history of the Harley ministry provided evidence enough between 1710 and 1714 that a Whiggish Bank directorate, even one that was hostile to the government's foreign policy, could not afford to keep up an incessant feud with an administration controlled by its political opponents.[88] Yet up to 1711, if not afterwards, there had seemed to be some justification for the prevalent Tory attitude. The 21-year extension of its charter by Parliament in 1707 and the huge new loan of 1709 had both strengthened the Bank's bargaining power considerably. Then, in June 1710, four of its directors, including Heathcote the Governor,[89] had made a direct attempt to deter Queen Anne from removing Godolphin and her Whig ministers, by trying to convince her that the nation's credit could never recover from such a shock. This seemed in Tory eyes a dreadful piece of constitutional sacrilege: the moneyed men were bidding fair to constitute a new estate of the realm: "the bank [as St. John observed] had been extravagant enough to pull off the mask".[90] High Tories like Beaufort (who set an example to his fellow magnates by offering to lend £5000 to a new Tory ministry to free it from such tutelage) were appalled at the treatment which the Queen had received at the hands of "four citizens". Oxford common-rooms agreed that "the insolence of these fellows is without example". A number of their brother directors actually disclaimed responsibility for the action of Heathcote and his clique; and even Harley, whom no one could accuse of class prejudice, thought it "a matter of very extraordinary nature, that private gentlemen . . . should have the presumption to take upon them to direct the sovereign".[91]

In the circumstances it is not surprising that Harley had an ulterior motive when he launched his great South Sea scheme in May 1711. The principal object of the project was to deal with the problem of the floating debt. But we cannot doubt that Harley also saw it as a chance to reward his own friends and supporters in the City, those hitherto excluded from the magic circle of the Bank and the East India Company:[92] a chance to fortify them with corporate privileges and a measure of official patronage sufficient to enable them to break into the circle, if not actually to rival the Bank itself. Parliament's authority was used to ensure that Whig stockholders were given no chance to influence the composition of the new company's first board of directors; and when the choice of directors had at length to be thrown open to election from the summer of 1712 the attempts of the City Whigs to infiltrate into the board-room in strength were strongly and successfully resisted by the Harleyite contingent.[93] Moreover, although the commercial basis of the South Sea Company proved in the end to be largely spurious, the ministry must have been well satisfied with its initial success as a new magnet for investors. Not only was it popular with Tory country gentlemen; even so hardened a speculator as James Brydges in 1711 thought "this Company to be by far the best way to lay out money in hopes of a great & suddain profit".[94]

If most Tories were angered by the political pretensions of the Bank many were alarmed at the electioneering activities of this and other great City syndicates and corporations. Again, much of this alarm was exaggerated. For one thing it overlooked the fact that in some of the really corrupt boroughs, such as Devizes and New Shoreham, the City magnates were cutting each other's throats rather than those of the neighbouring gentry. More important was the evidence that money alone could rarely guarantee anyone a seat in the Commons for any length of time. When Henry Cornish went down from London with £3000 in his pocket to challenge the ascendancy of Lords Abingdon and Weymouth among the burgage-holders of Westbury in 1710 he suffered the humiliation of polling a mere 3 votes against 42 and 40 for the Tory candidates, Francis Annesley and Henry Bertie.[95] Most of the London businessmen who regularly filled provincial seats, especially in the home counties, had to earn them by the purchase of a borough manor or a judiciously-placed estate: such was the method of the Claytons, the Newlands, the Parsonses and the Docminiques. Others, like the Bank director John Rudge, who sat for Evesham, already had local roots of some depth. Without such solid advantages or investments, or at very least the recommendation of a neighbouring nobleman or gentleman (such as "Vulture" Hopkins was fortunate enough to secure at St. Ives),[96] it often required an inordinate expenditure of money to disturb a well-established landed interest in a venal borough. Even with the advantage of the Duke of Grafton's patronage it cost Robert Baylis £3000 to oust Sir John Wodehouse from his seat at Thetford in 1708.[97] This was a bill which even the best-lined London pockets would not meet every two or three years without some guarantee of permanence; and as Baylis's experience proved — he spent less than 18 months in the House — success of this kind was often as ephemeral as it was expensive.

Above all, however, it is worth emphasising that most of the bankers, merchants, company directors and contractors who did sally forth from London to pit their resources against local landlords did so at their own initiative, or at least at their own private expense. Concrete evidence of electoral activity that was definitely initiated by organised syndicates is rare. But country gentlemen did not readily forget that the East India Company had run its own candidates in one General Election at the beginning of the century.[98] During the Commons' debates on the proposal for a new East India loan to the government in January 1708 the Company's directors were shocked by the viciousness of the Tory onslaught upon them, "as if they were the pest of the nation [one Court member recorded] and the corrupters of all the boroughs".[99] So we can be sure that St. John's dark hints in the House of Commons in December 1710 about "Societys" of financiers "that joint'd stock to bring in members", though unsupported by specific illustration, were accepted at their face value by his eager audience on the Tory benches.

Henry St. John's personal rôle in the conflict of interests in Anne's reign was an exceptionally important one. He was by far the most eloquent and persistent voice of Toryism in its resistance to the economic and political encroachments of the new rich. It was he who, after quitting the ministry along with Harley in February 1708, provided the pent-up prejudices and resentments of the Tory squirearchy with their most effective outlet; the more effective since this was the time when disillusionment with the Continental war reached its height. As early as October 1708 he was begging Harley to bring his own followers into the closest association with the Church party, for only thereby would they "be in condition whenever the propitious day comes to lodge power where it naturally should be, *with property*".[100] The persistent rumours that same autumn that the Whigs intended to raise by far the biggest government loan yet on the security of the land tax or even of the malt tax in perpetuity stirred him still further.[101] Unable to find a seat himself in the new Parliament he continued to brood in his country exile at Bucklebury on the grievances of those "private" landlords whose lot (for a while at least) he now shared. And to his old friend Lord Orrery in the following July he presented the *cahier de doléances* of the men of property with a fluency and compelling force that none of his contemporaries could quite equal, though also with his own inimitable brand of dramatic licence:

We have now been twenty years engaged in the two most expensive wars that Europe ever saw. The whole burthen of this charge has lain upon the landed interest during the whole time. The men of estates have, generally speaking, neither served in the fleets nor armies, nor meddled in the publick fonds & management of the treasure.

A new interest has been created out of their fortunes, & a sort of property wch was not known twenty years ago is now encreased to almost equal to the terra firma of our island. The consequence of all this is that the landed men are become poor & dispirited. They either abandon all thoughts of the publick, turn arrant farmers & improve the estates they have left; or else they seek to repair their shattered fortunes by listing at Court, or under the heads of Partys. In the mean while those men are become their masters, who formerly would with joy have been their servants.[102]

When St. John and his friends at length got back into office in August and September 1710 they found their freedom of action limited. Any hopes they may have cherished of prompt and spectacular steps to relieve the burden on the landed men, or to depress the pretensions of the Whig moneyed interest, were threatened with frustration by immediate exigencies. A credit crisis had to be overcome. A war had still to be fought; indeed the new government accepted the need to prosecute the war vigorously for at least one more campaign while new peace feelers were being put out to the French. So that however confidently the Tory squires in 1710 may have looked for "the golden age to come agen",[103] the land tax had to be kept at four shillings in the pound for two more years. Not until the 1710–13 Parliament met for its third session in April 1713, immediately after the signing of the Utrecht treaties with France, was there a real opportunity to reduce the tax; and the Oxford ministry reacted boldly if somewhat injudiciously to it. Sound fiscal judgement and some responsible Tory opinion advised a reduction in the rate of no more than a shilling.[104] But their own philosophy combined with the pressure of their long-suffering backbench supporters* forced the Tory ministers to take the much more drastic step of cutting the tax by half — a move which, by making the revenue from the malt tax indispensable, was to involve them in serious political difficulties later in the session. Meanwhile the credit crisis bequeathed by the Godolphin government had made an open breach with the Bank of England or the East India Company out of the question. After the new ministry's failure to capture the

* This pressure had been strongly exerted since the previous summer. E.g. a draft of the Beaumaris address to the Queen, *c.* June 1712, drawn up by the member for Anglesey, anticipated the near approach of "a Peace which will... in a short time ease us of our taxes, wch consequently will advance the Landed Interest". Baron Hill MSS. 6766.

Bank directorate in 1711 it significantly resisted attempts by Tory back-benchers to tie its hands in its future dealings with the Bank.* In this field all Harley could do was to reduce the government's dependence on Whig-dominated corporations as much as was feasible; and the measure of his success in satisfying Tory opinion on this score was the enthusiastic reception given to his South Sea bill by the High Church gentry, numbers of whom invested in the new company and one of whom[105] accepted a seat on the board.

Yet the clash of interests did have one notable and another really major political repercussion after the change of ministry in 1710. For one thing it clearly underlay a motion promoted in the House of Commons by the October Club Tories in March 1711, when the House voted by 186 votes to 115 that no person could be a Governor, Deputy Governor or director of both the Bank and the East India Company at the same time. A clause giving legal effect to this vote was soon afterwards inserted in an act obliging the Bank to cash Exchequer bills upon demand.† Far more important, the social conflict gave rise to the Qualifications bill, introduced into the Commons in December 1710 and eventually passed by the Lords on 22 February 1711. It was to this measure that the Tories looked for a future guarantee of protection in their constituencies from the competition of City carpet-baggers, and also of upstart army officers and the younger sons of Whig peers;[106] and it was one to which Harley and his colleagues, despite their other difficulties, were able to give official blessing. In fact, although it was a backbench bill in origin it soon became the special charge of Mr. Secretary St. John.

This was not the first time an attempt had been made to impose a property qualification on parliamentary candidates. In the middle of William III's reign two "country" bills had been brought in requiring members of Parliament to possess a significant amount of real estate. That of 1696 had been vetoed by the Crown in deference to the protests of the mercantile community, while that of 1697 had failed to pass the Lords. Six years later the Qualifications bill had been revived by the Tories in the flush of triumph

---

* E.g. the Court overrode Tory opposition to a proposed Bank loan of £1,200,000 in June 1713.

† 9 Anne, c. 7, clause 15. One Bank director, John Ward, was not unduly concerned. "The clause past in yr. late act", he told James Brydges on 24 Mar., "has made me transfer my stock in the Bank to my son who perhaps may be a candidate at the next election". John Ward, junr. duly took his father's seat in the board room. H.L. Stowe MSS. 58, vi, 118.

which followed their electoral victory of 1702 and the return of their champions to high office. The bill framed then had a number of features which distinguished it both from the two earlier measures and from that which became law in 1711. For one thing it was government-sponsored from the start.[107] In addition, the fact that Sir Richard Onslow took a hand in the drafting of the bill[108] shows that some Country Whigs still had no quarrel with the principle behind it. Important also was the insistence in the 1702–3 bill that it was necessary for members of the Commons not only to have "estates sufficient to support themselves in the execution of that great trust" but also to be "natives of this Realm, born within the Kingdom of England or dominions thereunto belonging"; two of its clauses, in fact, were clearly aimed at debarring from the House Dutch immigrant and French refugee businessmen, unless they had first been naturalised by Act of Parliament.[109] Finally the bill differed from those of 1696 and 1711 in fixing the estate qualification for county members rather lower, at £500 a year. It went through all its stages in the Lower House without a division. Then it came up against the opposition of Whig peers in the Lords. In February 1703 it was refused a Committee stage by 46 votes to 39 and it was subsequently rejected by a majority of 4.[110]

The bill that was brought in by Ralph Freeman in December 1710 stipulated that a candidate was only to be eligible for election as a knight of the shire if he had an income of at least £600 a year from "an estate freehold or copyhold for his own life", while the minimum qualification for a borough member was fixed at half that amount.[111] In common with most contemporary opinion, l'Hermitage, the Dutch agent in London, was in no doubt that the property qualification was a landed one — "en fonds de terre", as he put it.[112] And one Whig member who spoke against the bill in the Commons argued

that Corporations and Boroughs were erected chiefly to send up representatives to take care of trade and manufactures, which were then but in their infancy; yet now that trade was extended, and bore such a mighty proportion to land as to be in competition with it, to exclude those from Parliament who seem'd before to be the proper trustees for trade, and to commit the protection thereof to the Landed Men only, or in the common phrase, to the "Country Gentleman", seem'd a great alteration of our constitution, and what might very much turn to the detriment of trade and manufacture.[113]

Yet the key clause was so worded that the ownership of blocks of property in London, or even in some other large town, would have satisfied the legal requirement no less than possession of a country estate,* though obviously it was a far less likely contingency. Furthermore the bill's provisions did not extend to those contesting the four university seats or the forty-five Scottish seats; nor were the new qualifications to apply to the eldest sons of peers or to the heirs of country gentlemen of more than £600 per annum. Nevertheless most Tory backbenchers applauded the measure during its passage through the Commons and all seem to have entertained high hopes of its efficacy. No longer, they imagined, would the voting of revenue be at the mercy of men who "did not care how heavily land was tax'd, if they could keep the burthen off their own shoulders".[114] Some Tories even talked optimistically in 1711 of the disqualification of something like one third of the existing House of Commons at the next General Election, anticipating a rout of many professional placemen, lawyers and army officers as well as of the City cohort of the Whigs. Even experienced "Country" campaigners like Hanmer were astonishingly sanguine.[115]

In the event most of these rosy expectations proved illusory in 1713, when the Qualifications Act was first put to the test. The Whigs, who for the most part had accepted the measure with the minimum of protest in 1711 in the hope that it would deal with some of the more notorious cases without substantially affecting their party's election prospects,† were not unduly disappointed. At first sight it may appear highly significant that so many new members were returned in 1713: the Hanoverian minister in London obviously believed it to be so when he informed the Elector that the number exceeded 200.[116] But on closer scrutiny it becomes clear that most of the newcomers were replacing country gentlemen (frequently Tory gentlemen) who were not able to contemplate the expense of a new contest or another spell of residence in London, or who in some cases were simply defeated at the polls. The Whigs suffered their share of casualties, of course, as a direct result of the new qualification; but then, so did their opponents. Thomas Legh, who had sat for his elder brother's pocket borough of Newton for twelve years but now found himself disqualified, had been one of the hottest Tories in the Commons, and Josias Burchett, the invaluable Secretary to the

---

* The enacting clause stipulated "an estate freehold or copyhold ... in lands, tenements or hereditaments". The distinction was clearly important to some Tories, for John Dyer had forecast confidently in Dec. 1710 that no borough member would in future be qualified without an income of "300 l. p. ann. *besides* houses & hereditam^ts". B.M. Loan 29/321: Newsletter, 12 Dec. (my italics).

† Ostensibly orthodox Country Whig opinion still accepted in principle the necessity of imposing some kind of property qualification on members. See the evidence of Robert Molesworth (c. 1711) in *The Memoirs of John Ker of Kersland*, pt. iii (London, 1727), p. 205.

Admiralty, was unable to stand for re-election at Sandwich.[117] This was an Election which the Whigs were obliged to fight in face of the full blast of Court disapproval; and even if the 1711 act had never been passed it is doubtful whether they could have fared much better than they did. As it was, they could still show a significant City element among their successful candidates. The two Londoners John Knight and John Hopkins, banker and stockbroker respectively, held the favour of their Cornish borough electors. John London, a City cloth factor who had been unseated in 1711, was re-elected in the dissenting stronghold of Wilton, along with the Whig younger son of "Diamond" Pitt. William Cotesworth, the merchant, who had taken two goldsmith bankers with him in a bid to "infatuate" the electors of Boston in 1711,[118] recovered his old seat at Grimsby. Shoreham returned a West India merchant — a complete "foreigner" both to the borough and to Sussex[119] — and a Bank director, both solidly in the Whig interest. Most galling of all, perhaps, for the Tories was the fact that John Eyles, son of one of the four offending Bank grandees of 1710, came into the House as one of the new members for Chippenham in Wiltshire, although "a stranger to the said borough".[120] There was some consolation for the country gentlemen in seeing the Whig military and legal contingents slightly reduced; but even here they must have been irked to find how many escaped the net. The mayor of Bury St. Edmunds, who was in Lord Hervey's pocket, cannot have enquired too closely into the financial circumstances of Colonel Porter when he offered himself for re-election to that corporation; and though William Thompson, one of the leading Whig lawyers, stood and was returned at Ipswich, even his partner did not believe his claims that he had properly "qualifyd himselfe".[121]

One of the most remarkable features of the General Election of 1713, however, was the attitude of the Court to this question of property qualification. Leading members of the very ministry which had helped to promote the 1711 bill connived themselves in 1713 at a number of flagrant breaches either of the letter or spirit of the new law. When the petition of the two ministerial candidates for Brackley came before the Commons the following spring, John Scrope congratulated Oxford's cousin, Thomas, that "no objection was made about their quallifications".[122] Oxford himself put up his kinsman, Paul Foley, on the Holles interest at Aldborough, though William Jessop, the Whig M.P., had "heard it questioned whether he . . . hath enough to qualify him to stand for a Borough".[123] Sir Roger Bradshaigh, a client of Oxford's whose financial embarrassments were acute and whose legal right to membership was subsequently challenged in a petition to the House, could never have afforded to stand again at Wigan without a subsidy from the Treasurer.[124] Bolingbroke acted still more cynically in securing the return of his friend, William Collier, at Truro; for Collier, "a petty-fogging attorney" before he became manager of Drury Lane theatre, lacked even personal estate let alone land.[125] Infractions as blatant as these leave one wondering how far the power-politicians on the Tory side, as opposed to the country members, were genuinely convinced by their own professions. Did they really believe that they could make the political nation, any more than society itself, a kind of 'closed-shop', to which a firm stake in the land of the country would be the only ticket of admission? If they did — and it is hard to imagine a politician of Oxford's subtlety and experience failing to realise that the power of the patron and the ingenuity of the lawyer would together make strict enforcement of the Act of 1711 impossible — they were very soon disillusioned. By the time the next General Election, that of 1715, had been fought and lost by the Tories the act was already so much of a dead letter that the Tory lawyer John Ward, a veteran of six elections, could only dejectedly confess, "I never saw any like it. Between the Army and the City there's very little room left for the Country Gentleman."[126]

The character of politics in the age of Anne was thus moulded by social prejudices and economic pressures as well as by the forces of principle and power. Politics after 1701 was materially affected by a clash of interests in society for which at the time there were genuine and rational causes. Social conflict added fresh gall to a party struggle which even without it would have been bitter enough; though it also introduced some curious anomalies and inconsistencies into this struggle at a period when the Whig country gentle-man and the Tory "moneyed man" were far from being political freaks. In part because of these anomalies, and in part also because the social conflict itself was mainly the product of exceptional and short-term circumstances, its intrusion into politics between 1702 and 1714 usually generated a good deal more heat than light. So it may not be unduly surprising that by the end of the reign, even after four years of Tory supremacy, it had produced little more than stalemate. Certainly it had left behind no insurmountable obstacle to the organic development of the 'governing class' in the eighteenth century, along lines at least as broad as those open to it in 1702. Tory fears that their own eclipse as a political party would involve the automatic eclipse of the landed interest in the "councils of the nation" were proved after 1715 to have been ludicrously wide of the mark.

PART TWO

The Working of Politics

CHAPTER SIX

The Managers, the Queen, and the Royal Closet

I

WHILE we have been seeking to identify the various elements which made up the substance of politics during Anne's reign, and the forces which helped to mould its general character, it has only rarely been possible to escape from the confines of the two-party conflict. Thus far these have been in no way inhibiting. The very fact that this conflict of Tory and Whig was one in which considerations of ideology, policy, power, self-interest and class-interest were all involved, as well as being one which was complicated from time to time by the persistence of the older antagonism between Court and Country, has meant that within its confines we have been able to range freely and widely. Yet while these boundaries provide an indispensable framework for the understanding of political motives and political actions in this period, there are limits to their usefulness and to their validity. These become apparent as soon as we turn our attention from the character of politics to the actual working of the political system in the age of Anne. We have found that the heat produced by party enmity was the main source of energy and motion in British politics for a decade and a half after 1701. It was the fuel that drove the machine. What we have still to discover is how the machinery of politics was constructed and in what way it functioned. And in this fresh area of investigation terms of reference which are related *strictly* to the struggle between Tory and Whig are simply not adequate. The problems raised by the working of politics are problems that must be seen, in the first instance, within the broad context of the post-Revolution constitution.

The form of government which existed in Britain after 1688 has been described as 'legal monarchy' or as 'limited monarchy'. Both descriptions are equally appropriate, and the three constitutional elements which they pre-suppose — the legal foundation of the constitution, its central core of monarchical authority, and the superstructure of limitations on that authority — all contributed to shaping the pattern of politics in the early eighteenth century. Certainly there could have been no reasonable room for doubt in anybody's mind by 1702 that the constitution rested on a firm basis of law. Whatever the powers and prerogatives remaining to the sovereign, and they were considerable, they were plainly subject to the ultimate supremacy of statute law and common law. Never again would a monarch attempt to suspend the operation of a law or dispense with the statutory penalties of an act of Parliament in individual cases. Nor, after 1708, would he attempt to prevent a bill becoming law by the use of the royal veto (though it is worth recording that Queen Anne's rejection of the Scottish Militia bill in March 1708 produced not even a ripple of political excitement at the time, let alone a sense of constitutional 'occasion').* There was also the fact that the patents of English judges appointed after William III's accession contained a guarantee of tenure "during good behaviour", which meant that no judge who proved politically unamenable, either to the sovereign or to the ministry of the day, could henceforward be removed until the accession of a new ruler.¹ This particular development is an excellent example of a constitutional change which did more than limit the prerogative and strengthen the judiciary, for it was to prove of practical importance to both political parties during Anne's reign. It meant, for instance, that judges appointed at the behest of one party, at a time when that party was in a position to influence or control the executive, could continue to protect its members from persecution when the latter had ceased to enjoy government favour. Thus the presence on the bench in the years 1710–14 of such staunch Whigs as Lord Chief Justice Parker, Mr. Justice Eyres and Mr. Justice Dormer, all former M.P.s, was a frequent source of comfort to Whig journalists, pamphleteers and local officials whose work exposed them to judicial proceedings inspired by party malice. It also served as an occasional deterrent to, or a means of counter-attack against, their Tory counterparts.²

In its political repercussions, however, no change which the monarchy experienced after 1688 was more important than the new character of its title to the throne. The last two Stuarts ruled by virtue of a title that was in

* A member of the House of Lords, for example, recorded the event in his diary parenthetically, as something which to him seemed quite unremarkable: "[Thursday, 11 March] . . . They [the Lords] prepar'd several bills for the Queen, who came to them abt four and (haveing given the royal assent to several, and rejected that for modelling the militia in Scotland) acquainted both Houses that the Pretender was on the Suffolk-coast. . . ." Tullie House, Nicolson's MS. Diary.

essence parliamentary. However much Tory lawyers and clerics might try to gloss over this fact, it was simply inescapable, as Archbishop Sharp acknowledged with commendable lack of humbug immediately after the Queen's accession.[3] Anne succeeded to the throne only because in 1689 the Parliaments of England and Scotland had offered the crown conditionally — the Whigs would have claimed, contractually* — to her sister and her brother-in-law, passing over the direct hereditary heir in the process. What is more, Parliament in 1701 had made further statutory provision for the succession after Anne's death, in the expectation that she would have no more children. For all her own High Anglicanism, and the revival of royalist sentiment and reactionary political theory which her accession inspired, the Queen herself was always refreshingly free from any delusions about the source of her own authority. Tory peers may have squirmed uneasily when Lord Wharton reminded her to her face in the House of Lords that "the best title she had to the Crown was her parliamentary title, founded on the Revolution"; but there is no evidence that Anne herself resented this piece of plain speaking. On the contrary, when Lord Guernsey later in the same debate was earnestly "clearing himself of the Revolution" the Queen "riss & left them, wch so much confounded him that [he] had much ado to proceed".[4] Her first reaction to Sacheverell's notorious sermon of 5 November 1709, with its blatant assertion of the doctrines of divine right, passive obedience and non-resistance, was to admit quite frankly "that it was a bad sermon, and that he deserved well to be punished for it".[5] And even on the opening day of the Doctor's trial, when the Tory mobs milled round her coach linking her name with Sacheverell's in their shouts, she still maintained "that there ought to a punishmt, but a mild one . . ."† It was characteristic of Queen Anne that eight months later, when she read the loyal address from the city of London, fulsomely congratulating her on her recent change to a Tory ministry, "she immediately took exception to the expression that 'her right was Divine', and [reported the Duke of Shrewsbury] this morning told me that, having thought often of it, she could by no means like it, and thought it so unfit to be given to anybody that she wished it might be left out".[6]

Changes as fundamental as this, affecting the very basis of monarchy,

---

* See p. 60 above.

† Panshanger MSS.: diary of Sir David Hamilton, 27 Feb. 1710. Hamilton's opinion, based on a conversation with the Queen, was that it was fear of the "great commotions" caused by the mob, rather than sympathy for Sacheverell, which had converted her to the notion that a light sentence was advisable.

were bound to have some effect on the working of the political system. For the monarch was no longer after 1688 on a different plane from the political arena in whose dust and heat his subjects fought their battles. If the execution of Charles I had already subtracted much from the sanctity of kingship in England, the enforced "abdication" of James II and the settlement of the throne by a Parliament that was not even summoned by royal authority had completed the secularisation of monarchy. "Stripped of divinity", as one recent scholar has strikingly put it, "the King must take his chance along with other mortals".[7] One result of this increasing vulnerability was that however sincerely both William III and Anne may have wished to stand impartially aloof from party differences, such detachment was hard to preserve in practice. Both the major political parties after the Revolution sought at times to 'appropriate' the Crown: that is to say, they attempted to enlist the personal prestige of the sovereign as a permanent party asset. This was undeniably true of the Whigs in their attitude to William. Tom Wharton spoke not only for himself but for all "the honest old Whig interest" when he told him shortly after his accession that "Wee have made you king", and went on to enquire with typical bluntness, "if you intend to governe like an honest man, what occasion can you have for knaves [i.e. Tories] to serve you?"[8] It was equally true that the loyal churchmen who welcomed Anne's accession with undisguised relief and exultation in March 1702 did so in the hope, and in many cases the firm conviction, that she would be content to be "the Queen of the Tories". In the event, William III never succumbed entirely to these pressures, while Anne only did so fully in the last half-year or so of her life. Even then she only gave way after the Whig opposition to the Oxford ministry, despairing of ever regaining her favour, had adopted the practice that was later to become the favourite ploy of Hanoverian oppositions — turning to the heir to the throne for the countenance that would endow their constant obstruction of the policies of the Court with an air of respectability and even of patriotism.

Such manoeuvres on the part of the Whig and Tory leaders were not the sole consequence of the changed relationship between the sovereign and the politicians after the Revolution. With Parliament now an indispensable part of the machinery of state the ruler, for his part, was forced to come to some sort of terms with the political parties which dominated the legislature. He might reject the relationship which the parties themselves were anxious to thrust upon him; yet he had to establish some *modus vivendi* with forces in the nation whose existence he had to accept, however much he might deplore it. It was William, in his reaction against committed party men on both sides, who initiated the practice of employing intermediaries between the Crown and the parties: men who served the dual purpose of buffers, protecting the monarch as far as possible from the importunities and encroachments of the partisans, and of brokers, negotiating with the party politicians on the Crown's behalf whenever the King was forced to reconstruct his administration. In this capacity William was served above all, after 1692, by the second Earl of Sunderland,[9] and to a lesser extent by the Duke of Shrewsbury. These two men, despite a seeming partiality for the Whigs in practice, were both sufficiently detached from the extremists of either side to be well fitted for the rôle of middle-men. As Sir Keith Feiling first suggested forty years ago,[10] they must be regarded as the first of that breed of politicians peculiar to the period 1689–1714 whom contemporaries knew sometimes as "the undertakers", sometimes as "the Ministers", but more often as "the Managers" (the term by which we shall henceforward refer to them). These were statesmen whose philosophy was summarised in the words of their progenitor, Sunderland: "what matter who serves his Majesty, so long as his Majesty is served".[11] At the top level they were few in number. But to ignore their distinctive ideology, and to lump them together uncritically as 'politicians' along with the genuine party bosses, is to overlook one of the key parts in the operation of the politicial system at this time. The 'third force' in the working of politics from 1702 to 1714, besides the monarch and the parties, was the Managers. By comparison, other forces — the force of country sentiment, for example — were negligible in importance.

If William III had made use of Managers to some extent from choice, Anne did so from necessity. She turned first, naturally enough, to her friends Godolphin and Marlborough, two men whose Toryism had ceased by the time of her accession to be much more than nominal. Lord Godolphin, a man "never in the way and never out of the way", as Charles II had long before observed, had the temperament, political outlook and mental equipment of a natural bureaucrat. "I cannot think it for your service", he had once protested to King William, "to make changes in the management of your revenue, to gratify party and animosity."[12] He was a painstaking and scrupulously honest administrator, not least in his favourite sphere of public finance. In his various spells of office since the Revolution he had worked without apparent difficulty with Whigs as well as with Tories. In many respects, then, he was ideally qualified in 1702 to act as an arbiter between the parties. As a Manager, however, he was also to reveal some of the weaknesses of his virtues. Not only did he recoil from the excesses of party; he also lacked stomach at times for the free-for-all of the party arena in which he was inevitably involved. When, for example, the High Tories turned on him in 1705 and he was branded in a scurrilous pamphlet, *The Memorial of the Church of England*, as an enemy to the Established Church, Godolphin was both resentful and distressed. The Archbishop of York noted his parting words after an interview with the Treasurer soon afterwards: "... he said he hoped in his distress he might have recourse to me, or words to that effect. He was often, as I thought, in a great concern, and very near weeping".[13] Godolphin was, in fact, at once too touchy and too timid for the political maelstrom in which a fellow moderate like Harley could revel. Nor did he have the tact and delicacy of touch which were often needed for the extra-ordinarily trying job of managing Queen Anne. In short, he made rather heavy weather of politics. He was tempted to throw in his hand more than once in the various crises which confronted him between 1702 and 1710. That he never did so was due in the main to the stiffening provided by the Duke of Marlborough and the strength which the Treasurer drew from the latter's hold over the Queen.

The celebrated "duumvirate" of Anne's reign was essentially a partnership. It may not have been utterly rock-like. It did, for instance, suffer a period of intermittent strain between the winter of 1707–8 and the summer of 1710 which had its effects on political developments in those years, and which may even have contributed to the fall of the Godolphin ministry.* But for the most part it was a genuine partnership, based on close personal friendship, on mutual respect, and most of all on a remarkable identity of objectives.

---

* This is a controversial matter and one which merits detailed investigation. But it does seem that the first stresses in the alliance began to show after Godolphin had had cause to suspect his colleague of coming near to deserting him in the days of high drama just preceding Harley's fall in Feb. 1708. The strain was possibly renewed after Marlborough's first ill-advised application to the Queen for a grant of the Captain-Generalship for life in 1709, and certainly after Godolphin had failed to give the duke the support he counted on when he took his stand for Mrs. Masham's dismissal in Jan. 1710.

The evidence of Coningsby, the Vice-Treasurer of Ireland, which bears on these questions (B.M. Landsdowne MSS. 885, ff. 76–7, 79–82), has on the whole been rejected by scholars working on this period, or has been treated at best with strong suspicion and reserve. Yet the discovery of fresh evidence has proved him almost certainly right about the original cause of friction in 1708 (see Holmes and Speck, 'The Fall of Harley in 1708 Reconsidered', *E.H.R.* lxxx [1965], 687–9); and Coningsby was in close enough personal contact with both men, and was sufficiently trusted by both, in the late winter of 1709–10 to know the truth about their relations at this time. Moreover some features of his story — his own rôle in the crisis over the Essex regiment, for instance, and the disillusioned Marlborough's determination thereafter to leave the country at the earliest opportunity — can be substantiated from other sources.

Scarcely more than his ally at the Treasury was Marlborough of the stuff of which extremists are made. Both by training and temperament he was a soldier and not a professional politician. He was drawn closely into politics first by his marriage and later by his family connection with Godolphin. Yet paradoxically he proved in some ways a cleverer natural politician than the friend whom the Tories called "the fox". He had a cooler and shrewder eye for the realities of a political situation (he demonstrated this in the crisis of January–February 1708 and again in the summer of 1710); he was less liable than Godolphin to be deluded by false hopes; and he was generally the more resilient of the two in face of difficulties. One important clue to the relations of the duumvirs, and also to the workings of the political system in the period 1704–8, is that the duke was also the more genuine Tory. He was usually more wary than the Treasurer when the need arose to make fresh concessions to the Whigs.[14] Then again, as the hero of Blenheim and Ramillies he acquired a very real hold in the middle years of the reign, impermanent but while it lasted important, over many independent Tory beckbenchers: over men who were not his 'followers' in any strict sense, but who still respected and admired him and regarded his presence as the *sine qua non* of any ministry's stability and success. This was something Robert Harley well appreciated; and it explains why, when he was eventually forced to break with Godolphin in January 1708 and fight him for control over a ministry whose Whig element Harley was anxious to reduce, he made strenuous efforts to divide Marlborough from his "old friend" and to win him over to the new scheme.[15]

All the same the Captain-General believed just as honestly as the Lord Treasurer that Queen Anne's government must not fall under the tutelage of the party zealots on either wing; and his position, alongside Godolphin, in the centre of the field of political opinion and political manoeuvre, is well illustrated by his capacity to attract personal adherents who would un-hesitatingly have called themselves Whigs. Most of the small group of army officers who were in Marlborough's favoured inner circle and who also held seats in the House of Commons were palpable Whigs: such stalwarts as Generals Cadogan,[16] Meredith,[17] Daniel Harvey,[18] and Francis Palmes.[19] Also from the Whig ranks came the Duchess of Marlborough's secretary, Arthur Mainwaring, who had ties with the Junto going back to the early 1690's,[20] as well as Sir Thomas Wheate and Joshua Lomax, two of the civilian members who represented Woodstock and St. Albans respectively with Churchill backing. Neither the duke's notorious client, James Craggs,[21] nor his banker and agent for army remittances, Sir Henry Furnese, could conceivably have been classed as Tories; while their two sons, James Craggs the younger and Robert Furnese, both of whom came into Parliament later in the reign, were strongly committed Whigs. What was the case with many of Marlborough's followers applied equally to some of Godolphin's relatives in the Commons. His nephew, Hugh Boscawen, and his cousin, Lord Fitzharding,[22] were both Court Whigs. And from late in 1707, as will later appear,* Godolphin became the magnet for a new grouping of politicians in both Houses, especially in the Lower House, who came to be labelled "Lord Treasurer's Whigs".

It was Godolphin and Marlborough who supervised the construction of Anne's first ministry in 1702, and it was they who then proceeded to manage it as "the Queen's servants", and not as the servants of a party, through all its various metamorphoses down to 1710. When they finally lost the Queen's confidence Anne turned instead to Harley and to a lesser degree to Shrewsbury (recently emerged from a long political retirement) to take over the part which the duumvirs had played for more than eight years. There was never any question of Shrewsbury's being equal to Harley in real influence. Where any disagreement arose between them over the new ministry's early appointments Harley almost always prevailed.[23] Theirs was not a partnership, save perhaps initially, at all comparable with that between Godolphin and Marlborough. But what is of critical importance to any understanding of politics in the tumultuous last four years of Stuart Britain is that Harley and Shrewsbury — Harley above all — carried on the managerial tradition of their predecessors. Harley, furthermore, did so in spite of the fact that his previous involvement with the Tories had been far closer before 1710 than had that of the duumvirs before 1702, and that his personal following at the time of his coming to power was overwhelmingly composed of Tories of varying hues.†

The very special relationship which existed in Anne's reign between the Managers and the monarch made it almost inevitable that the former should become the keystones of the political structure. Henry St. John preferred a different metaphor. "As he [Harley] is the only true channel through which the Queen's pleasure is conveyed", he told Orrery in 1711, "so there is and must be a perfect stagnation till he is pleased to open himself, and set the water flowing".[24] In a period of transition between Managers the whole pattern of politics significantly became kaleidoscopic and confused. So it was for a while in the spring and early summer of 1710 after the Queen, acting

* Pp. 229–30 below.
† These associations are fully explored in Chap. 8, pp. 260–4 below.

on Harley's secret advice, had foisted the Duke of Shrewsbury on Godolphin as Lord Chamberlain. Godolphin, fearing that the ground was about to be cut away from under his feet, hastily offered to enter into joint-management or "strict confidence", as Coningsby put it, with his unwelcome new colleague, "with a moderate regard to all parties" (though with less regard, it may be suspected, for the Duke of Marlborough, who was at this time abroad in the Low Countries). At the same time the Tories, though fairly certain that prosperity for them was just around the corner, were for a while quite unable to decide whether Godolphin or Harley was now their best channel of "interest with the Queen".[25] The next ministerial change, however, Sunderland's replacement in June by the moderate Dartmouth, removed their remaining doubts; and with Harley regarded from now on as the natural heir-apparent, the party seesaw once again acquired a stable fulcrum. It was from Harley, for instance, even though he still had no official position in the ministry, that the Tory peer, Lord Weymouth, earnestly requested "directions how to govern myself" soon afterwards, for (he explained) "I would not thwart anything that may be designed, by ignorance or inadvertence".[26]

Robert Harley was the last of the great political managers in post-Revolution Britain. But he was also prime minister, as in a sense Godolphin had been before him.* And this again was a fact of more than constitutional significance. In it lies one of the most important explanations of the striking differences which can be observed between the political machinery of Anne's reign and that of her predecessor's. William III had consciously withheld primacy from even the most indispensable royal servants; Sunderland, for instance, actually remained outside the ministry altogether until he became Lord Chamberlain in April 1697. The change after 1702 arose not so much from the constitutional limitations imposed on the Crown by the Revolution Settlement as from the personal limitations imposed on Anne by her sex, her wretched health, and her inferior abilities. For one thing, the Queen's recurring bouts of illness made her incapable of any prolonged mental and physical effort. In her later years, indeed, her invalidism was taken so much for granted that we are inclined to forget just how debilitating it normally was. After a visit to Windsor in September 1713 the Hanoverian resident wrote almost lyrically of the intense joy felt by the whole Court when on the 13th the Queen had walked for the first time since the previous February. True, she had been carried to the Royal Chapel, but she had actually walked back, needing no other help except her Spanish cane in her right hand and the

---

* See pp. 440–2 below, "Appendix C: Robert Harley, Earl of Oxford, as 'Prime Minister'".

support of the Duke of Shrewsbury on her left![27] But it was not merely Anne's physical weakness which severely restricted her capacity for political, and above all for administrative, activity. In addition her sluggish, undisciplined mental processes normally put most of the complexities of public business, especially financial and diplomatic business, beyond her. It was therefore essential for Queen Anne always to have the help of some trusted servant who would assume the real responsibility for supervising the day-by-day functioning of the administration, and for that matter of the whole constitutional machinery, including the relations between the government and Parliament. She needed, in other words, a prime minister, in the widest sense in which that was possible within the existing structure of the constitution. And this necessity could scarcely fail to affect two at least of the distinctive relationships involved in the working of the political system after 1702: that between the sovereign and the Managers, for obvious reasons, and that between the Court and the Whig and Tory parties, for reasons which should emerge more clearly later.

II

Monarchy in Britain, therefore, in the years between 1702 and 1714 was undeniably 'limited'. But whatever the limitations imposed on it by law, by convention, or by reason of personal inadequacies, it was none the less still monarchy; and one should not forget for a moment that the monarchical element remained an essential constituent not merely of the machinery of government but of the pattern of politics. Inevitably it was not so vital a constituent as in the period 1689–1702; but in the person of Anne Stuart it was very far from negligible. It is just not possible to write the history of politics in this reign and leave out Queen Anne. No more is it possible to explain how the political system functioned by concentrating purely on the politicians and virtually ignoring the Queen.

The accession of a thoroughly native and Church-of-England Queen on William's death buoyed up the Crown on a wave of affection, loyalty and popularity which had still not entirely spent itself twelve years later. If Anne had been quite prepared to be a cipher the political significance of this emotional reaction might have been confined purely to developments in the field of party ideology. But neither at the beginning of her reign nor at any time in it was Anne resigned to such a position. This is not the place to discuss the Queen's character in detail, nor for that matter to embark on a full analysis of her political and religious ideas; especially as both questions have been fully explored elsewhere.[28] But there seems no reason to doubt that to certain cherished views and ideals in matters of Church and State Anne clung as tenaciously as any of her Stuart forebears. Nor can we question the deep sense of responsibility and obligation which she brought to her royal office. Whatever the limits of her capacity for detailed business, her sedulous attendance at meetings of the full Cabinet[29] and her jealous care for her prerogatives in the field of civil and ecclesiastical appointments both demonstrate how seriously the last of the Stuart monarchs took her duties and privileges under the Revolution constitution. When the House of Commons requested her in an address presented soon after the opening of her first Parliament to remove the Whig Bishop of Worcester from his post as Lord Almoner to the Queen, her first reply was non-committal as to the bishop but explicit and unequivocal on the general constitutional issue raised: "that it was her own undoubted prerogative to retain or displace those that attended her person".[30] It was a timely reminder that the "influence of the Crown" in the years ahead was to be more than just a collective phenomenon. There was still some exercise of personal sovereignty in the years 1702–14; and this was a fact that was always of political significance and could occasionally be crucial.

Valetudinarian though she was, and normally timid and apprehensive by nature, Anne could never be browbeaten by any minister, least of all by one against whom she had already hardened her heart. In the spring of 1704, for example, she decided on the removal of two Cabinet ministers, Lord Jersey and Sir Edward Seymour, after they had persistently obstructed the policies of Godolphin and Marlborough in and out of Parliament. What Seymour's reaction was we do not know. He was in the country at the time and a messenger was sent down to Wiltshire by Secretary Hedges to collect his white staff. But the affronted and much-astonished Lord Chamberlain, after failing to get satisfaction from the Treasurer, sought an interview with the Queen. "I argued my case a little with her Majty", Jersey told his friend, Richard Hill, "not for my Staff, but for my own justification"; but Anne would offer no explanation for a dismissal that was quite unexpected, save the curt remark "that some of her servants had taken measures she did not approve".* The Queen could and frequently did assert her full dignity and regality against the politicians. When her prime minister, Godolphin, gave

---

* Blenheim MSS. F. 2–16: Hedges to Marlborough, 21 Apr. 1704; B.M. Loan 29/70/9: Robert to Edward Harley, 22 Apr.; Jersey MSS., letter 154: Jersey to Hill, 5 May. Jersey's letter, written by one who had only just ceased to be a Cabinet minister himself (cf. Add. MSS. 29589, ff. 121, 143), contains conclusive evidence, confirming that of John Ellis in 1702 (Add. MSS. 7074, f. 119), that Seymour sat in the Cabinet Council from

her a blunt choice between accepting his resignation or Secretary Harley's in February 1708 she dismissed him from her presence almost contemptuously, telling him "he should doe as he pleas'd, wth all she could find enough glad of that staff". What is more, she salted the wound by granting him twenty-four hours in which to reconsider his decision — a special concession, she made it clear, in view of his six years of service as her Lord Treasurer.[31] One who could mete out such cavalier treatment on occasion to the great was not likely to suffer patiently the brashness of lesser men. So young Richard Hampden found to his cost in August 1710, when he was offered a place at the Treasury Board under Harley and tried to use the opportunity of his audience with the Queen to lecture her on the folly of dissolving Parliament. Anne merely cut him off short with the crushing remark "that tho' she offer'd him an employment yet she did not ask his advise".[32] A few weeks earlier Lord Coningsby, the Vice-Treasurer of Ireland, whose own post was already in jeopardy, had unwisely ventured to demonstrate to Anne the dangers involved in removing her Whig ministers. He, too, was stopped in mid-speech by the Queen, "rising from her seat & . . . with a very angry air".[33] Even more impressive was her reaction this same summer to an urgent and somewhat tactlessly worded representation from the Dutch government, warning her against changing either her Parliament or her counsellors. Behind this move she saw the hand of her Junto ministers; and when the representation came before the Cabinet on 2 July she dealt both with it and them in blistering fashion — "worthy of Q. Eliz.", as William Bromley joyfully told his Tory friends. Her reply to the States "was given in the Cabinet without consultation upon it, & in such a manner that there was not a word offered agst it".[34]

Not even Robert Harley, who clearly exercised far more influence over the Queen's mind between 1706 and 1713 than any of his contemporaries, could use that influence crudely or even incautiously. This is all the more significant because Anne, from the time she first began to sign her letters to him "your very affectionett freind" in the summer of 1705, steadily developed a warmer personal regard for Harley than she ever felt for any of her other political servants. By 1710, if not earlier, it was already stronger than the feeling she had had for Marlborough in the early years of her reign; understandably so, because after the death of her husband in October 1708 personal friendships were the only thing, apart from her faith in God, which

1702 to 1704. Although he was only Comptroller of the Household in these years no politician of Seymour's stature holding office could conceivably have been excluded from the Cabinet.

could lighten the burden of a singularly bleak and painful life. On that fateful Thursday in March 1711, when Secretary St. John brought to Anne the news of Guiscard's attempt on Harley's life at the Cockpit, she wept uncontrollably for two hours, passed a sleepless night, and was so distraught with anxiety for the next two days that she worked herself into a high fever, and four of her doctors had to be specially summoned to her bedside at 5 o'clock on the Saturday morning to administer emergency treatment.[35] Her solicitude for Harley's health and safety after his recovery from his wound, and after she had signified her thankfulness by raising him to the earldom of Oxford, became almost obsessive. When the Treasurer was convalescing after an illness in October 1711, for instance, she begged him in a series of anxious letters "not to fatigue yourself with buisnes till you are better able to beare it", on no account to come to Windsor "for feare of catching cold", and to take every precaution to avoid "more relapses before the meeting of the Parliament".[36] And in November 1712 we find her writing, again from Windsor: "When you com next pray order it soe that you may be hear by day light, and take more care of yourself. . . ."[37]

Harley was the last man wilfully to abuse this precious relationship with the Queen by trying to ride rough-shod over her private feelings and prejudices. But even his political touch was not infallible. In occasional moments of stress he strayed over the delicate borderline between offering respectful and persuasive advice to the sovereign and attempting (or at least seeming to attempt) to force her hand. Anne's reactions to these aberrations were thoroughly in character; for all her political dependence on Harley, they were essentially those of the monarch rather than the friend. "I told you my thoughts freely, as I have always, and ever will continue to do on all occasions", she told him, after one of their rare altercations in 1712. "You cannot wonder that I who have bin ill used soe many yeares should desire to keep myself from being againe enslaved; and if I must always comply and not be complyed with, [it] is I think very hard and what I cannot submit to, and what I beleeve you would not have me".[38] Still more illuminating is letter which she wrote to the Lord Treasurer in August 1713, at a time when Oxford, having temporarily routed his ministerial enemies, was probably at the very peak of his influence with the Queen.

I was very much surprised to find by your letter that, though I had told you the last time you weare hear I entended to give the Treasurer of the Chamber to Lord De Laware, you will bring me a warrant in blank. I desire you would not have soe ill an oppinion of me as to think when I have determined anything in my mind I will alter it. I have told Lord De Laware I will give him this office and he has kissed my hand upon it. Therfore when you com hither bring the warrant with his name.[39]

Such incidents are revealing enough in themselves. But Anne's political influence was far from being limited to spasmodic displays of queenly temperament or assertions of dignity. On the most vexed political question of the day, the relationship that should exist between the Crown and the parties, she not only knew her own mind but stubbornly adhered to it. Moreover it would be wrong to imagine that her political ideas amounted to no more and no less than the notions which were implanted in her by a series of professional politicians who were the 'powers behind the throne' — that she was simply indoctrinated, first by Godolphin and Marlborough, then by Harley, and finally by Bolingbroke. It is true that both Godolphin and Marlborough in the opening years of the reign sought to inculcate in her that concept of a "moderating scheme" and a "mixed" administration which Anne was to favour from 1704 until the closing months of her life. But not until the over-confidence of the High Tory leaders and the crisis of "the Tack" played into their hands between April and November 1704 were they able effectively to counteract Anne's initial bias towards the Tories. So pronounced was this bias at the start of her reign that Sir Richard Gipps, a Suffolk Whig turned out of the commission of the peace in that golden High Church summer, swore "that if matters went or were like to goe so, he cared not how soone there should be another coronation".[40] The pledge which Anne made in 1702, that she would "be Queen of all her subjects, and would have all the parties and distinctions of former reigns ended and buried in hers",[41] was one which for nearly eighteen months thereafter she made little real effort to redeem. Long before the resignation in April 1704 of Lord Nottingham, the senior Secretary of State in her first ministry, Marlborough and the Lord Treasurer had been aching to be rid of this most embarrassing Tory colleague. Yet when the final showdown came the Queen was exceedingly reluctant to part with him. At first she declined to accept the seals when he offered, or rather threatened, to surrender them. Indeed the very fact that Nottingham felt confident enough to make the issue of his resignation a virtual ultimatum to the Managers, presenting them with a choice between his services and those of two Whigs in the Cabinet to whom he was inveterately opposed, can only suggest that he believed Anne to be so well disposed to the Tories that she would give way, at the crunch, to their pressure.[42]

Nottingham, however, overplayed his hand; and his miscalculation opened the way to Anne's conversion to the principle of balanced, coalition government. But having completed the conversion Godolphin and Marlborough soon found the Queen too enthusiastic a convert for their purposes. By 1705 her passionate belief in the justice of the Spanish Succession war and her realisation that a nation distracted by party extremism could not hope for victory had proved more powerful than her natural sympathy for the "Church party"; it had even made her resolve never to employ the old High Tory chieftains again;[43] but it had not overcome her antipathy towards the Whig Junto. And when their own political necessities compelled the duumvirs thereafter to move closer and closer to the Whigs, Anne deployed their own political theory of the *via media* against them to their frequent discomfort. On 21 September 1706, for instance, protesting to Godolphin against their proposal to bring the Earl of Sunderland into the government, she wrote: "the making him secretary, I can't help thinking is throwing myself into the hands of a party ... You say yourself, they [the Whigs] will need my authority to assist them, which I take to be the bringing more of their friends into employment, and shall I not then be in their hands? If this is not being in the hands of a party, what is?"* Even Harley was to find, especially in 1710 and 1711, that the sheer intensity of her desire "that the names of parties and factions may be buried in oblivion" could be a source of considerable embarrassment to him.[44] At length, in 1714, the ceaseless prompting of Bolingbroke and an act of folly on the part of the Whigs as decisive in its way as those of the High Tories in 1704† virtually convinced Anne that a full partnership between the Crown and "the Church of England interest" was necessary. Yet even at the very last Bolingbroke was not quite certain of the Queen's willingness to identify herself completely with a single party: he could not be wholly confident that a habit of mind to which she had clung for ten years had indeed been shed. "I do not absolutely despond", he told the Primate of Ireland on 27 July, two days

---

* Coxe, ii, 10. She reiterated the same arguments in frustrating the attempt of the Junto to break into the ministry in strength between the fall of Harley in February 1708 and the General Election in May; and it was undoubtedly Anne, and not her two Managers as has been suggested (by R. Walcott, *English Politics*, pp. 147–50), whom the Whigs had to thank for their failure at this juncture. *Ibid*. ii, 209–18, *passim*; Blenheim MSS. E. 27: Mainwaring to Duchess of Marlborough, [7 Apr. 1708].

† Viz. the attitude of some Whigs during Anne's critical illness in December 1713. This varied from genuine anxiety in some quarters to eager anticipation in circles less discreet. Swift, *An Enquiry into the Behaviour of the Queen's Last Ministry* (*Prose Works*, 1923, ed. Davis and Ehrenpreis, viii, 154); *Bolingbroke Corr.* iv, 469; Lonsdale MSS.: Nicholas Lechmere to Lowther, 9 Jan.

before the beginning of the Queen's final illness, "nor yet flatter myself".[45]

Although Queen Anne's political influence is clearly traceable in the general course of power-politics between 1702 and 1714 — in the changing complexion of ministries and the alternating fortunes of parties — it can be measured with greater exactitude in more personal and specific terms. To a politician struggling to attain the highest peaks of power the Queen's favour was naturally a priceless asset. The experience of Robert Harley in 1707–8, in spite of his eventual failure then, and again in 1710, furnishes ample proof of this. But in addition Anne was capable of playing a positive rôle in the construction of her Cabinets, and one which was not always palatable to her Managers. A good illustration of this is her selection of the Marquess of Normanby (soon to be Duke of Buckingham) as Lord Privy Seal in the first ministry of her reign. Normanby had years before aspired to her hand; but he had few other recommendations. He was a suspected Jacobite who in William's reign had been on terms of close friendship with Tallard, the French ambassador, and his appointment was clearly unwelcome to Godolphin and Marlborough. Marlborough, in fact, made it quite clear to the Imperial minister, who had shown some concern lest Normanby should leak war secrets to the French, that he was anxious about this and other consequences of the Queen's action; "but it is not in my power [he stressed] to intervene in everything . . .".[46] Eight years later the Queen took an equally independent initiative in appointing Lord Dartmouth to the post of Secretary of State for the Northern Department, after her advisers, Harley included, had argued for weeks over various other contenders.[47]

More frequently displayed, however, was her negative influence over the choice of her ministers. Anne's disfavour was always a formidable obstacle to the realisation of personal ambition, and at times an insuperable one. It condemned Somers, the most distinguished Whig statesman of his generation, to remain in the wilderness until the end of 1708, mainly because of an "aversion . . . that was personal to that Lord".[48] It thrice blocked the return of the High Tory Earl of Nottingham to the ministry, once in 1710 and twice in the following year; not because of his high-handed action in April 1704 but because he had bitterly offended Anne in November of the following year by his support of the "Hanover motion" in the House of Lords, pressing for the Electress Sophia to reside in England.* It also kept Lord Jersey chafing in the wings for a full year after the Tories returned to power

---

* *Bolingbroke Corr.* i, 281. See also pp. 113–14 above. It may seem remarkable that although other leading High Tories in the House of Lords who were equally associated with the motion, such as Rochester, Buckingham and Anglesey, later recovered Anne's

in August 1710, until death completed the frustration of his hopes of high office.

Jersey's case is less well known that Nottingham's, but is equally instructive. Although he had been dismissed under a cloud in 1704, his expectations in the summer of 1710 were avid and undisguised. At the beginning of the reign he had found the Queen prepared to overlook the evidence of his Jacobite sympathies in appointing him Lord Chamberlain; he saw no reason why she should not be similarly disposed in 1710. But on this point not only he but also Anne's new Managers miscalculated.[19] From the beginning of September until well into November both Harley and Shrewsbury tried hard to accommodate him in the Admiralty, latterly as First Lord, but they had to give way against Anne's "objections . . . to Lord Jer, which [Shrewsbury admitted] are no ways to be overcome . . .".[50] When the Duke of Newcastle died suddenly in the following July Jersey soon established himself, with Oxford's backing and that of other Cabinet ministers,[51] as the strongest candidate for the vacant post of Lord Privy Seal. But again the Queen resisted him, and it is very doubtful whether she would have succumbed at all had not the Lord Treasurer begged her most earnestly to put the success of the peace negotiations with France (in which Jersey himself had played a vital, though entirely unofficial, part) before her personal feelings, at a critical stage of his ministry's life:

The traine of unhappy consequences wch attended K: Wm, & lasted so long [he reminded Anne], from the prejudices he had agst Sr Tho: Trevor in the disposal of the great Seale, make me wth humble earnestness submissively to entreat yr matie to ballance the case before you . . . I have no other views, no other attachmts, but yr honor & service: this great affair now upon the anvil [the peace] wil languish, if not miscarry; yr ministry wil crumble al to peices, & what is of the last consequence, I cannot have any one *to help me in your service* . . . Your matie is too wise not to weigh every thing & compare the convenience & inconvenience, & you are too just to let your affairs suffer for the fault of another. What has passd wil shew the world if [*sic*] yr matie brings him in, not by importunitys, but for the good of the service.[52]

favour, Nottingham put himself permanently beyond the pale. The reason why she could never forgive him, according to Dartmouth, was that, while in office from 1702 to 1704, it was he more than anyone else who had sought to impress upon her that "whoever proposed bringing over her successor in her life-time, did it with a design to depose her" (n. to Burnet, v, 233). Anne saw Nottingham's crime in 1705 not just as an unscrupulous pursuit of party advantage but as a piece of intolerable hypocrisy. This was the main reason why she "would not hear" of him as Secretary in May 1710 and why his hopes were blasted again in 1711, when he bid in turn for the offices of Lord President of the Council and Lord Privy Seal.

Even then it was only after a solemn promise from her prime minister "to prevent anything of the like nature of being uneasy to you for the future"[53] that the Queen reluctantly agreed to Jersey's return to the Cabinet. And when the earl obligingly died on the very day his appointment was to have been announced, and his place was filled by a blameless cleric, John Robinson, Bishop of Bristol, she was doubtless much relieved.

Her attitude to the Earl of Peterborough is as significant in its way as her attitude to Somers, Nottingham and Jersey. From the time of his recall from Spain in 1707 by a ministry out of patience with his wayward conduct Peterborough's political career was influenced less by his Whiggery than by his personal and professional grievances against Marlborough and his antipathy towards Godolphin and Sunderland. These resentments enabled Harley early in 1710 to draw him into the Court conspiracy against the Godolphin ministry. In fact he became one of the small "juntilla", along with Somerset, Shrewsbury, Rivers and St. John, with whom Harley worked most closely in the early stages of the ministerial revolution of that year. Yet although Anne consented in October to Peterborough's appointment as General of the Marines, she refused to consider him for any major domestic employment, least of all for the Admiralty, which he coveted; and he spent most of the period of Oxford's administration cavorting round Europe on a series of rather bizarre diplomatic missions.[54] The attraction of these soon began to pall, and in December 1711 he begged to be allowed to be "above all things ... made usefull" or, failing that, to be permitted to return "to York buildings, my bottle of clarrett & Dr. Swift". But the Queen was not to be budged. "Ld. Dartmouth proposed to me the sending him to Venice", she had just previously informed the Treasurer. "I think he should be sent some where, for I feare if he coms home while the Parliament is sitting he will be very troublesome".[55] The trouble in this case was that Peterborough's undoubted, though fitful and somewhat theatrical, talents could never compensate in Anne's eyes for the fact that he was the Joker in Harley's pack — a rackety sort of fellow, an inconoclast and a religious sceptic, with the kind of character which she considered unsuitable for her Court and certainly for her Cabinet table. The Queen preferred more solid virtues in her public servants. A blameless private life was a fair passport to her good opinion — one reason, no doubt, why Robert Harley, that model of domestic rectitude, kept her favour for so long, while St. John, who shamefully neglected his wife and chased after street-women even when Secretary of State,[56] never made the final break-through into her closest confidence.

Even the lower rungs of the ladder of preferment could be made very precarious for an aspiring young politician for whom Anne had developed some aversion. And indeed there were those who never did succeed, while her reign lasted, in establishing a foothold there. In the spring of 1708, for instance, Godolphin was anxious to appease the brilliant young Whig lawyer, Peter King, who had caused the ministry undue trouble in the Commons during the previous session. But Anne refused to appoint him Solicitor-General, or even made him a Q.C., as Arthur Mainwaring discovered through his private contacts with the Marlboroughs in March 1708:

> I find by your Grace's discourse [he told Sarah] that Mr. Eyres has the first promise of attorney or solicitor, as either shall become vacant; and that at all adventures Mr. King is to have nothing, being so very disagreeable to the Queen, upon account of what he did in the business of the Admiralty,* or rather of Mr. Harley's misrepresentations. . . . When I saw his Grace [Marlborough] last week, and he was speaking of a vacancy that would be among the Barons of the Exchequer, I mentioned a thing which he says he has told my Lord Chancellor [Cowper] of, who likes it; and that was the making the Recorder a Baron, and getting the city to choose Mr. King Recorder, who in that case would, however, have the obligation to the Court. And this I believe might do very well for the present; but he says he believes it is impossible to prevail with the Queen to let him be one of her counsel, which signifies very little more than having a place within the bar, though at the same time she is willing to give him a sum of money. If this be so, we are in a sad way, that even money shall be given privately, to prevent the shewing the least open favour to one that has appeared against this hopeful Admiralty.[57]

Although well over 40 at the time of the Queen's death, King never rose higher in her lifetime than that same Recordership of London which Mainwaring had regarded as a mere temporary palliative in 1708.† Yet under George I he was to sit on the Woolsack.

The Queen was not always successful in resisting party pressure to force unwelcome ministers upon her. But even in fighting a losing battle she used delaying tactics that were astonishingly pertinacious. These were particularly in evidence during the period of her long resistance to the Whig Junto

---

* King had taken his share in the Commons' attack on the administration of the Admiralty in December 1707. Ironically his part seems to have been more judicious than that of some of his fellow Whigs, like Hampden (in fact his parliamentary speeches were generally noted for their cool restraint). Yet Anne imputed to him a particular personal animus against her husband, the Lord High Admiral. *H.L.Q.* xv (1951–2), 38: Brydges to Cadogan, 24 Dec.; *Vernon Corr.* iii, 284, 293; *Letters of Thomas Burnet, 1712–22*, p. 40.

† He was elected Recorder after a contest with Serjeant Richardson on 27 July 1708. On 12 Sept. the Queen knighted him. Luttrell, vi, 327, 333.

between 1705 and 1709. Right through the summer of 1705 she stonewalled against the proposed appointment of William Cowper as Lord Keeper, a change pressed on the Managers by the Junto lords after Lord Chief Justice Trevor (the Harley-Newcastle candidate of whom Anne apparently approved) had declined the job.[58] Her own wish, as she made plain to Godolphin, was "that there may be a moderate Tory found for this employment" which carried so large a measure of control over church patronage.[59] In the following year Anne stood "firme agst all batteries", as Harley put it, for nearly five months while the duumvirs struggled to overcome her bitter personal and political objections to Sunderland's becoming one of the Secretaries of State; and her Managers only prevailed in December 1706, on the very eve of the opening of Parliament, after a serious threat of resignation from Godolphin and a passionate personal appeal from Marlborough on his return to England.[60] In 1708 the office of Attorney-General remained unfilled from the middle of February to the end of October while the Treasurer tried every argument he knew to break down the Queen's prejudice against Lord Halifax's brother, Sir James Montagu. That the prejudice was irrational made his task no easier. As Solicitor-General during the previous session of Parliament, Sir James had remained more loyal to the Court than most of his friends. Only in the debates on the controversial Scottish Privy Council bill, and in particular on the specific issue of heritable jurisdictions in Scotland, had he openly parted company with the ministry. And yet to this solitary straw the Queen clung unshakeably for month after month, to the anger and incredulity of the Junto lords, while poor Montagu struggled to do the work of both offices.

> I beleive [said Halifax] the Court has some times show'd their displeasure against the servants who have been for attacking ministers, arraigning the administration, or joyned in some violent proceedings, ... but was it ever attempted to turn out a lawyer for giving his opinion in a point of law, which the Queen had left to the Parliament and referred to their consideration in her Speech?[61]

After one of many long and fruitless audiences with her on this subject, Godolphin wrote in understandable exasperation the same night that he believed he and Anne would have been wrangling yet, "if, after the clock had struck 3, 41 [the Prince of Denmark] had not thought fitt to come in and look as if he thought it were dinner time".[62]

On the other hand, towards men already in office for whom she had conceived a real liking or respect, especially those men of temperate politics to whom she was especially addicted, Anne was capable of showing great loyalty. She battled hard to retain Sir Charles Hedges in the ministry in 1706, ignoring in the process both the pleas of her Managers and the Duchess of Marlborough's taunts that Hedges had "voted in remarkable things"* simply in order "that he might keep his place; and [that] he did the same thing in the late King's time . . .".† In the same way she stood by the Duke of Somerset, in face of constant Tory sniping, for seventeen months after he had ceased to attend the Cabinet in August 1710, even when at length Oxford began to press most strongly for his dismissal. And on more than one occasion she rescued the moderate Dartmouth from the wolves of both parties, for as she once explained quite simply to Oxford, "I beleev him an honest man and I think [his resignation] would be very prejudicial to my service".63

Towards her prime ministers, in particular, Anne's sense of loyalty was intensely strong; and, what is especially significant, it was shaken in the end more by personal than by political factors. The fall of both Godolphin and Oxford is attributable in origin to a breakdown in their special personal relationship with the Queen. Her alienation from Godolphin, Bolingbroke later testified, began with "the personal ill usage which she received in her private life,‡ and in some trifling instances of the exercise of her power; for indulgence in which she would certainly have left the reins of government in those hands which had held them ever since her accession to the throne".64 Even so, when the time for the break came in the summer of 1710 she found it desperately hard to take the final step. In May she made use of one of her doctors as an unofficial ambassador to the Treasurer in a last bid to persuade him to sever his connection with the Marlboroughs, or at least with the termagant Sarah: for that, she told him, "wd be one of the happiest things imaginable". A letter of dismissal which she drafted early in July was shelved for a further month.65 And when she finally parted with her chief minister on 8 August it is notable that the only specific reason she gave for doing so was a personal affront — "what you said to me personally before the lords [of the Cabinet]".66 In the case of Oxford, the cause of the breakdown of his private *rapport* with Anne — a quarrel with her over the title of Duke of Newcastle — was not even remotely political. The dukedom was an honour which he sought in September 1713 not for himself but for his son, Edward,

---

* I.e. supported the Court on major issues.

† Sarah to the Queen, N.D. [1706], printed in *Conduct*, p. 168. See also pp. 255–6 below for Hedges; Add. MSS. 7059, f. 116 for Anne's "approbation of his services" in 1706.

‡ Godolphin's attempts to heal the breach between Anne and Sarah, commendable but ill-advised, were probably a factor of some importance here.

immediately after the latter's marriage with the heiress of the Holles family. It was an act which, at least in part, was forced on him by the pressure of the dowager duchess, but which he later came to realise was one of "never enough to be lamented folly", an act from which his credit at Court never recovered.[67]

Oxford, of all the politicians of the day, was the one least likely to under-estimate the effects of such a quarrel; for the whole trend of his political thinking over the previous decade had been towards making the Queen the true heart of the whole political system. The Crown, he believed, was the one ideal mediator between the parties; only the monarch could provide politicians with a common loyalty, transcending their loyalty to Tory and Whig, because only she could bridge the gap between them. "The foundation of the church is in the Queen," he wrote in September 1706, "the foundation of liberty is in her! Let her therefore be [the] arbitress between them."[68] Since the first years of the reign it had been his constant theme in his con-versations and correspondence with Anne that only by asserting herself to the full limit of her lawful prerogatives, especially in the crucial field of appointments, could she shore up the Revolution constitution against the stresses imposed on it by party ambition and party violence. Again and again he had insisted that if only she would give the lead, many of the independent country gentlemen, whom he looked on as the backbone of the constitution, would gladly take their tune from the Crown instead of from the party leaders. As he once put it: "if the gentlemen of England are made sensible that the Queen is the Head, and not a Party, everything will be easy, and the Queen will be courted and not a Party; but if other-wise ———".[69]

It had been Harley's persistent coaching of Anne, his determination to "treat her like a Queen",[70] which had done more than anything else to nerve her for her struggle against the concessions to the Junto which Godolphin urged on her from 1705 onwards. It had also precipitated the crisis of January–February 1708, when she almost succeeded in jettisoning Godolphin after he had refused to support Harley's scheme for a remodelling of the ministry in favour of the Tories. Finally it had given her the impetus to break with the Churchill family and its allies decisively in 1710. Even in the dark days of his own eclipse in 1708 and 1709, when his friend, Henry St. John, was ready to write off the Queen as a political force and to "despair of any salvation from thence",[71] Harley had never lost faith in the Queen's potentialities. On the contrary, that faith had been strengthened by the evidence of her remarkable resistance to the combined thrusts of the Junto and the Managers between February and October 1708, for throughout this period she had stood completely alone, save for Abigail Masham and the Prince. He himself had been in no position to give counsel or to render aid:

no body can say [he had written on 16 October] that I have any hand in influencing her or rendring her incompliant with the solicitations of Sr. Cha. Pye & my Lady [Godolphin and the Duchess of Marlborough]. It is now eight months since I have had no sort of communication with her, & several months that I have been at this great distance, so that the dificultys (I am wel informed) they complain of are not to be imputed to me; & therefore they should consider that it arises from the un-reasonableness of their own demands, & my Aunt's [the Queen's] true judgment & right understanding.*

And so Robert Harley had continued to preach his old philosophy. "Act by her own judgmt . . . ", he wrote in a private memorandum before one of his audiences with Anne in 1710, "& I wil be ready to obey and promote it."[72] After Godolphin's removal he even tried to associate the Queen more personally with Treasury business by inviting her at first to attend meetings of the new Treasury board, quite apart from her normal attendance at the Cabinet Council.[73] From his ministerial colleagues in the years 1710–14 he always required strict adherence to the forms and courtesies of govern-ment where Anne was in any way concerned. She must never feel that she was being by-passed.[74] He himself, in four years as prime minister, very rarely strayed from his chosen path of patience and tact in fulfilling his own part as the Crown's chief counsellor. Not for nothing did he choose to head one of his last *aides-mémoire* for an audience with Anne with the precept "Let thy words be few — by long forbear[ing] is a Prince persuaded".[75]

Ironically the very persistency with which Harley applied himself to restoring the failing political health of the Crown after 1704 created its own difficulties for the physician. Anne's growth in self-confidence, together with Harley's own genuine conviction that with patient guidance she could be given her head, made his own tasks in 1710, both destructive and con-structive, much more complex than they would otherwise have been.† They

---

* Longleat MSS. Portland Papers, x, f. 55: to "Cousin K. Stephens" [Mrs. Masham], 16 Oct. The key to the code is in B.M. Loan 29/38/1. This vital letter, never published, destroys the popular myth (credited even by the Churchills) that Harley had secret access to the Queen via Abigail in the weeks that followed his fall in Feb. 1708, and makes it clear that he did not even see her in the course of his brief visit to London from Hereford-shire in July.

† This question will be examined more fully in the writer's forthcoming study of the Oxford ministry.

also created serious difficulties for him later when it became politically desirable to make decisive concessions to the Tories. "A through change", Poulet was to admit in December 1711, was something which "*none* of her servants could perswade her to at first".[76] Oxford's personal dilemma was later highlighted by Jonathan Swift: "he could not with any decency press the Queen too much against her nature", he pointedly observed in 1714, "because it would be like running upon the rock where his predecessors had split". And when Anne declined to make the changes for which "the warm members in both Houses" were clamouring, he found himself in the unenviable position of being able neither to "own his want of power nor fling the blame upon his mistress".[77]

Yet however much Harley may have suffered later from the logic of his own philosophy, not least because he practised in office what he preached in opposition, there is no doubt that he recognised more clearly and shrewdly than any of his contemporaries the great reserves of power latent even in so weak a vessel as Queen Anne by virtue of her crown. And the ministerial revolution of April-September 1710, which brought him to the climax of his political career, was, despite all its vicissitudes, the greatest vindication of his political theory. It demonstrated that no ministry, however able and however strongly supported in Parliament, could preserve its self-confidence and stability once it had cause to fear the irrevocable withdrawal of the Queen's confidence from it. The loss of nerve, cohesion and tactical sense which the members of the Godolphin administration so patently betrayed in the crisis of 1710 was largely attributable to the knowledge that it was no longer Godolphin and Marlborough but Harley, Shrewsbury and Abigail Masham who had the Queen's ear. With this knowledge came the numbing feeling that they had become the sport of circumstances outside their control. The pattern was repeated on a smaller scale in December 1711, when for two weeks the members of Oxford's own Cabinet, their leader only excepted, suffered similar demoralisation (and with far less reason) when they became convinced that Anne had forsaken them and was preparing to countenance a Whig *coup*, a 1710 in reverse.[78] Neither to the Whig leaders in 1710 nor to the Tories in December 1711 did their formidable parliamentary strength bring much solace. Parliaments, after all, could at any time be dissolved. Indeed, as the events of 1703-4 had earlier demonstrated, even a dissolution might not be necessary to effect the rout of powerful ministers if the Queen was determined and the government itself divided. For then the three leading High Tory grandees of the day, Rochester, Nottingham and Seymour, had all been forced out of office at a time when they and their henchmen virtually controlled the Commons and were strongly entrenched in the Lords. One fact which the politicians had certainly to reckon with as long as the last of the Stuarts reigned was that a large parliamentary majority at their backs was no insurance against disaster once the Queen's hostility had become implacable.

Yet the converse of this situation also held good. No ministry and no great minister fell between 1702 and 1714 as a result of loss of control over Parliament. Parliament was the one political battlefield on which Oxford had *not* been defeated at the time of his dismissal in 1714. By contrast, earlier in the reign Godolphin and Marlborough had been able to survive a succession of demoralising parliamentary setbacks between mid-December 1707 and 6 February 1708. In both crises it was the royal closet and to a lesser degree the Cabinet room, and not the Lords' or Commons' House, which held the real keys to the outcome. It is not altogether surprising, therefore, that the patience of all Queen Anne's political managers was strained at times by the inability or unwillingness of the sovereign to accept the logic of a parliamentary situation: that the duumvirs spent three years, for instance, in the middle of the reign trying to persuade her that Whig votes should be paid for by Whig places; or that it cost Harley many anxious weeks in 1710 before he eventually convinced the Queen that a new ministry would never be viable until the old Parliament, with its potentially hostile majority, had been dissolved.[79] And it does seem that a very important clue to this strange insensitivity was that Anne herself never felt overawed by a party majority in the Lower House, however formidable. This may be one reason for the panic among Oxford's Tory colleagues in December 1711, at a time when, whatever their difficulties in the Lords over "No peace without Spain", they still had complete control over the Commons. They no doubt recalled that in January 1710 their opponents had enjoyed a majority of over a hundred in the Commons, but that only a handful of their leaders — Sunderland, Devonshire, Lechmere and Walpole — had felt confident enough to propose using this majority to force the pro-Tory Mrs. Masham out of the Queen's service by a hostile address. They doubtless remembered too that the support which these zealots attracted had melted away when Anne began personally to canvass scores of members, Whig as well as Tory, against the address. As one of Nottingham's correspondents had remarked at the time, "observers say they never saw such a turn in their lives, & Lady Fretchvill says in 30 years she has served she never saw the like".[80] Even so strong a nerve as Wharton's had wavered at the thought of such a step, although his political sense must have told him that without it the

Whig future was far from secure.[81] This whole incident in fact reveals as strikingly as any in the reign just how far removed from a state of "bondage", the state which some Tories once piteously depicted as her lot,[82] was the normal position of Queen Anne in relation to the politicians. Rather does it seem to bear out the truth of what Harley had confidently proclaimed to Marlborough in 1704: that "there is no one party, nay not both of them, can stand agst. the Queens frowns".[83]

III

The history of the abortive address against Mrs. Masham also highlights the importance of another aspect of personal sovereignty in the years 1702–14. This was the part played in the politics of the period by the royal closet, and particularly by the Queen's favourites.

Some measure of 'bedchamber politics' is endemic to personal monarchy, and a female ruler is peculiarly susceptible to it, though Anne at least was free from the problem of male favourites. To assess the true political importance in Anne's reign of what contemporaries called "the backstairs" is far from easy; but it is at least obvious that most politicians of the day *thought* them important. The control which Marlborough and Godolphin established over the Queen's government in 1702 was widely anticipated in view of the friendship which the Churchills and their relations had shown towards the princess during her unhappy years of estrangement from William III. And it was generally assumed that their extraordinary influence with her thereafter, right down to 1707 at least, was sustained by Anne's affection for Sarah Churchill, Marlborough's wife, who became First Lady of the Bedchamber and Groom of the Stole on the accession of the new ruler. The High Tory opposition, for instance, saw in the duchess the chief source of all their frustration after the spring of 1704, and William Bromley was once so carried away in the House of Commons by the enormity of her offence that he compared her influence on the Queen with that of Alice Piers on Edward III.[84] Historical perspective, however, makes possible a cooler appraisal than this. In retrospect it seems fairly clear that the Duke of Marlborough's military triumphs, and to a lesser extent Godolphin's part in financing them, were a far more potent factor in the supremacy of the duumvirate than bedchamber influence. This was so even before the Queen's famous quarrel with the duchess; and the fact is underlined by the survival of the Godolphin ministry for many years after relations between Anne and Sarah had first become strained,* and for as long as three years after all true friendship between the two women had been destroyed by increasing tension, jealousy and mutual recrimination. It was only in 1710, when Anne had finally become convinced of the need for peace, that Marlborough ceased to be indispensable and Godolphin to be tolerable.

But even during the years of Sarah's hold over the Queen, when as she later confided to Lady Cowper "she had no reserve from mee nor would suffer any thing like ceremony",[85] her politicial influence was much exaggerated by those outside the inner Court circle. In the matter of appointments, especially, it was very limited. Of her own efforts from the early days of the reign "to get honest men into the service, and such as would not give us up to France" the duchess once told Burnet with complete candour: "I never, or very rarely succeeded in any endeavour of this kind, till the ministers themselves came into it at last . . .".[86] She managed to procure a peerage for her friend, John Hervey, in 1703 and the post of Constable of the Tower for a needy Whig, Lord Essex; and she also claimed (with less justification) that "a great deal of drudgery" on her part was a vital factor in Cowper's advancement in October 1705.[87] But it would seem that the only major appointment which was ever made essentially on her recommendation was that of the Earl of Kent to the office of Lord Chamberlain in 1704. What truth there was in the rumours that "the Bug" paid her £10,000 for her good offices on this occasion we can only surmise; but in any event, by promoting the interest of a political nonentity Sarah was scarcely striking a significant blow for the cause of Whiggery.† In 1706 she struggled in vain for months to get her son-in-law, Sunderland, into Cabinet office. But in the end, as we earlier saw, it was other pressures which broke down Anne's resistance, and not the nagging and histrionics of her First Lady.

From mid-1707, with Sarah spending most of her time at Windsor Lodge, her influence with Anne was virtually at an end, and her ill-judged attempts to recover it were a continual embarrassment to her husband and to Godolphin. And yet the myth of her power died hard indeed. Just as the Whigs had seen her as their most potent advocate between 1705 and 1707 — "I must say . . . very sincerely, and without the least compliment", Sunderland had once told her, "that if England is saved it is entirely owing to your good intentions, zeal, and pains you have taken for it"[88] — so they remained

---

* There seems little reason to question Sir Winston Churchill's judgement that Sarah's influence was already on the wane before the end of 1705 (*Marlborough*, ii, 32–3).

† See *Wentworth Papers*, p. 134; Bodl. MS. Add. A. 269, p. 6: Edmund Gibson to Bishop Nicolson, 16 May 1704; pp. 227–8 below.

convinced for at least two years thereafter that the duchess's influence could be retrieved by assiduous courtiership. ". . . for God's sake, madam, come to court again", implored Mainwaring in the spring of 1708, "and be assured that, as nothing will so much dark the hopes of your enemies, nothing will so please or revive your friends . . ."; if she could not "put an end to the senseless farce of Harlequin and Abigail", he thought, no one could.[89] Mainwaring was Sarah's secretary, and may be suspected of flattery. Yet Sunderland, who rarely flattered anybody, was developing much the same theme at precisely the same time, and what is more, he reiterated it two years later.[90] As late as November 1709 his Junto colleague, Halifax, could still say with apparent sincerity that Orford's promotion to the Admiralty, the last stage in the Junto break-through into the ministry, "was entirely done by [the duchess], as everything had been that was right since the Queen's reign".[91]

After the quarrel with the duchess Anne's craving for private companionship and advice led her to confide increasingly in her husband, Prince George; and there are some grounds for thinking that it was he who eventually persuaded her to take what was perhaps the most difficult decision of her reign — to resolve the political crisis of February 1708 by agreeing to accept Harley's resignation as Secretary for the North.[92] But since independent political judgement was more or less beyond that amiable but bone-headed gentleman there was a period in 1707–8 when the consort's 'shadow', George Churchill, Marlborough's Tory brother and the dominating figure on the Prince's Council of the Admiralty, was able to exercise a certain indirect influence in the royal closet. Godolphin even blamed the Admiral's backstairs manoeuvres for much of the obduracy which the Queen showed in resisting Junto pressure on behalf of Sir James Montagu and Sir George Byng in the spring and summer of 1708.[93] Churchill's independence of mind certainly caused his relatives embarrassment; but they probably rated his influence too high. In any event that influence promptly came to an end with the death of the Consort in October 1708.

Thereafter, as every student of the period knows, Anne was thrown more and more into the company of her dresser, Mrs. Masham, who as Abigail Hill had begun quietly to usurp Sarah's place in her affections well over a year previously. And this new relationship inside the closet was the more important to the Queen because Robert Harley, a remote kinsman of Mrs. Masham's, was for two and a half years deprived of official opportunities of gaining access to the royal person. The growth of Abigail's influence and her intrigues on Harley's behalf became in later years an accepted part of the gospel of Whig historians in explaining the collapse of the Godolphin administration in 1710. Their verdicts have seemed far too unsophisticated for most modern authorities, who have probed instead for much deeper political, economic and religious circumstances that would account for the fall of the Whigs. Yet the opinions of nineteenth-century scholars were no more than a reflection of all the dark suspicions and fears nurtured by Whig politicians at the time. The latter understood, better perhaps than some recent historians have appreciated, just how crucial was the Queen's personal attitude towards their party. What they did exaggerate, almost certainly, was Abigail's influence in governing that attitude.

As early as November 1708 Godolphin had been disturbed to find "that some of the Whigs are making up to Mrs Masham", and less than two months after this Marlborough was already afraid it would henceforward be "very difficult to persuade [Anne] to see any thing which Mrs Masham would not have her believe".[94] At the height of the crisis over the Essex regiment, at the beginning of 1710, the ministers' fear of Abigail became almost pathological. The duke, whose political judgement was normally cool, told his son-in-law "that all must be undone, if this poison continues about the Queen", while Mainwaring declared himself "quite sick allready of a countrey where it is thought possible that there can be a moment's competition between him [Marlborough] and a stinking chambermaid".[95] After the humiliation of hearing from the Queen's own lips that the coveted regiment of dragoons was intended for Mrs. Masham's brother, a junior colonel of infantry, and not for his own nominee, General Meredith, the duke withdrew with his wife to Windsor on 15 January, abandoning his duties both in Parliament and in the Council, and leaving neither the Queen nor any of his colleagues in doubt that he was prepared to leave the royal service unless Abigail was removed. There is even some evidence that he sympathised with Sunderland's plan for a showdown in the House of Commons. And though, after eight days of suspense, a compromise was patched up and Marlborough returned to town, his own relations with Anne and the Managers' standing in the ministry were never the same again.[96]

The fact remains, however, that Abigail Masham herself took a much more modest view of her power to sway the Queen's mind than did the men who so feared and detested her. Her surviving letters to Harley, written between July 1708 and March 1710, provide the most convincing evidence of this:[97] "they [the Whigs] come so fast upon her I have no hopes of her deliverance, for she will put it quite out of her friends' power to save her" — such was the pessimistic theme of one of her earliest letters. In September

1709 we find the favourite lamenting that the Queen "keeps me in ignorance and is very reserved", and she was nervous even of reading Harley's letters to her in the Queen's presence, though Harley clearly intended them for the sovereign's ear. Even as late as March 1710, after the Sacheverell trial and on the very eve of the ministerial revolution, it is astonishing to note the desponding tone of the woman whom the Whigs believed to be all-powerful behind the scenes. She seriously doubted whether her influence was adequate even for the relatively limited task of persuading the Queen to appoint two Tory bishops, and was full of apprehensions about the future: "for my part", she told Harley, "I should be glad to leave my aunt* before I am forced from her".[98]

It is in the last four years of the reign that Mrs. Masham's influence, and the political importance of the royal closet, can be seen in their clearest perspective. Early in the life of the Harley administration, when the favourite was being "visseted in crowds by Whigs & Torys", the Captain-General expressed the opinion "that in some little time the Tories will be desirous to lessen the power and credit of Mr. Harley; but as long as Mrs Masham continues they will find it very difficult".[99] Yet the new prime minister himself did not share this view of his kinswoman's indispensability to his fortunes. The Whigs might continue to rail against the insinuating influence of "that Pimplefaced Bitch". His own colleagues, great and small, might be as chary as they liked of offending Abigail, or for that matter any of her relations ("for one wou'd take care", Peter Wentworth wrily reminded his brother, "not to fall from the same *Hill* we have seen others before us").[100] But Harley himself, except at occasional moments of particular difficulty,[101] paid little more than token court to her from the time he was safely into the saddle in 1710 until the summer of 1713.[102] This can only suggest that during the years of his conspiracy against the Whigs he had recognised in Mrs. Masham a useful means of communication with the Queen, but not in any sense a key to the Queen's feelings and attitudes. Anne's relations with Abigail were in fact very different from her previous relations with Sarah. She was grateful to her for her companionship in the unhappy years from 1707 to 1710; and she remained grateful thereafter. But this was not a relationship between two friends so close that social barriers could scarcely affect them; nor was it one in which the Queen's freedom of will was to any significant degree sacrificed. When Sarah at length resigned all her Household offices in January 1711 the Queen conferred on Abigail only the least valuable and least prestigious of her posts, that of Privy Purse. Snobbery was

* The Harley-Masham code name for Anne.

one of Anne Stuart's least attractive traits, and she was always acutely conscious of her favourite's lowly social status. On these grounds she raised strong objections to Harley's suggestion, made more than once, that Mrs. Masham's husband should be given a peerage. "She took me up very short last night only for mentioning it", noted Harley ruefully in a memorandum which was apparently written some time in the summer of 1711.[103] Even when twelve new peers were urgently needed to meet a dire emergency in the House of Lords the following December, Oxford only included Masham in his reserve list, and put his name forward at the last minute only when the M.P. for Beverley, Sir Michael Warton, declined.[104] And Lord Dartmouth, who made the final proposal to Anne, still found her very hard to convince. "The queen told me, she never had any design to make a great lady of her [Abigail], and should lose a useful servant about her person: . . . but at last consented, upon condition she remained a dresser, and did as she used to do".[105]

Indeed, if anyone in the Queen's private circle succeeded in securing a measure of dominance over her mind in the first eighteen months or so of Harley's ministry it was not Abigail but the Duke of Somerset's red-haired Percy wife, who succeeded Sarah as Groom of the Stole and First Lady of the Bedchamber. Swift was not alone in believing her to be largely responsible for the Queen's apparent wavering at the time of the peace crisis in November and December 1711: "this is all your d———d Duchess of Somerset's doings," he complained to Stella. "I warned them of it nine months ago, and a hundred times since: the secretary [St. John] always dreaded it."[106] Such convictions explain why, when Somerset himself was dismissed from the government in the following January, his Whig friends begged him to change his declared intention of compelling his wife to resign her Court offices. Anne was pleading that "her health . . . wd be greatly injur'd, if it happen'd that the Duke woud not let her stay in"; and Lord Cowper and some of his Junto associates were not without hopes that "possibly some good may come of it".[107] In the event little further positive advantage did accrue to the Whigs from the duchess's position at Court, although the ministry's continued fear that it might do so is reflected in the strong rumours that Oxford had again pressed the Queen unsuccessfully to remove her in the summer of 1712.[108] While Dartmouth later maintained that she was still "by much the greatest favourite, when the Queen died", it was as "a credit and ornament to the court" rather than as a political wire-puller that she retained to the end both Anne's affection and the respect of all but the most inveterate of her Tory entourage.[109]

Oxford's comparative neglect of Abigail, meanwhile, cost him seemingly nothing; at least not until his quarrel with Anne in September 1713. Thereafter the Queen's dependence on Lady Masham did increase, and the fortunes of Bolingbroke, "ploughing with the same heifer" (or so the Whigs saw it) as Harley before him,[110] took a decisive turn. Bolingbroke's calculated investment in the favourite's influence in the closing year of the reign, enhanced by his procuring for her both legal and illegal profits from the South Sea trade,[111] in the end paid dividends. Only in the last weeks of his ministry, with his political existence hanging by a thread, did the Treasurer attempt to reply in kind: first by trying to revive the influence of the Groom of the Stole and mobilise it in his own interest;* and when this failed (less through the Duchess of Somerset's lack of favour than through her reluctance to make use of it on Oxford's behalf),[112] by a last and rather pathetic attempt to patch up his quarrel with Lady Masham through the Queen's mediation.[113]

On the whole, however, bedchamber intrigues had a peripheral rather than a central place in the normal pattern of politics between 1702 and 1714. The royal favourites occasionally played a negative or destructive rôle of real importance, but were never an indispensable positive factor in the success of any of Queen Anne's administrations. Oxford himself plainly recognised this when he told Lady Masham quite bluntly in May 1714: "You cannot set any one up; you can pull any one downe".[114] And yet even if contemporaries often exaggerated the importance of the royal closet, their preoccupation with backstairs manoeuvres does at least underline once again the point that government in these years was still very much *the Queen's government*, in practice as well as in name. It also serves to remind us that the working of politics in the age of Anne was continually being affected, if not in one way then in another, by this quite basic constitutional fact.

---

* B.M. Loan 29/10/8: notes for an interview with Anne, 8 June 1714, including the passage "Send for the D^chs of Somerset — no body else can save us". Kreienberg (S.H. Cal. Br. 24 England, 113a, f. 324) mentions a second approach to the duchess, this time via her husband, at the beginning of July.

CHAPTER SEVEN

Parliament and the Parties:
The Structure of the Whig Party

I

IN the previous chapter we observed one way in which the post-Revolution constitution helped to determine the working of politics. It was not of course the only way. Of even greater importance than the fact that government after 1702 was still the Queen's government was the fact that it was also, to an extent unparalleled before 1688, *government through Parliament*. Parliament after the Revolution became an indispensable part of the machinery of state. It would not be quite accurate to describe it as a 'permanent' part of the political scene. During the lifetime of the Harley ministry between August 1710 and July 1714, for instance, it was in session for only 21 months out of $47\frac{1}{2}$; and the long periods when Parliament stood prorogued, or between the dissolution of one Parliament and the first meeting of another, were often intervals of great political activity and importance. At the same time regular, annual sessions of Parliament were now the invariable norm, and the political effects of this were incalculable. One effect was the enhanced importance not merely of Parliament as a body but of the individual members who made up each House. By Anne's reign Parliament had become the surest road for the able young man of ambition to take into the favoured circle of office and power — a surer road than the royal bureaucracy or (Marlborough's case notwithstanding) than the armed services. It was parliamentary dexterity, not family connection or royal favour, that brought Robert Harley into the Cabinet in 1704. It was their stature in the House of Commons which made Walpole a junior minister after four years in Parliament, and St. John Secretary-at-War after only three, and which brought Wyndham into the latter office as a member of little more than eighteen months' standing. Under the more arbitrary government of the earlier Stuarts these men might well have had to take a different and more tortuous road to the top. It is conceivable they might never have attained it.

A consequence of very much wider significance which stemmed from Parliament's indispensability to government after 1688 was that its management became from now on a perpetual care of the Crown and its advisers. Even in the periods of respite when the Houses were not in session provision had always to be made against the next meeting of Parliament; and once that meeting took place ceaseless vigilance was the order of the day: "there's no such thing as safety", Godolphin recognised, "till the Black Rod knocks at the door".[1] In fact the overriding political problem confronting the Queen's ministers after 1702 was the forging of an effective working partnership between Crown and Parliament.

Not the least of the factors which influenced their calculations was the existence on the statute book since 1694 of the Triennial Act, which made it illegal for a sovereign to keep a Parliament in being for longer than three years. This change had profound repercussions on the working of politics as well as on the development of the constitution. It meant, for one thing, the holding of a General Election at least once every three years, with a probability that in practice the incidence of elections would be even more frequent. The occurrence of no fewer than ten General Elections in the space of twenty years between 1695 and 1715 was something quite without precedent in English history, and as things turned out it has had no parallel in the 250 years that have followed. The result was that throughout these two decades the political temperature at the grass roots of politics, in the constituencies, was rarely allowed to descend to normal; while in a large number of key constituencies (counties where the party balance was fairly even, cities and boroughs with large, volatile electorates, and many smaller incorporated boroughs where control of the council or even of the mayor was a crucial factor in commanding parliamentary seats) the temperature was feverishly high for much of the time. Far from exhausting party passions, as has sometimes been suggested, this atmosphere of hot-house intensity did much to sustain and stimulate them, and so added very materially to the problems of the political managers at Westminster.

The passing of the Triennial Act meant, secondly, that the Crown was now unable to hold on to a docile or amenable Parliament (supposing it were fortunate enough to acquire one) for longer than three years. The authors of the 1694 bill wanted no repetition of the experience of 1661–79. And in their anxiety to assert "the freedom of Parliament" they ensured that in addition to the problem of annual sessions the Crown would be presented with the further problem of a House of Commons whose complexion was subject to continual change. It is true that not all the General Elections and the frequent changes of membership which took place after 1694 were the result of statutory dissolutions. But the majority were; and even the dissolution of William III's last Parliament by Queen Anne in the summer of 1702, which was technically voluntary, could not legally have been postponed beyond the early autumn under the terms of an act passed in 1696.[2] It would be naïve to imagine that every dissolution between 1695 and 1715 was politically convenient for the Court. There is evidence that of the five General Elections held during Anne's reign at least one (that of 1713), and possibly another two (those of 1702 and 1708), would not have been held if the Queen's ministers could by law have avoided them.* At the beginning of 1708 many Whigs would clearly have preferred to hang on to the small but workable majority which by that time they enjoyed in the old Parliament, instead of risking setbacks in the new Election due in the early summer. It was strongly rumoured that proposals to suspend the Triennial Act were being aired in their "private cabals";[3] but before any decisions could be taken the Jacobite invasion attempt had played into the party's hands and made most of its supporters positively anxious to do battle at the polls. In 1713 the pressure to amend the law came from their opponents, rejoicing in the huge majority they had secured in the exceptionally favourable circumstances of October 1710.[4] But Cabinet ministers preferred in the end to let things take their statutory course, and to consider instead the repeal of the Triennial Act in the first session of a new and (they hoped) equally favourable Parliament.[5] Those who shouldered the main responsibility for carrying on the Queen's business between 1702 and 1714 were under no illusions about the effects of triennial Parliaments. It was obvious that in some ways they made the problem of parliamentary management appreciably more difficult than it would otherwise have been. They stimulated the divisive tendencies already present in the nation, and ensured that an essential instrument of government would not merely be divided into parties, but divided into parties whose relative strength was rarely the same for more than two or three years at a time. It is surely significant that on the one occasion when the Queen's Managers were presented with a legal loophole to avoid a dissolution, when the separate Parliaments of England and Scotland were abolished in 1707, they gratefully made use of it; although Secretary Harley protested that the arguments adduced in support of their decision amounted to no more than "gross and substantial nonsense".[6]

If the indispensability of Parliament to the working of government

* The evidence regarding 1702, the most interesting case of the three, is discussed in Chap. 11, pp. 367–8 below.

created problems for the Court, it would seem natural to assume that it created corresponding opportunities for the party leaders, bidding for political power. In some ways this was true. No opposition party after 1689 had to fear the effects on its cohesion or even on its very identity of a long period of non-parliamentary rule, which the Exclusionist Whigs had found so damaging between 1681 and 1685. Opposition leaders could be certain during Anne's reign of anything from $3\frac{1}{2}$ to $6\frac{1}{2}$ months in every year in which they could exploit what parliamentary assets they possessed to further their own claims to office. Yet if annual sessions opened up these opportunities, triennial elections undoubtedly made them more difficult to realise. They did so by the strain which they placed on party organisation, not only in the constituencies but in Parliament itself. The Whig and Tory chiefs could not effectively promote the policies and interests of their parties, nor successfully compete with their opponents for the all-important favour of the Crown, unless they could be sure of some measure of discipline among the rank and file of their parliamentary followings. Such discipline was unattainable without the elements of organisation, at least so long as Parliament was in session. Since neither Whigs nor Tories in Anne's reign possessed a leadership that was universally acknowledged throughout the party, still less a formal party machine providing 'whipping' in the modern sense, it would have been no very easy matter to supply this organisation in any event; but with the frequent changes of personnel that took place in the House of Commons between 1695 and 1715 the problem became even more taxing.

The efforts that were made to try to surmount these difficulties, the variety of ways (some of them astonishingly sophisticated) in which the party men of the period contrived to organise themselves, both to carry out policies and to compete for power, are in some ways the most intriguing aspect of early-eighteenth-century politics. In order to understand them, however, we must first look in some little detail at the structure and composition of both the Whig and Tory parties after 1702.

II

Broadly speaking the Whig party in Parliament during Anne's reign was an amalgam of three main elements: the Country Whigs, the Court Whigs and the Junto Whigs. At times, notably from 1703 to 1705 and again after 1710, these elements were so nearly fused that the Whigs came close to achieving the appearance, and for a while even the reality, of a united and homogeneous party. More usually, however, the three elements were distinguishable to contemporaries, if not always in the clearest of colours, and they certainly merit separate consideration in any historical analysis of the party at this period.

The Country Whigs were represented in all Post-Revolution Parliaments by a very variable number of independent backbench members of the House of Commons. In the Lords there was virtually no parallel to them, although a tiny handful of Whig peers did accept the austere code of the third Earl of Shaftesbury and make some effort after 1702 to perpetuate the old country traditions of the party outside the Commons. Shaftesbury's personal activity was drastically curtailed after Anne's accession by consistently poor health. But as the much-respected 'conscience' of the party his exhortations from Chelsea and St. Giles still carried some influence, and disciples like the first Baron Hervey and the second Earl of Warrington tried to follow his precepts. To Hervey it was intolerable that his party's leaders should ever disregard "justice and the safety and happyness of their fellow subjects" merely "to serve their Prince's turn",[7] while Warrington prided himself on his parliamentary independence: "[I] have never tyed myself to any sort of persons", he once claimed, "but consider'd things to the best of my small reason".* In the Lower House the Country Whigs, "the old staunch Whigs" as they like to be called,[8] had been a numerous and important body in William III's reign; but they unquestionably declined both in numbers and in independent significance in the course of Anne's. They enjoyed a brief but influential period of revival between 1705 and 1708. But following the General Election of 1708 their acts of independence became more isolated and less organised, so that James Craggs described them as "some few Whimsicalls" in 1709 and Francis Hare dismissed them even more contemptuously in 1710 as "a small handful", with whom no ministry could profitably or practicably "deal".[9] After 1710 it became extremely rare for these members not to follow the political lead given by the Junto lords and their lieutenants or by other recognised Whig chiefs. The reason for this seems plain enough. In the hour of tribulation these leaders had a stronger claim than they had ever had in the past to be representing party and not

---

* B.M. Loan 29/127: to Oxford, 11 May 1713. Although on one occasion in the 1713 session he voted with the Court against his party, having been promised the arrears of his father's pension, long overdue from the previous reign, he made it quite clear to the Lord Treasurer that he was not selling his soul. "I did not ask it of yr Ldp", he reminded him, "nor do I want it to buy my bread." *Ibid.*: 10 June 1714. See also p. 388* below.

merely sectional interests. "The nation, I believe", wrote Shaftesbury, "will be no more endangered from what was called a Whig cabal".[10] In the last four years of the reign, therefore, it was normally only on certain perennial country issues, such as Place bills, that the Country Whigs preserved their separate identity. The boast of one of their representatives, Edward Wortley Montagu, in 1715, that since "the Court Whigs had quite lost the esteem of the nation when my Lord O[xford] got into power, . . . the Country Whigs did everything that was done against the Court during that infamous ministry" was no more than a pathetic piece of self-delusion.[11]

The membership of the Country Whig group in the House of Commons was not confined after 1702 to a single social stratum. For one thing, it always included a small number of independent merchants, some metropolitan, such as John Rudge, but mainly provincial, like the Devonian John Dibble, Colchester's Sir Isaac Rebow and Sir Thomas Johnson of Liverpool.* Also active among the Country Whigs in Anne's reign were a handful of lawyers, such as Richard Vaughan, M.P. for Carmarthen, and. the more celebrated Peter King, M.P. for Beeralston, and even an occasional carpet-bagger like Sir John Cropley, a Londoner resident in Red Lion Square whose only claim to represent his Dorset borough was the friendship and patronage of Lord Shaftesbury. But, as one would expect, the great majority of Whig members who were associated with "country" attitudes and policies during Anne's reign were themselves country gentlemen. They ranged from wealthy county landowners at one end of the scale (such great local *seigneurs* as Sir Richard Onslow, John Morgan of Tredegar with his income of £7000 a year, James Lowther of Whitehaven and Richard Edgecumbe), through solid "middling" gentry like John Thornhagh, Sir Michael Biddulph and Peter Gott,[12] down to small fry of the stamp of Roger Tuckfield, the local squire who sat for the little borough of Ashburton in Devonshire between 1708 and 1711, and again after 1713. They ranged likewise from prominent and active House of Commons men, like Edward Wortley Montagu, Thomas Onslow and Richard Nevil, to relatively inert "occasional members" — the wealthy Sir William Bowes, M.P. for Durham, for example, or Henry Henley of Colway, who even when he sat for Lyme Regis in the years of peril for his party between 1710 and 1714 was

---

* The Country Whigs specified in this section have been identified partly on the basis of correspondence and of electoral interest, and partly on the more negative evidence of the Whig names missing from the list of Court voters in the key division on the "Whimsical clause" in 1706. This list is printed in *Bull. I.H.R.* xiv (1936), 30–33, and there are various copies of the original extant, e.g. in Bodl. Fol. θ. 591 (84).

absent from every key division on the Whig side of which we have a full record.[13] And the contrast was equally sharp between the warm, undeviating partisans among these gentry and the less committed, the more open-minded or the more wayward Country Whigs. At one end of the scale we meet such figures as Sir William Ellys (Grantham), Sir William Robinson (York), the Yorkes of Richmond and the Onslows of Surrey. At the other end we encounter Sir John Guise, who at the time of Sacheverell's impeachment "was so civil as to promise [the Dean of Gloucester] not to meddle in it, & kept his word"; or Daniel Wilson, the young Westmorland member whose conversion the Tory ministry was encouraged to hope for in 1710; or William Harris, of whom Sir Francis Drake wrote glumly after the 1708 Election in Devon: "after all my services I cannot tell what to make of him; we can have no comfort in bringing him into Parliament but that of turning Northmore [a Tory] out".[14]

The predominance among the Country Whigs of gentry elected on their own interests and responsible to no one but their constituents, and the consequent unpredictability of their attendance at Westminster, meant that their capacity for organisation was at all times somewhat limited. In fact, as we shall later see, they were able to operate really effectively as an independent force only when led by careerist politicians. Sometimes they would rally behind men who had donned a "country" mantle largely for the sake of political convenience, as was the case with the brilliant young Whig barrister, Peter King, and (more briefly) with Robert Eyres, the Recorder of Salisbury. At other times they were inspired by prominent figures who found themselves in temporary sympathy with the country interest on particular issues, as did Sir John Hawles, a former law officer of the Crown who none the less approved of Place legislation, and above all James Stanhope, who led the campaign for the "Whimsical clause" in the winter of 1705–6, and who supported a Place bill as late as 1710.[15] One of the most impressive tributes ever paid by one politician to another in the early eighteenth century was bestowed by that fierce independent James Lowther on Stanhope, one of those "military men" whose influence he normally deplored: "His honorable promoting of bills to lessen the number of officers in the House when he himself was one, because he believ'd one time or other they wld ruine the constitution, is a proof of his integrity that wil never be forgot."[16]

With a handful of exceptions such as King, Eyres and Stanhope, however, we would not normally expect to find the more active of the Whig politicians of Anne's day associated with the Country Whigs. We would expect to

locate them instead in one or other of two further categories: either among
those politicians who could conveniently be classed together under the generic
name of "Court Whigs", or among the leaders and followers of the great
Whig Junto.

The Court Whigs never formed a single 'group' in the accepted sense of
that word. Normally they were no more than a miscellaneous collection of
individuals who had certain qualities in common: principally, moderate
Whig views, a greater deference towards the monarch than most other
members of their party, a distaste for the domination of the Junto, and a
preference, all things being equal, for the comforts of office or other advantages of official favour rather than for any extravagant flights of party
principle. No one better expressed the central creed of the true Court Whig
at its simplest than Robert Monckton. At the time of the change of ministry
in September 1710 he came hurrying up to town from Yorkshire "to take
care of his place", and was so determined not to leave London again until he
was securely entrenched that he even conducted his electioneering at Aldborough the following month by correspondence.[17] To Peter Wentworth
he was quite frank about the reasons for his behaviour. He well knew "that
the party [would] be very angry with him", but was quite resolved that
"tho' he served them as long as he cou'd . . . he wou'd not fly in the Queen's
face for them".[18]

Five prominent Court Whigs served at various times as Cabinet ministers
during Anne's reign. Henry Boyle was Secretary of State from 1708 to 1710,
the first Duke of Devonshire was Lord Steward from 1702 to 1707, the
Duke of Newcastle Lord Privy Seal from 1705 to 1711 and the Duke of
Shrewsbury Lord Chamberlain from 1710 to 1714.* The longest spell in
high office, however, was enjoyed by the Duke of Somerset, who held the
post of Master of the Horse from 1702 to 1712 and was in the Cabinet for all
but the last eighteen months of this period. The one commoner among the
five (and it was no coincidence that there should have been only one) is an
interesting study. Henry Boyle had been retained as Chancellor of the
Exchequer by Godolphin when the Queen's first ministry was under construction in the summer of 1702, and he held this important House of

---

* Although Shrewsbury held office in Anne's reign only in a period of Tory supremacy
(1710–14) he never quite ceased to be suspect on the score of his pre-1702 party affiliations
(see, e.g., his letter to Oxford, 4 Apr. 1712, B.M. Loan 29/159). His appointment as Lord
Treasurer in succession to Oxford in 1714 afforded the Oxford Jacobite, Thomas Hearne,
cold comfort. "As for Shrewsbury," he wrote on 1 Aug. 1714, "he is a very great Whigg."
Remarks and Collections, iv (ed. D. W. Rannie, 1898), 388.

Commons' post not only while the tide of High Toryism was running at its highest between 1702 and 1704, but also thereafter, until his promotion to the Cabinet after Harley's fall in February 1708. Arthur Onslow later wrote of him that, although "acceptable to the whigs", Boyle was "without any party violence, and never engaged in mean things"; and he also commented that, as befitted a good Court Whig, he was "wary and modest in all his actions".[19] His reputation for cool and restrained political behaviour was indeed such that Arthur Mainwaring, who knew him well, was plainly astonished in the winter of 1709–10 to hear "Mr. Boyle's manner of talking this morning about the business of Sacheverell's sermon . . .; for he talked of it [he told Sarah] with another sort of warmth than ever I heard him".[20]

Normally, however, those Court Whigs who found their way into the highest offices of state were not able commoners like Boyle but great territorial magnates, noblemen who could well afford to affect an independence of the party chiefs. The Dukes of Newcastle and Somerset were classic examples. Both of them enjoyed considerable influence under Anne — very much more influence than their modest talents warranted. Newcastle owed this influence largely to the fact that he was the richest peer in Britain and a great electoral potentate, especially in the north of England. In the last two sessions of the Parliament of 1705–8 he had a tight personal following in the House of Commons of ten members, nearly all of whom were either mainly or entirely indebted to him for their seats,* and between 1708 and 1710 his clients were equally numerous.† But in part, at least, the duke was able to capitalise on another asset, his friendship with Robert Harley, which gave him a convenient foot in two camps. Newcastle's Whig colleagues, however, always found him more dependable in office than the treacherous Somerset with his Tory ancestry. Admittedly he was too easily flattered by the Queen's good opinion, and as Sunderland once said, "a place of 3000 l. a year [was] a temptation to his inclinations". But even when

---

* Viz. George Whichot (Lincs. Co.), Awnsham Churchill (Dorchester), John Digby (Newark), John Plumptre (Nottingham), Robert Molesworth and Sir Hardolph Wastneys (East Retford), John Thornhagh (Notts. Co.), Robert Monckton and William Jessop (Aldborough), Craven Peyton (Boroughbridge).

† After the 1708 Election Richard Sutton replaced Digby and Thomas White took over Molesworth's seat. Wastneys lost his seat at Retford and Thornhagh defected to the Country Whigs; but Newcastle gained an extra member at Nottingham, where Roby Sherwin joined Plumptre, and the intervention of the duke's "myrmidons" at Pontefract helped to confirm William Lowther in his seat there. Apart from his influence in all these constituencies Newcastle's interest extended to Sussex county elections, to Hull, and to the city of Westminster.

persuaded by Harley to stay in office after the ministerial revolution of 1710 the Lord Privy Seal could not be coaxed into opposing his friends in the House of Lords, a fact which no doubt reminded Marlborough that he had once opposed the Duke of Newcastle's introduction into the ministry on the ground that "he was too much a party man".[21]

Somerset's only personal claim to distinction, enshrined in his nickname of "the Sovereign", was the very dubious one of being by far the proudest and most insufferably pompous man in England. By contrast with Newcastle he owed his political influence in large measure to his wife's hold over the affections of the Queen; but an appetite (if not a talent) for politics, and an unflagging belief in his own capacity and cunning, certainly helped to keep him in the foreground. The infuriating thing about Somerset was that although contemporaries perpetually ridiculed him in private, or even abused him as "a nauseous creature" and "a mean worthless wretch",[22] they always found it difficult to ignore him. When Marlborough and Godolphin were struggling to prevent their High Tory colleagues from dictating vital policy decisions in 1703, Somerset, as the most active of the three Whigs still left in the Cabinet, was able to worm his way into their special confidence. In consequence, when he threatened to resign his office of Master of the Horse and leave the Cabinet, over an absurdly minute question of Court punctilio which he insisted on disputing with the Tory Lord Chamberlain, the Whig leaders hastened to smooth his ruffled feathers and flattered him into staying in the ministry.[23] More than once, however, in the years between 1706 and 1710, when they were first bidding for power and then trying to hold on to it, the lords of the Junto found "the proud duke" a niggling thorn in their sides as he followed his own wilful course. Mainwaring's prophecy in 1708 that he would be "very troublesom if . . . kept out of their secrets, & more so if he be let into 'em"[24] was amply fulfilled in the next two years; so that in 1710 it came as no real surprise to any Whig, but only as a further irritation, when Somerset allowed himself to be lured for six months into Harley's conspiracy to overturn the Godolphin ministry.

In Parliament the House of Lords was the chief stronghold of the Court Whigs. Between 1710 and 1713, for instance, something like thirty peers could have been fairly described in these terms, a remarkably large proportion of the members of the Upper House. They spanned a wide range of political types. On one wing were the close allies of the new Harleian régime: the brothers Argyll and Islay, Lord Rivers and the Earl of Peterborough. Then there were the assiduous courtiers like the Earls of Radnor and Cholmondeley and the one-time-Tory Duke of Kent. There were also a few political eccentrics, of whom the Earl of Scarborough and Lord Ashburnham were representative.* And finally, in the most numerous category of all, we find pensioners of the type of Grafton, Schomberg, St. Albans and the "changeling" Duke of Cleveland, together with other necessitous Whigs such as Lords Fitzwalter and Howard of Effingham.

Among a richly varied selection, however, it would be hard to find two choicer specimens than Kent and Cholmondeley. "The Bug" (Arthur Mainwaring once referred to Kent even more pertinently as "His Stinkingness") was not merely the most malodorous Household officer of his day but also the only Lord Chamberlain in Anne's reign — he held this office for six years — never to be summoned to the Cabinet. The reason was not far to seek. Lord Raby was not overstating the case when he described him on one occasion as a nobleman "of but indifferent parts".[25] "Dey never let me into any of deir politicks", Kent once remarked rather wistfully to Mainwaring, "& I must be civil to all the Queen's servants."[26] In April 1710 he surrendered his position in the Household in return for a dukedom. Not so Lord Cholmondeley, who through most of the life of the Tory Parliament of 1710–13 held on to the office of Treasurer of the Household to which Godolphin had appointed him in November 1708. The post-Sacheverell storm of 1710 caused him acute misgivings. "These times are as dangerous and uncertain for those that set their hearts upon holding places as perhaps ever were," he reflected. "For one that has neither superstition nor more religion than is absolutely necessary, a quiet mind is better than to embroil, plague and trouble myself amongst the kn—s and fo—ls about either Church or State."[27] When Harley tossed him the political lifebelt, however, he clung to it gratefully and floated comfortably enough on the relatively placid seas of the 1710–11 session in the House of Lords. Having received the Queen's assurance in June 1711 that he should keep his staff, Cholmondeley felt free to follow his conscience when the Lords took the critical votes on "No Peace without Spain" in December. In company with many other Court Whig peers he deserted the ministry; but with the Tories braying for his dismissal he came back rather abjectly into line at the be-

* Scarborough combined Whig principles with a pathological dislike of the dissenters — an odd combination — and he also joined the Tories in criticising the Treaty of Union in 1707 (Nicolson's MS. Diary, 15 Feb.). In the case of the 3rd Lord Ashburnham, "a tight Whig" in 1710 (see pp. 331–2 below), principle was a prey to an impressionable nature and subsequently, up to her death in Jan 1713, to the domination of a Tory wife and her Butler relations.

ginning of 1712.[28] The moment of truth eventually came, however, in April 1713, when the Privy Council was summoned to consider the immediate ratification of the treaties of peace and commerce with France. Now one of the few Whigs left in the Council, the Treasurer of the Household was moved to protest with untypical vehemence, and on the following day he was ejected from office.[29] For the remainder of the reign he was in opposition; and in 1714, when party men of every hue stood up to be counted, even Henry Grey, Duke of Kent, felt bound to join him there.

Although always more prolific in the House of Lords the Court Whig breed was far from being unknown in the Commons. Henry Boyle was only the most prominent of quite a large body of Whig members who combined place-holding, or at least an ambition for office, with fear or jealousy of Junto domination; men who accordingly were prepared on many issues, though rarely on the most contentious "party matters", to place their sense of duty to the Crown before their obligations to party leaders, if these should clash. Robert Monckton has already been mentioned as the archetype. But the picture which the Court Whig commoners as a whole presented was one made up of a series of subtly graded shades rather than of a single dominant colour; some members were more "Court" than Whig; others very much the reverse. Among those who held office at various times up to 1710 several names stand out. That of John Smith is an obvious case in point. He was successively Speaker of the House of Commons and Chancellor of the Exchequer between 1705 and 1710, and he "made his court so well" during the change of ministry in 1710[30] that he was granted a sinecure which he held under the Tory régime until 1712. Sir Thomas Littleton, like Smith a former ally of the Junto, clung on to the highly profitable post of Treasurer of the Navy through every change of administration between 1699 and his death in January 1710. Other notable Whigs, too, found their allegiances to a varying extent divided during Anne's reign between party and Court: Spencer Compton, Treasurer and Paymaster of the Pensions, 1708–13, was one;* also Hugh Boscawen, Lord Warden of the Stannaries, 1708–34;† Lord Coningsby, Vice-Treasurer of Ireland, 1692–1710; and Sir Thomas Frankland, who was Joint Postmaster-General right through from 1690 to 1715 and afterwards a Commissioner of the Customs. In the nature of things the Court Whigs in the House of Commons were more susceptible to organisation than their Country brethren. For one thing, a number of them,

* Previously Treasurer to Prince George of Denmark, 1707–8.
† Previously a Groom of the Bedchamber to Prince George, 1702–8.

notably the nominees of Somerset and Newcastle, were knit together by their common obligations to an electoral patron. But at least as important was the fact that most Court Whig commoners, being either in office or in hopes of office, were regular in their attendance at the House, and were therefore vulnerable to the particular pressures which the Court party (as we shall discover) was often in a position to exert on party men in alliance with it.

The most advanced degree of organisation imposed on Court Whigs in this period was that achieved by the so-called "Lord Treasurer's Whigs" in the winter of 1707–8; and theirs was an organisation essentially subordinate to the interests of the Court, rather than to those of the party. Boyle, Smith and Littleton, like Compton, Boscawen and Coningsby, were all prominent figures among the group of placemen and aspiring placemen who responded during that winter to the fervent appeals of Lord Godolphin. Joined for a while by <u>Robert Walpole,</u>* they agreed to stand by Godolphin and the government against what appeared to many of them to be the factious attacks of the Junto in the last session of the 1705–8 Parliament, and it was as "Treasurer's Whigs" that they thus became labelled by their somewhat contemptuous brethren.[31] Peter Wentworth, for instance, wrote of Coningsby that by the closing years of Godolphin's ministry he was "a meer creature of Lord T——r, & what he said in the house of commons was always look't upon as the sence of Lord T——r".[32] But in 1707–8 Coningsby and his friends were in good company. Associated with them were other Whig commoners of note: John Plumptre and John Pulteney, for whom ministerial berths had been found by Godolphin earlier in 1707; Sir John Holland, who was to be rewarded with the Comptroller's staff in 1709; Sir Harry Peachey, a friend of Lord Pelham, and Newcastle's Whig client George Whichcot.[33] The deal that was finally made between the Managers and the Junto in November 1708 naturally reduced the effectiveness of the "Treasurer's Whigs" as an independent force in the Commons. "Those that were engaged, as Smith, Compton & others, to be the heads of a new ministry & the managers of this parliament", remarked one Whig member at the time, "are prettily dropt and cant in my opinion be so well pleasd in coming under those they had set at defyance as they say they are".[34] Nevertheless, on a diminished scale this group retained something of its separate identity up to the winter of 1709–10. At that time there were still Court Whigs who could regard Godolphin "as a blessing fallen from heaven to us", and who would have agreed with Robert Molesworth that "if he

* See p. 234 below.

can be preserved ... from being ground between 2 parties like 2 millstones, or from going too deeply into the intrigues & private ends of any one of them, I look upon it as the greatest happiness that can possibly befall these nations".[35] Sacheverell's prosecution restored superficial amity between this Godolphinite rump and the rest of the party; but even in the early stages of Harley's assault on the ministry in 1710 — when, as Walpole vehemently protested to Boyle, it had become no longer a case of "striving for the second place under [the Managers], but for the whole" — a handful of Court Whigs were still more disposed to cold-shoulder than to welcome the Junto's attempts to conciliate them.[36]

Before we examine the third major element in the composition of the Whig party in the reign of Anne, the Junto Whigs, one contentious and rather confusing question requires an answer. In his book *English Politics in the Early Eighteenth Century* Dr. Walcott claimed to have identified a separate group of power-politicians among the Whigs by 1701 — a group independent of the Junto to which he gave the alarming designation of 'the Newcastle-Pelham-Townshend-Walpole connexion'.[37] Walpole's latest biographer subsequently expressed the gravest doubts about the existence of such a connexion in Anne's reign, and in particular about the links which Walcott purported to establish between Walpole and Newcastle.[38] We do need to know, therefore, whether the present state of the evidence permits this question to be resolved beyond further dispute. The answer, quite simply, is that it does; though there are still a few details of an unusually complex picture which can only be sketched in rather tentatively. More will be said in a later chapter of Walcott's method of presupposing a close political relationship between men on the strength of the slenderest genealogical evidence; but it will suffice here to say that the creation of this strange and semi-fictional combination of politicians — 'the Newcastle-Pelham-Townshend-Walpole' Whigs — is the *reductio ad absurdum* of this method.

At one point only can his thesis be substantiated, and indeed taken much further than he himself takes it. There are many indications that quite early in Anne's reign there was already a small but influential group of Whigs in the House of Commons who were particularly associated, by friendship, kinship and especially by local ties, with young Robert Walpole and with Walpole's friend and later brother-in-law, Viscount Townshend; and in this group it is feasible to recognise the nucleus of the big following which these two men were to build up after 1714. Basically it was a local group. Its nucleus was made up of the Whig members elected in the county of Norfolk, where the combined power of the Townshend and Walpole families so dominated the local party organisation that Defoe in 1712 called Norfolk "the territories of King Walpole".[39] Between 1705 and 1710, especially, this was a fairly numerous and very talented squadron. Apart from Walpole himself, who in these years was a member of the Admiralty Council, Secretary-at-War, and eventually Treasurer of the Navy, it included Sir John Holland of Quidenham, Comptroller of the Household from 1709 to 1711; Sir Charles Turner of Lynn (Walpole's brother-in-law), who became a Commissioner of Trade in April 1708; the Honourable William Feilding, who had inherited an estate at Castle Rising which gave him joint control over that borough with the Walpoles; Colonel Roger Townshend, the Viscount's younger brother, who died in 1709; Ash Windham of Felbrigg, who replaced Townshend as knight of the shire in 1708; and the two Norwich members, Waller Bacon and John Chambers. At the 1710 Election, however, the Whig cause in Norfolk suffered a severe setback. Robert Walpole himself came bottom of the poll after attempting to win one of the county seats in an election of great bitterness and violence. His two Tory opponents "had Dr. Sacheverell's picture carryed before them & the cry was No Manager,* No Scaffolder; but that was not all, for they pelted Mr. Walpole with dirt and stones & drove him out of his tent spoiling his fine lac't coat which they told him came out of the Treary".[40] He had insured himself against this disaster by standing also at both King's Lynn and Castle Rising, but when all the Norfolk elections were over only Sir Charles Turner and Feilding survived to accompany Walpole back to Westminster, and the Norfolk Tories boasted of their triumph "in turning two into nine".[41] The 1713 Election increased the size of Walpole's Norfolk group to four, with the first appearance in the House of his younger brother, Horatio, but at that tiny number it was destined to remain until 1715.

However, at various stages of Anne's reign other members of the House of Commons were drawn into an association with the Norfolk squadron, mostly by the personal friendships which developed between them and Walpole. The young Robert Walpole was a man of easy temper and almost limitless good humour, endowed with what James Brydges once called "the most friendly nature I have known".† The friends he made in London were many and close. One of the first to succumb to his spell was William

---

* Walpole had been one of the chief Whig managers at Sacheverell's impeachment.

† H. L. Stowe MSS. 57, iv, 157: to John Drummond, 26 Sept. 1710. When Walpole was a member of the Prince's Council he was dubbed "the chearfull admirall" by Harry Mordaunt (Lonsdale MSS.: to Wharton, N.D. [? 29 Nov. 1707]).

Cavendish, Marquess of Hartington. In the Parliament of 1701-2 Walpole found a seat at Castle Rising for Hartington, who was always a much more committed party man than his Court-inclined father, whom he succeeded in 1707 as second Duke of Devonshire and Lord Steward.[42] Early in Anne's reign Walpole's circle widened to include James Stanhope, the talented young soldier whom Somerset had nominated to a seat at Cockermouth in Cumberland; and though these two young hopes of the Whig party were temporarily to part company in 1705, when Stanhope became associated with the Country Whigs and Walpole accepted junior office, they remained on the best of terms again from 1708 to the end of the reign.[43] Equally important was a new connection which Walpole formed after the 1705 Election with William Pulteney, who at the age of 21 had just entered the House of Commons as one of the members for the Yorkshire borough of Hedon, and who quickly made a reputation as one of the most promising young debaters on the Whig benches. He and Walpole became close friends. It may well have been Walpole's influence which procured for Pulteney election to the exclusive Kit-Cat Club; and Pulteney's prominence as an opposition speaker after 1710, not least in defence of his friend when Walpole was pilloried by the Tories for alleged peculation in January 1712,[44] suggests that he would certainly have been in office long before 1714 had the Whigs remained in power in the later years of the reign.

A number of other friends and political associates of Walpole's deserve particular notice. One was General Thomas Erle, with whom Walpole developed a special relationship after taking over from St. John at the War Office in 1708.[45] One letter between them, written in September 1710, illustrates vividly how carefully Walpole tended the interests of his friends during parliamentary elections:

I understand that Sir John Cropley is like to have an opposition at Shaftesbury [he told Erle], where your interest is so very considerable that I must desire you will give Sr. John all the assistance you possibly ... can, & exert yourself in behalf of so honest a gentleman, who has all the merit that a steady perseverance in the true interest of his country can give, & is besides so particular a friend to honest Stanhope that I am sure he will forever acknowledge your civility to him ... Stanhope is set up for Westminster & it pleases me very much that I think his election is beyond a dispute ... [P.S.] Pray appear at Shaftesbury in person.[46]

Three other politicians of stature with whom Walpole was on terms of some intimacy were the wealthy Buckinghamshire baronet and army officer Sir Richard Temple of Stowe,[47] Lord Northampton's Whig brother, Spencer

Compton,[48] and "Jack" Smith, the member for Andover, who had been friendly with Walpole in the early years of the reign and who, after some years as a Court and Lord Treasurer's Whig after 1705, appears to have returned to his old associations after the eclipse of Godolphin.[49] Even some of the dour Scots who entered the House after 1707 — Sir Patrick Johnstone, the Lord Provost of Edinburgh, for one — were thawed by the warmth of Walpole's nature.[50]

The parliamentary solidarity of the Norfolk group and some of its outside associates can plainly be seen as early as the last session of William III's reign. We find Ralph Hare writing towards the end of this session to Walpole: "the members wee have to represent us [Sir John Holland and Roger Townshend] are both as worthy as wee can wish; their sentiments & principles are the same together with my Ld Hartington, yrself, Sr Charles Turner etc, & appear in all votes according to yr. wishes . . .".[51] Again, it was significantly the Walpole-Townshend Whigs on whom Godolphin chiefly depended in 1705 to sponsor Jack Smith's nomination for the Speaker's chair. When the Commons met to make their fateful choice of a Speaker on 25 October it was the Marquess of Granby, a friend and relative of Hartington's, who proposed the Court candidate to the House and Sir John Holland who seconded him, while Hartington, Turner, and Walpole himself were among the supporting speakers.[52] This can hardly be coincidental when there were somewhere near 200 Whigs in the House that day who voted for Smith and who *could* have spoken for him.

That there was even at this time a small and recognised group of influential Whigs in the House of Commons of which Robert Walpole was the centre is not then in dispute. But if we are to put Walpole and his friends in their appropriate place in the structure of the Whig party before 1715, two facts of key importance have to be taken into account. The first is that the purely genealogical connection which Dr. Walcott conjures up between the Walpole Whigs and the followers of Newcastle and Pelham had little if any basis in political fact. In Newcastle's case the evidence is almost entirely negative: the almost total absence of letters from either Townshend or Walpole among the duke's quite substantial surviving correspondence speaks for itself.[53] As far as the Pelhams of Sussex are concerned, and their relations and friends in the Commons like William Monson, George Naylor and Sir Harry Peachey, there may be slightly stronger grounds for suspecting some political integration between them and the Norfolk squadron,* but as a

* Townshend was Pelham's son-in-law; Monson is once known to have stayed with him at Rainham (C.U.L. Cholmondeley [Houghton] MSS. Corr. 588); and two or three

matter of sober fact it simply cannot be documented. The second fact to be emphasised is even more important. It is that the Walpole group was not only numerically small but, except for one brief period in the middle of the reign, almost always made common cause with the Junto Whigs.

As early as 1703 Halifax and Sunderland of the Junto were joining in "full committee" with Stanhope, Hartington and Smith to hurry Walpole up to Westminster for the parliamentary battle.[54] Professor Plumb has shown how Walpole owed his first experience of office, in the Prince's Admiralty Council, mainly to the friendship and patronage of Lord Orford of the Junto; and it was Orford's Junto friends who had elected Walpole to the Kit-Cat Club in 1703.[55] It is small wonder, then, if his patrons felt piqued during the stormy winter of 1707–8, when Walpole himself, Townshend and "the personal friends of Mr. Walpole" in the House of Commons[56] elected to stand by Marlborough and Godolphin against the five lords, defending them against attacks on the Admiralty, on the Scottish Privy Council, and on the conduct of the war in Spain. Some months later "Jacob Tonson in his cups, sitting between Dormer and Walpole" one night at a gathering of the Kit-Cat, "told them that he sat between the honestest man in the world and the greatest villain; and explained himself that by the honest man he meant Dormer, the other was a villain for forsaking his patrons and benefactors the juncto . . .".[57] The aberration, however, was short-lived. Already by the summer of 1708 Walpole's friends, Townshend and Devonshire, had begun to return to their Junto allegiances, and he himself had had a violent quarrel with Admiral George Churchill which lessened his sense of obligation to the Managers. In the early autumn Marlborough warned his brother that Robert Walpole would never again defend the present Admiralty Board against his old friends' assaults; and finally in October, we are told, the prodigal returned — "came over to the W[hig] lords", as Cropley noted, "before the change was made or the capitulation sign'd [between Godolphin and the Junto]".* Thereafter

letters between the families survive from the time of the 1705 Election (H.M.C. *Townshend MSS.* p. 331; Add. MSS. 33084, f. 177). The closest link in the chain was probably Newcastle's political ties with Pelham rather than Walpole's with either (e.g. Add. MSS. 33084, f. 165; H.M.C. *Portland MSS.* ii, 189), and indeed as late as 1711 the then Lord Pelham left his proxy for several months with the duke. Yet contemporaries generally considered the Pelhams to be markedly less moderate in their politics than Newcastle (see, e.g., H.M.C. *Portland MSS.* vii, 40).

* H.M.C. *Portland MSS.* iv, 493: [E. Lewis] to Harley, 17 June 1708; N.U.L. Portland (Holles) MSS. Pw2/23; Blenheim MSS. A. 2–38 (Godolphin to Marlborough, 6 July), E. 26 (*loc. cit.*); Chevening MSS.: Cropley to Stanhope, 27 Nov. 1708. A few of Walpole's

Walpole and Townshend rarely had occasion to part political company with the Junto, though the former always retained a personal sense of obligation to Marlborough, with whom he had worked closely and well during his tenure of the War Office.[58] By 1710 no one doubted that Walpole had emerged as a political figure of considerable stature in his own right: important enough, for example, to encourage first Harley and later Bolingbroke to bid for his support independently of his Junto friends. But in the bitter years of opposition after 1710 Walpole's small following and the very much larger Junto forces in the House of Commons worked together as a unit right from the start, and it is striking that contemporaries found it quite unnecessary in these four years to make any distinction between them.

One thing which no contemporary would ever have questioned for a moment, and no historian could possibly doubt, is that it was the Junto Whigs who represented by far the most important element in the party after the Glorious Revolution; or that in Anne's reign it was they who supplied the party with most of its driving force and most of its organisation. Their leaders, the "Junto" itself,[59] comprised by 1696 four of the ablest and most ambitious Whigs in Parliament: Sir John Somers, soon[60] to become Baron Somers and Lord Chancellor of England; Charles Montagu, who became Lord Halifax in 1700; Thomas Wharton, who had just succeeded to his father's barony of Wharton; and Admiral Edward Russell, the first Earl of Orford. Soon after Anne's accession "the lords of the Junto", as they now were (in the Queen's early years, especially, they were often referred to simply as "the Whig lords"), acquired a new associate in the person of the third Earl of Sunderland. As Lord Spencer he had sat in the House of Commons from 1695 until the death in July 1702 of his celebrated father, who outlived only by a few months the king he had served so skilfully in the highly complex, transitional political world of the 1690's. Of these five men, Somers, Halifax, the younger Sunderland, Orford and Wharton, only the last two had figured in any significant way in politics before the Revolution. Wharton indeed was the only one to have reached the age of 50 by 1700. Both these facts distinguished the Junto lords from most of the Tory chiefs at this time, for all of the latter apart from Harley (and Harley would not have

friends seem to have lagged behind him. Cropley mentions Spencer Compton and Sir John Holland. John Smith has been noticed already, and Sir Richard Temple was probably another who was reluctant to follow Walpole's lead at this point. Blenheim MSS. B. 1–10: Temple to Marlborough, 22 Oct. [1708]. Holland was always the most independent of the Norfolk Whigs, a colleague rather than a follower of Walpole and Townshend.

considered himself a Tory in 1700) were of a rather older vintage, and some emphatically so.*

The impeachments of 1701 are an accurate measure of the importance which its opponents by then attached to the Junto. Before the end of William's reign Somers, Halifax, Orford and Wharton had come to embody all that the Tories most hated and feared in Whiggery; and from 1701 until the vicious anti-Marlborough campaign of 1710–11 Tory pens and Tory speeches reserved a special venom for them and their junior partner, Sunderland. "Wee have nothing here but pamphlets & libells . . .", one of the Secretaries of State informed the King after the prorogation of the 1701 Parliament; "it looks as if . . . nothing would satisfy [the Tories] but the utter subduing of those they have sett themselves against . . . In all these writings my Lord Somers seems to bee the chief mark they aime at, tho others too are not spared".[61] When both Somers and Wharton fell seriously ill towards the end of the 1702–3 session, the reports of their physicians were discussed with ghoulish enthusiasm by their more implacable political enemies:

Lord Wharton is yet in a doubtful state [Atterbury told Bishop Trelawney]; nor can it certainly be judged whether he will live or die. Lord Somers is out of all danger: but he had much ado to escape; his old wounds had like to have made his new one mortal; and his body, the physicians say, cannot well hold out long; he hath an ulcer in his back. Some of his predecessors, your Lordship may remember, made a shift to live a few years by tapping.[62]

Of Wharton's illness Richard Steele said later that he had "heard the Tories curse Sir Samuel Garth for recovering him out of it, when it was all their hope as well as talk that he was irrecoverable".[63]

So awesome, in fact, was the reputation of the Junto lords in their own day, and so profound their influence on the whole development of post-Revolution Whiggery, that there is an obvious temptation to exaggerate their collective significance out of all reasonable proportion. They did not, as the older textbooks and even some not-so-old authorities imply, dominate and control virtually the whole Whig party in Parliament;[64] they assuredly did not hold such a commanding position 'throughout the whole of Anne's reign', as Dr. Trevelyan claimed,[65] though it may be argued that in the Queen's last four years they came very near to doing so. What the Junto did command was the largest and easily the most disciplined and formidable of the party groups on either side in the House of Commons. Many of its

---

* Sir Edward Seymour at the end of 1700 was 67 and the Earl of Rochester 59; Godolphin was 55, Nottingham 53 and Marlborough 50. By contrast Halifax was only 39 and Sunderland 26, and both Somers and Orford were in their late forties.

members may have been more notable for their proverbial obedience to their leaders than for their individual talents; indeed Sir John Cropley once complained (though with exaggeration) that the Junto preferred *any* strictly disciplined follower — "a tinker at the word of command", as he scathingly put it — to "any credit or fortune that is not so servile to them."[66] Yet it was also the case that a significant proportion of these followers had no personal obligation to the five lords, nor indeed any direct connection with them. Without such recruits the Junto Whigs in the Commons would still have mustered a cohesive force, but it would have been far less powerful than it actually was. "The Whig lords", however, had more in their armoury than this formidable weapon in the Lower House. For most of Anne's reign they also enjoyed the firm support of a numerical majority among the Whig peers. Taking the period 1702–14 as a whole, in fact, they were if anything stronger in the Lords than in the Commons. Even a hostile party critic like Coningsby grudgingly conceded that "in the House of Peers . . . the interest of the Lords (call'd the Junto) *only* prevail'd".[67]

As individuals the Junto lords, as their most recent student has made vividly clear,[68] were an oddly-assorted bunch. They were cemented together into the most effective political combination of their day neither by kinship nor by compatibility of character and temperament, but simply by the strength of the principles which they shared, the compelling force of their mutual quest for power, and a sense of loyalty to each other which in the circumstances of the time was astonishing. It is true that there were chinks in the armour even of this, the most tightly-welded of all the political combinations of the years 1689–1714. Quarrels among the five were not unknown. In 1703 Somers had much ado to keep the peace between Orford and Halifax during the parliamentary investigations into their accounts. In the session of 1708–9 Halifax differed from his friends over the controversial Treasons bill. More serious still, Somers and Wharton were thought to be in disagreement that winter over basic parliamentary strategy, the former advising moderation in face of the latter's more extreme counsels, though again the dispute was never allowed to get out of hand.[69] Moreover, even the Junto lords were reluctant to accept the full logic of mutual dependence and joint responsibility when in power. When forced out of office in 1699–1700 they resigned piecemeal. And in the early summer of 1710, when Robert Harley was sapping and mining under the outworks of the Godolphin ministry, they once again failed to resign *en bloc* when their colleague, Sunderland, was made the first victim of Harley's policy, though by September they had come to accept the necessity for such action.[70] None the less, their sense of personal loyalty to each other, and their concept of the exacting nature of party ties, were alike remarkable.

There is no more striking example of this than an incident involving the Earl of Wharton in the summer of 1708. Ever since March of that year the Junto had been trying to get Somers into the Cabinet as Lord President of the Council. For months Godolphin had badgered the Queen to give way, but she had remained adamant. Somers had led a parliamentary attack on the incompetence of the Admiralty during the previous winter, and in so doing had trodden on one of Anne's pet corns, since the Admiralty Council was nominally presided over by her husband, Prince George. To try and break the ensuing deadlock the Duke of Somerset, possibly with Godolphin's approval (though there is no proof of this), made a private approach to Wharton; and the proposal he put to him was roughly this: 'Lord Somers, as you can see, is quite unacceptable to the Queen; and by going on with this campaign you and your friends are only banging your heads against a wall. But if you will abandon Somers's cause, and agree to support the Court next session, your own personal claims to office will receive very favourable consideration from the Queen'. The temptation for Wharton to make a private bargain at this point must have been very severe. Not only was it obvious that Somers's prospects in the short run were gloomy, but Wharton's own need for the emoluments of office, which he had not enjoyed since he lost his Comptroller's staff in the Whig rout of 1702, was literally desperate. By the middle of 1708 he was almost bankrupt. And yet his reply to Somerset was absolutely straightforward and uncompromising. After indulging his love of irony in what he later described as "some preambles about his own unworthiness and insufficiency", he came straight to the point: which was "that he thought making distinctions among men of the same principle and interest was not the way to do the nation's business; that if he had ever been of any service, it was chiefly owing to the assistance of those friends, from whom he would never divide, nor could do it without making himself quite inconsiderable; that he thought it would be much more for the service and honour of his Grace and the ministers to put themselves at the head of the whole party, which would make them strong and carry them through all their present difficulties, than to think of dividing them again, which would only increase their troubles of last year . . .".[71] It will be appreciated that even in the early eighteenth century, at a time when party loyalties were more strongly developed than at any time in the next hundred years or more, this was a rather extraordinary statement.*

* It should be added that the loyalty of Wharton and his friends to their close followers

What made the Whig Junto such a superbly effective political force, however, was not merely their cohesive qualities but the fact that their individual talents and assets were so complementary. Each made his own distinctive contribution to the common cause. Somers, who was the leading figure in the Junto in William's reign and remained so for all but the last few years of Anne's, when his health broke down, was a man whose greatness had to be acknowledged even by the Tories.[72] One of the most distinguished lawyers ever to sit on the Woolsack, he contributed the finest intellect in the party, and also qualities of integrity and moral strength in which some of his colleagues were at times deficient. Halifax, a vain and prickly little man with a restless, ambitious, striving spirit which may well have had its roots in an inbred sense of inferiority,[73] was in many ways the least reliable of the five as a colleague, especially when (as in 1709–10) power did not bring him the rewards he hoped for and expected as his due. "His old friends", Godolphin observed at that time, ". . . are not quite secure how farr his own naturall inclinations to bee employd, & his expectation of future favour, may engage him out of his depth."[74] Yet on the credit side he was a superb debater, bringing into the House of Lords after 1700 the same devastating (and, to many of the traditionalists, dubious) techniques which he had developed so brilliantly in the Commons during the 1690's.* And in addition, Halifax's grasp of public finance, first demonstrated by a spectacular career at the Exchequer and Treasury Board under William III, together with his "great interest in the City", ensured that he would always be heard with respect on fiscal questions in the Lords,[75] and that his advice would be privately welcome even to Harley and his Tory colleagues after 1710.

The Earl of Orford was no longer an active parliamentarian by Anne's reign. He attended the Lords regularly enough, but he no longer took a prominent part in their debates, and in 1705 (with more than a touch of false humility) he remarked to Somers: "I signify nothing anywhere, much less at the opening of a Parliament".[76] The truth was, however, that Orford still signified a good deal to the Junto cause. His personal following in the House of Commons, made up partly of Russell relatives and in-laws[77] but mainly of naval officers and admiralty officials, was a most valuable asset; and

on the whole matched their loyalty to each other. The Junto, as Peter Wentworth admitted in 1710, looked after its own. *Wentworth Papers*, p. 156.

* Even Dartmouth, though younger than Halifax, was primly shocked by what he called the "familiar style" which both he and Wharton brought up with them from the Commons, with its tradition of "free speaking". See Burnet, v, 234n.; Dalhousie MSS. 14/352: Balmerino to Harry Maule, 30 Jan. [1711].

so too was the earl's own naval experience, acquired as the victor of La Hogue and during two spells as First Lord of the Admiralty. Lord Sunderland's contribution to the influence of the Junto, by contrast, was less particularised. It was compounded from a store of boundless, if at times misdirected, energy; an incurable optimism that could never envisage defeat, not even before the electoral holocaust of 1710; a keen appetite for parliamentary management;* and a zeal for Whiggery that was loyal and sufficiently disinterested to make him spurn the pension of £3000 a year which Anne offered him on his removal from the Secretaryship in 1710.[78] If his political indiscretions made him on occasion an uncomfortable bedfellow for his colleagues, as well as a vulnerable target for his opponents (as he proved in 1710), he compensated in part for this by providing his friends during Anne's reign with a valuable connection with the Marlboroughs, whose son-in-law he was.

Finally there was Wharton — not merely the most colourful personality among the five lords of the Junto but in many ways the most vivid character of his age. Two great qualities he put at the service of his friends and of his party. One was a mastery of the art of electioneering without equal in his own day, and reinforced by an income of £16,000 a year which he placed unhesitatingly and consistently at the service of the "honest interest" in seven shires and well over a dozen constituencies from Cumberland to Wiltshire. The second was unlimited courage and resilience, qualities which made him quite invaluable in opposition, especially when things were going badly. There were times, it is true, when some Whigs considered Wharton a mixed blessing to their party. His moral reputation was appalling. As adulterer and rake he was still by 1702 (at least on reputation) unchallenged in a field he had made as much his own as the field of electioneering. And although the vicious barbs which Swift directed against him after 1710 have tended to obscure the fact that by the second half of Anne's reign Wharton's days of spectacular depravity were over, he nevertheless retained to the end that strange compound in his character which never failed to mystify Lord Shaftesbury, a compound "of the very best and the very worst". The coarse-mouthed womaniser, and the frank atheist who loved to bait the High Church Tories in the House of Lords, and not least the Tory bishops, by quoting the Bible at them with great relish and great facility, always remained to his own party — and deservedly so — "honest Tom Wharton". Moreover his

---

* N.U.L. Portland (Bentinck) MSS. PwA. 1186: Somers to Portland, 21 June 1708. See also p. 18 above.

reputation for staunchness and for unwavering political principle where the essentials of Whiggery were concerned meant far more to Wharton than high office or royal favour, neither of which he ever sought for their own sake.

The charge which their opponents, even their Whig opponents, frequently levelled at the Junto lords — namely that they were a narrow clique, trying arrogantly to force both their policies and their exclusive leadership on the whole Whig party — was an unfair one at any stage of Anne's reign. Yet there was just sufficient truth in it during the first half of the reign for their experiences in the session of 1707–8, when there was a major Whig revolt in both Houses against their factious anti-ministerial tactics,* to have a noticeable effect on the Junto's willingness to expand the hitherto tight inner circle of their leadership. Apart from their chief lieutenants in the House of Commons, where Nicholas Lechmere, Sir James Montagu, Sir Joseph Jekyll, Harry Mordaunt, Lord William Powlet and Sir William Strickland all figured prominently, there had always been a number of peers of vehement Whig principles who from the start of Anne's reign had been not so much followers of the Junto as what might be termed 'junior associates'. The most notable were borough patrons of real importance to the party cause like the Duke of Bolton, the Earl of Carlisle, and to a lesser degree Lords Derby and Cornwallis. These men would normally be kept informed of day-to-day decisions concerning parliamentary tactics during sessions, and they played a vital part in the great Junto network which operated during General Elections. But what little evidence we have about those who attended the major Junto conferences on party strategy, especially those held between sessions at Newmarket (a favourite haunt of the five lords) or at Althorp, Winchendon, or another of their great country houses, suggests that men like Bolton and Carlisle only rarely attended. However invaluable Bolton was to the Junto as a beneficent provider of parliamentary seats in Hampshire and Cornwall, to describe him, as Dr. Walcott does, as one 'of the inner group' or as 'practically a sixth member of the Junto'[79] is rather to exaggerate his influence on policy-making and his general political stature; he was, for instance, an infrequent and notoriously bad parliamentary speaker,[80] and the few letters of his which appear to have survived impress one neither by their intelligence nor their literacy.[81] As for Lord Carlisle, he was very occasionally allotted a parliamentary rôle of some importance — "puft up [Berkeley once

---

* The dissident Whigs objected most of all to the readiness of the Junto squadron to enter into *ad hoc* combinations during this winter with the High Tory opposition in order to bring the Queen's Managers to terms.

said] by a flattering party for their own ends";[82] but this clearly conferred on him no permanent passport to the Junto's innermost councils.

The big change which came over the Junto's party policy after the summer of 1708 was reflected less in its attitude to these junior partners, or to others of similar status like Dorchester and Mohun, than in its greater willingness to take into its confidence, and associate with its decisions, certain politicians of real ability: committed party men like themselves, who fitted naturally neither into the "Court" nor "Country" groupings of the Whigs, but who had never hitherto been fully assimilated by the Junto. Three conspicuous examples were Lord Cowper (formerly William Cowper), who was Lord Keeper and later Lord Chancellor from 1705 to 1710; the second Duke of Devonshire (the former Hartington), who sat in the Cabinet as Lord Steward from 1707 to 1710; and Viscount Townshend. At times during the winter of 1707–8 all three had been at loggerheads with the main Whig leadership in the House of Lords, especially during the enquiries into the conduct of the Admiralty and the debates on the bill for terminating the Scottish Privy Council.[83] The point was taken; and subsequently a real effort was made to consult with them and secure their support on major policy decisions.[84] By the summer of 1710 this policy had achieved such complete success[85] that right through the last four years of the reign Devonshire and Cowper were every bit as closely identified with the Junto as was Orford;* and the same was true of Townshend after his return from his embassy at The Hague† in 1711. They were all invaluable acquisitions, and without them the Junto's opposition in the House of Lords to the policies of the Oxford administration must inevitably have been less well co-ordinated and less effective. But Cowper's support was particularly precious, for he was not only a polished and persuasive orator in the Somers tradition — "much the finest speaker of all the lawyers if not of all others in England", James Lowther had thought him in 1705 — but also a man whose charm, honesty, and eminent fairness of mind could disarm even political opponents as bitter as Bolingbroke.[86]

One other group of Junto associates merits particular mention: the group of Scottish politicians known to contemporaries as the Squadrone. Although

---

* The only major parliamentary occasion from 1710 to 1714 when either openly differed with the Junto lords in the Upper House appears to have been the Hamilton vote on 20 Dec. 1711 (see p. 37 above), when Cowper's tender political conscience was offended by the unscrupulousness of his colleagues' tactics.

† A mission for which he had been sponsored by Somers in 1709, during what Raby later called "his friends' the Junto's reign". H.M.C. *Portland MSS.* ix, 293.

their leaders were mostly peers, of whom the Dukes of Roxburgh and Montrose were the most prominent after the Scots entered the Union Parliament in 1707,[87] the main strength of the Squadrone, numerically and at times tactically, lay in the Commons. There were only four Squadrone peers in the Parliament of 1707–8, three in that of 1708–10,[88] and none whatever between the General Elections of 1710 and 1715; whereas in the Commons Squadrone M.P.s, led by stalwarts like Baillie of Jerviswood, John Cockburn and John Haldane, always represented a useful proportion of the total Scottish membership of 45. There were at least eleven Squadrone members in the Lower House in 1707–8, and eight or nine between 1708 and 1710.[89] Even after the Tory triumph of 1710 there was a hard core of some half a dozen returned to the Parliament of 1710–13, on to which were soon grafted in opposition to the Court other strong Whigs, like Robert Monro, Sir Patrick Johnstone and Sir Robert Pollock, who previously had not been strictly associated with the Squadrone. Indeed in the last four years of the reign, any Scot who deviated in the House of Commons from the strict Court or Episcopal Tory line was almost certain to be accused, as was Sir David Dalrymple, of "caballing with [the] Squadroni".[90]

Although the leaders of the Squadrone and the Junto had been in correspondence for some years before the Union,[91] theirs had been a wary relationship to begin with, especially on the side of the Scots. Early in 1705, for instance, Roxburgh was still for putting no trust in any of the Whigs, "since its tools they want" (he was convinced).[92] The close parliamentary links between the two groups were forged in the session of 1707–8 as a mainly tactical arrangement, initially, developing out of Junto support for the abolition of the Edinburgh Privy Council, a body dominated by the Squadrone's bitter rivals, the Queensberryites. Subsequently a more genuine alliance became possible, as common "Revolution" principles,[93] devotion to the Protestant Succession, opposition to the Tory peace with France after 1710, and the Junto's support of the interests of the Presbyterian Church in Scotland in 1711–12 all combined to draw the two groups together. Yet until 1713, when the apparent threat to the Hanoverian succession acted as a cauterising agent on all Whigs, north and south of the border, the relationship between the Junto and the Squadrone was never a fully-integrated one and it was subjected to a series of strains.

These vicissitudes can be clearly traced in the papers of the Duke of Montrose, especially in the letters written to him between 1708 and 1713 by Roxburgh, who was generally enthusiastic by this time for closer ties with the English Whig leaders, and by George Ballie, who remained distinctly suspicious of the Junto until as late as 1712. During 1709, for instance, there was a marked cooling of relations between the two groups. This was in part the result of disputes over the government's Treasons bill, which was aimed at bringing Scottish procedure in the trial of treason charges more into line with English, and in part the outcome of the Junto's failure to secure the newly-created post of Third Secretary (or Scottish Secretary) for Montrose instead of Queensberry.[94] Montrose and Roxburgh were at length placated, with the help of the former's appointment as Keeper of the Privy Seal in Scotland and the latter's nomination as a privy councillor. But Baillie at first turned down the Junto's offer to make him a Commissioner of Trade, in spite of Sunderland's assurances that "care should be taken to shew that greater equality was meant for the future". In fact he did not accept the post until April 1710 — long after Montrose had assured him that it was only in alliance with the Junto that the Squadrone could hope to achieve their Scottish policies and that "a refusall, if it should come to that, would be such a *rompre en visiere* as were not to be repaired".[95] The terms on which Montrose understood the alliance to rest from the summer of 1709 until the end of this Parliament in the autumn of 1710 are interesting. They did not, to his mind, imply a purely subordinate relationship on the part of the Squadrone group. Sunderland had asked only that its members, and Baillie in particular, should "freely and heartily enter into measures" with the English Whigs, and this to Montrose seemed "to import no more to ane honest man then to enter into honest measures with ones freinds freely and heartely. If bad measures are proposed [he concluded] no honest man I suppose is bound to go into them."[96] On this footing the two groups co-operated satisfactorily enough during the session of 1709–10, through the Sacheverell affair, and the ministerial crisis of the following summer, and during the subsequent General Election.

In 1711 and 1712 Squadrone members in the House of Commons, supervised and encouraged from the sidelines by Roxburgh, who was in London for much of the time though no longer in the House of Lords, seem generally to have acted and voted in harmony with their Junto counterparts.[97] By October 1711 the most charitable comment the Earl of Islay felt able to make about Lord Polwarth, Marchmont's son, was that "he . . . has never been so much dipt in the service of the Junto as the rest of those we nick name by the word *Squadrone*".[98] But the partnership was still not entirely free from friction, if the continued misgivings of George Baillie are a reliable guide. For instance, Junto opposition to the Duke of Hamilton's patent in 1711 — the test case which was to decide the right of Scots holding British peerages to enjoy hereditary seats in the House of Lords — understandably upset the Squadrone: so much so, that some of its members were at first uncertain whether to lend their full support to the Whig attack on the ministry's peace policy, due to be mounted in December 1711. Baillie's letter to Montrose explaining their quandary illustrates very well how far he, for one, still regarded the Squadrone as an independent political unit:

What part your friends here should act in the matter is not easy to determine considering how we are stated (*sic*) with Court, Whig and Tory. The Whigs and many of the Tories are to oppose D.H. patent, and I must own that to assist them goes against the grain with me, and yet for one to act from resentment against his country in so weighty a point is a heavy thing and what I can not well think of, and I am sure we owe no such favour to the ministry. At best our case is hard.[99]

Six months later, when the Junto attacked the government in both Houses over the "Restraining Orders" sent to the British commander-in-chief in the Low Countries, and was badly repulsed, Baillie could not disguise his dissatisfaction with a tactical move he had not approved of, and about which the Junto's managers in the Commons had clearly not consulted him.[100] And when the Lower House was asked a few days later to approve the specific French peace offers made at Utrecht he spoke disparagingly of the "profound silence" of "those gentlemen who made a bustle all winter" against the peace.[101] It was only perhaps in the last two critical sessions of the Queen's reign, those of 1713 and 1714, that the Squadrone committed themselves quite unreservedly to battle under the Junto colours.

In this they were at one with almost every important section of the party, and with all but the tiniest handful of individual Whigs, in both Houses of Parliament. For in the last eighteen months of the Queen's life the Whigs, both English and Scottish, achieved a homogeneity that was truly astonishing. Both parties in Anne's day found unity, or something approaching unity, a more practicable goal in opposition than they did in power; and the Whigs, always the more coherent of the two, came much nearer to realising that goal between 1702 and 1705, and again between 1710 and 1714, than their opponents did at any time. In these years the separate identity of the different elements we have distinguished in this chapter — Country Whigs, Court Whigs, Walpoleans, Junto men, and latterly Squadrone men — was to a large extent merged in the common aims and attitudes of "the honest interest". In 1713–14, however, in a political world almost totally overshadowed by the succession question, the fusion became virtually complete. Analysing the political forces as he found them at the time of his return to

England in March 1714, Sir John Percival first explained the various divisions among the Tories. He then added, without elaboration or qualification, "As to the Whiggs, they were intire . . .".[102] These words were a simple but impressive recognition of an almost unique state of affairs. For us they are a reminder that in the months preceding their final triumph at the accession of George I, the Whigs of the age of Anne achieved not only an unbroken unity of front but an underlying solidarity of purpose which was not to be approached again by any political party in Britain until well into the nineteenth century, and was possibly not equalled until the twentieth.

CHAPTER EIGHT

The Structure of the Tory Party

IN structure the Whig and Tory parties of the age of Anne had certain features in common. In this chapter we shall encounter among the Tories at Westminster "Country", "Court" and organised power elements which suggest obvious parallels with those already identified among the Whigs. But we shall also find that the relative importance of these three elements in the parliamentary party contrasts sharply with the corresponding distribution of influence on the Whig side; and what is equally significant, the character of their relationship with each other, and above all the fragility of the ties between them, and even within them, is unmistakably distinctive to the Tories. Indeed the working of politics in this period was affected far more by marked differences in the composition of the two great political forces than by their superficial similarities.

It requires no very deep analysis of the Tory party to reveal a confederacy very much looser than that which held the Whigs together for the greater part of Queen Anne's reign. The divisive, at times centrifugal, forces that were exerted within the party in the early eighteenth century have not escaped the notice of its twentieth-century students. But recent work has tended to concentrate on divisions of a very specific kind. It has postulated a clear distinction between four major Tory connections, organised on a 'family and personal basis', which competed with each other as well as with the Whigs.* This new emphasis has been valuable to modern scholars, none of whom would deny that differences of this kind existed and few of whom would dispute their importance. And yet amid all the detail that has been

* R. Walcott, *English Politics*, pp. 51–68. Professor Walcott identifies these groups as being led by Nottingham, Rochester and Seymour, Harley, and the Marlborough-Godolphin alliance respectively, though he is doubtful (and with reason) how far the followers of Marlborough and Godolphin can be considered an integral part of the Tory party after 1702.

accumulated about these ambitious, 'dynastic' groups and their various ramifications one can search in vain for a really convincing explanation of the great Tory dilemma of the age. One is still left wondering why a party which was so manifestly the natural majority-party in the country failed to establish and maintain its dominance consistently under a Queen who, in so many respects, was an instinctive Tory. Least of all can one discover in the labyrinth of faction why this same party should have gone so far towards destroying itself in the critical last months of Anne's life, even with a huge majority in the House of Commons, that by the end of 1716 it had ceased for good to be a serious competitor for political power.

That the Tories did command a natural majority of supporters in the political nation was a fact which few of the Queen's subjects would have seriously disputed. It was not only the fiercely committed partisans like St. John who recognised the contrast between the "fictitious" supremacy attained by the Whigs between 1708 and 1710, a supremacy achieved only on the high tide of Court favour, and the "natural genuine strength" of the Tories evinced in the 1710 Election.[1] "It has always seemed to me very plain", agreed the shrewd and balanced Francis Hare, "that the spirit of the gentry of the nation is Toryism, and that nothing but the influence of the Court has made it otherwise in any Parliament."[2] This was a recurring theme of Harley's, too, particularly in the years between 1705 and 1710 when the Whigs were mounting one attack after another on the places of power and profit in the administration. "Those who call themselves Whigs [even] if united are the inferior number", he warned Godolphin; only "by activity and by the interest of the Crowne" could they "supply their want of credit" in the country at large.[3] In the summer of 1708, when the Junto was at last within sight of total victory at Court, he lamented to Bromley "how those who are the smaller part of the nation have made themselves formidable & terrible to the greater".[4] Harley's diagnosis of the causes of this Whig triumph points by implication at the Achilles' heel of the Tories, suggesting why more than once in the course of Anne's reign, and in the end fatally, they came to squander all their innate advantages. The Whigs, he claimed, had turned the tables because "tho' they hate one another yet *they unite together to carry on their designs*".[5] By contrast the Tory party was so fissile that, in Harley's view, it was delivering itself into the hands of its more disciplined and cohesive rivals.

Part of the reason for its vulnerability undoubtedly lay in the basic lack of unity among the power politicians. For one thing, the number of organised or semi-organised Tory connexions was far higher than the number of similar groups among the Whigs.* More important, what divided these Tory groups was not merely their mutual rivalry in the scramble for office and place but often grave differences of policy, even of fundamental principle. But place-hunters and policy-makers alone did not hold the keys to the Tory dilemma of Anne's day; for they did not provide the bedrock on which the foundations of the party structure rested, in Parliament any more than in the country. Invariably the largest and usually the most significant constituent of the party in every Parliament of this period were the independent Tory gentlemen in the House of Commons.

The Country Tories, "the gentlemen of England" as Harley called them, always formed much the largest single political group on either side in the Commons. The word 'group' is used for want of a better, but it is really a misnomer when applied to the most amorphous political phenomenon of post-Revolution England. If a natural resistance to organisation was a fairly common characteristic of Country Whigs, it was the special hallmark of the independent gentlemen who sat across the chamber.† On those benches clustered a high proportion of rustic squires, to whom a seat in the House of Commons was largely a matter of social distinction and local prestige. Such men did not regard membership of the House as a vehicle for an active personal career in politics; still less did they see it as entailing an obligation to accept a rigidly disciplined course of service to their party. This type of Country Tory — and it was represented by scores of members in every one of Anne's Parliaments — would have quickly reduced any modern party whip to a state of nervous prostration. "The gentlemen of England" were notoriously dilatory, for instance, in coming up for the start of a session. So sluggish were they in October 1704 that the government was almost

* As we shall later see, it was also far more, taking the reign as a whole, than the four groups which Dr. Walcott distinguishes on the Tory side.

† The polarisation of politicians late in William III's reign and early in Anne's was reflected in the growing tendency of party men of like views to congregate on their own side, or in their own "corner", of the House of Commons. John Toland, writing in 1701, re-marked that "you may know the several partys (they say) by their very seats in the House of Commons, where they have their peculiar sides and corners. . . ." "It was a new thing to me", wrote a Scottish member in November 1710, "to see all the bussiness of the House come from the [Tory] corner, and not one word from the opposite corner." We should not, however, assume that seating arrangements were rigid. During one sitting in January 1708, for example, it is clear that Harley, the senior Secretary of State, was only a few seats removed not only from a humble Tory backbencher, William Clayton, but also from Clayton's fellow Liverpudlian, Thomas Johnson, an independent country Whig. Toland, *The Art of Governing by Partys* (London, 1701), p. 63; Auchmar MSS.: Mungo Graham to Montrose, 25 Nov. 1710; *Norris Papers* (London, 1846), p. 161.

reduced to a further prorogation for lack of a quorum "to go upon business"; and in the first division of this session, in the committee on the Address, less than 40 Tories were present to vote out of a total of over 300.[6] The slowness of many Country Tories in arriving in town at the beginning of a session was matched only by their eagerness to depart long before the end. The Commons' Journals abound with requests granted to this Tory backbencher or that "to go into the country for four weeks [or five, or sometimes six] upon extraordinary occasions". How "extraordinary" these sometimes were can be judged from a delightfully frank letter written, probably in 1705, by Sir Edmund Bacon to his fellow representative for the borough of Orford in Suffolk: ". . . I perceive the sessions is drawing to conclusion as fast as may be", he observed optimistically [Parliament still had, in fact, six weeks of work before it], "and I hope I shall be excused for not coming up. It is very good hunting weather & I make the best of it I can . . . ".[7] At a critical juncture of the 1713 session Lord Weymouth was dismayed to find his friend Sir Richard How, one of the most experienced High Tory backbenchers in the House, "positive in his resolution" to return to his native Wiltshire, "though I believe he will be wanted [he told his daughter], the Scotch in both Houses being [so] enraged at the Malt Tax, that they will move on Monday to have the Union dissolved".[8]

When party stalwarts like How felt justified in following their personal whims and ignoring the advice of friends in the ministry, far less prominent Country Tories were understandably reluctant to put the fatigues of a long session, especially when it extended into the spring and summer months, before their country-house comforts and rural pleasures. Such a one was Sir Thomas Cave, the young baronet who sat as knight of the shire for Leicestershire from 1711 until his early death in 1719. From the Verney papers at Claydon House a splendid picture emerges of the reluctant "occasional member", whose interest in politics was mostly local and always spasmodic. Occasionally, as during the 1714 session when he believed the ideals of the Tory gentry to be seriously threatened by the dangerous combination of the Whigs and the "Whimsicals" in the House of Commons, Cave stuck nobly to his post in what he termed "the Westminster Hell"; so that his father-in-law Lord Fermanagh, whose attendance (admittedly hindered by ill health) was even more perfunctory than Cave's, chaffed him with loving London "like the Women". But always, to leave "that stinking London" was Cave's idea of a "return to Paradise"; and after the session of 1714 had been in progress little more than a fortnight, and Easter was in prospect, he was already heading for Leicestershire — pursued by the recriminations of a

Tory aunt who (as he told Fermanagh) "declares us both knaves to the Queen and Country, Dutch deserters, and what not; but I come off the better by your leading the vann. Sheel never forgive you and me". He was back again, under duress, on 13 April; endured "this dusty place" valiantly for another month; and then apparently gave up the unequal struggle for the remainder of the session, ironically heading one letter to a relative on 7 June (when the session still had a month to run) "from the House of Commons at Stanford".[9]

However, we should gravely misjudge the importance of the Country Tory element in the Commons if we took the undisguised distaste for routine parliamentary business and for town life of men like Bacon, Cave and Fermanagh as the main criterion of our assessment. Two constant features of this section of the parliamentary party, its sheer size and the extreme political opinions and prejudices of a majority of its members, guaranteed it a high priority in the calculations of the leading politicians of the day. In both respects it presented a complete contrast with the country wing of the Whigs. Its extremism was a particularly important factor in the political situation; for whereas it was the Junto's followers who were normally associated with the more partisan policies advocated by the Whigs, it was country members like Sir John Pakington and Sir Simeon Stewart who frequently made the most virulent speeches from the Tory side.[10] The Country Tories, then, were at all times a power to be reckoned with, even when the bulk of these High Church gentlemen were essentially unorganised, as they were for the first nine years of Anne's reign (apart from the brief interlude of the campaign for "the Tack" in 1704). Even in these years from 1702 to the beginning of 1711 it is remarkable how rarely the most adroit Commons' manager of the day, Robert Harley, took any major political step without a wary eye on the reactions of the Tory independents.* But in the early years of Harley's own administration the importance of "the gentlemen of England" increased still further. In 1711 and 1712 the Tory backbenchers in the Commons for the first time acquired not merely a corporate feeling but a genuine organisation of their own, one that was independent of the party leaders and equally independent of the Court. This organisation, supplied in 1711 by the October Club and in 1712 by the October and March Clubs together,† involved at times that "embodying of gentlemen" against the ministry itself which Harley had dreaded ever since he entered the Queen's service; and the formidable force which the Country

---

* For the part these men played in conditioning Harley's political thinking as well as his parliamentary strategy, see pp. 372–3 below.

† These phenomena will be examined at more length in Chapter 10.

Tories came to exert in these years in the working of politics proved his earlier apprehensions[11] more than justified. Even in 1714, when the clubs had lost their importance, it did not escape remark that Tory ministers and their supporters in the House of Commons were much embarrassed when 'a considerable Country Party among the Torys" failed to "speak to things in the House as they us'd", but rather "sat still, and left the Ministry's freinds to battle matters with the Whigs".[12]

The Country Tories bulk so large in our picture of the Commons in the early eighteenth century that it is easy to overlook the corresponding element in the House of Lords. This was largely made up of backwoods peers who had no close connection with the major family groups, who had neither the talent nor the ambition to aspire to government office, and who could afford to be disdainful of Court *largesse*. Over a dozen of these aristocratic independents can be identified with little difficulty: the Earls of Salisbury, Exeter, Sussex and Berkshire, for example, and also the Earls of Yarmouth and Plymouth; the fourth Lord Coventry and Viscount Saye and Sele; the Lords Ferrers, Chandos, Leigh and Maynard; and the Marquess of Annandale among the Scots. Most of them were of a fairly "high" political colour, and in irregularity of attendance and unpredictability of behaviour, too, were not unlike their fellows in the Lower House. A case in point was Lord Leigh, who had nursed a gouty foot in Warwickshire for years before 'is death in November 1710, and who therefore caused no little surprise when in the winter of 1709–10 "he made a shift to come up to Town that he might have an opportunity of shewing his zeal for the Church in voting for Dr. Sacheverell".[13] As a body the Country Tory peers mustered a very useful tally of votes; but no Tory leader, in or out of office, ever managed to control or command them as successfully as the lords of the Junto maintained their sway over similar figures in the Whig ranks.

One crucial reason, therefore, why the Tory party never capitalised effectively on its natural majority in the nation was that it never solved the problem of harnessing the full potential strength of its country members and its country peers. A still more basic reason was the radical disagreements on questions of policy and principle which divided different sections of the Tories. That is why it is quite impossible to dispense with the contemporary distinction between "moderate" and "high" Tories, or with some kind of terminology which roughly conveys the fact of this distinction, in any analysis of the party in the period 1702–14. Such terms as 'Tory moderates', 'Tories of the centre' or 'the Tory right wing' may occasionally mislead by concealing finer shades of opinion. But they broadly correspond with the facts of a political situation which was widely recognised at the time and was of continual relevance to the operation of the whole political system.

When Queen Anne wrote to Godolphin in July 1705, expressing a preference for "a moderate tory" replacement for Sir Nathan Wright as Lord Keeper,[14] both she and her Lord Treasurer understood perfectly well what she had in mind. She wanted to place the Great Seal of England in the keeping of a man who would be firm in his support of the war, especially the war in the Low Countries, and who would support the Queen's business in Parliament and in the Cabinet without being deflected either by vindictiveness towards the Whigs or by a determination to press partisan legislation regardless of the country's circumstances. She was looking for a man who was sufficiently tolerant in his religious views to accept the privileges accorded to Protestant dissenters, and sufficiently firm to the Protestant succession to accept the settlement of the crown on the House of Hanover made in 1701; but at the same time for a man with a known affection for the institution of monarchy and for the established constitution; and above all for a sound Church of England man, who as Lord Keeper could be depended upon to make wise use of the ecclesiastical patronage at his disposal. A High Tory in 1705 would have passed the final two tests with flying colours; but he could not have been relied upon to meet any of the other requirements the Queen had in mind.

The smallest of the three main elements in the structure of the Tory party, the Court Tories, consisted almost entirely of men who were by definition "moderates". In the House of Lords the tall, spare figure of "Long Tom" Herbert, Earl of Pembroke, personified the type to perfection for twenty years: a man of mild Tory sympathies, but with so natural a gravitation towards the government of the day that he always fitted usefully into the centre of any coalition ministry.[15] Between 1689 and 1709 Pembroke was never once out of office, and for the greater part of the time he was in high office. In William III's reign he had had one spell as a Commissioner of Trade, one as Lord President of the Council, and no less than three spells as either First Lord of the Admiralty or Lord High Admiral. Most striking of all, right through the period 1692–9, a period for the most part of Junto predominance, he had comfortably filled the post of Lord Privy Seal. When Godolphin and Marborough were casting about them in the spring of 1702 for ways of counterbalancing the heavy weight of High Tories in Anne's first Cabinet, it was an obvious step to keep Pembroke in the Council and make him once again Lord President. No Tory could object to him, and no Whig could consider his presence there in any way threatening.[16] Through all the many changing phases of the Godolphin ministry in the next seven and a half years Pembroke remained the one constant factor, apart from the Managers themselves. In 1707 he acquired the Lieutenancy of Ireland in addition to the Lord Presidency, a most lucrative combination of offices; and when he surrendered both to the Junto in November 1708 he was immediately compensated with the post of Lord High Admiral. For the next twelve months his political existence became for the first time, in Burnet's words, one of "great uneasiness":[17] not so much because he was now the only Tory left in the Cabinet — a fact which probably did not worry him unduly — but because he was well aware that the Junto lords now regarded him merely as a stop-gap until the Queen was ready to accept Orford as head of the Admiralty. This she was eventually persuaded to do in November 1709, and Pembroke, encouraged by a 'golden handshake' of £3000 a year, passed at last into private life.*

Three peers whose careers illustrated the subtle variety of political shades that could be found within the spectrum of Court Toryism in the House of Lords were the Earl of Dartmouth, the Duke of Northumberland and Lord Berkeley of Stratton. Dartmouth was much the most important of the three — a Cabinet minister during the last four years of Anne's reign he was advanced from a barony to an earldom in 1711) and a member of the Board of Trade continuously throughout the first eight. The fact that in 1700 Dartmouth became a relation of the Earl of Nottingham's by marrying the daughter of Nottingham's brother, Heneage, encourages Dr. Walcott to place him in the High Tory 'Finch connexion'.[18] But his whole political record in Anne's reign belies this. He both regarded himself, and was regarded by all contemporary politicians, as a plain middle-of-the-road Tory — "no zealous party man", as he himself later said. It was such known qualities, outweighing an undistinguished administrative record as a trade commissioner, which made him an acceptable compromise candidate for the post of Secretary of State in June 1710 (a post for which Nottingham was a candidate);[19] and the same "moderation" prompted him in February 1711 openly to denounce what he considered to be Nottingham's factious attempts to force extreme policies on Oxford's administration.[20]

If Dartmouth's political opinions put him roughly in the middle of the Court Tory range, Berkeley of Stratton and Northumberland each have

---

* Though his record of office-holding may seem to belie the fact, Pembroke was not without principles. His firm belief in the necessity of a Hanoverian succession, for instance, was to take him into opposition to Oxford's Tory ministry from 1711 until the Queen's death.

their niches on opposite flanks. Lord Berkeley, who was Harley's surprise choice as Chancellor of the Duchy of Lancaster in September 1710, was almost as apologetic a Tory as the Duke of Kent was a Whig. His opinion of the leaders of both Whigs and Tories was equally severe — they all ('made but tools of th'others" in their parties — and he preferred to take his cue from a man of Dartmouth's kidney.[21] Besieged by Tory requests for his patronage after his appointment to the Duchy, he soon made it clear that his intention was to turn as few men as possible out of their jobs. "My chief aim, all parties laid aside", he explained, "is to find out the fittest men for their offices, and that will do the best service to the country."[22] Not surprisingly he was employed for a while by George I as a Commissioner of Trade, until his place fell prey to the voracious appetite of the Whigs in 1715. Northumberland, on the other hand, was that very rare bird, a High Church) courtier. A holder of convinced Tory principles, and indeed a friend and patron later in Anne's reign of one of the most active of Jacobite M.P.s, Charles Aldworth,[23] he nevertheless acknowledged such obligations to the Churchills and displayed so marked a deference for the Queen (an attitude which contemporaries would not have considered improper in one who was colonel of the Royal Horse Guards and Constable of Windsor Castle) that right up to the time of the Sacheverell trial he lent general support to the Godolphin ministry in the House of Lords, even in the years when it was dominated by the Junto. This explains why Marlborough had Northumberland in mind for the prized Lieutenancy of the Tower when the post was vacated by the death of the Whig Earl of Essex in January 1710.[24]

The Dartmouths, Northumberlands and Pembrokes in the Tory party of the early eighteenth century had their counterparts in the House of Commons. Sir Charles Hedges, for instance, though his career in the Queen's service was in one respect the reverse of Lord Dartmouth's, was a politician of very similar stamp. He spent the first four and a half years of the reign as a Secretary of State; and when eventually he was forced to give way to Sunderland in December 1706 he was amply compensated by the grant of a pension and two lucrative legal offices. These continued marks of Court favour kept him fairly steady in the government interest until 1712, when his Hanoverian sympathies led him to associate increasingly with the "Whimsical" Tory opposition to the Oxford ministry. Although he probably got his Secretaryship in 1702 because Rochester looked on him as a useful satellite,* Hedges soon carefully dissociated himself from the wilder element

---

* See *The Conduct of the Dowager Duchess of Marlborough* (1742), p. 170; B.M. Sloane MSS. 3516, f. 49. The evidence on which Walcott (*op. cit.* p. 98) classes Hedges as a

in Anne's first Cabinet and settled down to an unspectacular career in office and a prudent one in Parliament. He made it a rule to toe the Court line in the House of Commons whenever important or controversial issues were under discussion. Thus he tried to block the introduction of the second Occasional Conformity bill in November 1703,[25] opposed the "tack" of the third bill in 1704 and supported the election of John Smith as Speaker in 1705; and predictably, during the later summer and autumn of 1706, Anne fought hard to keep him in office.

If Hedges may be said to have represented roughly the political 'centre' of the Court Tories in the House of Commons, Edward Nicholas, M.P. for Shaftesbury, may be taken as equally representative of the 'right' of that body, and Sir Edward Northey (Attorney-General for all but three years of Anne's reign) as the epitome of the ultra-moderate element. "Ned" Nicholas was always a reliable government man as long as the Tories were in office. In 1704 he supported Godolphin loyally against the High Tory Tackers, just as in 1711 and 1714 he stood by Harley, first against the excesses of the October men[26] and then against the Whimsical Tory rebels. *A Numerical Calculation of the Honourable Members*, published just after the 1705 Election,[27] describes Nicholas as a "High Church Courtier". But his Church principles did not prevent him from voting for a Whig Speaker on the government's directions in October 1705, and this despite a passionate appeal from his Tory friend Lord Digby:

Br[omley] is gone up I believe, & has been told by severall he may depend upon your vote. I hope he will not be deceived, for your sake, for this I find will be made the test of mens integrity. Your opinion is so well known, & if your vote should not go with it, the world will ascribe it to something that is not very honourable . . . This I know you are sufficiently sencible of . . . but what passd between us at S——ry upon this subject had made me a little uneasy, & given me some apprehensions lest a wrong notion of gratitude, or some other false argument, should mislead you in a thing of so much concern both to your self & your country. For I do think a great deal more depends upon this than the having a Sp[eake]r our freind . . .[28]

For a man whose "opinion" was so decided as Nicholas's his decision to support the Court on this occasion must have been an agonising one. And the more the Whigs got the upper hand in the ministry thereafter, the more difficult did he find it to continue his support of Godolphin, so that in April 1707 he was at length removed from the post of Treasurer to Prince George

Nottinghamite is not convincing; cf. Hedges's stiffly formal letters to Nottingham, 1702–4, in Add. MSS. 29588–9, *passim*.

which he had held since 1700. When, however, the Whigs formed designs on his Dorset borough seat at the next General Election, Lord Shaftesbury advised against the attempt; for "Mr. Nicholas [he told them] is so supple a Tory, so experienced in doing all desired tho never so much agt principle, that the Court will never heartily help agt such a sure tool".[29] After three years in opposition, when he was at liberty to vote freely for the Church interest on major occasions, as in the Sacheverell divisions, and after a further year of loyal service in the Commons to the new Tory ministry after November 1710, Nicholas gained his reward by re-entering the Queen's service in December 1711 and remaining a placeman until 1715.[30]

Sir Edward Northey was a different kind of political animal, a professional lawyer and civil servant first and foremost, with his ultra-mild Toryism coming a very poor second in his priorities. Indeed, he seems to have had only a limited interest in politics, as such. Although Attorney-General under Godolphin from 1701 to 1707 he was not even at this time a member of the House of Commons. The first time he sat in the House was in 1710, when he was elected for Tiverton after Harley had reappointed him Attorney-General on the removal of Sir James Montagu. When the Oxford ministry fell in 1714, and Lord Cowper, as the new Lord Chancellor, had the task of counselling George I on a wide range of legal appointments, he believed that, on balance, the King's service would not suffer from keeping Northey in office. "The Attorney General", wrote Cowper in an admirable memorandum, ". . . is an excellent Lawyer, and a man of great abilitys in the Law, a moderate Tory, and much respected by that Party, and no further blameable, then by obeying those who could command him, if he kept his place".[31] The King took Cowper's advice, and Northey remained the chief law officer in the House of Commons until, "old and infirm", he was retired in 1718 with an annual pension of £1500 — a fitting quietus for a politician of his temper and breed.

The ambitious or careerist element among the moderate Tories thus included a prominent minority whose links were primarily with the Court rather than with any individual party leader. Most Tories of this stamp, however, found their way after Anne's accession (and in some cases before it) into one of two personal connections: either they attached themselves to Marlborough and Godolphin or, more frequently, they became Harleyites.

Marlborough and Godolphin were so synonymous with the Court throughout the years 1702–10 that it is not easy to distinguish confidently between those who could be counted among their personal adherents and those who were in reality just Court Tories or even pure Courtiers. The

strictly personal following the two Managers commanded was probably
fairly small; and as we earlier saw,* the longer the reign went on, the more
attenuated the Tory content of that following became. Admittedly, it was
some years after 1702 before the Whig leaders ceased to regard the duke and
the Lord Treasurer themselves as Tories. Looking back early in 1705 at the
struggle for power between the duumvirs and the High Church grandees,
which had only recently ended in victory for the former, Lord Somers still
argued that the Tory party "was their own party", whatever their current
disagreements with its other leaders.[32] But between 1705 and 1710, the
years of the Managers' growing dependence on the Whigs for getting the
Queen's business through Parliament, the few genuine Tories who appear
to have stayed in the Marlborough-Godolphin camp fell mostly into two
small categories. On the one hand were the close kin of the two ministers
themselves; on the other were the relatives and clients of Sir Jonathan
Trelawney, the Cornish landowner-prelate, who was weaned from his old
High Tory allegiances in 1704–5. Trelawney was later placed so heavily in
the ministers' debt by his translation from Exeter to Winchester (1707) that
he put his electoral and parliamentary influence entirely at their disposal
until Godolphin died and Marlborough left England in 1712.

Marlborough's two brothers, Charles and George (the latter a "high"
and somewhat wayward follower, the former by 1710 a drunken recluse),[33]
along with Godolphin's cousin, Sidney, and his son and heir, Lord Rialton,
comprised the core of the first group in the House of Commons. The
second group included General Charles Trelawney, Sir Harry Trelawney,
and John Mountstevens (until his suicide in 1707).[34] The most prominent of
Bishop Trelawney's nominees in the middle years of Anne, John Dolben,
came from a Tory family — his father being a former Archbishop of York
and his elder brother a prominent High Church lawyer-politician — but
his own views and associations made the "Treasurer's Whigs" and not the
moderate Tories his natural political brethren.† As for the rest of the Marlborough-Godolphin connection after 1705, it contained a tiny handful of
members who, if they were party men at all, had mild affiliations with the
Tories (Adam de Cardonnel, the duke's faithful secretary, Admiral Killi-
grew, his nominee at St. Albans in 1705, and Walter Chetwynd, the
Godolphinite Master of the Buckhounds from 1705 to 1711, were three

---

* Pp. 191–2 above.

† "A great stickle for Lord Treasurer in the house of Commons" (*Wentworth Papers*,
p. 73), Dolben sat for Liskeard, 1707–10, and was latterly in the van of the attack on
Sacheverell.

such); but its main source of recruits was unquestionably the Whig party.

It was the personal following of Robert Harley which from relatively early in Anne's reign attracted most men of moderate Tory inclinations who were interested in place and power. In the late 1690's Harley's "New Country Party" had offered a fresh and attractive political home to those whose old Tory philosophy could no longer satisfy their aspirations; and after 1702 Harley likewise became a magnet for a number of ambitious Tories of the younger generation who supported the war with few reserves and accepted the toleration of Protestant dissent. That the Harleyites should have become by 1704 a power-group in the Tory party, and a group that was beginning to approach in importance even the big High Church followings of Rochester and Nottingham, was none the less a curious development, and in more ways than one. It was curious because the core of the group — the close-knit family alliance of the Harleys, Foleys and Winningtons* — consisted exclusively of men who were Revolution Whig by political tradition and nonconformist in their religious background; and as late as 1703 one of the most jealous guardians of this Whig tradition, the third Earl of Shaftesbury, could still say to his friend Benjamin Furley: "your judgment about R. Harley is perfectly right. He is ours at the bottom".[35] It was equally curious because the original *raison d'être* of Harley and his friends in the 1690's had been as "Old Whigs", carrying on the country traditions of that party in opposition to the corrupting, Court-tainted influence of the Junto; they had been essentially critics of administration rather than aspirants to a share in its responsibilities and its rewards.

The transformation of a Country Whig group into one that by the early years of Anne's reign had become both Tory in association and Court in sympathy was the result of a variety of factors. One was the protracted alliance of convenience between the Harleyite nucleus and genuine Tory elements in the Commons during the Parliaments of 1695–8 and 1698–1700. Another factor, one that has not always been appreciated, was personal and religious. Harley was a man of deep and sincere Christian convictions.† When the stresses in the post-Revolution Church came to the surface and produced the open rift between "High" and "Low" churchmen in the years 1699–1701 he found himself involved in an awkward dilemma. He had little sympathy with the intolerant spirit or the reactionary politics of the

---

* For an excellent account of their ramifications see Walcott, *op. cit.* p. 67.

† His family letters bear constant testimony to this. One of many striking examples is his letter to his sister, Abigail, on 17 Apr. 1711 — his "first essay with a pen" after Guiscard's attempt to assassinate him (B.M. Loan 29/67/5).

true highflyers, whose cause the old Tory leaders espoused. Yet he felt that, on balance, both the Establishment and the spiritual and moral health of the country were safer in their hands than in those of latitudinarian clergy who looked for lay support to Whig magnates of dubious religious principles. Without doubt Harley exaggerated the threat to doctrinal orthodoxy from an unqualified Whig-Low Church supremacy; but that he believed in it is evident from a passionate letter he wrote to Archbishop Tenison in 1702.

I must tell you [he wrote at one point] what you have nobody else faithful enough to do it, you are entirely under the influence of those who have not only dischargd themselves from al obligations of religion, but also have for many years been promoting, first Socinianisme, then arrianisme & now deisme. In the state they have propagated notions wch destroy all governmt. In order to perfect that, they set up for notions wch destroy al religion & so consequently dissolve the bonds of all society.[36]

Among essentially political events, however, those which did most to shape Harley's personal development and also to bestow on his followers both a new rôle and a new importance in the working of politics, took place in the year 1701. In that year the necessity of facing up to two vital decisions, the imperative need to settle the succession by law on a Protestant heir and the equally urgent need to recognise that Louis XIV was again threatening Western Europe with the prospect of Bourbon domination, opened up a gap between Harley and his friends and the more extreme Tories which was never subsequently closed;[37] at the same time it converted the Harley connexion into one that from now on was normally pro-Court rather than anti-Court, responsible rather than destructive, composed of potential servants rather than truculent opponents of the Crown. Harley himself in later years was fully conscious of the momentous change in his political direction which took place in 1701, more conscious perhaps than he had been at the time; for his own distrust of William III, and the distrust which he in his turn inspired among William's friends and allies, lingered on till the King's death, prompting him even to oppose the dissolution of the most troublesome of all William's Parliaments in the autumn of 1701.[38] It was only of Queen Anne that Robert Harley could truly say: "she is the first Prince I ever did belong to".[39]

We have observed that the nucleus of Harley's following was formed by what was essentially a family group. It was also very much a local group. Its cohesion rested on the electoral dominance in three of the border counties (Herefordshire, Worcestershire and Radnorshire), and the influence in at least two boroughs* in neighbouring Shropshire and Staffordshire, of the Harleys themselves — Robert, his brother Edward, and his cousin Thomas — and their kinsmen by marriage, the Foleys and the Winningtons.† But already associated with Robert Harley in 1702, either by remoter kinship or personal friendship, were a number of other politicians who were marked out as coming men in the Tory party. The most notable among them was an old school-fellow of Harley's, Simon Harcourt,[40] at this time 41 years old and, with the possible exception of Heneage Finch, the most brilliant lawyer on the Tory benches in the Commons. Thanks to Harley's influence with the new Managers Harcourt became Solicitor-General in Anne's first ministry,[41] and this appointment was the first official prize to fall to the Harleyites in their new capacity as "Queen's servants", although their leader accepted the government nomination to the Chair of the House in 1702. Another and younger Tory who had attached himself firmly and whole-heartedly to Harley by 1702[42] was Thomas Mansel of Margam, son and heir of the biggest landowner in Glamorgan[43] and already, at the age of 34, a power in the political world of South Wales. Through him Harley acquired a special influence over the Tories in Glamorgan and other neighbouring counties, notably Cardigan and Pembroke, a measure of which he retained right through the reign. What is of particular interest is that neither Mansel nor Harcourt were lukewarm Tories; Harcourt, indeed, had been the spearhead of the impeachment of Somers, while Mansel under a different leader could well have developed into a backbench troublemaker.‡ Their early association with Harley illustrates one very significant feature of his connection which deserves some emphasis. Although it always contained a large proportion of genuine moderates, its members included a number of very active partisans. But theirs was a new and essentially post-Revolution brand of Toryism. Their creed was that of a new generation, one which had little interest in re-fighting the political battles of Charles II's and James II's

* Bishop's Castle and Stafford.

† Robert and Edward both married Foleys — two of the daughters of Thomas Foley of Witley and sisters of Thomas, junior, M.P. for Stafford 1694–1711, who was created Baron Foley in December 1711. Another of the latter's sisters was married to Salwey Winnington, who represented Bewdley in every Parliament but one between 1694 and 1715. Robert Harley's first wife, Edith Foley, died in Nov. 1691 and he subsequently remarried. See Walcott, *loc. cit.* and app. III, pt. viii, for the constituencies controlled or influenced by this formidable electoral alliance.

‡ Mansel's friendship with Frank Gwyn in the 90's could easily have led him into Rochester's camp, and Godolphin was significantly grateful for Harley's influence over him in the early years of Anne's reign. B.M. Loan 29/191, f. 38. On the other hand, the Harleys' other main recruiter in South Wales, Sir John Philipps of Picton Castle, was a moderate, staunchly Anglican Whig.

reigns and which had little in common with the "old Tories", those High Church zealots who looked for leadership to the Hydes, the Finches and the Seymours.

Two more friends of Harley, who became associated with his group in the early years of Anne's reign, were equally representative of this new spirit though more obviously moderate than Harcourt and Mansel. One was the Honourable Henry Paget, knight of the shire for Staffordshire since 1695 and a relative by marriage both of Harcourt and Thomas Foley. A protégé of the Whig Duke of Newcastle, he was so pallid a Tory that in December 1701 it had even been rumoured that for the sake of office he had "gone in to my Lord Summers party and measures".[44] It was Harley, however, who first pressed Paget's claims to government favour on Godolphin in 1703, shortly after beginning his own wooing of Newcastle;[45] and his status as Paget's patron and mentor was naturally confirmed in 1704 when the latter was appointed to the Prince's Council of the Admiralty.[46] A slightly earlier acquisition to the Harleyites, and a more valuable one, was Lord Poulet. A relation of Paget's, "Swallow" Poulet was a Somerset nobleman with a shrewd political brain, extensive estates and useful electoral influence in the west country which was always (as he once avowed) "with out reserve devoted" to Harley;[47] and in addition to these assets he also brought to Harley, through his kinsman and client, James Johnson, worthwhile contacts in Scotland.[48] Like Paget, he was in his late thirties in 1702.

It is often forgotten that the friendship between Harley and Henry St. John, which for some five or six years in the middle of the reign was to be a key factor in the working of politics, and was to bring Harley valuable reinforcements from St. John's private circle of associates and boon companions, had not matured by the time of the Queen's accession.[49] On the contrary, in his spectacular first three years in Parliament from 1701 to 1703 the young member for Wootton Bassett seemed to most observers of the Westminster scene to have carved out a special niche for himself on the right of the party: a niche alongside other prominent young zealots, such as William Bromley of Baginton, who had just entered on a 30-year parliamentary association with Oxford University,* and Sir Thomas Hanmer, the 25-year-old Suffolk baronet who was already one of the wealthiest commoners in England. The violent partisanship he showed at the time of the impeachments of 1701 was scarcely the attitude of a man of "moderation".[50] And while it is true that he struck up a correspondence with Speaker Harley in December of that year, this seems to have remained for some time a rather

* Bromley had begun his parliamentary career, however, back in 1690 at the age of 26.

desultory affair, on Harley's part at least.[51] Few people would have cared to prophesy in November 1702, when St. John warmly seconded Bromley in sponsoring the first Occasional Conformity bill in the Commons, that this volatile, compelling young man would within two years be drawn into the Harleian orbit as an apostle of Tory "moderation", a vigorous supporter of the war, and a strenuous opponent of the Tack. But Robert Harley, in these early years of the new reign, came to exercise an oddly magnetic hold over a passionate young politician whose idealism and capacity for hero-worship had not yet been warped by overweening ambition and the corrupting influence of office — over a St. John who was able, without the slightest self-consciousness, to regard the Speaker as his "dear Master" and to sign his letters to him "yrs everlastingly".[52]

Although by October 1703 St. John was already professing himself Harley's "faithful unalterable friend", it was the session of 1703–4 which transformed such professions into political links of exceptional strength. At the beginning of that session St. John's ties with the High Tories were still close enough to draw him for a second time into the promotion of the Occasional Conformity bill, in company with Bromley and Musgrave and in opposition to old friends like James Brydges as well as to Harley. But in January 1704 he broke with the highflyers over their obstruction of war supply,[53] and by the spring, when Harley himself entered the Cabinet in place of Nottingham, the Harleyite group in the Commons had been strengthened not only by the accession of St. John himself, who was made Secretary-at-War as soon as the session ended, but also by the association with it of a number of St. John's particular cronies. The included Tom Coke, the randy young knight of the shire for Derbyshire, who also entered the Queen's service for the first time in 1704;* Arthur Moore, a sharp City businessman of somewhat disreputable Irish parentage who was similarly floated into office on the Harleyite tide[54] after the fall of Nottingham and Seymour; and St. John's cousin, Brigadier Webb, who had imbibed something of Harley's political philosophy and who in this Parliament sat for Ludgershall in Wiltshire along with his father, Edmund.[55] But of the new recruits which St. John brought into Harley's camp easily the most important, in the long run, was another young Tory still in his thirties in 1704, George Granville. In his first extant letter to Harley, written on 25 July 1704, Granville wrote: "I take the liberty to offer myself to your friendship, upon which only I rely,

---

* As a Teller of the Exchequer. For his correspondence with St. John see H.M.C. *Cowper MSS.* iii, 49 *et seq.* In 1706 Coke was made Vice-Chamberlain of the Household and from then on became progressively more of a Court member and less of a Harleyite.

and to put you in mind of one who will never forget the obligation";[56] and he did not lack the wherewithal to repay his political debts. He was heir to a great electoral interest in Cornwall, an interest based largely on five centuries of intermarriage between the Granvilles and almost every other Cornish family of note, and one which he had been effectively managing on behalf of his cousin, John, since 1702.[57] By 1708, the year after his cousin's death, George was already acting as unofficial 'whip' for the Harleyites among the members for the south-western counties. But it was not until after the 1710 Election that Harley reaped the full harvest in the House of Commons of Granville's friendship,[58] or that his ally received his rewards — the Secretary-ship-at-War and the barony of Lansdowne.

Kinship, friendship and electoral interest: these, we may conclude, were the three factors which, common opinions apart, did most to group and hold together those younger Tories whom soured High Churchmen later dubbed "the Harlequins" or "Harlekins".[59] Their significance can be illustrated by analysing the membership of the first House of Commons to be elected after Robert Harley himself became the first minister of the Crown. In the session of 1710–11 the House contained three Harleys, three Harcourts, three Foleys, two Winningtons and two Granvilles, not to mention a flock of Cornish members who owed their seats to George Granville — among them Jack Hill,* Tom Coke and John Manley — and others, like George Courtenay and Alexander Pendarves, who took their cue from him and regarded him as their channel to official patronage. St. John, of course, was there as Secretary of State for the South; and so were his nominee for Wootton Bassett, Richard Goddard, his young fellow member for Berkshire, Sir John Stonehouse, over whom he quickly acquired great influence,[60] and his intimates, Moore and Webb (the latter bringing in on his coat-tails another Tory general, Thomas Pearce, as his partner at Ludgershall). But by this stage there were others who, from Harley's point of view, were more dependable than St. John's immediate coterie. In this same Parliament sat also Sir Thomas Mansel, Harley's "dearest friend"[61] and faithful lieutenant to the end of his ministry, along with his various Welsh friends;† Poulet's kinsman James Johnson (returned for Calne), his Somerset neighbour Nathaniel Palmer (Bridgwater) and his nominees at Ilchester, Edward Phelipps, Samuel Masham and Sir James Bateman;[62] the Harley candidates for Bishop's Castle and Leominster, Sir Robert Raymond and Edward

* Abigail Masham's brother.

† Notably John Meyrick and John Laugharne (Cardigan and Haverfordwest), and Sir Edward Stradling (Cardiff Boroughs), who was Mansel's brother-in-law.

Bangham; and a number of other members based in the West Country such as John Blanch, whose election Harley had supported at Gloucester, and Charles Coxe (Cirencester), a Welsh judge who had owed his appointment partly to Harley's influence in 1704 and who had been saved by him from dismissal in 1707.[63] The new member for Buckingham, Thomas Chapman, seems early to have put himself under Harley's wing and to have remained faithful to the prime minister even in his hour of disgrace in 1714,[64] and the latter's squadron was completed by a Scottish contingent headed by Lord Dupplin (Harley's son-in-law), Sir John Malcolm, and other relatives and friends of the Earl of Kinnoull. In all there were at least 40 members on whose loyalty — so long as St. John behaved himself — Harley could absolutely depend in this first parliamentary session of his ministry.

Yet to appreciate the full range of his influence in the Commons between 1702 and 1714 one must bear in mind that three further factors helped on occasion to extend it well outside this close inner network of kinsmen, personal friends and electoral clients. One was the fact that in spite of his chequered career in the middle of the reign, which lost him most of his former High Tory friends, a number remained very much attached to him for many years thereafter. While they would not always vote with him when their most cherished party principles were at stake, High Church gentlemen like Sir Robert Davers, Sir Michael Warton, Charles Caesar and Tom Conyers, or James Grahme, Lord Cheyne, Tom Rowney and Sir John Bland remained susceptible to Harley's influence and were often ready to rally to his defence when he was in political difficulties.[65] The second point to remember is that Harley had an astonishing number of relations in the Commons. Many of them, it is true, were very distant cousins; but however remote they were he always regarded them as potential allies worth his cultivation, whether they were Tories like Cheyne, John Prise of Wistaton and the Cornwalls of Herefordshire, or whether they were Whigs like Richard Hampden, Paul Methuen, Sir Henry Ashurst, the Robarteses of Cornwall, the Newports of Salop, or the Ashes of Heytesbury.[66] The third and the most important factor in Harley's extraordinary parliamentary influence is a far more elusive one for the student of the period to capture and a far more difficult one to assess: this was the personal calibre of the man himself.

Robert Harley's emergence as a party leader late in William's reign and early in Anne's, and particularly as the leader of men of such glittering talents as Simon Harcourt and Henry St. John, has puzzled many historians. We are frequently told that he himself was not, in any obvious way, outstandingly endowed, and up to a point this generalisation can be justified. Harley certainly lacked the wealth that often attracts a circle of hopeful clients; until he became Speaker in 1701 his private means were no more than modest. He was physically unprepossessing: a small, dark, shifty-looking man. His manner outside his domestic circle lacked "that grace and openness which engages the affection".[67] Nor were his intellectual powers exceptional. His letters and memoranda are almost all written in that peculiarly muddy and laboured style which every scholar working in this field soon comes to recognise as authentically Harleian.[68] As a parliamentary speaker he was not to everyone's taste; his style was too oblique and too lacking in oratorical flourishes to have general appeal, though he was an adroit debater, well-equipped to handle constitutional, procedural and (after 1710) financial questions, and he would sometimes surprise both his friends and his opponents by rising to an occasion superbly.[69] His administrative record from 1704 to 1708 as Secretary for the North, a post into which (to quote his own words) he was "unfortunately pressed",[70] was an improvement in some respects on that of his predecessor, Hedges, but it was a record of hard-working competence rather than of distinction.[71] Only in his organisation of government intelligence did he achieve extraordinary success,[72] and this first spell of office ended under the dark cloud of the Greg affair, which exposed Harley's culpable slackness in failing to guard against security risks in his department. His work at the Treasury from 1710 to 1714 was more notable; certainly it did not merit some of the harsh strictures it has subsequently received.[73] But to depict him as a Pitt or a Gladstone, or even as a Montagu, would be absurd.

All this may suggest a somewhat commonplace figure. But Harley was very far from being that. In many ways he was the key political figure of the whole period from 1695 to 1714. In an age that was lavishly furnished with political talent, an unwavering but level-headed Whig could write of Harley in 1712, with a mixture of respect and apprehension, "Nor have we had (in my opinion) a genius equal to oppose to him".[74] One secret of his great personal influence we have touched on earlier: namely, that after 1702 he perceived more clearly than any of his fellow politicians the great reservoir of power still in the keeping of the Crown and that he plotted his course accordingly. He was also an expert parliamentary manager, a man who revelled in the under-cover work of politics, in the conspiratorial whisper behind the Speaker's chair, in the assiduous canvassing and manipulation of votes and voters. This talent, more than any other, brought him to the front rank of politicians in the 1690's, and it was appropriate that it should also have enabled him for many months to stave off the final collapse of his ministry in 1714. St. John, whose gifts were in so many respects more brilliant, could never equal him in this very necessary qualification for success. A third clue to Harley's magnetic influence lies in his family connections and breadth of interests. These gave him an astonishing range of contacts, both inside and outside the political world: among industrialists and City financiers, among lawyers, among scholars and journalists, among clerics of every hue, from Highflyers like Atterbury to Presbyterians and Quakers like Calamy and Penn, as well as among his own class of country gentlemen. These contacts helped him to keep a sensitive finger on the pulse of public opinion outside Westminster, and at the same time to be equally expert at taking the temperature of the House of Commons (he was never quite as sure in his touch after November 1711 in the House of Lords). He had qualities of character, too, which were invaluable political assets. Like his predecessor at the Treasury, Godolphin, he was utterly incorruptible. The stinging rebuke he administered in 1707 to a place-hunter who had tried to oil his palm deserves quoting:

I must tell you very plainly I resent your going about to offer me mony, and much more your continuing to insinuate it in your last letter even after I had told you so plainly before I would hear nothing of it. I told you before that you did not know me when you went that way to work ... I now repeat again to you that until you are cured of thinking to bribe me I shall never think my self capable to serve you.*

Scrupulous in his concept of public duty, he was also imperturbable and courageous in discharging that duty. His phlegm, even at times of acute personal crisis in 1708, 1711 and 1715, was truly remarkable. Under attack he was "as easy as a lamb"; and for criticism, Swift once said, he "cares not a rush".[75]

At the very root of Harley's success, however, lay a further quality, more intangible yet more important than any other. He was an *instinctive* political animal, ever fertile in resource and expedient, and possessing that rarest of gifts which Sir Keith Feiling once so memorably described as the 'power of knowing the individual motive next every politician's heart'.[76] The impression he regularly gave of being one move ahead of everyone else in the game, together with the vapour cloud of mystery he perpetually (and not always

---

* B.M. Loan 29/127/7: to William Brenand (copy), 28 June 1707. For Erasmus Lewis's testimony to Harley the incorruptible see Add. MSS. 31143, f. 508 [July 1710]; cf. Oxford's glowing praise of his brother Edward for refusing a proffered bribe in 1713 in B.M. Loan 29/70/9: 25 July.

consciously) trailed throughout his career, earned him his reputation as "the Sorcerer" of post-Revolution politics.[77] This reputation, however, was not an unqualified blessing to him. In the years from 1698 to 1702 it held spellbound scores of High Anglican country gentlemen who might well have been expected to regard an ex-Whig and an ex-dissenter with the gravest suspicion. Andrew Archer, the Warwickshire squire, rejoiced when Harley was re-elected Speaker in William III's last Parliament,[78] and many other Tories shared his exultation. But once the Harleyites had betrayed the cause of the Church party in 1704 over Occasional Conformity and "the Tack", their leader's reputation for wizardry and enigmatic behaviour began to work against him; and although there were many times in the next decade when the High Tories were forced into a grudging respect for Harley, few of them ever fully trusted him again. The unfortunate lack of frankness and openness which so often afflicted him in his day-to-day political dealings (a strange paradox in one who was so relaxed and warmly affectionate among his intimates and in his family circle) made it all the harder for him to dispel this distrust. "He passes for a tory", one contemporary said of him in 1710;[79] and perhaps this was the most that could have been said. For the bulk of the party could never after 1704 accept him as one of themselves, not even on the eve of his greatest triumph in 1710,[80] and he, for his part, could never whole-heartedly accept the mantle of a party leader which some of his friends were anxious to thrust upon him.* All the same, his unenviable nickname of "Robin the Trickster" was not entirely warranted. Like most successful politicians Harley was an opportunist; yet in his devious way he maintained a remarkable consistency in holding firm to his political ideals and attitudes right through from 1701, when he shepherded the Act of Settlement through the Commons, to the fall of his administration in 1714. He was not being hypocritical when he told his Christ Church friend William Stratford: "I took up my principles not to lay them down because they please not the factious & humoursome".†

As a major political group within the Tory party the Harleyites held together a surprisingly long time: longer, at least, than might have been predicted in view of inherent flaws in their structure, weaknesses of a kind which the Junto Whigs, for example, never had to contend with. In part

* This point is developed in Chapter 11.

† B.M. Loan 29/171: 16 Oct. 1705. Of particular note is Harley's proud and patently sincere claim about his undeviating attitude to the succession question, made to his cousin Thomas in March 1714 (Add. MSS. 40621, f. 178) and again to his brother Edward, in a letter written from the Tower, on 24 Mar. 1716 (B.M. Loan 29/70/10).

these were the weaknesses of the Tory party at large: symptoms of the political schizophrenia of a party which could never fully and finally come to terms with the betrayal of its traditional principles involved in the Revolution, in the Toleration Act, in the Act of Settlement, and in the Oath of Abjuration. But more specifically they were the stresses and strains at work within a body of men who held diverse views on certain major questions, especially on religious problems, led by an individualist who defied classification in any normal party terminology. In the end these pressures proved too much even for a connexion which had astonished the political world in 1708 by its solidarity, when its four leading figures all resigned from the ministry in the space of two days. By 1711, when they became personalised in the famous quarrel between Harley and St. John, they had already begun to open up cracks in the Harleyite fabric, and in the last year of the Queen's life they were to split it down the middle, with dramatic effects on the working of politics.

The Harley-St. John conflict is often seen in terms of personal rivalry, but there was more to it than this. Its origins can be traced as far back as a fundamental difference of opinion on political strategy which followed the fall of the Harleyites in 1708. For Henry St. John the break in 1704–5 with his "old friends" of the Tory right had been infinitely more painful than for Harley, and it had been the old chieftains and not the principles of the party he had then rejected.[81] After their resignation from the government in February 1708 it was not long before he was begging his leader to come to terms with the younger High Tories in the House of Commons under Bromley and put himself at the head of a reunited "Church of England party".[82] He found, however, that Harley was still resolved to steer clear of any irrevocable commitment to the High Churchmen. The "Master" preferred to go to work in his own distinctive way to undermine the Godolphin administration, using his favourite weapons — the influence of the Queen and the privy-stairs — and indeed any useful tools that came to hand, especially the help of discontented Whigs. But this way was not for St. John. By the autumn of 1709 there were already rumours of a cooling between the two men, regarded with some concern by their friends.[83] Relations were aggravated that winter by the paradox of St. John's continued intimacy with Marlborough,[84] and in the following spring and summer by the younger man's well-founded suspicions that when the Tories re-entered the Promised Land Harley designed to keep him out of the Cabinet.[85] The disputes in 1711 over the Quebec expedition, over St. John's tampering with the October Club and his tactless behaviour after Guiscard's attempt on Harley's life, and again in 1712 over St. John's promotion to the House of Lords, added fresh fuel to the flames.[86] From then on there were only brief interludes of reconciliation.

Not until 1713–14, however, did St. John (now Viscount Bolingbroke) at last emerge as the leader of a new party group of his own in Parliament, committed to an out-and-out Tory programme and to a succession policy that, to put the most favourable construction on it, was frankly opportunistic. In building up this following Bolingbroke drew off from the Harleyites some of their more right-wing members like the Harcourts, Lord Masham and Sir John Stonehouse, as well as carrying over some of his old friends such as Moore and Webb.* But he also attracted a large number of hot Tories (including many Jacobites) who had previously had no special connection with Harley: in the Commons, Sir William Wyndham, Henry Campion, William Collier, Sir Edward Knatchbull, Richard Cresswell, Sir William Barker, and many more of a similar complexion; and in the Lords, Bishop Atterbury, Lord Lexington and that ill-disguised Jacobite, the Duke of Beaufort. Beaufort was not the least of Bolingbroke's assets; for though something of a figure of fun in Parliament, his electoral influence — extending to six counties and at least a dozen boroughs[87] — was more widespread than that of any other Tory magnate in the last two General Elections of the reign, and he had a substantial personal connexion in the Commons to add to the Secretary's other followers in the session of 1714.

One of the ironies of Augustan politics is that in the final crisis of the reign, when the fate of the Protestant Succession appeared to many to hang on the outcome of the struggle for supremacy between Oxford and Bolingbroke, senior members of the House of Commons who in the earlier years of Anne had been lieutenants of the old High Tory chieftains, ex-Rochesterites like Frank Gwyn and Seymour Portman, or erstwhile friends of Harley's bitterest foe Nottingham, like Bromley and John Sharp, chose on the whole to support the Lord Treasurer, the arch-apostle of "moderation". Bolingbroke, who back in 1705 had scourged the old Church Tories as a collection of "all the knaves and fools in England",[88] ended up as the champion of the extremism of a younger generation of party zealots.

So radical a regrouping of Tory forces as this could never have taken place but for an earlier development of basic importance. This was the disintegration of the three great personal connexions which in the first half of

---

* Granville, however, never deserted Oxford, while Coke played a safe Court game throughout.

Anne's reign had absorbed so many High Tory politicians whose sights were set firmly on place and power. The change was already under way by the years 1705–8, when Sir Edward Seymour, by then a victim of diabetes and a very sick man, lost the dominant position in the House of Commons which he had held for so long.* It was accelerated by Seymour's death in April 1708. It was carried a significant stage further by the alliance which was forged in February 1711 between the Earl of Rochester and Robert Harley against the excesses of the October Club and the disrupting influence of St. John; an alliance which was abruptly ended by Rochester's sudden death in May of that year, but which bequeathed to Harley the continued support of many of Rochester's former adherents.[89] And it was completed in November and December 1711, when Daniel Finch, Earl of Nottingham, staggered the Tory world and shattered his own personal following by his incredible decision to strike a bargain with the Junto and go into permanent opposition to a Tory ministry.

When Queen Anne came to the throne most of the really active Tories "of the higher sort" who had been closely engaged in the political battles of William's reign, and who were still in the field, were already attached to one or other of these three great chiefs: to Rochester and Nottingham, who led important groups in both Houses, and to Seymour, whose interest was naturally concentrated in the Commons. Danby, now Duke of Leeds, had retired from the competition in 1694. Three High Tories of Cabinet status — Jersey, Ormonde and Buckingham — preserved some degree of independence.[90] But the vast majority of the remainder, including even sturdy veterans like Francis Gwyn, Sir John Leveson Gower and Sir Christopher Musgrave, were absorbed into the three big groups which together provided the power-house of the "Old Tories". In the working of politics these three Tory connexions exercised their maximum influence in the first two years of the reign. By the spring of 1704 their leaders had lost their battle with Marlborough and Godolphin for control over the ministry; and for the next six years High Toryism became very largely, if not wholly, an opposition force in British politics. Rochester and Nottingham continued to be its principal champions in the House of Lords right down to the change of ministry in 1710. But in the interim even they, as well as the ailing

---

* He remained indispensable up to the winter of 1704–5. Nicholas Pollexfen could still describe him as "the general" of the Tory army in the Commons in Nov. 1704, at much the same time as Godolphin was writing to Harley: "S^r. E: S^r being at last come to town, I hear tuesday next is designed for the day of battell". Norris MSS. 920 NOR. 1/266: Pollexfen to Norris, 4 Nov.; B.M. Loan 29/64/4: 12 Nov.

Seymour, lost something of the authority they had previously exercised over the politically ambitious Tory extremists in St. Stephen's Chapel. With Musgrave dead before 1705, and John Granville and Leveson Gower removed from the Lower House by promotion to the peerage, leadership there began to pass to younger men: to William Bromley, in particular, Seymour's heir-apparent since early in the reign,[91] but also in some measure to Sir Thomas Hanmer, a man of greater wealth and loftier oratorical style than Bromley, who had attracted the attention of the powers-that-be in 1702 and who by 1708 had made himself indispensable in opposition.[92] Between 1707 and 1710 even Bromley and Hanmer began to be challenged by another candidate, Arthur Annesley, whose fiery speeches frequently inflamed the back benches in the middle years of the reign and whom James Brydges thought "equal to any there" by 1710.[93] However all these new leaders remained on good terms with the "great men" in the Lords, and particularly with Nottingham, with whom all had had fairly close associations in the past.

There is little profit in trying to submit the composition of the main High Tory groups of the years 1702–11 to minute analysis. Scarcity of information from surviving correspondence, by contrast with the abundant material available for identifying the Harleyites, makes such an exercise extremely difficult if not quite impossible.* However, such evidence as we do possess strongly underlines certain general facts of great significance, affecting our entire assessment of the relative importance to early-eighteenth-century Toryism of the 'organised' element in the Church party. It warns us constantly against exaggerating either the size of any of these High Tory groups, or the consistency of their composition, or indeed the discipline governing the political conduct of their members. On negative evidence alone, as we shall later find,† we are entitled to conclude that they were certainly smaller, and probably very much smaller, than Professor Walcott — with his estimate of 111 M.P.s of this category elected in 1702 — has suggested; and also that individual connections were far less rigid both in membership and in parliamentary conduct than might be supposed.[94] In addition, the sources do yield a number of specific facts of particular interest about the Nottinghamites, the followers of Seymour, and those whom contemporaries knew as "Lord Rochester's friends" which do something to clarify their place in the structure of the Tory party at this period.

One such fact is that Nottingham's following was the smallest of the three in the House of Commons but the most important in the House of Lords. Nottingham himself, the senior Secretary of State early in William's reign

* Some of the problems involved are discussed in Chapter 10.   † See pp. 333–4 below.

and again from 1702 to 1704, was a solemn, excessively moral, pillar of the Anglican Church, whom Wharton unforgettably christened "Dismal". In an age when long formal speeches were the order of the day in the House of Lords Nottingham's staying-power comfortably exceeded that of any of his fellow peers, with one notable exception (this was his friend Lord Haversham, who could be depended on to deliver an "annual speech" of unbelievable prolixity which he then had printed for the edification of those not fortunate enough to have heard the eloquence of the original). In the Lords Nottingham marshalled a powerful squadron of relatives and friends. Apart from Haversham, a convert from Whiggery and a political eccentric, there was Daniel's brother Heneage, created Lord Guernsey in 1703, his cousin Winchilsea, his kinsman Hatton, and his friends Weymouth, Thanet, North and Archbishop Sharp.[95] Through his friendship with Bromley in the early years of Anne's reign Nottingham also acquired influence with midland peers like Stawell and Scarsdale. When he was under severe fire from the Whigs during the Lords' enquiry into the "Scotch plot" in December 1703 it was Stawell who wrote urgently to Weymouth:

I hope you will excuse this hasty scribble. 'Tis to let you know that Lord Nottingham is attacked & they are doeing their endeavour to pass a scandalous vote on him as to his proceedings in examining the Plot, and to tell you if you can come it may be of service to him.[96]

Two young Tory noblemen, the second Earl of Abingdon, who had entered the House of Lords in 1699, and the fourth Earl of Anglesey, who took his seat just before William III's death, also gravitated towards Nottingham as the leading lay champion of the Anglican Church in the Upper House. Whether they could have been accounted his adherents in the strictest sense is more doubtful. Some facts admittedly point to a fairly close association between Abingdon and Nottingham: their mutual friendship with Weymouth, for example,[97] and the apparent co-operation of the Berties (Abingdon's relatives) with known Nottinghamites in the House of Commons on critical occasions between 1702 and 1711 — "the Tack" being an obvious case. At the same time there is virtually no correspondence in the Finch papers to substantiate the relationship, and we know that in the years of High Tory opposition from 1704 to 1710 Abingdon's loyalty sometimes fell short of "Dismal's" exacting standards.[98] As for Anglesey, he was clearly on good personal terms with Nottingham;[99] but much of his time in the early years of Anne was spent in Ireland, and by 1710, if not earlier, he had achieved a stature in his own right in the House of Lords independent of the older man[100] — which was one reason why Harley was so anxious to bring him into his new Cabinet in 1710.

Nottingham's authority in the Commons, circumscribed as it was by his limited electoral influence, which did not normally extend beyond the county of Rutland, and by the misfortune of having very few close relatives in the House before the election of his nephew and eldest son in 1710,[101] depended very much on his prestige as the most respected representative of the High Anglican laity. Apart from cementing his friendship with Sharp (who could himself influence several votes in the Commons in addition to that of his son, John),[102] this prestige was one of the main factors which brought Nottingham and William Bromley together. It was Bromley who promoted the earl's Occasional Conformity bill in the Commons in three successive sessions between 1702 and 1704, and the personal and political links between the two men held firm for over six years thereafter. Even when Nottingham deserted his party in December 1711 the Canon of Christ Church, who knew Bromley well, thought him still the likeliest person to affect a reconversion.* Apart, however, from the general asset of his high standing with good Church of England men in the House of Commons, the earl enjoyed a more particular advantage there for much of Anne's reign. This accrued to him as a result of his daughter's marriage in 1704 with Sir Roger Mostyn of Mostyn, who represented Cheshire and both the county and boroughs of Flint between 1702 and 1714. The alliance opened up for Nottingham a new network of connections centred on North Wales and on the counties of Cheshire and Lancashire. Hence the subsequent closeness of his relations with Sir Thomas Hanmer (Mostyn's cousin and Flintshire neighbour),† with Sir Henry Bunbury and Sir John Conway (brother-in-law and friend respectively of Hanmer), with those two staunch Cheshire Tories, Peter Shakerley and Sir George Warburton, with John Ward of Capesthorne, who became the Finches' most loyal lieutenant in the Commons in the middle years of the reign, and with the Leghs of Lyme (cousins of Bunbury), who controlled the borough of Newton in Lancashire.[103] Outside this network, Nottingham also had a claim on the allegiance of a few other relatives or friends of relatives in the House, among them Edward Knatchbull, his

---

* H.M.C. *Portland MSS.* vii, 80. There had, as Stratford rightly told Lord Harley, "been a great correspondence betwixt them", part of which is still preserved among the Finch MSS.

† *Hanmer Correspondence* (London, 1838), pp. 123, 125–6. Hanmer, it must be stressed, was far too much the *grand seigneur* and the epitome of the wealthy, independent country gentleman to be in any sense a *client* of Nottingham's.

cousin and "creature", who held Kent seats in two of Anne's Parliaments, and Morgan Randyll, "a bosom friend of Ld Guernsey's", who represented Guildford in four.[104]

A further conclusion which present evidence strongly suggests about the old High Tory groups, though it cannot be established as a cast-iron certainty, concerns the two other connexions, those centring on Rochester and Seymour. It has been said that these were so closely dovetailed as to constitute in effect a single formidable interest.[105] The truth would seem to be that their association was nothing like as complete as this. Sir Edward Seymour, of course, had ties with Rochester that went back to Charles II's reign, and these were strengthened by the marriage of one of Seymour's sons to Rochester's daughter. Moreover in the first two sessions of Anne's first Parliament it was Seymour and his allies, as often as not, who appeared to be doing most to force on the Commons the particular policies or prejudices Rochester was pressing or indulging in the Lords and in the Cabinet: obstructing the voting of provisions for a large army in Flanders, for instance, criticising the allies, and furthering Rochester's personal vendetta against the Duke of Marlborough. Yet Seymour, we must remember, was a highly independent magnate. His "Western Empire" among the decayed boroughs of Cornwall and Devon, where (it was said) he "swears and swaggers amongst the seamen",[106] together with his shoal of relatives, many of whom held safe parliamentary seats, gave him a bargaining power that made him anything but an easy partner; his local interests by no means always coincided with those of the Hydes;[107] and there were prominent political issues — "the Tack" being a notable one — on which Seymour's clan and part, at least, of Rochester's following clearly did not follow identical courses. On that occasion — and it was not the first instance of its kind in Anne's reign — Seymour appears to have been temporarily closer to Nottingham and his brother Heneage than he was to Rochester.[108]

Seymour, in fact, was a law unto himself. "A man of so many passions and perturbations", as a Devonshire neighbour described him,[109] his political talents may have seemed formidable to some of his fellow partisans but they were imperfectly disciplined and very largely destructive. Far too often, in consequence, he carried his negative parliamentary activities to the point of utter irresponsibility: and this is a charge which cannot fairly be brought against Nottingham, except for a few brief interludes of factious wrecking which disfigured his career in 1705–6 and in the spring of 1711, nor even against Rochester, for all that his passionate temper and thwarted ambition sometimes drove him along reckless paths. In the twilight of his life, as Lord

President of the Council in the Harley administration in 1710–11, Rochester brought qualities of consideration and restraint to public affairs which as a private individual this "good natur'd man, tho' hot" had always possessed;[110] and at the same time he achieved a degree of statesmanship that would have been quite beyond the essentially backbench mentality of "Tsar Seymskie". Even in the opening years of Anne's reign, when Marlborough's exasperation with Rochester was considerable, it never drove him to say, as he once did of Seymour, that "We are bound not to wish for any body's death, but if 14 should die, I am convinced it would be no great loss to the queen nor the nation".[111] On those occasions when they did act jointly, however, Seymour and the Hydes unquestionably commanded considerable support in the Commons. In the Lords their influence was slighter, and rather overshadowed by Nottingham's, although Rochester's hand was strengthened there after 1703 by the promotion to the peerage of three of his friends and allies, Lord Granville, Lord Gower and Lord Conway, to join Viscount Hereford and a handful of other Rochesterites in the Upper House.[112]

If concert between Rochester and Seymour was by no means automatic, the difficulty of ensuring co-operation between Nottingham and Rochester, and united action by their parliamentary followers, presented a major problem to the High Church Tories in Anne's reign. Unfortunately for the party such unity was always more attainable when the Tories were out of favour than when their leaders were either in office or in hopes of office. Between 1705 and 1710, for instance, Rochester and Nottingham only rarely followed divergent courses in the House of Lords, frequently speaking on the same side in major debates and at times leaving no room for doubt that their tactics had been carefully concerted. Yet the differences between the two leaders when the Tories had dominated the Cabinet in the early part of the reign caused several serious splits among their parliamentary adherents. These were especially obvious in the sessions of 1702–3 and 1704–5. In the first the Nottinghamites generally behaved much more responsibly than the Hyde faction in their attitude towards the war and the allies.[113] In the second a number of Rochester's closest followers refused to support Nottingham's plan to force through the Occasional Conformity bill by a dubious constitutional device, and even his son "sneaked" out of the House before the crucial division on the Tack was taken.* After the Tory triumph in the

---

* Rochester's eldest son, Lord Hyde, is among 30 "Sneakers" listed in the contemporary list of members returned in 1705 (B.M. Stowe MSS. 354). Rochester's own attitude to "the Tack" is not absolutely clear. Godolphin believed that this was "a measure settled

1710 Election these parliamentary divisions quickly reappeared. Rochester, restored to the Cabinet, kept his Commons' followers generally in line in support of the Court during the critical late winter and spring of 1711; but Nottingham, who had been passed over in the disposal of the spoils in 1710, encouraged his supporters in the Lower House to support the destructive activities of the October Club, while he and his friends in both Houses supported legislation (like the repeal of the Naturalization Act) which the ministry was known to view with disfavour.

The death of Rochester in May 1711 and the desertion of Nottingham to the Whigs at the end of the same year created a vacuum in the leadership of the more extreme Tories in the House of Lords, a vacuum which for the rest of the reign was never properly filled. In the Commons, however, these changes only enhanced the already considerable authority of William Bromley, by now the Speaker of the House, and underlined the importance of the partnership with him which Harley had been quietly consolidating since the winter of 1709–10. Not that Bromley's influence was confined entirely to the Lower House. Among his neighbours in the midlands was a covey of Tory peers who could be expected to respond to his promptings. It comprised Lords Leigh, Denbigh, Craven, Digby and Willoughby de Broke, while the Speaker's brother-in-law, Lord Stawell, appears to have come to roost here in the later years of the reign. Even the most substantial of the midland noblemen of Tory sympathies, the Earl of Northampton, sometimes deferred to Bromley's judgement.[114] But naturally it was in the Commons, where he had been the chief standard-bearer for the High Churchmen since 1704, that Bromley's real power lay. It was a power which owed less to ties of blood and marriage than that of any other Tory leader of this period, and virtually nothing to influence in the constituencies. It derived in the main from comradeships forged through years of fighting common parliamentary campaigns, backed by the general respect of virtually every Tory for Bromley's integrity and intellect, for his unblemished "country" record up to 1710, and for his status as "un des arcboutems [pillars] du Party des

among the heads of them [the High Tories] in our house, or else so many of the herd would not run blindfold into it at this time" (Longleat MSS. Portland Misc. ff. 134–5: to [Harley], "Monday at 2" [27 Nov. 1704]). Yet three of the members closest to Rochester in the House of Commons, Lord Hyde, Frank Gwyn and William Ettricke (the last two being Hyde nominees for Christchurch borough) all acted differently, the first abstaining, the second voting for and the third against. At the 1705 Election the earl was said to have deliberately switched his interest at Oxford University from his friend George Clarke to Bromley and Whitlock "because Tackers" (Add. MSS. 28893, f. 113), but this may have been an electoral gesture to retain popularity in a High Church stronghold.

Anglicans Rigides", as one foreign newswriter described him in 1709.[115] His friendships knew no local boundaries. Although his seat at Baginton gave him exceptional sway in Warwickshire, over men like Sir John Mordaunt, Sir William Boughton, Andrew Archer, Charles Leigh and the Greviles, we find him after 1710 using his new interest with Harley on behalf of political friends in Northamptonshire, Derbyshire, Cheshire and Westmorland. Harley regarded him as an expert source of information on Toryism in the northern counties, where one of Bromley's intimates was Colonel Robert Byerley, M.P. for Knaresborough and a leading figure among the High Church gentry in Yorkshire.[116] The other remarkable feature of Bromley's influence was that it sometimes cut clean across the lines of other political clans. He was on terms of equal friendship with Rochester's Gwyn or Nottingham's Ward; with Frank Annesley, a key figure in the Anglesey connection; or with James Grahme, who had a foot both in Nottingham's camp and in Harley's. Small wonder, then, that Canon Stratford thought Bromley's support absolutely vital to Lord Oxford when the latter's conflict with Bolingbroke burst into the open in 1713: "for whilst you have him, you are sure of a standing body of the church and gentry with you".[117]

By this time the yawning gap in the High Tory leadership in the House of Lords which had existed since 1711 had been at least partially filled. The further growth in stature of Arthur Annesley, who in September 1710 had succeeded his brother John* in the earldom of Anglesey, was the main factor in this development. Anglesey was a fiery parliamentary speaker in the Rochester mould, a sound High Churchman who had some claim in this respect to have inherited the mantle of Nottingham,[118] and the head of a far-from-negligible connexion in the Commons. Yet he was to prove no more capable than his predecessors of uniting the "old Tories". He was not altogether to blame for this: not only was the whole party by 1713 in the grip of the ideological conflict which was finally to paralyse it, and of which Anglesey's own rise to prominence was in part symptomatic, but he had to contend with the competition of Bolingbroke, Oxford, Bromley and even Hanmer for the remnants of the old Rochester and Nottingham connexions. All the same, Anglesey had personal qualities which were unquestionably damaging to the Tory cause in the last year of the reign. His character was more suited to the leadership of an opposition faction than of a party which was nominally, at least, in partnership with the Court. He was able enough, with what a fellow Irishman called a good "working head"; but he was

* See pp. 273–4 above.

greedy, self-centred, wayward and unscrupulous.[119] In the session of 1714, when the Tory party faced its greatest internal crisis since 1689, Anglesey steered a wildly erratic personal course and proved a bewildering pilot for the many pro-Hanoverians in the party who tried to follow in his wake. In the great series of debates on the succession, the peace treaties and the enquiry into trade with Spain, which occupied the Lords from April to July, he tacked now towards the Whigs, now towards Oxford, now towards Boling-broke, and finally towards the Whigs again, in a manner which suggests that his ambition for the viceroyalty of Ireland[120] was more important to him than any of the causes he was ostensibly, and often eloquently, espousing. In this respect there is a very marked contrast between Anglesey's conduct and the consistency of Sir Thomas Hanmer, who in 1714 was the other leading champion of the Hanoverian Tories.

Since the last pretensions of the Tory party to coherence were destroyed in this final phase of our period by its fundamental disagreement over the succession of the House of Hanover, our analysis of the party's structure would not be complete without some reference to the two new groupings of Tory politicians which this question threw up in 1713 and 1714. It was then that for the first time the staunchly pro-Hanoverian and the solidly Jacobite elements in the party broke away from their previous associations and operated to some extent as independent forces.

With the Jacobites, most of whom had previously found a congenial spiritual home in the October Club, this development seems to have been delayed until the 1714 session. We know that after the 1713 Election the committed supporters of the Pretender in the House of Commons numbered at least 80. It is impossible to be precise as to the total figure; but it was probably in the region of 100, and, as one of their leaders noted, it undoubtedly included "a great many young members, keen and eager and wanting only to be led on to action".[121] Only 40 to 50 of these Jacobite M.P.s, however, under the leadership of Sir John Pakington, George Lockhart and Will Shippen, acted as a genuinely independent unit throughout the session, choosing either to support or oppose the ministry as tactical considerations seemed to dictate.[122] Many of the remainder, including one of the ablest of the backbench Jacobites, Henry Campion,[123] were steadily drawn off into the Bolingbroke faction, seeing therein the best hope for the realisation of their chief immediate aim, which was to chivvy the government into renouncing or by-passing the Act of Settlement. A group of Scottish members, notably John Carnegie, the Solicitor-General for Scotland, James

Murray and Sir Alexander Cummings, were prominent in this pro-Boling-broke phalanx; so also, it seems, were a number of the Duke of Beaufort's clients and nominees among whom were conspicuous Jacobites like Sir Charles Kemys;[124] and it is probable that yet another of its leading recruits was the fire-eating Charles Aldworth, the friend of one of Bolingbroke's principal allies, Lord Masham.[125]

The evolution of the Hanoverian Tories as a distinct group, not merely in the Commons but in both Houses of Parliament, was a more complex process and one that started earlier. Not until 1713 did they emerge as a really powerful force with a recognised leadership of their own. But ever since the peace crisis of December 1711 there had been a number of Tories so fearful of the implications of government policy, and especially of the Oxford ministry's private deal with France the previous September, that they had opposed the Court either spasmodically or fairly consistently.[126] Promi-nent commoners like the Admiralty commissioner, John Aislabie, "Long Glory" Lawson,* Thomas Pitt of Old Sarum and George Pitt of Hampshire, and Robert Heysham, the London merchant who sat for his home town of Lancaster, had already earned a reputation as rebels before 1713; and so, to a lesser degree, had a few Tory peers — Guernsey, Thanet and Carteret, for instance. For a short while in the spring of 1712 the Hanoverian Tory interest in Parliament found a measure of organisation through the March Club. But although there were reckoned to be over 40 Tory members in the Commons alone by June 1713 who had been "very Whimsicals indeed" during the past two sessions,[127] it was not until Sir Thomas Hanmer and the Earl of Anglesey quarrelled with the ministry at this juncture over the commerce issue that the "Whimsical" Tories found leaders of real weight. Both denounced the treaty of commerce with France not only because they shared the prevalent fear about its effect on the British cloth industry but because they thought it symptomatic of a dangerously pro-French trend in government policy which other "Hanoverians" had long been suspicious of; and although neither broke decisively with the Court for some months thereafter,[128] it was Hanmer and Anglesey who clearly stood out in the van of the Hanoverian Tory forces in Parliament by 1714.

In the House of Lords Anglesey was by then the leading figure among a small group of dissident peers which included Archbishop Dawes of York, Lords Windsor[129] and Conway (both close followers of Anglesey), Lord Carteret, and above all the Earl of Abingdon, with whom Anglesey co-

---

* Gilfred Lawson, M.P. for Cumberland. See Clavering Letters: Ann to James Claver-ing, 21 Jan. 1709[-10].

operated from the summer of 1713 onwards. In the Commons both the "Whimsical" leaders could reckon on significant personal followings. That Hanmer could directly control as many as 40 or 50 votes in the Commons by 1714, as was reported at the time,[130] seems a little doubtful. When he led the Tory revolt on the Commerce bill the previous June he had "carryed over wth him 20 voices all agree, some say above 40";[131] but not all these members were re-elected to the next Parliament,[132] and some of those who were, and who had been primarily concerned with the trade issue itself in 1713, returned to their government allegiance. Hanmer's influence is difficult to assess accurately because, rather like Bromley's, it was based so much more on friendships built up over the past decade, and above all on his personal prestige and authority (further bolstered now by the influence of the Speaker's Chair, to which he was elected in February 1714), than on kinship or clientage. What is certain is that Sir Thomas included among his followers in 1714 some notable parliamentarians: Ralph Freeman, member for Hertfordshire and Chairman of the Committee of Elections in the previous Parliament, who was perhaps his closest ally; Heneage Finch (Guernsey's son) whom Bolingbroke considered "the busiest spark amongst them";[133] Peter Shakerley, the hard-working representative of the city of Chester;[134] and John Ward of Capesthorne, the able Tory lawyer who was one of those to speak in support of Hanmer in the critical debate in committee on the danger to the succession on 15 April 1714.[135] Under the Speaker's standard, moreover, a number of other former Nottinghamites who had declined to follow their old leader into opposition as early as December 1711 (Sir Roger Mostyn, Sir Henry Bunbury and Lord Barrymore are three instances) were now able to rally. Hanmer may never have been the centre of a 'connexion' in the strict sense in which Harley was, or Newcastle, or Seymour, but in 1714 he plainly led an independent party group of considerable importance.

Of Anglesey's supporters in the House of Commons in this session the term 'connexion' would be an apt enough description. They were recruited from several sources. Anglesey had considerable influence among Tory members with Irish estates or associations, of whom Edward Southwell was a typical example. In addition, helped by his former university associations, he was particularly powerful in Cambridgeshire, and his interest also extended into Sussex, Norfolk and Lancashire.* But his chief asset in the Commons

---

* Among his close followers in 1714 can be counted Dixey Windsor, one of the current representatives of Cambridge University, Andrews Windsor (Dixey's brother), who sat for Bramber in Sussex, and Lord Hawley, an Irish peer whom Viscount Windsor had nominated

was his cousin Francis Annesley, a former October Club leader and one of the Commissioners of Public Accounts, who served as an invaluable link between the earl's personal following and the Abingdon 'clan'. Annesley sat for the Bertie pocket borough of Westbury, and was thus able to keep up to the mark not only his fellow member, Henry Bertie, Lord Abingdon's uncle, but also two of Abingdon's brothers who sat in the House in 1714,[136] a Bertie cousin (Charles) who represented Stamford, and Abingdon's Hanoverian Tory brother-in-law, Sir William Courtenay, who was one of the knights of the shire for Devon.*

Because the Hanoverian Tories had two leaders of widely acknowledged ability and could muster a fairly impressive array of debating talent, their importance in the House of Commons in 1714 was at the time, and still is, liable to exaggeration. In practice it was limited by two factors: relative weakness in numbers and an unco-ordinated parliamentary strategy.

After the great debate on 15 April on the Court motion that the Protestant succession was not in danger under the Queen's administration, Sir John Percival, who heard the whole debate and witnessed the division, put the number of Tories voting with the Whig opposition at "four score and odd".† This was a rough-and-ready estimate, and no division list has survived to confirm it. We do know, however, that the total opposition vote that evening was 208 and that the total attendance of members at the time the division was called was 467, the highest turn-out of the whole reign.

to the second seat at the same borough. There was also a sizeable East Anglian contingent in his connexion, including George England, M.P. for Great Yarmouth, at least two of the Cambridgeshire members (John Bromley and John Jenyns) and possibly a third (Samuel Shepheard, junior). All these members had a "Whimsical" voting record in 1714 (see Worsley MSS. 1) and it seems no coincidence that at the time of the great debate on the motion condemning Marlborough for peculation back in Jan. 1712 Oxford had relied on Anglesey to mobilise the votes of Bromley, Jenyns and England for the Court (see his canvassing list in B.M. Loan 29/10/3). The position of Dixey Windsor's fellow University member, Thomas Paske, who also had old associations with Anglesey, is not so clear in 1714, but the earl gained a new recruit in the person of one of the Lancashire county representatives, Richard Shuttleworth, a March Club rebel in 1712 (B.M. Loan 29/310: Bromley to Oxford, 4 Sept. 1713).

* In addition to being the head of a sizeable family clan in Parliament, Abingdon was unquestionably the leading figure among the Oxfordshire Tories, and both the county members in 1714, Sir Robert Jenkinson and Francis Clerke, had been elected with the powerful support of the Bertie interest. The same was true of Thomas Renda at Wallingford.

† Add. MSS. 47087: to Philip Percival, 17 Apr. In the parallel division in the Lords on 5 Apr. there had been "6 deserters" from the Tory side. Add. MSS. 40621, f. 201.

On such an occasion it would be distinctly surprising if the Whig vote had been quite as low as 130, or even less, as Percival implies, for such a vote was nearly 50 below the party's maximum strength at this stage of the session. It is a reasonable inference, then, that Percival's figure was a slight exaggeration.[137] Fortunately we are not dependent in this case merely on inference, for it happens that sufficient evidence exists about Anne's last House of Commons to enable us to analyse its political behaviour with very much more confidence than would be justified in the case of some earlier Parliaments. Such an analysis, based on the invaluable Worsley list and the division list on the condemnation of Richard Steele on 18 March,[138] and supplemented both by biographical material and by detailed information about the rôle of individual members in the key debates of the 1714 session,[139] yields an absolute maximum of 75 Hanoverian Tories (men, that is, who felt sufficiently strongly about the necessity for a Protestant succession to be prepared to speak and divide against their friends, and if necessary against the government, in order to try and safeguard it).*

As for the unity and cohesion of the "Whimsicals" of 1714, it is striking that a contemporary observer of the great Succession debate in April drew a clear distinction between the different elements which made up the Tory opposition: "All my Ld Anglesea's interest, with the Duke of Arguile's, the Earl of Abingtons & Sr. Thomas Hanmer['s] voted against the question".[140] Although on this occasion they acted in concert, too often the co-ordination between the three main "Whimsical" connections, especially between Hanmer's squadron and the Anglesey-Abingdon group, was inadequate. Not even the rehabilitation of Lord Nottingham in the eyes of many Tories, and his attempts to mediate in 1713–14 between his old friend Hanmer and his new friend[141] Anglesey, could bring genuine harmony to the Hanoverian cause. The position was further complicated by the activities of independent "Whimsicals", including prominent speakers like Archibald Hutchinson, Thomas Pitt and John Aislabie, who seem to have co-operated more closely with the Whigs than with any of the "Whimsical" groups as such. These were undoubtedly the main reasons why the Hanoverian Tory vote remained from start to finish of this epic session so variable and unpredictable a factor, and why as a result the Whigs could never quite close the crucial gap in the House of Commons between the forces of government and those of opposition.

They are facts worth emphasising, for they serve as a final comment on the basic problem posed at the start of our examination of the Tory party of

* The figure of 75 includes some doubtful cases and 70 might be more realistic.

Queen Anne's reign: the problem of why the Tories were so rarely able to capitalise to the full on their command of a natural majority in the political nation. They demonstrate how the seemingly limitless Tory capacity for fragmentation could triumph at times even over the most obvious community of interest. Given a firm ideological basis for unity at least in a section of the party — and both the Hanoverians and the Jacobites obviously experienced such an advantage, in their wholly different ways, from March to July 1714 — the achievement of common parliamentary action still proved an elusive goal, unattainable by the latter and only spasmodically approached by the former. And herein lay the fundamental difference between the structure of the two great political parties of early-eighteenth-century Britain. For whereas the few basic elements in the composition of the Whigs — Country, Court and Junto — were always capable of fusion, at least under stress, into a genuine compound, the more numerous and diverse elements in the Tory party made up at best an imperfect amalgam, whose innate tendency was towards disintegration rather than towards synthesis.

CHAPTER NINE

The Parties in Action:
Direction and Organisation

FROM our scrutiny of the composition of the two great parties of Queen Anne's day two further general conclusions have emerged that are of obvious relevance to the working of the political system. One is that the structure of both parties was complex, and that of the Tories peculiarly so. The other is that Tories and Whigs alike, and especially the former, were at all times heavily stocked with "Country" politicians — many of them with independent fortunes and independent minds, and some of them with no very exacting concept of the duties and obligations which membership of Parliament entailed. Together these two circumstances do much to explain the preoccupation of party men in the early eighteenth century with the perpetual problem of organisation: the problem of how to harness for effective political action the abundant energy which both Whigs and Tories were able to generate in a divided and fiercely competitive society. In the localities as well as at Westminster this period saw a whole succession of experiments with different media and techniques of organisation. Some were derivative (owing an obvious debt, for instance, to the experience of the Exclusion struggle), others essentially original; some were hurriedly improvised, others remarkably sophisticated. All are a testimony not merely to the difficulty of the problem they were intended to solve, but also to its urgency.

Long before Queen Anne's death most men actively engaged in parliamentary politics had come to recognise, if not always with enthusiasm, that in the Britain of their day organisation was the main stairway to power. It could not provide men with an automatic passport through the door to political authority; for this, royal favour or acquiescence was still indispensable; but at least it could bring them to the threshold. And since not even "Country" politicians after 1701 could accept with equanimity the prospect of power being monopolised by the leaders of the rival party, they too, as well as the hundreds of career-politicians concerned, found it increasingly necessary to co-operate with their fellows at all levels and to accept some diminution of their individual freedom in consequence.

To appreciate the pressures at work on the party men of the period we need only reflect on why it seemed so important even to the least ambitious country squire or backwoods peer in Parliament that power should be securely lodged in the hands of his own "friends". It was important because it promised to be a guarantee of certain essentials: a guarantee to the Country Tories, for instance, that the privileges of the Established Church would not be eroded, that the nation's commitments to its European allies would be limited, and that the special interests of the landed classes would be safe-guarded; a guarantee to the independent Whigs that the war would be vigorously prosecuted, the Toleration defended, the Bank and other pillars of the national credit structure protected, the Protestant succession secured. And because power was such a precious commodity — and in a distracted, unstable political world such a transient one — it seemed imperative even to the country member without personal ambition that its possession should never be wasted. John Harpur, a Tory who represented the town of Derby in the first three years of the Queen's reign, expressed what scores of ordinary backbenchers felt even then, when he wrote in 1703:

others have a prospect, if we neglect to make use of those blessings that are in our power. If we carelessly let slip those days that offer us happiness, and by an accident lose our moment, how will those who are now as industriously as ever struggling for power and interest, despise our neglect and triumph over us. Nay, the very omissions that we have been guilty of will be a warning to them not to fall into the same errors.[1]

If these were the thoughts of relatively humble members, it is not surprising that to the leaders of the two parties and to their lieutenants the allurements of power seemed correspondingly greater.

But if they were to be in a reasonable position to compete with their opponents for the favour of the Court, or to resist attempts to wrest that favour from them, the political leaders simply had to be sure of a measure of discipline and co-operation among those who accepted the same party name as they did; and what is more, they needed to maintain such co-operation both while Parliament was sitting and in the often-long intervals between sessions. This they had to do without most of the more obvious advantages enjoyed by a major political party in modern Britain. Neither the Whigs nor the Tories of the Augustan period had at any time a single, acknow-ledged leader commanding universal allegiance (Somers, in the years up to 1712, approached nearer than anyone to this lofty eminence, but his authority over the Whigs was very much less than that of a twentieth-century party leader); neither possessed a party 'machine' in any strict sense, nor the regular income needed to maintain one; neither employed a system of official whips whose authority was generally recognised. Yet party organisation of a kind was undoubtedly achieved in the years from 1702 to 1714, more susceptible to failure, inevitably, than its more streamlined and formalised modern equivalent, but also capable at times of surprising effectiveness. The purpose of this chapter, and of the following one, is to show how the Whigs and the Tories of the age of Anne served their apprenticeship in this toughest of all political trades, and to illustrate the numerous and fascinatingly diverse forms of organisation which these years of experiment and developing experience produced.

I

The problem of organisation began at the top, within the High Commands of the two parties. It hinged there on the attempts made by the principal leaders of each party to achieve some uniformity of action among themselves; on their efforts to agree on common policies and on the means of carrying them out. Unfortunately it may never prove possible to reconstruct a really detailed picture of the parties in action at this level. Even to judge how far co-operation among the leading politicians on either side was genuinely 'organised' is no simple matter. In the main this is because of the freaks that govern the survival of historical manuscripts. All too few of the outstanding party figures have left private papers of any real value for this period. Harley, Godolphin and Marlborough, with their massive legacies, are conspicuous exceptions; but only Harley's papers allow us much of an insight into the workings of party leadership. A certain amount of the correspondence of Nottingham and Cowper has been preserved, as well as the latter's political diary, and so has a useful collection of the first Duke of Newcastle's papers. But even on the Tory side there are vital missing links in the chain of evidence; there are virtually no letters to Bromley, none for Anne's reign to Rochester or to Seymour, only a handful to Hanmer and none so far traced to Anglesey. On the Whig side the tale is still more dismal. Of the letters and memoranda of the Junto lords, fires and other vagaries of the intervening centuries have accounted for all but a part of Sunderland's correspondence and a few tantalising fragments of the papers of Wharton and Somers. The loss is incalculable. The destruction of Lord Somers's papers alone was a major tragedy: one has only to read a few lines of the preliminary report which Charles Yorke sent to his brother after the collection came into the possession of the Earl of Hardwicke to realise this. He writes of "the quantities of letters, etc, contained in the boxes which I have searched", a mass of material which had to be seen to be believed. "Indeed there were such numbers that tho' I spent a fortnight at Bellbar, & some hours every day in perusing & sorting them, yet I could make but a small progress in examining them & so contented myself with a superficial view of the matters they related to".[2] The one minor consolation in all this for the political historian is that even if there did exist very much more correspondence between the great party figures of Anne's day, it is likely that it would tell us mostly about consultations held and plans made while Parliament stood prorogued or was in recess. Men rarely wrote to arrange meetings when they normally saw each other every day in Westminster Palace, or in St. Stephen's Chapel, or in Whitehall.

However, what slender evidence we do have about top-level organisation on both sides nearly all bears out one conclusion that our earlier investigation of party structure has already suggested: namely, that the Whig leadership was in general much the more closely co-ordinated. The Whigs enjoyed two crucial advantages over their opponents. The first was the ability of the five Junto lords to maintain an effective liaison with each other. The second was their success, especially at periods of particular stress, in bringing other Whig leaders into line with their own thinking.

The automatic regularity with which "the Whig lords" conferred with each other while Parliament was in session is something that can be deduced both from the nature and the success of their parliamentary tactics. Their record in the House of Lords, in particular, speaks for itself. It obviously did so to their contemporaries. Bishop Nicolson found that even the most minor parliamentary motions which the Junto sponsored, such as one in 1704 requiring the government to bring pressure on the French to alleviate the hardships of Protestant galley-slaves, were "manifestly concerted".[3] One Tory backbencher gloomily predicted that the triumph of the Junto at Court in November 1708, following the Whig electoral victory earlier that year, would render Parliament more or less ornamental; "for all matters which used to be its business are now arranged in private meetings".[4] Lord Treasurer Godolphin, on the other hand, was more concerned with another hazard latent in the exceptional solidarity and political expertise of the Junto lords. In their years in office he had occasion to complain at least once during sessions that the very efficiency of their well-oiled political machine impaired their usefulness as administrators and councillors. "I have pressed

Lord Sunderland all I can to dispatch Palmes's instructions", he told Marlborough in February 1709; "but so much of his time is applied to caballing and Parliament meetings, that I can't obtain one meeting about this affair . . .".[5]

During the long months from early summer to late autumn which divided most sessions and most Parliaments between 1702 and 1712, and again through the winters of 1712–13 and 1713–14,* the Whig leaders continued to keep in very close touch. We read, for instance, of formal "councils" of the Junto, such as that arranged to meet at Newmarket at the beginning of October 1708 to determine parliamentary strategy over the forthcoming election of a Speaker, or those held in October 1710 and October 1713, in the same relaxed surroundings, to discuss the political situation in the light of General Election results.[6] Still more frequently do we catch glimpses of the round of country-house parties, attended by all or most of the five lords whenever they were in England,† which obviously fulfilled an important function in binding together the Whig upper crust. Other Whigs of wealth and influence whom the Junto was particularly anxious to placate or recruit were invited from time to time to these distinctive gatherings; indeed the only frequent absentee of note in the second half of the reign seems to have been Lord Somers, whose health after 1704 was rarely robust enough to stand up to the days of travelling which the house-parties involved, and who preferred whenever possible the quiet of Belbar to the dusty summer roads, relying on letters and periodic excursions to London to maintain contact with his colleagues.[7] When events of unusual importance required their presence in town between sessions, the Whig chiefs would hold special meetings there. There was a momentous gathering in London immediately after Godolphin's dismissal in August 1710; another at the end of October that year, for the purpose of drafting a reply to Marlborough, who had sought Whig advice about the wisdom of returning at once to England; and yet another in January 1714, called to debate future policy in the light of the serious deterioration in the Queen's health.[8]

We have noticed already‡ how after the winter of 1707–8 — the one period in the reign when the Junto seriously lost control over an important section of the parliamentary party — there was a marked tendency for its

---

* The last two parliamentary sessions of Anne's reign broke with tradition by not opening until the spring.

† Sunderland and Halifax each had one brief spell abroad in 1705–6, while Wharton spent two summers in Ireland.

‡ Pp. 241–2 above.

meetings, both in town and country, to lose the character of close, exclusive conclaves. Henceforward their doors were opened to many more men of weight in the party. In 1708, for instance, the Squadrone leaders were earnestly pressed to attend; the Duke of Bolton and the Marquess of Dorchester, both admittedly Junto auxiliaries for many years, were called to a key conference with Godolphin at the Bishop of Ely's Cambridgeshire house to discuss the terms on which the Lord Treasurer would be guaranteed Whig support in Parliament the following session (and Bedford, too, might have been there, had he been willing to "stir" his indolent frame as far as Newmarket that autumn); while another similar conference held soon afterwards in town significantly met at the house of the Duke of Devonshire.[9] The totally unexpected bombshell tossed into the Whig camp in April 1710, when Shrewsbury was brought back into the Cabinet at Harley's instigation, necessitated what Roxburgh described as "a great meeting" of the party magnates in London;[10] and late in October 1711, when the Junto was preparing for its full-scale peace offensive in the House of Lords against the Oxford ministry, no fewer than seventeen influential Whigs were invited to a high-level discussion at Chippenham, the Earl of Orford's Cambridgeshire mansion.[11]

One point which remains obscure is how regularly leading Whig commoners were associated with these major consultations on party policy. While Parliament was sitting, of course, the Junto lords never overlooked the importance of close co-ordination with the Commons. When their motion requesting the immediate dispatch of Marlborough to the Continent was suddenly introduced into a surprised House on 15 February 1710, it was obvious to any experienced observer that the Junto spokesmen who made the first three speeches in its support, Sir Gilbert Heathcote, Sir William Strickland and Sir Joseph Jekyll, had been carefully briefed.[12] In May 1712, when the shock news of the Restraining Orders reached them from the Continent, the Whig leaders at once arranged an emergency meeting at Orford's London house to discuss parliamentary action; and since Walpole, incarcerated in the Tower, was unable to attend, young William Pulteney was invited to move an immediate address of protest in the Lower House parallel to the one which Halifax planned to move in the Lords.[13] On the other hand, there is nothing to suggest in the meagre evidence that survives that Whig M.P.s were normally present in any strength at Junto conferences held when Parliament was not sitting. The summit meeting at Althorp in August 1707, the purpose of which was "to fix measures for the approaching Parliament" was attended (as far as Edmund Gibson could discover) by none of "the

Whig-commons", despite the patently restless mood which prevailed among them at this time.[14] Between the General Elections of 1710 and 1713, when the party was too weak in St. Stephen's Chapel to undertake more than a rearguard action, prior consultation with its leading representatives there about major policy matters became less necessary; though even so it is surprising to find that the sole commoner whose presence at the great Chippenham congress in October 1711 can be verified for certain was Robert Walpole, who was deputed to lead the forlorn hope against the peace preliminaries in the House of Commons.[15] After the shock defeat of the government's Commerce bill in June 1713 and the slight improvement in Whig prospects in the Commons as a result of the 1713 Election the House naturally assumed a rather more important place in party strategy, and this may have been reflected to some extent in the organisation of the Whig hierarchy. At least it seems likely that the numerous gathering of Whigs which assembled at Sunderland's Northamptonshire house in September 1713, to hold a post-mortem on the Election and to plan the new campaign to safeguard the Protestant succession, included several commoners.* At no time did the Whig leaders cast a wider net, however, than *before* General Elections. Then they were at obvious pains to bring into their consultations their friends in the City as well as in the House of Commons. Their efforts to build up a campaign fund in advance of the great struggle in 1710 were exceptionally strenuous: "Twice a week [Sir Michael Warton reported] great meetings at Putney bowling green and at nights at my Lord Sun[derland's] and Orford's, and elsewhere".[16]

Because of the dearth of correspondence between the great High Tory figures of Anne's reign which is the sorry legacy of the past 250 years, even less is known about organisation at the highest level of the Tory party than can be ascertained or deduced about the Whigs. But again there are some significant pointers in the fragments that can be pieced together. They appear to indicate that the organisation of the High Tory leadership was, by Whig standards, decidedly primitive. They also suggest that efforts to effect a common front between the Highflyers and the more moderate Harleyites, notably after the latter left the government in February 1708 and joined the Tory 'right' in open opposition, were very seriously hampered by the absence

---

* Sunderland told Nottingham on 14 Sept. that he was "greatly burdened with company" (Finch MSS. G.S., bundle 24). Cadogan and James Craggs were certainly among that company (B.M. Stowe MSS. 225, f. 196; Charborough Park MSS.: Craggs to Erle, 21 Sept.) and it seems unlikely that they were the sole representatives of their order.

of any recognised machinery for consultation and discussion at the apex of the party pyramid.

What is particularly evident is that the maintenance of contact between prominent High Church politicians when Parliament was not in session was more often casual than planned. There were no parallels to the regular Newmarket councils or the Althorp or Winchendon house parties of the Whigs. Very occasionally one stumbles across references to isolated *pourparlers*: to the pilgrimage of Rochester and Musgrave to Bath to see the convalescent Seymour in May 1703; to the scent of "little cabals & meetings" which Harley's keen nose sniffed out in June 1704; or to the visit paid by Hanmer and Arthur Annesley to Nottingham's house in the summer of 1709.[17] But the events of the autumn and early winter of 1708, when the Tories appeared for a while to have an excellent chance of profiting in the new Parliament from divisions among their opponents, illustrate some of the difficulties under which the Tory right-wing laboured as a consequence of its divided leadership. Preserved among the Finch papers is an exceptional series of letters and draft letters between Bromley and Nottingham, beginning on 2 October 1708 and ending on 31 December; and this correspondence reveals the astonishing fact that for several weeks before Parliament met, and for at least seven weeks afterwards, Nottingham flatly refused to leave his country house at Burley to discuss major strategy with Rochester or Haversham or anyone else; and this in spite of Bromley's repeated and eventually urgent pressure on him to do so. What is more, "Dismal" poured nothing but cold water on Bromley's tentative plans for a closer liaison with Harley and his followers, plans which had seemingly been broached during a brief visit which Bromley had paid to Burley in the early autumn. By the eve of the opening of Parliament a note of mild reproach had understandably crept into the younger man's letters: "You'l give me your pardon for saying, I am sorry to find yr. Lordship so much determined agt. coming to town at a juncture when all advice & assistance are wanted, & when I am sure the ablest is absolutely necessary to preserve us"; and by 7 December he was prepared to say that only Nottingham's presence and counsel could appease the "restlessness and dissatisfaction" which had by then afflicted the Tories. Yet to all these appeals Nottingham's ear remained obstinately deaf.[18] It is impossible to conceive of the Whig leaders, presented with similar opportunities, acting so negligently and unconcertedly.

The same lack of concert within the High Tory hierarchy was betrayed during the ministerial revolution of 1710, engineered by Harley. Bromley (worried, it is true, by his wife's health) stayed in Warwickshire throughout the summer and early autumn. His letters to his friend James Grahme at Levens Hall show him to have been almost wholly dependent on correspondence, and on reports of variable authenticity, for his information about the critical developments that were taking place at Court and inside the Cabinet room. A visit to Baginton by John Ward, en route to Lancashire from London, was avidly awaited — "it is a great comfort", Bromley confessed, "to see any friend to discourse with at this time" — but more often than not he was reduced to anguished speculation about each fresh or rumoured turn of events.[19] Meanwhile Lord Nottingham, again closeted in his Rutland home, was even more isolated and aloof than Bromley; and Rochester's eventual push to exert pressure on Harley in July and August, to try to ensure for the Tory zealots a prominent place in "the new scheme", seems to have been made purely on his own initiative. Three years later, Lord Berkeley of Stratton found the new generation of High Tory leaders, as represented by Hanmer and Anglesey, no improvement on the old. "The Whigs . . . must have this justice done them," he confessed to the First Lord of the Admiralty, "that they observe better discipline; but the others all think themselves fit to govern."[20]

II

Once we switch our attention from the highest level from which party policies were directed to the far wider area covered by general party organisation at Westminster, there is happily very much more material on which conclusions can be based. It is possible to gauge, at least roughly, how much co-ordination existed between the high command on both sides and the lower ranks; and it is certainly possible to say how this co-ordination was achieved. Broadly speaking there were two separate problems here for both Whig and Tory leaders: first, the problem of getting their own agreed policies endorsed by their supporters in both Houses of Parliament; and second, the problem of ensuring the actual attendance and votes of as many members and peers as possible on specific occasions, in pursuit of these agreed policies.

The first stage as a rule presented fewer difficulties. Once a policy had been agreed on by the party chiefs, or even by a group of them, a variety of channels was available for making that policy widely known and understood and for organising a fairly general body of support for it within the party. One method, especially popular among the Tories, was to arrange mass meetings between the leading commoners of the party and its backbenchers

immediately before, or just after, the start of a new session, and if necessary
to reconvene them at fairly lengthy intervals as long as Parliament was
assembled. The practice of holding these "general meetings", as they were
called, was firmly established among the Tories by the winter of 1703–4,
and there were precedents going back at least as far as 1701.[21] At the beginning of October 1704 John Ward of Capesthorne, who as a trusted auxiliary
both of Bromley and Nottingham filled a valuable link rôle for the Tories in
the Commons, informed the member for Appleby that "Mr. Bromley &
some other members will observe the agreement at the last general meeting
at the Fountain, wch was for all to meet there again a full week before the
next sitting of the Parliament [due in a few weeks' time]".[22] The Fountain
Tavern in the Strand became for many years the favourite venue for these
great Tory councils. Following the pre-session gathering anticipated by
Ward, 150 Tories met there again on 6 November 1704, a fortnight after
the meeting of Parliament. Their purpose was primarily to discuss what
tactics could best ensure the passage of the third Occasional Conformity
bill, and it was at this meeting that a decision was reached that may not have
been prompted from above (for it was soon to be rejected in favour of Nottingham's more controversial expedient of a "tack") — a decision to hold
up supply until their "darling" bill was safely through both Houses.[23] In
October 1705, a diarist records, a "great number" of the High Tories who
had come up to town early that month at the urgent instance of their leaders,
pledged to support the election of Bromley for Speaker, met at the same
tavern three days before the opening of the session "to consider of their
strength".[24] In view of the massive attendance at the House on the 25th the
number present at this council of war was probably not very far short of 200.
But the largest Tory attendance at a Fountain meeting which can be
documented was recorded at the very outset of the Parliament of 1710–13.
Two mass meetings were held under the same accommodating roof within a
week; and at the first of them, a rather turbulent assembly held on the third
night of the session, one member who was present counted about 200 in the
room; "& I don't know [he added] of one Whigg amongst us".[*]

When new issues of moment arose in the course of a session a general
meeting of this kind was not always practicable or desirable. Some more

---

[*] Claydon MSS.: Fermanagh to Ralph Verney, 30 Nov. 1710 (cf. *Verney Letters*, i, 305,
the printed version of the above, in which the number is wrongly put at 300, which was
probably beyond the seating capacity of a single room in any tavern in London). Swift
confirms the figure of 200 and discusses the business of the meeting in a letter to King of
28 Nov. (*Swift Corr.* i, 221).

selective procedure was often preferred, by which Whig or Tory leaders could outline their policies to a smaller, though if possible representative, caucus of party stalwarts — a group which, if necessary, could also be regarded as a soundboard, transmitting the general tone of party feeling to the *élite*. When the House of Lords was involved in sudden changes of strategy its limited membership made special meetings of such key figures relatively easy to arrange, even at the shortest notice. Soon after the opening of the new Parliament in 1705 the High Tory chiefs decided to make use of an early debate in the Lords on the State of the Nation to call, through Lord Haversham, for the Electress Sophia to be invited to England. This move, ostensibly designed to provide for the security of the succession but in reality a factious manoeuvre, was embarrassing in the extreme to the government and to the Whigs. With little more than twenty-four hours to spare the news leaked through to Godolphin. At once he wrote to the Lord Privy Seal, Newcastle: "Believing it may bee necessary to prepare ourselves wth some defences against my Ld Haversham's great guns tomorrow, I beg leave to offer to your Grace . . . that you would please to send to the D. of Bolton [a right-hand man of the Junto lords], whose house lies in your way & is convenient for this purpose, to desire his Grace to send to such lords as you and he shall think proper to meet you there tomorrow morning before you go to the House, that so you may have opportunity of considering wth them what is proper to bee done when you come thither. . . ."[25] As a result of this critical meeting the Whig peers were prepared to meet Haversham's attack, first with shrewd delaying tactics and then with the brilliant counter-stroke of the Regency bill.*

How many attended at Bolton's house on this particular November morning we do not know. But it is clear that when the Junto lords needed to rally support on issues where the attitude of the Court Whigs was considered questionable, as they did at the time of the Place bill and the Land Grants bill in 1712, quite minor peers of the 'centre' group could sometimes expect invitations to these councils. In February 1712, for instance, Lord Oxford learned much to his bewilderment that Portland, Longueville, Cholmondeley and Kent had been summoned to "a great consult . . . from seven this night until past ten at Lord Halifaxes", along with six other peers, including the two rebel Tories, Nottingham and Guernsey;[26] and the conclave held at the end of May 1713, described by one source as "a great meeting", at which the Junto lords explained their controversial plans to deal with the Malt Tax crisis and the threat to the Union with Scotland,

* See Chap. 3, pp. 84, 114 and n. * above.

significantly took place, not in one of their own houses, but under the august roof of his Grace of Somerset.[27]

Where the House of Commons was concerned the leaders of both parties approached many of their biggest hurdles by organising selective meetings of senior members. Three examples, taken at random over a period of nine years, serve to illustrate this technique. On 11 November 1702 a group of the most vigorous and outspoken critics of Occasional Conformity in the House met the government's representatives at the Cockpit, at the instigation of Lord Nottingham, to smooth the path of the first of Nottingham's bills to prevent this abuse. Three years later the Whig helmsmen took comparable pains in steering their Regency bill through the Lower House. When the Bishop of Carlisle called on Lord Halifax on the morning of 5 January 1706 and again two days later, he found his friend's house seething with Whig M.P.s and had to leave without seeing him; had he reflected that the Commons were due almost immediately to go into committee on this vital bill he might have spared himself two fruitless journeys. Harley, too, made use of this kind of liaison when in power after 1710. On the day before his South Sea scheme was to be unfolded to the House in May 1711, some forty to fifty important Tory members were called together and privately sounded by the Chancellor's lieutenants in order to assess party reactions to the plan. The results were highly gratifying.[28]

Quite frequently, however, the media of communication between the party hierarchs and the most influential of their prospective supporters in both Houses were as much social as political. This was a form of organisation which was to the particular taste of the Whigs, although it was their opponents, curiously enough, who boasted the two largest of the politicians' clubs to flourish in this period. These were the Vine Club, which met for a while at the Vine Tavern in the middle years of Anne's reign, and the much more celebrated October Club, founded in the winter of 1710–11. But the Vine Club was a shadowy affair about which very little is known, and the October Club — at least in its earliest and most active phase — was the very opposite of a convenient instrument in the hands of the Tory leaders for effecting policy. Its real significance, as the next chapter will show, was as a backbench pressure-group representing the most extreme opinion in the party. Also on the Tory side, there existed from the summer of 1711 the Brothers' Club, formed by Henry St. John round a nucleus of leading Harleyites (though by an odd freak excluding Harley himself), and from the summer of 1709 the similarly-named Society of the Board of Brothers, sponsored by the Jacobite Duke of Beaufort. The two societies could scarcely have been more different in character, but neither was designed to put business before pleasure. St. John's Club, apart from being most exclusive (by the middle of 1712 scarcely any of its members still sat in the Commons), soon lost the political teeth with which it had originally been endowed;* while the Board, though at one time or other including as full brothers or "adopted nephews" some thirty Tory peers and M.P.s, was primarily and quite unashamedly a boozing club. The third entry in its minutes, on 21 July 1709, suggests that at least one London publican decided very early that its members' patronage would not compensate him adequately for the cost in breakages.[29] Its links with the higher echelons of the party were fairly tenuous. Indeed the only strictly parliamentary reference to be found in its minute-book occurs on 25 January 1712, the day after the Tories in the House of Commons had carried their vote of censure against the Duke of Marlborough, when the secretary noted: "By order of the Board, Mr. H. Bertie: Mr. Griffith: Mr. Pendarvis: Sr. J. Walter: Sr G. Parker: Sr W. Pole: Mr. Dashwood: Mr. Strangeways. The Honourable members of the House of Commons that have received the thanks of the Board for their good attendance & service. Jan 24 1711/12".[30]

The great Whig politico-social associations were of a far more formidable character. No mark of social distinction was more highly prized than admission to the famous Kit-Cat. But the roll of the club's members suggests that it also played an invaluable part in keeping the party's political wheels well lubricated while Parliament was sitting. Its members were certainly admirably representative of many of the influential sections of the parliamentary party: of the Junto lords and their closest associates; of the great Whig magnates in the House of Lords; and of some of the most promising and active Whigs in the Lower House. Thus in 1711 there were included in the first category Wharton, Somers, Halifax and Sunderland, along with Cowper, Devonshire, Carlisle, Manchester and Mohun. In the second category were to be found the five Dukes of Newcastle, Richmond, Grafton, Montagu and Somerset. The third group was represented by Walpole, Pulteney, Mainwaring, Stanhope (still a prisoner in enemy hands), Edmund Dunch and Joseph Addison.[31]

Although the occasional parliamentary aberration on the part of individual Kit-Catters could be overlooked,[32] in a conclave so close to the political heart of the Whig party the slightest suspicion of real treachery was enough to terminate the membership of the suspect. In April 1710, for instance, it came to the ear of James Brydges that "The Duke of Somerset (Thursday

* See p. 21 above.

was sevennight) was expellet the Chitcat [*sic*], by a vote brought in ready cut
& dried by Ld. Wharton: the crime objected, the words of the vote say, was
for being suspected to have held conferences with Robin the Trickster".[33]
The meeting was a special one, convened after due notice by the Duke of
Richmond for the specific purpose of investigating Somerset's conduct; for
with so many club members out of town at the end of the session it was
thought essential for "a thing of that consequence to be done in a full
House".[34] Unfortunately, in the tragic absence of a minute-book, evidence
that would enable us to pinpoint the contribution of the Kit-Catters to
particular Whig moves, in or out of Parliament, is extremely sparse. It was
under the club's auspices that plans were made in 1711, and sums raised that
were estimated at anything from £200 to £2000, for the abortive public
demonstration against the Tory peace policy on the anniversary of Queen
Elizabeth's birthday, plans which envisaged an elaborate procession, effigy-
burning, and the raising of the London mob. There is also good reason to
believe that it was in the rooms of the Kit-Cat that the first secret Whig
military preparations were set on foot in 1714, some months before the
Queen's death, to counter a possible Jacobite rising supported by a French
invasion.[35] It is possible, too, though far less certain, that the crucial question
of whether to proceed against Dr. Sacheverell in December 1709 by the
ordinary processes of law or by parliamentary impeachment was originally
debated at one of the club's meetings before it was discussed more widely
and more authoritatively.[36]

Conferring less prestige than the Kit-Cat in the social sense but perhaps
even more valuable as an integral element in Whig organisation during the
later years of Anne was the Hanover Club. Founded in the summer of 1712,
it held weekly meetings in rooms at Charing Cross for the rest of the reign
and during the early months of George I's reign. It was very much a political
action group as well as a congenial social gathering, and in that respect, at
least, its membership was "more select" (as Steele put it) than that of the
Kit-Cat. The Hanover men — mostly commoners though the club included a sprinkling of peers* — were pledged to offer the Tories and Jacobites
"all the opposition they could in their several stations, and every member
. . . to take his part in the Upper or Lower House, for detecting the sophistry
of such as endeavour'd by it to impose on their majority, that they might not

---

* A list of members of the Hanover Club on 4 Nov. 1713, for instance, contains the
names of 4 peers, 19 Whigs who had been elected to the House of Commons in the
autumn General Election, and 2 more who had sat there in the previous session but had
not been re-elected. Oldmixon, p. 509.

carry their votes by reason if they did by numbers".[37] To make this opposition the more effective the club evolved a characteristic technique of 'close marking' in parliamentary debates, with each member allotted a specific Tory opponent whom it was his duty to harry persistently. Of more general value to the Whig organisation, however, were the important links that existed between the Hanover Club and both the Kit-Cat and the Junto. In November 1713, for example, William Pulteney, the Duke of Montagu, Lord Lincoln and Richard Steele were members of both clubs, and soon afterwards it would appear that Lord Wharton, too, joined the Hanover Club.[38] At the same time both the Walpole family and the Lumley family had a representative in each society. Among the Hanover men in the House of Commons were a number of staunch Junto followers: George Montagu (Halifax's nephew), Paul Methuen (recently elected for Brackley on the Wharton-Bridgewater interest), William Strickland, Robert Furnese, Tom Frankland, and not least Lord Castlecomer, who both by his political and his amorous proclivities proved himself a true disciple of Wharton. Something of the importance which the Junto lords themselves attached to their connexion with the Hanover Club can be gauged from their alarmed reaction to the news that dissension had broken out in the club at a crucial stage of the 1714 session, and from the fact that Lord Sunderland was hastily called in as mediator.[39]

Less formal social contacts than those made through the societies and clubs also made an effective contribution to party organisation during sessions. Those coffee-houses and chocolate-houses which were the favourite haunts of "a particular set of men" had an obvious part to play here. But so too had the common habit of making morning calls on one's friends of like persuasion, especially since these calls so often preceded afternoon parliamentary sittings. Some idea of the extensive network that could be covered by this particular medium of informal contact, and of the use which the Junto in particular made of it, can be deduced from the London diaries of two of the most politically-active bishops of the period, Wake of Lincoln and Nicolson of Carlisle. In little more than two months of the 1710–11 session Lord Somers alone, quite apart from Halifax, Sunderland, Cowper and other Whig leaders, paid two morning calls on Nicolson and one on Wake, was in turn visited once by Nicolson and twice by Wake, and had an additional meeting with Wake at the Bishop of Ely's house when they both called there on 18 February.[40] More obvious, though not necessarily more valuable, were the political benefits which accrued from the frequent dinner engagements which occupied the winter evenings of every politician of note in town. That austere critic of his party's principles and standards, the Earl of Shaftesbury, might counsel the younger Whigs, the bright new hopes of the Good Old Cause, to beware of "that gulph of quality-entertainments, I mean the invitation-dinners and suppers of our Whig-grandees . . .";[41] but it was a question of priorities. Without them Whig livers would no doubt have been the stronger; but Whig organisation would assuredly have been the weaker.

*   *   *

The maintenance of contact with members of both Houses as long as they were in town was clearly not beyond the resources of the party leaders of the early eighteenth century. But the problem of organising the rank and file was only half solved by keeping them abreast of new parliamentary moves and measures, or by ascertaining their views beforehand on changes of policy or tactics. Whether they could then be persuaded to attend at Westminster as and when required, whether they could be relied upon to vote as their leaders wished, and whether they could be disciplined in any way if they did not so vote, or if they persistently strayed from the straight path of party virtue — these were very different questions. It was these problems of attendance, voting, sanction and discipline which most taxed the ingenuity of the great power-politicians of the age of Anne. Only to a limited extent, of course, were they able to anticipate the solutions which British political parties of our own day have devised to solve these problems. Yet even at this level of organisation there are interesting parallels as well as patent differences between the two periods. There was undoubtedly 'whipping' of a sort in both parties between 1702 and 1714; less formal and far less rigorous than modern practice, but never wholly ineffectual, and frequently very successful. In addition, there were various forms of discipline which could when necessary be applied by the party leaders to reluctant or recalcitrant followers.

A highly individual feature of Tory organisation in Queen Anne's reign was the use made of a number of recognised regional 'whips', men entrusted by their leaders with a responsibility for certain areas of the country. It may be that the Whigs evolved a similar system; but this is something we cannot know for certain, and are unlikely ever to discover, unless we can unearth a great deal more correspondence of ordinary Whig M.P.s, comparable with the relatively rich collections of the papers of Tory country gentlemen which have survived from this period. On the Tory side we are fortunately able not only to trace the system in outline but to fill in many of the details as well. One of the main functions of the regional 'whip' (as we shall later see, it was not his only one) was to ensure a good attendance in the House of Commons at the very beginning of a session. To this end William Bromley and Sir George Beaumont looked after most of the midland Tories known to be in the "church interest": Warwickshire, Leicestershire, Northamptonshire and at times even Derbyshire were all within their field of operations.* Peter Shakerley (M.P. for Chester) had an unofficial responsibility for Cheshire, Lancashire, and to some extent for Staffordshire, Sir Richard Myddleton for much of North Wales and for Shropshire, and George Granville, by the middle of the reign, for Cornwall and Devon.[42] In addition, in Anne's early years at least, the party leaders looked to Colonel Grahme of Levens to "muster up" the Tory troops of the extreme north of England.[43] Since one of the most important cohesive elements in the political parties of this period was local loyalty, there were rational foundations for this type of organisation. Groups of members within both parties developed close associations based on neighbourliness and the sharing of common local interests. The tight knot of Norfolk Whigs which accepted the primacy of Walpole and Townshend was an obvious example. The South Wales Tories, grouped round the Mansels of Margam, provided another. A "Suffolk Club" in London in the early years of Anne's reign seems to have catered for the local patriotism of that county's ten Tory representatives in the Parliament of 1702–5.[44] The Devonians and Cornishmen experienced this sense of common identity to an unusual degree, so that it comes as no surprise to read that when James Bulteel, the sitting member for Tavistock, gave a dinner party in his London lodgings in April 1711 he chose no fewer than nine Cornish M.P.s as his guests.[45] Wherever such natural flocks existed a watchful, hard-working regional shepherd could perform a priceless service for his party.

In normal circumstances problems of distance and inadequate communication inevitably put a heavy strain on a rudimentary organisation before the start of a session. How effectively these problems could be overcome by a heavy dependence on regional 'whipping', supplemented by impromptu variations to suit the circumstances and a full use of the party grapevines, is admirably illustrated by two remarkable political operations of the early eighteenth century. One was the success of both sides in assembling their forces for the vital choice of a Speaker in 1705; the other was the Tory preparations to run William Bromley for the Chair before the opening of the

---

* Beaumont, M.P. for Leicester throughout Anne's reign, was a prominent figure on the Tory back benches until 1711 and in the service of Oxford's ministry thereafter. For his activities see p. 307 below.

Parliament of 1708–10. In October 1705, admittedly after having had some weeks' notice of an impending clash, the party managers achieved on the initial day of a new Parliament the largest recorded attendance on any day in the House of Commons between the great vote on Somers's impeachment in 1701 and 15 April 1714, the day of the debate on the danger to the Protestant succession. It was not even surpassed in January 1712, when 439 crammed into the chamber before the first of the votes against the Duke of Marlborough; and indeed, as far as John Evelyn's memory could recall, "There had never ben so greate an assembly of members on the first day of sitting".[46] So feverish was the activity up to the fifty-ninth minute of the eleventh hour that the Bishop of Carlisle, spending the night before the vote in an inn at Peterborough "weary'd with the fatigue of a wearysome journey in bad weather", could scarcely get a wink of sleep for the perpetual "posting up of Commoners in the night", clattering in and out of the inn yard on their way to London.*

In some ways more astonishing still was the success of the Tory leaders in organising their next bid for the Chair three years later, when surprise rather than a frontal assault was their only hope. This time they contrived to bring up to town very nearly a maximum complement of their supporters, "moderate" and "high", in the teeth of the discouragement of an election setback the previous summer and despite the expectation that on this occasion most backbenchers would "stay till business, as they cal it, comes on".[47] But their greatest triumph of organisation in 1708 (and the greatest tribute that could be paid to the efficiency of their regional 'whips') was the fact that they achieved all this without ever communicating the precise reason for the summons. Since secrecy was an essential part of the Harley-Bromley plan to outmanoeuvre the Whigs and the Court,[48] and Harley was in fact doing everything he could deliberately to deceive the Whigs into expecting a small Tory turn-out at the start of the session,[49] even some of the 'whips' themselves could not be entrusted with the object of the exercise. James Grahme was simply told that "some of our best friends who have taken all possible care to inform themselves conclude there will be some very material points

---

* Nicolson's MS. Diary: Thursday, 25 Oct. 1705. An example of the kind of circular sent round to leading Tory M.P.s up and down the country is the unsigned letter, written in a clerical hand, received by Sir John Mordaunt (knight of the shire for Warwickshire). It begins: "Its desired that you will take care to engage all in yor county to be in Towne some time before the choice of the Speaker wch will certainly be the 25th of October, for its found upon the stretest calculation that there is a majority suffitient to place Mr. Bromley in the Chaire if those in the interest of the Church will give their early attendance . . ." Walton MSS. iii, 93: N.D.

at first opening & agree to press all friends accordingly", and Peter Shakerley's and Sir Richard Myddleton's instructions were equally mysterious.[50] Nevertheless, when the House assembled on 16 November it was "very full [Dyer reported], 413 having been sworn besides many more that were not".[51] It is clear, however, that many Tory members, accustomed to a more casual routine, found this second great effort in three years a considerable strain; and when the promised display of rockets ended only in the dampest of squibs, with Bromley's nomination being dropped for tactical reasons,* there were rumblings of protest. One of the loudest came from the representatives of the city of Oxford, one of whom confided to a Fellow of All Souls: "My brother, [Sir John] Walter, as well as Sr John Stonehouse with several others [are] displeased at their journey to London . . . I believe the gentlemen will be better informed of an opposition before they will venture such another journey. Where the trouble lies I am not a judge, but am satisfied we have been made fools of. . . ."[52]

The party machinery of Anne's day was not so crude that it was incapable of being geared to the demands of the *exceptional* occasion, when that occasion could be reasonably foreseen: that is surely the moral of the events of 25 October 1705 and 16 November 1708. But, as one would expect, efforts to secure a high turn-out of party members at the start of a session were usually affected much more than they were in 1708 both by the political climate at the time and by the current state of party morale. When the prospects of one party seemed dim, or enthusiasm and excitement were at a lower than average level, it was always difficult to achieve a good "appearance". In the first division in the Commons in the winter of 1709–10 only 54 Tories voted, and one of their supporters admitted that "most of the countrey members are grown sullen & doe not com to Towne".[53] In April 1713, by which time the Whigs had given up the struggle for peace as lost, there were only 300 members out of 558 in London for the opening of the last session of this Parliament, compared with the 460 who were there for the opening of the first in November 1710. It was only after a few unexpectedly close divisions in May that both sides began calling up their forces from the country.[54]

Once a session was under way the success with which the party chiefs could keep their supporters up to the mark and persuade them to attend important debates in large numbers depended on a great many variables; but

---

* By the time Parliament met the differences among the Whigs, and between the Whigs and the Court, which had given the Tory leaders their hope of success had been composed, and Bromley preferred to use his strength in other ways.

an unexpected run of parliamentary victories by either side, or a series of closely-fought divisions (as in 1713) which sent up the mercury in the political barometer, were always a godsend to the Whig and Tory leadership. The Tories reacted impressively to such stimuli in the House of Commons early in the sessions of 1705–6 and 1708–9, as did the Whigs in the second half of the 1713 session and at the beginning of that of 1714, and in every case their opponents were forced to respond in kind. On the other hand a long-drawn-out session almost invariably caused attendances to fall away badly and made organisation for special parliamentary efforts in the latter half of the session very difficult. The most frequent cause of a prolonged Westminster "campaign", something which no ministry welcomed but which was at times unavoidable, was a protracted struggle over ways and means; and there was no aspect of Parliament's work which the average backbencher found more tedious and unpalatable than this. "The House of Commons", complained one of its Scottish members after the Union (with perhaps just a touch of national prejudice), "is represented as a wise and august assembly; what it was long agoe I shall not say, but in our days, it is full of disorder and confusion; the members that are capable and mindful of business are few in number, and the rest mind nothing at all. When there's a party job to be done, they'l attend and make a hideous noise like so many Bedlamites; but if the House is to enter on business, such as giving of money or making of public laws, they converse so loud with one another in private knots, that no body can know what is doing, except a very few, who for that purpose sitt near the clerks table, or they leave the house and the men of business, as they call them, to mind such matters".[55] This picture probably does scant justice to a minority of backbench squires who were genuinely concerned to discharge their duties as makers of laws and voters of taxes conscientiously. But even they, with the best will in the world, must often have found the complexities of fiscal business in war-time a sore trial. When, for example, the first great money bill of the Spanish Succession war at length reached the table of the House of Lords, one peer noted to his horror that it contained "206 sheets of parchmt. haveing the names of 32000 [*sic*] commissioners".[56] One can only sympathise with the plaintive cry of a Liverpool member some years earlier: "it will puzzle a more politick noddle than mine to find out wa[y]es and means to carry on the war".[57]

On the whole the Whigs seem to have been rather more successful than their opponents in resisting the tendency for interest to sag and numbers to dwindle away in the course of a session. Harley's amendment to the Whig ministry's Treasons bill in April 1709 tested this capacity to the full. In a thin House, such as could normally be expected so close to a prorogation, it would have had an excellent chance of success, especially as it commanded general support from the Scottish members, whose interests were very much involved. Yet in the event it was defeated by six votes after the Whigs had "assembled all their forces, the lame and blind and all".[58] Even as a heavily outnumbered, struggling minority in 1711 the Whigs still retained the knack of being able to get a good complement of members into the House of Commons in an emergency. After rumours of an exceptional canvass of High Tory M.P.s during the Easter Recess, "they did not fail [Peter Wentworth observed] of giving their attendance to[o]" on the day Parliament re-assembled, "in expectation that some state mine was to be sprung and somebody or other blown up . . .".[59] Yet Whig organisation could be just as vulnerable as that of the Tories to the two prime bugbears of the party manager of Anne's reign: the snap vote forced by his opponents, and over-confidence among his own supporters. When a number of ex-officials of the Prize Office were censured by the Tories in the House of Commons in February 1705, one of the unfortunate Whigs concerned insisted that a grave injustice had been done, in that William Bromley and the two members for the county of Northampton "did by their whispering and interest with the Speaker procure that vote to be pass'd, in a thin House, when it was pas[t] five a clock, and when there was not an hundred members left in it, and most of my friends gon out to dinner".[60] A surprise attack was potentially dangerous even to the majority party, particularly in the latter part of a session. Lord Oxford was normally the most phlegmatic of men; but even he grew jittery in March 1712 after reports of many meetings among the Whigs, and began to suspect an ambush in the House of Lords.[61] Nervousness, however, was always preferable to complacency. This was the moral pointed in the most famous cautionary tale in the whole chronicle of Augustan politics, the case of the Westminster election.

In December 1708 the petition of the Whig Sir Henry Dutton Colt against the return of Thomas Medlicott for the city of Westminster was heard at the bar of the House of Commons. Colt had a strong case, for the Tory bailiff of Westminster had shown blatant partiality for his rival, and there was scarcely a Whig in Parliament who did not take it for granted that the seat would be captured. On the second day of the hearing, a Saturday, after hours of evidence and debate, most Whig members rashly assumed around 5 p.m. that the case was certain to be adjourned until after the weekend, and a flock of 35 of them absconded to Covent Garden, where Nicolini was performing in a new opera, *Pyrrhus and Demetrius*. They should have remembered as they hurried out of the chamber that only a few days earlier Bromley had "scandalously surpriz'd" them by carrying a sudden vote on the battle of Wynendael, taking advantage of the fact that some of the leading Whigs in the House had been called away to a special ministerial meeting to discuss the Recruiting bill.[62] However, this warning went unheeded; the revellers departed; the High Tory leaders saw their chance and took it; a Junto henchman, Lord William Powlet, so far miscalculated his party's remaining strength as to support the call for a division at about 7 o'clock; and the result was a humiliating defeat for Colt and the Whigs by 12 votes, though their normal majority was probably around 60. When the tidings reached the opera house towards the end of the second act it utterly ruined the evening's entertainment for the "honest interest", and transported the Tories, who found the sudden change on the faces of their rivals as the news spread round the theatre well worth the price of admission in itself. "These gentlemen", wrote Joseph Addison of the offending members, ". . . have been so reproached by their party for this piece of negligence, that it will have a good effect upon 'em for the remaining part of the parliament"; and so it proved.[63] But the capacity to deal with the unexpected remained to the end of the reign the greatest test of any party leader's skill as a parliamentary manager. Even a start to a session that was far more tranquil than that of 1708 was no guarantee against sudden and violent squalls later on. Speaking from long experience, the Duke of Shrewsbury once remarked: "so many things unexpected fall out in a sessions, that I have often found those most difficult, who at first had the greatest appearance of easyness".[64]

If the effectiveness of party organisation during sessions was governed by many variables, it was nearly always subject to one constant factor. One thing on which the leaders of both parties could generally rely was the basic unreliability of the independent country gentleman. Even when in town many country members would only attend spasmodically; and not all were as considerate as Sir Michael Warton, who made special arrangements with Harley in 1709–10 to be kept informed of any urgent business requiring his vote. But the real trouble with such members (as the Cave-Fermanagh saga illustrated in the previous chapter) was that they took every opportunity of drifting out of London when either the climate or the expense or the drudgery of their parliamentary labours became too much for them. It was normally not too difficult to keep in contact with absentees whose constituencies or country houses were within reasonable distance of Westminster. Sir Richard Onslow, taking the air at Clandon in the summer of

1713, received a special summons from the Duke of Somerset to return before the Whigs sprang their devastating "Lorraine motion" on the House of Commons on 1 July.[65] And when the news of the successful Lords' amendments to the Schism bill in 1714 was sent to two Kentish Whigs, who were quietly rusticating in the third week of June, they proved equal to the occasion by riding the fifty miles or so up to the House at "full speed" in the hope of contributing to the bill's defeat in the Commons. (It should be added, though, that having made this heroic gesture, they could not be persuaded to stay in town, despite the fact that the urgent business of the Spanish commerce enquiry was still pending).[66] Keeping control over members more distant from London was a well-nigh insoluble problem; though even here the party managers of the day were nothing if not resourceful. A "call of the House" would quite often be deliberately moved, as a spur to the absentees or as a deterrent to fresh desertions.[67] The regional 'whips' would occasionally be called into action during as well as before a session. Thus the Tory member for Peterborough wrote to the absent Sir Justinian Isham at the beginning of June 1713,

I am desired by the Speaker [Bromley] to acquaint you that your appearance on Saturday next will be very kindly taken on the account of the Trade-bill which has many enemys, their number being increasd by the apostacy of the Scots;

while Sir George Beaumont, appropriately nicknamed "the Serjeant", who kept in touch with the members of his and Bromley's platoon even when their presence was not required in the House, and "never failed" to send them his "usuall summons" when it was, sallied forth into the midlands in April 1714 to round up some of his straying Tories in person.[68] Tory inventiveness once went so far as to provide a specially-constructed "wyre cage" to convey gouty members up to town at short notice with the minimum of discomfort.[69]

When Parliament was in session the House of Lords generally presented less difficult problems than the Commons. The great advantage which party leaders enjoyed here was the proxy system, which meant that a tighter organisation could be maintained both during periods of excitement and during periods of relative, and perhaps deceptive, quiet. A study of the House of Lords' proxy book is guaranteed to dispel any lingering illusion that parliamentary management in the age of Anne was haphazard or unscientific. It shows, for instance, how the Junto extracted the maximum possible value from the system after 1710, in keeping up pressure on the Harley ministry. The Junto lords themselves, like every other peer, could hold no more than two proxies each at any one time; but in cooperation with a dozen or more completely dependable allies — men like Devonshire, Townshend, Mohun, Carlisle, Cornwallis, Dorchester and Bolton — they were able to ensure that scarcely a single reliable vote escaped them. During the sessions of 1710–11 and 1711–12 alone (they are the only sessions of Anne's last two Parliaments for which detailed information survives) this astonishing network embraced no fewer than 42 Whig peers. Another advantage of the proxy system, in the hands of the Whig chiefs, was that it allowed them to take occasional 'refreshers' themselves, carefully staggered to leave a quorum of experienced debaters always on hand. Even the irrepressible Wharton took care to recruit his strength occasionally at Newmarket and Winchendon; in 1711, for example, he took ten days off in February, a fortnight in April and another fortnight at the fag end of the session in late May and early June — his proxy duly entrusted to the "honest" hands of Dorchester and Mohun.

That the Tories were rather less systematic in their marshalling of proxies, at least before Harley went up to the Lords in 1711, is not altogether surprising. In most aspects of House of Lords' organisation they lagged behind their opponents. Until Oxford not merely brought into play his own capacity for management but recruited a few hard-working and enthusiastic Tory peers, like Dartmouth, Poulet and Masham, to help in whipping up a good attendance on special occasions,[70] the Church party could show nothing to compare with such Whig *coups* as the defeat of the second Occasional Conformity bill, a triumph of methodical, energetic organisation. Early in December 1703 it became clear that the Tory sponsors of that bill were planning to rush it up from the Commons much more quickly than expected in the hope of catching the Junto unprepared and taking the Upper House by storm. The Whigs took their measures accordingly. On the 8th Godolphin acknowledged that they had been "very industrious to gett proxy's & tell noses"; on the 9th, Atterbury found that "nineteen proxies were yesterday brought into the House of Lords against the bill, and but six for it", and an exultant Wharton openly "brag'd that by proxies his party was now able to fling out the bill . . . shou'd it be now sent up".[71] When the crucial vote was taken six days later seven more Whig peers had arrived in town, so that the Junto had to deploy only 12 of its original 19 proxies. The margin of victory was precisely 12. Time and again one is impressed by the forethought which the Whig chiefs gave to their organisation in the House of Lords and the pains they took with it. When a brief race-meeting at Newmarket coincided with a very quiet period of the 1712 session, only the Whigs would have thought to provide against parliamentary emergencies by arranging for supporters temporarily involved in these diversions to have relays of horses ready along the London road to carry them back to town at short notice.[72] At the first suggestion of possible trouble, Lord Townshend sent an express to his friend, Devonshire:

My Ld Marlborough is of opinion that the French ministers at Utrecht gave in their answer on Wednesday last & that we shall have it here by the next pacquett either to morrow or on Saturday. All the intelligence we can have in this case must be very uncertain, but I am persuaded yr Grace & our friends at Newmarket have the affair of Peace too much at heart to be absent at this criticall juncture, & that we shall have the happyness of yr. company here on Sunday next [4th May] at farthest. . . .[73]

The alarm on this occasion proved to be entirely false; but for all that, Devonshire, Wharton, Bridgewater and Somerset were back at their posts by Monday, Orford by Wednesday and Dorchester by Thursday.

In the enforcement of a measure of discipline over their supporters, the leaders of the party which happened at any time to be in alliance with the Court automatically enjoyed certain notable advantages over their opponents. One was that the government usually had its own 'whips' — Harley dubbed them "orderly men"[74] — on whom it relied to keep placemen to heel in the House of Commons when important issues were being debated. William Lowndes, the non-party Secretary to the Treasury, was throughout this period the indispensable figure among them. A year before "the Tack", when the ministry was secretly hoping to rally enough moderate support in the House to prevent the introduction of the second Occasional Conformity bill, it was Lowndes who was instructed by the Lord Treasurer "to ply his coffee house, & to diffuse";[75] and during the hectic days preceding the Tack itself he claimed to have performed "miracles" with office-holders at large, as well as discharging a specific responsibility for enforcing the attendance of all the officials of the Prize Office.[76] In performing such functions he normally had the assistance of a few moderate party men who were either in the ministry themselves or closely attached to it; and as the party complexion of the government changed, so did the identity of those who shared responsibility for marshalling "the Queen's servants" in the House of Commons. Apart from the ubiquitous Lowndes, Speaker Harley and Admiral Churchill were the most active members in the early years of the Godolphin ministry. Later Godolphin was well served by Harley's successor in the Chair, John Smith, and by two other prominent "Treasurer's Whigs", Boyle and

Coningsby. After 1710 Edward Harley, the Joint Auditor of the Exchequer, was Lowndes's chief coadjutor.

There were certain parliamentary occasions in Anne's reign so important to the government in power that it felt bound to undertake a complete individual canvass of all its prospective supporters in the House of Commons, and of all doubtful quantities as well, whether "in place" or out of it. By great good fortune the canvassing lists for two of these occasions — the attempted "Tack" in November 1704 and the censure of the Duke of Marlborough in January 1712 — have been preserved;[77] and in spite of the fact that the second list is torn and defaced, they allow an intriguing glimpse of an aspect of early-eighteenth-century political organisation in which party and Court pooled their resources to achieve maximum effectiveness. Almost every important minister of the Crown was clearly expected to play some part on both occasions; and in 1712, while the Lowndes–Auditor Harley net was spread to bring in minor placemen, law officers, and those members with financial or commercial interests who would not wish to offend the ministry unnecessarily,[78] the Lord Treasurer also called into service the Tory regional whips to make certain of the attendances of large numbers of party backbenchers. George Granville (now Lord Lansdowne) received his usual commission to muster up "Trevannion* & al Cornewal"; Sir George Beaumont was the obvious man to see that the Leicestershire members came to the House on the vital day; and Mansel, with some help from Oxford's old friend, Judge Price, was naturally made responsible for most of the Welsh brigade.†

As well as being able to call on the government's special facilities for 'whipping' and canvassing, party leaders in office or in alliance with the Court enjoyed a further advantage over those in opposition when trying to enforce the attendance of their supporters. The disciplinary powers of the Crown were, of course, considerable. When the parliamentary situation warranted it office-holders could not merely be pressed but *commanded* to present themselves and vote as required. Edward Harley thought this quite in order in April 1712, for instance, at a time when there was a prospect of another tack to force through a controversial bill on land grants.[79] These

---

* John Trevanion, one of the knights of the shire for Cornwall in this Parliament.

† In addition John Pringle, now the safest of the Scottish Court members, shared with Oxford's son-in-law Lord Dupplin, a Teller of the Exchequer, the no more enviable task of drumming up as many Tories as possible from north of Tweed. This is not the only evidence from the period that a tellership, while "a fat sinecure" in the administrative sense (H.M.C. *Portland MSS*. iv, 84), could involve its tenant in parliamentary chores.

instructions to placemen always carried with them the threat, implicit if not explicit, of dismissal in the event of non-compliance; and at the same time members of Parliament in hopes of place could be given to understand that their chances of success were contingent upon good parliamentary behaviour. Threats or warnings of this kind were not always decently veiled. A number of Court Whigs who would have preferred to abstain or vote against their party during the passage of the Treasons bill in April 1709 "were dragoon into't", according to Peter Wentworth, "and sent possitively word that if they did not vote as desired they shou'd be turn'd out of their places". [80] Nor could placemen afford to treat such admonitions as idle threats. Immediately after the defection of a tiny group of "Queen's servants" in the vote on the Tack the Lord Treasurer told Secretary Harley: "it will bee fitt to consider when I see you next, what men shall be pitched upon to bee made examples"; [81] and among those soon afterwards victimised was John Manley, who had openly rebuffed a directive from Lowndes to abandon his High Tory friends. Very heavy pressure was put on Tory office-holders to vote for the Whig Speaker countenanced by the government in October 1705, and one of those who had made it clear that he would disobey, George Clarke, received notice of his dismissal from the Admiralty Council in the lobby of the House on the very morning of the election. A further seven who rebelled on this occasion were granted stay of execution; but on continuing (in Godolphin's phrase) to play the fool, were sacked either at the end of the session or shortly afterwards. [82]

Opposition members, or those government supporters who neither held office nor aspired to it, were naturally more difficult to constrain. With them their leaders had to rely to a large extent on the self-discipline that stemmed from party zeal and from mutual loyalty and solidarity. The one sanction that could be imposed on such a member was the threat, or the fear, of the loss of his seat in the House of Commons. If he happened to owe his election in whole or in part to one of the party magnates it was a sanction that could occasionally be very effective. Spencer Compton paid for his frequent sallies against the Junto in the years 1707-9 by losing his seat at Eye in Suffolk, which he owed to Lord Cornwallis, and it was not until 1713 that, as a reformed character, he re-entered the House as a member for East Grinstead on the Sackville ticket. More fortunate was the renegade Craven Peyton. In 1710 the Junto pleaded in vain with his patron, Newcastle, to drop him at Boroughbridge in favour of a sounder man. [83] It was not until the young Lord Pelham succeeded to the Holles interest in Yorkshire before the 1713 Election that nemesis at last overtook Peyton, and also claimed another victim in Robert Monckton, a seasoned Court Whig placeman whom Pelham turned out of his seat at Aldborough for voting against his party on the French Commerce bill.[84] Only Lord Stamford's intercession saved "Vulture" Hopkins from ejection at St. Ives in the same Election after his patron, Sir John Hobart, had declared himself "not pleased with his voting".[85] Tory borough-mongers could be just as ruthless at times with their nominees, and sometimes on less provocation. Both William Blathwayt and Edward Brereton lost the favour of their patrons and their seats, the first in 1710, the second five years earlier, not because of an injudicous vote but simply because of a misleading report of such a vote;* and Jack Dolben's part in the attack on Sacheverell might well have cost him his safe berth in one of Trelawney's pocket boroughs in 1710, had not he saved the bishop the embarrassment by conveniently dying before the General Election took place.[86]

III

Parliamentary battles were not, of course, the only ones which called for careful planning and organisation from the political parties. Five times in the twelve years of Anne's reign, and eight times between 1701 and 1715, the ability of the parties to marshal their resources was subjected to the severest trial of all, that of a General Election. It would be quite wrong to imagine that the forces of either Tories or Whigs went into Elections with no constituency organisation and with a complete absence of co-ordination between electioneering magnates of the same party. The effort of both sides in the great contests of 1702, 1705, 1708, 1710 and 1713 represented far more than the mere aggregation of hundreds of individual "interests", even though the recruitment of interest, both great and small, was always the basis of every campaign. In scores of constituencies the length and breadth of the country, but especially in boroughs, each party was able to launch its attacks from well-established and well-prepared positions. Bishop Burnet wrote in the summer of 1708: "The parties are now so stated and kept up, not only by the elections of parliament-men, that return every third year, but even by the yearly elections of mayors and corporation-men, that they know their strength; and in every corner of the nation the two parties stand,

* H.M.C. *Dartmouth MSS.* i, 297; Chirk Castle MSS. E. 1000, E. 6066. Blathwayt, who had topped the poll at Bath both in 1705 and 1708 with 25 and 20 votes respectively from a total of 28 corporation electors, slumped with the loss of the Duke of Beaufort's support to bottom of the poll, with only 12 votes. John Rylands Lib. Eng. MSS. 330, p. 243; Dyrham Court MSS. D. 1779 x 9.

as it were, listed against one another".[87] Burnet's picture may be a little overdrawn. But there is ample evidence of rival personal and party interest steadily at work between one election and another in a large number of incorporated boroughs.

Bewdley, Bury St. Edmunds, Portsmouth and Buckingham were all towns with a very narrow corporation franchise. In all of them party warfare was more or less endemic throughout the reign, or at least for years on end. In all of them the local party champions were constantly on the watch for every opportunity that was presented to change the composition of the governing body and so directly influence the political disposition of the electorate. In Bewdley the outcome of the battle for supremacy between Tories and Whigs hinged on the legality of the borough charter of 1685; and the crippling cost of a protracted struggle that was not only local but judicial and parliamentary had by 1714 reduced the Winningtons, the leading Tory family in the area, to serious straits and had virtually ruined the Herberts, who headed the opposing interest.[88] Party leaders, ever on the look-out for seats that could be rendered safe by judicious attention, were quick to reinforce the efforts of local partisans when possible. The Junto, through the medium of Orford and Bolton, threw its weight behind the Portsmouth Whigs,[89] and Tory leaders became involved in the struggle for Bury and Bewdley, as well as Portsmouth, in the closing years of the reign.[90] In the last resort the conflict could be, and often was, taken on to the floor of the House of Commons itself, by petition and counter-petition, and the machinery of central party organisation there brought into action in support of the borough protagonists. In Buckingham the Whigs used the press to enhance their parliamentary prospects in 1713–14,[91] while the culmination of the battle for Bewdley in the Commons in December 1710 aroused such general excitement that it led both sides to deploy the talents of some of their star debaters for the occasion.* But the common denominator in all these four boroughs, as in other hotly contested restricted corporations such as Brackley and Marlborough, was permanent local organisation.

A comparable degree of organisation was a prerequisite for success in some of the freemen boroughs, also; and the frequent creations of large numbers of new burgesses and freemen in such boroughs, at the instance first of one party, then of another, in a bid to remould the electorate before a new General Election, furnish adequate proof that such organisation was

---

* On the Tory side, St. John, among others. On the Whig side "Sr Jo. Jekyll, Mr Lech[mere], etc, & honest R. Walpole". *Cowper Diary* (1833), p. 50; Clavering Letters: Ann to James Clavering, 21 Dec. 1710.

often forthcoming. The creation of 200 new freemen in the Whig interest at Norwich in 1701, the swearing of 125 freemen (including 80 "foreigners") in the watches of the night two days before the 1705 election at Colchester, and the subsequent confirmation of their freedoms in 1711 — these were scarcely acts of improvisation.[92] The bitter struggle between the rival parties to establish control over the electorate of the Carnarvon boroughs between 1708 and 1713 could only have been sustained by a systematic campaign on both sides.[93] In smaller towns, like the two Devonshire boroughs of Plympton and Okehampton, operations, if necessarily on a smaller scale, were just as well organised. In Okehampton, indeed, the local Whigs had a regular machinery for manufacturing freemen. A Tory petition against the return of John Dibble in 1710 complained that the late mayor of the town, Christopher Yendall, "and several preceding Mayors, by confederating themselves together, have yearly, as they were Mayors, purposely [advanced] the interest of John Dibble . . . upon whose account . . . 135 freemen were made, a great many of which were waggoners and carters of Mr. Dibble's . . .".[94]

In incorporated parliamentary boroughs control of the mayoral seat was at all times a primary objective of the local parties. The powerful voice which the mayor could exercise in the election of new burgesses or honorary burgesses was but one reason for his political importance. More vital could be his function as a returning officer in parliamentary elections. Frequently the tussles between Whig and Tory interests over the choice of a mayor in the autumn before an election were fiercer than the election itself. For the borough caucuses, they were not merely a dress rehearsal for the second contest but also an essential part of it. Thus in 1712, with the dissolution of Queen Anne's fourth Parliament certain to take place by the following summer, the Whigs made strenuous efforts in borough after borough to guarantee their candidates a favourable returning officer. In some towns their cause was hopeless from the start. The Tory sitting members at Cambridge, Shepheard and Cotton, had long had the backing of an efficient organisation, based on the Rose Tavern Club and controlled by a local 'boss', Alderman William Rumball, which had the borough corporation in its pocket. The choice of a mayor here was a formality.[95] But in the south-west, at Truro and Marlborough, as in the north, at Wigan and Pontefract, canvassing for rival mayoral candidates in 1712 was vigorous and unscrupulous, and money and ale alike flowed freely on both sides.[96] In the largest urban constituency of all, London, both mayoral and corporation elections in Anne's reign were major events of more than local importance, carefully watched by the political pundits between General Elections for signs of a shift in public opinion. In London party organisation existed down to ward level[97] and there also appears to have been an accepted method of choosing parliamentary candidates. "The two parties in this city have had meeting", Luttrell noted in April 1708, "and fixt upon the gentlemen they design for their members of parliament . . .".[98] Who attended these nomination meetings and how large the gatherings were it would be very instructive to know. Across the river in Southwark, where party passions were rarely allowed to cool, both sides "knew their strength" so well by 1710 that when the Tories called a general meeting in September of that year to nominate two new candidates and to guarantee them support they had no difficulty in getting several hundred electors to attend.* When mass party meetings were arranged in London they could be huge affairs; one campaign meeting alone held by the Whigs in 1713 attracted nearly 1500 supporters.[99]

Lacking the constant stimulus to organise which annual municipal elections and the opportunities for creating burgesses provided in many boroughs, the contending party forces in the county constituencies rarely developed a comparable machinery. Yet even here there were attempts, and sometimes successful attempts, to put organisation on a permanent and at least a semi-formal footing. Party clubs existed in a number of shires, in which the country gentlemen met regularly to discuss local business, including that most important of all local business, the choice of candidates for the next election and the planning of their campaign. The Royston Club in Hertfordshire, carefully tended by Ralph Freeman, provided the Tories in that county with a permanent committee which must have made a considerable contribution to their near-monopoly of the shire seats throughout the years 1702–14. The St. Nicholas Club, "very tite" thanks to the efforts of a group of devoted squires, kept Glamorgan generally safe for the Church interest.[100] A similar society in Derbyshire, the Swarkeston Club, was revived in 1710 after having lapsed for several years, and at its first meeting it refused to readopt one of the sitting Tory members, Thomas Coke, whose recent parliamentary behaviour had soured many of his High Church constituents.†

---

* *The Supplement*, No. 422, 25–27 Sept. In another large popular constituency, Coventry, invitations to Whig candidates to stand might be signed by as many as "betwixt 20 and 30 of the cheife of wigg interest" in the city. Blenheim MSS. D. 1–32: G. Lucy to Sunderland, 21 Feb. 1705.

† H.M.C. *Cowper MSS.* iii, 71, 85. Not every Tory club was fully representative of the local pillars of the party: e.g. the "Cycle of the White Rose", founded in June 1710 by

In most counties, however, the partisans kept their media of association more informal. This did not necessarily mean a loss of efficiency or a lack of preparedness; long before the 1710–13 Parliament had run its course, for example, indeed before it had even begun its final session, the Tory gentlemen of Surrey had arranged "to meet & dine together at Epsom [at the expense of the sitting members] . . . in order to settle matters for the next Election".[101] What it did mean was that the leading Whig and Tory figures in the majority of counties preferred the country-house round, the mellow atmosphere of the dinner-table at some convenient hostelry, the local race-meeting, and above all the Quarter Sessions and the Assizes, as their forum. At the Sessions and the Assizes the local parties flexed their own muscles and assessed the strength of their opponents before deciding to go ahead with the expense and trouble of a county contest. Occasionally this muscle-flexing became too literal, and at Worcester sessions in July 1702 the swords of the rival candidates and of some of their supporters were drawn.[102] Sometimes agreement was reached, amicably or grudgingly, to share the representation between one Whig and one Tory knight. At other times, as at the Shrewsbury Assizes in 1701 or the Worcester Assizes in 1707, a great deal of preliminary skirmishing and manoeuvring for position failed in the end to produce the hoped-for truce.[103] Often enough, however, there was never a hope of compromise and the struggle was carried through to its bitter and costly end. It is worth remembering that 26 of the 40 English counties went to the polls in 1705 and 23 in 1710; and that Gloucestershire, Buckinghamshire and Surrey each had five contests between 1702 and 1713.

The one safe generalisation that can be made about the pattern of local organisation in the counties is that there was nothing standardised about it. In fact its whole essence, especially in areas where contests were frequently in prospect, had to be variety and adaptability. It is true that, in the normal course of events, Tory candidates could expect to be formally nominated in a full gathering of "the Gentlemen of the Church party", either at the last Quarter Sessions or at the last Assizes preceding an election;[104] and they might then have their nomination endorsed by the Grand Jury of the county, provided this body could be so packed with Tories that it was ready to oblige.[105] But so leisurely a procedure was not always geared to the need for swift action, and in emergencies resource and flexibility proved not to be beyond even the conservative county squire. The Northamptonshire Tories

Tory gentry in Denbighshire and Flintshire, was frankly Jacobite, and for this reason was not patronised by the great Sir Richard Myddleton of Chirk. See P. D. G. Thomas, 'Jacobitism in Wales', *Welsh Hist. Rev.* i (1962).

were only momentarily shaken in August 1706, when they found that their opponents had already put two prospective candidates into the field for the next election (a contingency that was still two years ahead if Parliament lasted its full term). "I am sorry to find we are like to begin canvassing for another election so soon", Thomas Cartwright told his fellow member, "but since the other party doe it, it will be necessary for our friends to consider who to set up. I will send to as many as I can to meet at Northampton on Munday where I will wait on them, & whatever the gentlemen agree on I shall submit to".[106] The ingenuity of the Worcestershire Tories in the summer of 1707 on the death of one of the sitting county members, the Whig William Bromley of Holt, took even a hardened Junto man like William Walsh aback: "they had resolved [he told Somers] . . . to settle the election at Mr. Bromley's funeral, & put it to the votes of the gentlemen, who were all of their own inviting", though they subsequently abandoned this plan in favour of a rather more decorous expedient.[107] Even in Leicestershire, where the traditional Tory methods of consultation and agreement were very strongly rooted among the gentry,[108] a sudden call to action in the middle of a session did not find the party wanting. When the Duke of Rutland died in the winter of 1710–11, and his son Granby, one of the sitting knights, went up to the Lords, Sir Thomas Cave was promptly "petitioned by Lord Denbigh, Lord Ferrars, Lord Crewe, Lord Guernsey and several other gentlemen in town to stand this vacancy . . .". Back in the midlands, meanwhile, a few of the local Tory notables had met and made a different choice. But their nominee was eventually persuaded to stand down; for it was unthinkable to men like Sir Justinian Isham, who had spent years holding at bay "the adverse party" in the next county, "that two gentlemen both of the same principles shou'd oppose one another".[109]

Generally speaking, the Tories relied far less than the Whigs for the direction of their county election campaigns on the lead given by big aristocratic landowners. The Tory peer was rarely more than *primus inter pares* in his own area. Where evidence of any detail survives about the *ad hoc* committees convened to thrash out Tory policy for an approaching election it suggests that they were genuinely broad-based. "A List of the [49] Names of the Gentlem[n] who mett at the Swan in Warwick the 25th of Nov[r]. 1701 to consult abt. choosing Representatives in Parl."[110] was headed by the High Sheriff, 4 peers[111] and 2 peers' sons. Next came 8 baronets, 3 knights and 22 squires. At the foot of the list were 9 plain "gents", who sat no doubt at the bottom of the table but who were none the less granted a say in the nomination of their party's candidates. Except perhaps in Monmouthshire, where the

Beaufort interest prevailed,[112] there was no county where Tory fortunes depended almost exclusively on aristocratic support, as the Northampton-shire Whigs, for instance, depended on the efforts of Sunderland, and to a lesser degree on those of Halifax and Rockingham. Yet there were times when the more hierarchical system worked conspicuously well. If the impressive aristocratic "cabal" summoned to Althorp in 1710 to promote the Whig campaign in Northamptonshire proved a fiasco,[113] a similar meeting held at Welbeck a little earlier, presided over by Newcastle and Dorchester, not only launched but successfully promoted Lord Howe as the Whig candidate for Nottinghamshire.[114] In Bedfordshire, where the power of the Russell family was by far the greatest asset of the Whigs, the party managers were so efficient that they had a new prospective candidate ready, and had actually begun campaigning for him, only a fortnight after the 1710 election, at the first notice that one of their newly-chosen members, Lord Edward Russell, had fallen dangerously ill.[115] In Cumberland and West-morland the Tory gentry, though heavily outnumbering the Whigs, were forced to concede that the organisation of their opponents, based on the territorial power and unified control of three great electoral families (the Howards, the Lowthers and the Whartons), was more effective and more liberally financed than their own.[116] How much Whig organisation in Buckinghamshire normally owed to Wharton's peerless brand of personal supervision was emphasised in 1710, the one General Election of the reign in which his activities were unavoidably limited; for the blunders of the Whig agents on this occasion, which presented the Tories with one of the county seats, would scarcely have escaped the eagle eye of "King Tom".[117]

Quite apart from its strictly local advantages, the dominant rôle played by the party magnates in Whig organisation in many parts of England also gave the Whig leaders distinctly more control over electoral strategy and tactics than the more democratic but more loosely-knit associations of the local Tory squirearchy. At the same time it opened up more opportunities to ensure seats for men of their own choice in the House of Commons. The capacity to provide 'reserve' constituencies for key members whose election prospects were uncertain, or to make subsequent arrangements for candidates who had taken an unexpected tumble at a General Election, is one excellent criterion of the comparative effectiveness of the electoral organisation of the two parties in a broad, national context. In 1702, when the cards were heavily stacked in favour of the Tories, only two of that party's front-rank commoners were thought to be in serious danger of defeat, both of them contesting county constituencies. Both were offered safe alternative seats;

but it is not without significance that they were accommodated in the west country, where the influence of a few great Tory families — the Seymours, Trelawneys, Granvilles and Hydes — was exceptionally strong. Sir Christopher Musgrave was guaranteed a secure passage to Westminster by way of Seymour's "Western Empire", in case he should fail to carry Westmorland;[118] and Jack Howe, a particular target of the Whigs, found a haven with Trelawney's help at Bodmin since his prospects in Gloucestershire seemed doubtful.* One or two Tories of rather less imposing reputation but of obvious value to the party either as debaters or legislators also found refuge in this same area in 1702: Sir Thomas Powys, the lawyer, was nominated at Truro, for example, because his fate in his native Shropshire seemed uncertain.[119] Even where the big electoral magnates were unready or unable to lend a hand, the Tory first-aid system in elections undoubtedly had its successes. Its most notable occurred in February 1710 when Lewis Pryse, a power in Cardiganshire but a nonentity in the Tory party at large, made it possible for Sir Simon Harcourt to return to the House of Commons as member for Cardigan, little over a year after his scandalous expulsion from his seat at Abingdon.[120] But to be weighed against the successes were some spectacular failures. Jack Howe, though rescued in 1702, was left to sink in 1705.[121] More incredible was the experience of Henry St. John. Early in 1708 it became clear that he would not be re-elected at Wootton Bassett in the spring. Yet although many would have considered him the brightest star in the Tory firmament, no seat could be found for him either then or for two years thereafter. "After I had taken the resolution of not appearing at my own borough I did all I could to get myself elected in some other place", he told James Grahme in July 1708, "but found it utterly impossible".[122] Both then and later he clearly felt some sense of grievance against his party friends for not providing for him; but in this he did less than justice to the efforts of the Harleyites, who explored the possibilities of at least six alternative constituencies — all without success.[123]

The Whigs' network of private interests and large-scale borough patrons was both more extensive than anything the Tories could offer and better co-ordinated by their leaders. It was never more impressive in operation than in the last two Parliaments of the reign, when the electoral tide was flowing strongly against the party and threatening to engulf many of its champions

* H.M.C. *Cowper MSS.* iii, 13; Add. MSS. 29588, ff. 68, 74, 76. Howe also took out a second insurance policy, at Newton in Lancs., thanks to Lord Nottingham's influence with the Leghs of Lyme. *Ibid.* f. 78; Legh of Lyme MSS. Box 59: Howe to Peter Legh, 12 July 1702.

in the Commons. After the disaster of 1710 seats were in desperately short supply for the Whigs. Sir Richard Onslow, unexpectedly put to rout in Surrey, was hastily procured a "city of refuge" in Cornwall before the Election itself was over;[124] and the Duke of Somerset had fortunately held Cockermouth in reserve for Stanhope, who was decisively rejected in a turbulent contest at Westminster. Patiently the party leaders waited for their opportunities to bring back other notable casualties into the firing-line. In December 1711 Richard Hampden and Serjeant Pratt, defeated in Buckinghamshire and at Marlborough the previous year, were successfully recommended to electors as far apart as Berwick and Midhurst. Paul Methuen, ousted at Devizes, was strongly pressed to accept Somerset's patronage at Marlborough in the same winter, but preferred to bide his time until the next General Election.[125] When that Election came, leading Whig commoners gave few hostages to fortune. Methuen accepted Wharton's interest at Brackley. Grey Nevil stood in two places, Hampden in three, and Boscawen (it was said) in no fewer than five.[126] Matthew Ducie Moreton, narrowly defeated in Gloucestershire, was urged by his own constituents to "accept of a burgess place" instead, and exhorted by Wharton, who was soon at work negotiating such a place for him at Cricklade in Wiltshire, "to remember that yr. country wants yr. service".[127] But not the least remarkable feature of this Election was the way in which England (and even Scotland) was ransacked from north to south by the Whig hierarchs to uncover a suitable bolt-hole for Stanhope, whose luck at Cockermouth had finally run out. Sutherland, Derby, Andover, Salisbury, Poole, Dorchester, Guildford and even Southwark came at one time or another into the reckoning; but eventually it was left to the tiny borough of Wendover, at a by-election in 1714, to redeem the honour of an "England so degenerat as not to reguard so much vertiue & honor as Mr. Stanhop".[128]

Friction occasionally developed in parts of this elaborate Whig election mechanism. Stanhope's plight in 1713 ironically need never have arisen had not he (standing with Somerset's backing) and Lechmere (with Wharton's) found themselves in the unhappy position of competing against each other for votes at Cockermouth.[129] Three years earlier the two Whig patrons at Beeralston had quarrelled, with the result that Lord Cowper's brother Spencer, a valuable member of the party's debating-team in the two previous Parliaments, lost his seat and could not regain it until 1715.[130] Yet for a system which depended so much on voluntary co-operation, and on the willingness of a score of individual patrons (including self-willed grandees like Somerset) to subordinate personal whims and preferences to the common party good, its record of success was remarkably high. In common with so many of the forms of political activity and association we have been reviewing in this chapter, it represented the triumph of enthusiasm, energy and ingenuity over formidable practical difficulties. Like them it underlines what is surely one of the most impressive facts that recently-uncovered evidence has revealed about the parties of the age of Anne. However much their methods of organisation may have lacked the formal manifestations, the professionalism and some of the accepted techniques of a modern party machine, they were frequently flexible enough and imaginative enough, and at times rigorous enough for the purposes for which they were designed. Without them it would have been virtually impossible to transform into effective political action, either at Westminster or in the localities, many of the aspirations and the animosities of the tens of thousands of Britons who in these years called themselves either Whigs or Tories.

CHAPTER TEN

The Parties in Action:
Power-Groups and Pressure-Groups

ALTHOUGH there existed means of consultation and communication that were equal to the task, the marshalling of a party's full parliamentary strength, or even of something approaching it, was only rarely attempted in the early eighteenth century. Such an effort had to be reserved for occasions of exceptional importance; for in the nature of things, neither the impetus nor the degree of general organisation which the effort demanded could be sustained for any length of time. Given the heterogeneous composition of both the Whig and Tory parties, it is not really surprising that over protracted periods it was in relatively small and manageable units that the politicians of Anne's day found their most serviceable instruments of parliamentary organisation. Among these units two types predominated. In character they were radically different, yet each in its distinctive way made a notable contribution to the vitality of the parties in action. One type we must think of as the 'power-group', the other as the 'pressure-group'. The first was normally subject, directly or indirectly, to the control of the party leaders. The second sought rather to exert influence than to submit to it.

I

Within each party in the years from 1702 to 1714 there existed recognised associations of peers and members of Parliament which owed a particular allegiance to one leader or group of leaders in addition to their basic party allegiance. Contemporaries had no one word to describe such combinations; more often than not they referred to them simply as the "friends" of Lord X or of Mr. Y. Subsequently a useful label was found for them in the word 'connexion'. The connexion was by its very nature a vehicle of power politics. Not every such group may have come together in the first place with the principal object of pursuing profit and influence through official favour. Harley in the 1690's and Hanmer in 1713–14 both owed their original nucleus of followers to other incentives. But sooner or later almost all connexions became involved in the struggle for power. How many of these power-groups the Whig and Tory parties of this period contained, and roughly what strength each could deploy, are questions which have been considered already. But only by asking much more searching questions about the structure and working of connexions in practice is it possible to estimate the value of their contribution to party organisation.

The special cohesive quality which in ordinary circumstances distinguished political groupings of this kind from the parliamentary legions as a whole could be supplied by as many as four cementing agents. One was the close dependence of the nominee on his electoral patron. A second was a variation of the patron-client relationship, based on professional rather than electoral obligation, and involving particularly army and navy officers and lawyers. A third — more easily overlooked but unquestionably important — was the force of personal friendship. Finally, there was the element to which recent studies of the eighteenth century have given particular prominence, the links provided by kinship and marriage. To party leaders these distinctive relationships seemed to offer the best guarantee that a substantial body of their adherents would attend at Westminster on a given day to vote in a particular way. To what extent their expectations were justified can only be judged by trying to gauge the strength of the four bonds which brought and held together the members of connexions in Queen Anne's Parliaments.

Electoral obligation was the bond which contemporaries took most for granted. It was understandable that they should, for a member with any ambition for re-election would always think very hard before deliberately offending the patron to whom he owed his seat. Sir Jonathan Trelawney's right of nomination to a batch of borough seats in the west country — at East and West Looe, Plymouth, Liskeard, and at times elsewhere — gave to his following in the opening years of the century an impressive solidarity: Godolphin, at least, does not appear to have doubted it when in December 1701 he wrote urgently to the bishop "to muster up his squadron so as to have them here [in London] by the 30th".[1] The electoral magnate incurred some measure of responsibility for the parliamentary behaviour of his nominees, and his party colleagues expected him to take that responsibility seriously. Trelawney himself, for instance, took obvious pride after the 1702 Election in having sent to Westminster "11 members (whereof I wil answer for all but one, wch: I need not becaus the court must answer for him)".[2] When organising their two campaigns for the Speaker's Chair in 1705 and 1708 the Junto looked to the Duke of Newcastle to ensure them a bloc of safe votes from his nominees in the north of England. Somers's compelling request in 1705 "that yor Grace would *absolutely require* all yor freinds to be present the first day at the choice of the Sp." was dispatched more than two months before the event.³ Three years later, when the issue was less clear-cut, it was late October before Sunderland was able to write to Welbeck:

I am now desir'd by those Lords yr hble servants . . . to beg you would either speak or send to Mr. Jessop about this matter of the Speaker, to engage him for Sr Peter King, & that he would take what pains he can among the northern members, among whom he has a generall acquaintance, besides the weight in using yr name. They beg too that you would write upon this occasion to Mr. Monckton and Mr. Peyton.

Nine days later, when the Junto lords in return for the Queen's promise of two Cabinet posts had agreed to switch their support from King to the Court Whig nominee, Sir Richard Onslow, Newcastle was still out of town and had not been consulted. But Sunderland was confident that "if yr. Grace is of the same mind, & approves what they have done, you will please to lett yr friends of the house of Commons know it, in the manner you shall judge properest".⁴

Expectation, of course, was not always fulfilled. Even clients whose seats were absolutely at the mercy of a borough-owner occasionally played their patrons false. We saw earlier how Spencer Compton and Craven Peyton betrayed the trust of Cornwallis and Newcastle in the Parliament of 1708–10, and how John Dolben put party before patron when his loyalties were in conflict at the time of the Sacheverell affair.* Other nominees were guilty of negligence, if not of apostasy. Colonel Aubrie Porter, a Whig who sat for Bury St. Edmunds after December 1705 on the interest of his brother-in-law, Lord Hervey, failed to attend the House at all in the winter of 1709–10, offending in the process not only his noble relative (to whom he did not even bother to tender an excuse) but also his constituents.⁵ It is true that men like Cornwallis and Hervey were not great party figures. But even the great had on occasion to allow for the presence of a black sheep among their own flock of electoral nominees. Among Whigs elected directly on the interest of one of the Junto lords defaulters were rare indeed; but the division lists do reveal one notable case, the defection of Charles Godfrey, a member for Wharton's pocket borough of Wycombe, in the vote on the Commerce bill in June 1713.† Lord Rochester had a similar shock in 1705 when William

* See p. 312 above.

† Wharton's reaction was to sever Godfrey's 23-year connection with the borough at the next election in August.

Ettricke, who enjoyed the patronage of the Hydes at Christchurch, voted against Bromley in the election of a Speaker. In general, however, the strength of the link of electoral obligation only became suspect when the debt involved was less than total. Every House of Commons in Anne's reign contained dozens of members who had received some measure of assistance from the chief of one of the big power-groups — even perhaps the formal backing of his name as sponsor — yet whose election had been due at least as much, if not more, to the help of other interests including his own. It was in trying to forecast the behaviour of these marginal, semi-independent M.P.s that the computations of the party leaders became particularly liable to error; and the task was made no easier by the understandable tendency of electioneering enthusiasts like George Granville to exaggerate their influence and the number of their adherents with a view to raising their own political stock.[6]

Although it was not so common as the electoral tie, a professional relationship between a patron and his client could be an equally strong cohesive force in any connexion. The Earl of Orford's friends in the Admiralty, and his clients among the serving officers of the navy, were certainly among the loyallest of the Junto's supporters. Sir George Byng and Sir John Jennings were two such stalwarts — "the particular friends and servants of Lord Orford [Mainwaring once said of them] and raised by him, who has one merit really very great and unquestionable, to have always preferred the best officers in the service".[7] Reference was earlier made to the vital part played by military patronage in the solidarity of the Marlborough-Godolphin group. Argyll's influence among some of the Scottish members, especially after 1710, owed not a little to the same factor, while on a smaller scale the relationship between Earl Rivers and the Bradshaigh brothers is equally suggestive of the political possibilities of army patronage. Rivers's appointment of major Henry Bradshaigh as his *aide-de-camp* enabled him to command not only this officer's personal vote but that of Sir Roger Bradshaigh, his partner at Wigan from 1708 to 1713.[8] If the Whigs were the main beneficiaries from naval and military patronage, they also profited more than the Tories from associations based on the Inns of Court and the Bar. One reason why the Junto attracted to its standard so many able young lawyers, among them men (like Sir Thomas Parker, M.P. for Derby and Lord Chief Justice after 1710) who had neither constituency nor family links with the five lords, was clearly the unchallenged personal eminence of Lord Somers in the legal profession.

Personal friendships were the most intangible of the bonds which held together political connexions in the early eighteenth century, and on the whole they are the least well documented. Yet their importance is plainly manifest through all the limitations of the evidence. As we saw earlier with Walpole and Townshend, there were some leading politicians who had the gift of making close friends easily; and firm friendships such as theirs, annealed in the furnace of parliamentary controversy, could be more impervious to the alternating stresses of triumph and disaster than any other links in the party organisation of the day. There is a certain paradox in the fact that the less controversial figures among the heads of power-groups, like Godolphin and Newcastle, generally lacked the magnetism which attracted strong personal loyalties, while those who made countless public enemies, the St. Johns and the Whartons, also made large numbers of private friends. The paradox extends even to Harley, in spite of "that humour of his which [as those who did not share his intimacy were wont to observe] was never to deal clearly or openly, but always with reserve".[9] Although everyone recalls his famous quarrel with Bolingbroke in the closing years of Anne's life, it is seldom remarked how many of Harley's friends — Lansdowne, Poulet, Mansel, Dartmouth, Lewis — stayed faithful to his declining interest in 1714, despite every discouragement, and so helped him to preserve a large measure of his parliamentary influence to the end. Harley's friends, of course, were always reinforced by an ample stock of kinsmen and borough nominees. Even Walpole's personal influence depended to some extent on relationships of blood and marriage. But there was at least one party leader of the day whose interest in the House of Commons was based almost exclusively on personal friendship and political comradeship. This was William Bromley.[*] His case is the most salutary reminder we have that connection in the early eighteenth century should never be thought of purely in terms of kinship and specific obligation. To envisage it in these terms must inevitably lead to misunderstanding of the forces involved in the working of politics, and in Bromley's own case to a ludicrous undervaluation of the importance of a major political figure.[†]

This is not to say that friendship was totally immune from the strains imposed on it by conflicting principles or the pull of self-interest. Principle, for example, involved Archbishop Sharp in a number of sharp disagreements

[*] See pp. 277–8 above.

[†] This seems to explain why Dr. Walcott has so completely misjudged Bromley's stature in the House of Commons. It is quite remarkable to find in *English Politics in the Early Eighteenth Century* only a single reference to Bromley, and that merely to the effect that he 'voted consistently with the Finch connexion'. (p. 101, n. 1).

with his old patron and close friend, Lord Nottingham. Although both believed by 1702 in the justice and necessity of a bill against Occasional Conformity, Sharp refused to countenance the tacking of such a measure to a money bill when Nottingham pressed this device on his followers in the Commons in 1704. In November 1705 Sharp also dissociated himself from the mischievous motion inviting over the Electress Sophia, and for the most part he took an equally independent line over the Regency bill in the same session.[10] Many other Tory friendships were rudely jarred in the years 1704–6, years of great friction between those of moderate and those of extreme opinions in the party, and even between the responsible and the irresponsible elements on the Tory 'right'. Harley's Suffolk "rosebud", Sir Robert Davers, remained deaf to his friend's appeals to abandon his support of the tackers, while Sir Simon Harcourt's efforts to convert his own "old freinds" on the same issue only led (as he soon found) to his former influence with them being "entirely lost".[11] Dr. George Clarke's intimacy with Harcourt, which went back, as he tells us himself, as far as their Oxford days "in the year 1677, when we were appointed to speak verses in the theatre at the Act of that year",[12] was another of Harley's potential assets which we know to have proved unproductive in these years of exceptional stress inside the Tory party. Even the closest regard for his "very good friend" could not persuade Clarke to follow Harcourt and other Harleyites in opposing a High Church Speaker in 1705. There were times when on the Whig side, too, friendships were severely tested: in November 1708, for instance, Sir John Cropley noted that neither Spencer Compton nor Sir John Holland had by that time followed Walpole and Devonshire in making their peace with the Junto.* All the same, the effectiveness of party organisation over the reign as a whole would have been strikingly reduced without the stiffening regularly supplied within both parties and groups by relationships such as these: relationships that were freely entered into and were maintained through mutual respect and attraction and through common interests that were private as well as public.

In addition to the force of electoral, professional and purely personal attachments there was a further element in the composition of almost all the organised 'power-groups' in Anne's Parliaments. This was the cement supplied by blood-connections and marriage-connections. Its possibilities in the context of this period have been explored so exhaustively by the author of *English Politics in the Early Eighteenth Century* that extensive comment in the present study may appear superfluous. The case, however, is just the

---

* Chevening MSS.: Cropley to Stanhope, 27 Nov. Cf. pp. 231–4 above.

reverse. Dr. Walcott's work has made fresh consideration of this aspect of political organisation more necessary, not less.

Evidence that family relationships figured quite prominently in most connexions of any size is certainly not lacking. The groups which attached themselves to Godolphin and Marlborough, to Rochester, Nottingham and Seymour, to Harley and Anglesey, and to the Junto lords all contained a nucleus of relatives. At the heart of each was a knot of men whose political loyalty to their chief can be as convincingly established from letters, voting-records and electoral data as can their kinship from his family tree. Some of this evidence, as our survey of each party's composition has revealed, is plentiful. In other cases, as with the Junto, it has to be pieced together very carefully in the absence of large collections of correspondence. Obviously it is no coincidence that four of Wharton's kinsmen, quite apart from his brother Goodwin, sat at various times in Anne's reign for boroughs where the earl's influence was particularly strong;[13] or again that two members of the Cocks family, closely connected to Lord Somers by marriage, enjoyed his interest at Reigate and Droitwich. Neither can we ignore Arthur Mainwaring's forecast to the Duchess of Marlborough in the summer of 1709 that the consequence of passing over the Earl of Orford in the event of a new admiralty commission being issued would be that "the relations of Orford will be all dissatisfied, some of which are very considerable, such as the Duke of Devon and Lord Granby; and even the duke of Bedford will be more so every day, for he is quite recovered from the infatuation of Lord Granville, and is returned to the principles of his family . . .".[14]

When all the main political families are thoroughly investigated examples such as these, backed by similar types of evidence and confirmed by information on voting behaviour, can be multiplied many times over. The real problem, as far as party organisation is concerned, is to decide what conclusions we are entitled to draw from these cases, and more particularly how far these conclusions can be extended. For every one family connection, existing between two members of either House of Parliament, which can be *proved* to have involved a parallel political association, one can point to three or four about which nothing can be satisfactorily established beyond the bare fact of a blood or marriage tie. When our only information about such a relationship has been picked from the branches of a family tree, how much are we justified in deducing from it, even where there is a record of one or two parliamentary votes to indicate at least a common party allegiance? To this question Dr. Walcott has given a very definite answer. Unless there is concrete evidence to the contrary, or at the very least evidence with strongly negative implications, he is prepared to *assume* that a bond of kinship was matched by a corresponding political bond that was proof against all strains imposed upon it.[15]

This, however, is an assumption which can and must be challenged. And it will at once be apparent that if it can be proved to be unwarranted the consequences of its rejection will affect far wider aspects of the interpretation of Augustan politics than the specific field of organisation with which this chapter is primarily concerned. For it is largely because Walcott relies so heavily on genealogical evidence in determining the composition of party groups or factions that these connexions achieve such an impressive numerical strength and in consequence take on such immense importance in his whole thesis. In the 1701 House of Commons, for instance, he puts the total membership of the 'organized parliamentary groups' (excluding what he calls 'the Government interest') at 212. No fewer than 96 of these 212 M.P.s are allocated to one or other of the party groups apparently on no other basis than that of kinship: in only 116 cases is a more tangible link, such as clientage or electoral obligation, explicitly established.[16] But if the basic assumption on which these calculations are based is at fault, few of these groups can have been so tightly-knit or so rigid in their membership as we are encouraged to believe (a point of obvious relevance to their contribution to party organisation), while together they are likely to have absorbed a decidedly smaller proportion of the House's total complement than the figures suggest.

Let us look for a moment at some of the practical implications of the hypothesis that kinship (however remote) and political alliance can be regarded as synonymous, unless proved otherwise. We are asked, for instance, to accept that the member of Parliament for Middlesex, Warwick Lake, as the first cousin of Lord Nottingham's first wife (a consort who died, be it noted, well before the Revolution of 1688) must automatically have followed Nottingham through thick and thin during the seven years he spent in the Commons between 1698 and 1705; or that Lord Guilford was no less faithful to the Finch family interest on the strength of his being a second cousin of Nottingham's second wife. We are invited to allocate Sir John Pakington, a Worcestershire landowner of considerable wealth and prestige, to the 'Hyde-Seymour' group in Anne's reign, because his first wife, Frances, who had perished six years before the Queen's accession, had been a second cousin of Rochester's. Moreover assumptions of this kind, frail though they may appear, contrive to breed fresh suppositions more wraith-like still. Thus, on the basis of the tenuous Guilford-Nottingham relationship (and despite the bad blood which, Burnet assures us, existed between the Norths and the Finches), Dr. Walcott tacks on to the Nottingham connection not merely Guilford's son, Charles North, but his father-in-law, Lord Brooke, and his two brothers-in-law, Francis and Algernon Greville.[17]

In sober contrast to these highly speculative exercises, and many others like them, an array of incontestable facts can be set in the balance. They repeatedly warn us against taking for granted that genealogical and political links would normally coincide. They sometimes remind us that even where the two links did coincide they were none the less vulnerable to the shock of a genuine disagreement over policy or principle. There is no need to look further than some of the leading aristocratic families in Queen Anne's England to find striking examples of the closest blood relations pursuing widely divergent political courses. The Comptons, for instance, had a strong royalist-Tory tradition. The fourth Earl of Northampton, who was head of the family, his uncle Henry, Bishop of London, and his son Lord Compton all personified this tradition. But the earl's younger brother, Spencer Compton, was one of the most active Whigs in the House of Commons, the nominated member up to 1710 for a Junto-controlled pocket borough. Two other High Tory peers, Lord Denbigh and the ex-Catholic Earl of Cardigan, had similar crosses to bear. William Feilding, Denbigh's younger brother, preferred the sovereignty of "King Walpole" to that of "Tsar Seymskie",* and James Brudenell, Cardigan's son, stood for Chichester in 1713 as a Whig and supported the Whigs in the Commons in the next Parliament.[18] More enigmatic still was the Bertie family — Lord Abingdon, his uncle Robert, Marquess of Lindsey, and their shoal of close relatives. Nine Berties sat in the Lower House between 1702 and 1714 while a tenth stood unsuccessfully for Boston, and seven of them were Tories, mostly fervid High Churchmen. On the other hand, one (Lord Willoughby, M.P. for Lincolnshire) was a waverer with Whiggish inclinations, and two (Peregrine and Albemarle) were committed Whigs. The latter hardly took their cue from Lindsey; for although he veered away somewhat in Anne's reign from the Court Toryism he had favoured under King William, the vaguely Whiggish principles he professed after 1704 were only fitfully practised.[19] The zealous Whiggery of Peregrine and Albemarle Bertie, by contrast, made each *persona grata* with the Junto; indeed if family ties mattered at all in their case, the significant fact may have been that their mother was a Wharton, and not that their father was a Bertie.

Two further cases of political schism within important parliamentary

* See p. 231 above.

families will suffice to make our point. The Walpoles, as we have seen, were one of the two great pillars of the "honest interest" in Norfolk. In the 1714 Parliament the Whig cause was championed by Robert, his brother Horace, and his two brothers-in-law, Turner and Townshend. But there was a nigger in the family woodpile: uncle Horatio, a Tory placeman[20] whose consistent efforts to frustrate the efforts of his relatives in local elections had at length lost him his seat for the Walpole borough of Castle Rising in 1713. The record of the Finch family during Anne's closing years is also revealing. Nottingham, his cousin Winchilsea, and his brother Guernsey were all Tories by inclination and history. Yet in December 1711 the Finches came to the parting of the ways, when Nottingham declared against a Peace without Spain. "Dismal" and his heir, Lord Finch, chose one path; Winchilsea chose another that was diametrically opposite; while Guernsey and his son, between then and 1713, unhappily tried to follow an indeterminate track somewhere between the two.

The Comptons and Feildings, Brudenells and Berties, Finches and Walpoles all have one thing in common: because they were prominent families, their political disagreements are well known and easy to authenticate. In some of these cases, as well as in others that are almost equally well documented, Walcott frankly recognises exceptions to his rule. What is so hard to understand is why he makes virtually no allowance for similar divergencies in classifying scores of lesser politicians who have left little if any record of their activities. Why should it be supposed that such men were less likely than a Spencer Compton or a William Feilding to put conviction before clan? If the fragments of specific evidence that do survive are any guide, there is no reason whatever to assume a more predictable pattern of behaviour among the obscure than among the notable.

Referring in 1714 to the family of "Diamond" Pitt, three members of which sat in Anne's last House of Commons, that knowledgeable Tory John Ward remarked that "there is among them in the eldest son [Robert] the greatest instance I know of a son voting agst his father".[21] There is also the strange case of the Ashburnhams. The Tory holder of the barony died in 1710, to be followed shortly afterwards to the grave by his eldest son. The title had consequently passed by the time of Godolphin's fall in August to the second son, who was of such violently contrary opinions to those of his two predecessors that his reply to Lord Poulet, when the latter solicited his support for the new ministry against the next meeting of the House of Lords, must rank as one of the gems of the age: "may my estate sink under ground, my tenants be ruin'd, my family perish, & myself d—mn'd if ever I give you a vote". It is no wonder that the young Miss Clavering was enraptured. "Is this not a tight Whig?", she asked; "thank God his br[other] made room for him"![22] Sir Robert Pollock, who represented the county of Renfrew from 1710 to 1714, was described by the leader of the Scottish Jacobite members, George Lockhart, as "my near kinsman and personall friend". Yet Lockhart also records, without a hint of surprise or rancour, that Pollock was "a true staunch Whig".[23] Lockhart himself, by a delicious irony, was the nephew of Wharton, "with whom [he tells us] . . . I liv'd in good terms, notwithstanding our being of different principles".[24] Nobody, one imagines, has ever dreamt of describing Lockhart as a Junto follower. But what is the genealogist-historian to make of Sir Charles Kemys, who sat in only one Parliament in Anne's reign and whose name appears in no division-list before 1716? He, too, was a nephew of Wharton; but he was also a first-cousin of Mansel. Was he a Junto man or was he a Harleyite? Fortunately the awful dilemma is resolved by the survival of a letter of the Duke of Beaufort's which leaves no room for doubt. It was as *his* nominee that Kemys stood and was elected for Monmouthshire in 1713.[25] The answer to our problem, in fact, is that Kemys, like Lockhart, was a Jacobite!

The politicians of Anne's day were normally rather more ready to respond to the calls of kinship in elections than inside the walls of Parliament. John Bridgeman's Whiggery did not prevent him from judiciously dividing his electoral interest in Salop between his two brothers-in-law, the Whig Richard Corbet and the Tory Robert Lloyd, when they both stood for the county; and Lord Fermanagh admitted in 1712 that one of his reasons for not contesting the borough of Buckingham against the Whigs at the previous election was "that Sir Richd Temple and Alex Denton were the late Members and both my kinsmn., and that I thought it not handsome to indeavour to josle either of them out".[26] A more striking case was that of Thomas Medlicott, M.P. for Westminster, whose interest at Milborne Port in Somerset was put at the disposal of his brother James, though the two men espoused different parties in the House of Commons. Yet significantly Horatio Walpole found this rather shocking: ". . . had I a corporation intrest to elect a member", he protested, "I would not chuse my bro[r] if he was a Whig, wch he has don, even att the most criticall junture".[27] Contests were frequently too close, and the principles at stake in them too vital, to allow co-operation between relatives of opposite convictions even at local level. In Lincolnshire in 1705 the Marquess of Granby found that "Lord Kingston, tho related to one or both the old ons, gives his interest against them, they being tackers". Sir Thomas Hanmer found his activities in

Suffolk, both in county elections and in the borough of Thetford, regularly in conflict with those of his stepson, the Duke of Grafton; and when Tom Coke fell foul of his Tory neighbours in Derbyshire in 1710, after deserting "the Church interest" in Sacheverell's impeachment, no one was more zealous in hounding him from his county seat to a Cornish refuge at Grampound than his own brother-in-law, Godfrey Clarke, who was elected in his stead.[28]

There is therefore only one safe working rule for the student of early-eighteenth-century politics when trying to assess in any detail the importance of kinship: he should never accept it as evidence of a close political association unless there is reasonable confirmation from other sources. This is not to question the fact that the presence in the same Parliament of so many inter-related members and peers was of great importance to the working of politics. Without the network of ties which this ensured, the contribution which connexion was able to make to party organisation in the age of Anne would have been far less valuable. But to estimate the value of this contribution in precise, quantitative terms becomes quite impossible, once one accepts that kinship was so variable, so unpredictable a factor. One simply cannot say *how many* party men on either side, even on paper, were capable of being mobilised and organised through the medium of connections. It is generally possible, by correlating what is known about the family relationships of the party magnates with information on their electoral interests and with the records of division-lists, to identify the *nucleus* of every major power-group with some confidence. But the data on elections is too incomplete, and, above all, the division-lists are far too few, to go much further than this without the essential confirmation which only a major collection of correspondence can provide; and all too rarely are such collections encountered where they would be most valuable. In two cases only — those of the Harleyites and the followers of Marlborough and Godolphin — can the full strength of a group be fairly accurately documented in this way.*

With these exceptions, or unless there is a reliable contemporary estimate on which to base a calculation (a freakish contingency), it becomes a hazardous and rather futile exercise to attempt an exact assessment of the membership of any of the big power-groups in any Parliament of Anne's reign. To state, as Dr. Walcott does, that Nottingham had 45 followers in the House of Commons in the session of 1702–3 and that the 'Hyde-Seymour' combination had 66[29] is to assert what cannot conceivably be

---

* One could add the Duke of Newcastle's following to these two, but it was built, of course, on a much smaller scale.

proved on the basis of the evidence at present available. Since the part played by genealogical data alone in the author's allocation of members to these two groups is so very considerable, the only certainty about both totals is that they are too high. Most probably they are a great deal too high; for nearly all the indications are that, apart from the adherents of the Junto and the members who were arrayed behind Harley after 1710, the organised power-groups of this period were fairly small in size.[30] Indeed it would be hard to reconcile any other conclusion with the indisputable fact that groups of this kind (as we saw at the very outset of this study) figure so fleetingly and inconspicuously in the political vocabulary of the day.

In one further respect the contribution which connexion could make to party organisation was limited. In normal circumstances the solidarity of these groups was a great asset to party leaders. But under special stress this solidarity could crumble. The control of a party chieftain over his personal followers could be temporarily vitiated by exceptional parliamentary circumstances: by such circumstances as the Tack, which seriously split "Lord Rochester's friends" in 1704, or (on a less serious level) the proposed French claret bill, which disturbed the unanimity both of the Junto Whigs and the Walpoleans in the session of 1708–9. "I am told this transaction in the House of Commons has in some measure resembled a Civill War, & sett brother agst brother", wrote George Clarke of the bill to sanction the import of French wine; "Bridges agst Ld William [Powlet], Pulteney against Turner".[31] Cohesion was also a prey to the personal eccentricities of individual members of a group, especially of those who were not susceptible to the moral or practical sanctions involved in clientage: even the Junto Whigs in the House of Commons, whose standards of discipline were unequalled, suffered occasionally from the defections of quixotic spirits like Jekyll and Hampden.[32] Most serious of all was the permanent damage to the unity of a group which could be inflicted by the political aberrations of its leader. This lesson was driven home in 1713–14 when the Harleyites split irretrievably into two factions, the seceders having lost confidence either in the policies their leader insisted on pursuing or in his ability to keep the Queen's favour. But the most dramatic demonstration by far of the ultimate frailty of the power of connection was provided by the aftermath of Nottingham's great apostasy in December 1711. If politics in the age of Anne had really worked as Walcott would have us believe, we would expect to find the whole of Nottingham's faction in the House of Commons and the earl's many friends in the House of Lords obediently following his example in opposing the peace policy of the Oxford ministry. Yet on the first day of his revolt,

7 December, only one M.P. (his son and heir) and not a single peer was prepared to follow him.[33] A handful drifted over to him later in the session, and more still in 1713;[34] but it is perfectly plain that they did so only when convinced (as they had not been in December 1711) that real questions of conscience and principle with which they could sympathise were at stake in their leader's desertion of the Court.

The most revealing thing about the events of December 1711, however, is not the behaviour of the Nottinghamites but the reaction of other Tories to it. This was one of some relief, naturally, but of no great surprise. It was Nottingham's action which caused shock and astonishment, not the action of his followers. No connexion was expected to stand up to a blow as cruel and unexpected as this. The moral of this whole incident and of the others we have noticed seems fairly obvious. So long as a group of power-politicians, whether Tory or Whig, was satisfied that its own leader or leaders were pursuing ends consistent with party principles or were advocating policies which offended few individual convictions, its cohesion could for the most part be preserved; and it could then play its part, along with other groups in the same party, in ensuring disciplined parliamentary action. But with many politicians of this period personal obligation or attachment, in the final reckoning, would take second place to overriding party loyalty or to the scruples of the individual conscience; and this was a truth which no one concerned with the problems of political organisation at the centre of affairs could afford to ignore.

II

The connection was not the sole form of organisation familiar to the party men of 1702–14 in which the independent parliamentary unit, with a recognised membership and character, was the distinctive feature. Within each of the two great parties at various stages of Anne's reign politicians of like mind entered into close association with each other for the achievement of certain specific policies, and not simply to enhance their bargaining power in the competition for favour and office. There thus came into being a series of 'pressure-groups' of one kind or another, varying considerably in the extent, the formality and the permanence of their organisation, but all committed to the defence of certain special interests and ideals, or to the realisation of certain definite and often limited aims — if necessary in the teeth of resistance from the leaders of their own party.

There were occasions when party figures of great importance, including office-holders, played the dominant part in creating and preserving such associations, with ordinary backbenchers merely supplying the bulk of their voting power. The most striking example of such a development in the early years of the reign was the emergence and spectacular (if brief) career of the Tackers. The 134 members who voted in the Commons for the tack of the Occasional Conformity bill on 28 November 1704 included a whole galaxy of High Tory stars: Seymour, Bromley, Hanmer and Gwyn; Freeman, Byerley, Annesley and Pakington. Understandably the group's initial organisation was of a high order; it was "partly by surprise" (as Harley realised) as well as by quality of leadership and numerical strength that they hoped to carry the day; and in any case, they were looking to the future as well as to the present — trusting, whether their immediate objective succeeded or failed, to "lay the foundation of a considerable opposition during the whole course of the Queen's reign . . .".[35] In the months that followed their act of defiance this band of zealots retained their common identity to a marked degree, undiscouraged by the heavy defeat of their original policy, and contrived to keep up their pressure on Godolphin's administration. Their successes were few — distressingly few to their many sympathisers in the country;[36] yet the very fact that in the 1705 elections the Tackers were singled out as the special target of both Whig and government forces illustrates how much they were feared by their opponents, and High Tory newswriters like Dyer recorded their fortunes at the polls with a devoted fervour and reverence which seemed to place them on a plane not far below the Holy Apostles and Martyrs. Moreover the sense of solidarity which still permeated the group during the course of the General Election, and even in the early months of the next Parliament,[37] to which 89 of its members were re-elected, argues the successful maintenance of a fairly high degree of organisation right through the session of 1704–5. Unfortunately hardly any specific evidence appears to have survived as to the form which this organisation took. We do not know for certain that the Tackers held regular meetings to plan tactics between the end of November 1704 and March 1705; probably they did, but there are no clues as to where or how frequently they met, nor as to the steps they took to ensure a good attendance of the faithful on important occasions.

Information is very nearly as sparse on the organisation of the two rival pressure-groups, the Hanoverian Tories and the Jacobites, which developed inside the Tory party in the last Parliament of the reign. Of the Hanoverian Tories something has been said in a previous chapter. Their nucleus was formed from a combination of two or even three separate personal connections, the one led by Hanmer and the other by Anglesey in alliance with the Earl of Abingdon; and it was to this fact that the group probably owed such coherence as it managed to achieve. Its distinctly erratic parliamentary course during the 1714 session suggests, however, that whatever machinery existed to co-ordinate the policy of the two "squadrons", and to associate with them the many independent "Whimsical" backbenchers who shared their broad objectives but had no concrete ties with any of the three leaders, was not strikingly efficient. The opposing Jacobite group, by contrast, having no major connexion to depend on, formed in 1714 a "club" which appears to have met from time to time to discuss policy. The origins of the club are obscure. Possibly it owed its birth to a big meeting of Jacobite M.P.s held shortly after the unpalatable election of Sir Thomas Hanmer to the Speaker's chair in February. This was a meeting which ended with the passing of a resolution that "no more time shoud be lost in accomplishing the Kings restauration, at least in having matters put on such a footing, as might naturally introduce and pave the way for it, when the Queen died", and which deputed Sir John Pakington and Lockhart of Carnwath to approach Secretary Bolingbroke for his support.[38] Over 80 Tories are said to have attended one meeting of the Jacobite club during May, at which Pakington unsuccessfully proposed that they should move in the House of Commons to open "the black box", the receptacle containing the names of the members of the Regency Council nominated by the Electress Sophia to take over the interim administration after Anne's death.[39] But it was left to an action-group of roughly half this number to achieve for a short while in the following month a really "close concert, solemnly engaging to take and follow joint measures", more particularly through the deliberate obstruction of financial business in the hope of forcing the ministry to a positive declaration in favour of the Pretender. Attempts by Bolingbroke to win over two of their leaders were met with the cool response that they were "engag'd to prosecute joint measures with a sett of gentlemen" whom they "neither cou'd nor wou'd desert"; and it was only after a majority of the group had formally debated the Secretary of State's proposition that its opposition to the ministry was at length abandoned.[40]

During their first three years at Westminster, from 1707 to 1710, there were few signs that the 64 Scots in Parliament,* or even a section of them,

---

* As well as the 45 commoners and 16 peers who sat by right of the Treaty of Union, Argyll and (from 1709 to 1711) Queensberry enjoyed hereditary seats, and James Johnson sat for the English borough of Ilchester. In the next Parliament (1710–13) 2 more Scotsmen were elected for English boroughs, Lord Dupplin (Fowey) and Wm. Kerr (Berwick).

would ever be able to sink their private differences for long enough to form a pressure-group capable of advancing interests common to them all. The embarrassment caused to the government by their opposition to the Treasons bill in 1709 had indicated the possibilities of a situation in which the Scottish representatives were for the most part united* and were able to enter into an *ad hoc* alliance with whichever English party was in opposition at the time. But the lesson was only slowly absorbed. A move early in 1711, for instance, to arrange weekly dinners for the sixteen peers at which parliamentary tactics could be concerted had merely borne out the sceptical forecast of Balmerino, who at the outset had professed himself "convinc'd we will all of us agree to dine very well (at half a guinea the head beside our wine), and never mind or agree in any thing else".[41] It is true that one new development of some significance did take place in the winter of 1710–11. Five prominent Tory commoners from north of the border, headed by the Lord Lyon (Sir Alexander Erskine) and George Lockhart,† and acting in close concert, made a bid for the support of the bulk of the Scottish contingent in the Lower House over the heads of its natural leaders among the representative peers, whom they believed to be too servile to the Court and too self-interested. For a while, Lockhart recorded, "we succeeded so well therin, that our opinions were askt and follow'd in most matters relating to Scotland; and the Ministry applyd directly to us in what they expected or desir'd from us and our countrymen . . .".[42] During this session, however, neither of the two major projects with which the group became concerned — the marshalling of support behind the Reverend James Greenshields's appeal to the House of Lords[43] and a proposed bill for the toleration of episcopacy in Scotland — was able, for obvious reasons, to attract the support of the Presbyterian minority in the Commons; and this fact, together with the understandably lukewarm reactions of most Scottish peers towards the group, limited its effectiveness.[44]

It was not until the interests of their own order were directly challenged that "the sixteen" were able to attain some measure of corporate identity independent alike of party and Court. The necessary goad was applied on 20 December 1711, when the House of Lords rejected the Duke of Hamilton's right to sit in Parliament by virtue of his new British title of Duke of

---

* "On the side of the dyeing laws of Scotland", wrote Bishop Nicolson, after hearing one of the debates on the bill, "appear'd Sr David Dalrymple, Mr. Baillie, Mr. Carnegie. Mr. Dugal Steward, Mr. Cockburn . . ." — a representative cross-section of the main parties and interests among the Scots commoners. Diary (1709–10), 5 Apr.

† The other 3 were John Carnegie, James Murray and Sir Alexander Cumming *Lockhart Papers*, i, 338.

Brandon. The last days of December saw a number of urgently-convened meetings of the incensed Scottish peers in London, at one of which, at least, the Squadrone Duke of Roxburgh attended (though he was not himself a member of Parliament) to demonstrate the solidarity of all parties on an issue which affected the prospects or future aspirations of scores of Scottish landed families. The immediate outcome of these meetings was a conference with the commoners and the presentation of a joint memorial to the Queen on New Year's Day by six peers and four commoners.[45] There was nothing that could be done in the Lower House to retrieve the situation, but the peers continued with their meetings daily for much of January; and even after Annandale and Balmerino had withdrawn from these "secret committees", the remnant struggled to preserve a united front in the hope of prising satisfactory terms out of either the ministry or the Whigs.[46] They even organised an intermittent boycott of the Lords between the 7th and 26th of February to try to increase their bargaining power. But once this had ended in rather abject failure their solidarity crumbled, and by mid-March George Baillie was deploring that "the affair of the Scots peers [was] quite a sleep".[47]

A more serious proposition was the Scottish reaction at Westminster to the attempt of Oxford's ministry to impose a malt duty on Scotland in the summer of 1713. This time the initiative was taken in the Commons, with Squadrone, Presbyterian and Episcopal Tory members "uniting cordially" not only in voting against the measure itself at its various stages, but also (as Bolingbroke sourly observed) in joining with the English Whigs "to a man" in several other divisions. At the same time the commoners called on Lord Balmerino to arrange a council of war with the sixteen peers "at a great tavern" on 12 May; and this proved to be the first of a series of joint conferences which eventually produced on the 26th the dramatic decision to move for a bill to dissolve the Union. "Every body knew the divisions in England", Lockhart told them, "and if matters were right manag'd, it was not improbable that some considerable party might take us by the hand and carry our business thorough". In this hope negotiations were undertaken with the Junto and its allies, and it was not until the attack on the Union had been delivered and repulsed on 1 June and a final attempt to block the Malt bill had narrowly failed in the Lords a week later that the most formidable of the Scottish pressure-groups of the years 1707–14 ran out of steam.[48]

Some of the most impressive parliamentary campaigns of Anne's reign which had specific policy objectives in view were conducted by independent party groups consisting almost entirely of backbenchers. Such a group were the "Whimsical Whigs", a body of Whigs who skilfully exploited the even balance of forces in the House of Commons after the 1705 Election to further a broadly Country programme. Neither their leader, Peter King, nor two of the three men on whom initially they most relied for support, Sir Richard Onslow and Robert Eyres, had a place in the ministry or for that matter in the close confidence of the Junto.* Yet in the sessions of 1705–6 and 1707–8 King and his friends achieved a temporary influence in Parliament out of all proportion to their numbers and political stature. They owed it in large part to careful planning of tactics and, at the height of their activity, to the achievement of a measure of discipline that was truly surprising in members whose natural inclinations were antipathetic to discipline. There had been a foretaste of what was to come for the Court and Whig leaders in the closing weeks of the previous Parliament, sufficient to convince them by November 1705 that it was worth their while to try to conciliate King or at least appeal to his sense of party loyalty.[49] But it was the epic battle for the "self-denying clause" of the Regency bill in January and February 1706 which saw the full development of the Country Whigs as an organised pressure-group. At one stage over 50 strong, the "Whimsical Whigs" preserved their strength and cohesion virtually intact until just before the last crucial shots of the battle were fired; and even after the defection to the ministry of a splinter-group headed by Robert Eyres, and the consequent success of the Court in inserting their own compromise place clause in the bill,† Sir John Cropley was still able to write with conscious pride: "our squadron is the most formidable now in the House (that is excepting the 2 great ones of Tory & Court) consisting of about 30 sufficient to turn the scale; and, for all we lost the day, 'tis visible what our power is by the court & by the submision made to us so conqured".[50]

After a lull in their activity in the winter of 1706–7, when in the aftermath of Ramillies and Turin all Whig hands were bent to the necessary work of prosecuting the war and completing the Union with Scotland, the Country Whigs resumed their organised efforts as an independent unit in December 1707. By joining sometimes with the Tories and sometimes with the Junto Whigs in a series of attacks on ministerial policy, they contributed almost as much as the more numerous followings of the power-politicians to

---

* Stanhope, King's other ally of real importance in 1705–6, was an army officer. For the identification of Onslow, Eyres and Stanhope with this group, Chevening MSS.: Cropley to Stanhope, St. Giles's, 28 July [1705]; P.R.O. 30/24/20/112–4: Stanhope to Cropley, 17, 24 Feb. 1706; Cropley to Shaftesbury, end. "Feb 1705–6".

† See p. 133 above.

the acute discomfiture of the Godolphin administration in the first half of this eventful session. In December they backed the demand for an enquiry into Admiralty negligence, and used their votes to defeat a Court move to preserve heritable jurisdictions in Scotland. In January they joined with the Tories to inflict a surprise defeat on the government's Recruiting bill, and immediately afterwards played a big part in the final success in the Commons of the bill abolishing the Edinburgh Privy Council.[51] King and his friends were also prominent among the ministry's critics in the first two debates on the battle of Almanza on 29 January and 3 February; but although most of the group's well-drilled manoeuvres during this winter could be broadly justified as part of a general policy of laying bare official mismanagement and curbing the undue influence of the Crown and its ministers, the Almanza enquiry, it was soon realised, had more dangerous and disturbing implications. Before the third and decisive debate took place most of King's disciples, even his chief ally, Sir Richard Onslow, had recoiled from the possibility that the enquiry might get out of hand — that it might even end by opening the door for the Tories to return to office; and when on 24 February "Mr King voted for the question [censuring the ministry] but did not speak to it", all but two of his followers left him in the lurch.[52] The discipline of the "Whimsical Whigs" was broken.

By that time former champions like Stanhope, Eyres and Sir John Cropley had already enlisted with the "Treasurer's Whigs", and the final disappearance of the group as an effective parliamentary force became inevitable when its last leader of outstanding capacity, Peter King, was reconciled to the Junto in the summer and autumn of 1708. The success of all backbench pressure-groups depended in no small measure on the generalship of a few able and active career-politicians who, either from choice or necessity, operated outside the framework of the main organised connexions; and the "Whimsical Whigs" were especially vulnerable in this respect. It was the desertion of Eyres, "to his eternal infamy", and the enforced departure of Stanhope for Spain at a critical stage of the Regency bill, that probably proved decisive in the loss of the self-denying clause in 1706.[53] And Arthur Mainwaring proved quite correct in the spring of 1708 when he prophesied that if King "were engag'd, the Whymsical Whigs, as they call em, wou'd have no head to govern them, & having generally very indifferent ones of their own, cou'd do no great mischief".[54]

The failure of the Tory March Club to make any spectacular impact on Parliament in the spring and summer of 1712 can very largely be traced to the mediocrity of its leadership. This was an association of highflyers who broke away from the October Club in March 1712, committed to a pro-Hanoverian, anti-French and Country platform. The new club learned a good deal from its parent body about the lessons of backbench organisation. It met weekly, every Monday night, to deliberate on policy and tactics, and as its membership rose rapidly from an original 35 to a strength of well over 50 its supporters hoped for much from it, and the Court viewed it at the start with understandable apprehension. Yet although the March men scored a few early successes, inflicting in April a personal defeat on a prominent minister, Arthur Moore, in a case of privilege, and even successfully blocking a proposed tack of the Land Grants bill to a money bill early in May,[55] they accomplished little or nothing through their original organisation which had any direct influence either on the government's foreign policy or its succession policy. A group with the ambitious objectives of the March Club needed inspiration and debating talent that were beyond the resources of its nominal leader, George Pitt, and of independent county members of the stature of Charles Cholmondeley and Richard Shuttleworth, who filled its upper echelon.*

Far more impressive had been the record of the October Club in the previous session. In 1711, before it lost its pristine vigour and many of its first recruits, the October Club became unquestionably the largest and the most powerful of all the parliamentary pressure-groups to develop within either party in the years before 1715. Its members were pledged at this time to force partisan Tory policies on the Harley administration and to institute an anti-Whig vendetta, and they were fully prepared to use fair means or foul to attain these ends, including the systematic obstruction of supply and ways and means. The desperate anxiety which the Octobrists caused for at least three months after the beginning of February 1711, not only in government circles but in the minds of many responsible Tories outside the government, testifies more vividly than any other political passage in Anne's reign to the enormous potential power of the independent backbencher, when that power was properly harnessed and directed.

Some of the October Club's original leaders, surprisingly enough, were relatively inexperienced: Henry Campion, Charles Eversfield and Sir Simeon Stewart, three of its most prominent spokesmen in that tumultuous February when the club first exploded into parliamentary life, were all relatively unknown quantities in the House of Commons. The bulk of the club's original members, moreover, were decidedly raw: for many of them

---

* The parliamentary activities and policies of the March Club will be examined at greater depth in my detailed study of politics in the years 1710–14.

this session was their first experience of Parliament.[56] Yet these apparent disadvantages were more than cancelled out by three great assets. The first was sheer weight of numbers. The club's membership stood at 70 or 80 at the beginning of February,[57] rose to well over 100 by the end of that month, and was in the region of 150 by April. The second of its assets was the clockwork regularity of its meetings. Although at first the members met almost nightly, the custom was quickly established of holding meetings every Wednesday evening right through the session, usually at the Bell Tavern in King Street, Westminster.[58] The venue made it possible to strike a nice balance between social conviviality, calculated to retain the interest of "old beer-drinkers, as Sr Thos. Willoughby etc",[59] and political debate, in which democratic procedure and the dictation of policy by the majority vote gave even the rawest and most inarticulate member an unusual sense of participation.* But the quality which most distinguished the October Club from all other comparable groups was the fiery, crusading zeal which inspired so much of its parliamentary activity in the early months of its life — activity which every October man could identify with fundamental Tory principles and prejudices even when it was frankly obstructive or downright piratical. Although some of the club's sharpest teeth had been drawn by May 1711, with the reconciliation of some of its older and weightier members with the Court,[60] it remained dangerous to the very end of the session. This it demonstrated during the framing of the Commons' Address to the Queen, presented on 1 June, which lashed with impartiality both the preceding and the present administration; the former for its alleged abuses and mismanagements, the latter for its equivocation and its favour towards the Whig enemies of the Church and country interest.

It was no coincidence that one of Lord Oxford's chief concerns in the anxious days before the peace storm broke about his ears in December 1711 was to come to some agreement with the leaders of the October Club. The bargain which he struck did more than ensure their general support for his ministry for the rest of that session; it marked the beginning of a progressive decline of the club as a pressure-group. Not that it lost all its independent significance in the House of Commons, even after the break-away of the

* "What has once been carried by the majority of their club", Peter Wentworth noticed on 20 Feb., "they will stand to to a man in the house" (*Wentworth Papers*, p. 180). Swift (*Prose Works*, viii, ed. Davis and Ehrenpreis, 125) and George Lockhart (*Lockhart Papers*, i, 324) also comment on the procedure of the club. As a leading light himself, Lockhart's evidence that it became established that "the minority should yeild to the majority" is unimpeachable.

March men in 1712. Its organisation remained potentially formidable. In April 1712, for example, on the occasion of its only major revolt against the government this session, its leaders were said to "solicit ever[y] member in the House" on behalf of their plan to tack the Land Grants bill to the Lottery bill.[61] It was capable of isolated acts of rebellion in the Commons as late as 1713,[62] and as a club remained in existence for another three years at least thereafter. Yet its days of real power were over by the end of 1711. Only then did it fully justify l'Hermitage's memorable description of it as "le troisième parti".[63] Nevertheless, through the dramatic impact which it made on the House of Commons between February and April 1711 the October Club wrote a chapter all its own in the political history of the early eighteenth century. By any standards it was a remarkable experiment in political organisation, outstanding even in a period as fertile as the age of Anne in producing expedients to recruit and discipline the potent forces of party.

CHAPTER ELEVEN

The Court and the Parties
in the House of Commons

THE pattern of politics revealed in the past four chapters has been the familiar pattern of conflict: conflict in which the vast majority of politicians were deeply involved as men committed to one great party or the other, many in disciplined units, more still as independent combatants, a few as mercenaries; conflict in which the organised engagement was more common than the haphazard skirmish; conflict which was for the most part between the parties but at times within them. There were, however, a handful of politicians between 1702 and 1714, foremost among them being the men we have called the Managers, whose main concern, like that of the Queen herself, was not to further conflict but to promote harmony. At the very least they hoped to keep conflict so far within bounds that the essential business of government in these years — the raising of money, the waging of war and the making of peace — could be carried through without serious obstruction. The part which this tiny but active minority played in the working of politics was at all times a central one; but it naturally became of cardinal importance whenever party hostilities encroached (as frequently they did) on the territory occupied by the executive power. If we are to understand it we must remind outselves of one basic fact about the political system of Anne's day which preoccupation with the parties may easily have obscured. Although this system was so obviously the product of an acutely divided society, it was no less the product of an uneasily balanced constitution.

By the first decade of the eighteenth century two protracted foreign wars and the hardening of party divisions in Parliament had combined to produce a constitutional situation which it is certain the revolutionaries of 1688–9 never envisaged. Essentially it was an anomalous situation. Although in the years 1702–14 government could only be carried on in practice with the full co-operation of the legislature, and this necessitated keeping Parliament in session for an average of five months in every year, the logical implications of 'parliamentary government' were far from being accepted or even understood. It remained the Queen's undoubted prerogative to appoint, retain and dismiss ministers at her own pleasure, and not at the whim of whichever party the triennial seesaw had temporarily placed in the ascendant; and since Anne, acting at times on her own initiative and at times at the prompting of her advisers, consistently tried to exercise this power, the party politicians were forced to pay more than mere lip-service to the idea of "the Queen's government". And yet with every year that passed it became more evident to them that the crucial issues in dispute between Whig and Tory could only be decisively settled if one side or the other could establish positive control over official policy as well as over the votes of the House of Commons. It was out of this situation that there developed the most complex and the most distinctive feature of the working of politics in the reign of Anne: the relationship between, on the one hand, the two parties whose rivalry distracted the legislature, and on the other, a government which they sought to possess but which resolutely resisted possession.

The key figures in this relationship were the Managers: Marlborough, for a brief period Shrewsbury, but above all Godolphin and Harley, who for eight years and four years respectively controlled the Treasury. As the natural intermediaries between the Queen, over whose government they presided, and the party men who held sway in Parliament, Godolphin and Harley shouldered the main responsibility for ensuring a harmonious working partnership between the executive and the legislature. Already hindered more than helped by the constitutional legacy of the Revolution, their mission was made the more difficult because neither Godolphin in the first few years of the reign nor Harley at any time was able to stand wholly aloof from party associations. Harley's position, in particular, was ambivalent. After his break with the duumvirate in February 1708 he was under persistent pressure from some of his nearest disciples to put himself at the head of "the gentlemen of the Church of England", and almost to the end of his ministry in 1714 this pressure was maintained.[1] Nevertheless he resisted it. Seeing himself first and foremost as the servant of the Crown, he felt obliged, like Godolphin and Marlborough before him, to walk the narrow tightrope between the parties; he wobbled from time to time in the Tory direction, but never quite lost his balance. After the General Election of 1710 he occupied a unique position in Parliament, a position basically the same as that held by Godolphin and Marlborough in the previous eight years and essentially distinct from that of the party leaders. As well as being at the head of his own tightly-knit personal connection, he was the natural focal point of those forces in both houses of Parliament whose primary allegiance was to the Court rather than to either party. He managed not only the business of the Crown in Parliament but also all those supporters of the Crown who formed what can most accurately be described as the 'Court interest' or 'government interest'.

Since the relationship between the government of Queen Anne and the Whig and Tory parties hinges so much on the special rôle of the 'Court interest' both in the House of Commons and in the House of Lords, it can easily be misjudged without a clear misunderstanding of what this term implies; and here contemporary usage, for once, can be seriously misleading. Contemporaries were too apt to use the words "Court" and "Ministry" as though they were synonymous, in the process confusing each other almost as much as they have confused historians. In these final chapters it becomes imperative to differentiate between these two terms, for whereas "the Court" is *sui generis* in the structure of early-eighteenth-century politics, "the Ministry" represents a phenomenon altogether less distinctive.

The ministries of Queen Anne were heterogeneous bodies. Even at periods when most offices of the first rank were filled by men of similar political persuasions, strong and conflicting party loyalties were often the rule among junior ministers and dozens of minor placemen, who in consequence by no means always acted as a unit in Parliament. Their jars and divisions were capable of afflicting even the tenderest point in any government's programme, the voting of revenue. "I find by the stopping of the money bill today", the Lord Treasurer told the Speaker in January 1703, "the Queen's servants in both Houses are vying who shall bee maddest".[2] On 29 January 1708, when three Tory ministers in the Commons were in great difficulties, trying to defend the ministry's record in Spain against a sudden onslaught from the back benches, the Whig Solicitor-General felt under no obligation to support them; he even found time to leave the House at the height of a long and furious debate to convey the news of their discomfiture to the Junto leaders, who were dining at his brother's house (and possibly to receive their directions on how he and other Junto Whigs, whether in office or not, should vote at the end of the debate).* If junior ministers could at times oppose or desert each other where essential government business or the government's reputation were at stake, they were hardly likely to close ranks when "party matters" were debated. Controversial legislation and disputed election cases,

---

* Nicolson's MS. diary, 29 Jan. 1708. The Solicitor-General was Sir James Montagu, Halifax's brother.

for instance, frequently threw the lower echelons of the administration into total disarray. Senior ministers were less prone to air their dissensions in public — some actually felt that they had a positive duty not to do so[3] — but even the members of the Queen's Cabinet Council sometimes carried their conciliar disagreement on to the floor of the two Houses of Parliament. In December 1702, in spite of "great professions" to the contrary, the High Tory Sir Edward Seymour, Comptroller of the Household and the leading Cabinet minister in the Commons, associated himself with the opposition there to Anne's proposed grant of £5000 per annum to Marlborough and his heirs — an opposition that was led by Seymour's friend, Sir Christopher Musgrave.[4] In March 1704 the Master of the Horse, Somerset, so openly attacked his fellow Cabinet-councillor, Lord Nottingham, during the Lords' enquiries into the so-called "Scotch Plot" that Nottingham protested to the Queen "that the keeping the Duke of Somerset in the Cabinet Council after what had past would render the Government contemptible".[5] And four years later a correspondent of Lord Manchester thought it "remarkable" that, while most members of the Cabinet were striving in the Upper House for the continuance of the Scottish Privy Council, "Lord Sunderland [Secretary of State for the South and Marlborough's son-in-law] stuck to Lord Somers and Halifax, and the party that opposed it".[6]

The "Ministry", then, and on occasion even the Cabinet, might present a disunited front in Parliament. But not so the "Court", as represented by the Queen's Managers and the irreducible nucleus of politicians who would invariably support them. The foundations of every ministry in Anne's reign — those of 1702–4, 1704–5, 1705–8 and 1708–10 which were presided over by the duumvirs, and that of 1710–14 which was managed by Harley — rested on this solid base. Within each ministry and attached to each was a body of peers and commoners, ranging from trusted royal councillors to Household officials and from civil servants to backbench friends and relatives of the Managers, which preserved an identity distinct from the genuine party men in the administration. Later we must analyse the composition of this group of politicians in some detail and gauge its numerical strength. The point emphasised here is simply that the mere existence of such a group, of men immune for the most part from the vagaries afflicting the parliamentary behaviour of many of their ministerial colleagues, introduced one vital element of stability and continuity into the shifting pattern of parliamentary politics between 1702 and 1714. It is, in other words, as a constant in the various political equations of the period that we must see "the Court"; only thus can we make sense of its relations with the Whig and Tory parties both in the Commons and in the Lords, which is the theme of these last two chapters.

*   *   *

The House of Commons is the appropriate starting-point for investigation. It was here that the delicate constitutional mechanism produced by the Revolution suffered the greatest strain. It was here that the forces of party subjected the political system to the severest pressures — pressures which the slighter, if well-disciplined, resources at the disposal of the Court were perpetually being called on to contain. The problem confronting the Managers in the Lower House of Parliament was indeed a formidable one, given the political climate of later Stuart Britain. Their difficulty lay in reconciling two aims. They had to ensure, session after session, a degree of co-operation between Parliament and the executive sufficient to allow the essential business of government to be promptly despatched. But they had also to accomplish this, as far as possible, without permitting the Queen's administration to fall under the complete control of either party, because for much of the reign the concept of 'party government', of a 'two-party system' in anything like the modern sense, was as unacceptable to the Queen as it was alien and distasteful to the Managers themselves. Although the struggle to reconcile these two aims continued almost to the end of the reign, hard experience had shown by that time that only in certain circumstances were they genuinely reconcilable. "As long as the Parlt. give wt. ever is propos'd by the Court Managers and the Parliament askes nothing", one Tory wrote ironically, "without doubt ther will ever be a good corispondence betwixt the Court and Parliament".[7] But unfortunately for the Court, Parliament (or rather the parties that dominated it) had a great deal to ask in return for voting-supply and giving their blessing to government bills. And the price demanded was often one that neither the Queen nor her leading advisers were willing to pay.

It is true, of course, that in seeking a harmonious relationship with Parliament the Court did not lack certain valuable advantages. The most obvious was the fact that political dependence was not one-sided but mutual. If the Court had to work with and through party, the parties could only hope to achieve their own ends for any length of time with the countenance of the Court. Difficult though it was on occasion for the Managers to keep firm control of the reins, it was they who occupied the box: " 'tis plaine", one shrewd old Tory recognised, "without the concurrence of the ministers nothing can be done in soe divided a nation as this".[8] In addition, however, there were a number of more specific resources on which the Managers could draw in their efforts to maintain the co-operation of the House of Commons. One was the power of dissolution — a purely negative asset, but an indispensable one. As a result of the Triennial Act the sovereign could no longer hang on to a docile Parliament;* yet he was always at liberty to dissolve a fractious one, or one that had become politically unacceptable. King William exercised this right to good effect in November 1701, Anne to even better effect in September 1710. There were also at least two occasions, one in the summer of 1704 and the other in February 1711, when un-amenable elements in the House of Commons were threatened with a premature dissolution; and the second of these threats had a temporarily sobering effect on the more responsible members of the October Club.[9]

A more positive weapon was the considerable electoral influence which the government of the day could now wield, if it so wished: not yet as much influence as it was to enjoy in the heyday of Walpole and Newcastle, but enough to guarantee any set of ministers a highly important hand in shaping the general character of a fresh House of Commons. "Both parties talk very confidently of a majority", observed one Whig candidate before the General Election of 1710, "but the times are so corrupt, they must know very little that don't think a Court can give either side a majority to plague one another by turns . . .".[10] Lord Cowper told George I in 1714, on the strength of "repeated experience", that "the parties are so near an equality, and the generality of the world so much in love with the advantages a King of Great Britain can bestow . . . that 'tis wholly in your Majesty's power, by showing your favour in due time (before the elections) to one or other of them, to give which of them you please a clear majority in all succeeding parliaments".[11] Even a clear knowledge of the sovereign's personal inclinations, as Burnet had ruefully noticed as far back as 1702, "wrought on the in-constancy and servility that is natural to the multitude".[12] As for "the influence of the Crown" in its wider sense, the politicians of the day may have differed in their opinion of whether it could triumph at a General Election over a thoroughly adverse current of public opinion,[13] but all agreed that it was invariably a powerful factor in moulding public opinion in advance of an Election as well as directly affecting the result in many individual constituencies. A generous disposal of major offices on the eve of a General Election to whichever party the Court chose to favour — especially of those

---

* See pp. 218–19 above.

offices which bestowed direct electoral patronage* — and a corresponding reallocation of the Lieutenancies and Commissions of the Peace thus became a recognised prescription for the success of candidates acceptable to the ministry.

In theory, then, the Court could always look forward to the election of a House of Commons in which initially a majority of members were favourably disposed to it. But between theory and practice there was considerable disparity. It is abundantly clear that from one motive or another Queen Anne's prime ministers were generally unwilling to employ to the full the electoral powers they technically possessed. If this fact was not so clear to contemporaries, this was mainly because of the natural anxiety of the defeated party at every General Election to blame its discomfiture on the weight of official influence which had been thrown into the scales against it. Such was Lord Shaftesbury's explanation of the setbacks suffered by the Whigs in 1702: "the Justices of the Peace, the Sheriffs, the officers of all the militia . . . with all the rest of the civil and military offices were in the hands of the High-Church Party", he complained, "and the changes reserved to the very instant of the Elections . . .".[14] Yet there is evidence that the new Lord Treasurer, Godolphin, was less active in promoting Tory successes through government patronage than Shaftesbury believed. Both before and during the campaign several Tories had plainly suspected him of dragging his feet. Lords Weymouth and Winchilsea both complained of official "discouragements",[15] and John Bromley, while rejoicing in Tory successes, was certainly not disposed to lay them at the government's door: "I hope others whom it most concerns", he wrote, "will consider what little help has been given us, and from thence make a right judgement of the true strength and interest of this kingdom".[16] Three years later it was the turn of the Whigs to criticise the Court for acting "with such caution and coldness" that their party "had very little strength given them by the ministers in managing elections".[17] Godolphin's inactivity in this field during the winter of 1707–8, while preparations were afoot on all sides for the contest due in the spring, was the despair even of some of his greatest admirers. "Alass for elections", bewailed Sir John Cropley, "here is nothing like what I have known. Not an election in the kingdome but [the] former ministry they laid great stress & management on. These ministers will not venture to be concernd in any. If they doe dabble a little in a few particular places [to] enfluence, 'tis so gently done & unseen & so as really to signify very little.

* E.g. places in the Admiralty Commission, the Chancellorship of the Duchy of Lancaster, the posts of Warden of the Cinque Ports and Governor of the Isle of Wight.

Uppon my word, in judgment 'tis wrong to over doe this part...".[18]
Harley's electoral tactics after he took over the Treasury from Godolphin in
August 1710 were equally puzzling to his friends. After the remodelling
of a few county commissions of the peace in favour of the Tories,[19] the
removal of a tiny handful of Whig lords lieutenant, and a belated change in
the Duchy of Lancaster,* the springs of Court influence suddenly dried up
several weeks before the opening of the 1710 General Election, and most
Tory candidates were left to fight their campaign without official local support.[20]

This plain reluctance at times on the part of the Managers to unleash the
full power of the Crown in General Elections need not be explained by the
conscientious scruples which Cropley attributed to Godolphin: "Ld
Treasurer declared to all & so he did to me", he wrote in December 1707,
"[that] the Q. Ministry will never influence & concern in elections, & on
that pretends merit too".[21] In reality both Godolphin and Harley were
pragmatists in their approach to this whole question. Oxford in 1713, for
instance, was much more uninhibited in his exploitation of the Court's
electoral advantages than he had been in 1710. The reason for the change
was quite simply that at the time of the 1713 Election he believed the popular
tide to be flowing more strongly for the Whigs than in October 1710, and
therefore thought it necessary to harness the influence of the Crown more
effectively in the constituencies to the Tory interest, which he wished to see
in the ascendant in the new House of Commons. In 1710, however, when
there was clearly some possibility of a Tory landslide occurring even without
government assistance, Harley was more concerned to restrict the influence
which the government could exert, since a House of Commons dominated
by a Tory majority of quite unmanageable proportions was the last thing to
be desired by one who had always preached that no administration should
become the slave of a party. What the Managers attempted to do at the five
General Elections fought between 1702 and 1713 was thus to regulate the
extent of official influence on each occasion, and to do so in such a way as to
leave one party victorious in the Commons *but not uncontrollable*. But the
changing moods of a volatile electorate, an electorate just as susceptible to
party propaganda as to the promptings of the Court, made such an objective
extremely difficult to achieve. Godolphin discovered this to his cost in 1708,
when the fervent hopes of one government supporter in mid-campaign that

---

* The Whig Earl of Derby did not receive the Queen's orders to return the Chancellor's
seals until 15 Sept., little more than a fortnight before the Election began. Kenyon MSS.:
Derby to George Kenyon, Lathom, 15 Sept.

the new Parliament would be "a Parliament for the Court, a Parliament that may be guided" proved in the end illusory.* Harley's experience in 1710 was even more chastening. "Those who got the last Parliament Dissolved", Addison assured Wharton as the trend of the early results was remorselessly confirmed, "are as much astonisht and they say troubled, for the Glutt of Tories that will be in the next, as the Whigs themselves".[22] Lord Weymouth, who by 1710 had seen many elections come and go, had good cause to remark that he "never knew undertakers for Parliaments come off without some scratches";[23] for it was only after one General Election in Anne's reign, that of 1705, that the margin between the Whig and Tory parties in the Commons was narrow enough to allow those members who were committed essentially to the Court, rather than to either party, to hold the balance of power.

In any case, the return of a new House of Commons, even a House that was favourably disposed at the start towards the Court, was only the first step along the road towards solving the eternal problem of management. The heart of the problem was how to keep a majority of the new members well-inclined to the government: not for a few weeks, or even a few months, but if necessary for three years. And here the crucial handicap under which all Queen Anne's political Managers laboured was the fact that the 'government interest' in the Commons, the group of members which in almost all circumstances could be depended on to support the Court rather than follow the lead of the party chieftains, was so very small.

To appreciate just how small it was involves making full allowance for that confusion between "Court" and "Ministry". referred to earlier, which so bedevilled contemporary political terminology. When the politician of the early eighteenth century referred to "the Court Party" or to "the Queen's Servants" he very often envisaged all those members and peers who had material obligations to the Crown, in the shape of places or pensions or commissions in the army and navy. It was such members of the House of Commons whom Godolphin had in mind, for example, when he calculated in 1706 that the 450 M.P.s who had taken part in a key division in the previous autumn could be broken down into "Tories 190, Whigs 160, Queen's Servants 100".[24] A recent minute analysis of this very division has shown that the number of placemen, pensioners and serving officers who actually voted in it was 98, and that upward of 20 more such members

* Blenheim MSS. B1–7: Anthony Hammond to Marlborough, 17 May. Later, when all the results were in, Sunderland was to call this "the most Wig Parliament has been since the revolution". B.M. Lansdowne MSS. 1236, f. 243.

could have done so had they been able or willing to be present.[25] The total number of "Gentlemen . . . in Offices, Employments, etc"[26] who held seats in the House of Commons at the end of the previous Parliament, that of 1702–5, was put at 126 by one industrious contemporary researcher. Had a similar list been compiled three years later, in the spring of 1708, it would have been very slightly shorter.* Subsequently the creation by Lord Oxford of certain new offices which were made legally compatible with the holding of a parliamentary seat (such as the Scottish Commission of Chamberlainry and Trade), and also such temporary expedients as putting first the Treasury and then the Privy Seal in Commission in 1710–11 and 1712–13, led to further fluctuations. But a broad and safe generalisation would be that after the Union of 1707 somewhere between one quarter and one fifth of the House of Commons was made up of men who could technically be described as "Queen's Servants".

On the face of things, and certainly to students accustomed to the more static conditions of Hanoverian politics, so numerous a body may seem to have offered an admirable basis for any machinery of parliamentary management which the Court cared to operate, as well as providing the chief ministers of the Crown with a most effective counterpoise to the pressure of Whigs and Tories. But politics under the last Stuart sovereign could never work as neatly or as simply as this. The chief reason for this, as we have already suggested, was simply that at all times the so-called "Court Party" included a great many politicians whose first obligation on most controversial issues was to their own party, be it Whig or Tory, and not to the Court. Thus Godolphin was convinced that if all the Tories in the Queen's pay "had thought fit" they could have prevented the introduction of the third Occasional Conformity bill into the Commons on 14 November 1704; but instead they obeyed their instincts, and so involved the Court in all the anxiety attendant on the subsequent progress of "this Noisy, Mischief-making, Party-driving, Good for nothing Bill".[27] In October 1705 at least 39 Tories in the Queen's employment were given strict orders to attend the Commons and vote for the government's nominee for the Speakership, John Smith; but Smith was a recognised Whig, and on the day of the election only 19 of the 39 Tory placemen could bring themselves to vote for him.[28]

---

* Two important changes had taken place in the meantime: (1) new categories of officials had been disqualified from membership of Parliament by the Succession to the Crown Acts (or Regency Acts) of 1706 and 1708. (2) the passing of the Act of Union had partly made up for these depredations by admitting into the Commons a number of Scottish placemen and army officers from the session of 1707–8 onwards.

One final and more spectacular example will suffice to underline this crucial fact of early-eighteenth-century politics — the essential unreliability of many of the "Queen's Servants". At the beginning of the session of 1711–12 106 votes were cast in the House of Commons against the Tory ministry's policy of abandoning Spain and the Spanish Empire to a prince of the House of Bourbon; an astonishing proportion of these votes — a fifth of them, in fact — were cast by Whig placemen and pensioners, precarious survivors of their party's rout in 1710 and of a fresh purge in June 1711, yet still following the dictates of their party chiefs and rejecting the lead of the Court.[29]

This much at least is evident: at no time during Anne's reign did the total number of "Queen's Servants" sitting in the House of Commons provide any kind of criterion for assessing the strength of the true 'government interest' in the House. From what elements, then, could such an interest be built up? Where could the Managers expect to find members who could be depended on to remain consistently firm in their support of the Court, no matter how contentious the party issues involved? There were two basic sources of supply. The close friends and personal dependants of the Managers themselves — of Marlborough and Godolphin up to 1710 and of Harley and Shrewsbury thereafter — constituted the first. The strictly non-party group of placemen which was to be found in every Parliament furnished the second. In the nature of things most recruits from the first category who were not already in the armed forces found their way into office sooner or later, under the aegis of their patrons. But a minority were technically "independent"; and it was a valuable minority if we are to believe James Brydges, who "observ'd that Ministers of State & Great Men are with the best Grace & most effectually serv'd by such of their Personal friends as are independent, & estim'd to be on the same foot with the other Country Gentlemen".[30] As a *habitué* of every government interest between 1702 and 1713, Brydges was well qualified to pontificate on such matters, although he himself was a classic representative of the second basic constituent of this interest, the genuine 'government members'. This was always the smaller element of the two. Indeed the crux of the Managers' problem in the House of Commons between 1702 and 1714 lay in this very fact: that the number of 'government members' was invariably so meagre.

In every one of Anne's Parliaments were to be found such men as Anthony Hammond, who has left us with this brief and endearing self-portrait: "In public affairs he is naturally moderate, something uncertain in his opinions, from wch two causes he has been thought to be of both sides or sometimes of one & sometimes of the other, tho' as to the jacobites in his heart he never was inclined to them . . .".[31] But "Harmonious Hammond" and his kind, the members with no real party attachments and consequently with a built-in disposition to vote with the administration of the day, whatever its complexion, were conspicuous mainly because they were freakish deviations from the norm. Those M.P.s who had supported the Godolphin ministry right down to August 1710, even in its final and most Whiggish form, and who then promptly switched their allegiance to Harley numbered, for example, no more than two dozen; and of these by no means all were pure Courtiers. They included some "half a score half crown Whigs", as Lord Poulet dubbed them — Court Whigs who had chosen, for the time being at least, to follow the rising star;[32] so that in the first two sessions of the 1710–13 Parliament it is doubtful whether more than 15 men sitting for English constituencies would have been regarded as plain 'government members', men in the employment of the Crown to whom no party label, or at most a purely nominal one, could have been attached.

Even this tiny group was not entirely homogeneous. It was composed of a handful of inveterate placemen, adepts at riding out every political storm, of a few authentic Civil Service members whose administrative or diplomatic experience was gratefully utilised by every ministry, and of a residue of professional soldiers and sailors. James Brydges, an Admiralty Councillor from 1702 to 1705 and Paymaster-General of the Forces Abroad from 1705 to 1713, most clearly personified the first group;[33] but it also included Vice-Chamberlain Coke,[34] Francis Robartes, who held lucrative office continuously throughout Anne's reign, either in an Exchequer sinecure or in the Irish Revenue Commission,[35] and William Bridges, M.P. for Liskeard and Surveyor-General of the Ordnance from 1702 until his death in 1715. The civil servants were usually elected with official assistance in boroughs where strong government influence could be brought to bear. They had suffered two notable casualities at the 1710 Election, with William Blathwayt losing his seat at Bath (where the Crown had no influence) and John Ellis, seeking re-election after two years out of the House, failing at Rye. But there still survived the invaluable William Lowndes, the Secretary to the Treasury; Josias Burchett, the Secretary to the Admiralty and the Marines; the Henry Vincents, father and son, who between them monopolised a seat at the Victualling Board from 1699 to 1719;* Kenrick Edisbury, also of the

---

* They sat for Truro on the family interest. When the elder Vincent was ready to relinquish his post in 1711 he hoped to be succeeded by his youngest son, Nicholas, who had "been bred up to business", but Oxford preferred to keep the office not only within the

ce, who sat for the government borough of Harwich; and
, formerly an army officer and now a diplomat.[36] Among
elsh members in the years 1710–12 the number of serving
orces who could have reasonably claimed to be non-party men
but there were one or two in comfortable berths which they
ed to keep, such as Admiral Leake;[37] while others, like
Goring, M.P. for Steyning, and Brigadier Richard Sutton,
ected for Newark in January 1712, were too anxious about
of promotion to worry overmuch about party principles.[38]

her, managerial dependants and non-party officials could provide no more than a tiny nucleus of the majority which every ministry
House of Commons. How far was this nucleus capable of
r some two and a half years in the middle of the reign,
and 1710, it acquired a welcome reinforcement in the shape
us adherents of the old Scottish Court Party — the relations
of Queensberry, Seafield and Stair. They dominated Scottish
in the House in the first post-Union Parliament, and remained
ortant single element among the 45 Scottish members even
lost ground to the Squadrone in 1708.[39] But the ministerial
and the General Election which followed it largely destroyed
Court party as an important force in the Lower House, in-
both Whig and Tory. Seafield (though only temporarily) and
d true to the interests of the old ministry, and although
Queensberry stayed in office under Harley until his death in 1711 he was in
an invidious position which greatly impaired his old prestige.[40] Those of
their followers who survived the 1710 Election were mostly absorbed
thereafter by the Whigs.* In fact John Pringle, who was Under-Secretary
of State under Queensberry and later a Joint Keeper of the Signet, and (more
belatedly) Alexander Abercrombie of Glasshaugh were the only two Scottish
Court members of note who transferred their allegiance to the new masters,
unless one includes the few Argyllite Whigs who followed their chief into
alliance with the Harley administration in 1710 and out of it again in 1713.†

family but within the House of Commons. B.M. Loan 29/311/1: George Granville to
[Oxford], 27 May, 3 June 1711.

* E.g. Sir David Dalrymple, Brigadier Grant, Sir Robert Pollock, Sir Patrick Johnstone, and John Stewart of Sorbie. In the Parliaments of 1710–14 they generally co-
operated in opposition with their old rivals of the Squadrone.

† Pringle was a fairly orthodox professional placeman by 1709, though his earlier
associations seem to have been with the Squadrone and he showed some sympathy with

Later in the eighteenth century the government interest in the Commons, 'the Court and Treasury Party' of Walpole and the Pelhams, would have been swollen quite considerably by reinforcements from three further sources: government contractors, pensioners, and official nominees to seats where the patronage was in the control of a government department, minister or dependant. But in Anne's reign the Court was not so fortunate. Contractors and pensioners with seats in the Commons were erratic, at best, in their loyalty, and pensioners in any case were few in number; the representatives of 'government boroughs' were of more value, but even their contribution was surprisingly limited.

In August 1710 Alderman John Ward, one of the four members of Parliament for the city of London, turned down the government's offer of a valuable contract for supplying the army in Portugal: "my aim", he said, "has always been to have no byass or obligation".[41] Yet the case histories of ten navy contractors, most of them involved in the supply of timber or sail cloth, who sat in the Commons for all or part of the period 1710–14, does not suggest that the "obligation" they incurred did much to affect their parliamentary record.[42] Only one* appears to have consistently supported the Court and he was a convinced Tory in any event. Three of the other contractors were Tories, but all three gave Oxford's ministry cause for anxiety at one time or another: Charles Eversfield as a leading October man in 1711 and 1712, Sir John Parsons as a Hanoverian Tory in 1713–14, and John Ward of Hackney, whose record in 1714 (so far as it can be traced) suggests "whimsical" tendencies.[43] The other six contractors were all Whigs. John Dibble and John Wicker were absent at the time of the two great divisions on No Peace without Spain and the Commerce bill, and this could conceivably indicate a reluctance to offend the ministry on major issues. On the other hand there were many Whig absentees on both occasions who owed nothing to government favour, and the fact that both Dibble and Wicker lost their seats to Tories at the 1713 Election hardly argues in either case a sound Court record in the previous Parliament. Two other Whig contractors, Owen Buckingham and Sir Thomas Johnson, have left unquestionable evidence of their imperviousness to government influence, even though Buckingham's Reading workshops were the navy's most important supplier of sail cloth. The remaining two, Sir Thomas Webster and John Ridge, were intransigent enough to be turned out of the House of the Commons by a

the Hanoverian Tories in 1714. Abercrombie's record after 1710 was remarkably mixed, as befitted a client of that proficient courtier, Seafield.

* Thomas Vernon (Whitchurch).

partisan Tory majority — the former on two occasions for alleged electoral malpractices at Colchester, and the latter, a Portsmouth brewer sitting for Poole, for abuses connected with his Admiralty contract.

The pensioner members of the House of Commons in Queen Anne's Parliaments seem as a body to have been scarcely more reliable as pro-government voters than the contractors. Despite the stock complaints of country members of both parties, there is no evidence whatever that the granting of pensions to sitting M.P.s by either Godolphin or Harley was part of a deliberate and sinister attempt to build up the influence of the Crown against either Whig, Tory or "Country" interests. For one thing the number of grants made to M.P.s between 1702 and 1714 was remarkably small. It will be recalled that Dr. Walcott's meticulous analysis of the 1701 Parliament detected no more than six pensioners then sitting in the House of Commons, only one of whom, Anthony Henley, enjoyed a pension of more than £600 a year.[44] The contemporary *List of Gentlemen that are in Offices, Employment, etc.*, published in 1705 and relating to the final session of the Queen's first Parliament, names only eight, two of whom — Henley and George Sayer — had been present in 1701.[45] A second point worthy of emphasis is that both Godolphin and Harley, as successive heads of the Treasury under Anne, had far too many urgent financial commitments, with a war of unprecedented cost on their hands, to indulge for their political convenience in anything approaching a policy of indirect bribery of members of Parliament at the public expense. In the case of Harley — often in his day the subject of wild, unsubstantiated charges of bribery[46] — the restraining factors were particularly strong: his own natural parsimony; the "good husbandry" which, from the very start of his administration, he prided himself on bringing to the Queen's service; and not least the really critical financial situation which threatened him during his first year in office. "The first [thing] that the Comsr of the T[reasury] did", remarked one close observer soon after Godolphin's fall, "was to take away Harry Guys pention, & 'tis said they give [out] they will be such good husband[s] of the Queens mony that no useless persons shall have any".[47]

In any case, any attractions which the prospect of a body of dependent pensioners, tied to the government interest, might still have retained in the eyes of the Court Managers had been effectively dimmed by the passing of the Regency Act in 1706. One of the provisions which country members had been able to insert into this Act had been the exclusion of "pensioners during pleasure" from sitting in the House of Commons. The award of a pension "during pleasure" was naturally the most reliable means of ensuring that the recipient behaved himself to the liking of the Court. Grants for life, or during the Queen's life, were almost invariably regarded by the pensioner as a recognition of past services to the Crown, or perhaps as compensation for the loss of an office, rather than as a pledge of good conduct in the future. Between 1707 and the death of Anne such grants, not surprisingly, became exceedingly rare. When Lieutenant-General Webb (M.P. for Ludgershall) was awarded a yearly pension of £1000 that was technically "for life", after being maimed at Wynendael in 1708, it was on the clear understanding that it would be discontinued if or when he was given an office by the Crown; and one of Harley's first appointments in the autumn of 1710 saw Webb promoted to the Governorship of the Isle of Wight.[48] During Harley's own premiership I have been able to trace only one life pension that was granted to a sitting member of the Lower House. This was the award of a *douceur* of £1000 a year to Sir James Montagu, M.P. for Carlisle, when he was eased out of the office of Attorney-General in September 1710. Montagu, brother to Halifax of the Junto, was the stoutest of Whigs, and there is not a shred of evidence to suggest that his pension led him to abate his opposition to Harley's ministry in the slightest degree in the Parliament of 1710–13.

The extreme paucity of the grants made to commoners between 1702 and 1714 naturally limited very severely the contribution which pensioners could make to the Court interest in the Lower House. What made this contribution not merely small but entirely negligible, however, was the political behaviour of the recipients. Harley, for example, apparently inherited seven pensioner members from his predecessor in November 1710. Four of them, three Whigs and one moderate Tory, subsequently followed a parliamentary course completely independent of that plotted by the new ministry. Such independence was particularly courageous in the case of William Palmes, the Whig M.P. for Malton, who had been granted a pension of £1000 a year in 1702 (when his son Guy lost his Tellership of the Exchequer to Sir Christopher Musgrave) and had subsequently had this "settled for life" in 1708; for Palmes was in serious financial difficulties after 1710, and Harley was never loth to hold up the payment of pensions for years on end from tactical motives.[49] Equally unco-operative, though at less risk, were William Cotesworth, who had £500 a year on the Secret Service account, Sir Charles Hedges, the Tory ex-Secretary of State who broke with the ministry from 1712 onwards, and Wharton's Junto nephew, Edmund Dunch.[50] In the case of two other Whig pensioners, Anthony Henley (who had enjoyed £2000 a year from the Crown since William III's reign) and George Rodney Bridges (£1600 a year on the Irish establishment) evidence is inconclusive; but both had been stout Whigs before 1710, Bridges being a friend of the Duke of Bolton's and a Junto man, and

Henley passing even Sunderland's stringent test of "constant steadiness",[51] and there is no reason to suspect that they lapsed thereafter. Only one of the seven, Jack Hill, the Tory brother of Abigail Masham,* clearly earned his keep by his services in the House of Commons after 1710, when his military duties allowed him to do so.

Harley, as we have seen, reaped no political benefit from the sole life grant (Montagu's) which he himself procured for a member of House. But he did find two ways during his ministry of circumventing the anti-pensions clause of the Regency Act. One was to make large single payments in the form of bounties, equal to two or three years' income from an average-sized pension, to a few deserving individuals. The second and more dubious method was to grant pensions "during pleasure" to M.P.s under bogus names, and charge them to the Civil List of Ireland. But both expedients were used sparingly in the extreme. Only two substantial bounties were granted to House of Commons' men between 1710 and 1714, and both beneficiaries were men who would have supported the government anyway, without needing further inducement.† The only payment of a secret Irish pension which can be firmly authenticated was the £800 a year awarded in 1711 to Sir John Pakington, under the fictitious name of "Thomas Edwards",[52] although two other charges recorded on the Irish Civil List account, dating from 1712 to 1713,[53] could conceivably conceal similar manœuvres.‡ At best it was a precarious form of reward (or bribe), as Pakington himself was only too well aware:

I am highly sensible of the obligation I owe to your Lpp. & the Duke of Shrewsbury [he told Oxford in June 1712] for the grant you obtain last year of her Majesty's favour. But I fear the continuance of it in the method propos'd may take air, & by being known I should be precluded by an Act of Par^t· from sitting in the House of Commons, & consequently be disabled from doing her Majesty that service my duty & my inclination would always lead me to.

A "publick mark of the Queen's favour", he reminded his benefactor, would make him "much prouder".[54]

---

* Granted a pension of £1000 p.a. in May 1710 at a time when he was not a member of Parliament: he was elected for Lostwithiel in the following October.

† This was certainly true of Edward Nicholas, who was given a bounty of £1500 in June 1714, and very probably true of General William Seymour (younger brother of the late Sir Edward), who received a grant of £2000 in August 1710. Cholmondeley (Houghton) MSS. 53, f. 11.

‡ It has since appeared, from evidence in the Blenheim MSS, that the recipient of the smaller of these two pensions (£500 p.a.) was indeed Sir Thomas Hanmer, though it may well be he held it in trust for an indigent friend. See D. Hayton, 'The "Country" interest and the party system, 1689–c. 1720' in C. Jones (ed.), *Party and Management in Parliament 1660–1784* (1984), pp. 69–70.

Of distinctly more importance to the Managers than contractors and pensioners were those members who, though recognised party men, nevertheless owed their seats in some measure to official nomination or backing in those constituencies which Dr. Walcott has described as 'government boroughs'. 'At some twenty-five constituencies', he explains, 'the proximity of military, naval, or administrative establishments, together with the extensive patronage involved enabled the government to set up official candidates with every expectation of success'; and, backing this up in an appendix with a fifteen-page catalogue of such official nominees, he manages to convey the general impression that a large and very important contingent of members was tied to the Court in this way. 'All in all', he tells us, to emphasise the point, 'thirty-eight members of William's last Parliament were returned from these "government boroughs" — the majority owing both their offices and their seats to government influence'.[55]

Over the period 1702–14 as a whole, however, no ministry could possibly have afforded to place so inflated a value on the contribution of these boroughs to its management of the Commons. There were always three considerations to restrain its optimism. First, the Court had to recognise that in constituencies like Arundel, Shoreham and Rye (all included in Walcott's list of so-called 'government boroughs') its influence was never more than precarious, and towards the end of the period quite insignificant. At the General Election of 1713, for instance, at a time when the Oxford administration was overwhelmingly Tory, these three boroughs returned six Whigs.[56] Secondly, ministers had to take a realistic view of official prospects in several other towns where convention allowed the Court no more than a half-stake in the representation; and this meant accepting that not even one member could invariably be taken for granted, and that further encroachment required exceptionally favourable circumstances. The electors of Rochester, Preston, Dover, the three Isle of Wight boroughs, and even of Plymouth would never have admitted that the government had a clear right to nominate to *both* their seats.* In practice there was often a compromise arrangement in these constituencies whereby the representation was shared between a government candidate and either a local gentleman or an enterprising carpet-bagger. Preston affords a good illustration of this kind of convention. There the Chancellor of the Duchy was "complimented" with one nomination, but the other seat was open to contest among the neighbouring gentry, with the Tory squire Henry Fleetwood and the Whigs Edward

* All 7 constituencies are elevated by Walcott to the full status of 'government boroughs'.

Rigby and Sir Henry Houghton as the chief contestants.* Rochester provides an equally choice example. One seat here was invariably filled by an Admiralty nominee by virtue of the Chatham dockyard interest: and William Bokenham, Sir Stafford Fairborne, Sir Cloudesley Shovel and Sir John Leake were all successful government nominees in Anne's reign. The second seat, as at Preston, was reserved for a local landowner — Edward Knatchbull filling it in one of Anne's Parliaments and William Cage in three. The only time this agreement was seemingly broken was in 1705, when both Shovel and Fairborne were elected. But some fine hairs had to be split on this occasion to enable the two admirals to carry it off, Sir Stafford contriving to persuade the electors of the borough that "Sir Cloudesley is a very good county gentleman, having an estate in that county", and desiring that "he may be accounted the sea officer".[57]

The third and in some respects the most serious practical limitation on the value of 'government boroughs' to the Court was the absence of any guarantee that an official nominee would subsequently prove a safe pro-administration voter. Thus Richard Topham, Keeper of the Tower Records, whose election for Windsor in 1710 was officially sponsored, became a member of the opposition to Harley in the new Parliament. So, too, did young Thomas Frankland, elected on the Post Office interest at Harwich in the same year.[58] It was also quite possible for a man to establish an interest in a borough through government backing but maintain it subsequently by personal influence and careful cultivation of the constituency, in spite of a change of ministry unfavourable to his party. This was the experience of George Doddington at Winchelsea, Admiral Aylmer at Dover, and of Aylmer's son-in-law, Sir John Norris, in the course of Anne's reign. Norris, for example, first represented Rye on the Lord Warden's and Customs House interest in 1708; but in spite of being a Junto Whig, he held his seat there right through to the end of the reign.[59] In short, the most the Court could expect from the 'government boroughs' in the early eighteenth century was a useful rather than an abundantly fruitful source of recruits. In the Parliament of 1714, for example, official influence in these twenty-four constituencies helped to accommodate a few non-party placemen like Lowndes, Leake and James Worsley, who would have supported the Court no matter where they had been elected, and it also offered a means of cementing a

* Chatsworth MSS. Finch-Halifax Papers, box 5, bundle 11: Sir C. Musgrave to Guernsey, 19 Oct. 1714. In 1710 the replacement of Derby by Berkeley of Stratton as Chancellor came too late to prevent Houghton and Fleetwood sharing the representation between them.

dozen Tories, at most, to the ministry.[60] But all the other Tories representing such boroughs in this Parliament came to Westminster essentially as back-benchers, as men elected on their own interest and without any Court assistance. At least two of them, it is of interest to notice, were Hanoverian Tories and played a prominent part in opposition in the Commons during the 1714 session.[61] Still more revealing is the fact that these same twenty-four boroughs returned sixteen Whigs to the House in 1713, even though the number was later reduced by two as a result of the work of the Committee of Privileges and Elections.

We can now appreciate why Queen Anne's Managers found it so un-rewarding to strive for command of a large number of votes for the Court in the House of Commons regardless of party affiliations. The extraordinary scarcity of genuinely non-party members in the House after 1701, the political ingratitude of most government contractors and pensioners, and the limitations to which direct Court patronage in parliamentary boroughs was subject — all these factors militated strongly against the independent influence of the Crown. The perpetual complaint of country members since the 1670's — that the "King's servants" were so much lobby fodder for the administration of the day — had become almost pure myth by Anne's reign. At least half the "officers", the 120 to 140 members of the House of Commons who in the picturesque contemporary phrase "ate the Queen's bread", and who occasioned a stream of Place bills and clauses in the early eighteenth century, were always liable to be drawn away from the true government interest and from the Managers' orbit by the magnetic pull of party allegiance. An acute outside observer, writing in September 1705, estimated that there were normally no more than 50 or 60 members of the House of Commons "qui dépendent entièrement de la cour par leur charges et que la Cour puisse obliger a voter comme il luy plaist".[62] What appears to be a remarkable later endorsement of this assessment comes from the pen of the man who for almost four years at the end of the reign was the Queen's chief minister. Calculating the party strengths in the Commons before the opening of the 1714 Parlia-ment, Lord Oxford supposed the backbenchers of both major parties to be divided roughly in the proportion of 5 to 8: 151 Whigs to 240 Tories. But of the balance of 167, made up presumably of placemen, serving officers of the forces, pensioners and contractors, and also those personal adherents of the ministers who would follow the Court line even without the extra inducement of employment, he put the "dependants on the persons of the Queens service" only as a "certaine fifty or 60".[63]

This figure was undoubtedly capable of being increased at particular times and in particular circumstances. It was appreciably higher in the session of 1707–8 when the Managers had the temporary support of the "Lord Treasurer's Whigs" as well as of a solid corps of Scottish Court members. It rose again for a while after 1710 thanks to the size of Harley's personal following. In addition there were the 'fair weather votes' which any government could expect to pick up at quiet periods of any session from the Court wings of both the Whig and Tory parties: most of them came from placemen, but some from the back benches, where there were always those who preferred, all things being equal, to go with the ministerial tide. It was such men Grey Nevil had in mind when he explained to the Duke of Montrose in 1708: "My Lord the absence of our friends [at the opening of Parliament] wil be attended with dismall consequences, for if the Court carry 4 or 5 points att the beginning, they will draw in some fools who love to be on the side of the maiority & the labouring oar wil be on our side".[64] Competent organisation was needed to make the most of such limited and fluctuating assets, and this the Queen's Managers were generally able to supply. The efficiency of the Secretary of the Treasury, supplemented on big occasions by the efforts of more senior ministers, guaranteed them an adequate system of 'whipping', and the prospect of dismissal could be relied on to deter at least some of the needier office-holders from constant disobedience.* To ensure moreover that ministerial policy and tactics were clearly understood and coherently executed, there developed under Godolphin a system of regular meetings of those the Treasurer called "the gentlemen of the House of Commons", a select group of perhaps fifteen to twenty of the most dependable and active of "the Queen's Servants" assembling at the house of one of the Secretaries of State or of the Chancellor of the Exchequer.† Although he rarely attended in person, Godolphin clearly attached great

* See pp. 309–11 above for a discussion of these aspects of Court organisation.

† These meetings were usually held at the house of Sir Charles Hedges from 1703 to 1705, although it is fairly clear that Harley was their moving spirit. For the apparent initiation of the system in Nov. 1703 and subsequent examples of the system in action in these years see H.M.C. *Portland MSS.* iv, 75; Longleat MSS. Portland Misc. ff. 126, 132–3, 196. By 1707 at the latest (*ibid.* f. 186), and probably from the time of Hedges's dismissal in 1706, the "gentlemen" were assembling at Henry Boyle's. A list of 16 members of the Commons summoned to one council in the session of 1706–7, which has fortunately survived among Harley's papers (B.M. Loan 29/12/1), is made up entirely of office-holders — civil, military and legal. But very occasionally, it would seem, backbenchers were invited to attend. The 19 M.P.s summoned to Boyle's to consider the Recruiting bill in Dec. 1708, like those invited the previous March to deal with the same contentious business, apparently included a few Country Whigs. Blenheim MSS. B.1–1/2: Walpole and Boyle to Marlborough, 30 Mar., 10 Dec.

importance to this aspect of organisation, insisting to Harley during one particularly hectic period for the Court that "unless those meetings bee kept up constantly, and those who are called come willingly to them, & with a desire to agree, I cannot think tis possible to succeed".[65] For some reason the system was allowed to lapse in the first two years of Robert Harley's own ministry, when the prime minister seems to have relied more on informal consultations with his own personal followers; but he revived it in 1713 and 1714, on the advice of his brother Edward, increasing the size of meetings to around 30 in 1714 and introducing, by contrast with Godolphin's custom, a generous sprinkling of backbenchers.[66]

In all these ways the 'government interest' in the House of Commons during Anne's reign was adequately mobilised and co-ordinated. But no amount of organisation could compensate in the long run for sheer lack of numbers. If we discount the occasional bonuses which came their way and take a figure in the region of 60 members as the irreducible minimum on which the Managers could safely rely (a figure which must seem startlingly small to the student of the more stable political world of mid-Hanoverian Britain), it becomes obvious why Poulet lamented to Harley in May 1711 that "the Crown is reduced so low",[67] and why this harsh reality became in some ways the most important determining factor in the working of politics between 1702 and 1714. Having at their disposal so small a "Court party" involved the Managers in an almost continual dilemma in their dealings with the two major forces in the House of Commons, the two competing parties of Whig and Tory. It left them no alternative but to come to terms with one if not both these parties; at the same time it made it desperately difficult for them to avoid being asphyxiated by the overpowering weight of numbers which the party leaders could muster.

* * *

In its simplest terms, the basic problem of parliamentary management which faced Godolphin and Marlborough, and later Harley and Shrewsbury, was this: they had to find an acceptable method of harnessing the immense and organised power of party to the influence of the Crown without having control seized from their hands by the great power politicians, whether Whig or Tory. "It is impossible that a government can be glorious or usefull that is forc'd to take laws from the zealots of any faction", wrote that canny Scot, Sir David Dalrymple, in 1711. "I hope there will allways be found a sufficient number to support the Queen's servants in a plain & easy way".[68] The Managers shared this hope most fervently. But where was this "sufficient number" to be found, and how could it be grafted on to the stock of the government interest in the House of Commons? This was the question they had to answer.

There were two main solutions open to them. One was to try to preside over a coalition between the government interest and the moderate wings of both parties — those elements nearest to the 'centre' of political opinion. This solution meant giving office to party men, but as far as possible only to those who owed no direct allegiance to the chiefs of the great power-groups on either side. It meant, for instance, giving places to the personal dependants of the Managers themselves; to Court Whigs who refused to succumb to the dictatorship of the Junto; and likewise to moderate Tories who had no personal obligations to men like Nottingham, Rochester, Seymour and Bromley, and who had little sympathy with the extreme High Church policies which they advocated. There was a further condition involved in this strategy: it entailed preserving a reasonable balance, a roughly equal "mixture" as contemporaries liked to put it, between Whig and Tory elements at each level in the administration.

"A cautious and prudent management between parties", Somers once said, was Godolphin's "ordinary road";[69] and it is well known that this was the road which he and the duke tried to follow in the years from 1705 to 1708. What has generally been overlooked is that this was also the road along which the duumvirs would most probably have preferred to travel when they first took up the reins of management in March 1702. There is strong evidence to suggest that in the early weeks of the new reign their first thoughts were directed towards some kind of bipartisan coalition of moderates. Marlborough's early letters to Heinsius at The Hague were full of assurances of the Queen's inclination to moderation and of his expectations of an administration that would be "mutually acceptable".[70] As late as 21 April, by which time Normanby had just followed three other leading High Tory figures, Rochester, Jersey and Seymour, into Cabinet office, the duke was still prepared to guarantee that the limit of the swing in favour of the Church party had almost been reached: that Anne was "resolved very quickly to shut the dore upon any other alterations".[71] More significant still is a hitherto-unknown letter of Godolphin's, written at the end of April, which implies that he and his colleague were far from happy at the prospect of having to hold a General Election soon after the Queen's accession, because of the enormous advantage this was bound to confer on the jubilant Tories. "Many people, friends as well as others", he confided to the Speaker, "are still very full of giving the Qu[een] a power to continue the present parlt.

another session, to gain time for settling things & to avoyd heats".[72] Within four months of King William's death, however, a combination of Anne's personal bias towards the employment of sound Church-of-England men and the irresistible pressure exerted upon the Court by Tory politicians temporarily restored to popular favour[73] had compelled the drastic modification of the Managers' original plans. By May they had accepted the necessity of a qualified alliance with the Tory leaders, and at the beginning of July they agreed to the dissolution of the old Parliament. They had no illusions about the risks involved in a definite commitment to the Tories, and a General Election which left that party with almost a two-to-one majority in the Commons did not relieve their uneasiness;* but as Lord Shaftesbury put it, "the experiment must be tryed; it may be dangerouse, but it must be tryed".[74]

By the spring of 1704 both the chief ministers were convinced that the experiment had failed, and by the following winter they had converted Queen Anne to the view that a coalition of the centre was the best practical solution to their problems. "Making the bottom broad enough to be durable"[75] was to remain the basis of managerial policy, both in Parliament itself and in parliamentary elections, from the spring of 1705 to the late winter of 1707–8; and during these three years the ideal came nearer to realisation in practice than at any time in the reign. To take only one example: the caucus of placemen on whom Godolphin relied, as we saw earlier, to watch over the interests of the Court in the House of Commons was divided almost equally in the winter of 1706–7 between Whig and Tory members; it contained only one zealous Tory and no more than three Whigs who had any close associations with the Junto.[76] For three years the Managers battled hard to keep extreme partisans in the ministry to a minimum; and although even in the Cabinet they were forced to give a little ground by admitting Sunderland in 1706, in this respect they achieved a large measure of success. But the maintenance of a genuine *balance* between Whig and Tory in the administration proved far more difficult, and by the autumn of 1706 Godolphin, at least, had acknowledged that if the balance had to be tipped towards one side rather than the other in order to preserve harmony in Parliament it must be towards the Whigs, since "wthout them, & their being intire, the Queen cannot be served".[77]

* Marlborough's gloomy comment to Godolphin when the bulk of the election results had reached him — "I could wish that a majority wou'd be reasonable but I am afraid that is what wee must never expect to see" — is indicative of their apprehension. Blenheim MSS. A. 1–14: 10/21 Aug. 1702.

One can well understand why a "moderating scheme", based on a bi-partisan coalition, was so alluring in theory. But experience proved that as a practical expedient for ensuring co-operation between Crown and parties in the House of Commons it was only workable given three essential conditions. First, the parliamentary situation had to be exactly right: the policy of coalition was suited only to a situation in which neither party had a decisive majority in the Commons. Such a stalemate did exist in the last Parliament of William III (hence Godolphin's willingness to listen to arguments for not dissolving it). It also existed for a while after the General Election of 1705, which left the small government interest in a strong tactical position,[78] though oddly enough Marlborough and Godolphin were not at first entirely happy with the election results, fearing that the right-wing element was too strongly represented on the Tory benches for the ministry's comfort.[79] In actual fact the real threat to the precarious equilibrium of 1705 came from the Whigs. It was they who, during the three-year life of the new Parliament, gradually began to build up a small but decisive majority over their opponents: they did so by carrying most disputed election cases for their own candidates, by making important gains at by-elections, such as those for Chichester, Bury St. Edmunds, Newcastle upon Tyne, Preston and York-shire,[80] and by an alliance with the Scottish Presbyterian and Squadrone members who entered the Commons in the session of 1707–8. The further this process went, the more the hand of the Whig leadership was strengthened in urging its own claims to high office, and the weaker one of the essential props of coalition government inevitably became.

A second necessity if a genuine coalition ministry was to hold together was that the Court should succeed in keeping down the general temperature of politics and should manage to keep controversial party issues as far as possible out of the parliamentary arena. For two sessions at least, those of 1705–6 and 1706–7, the Marlborough-Godolphin ministry was fairly successful in doing this, aided by military triumphs in the Low Countries and in Italy which consolidated the great advantage won at Blenheim. In these sessions the two Managers, with the help of Harley, contrived to hold their heterogeneous body of "Queen's Servants" together by concentrating all their parliamentary efforts on financing what they hoped would prove a decisive effort in the land war, passing the Regency Act, and steering through both Lords and Commons the Union with Scotland. The problem of dissent was kept in the background after the defeat of a Tory attempt to vote "the Church in danger" late in 1705, and the Commission of Public Accounts, whose partisan investigations into "mismanagements" had provided material for so many inflammatory debates in the first Parliament of the reign, was mercifully left in abeyance.

The third condition vital to the success of a "mixed ministry" was that the centre groups which composed it should be able to provide enough administrative talent to carry on the Queen's government competently, or at least without any major fiasco. Here, as with the hard arithmetical facts of the disposition of party forces in the Commons, the cards were stacked heavily against the Godolphin concept of non-party government. By their very success after 1704 in excluding from office "the warm men" of both sides, and especially in excluding them from the policy-making and chief executive posts in the ministry, the Managers were inevitably depriving themselves of an invaluable source of political and administrative experience which they could ill afford to lose. The Cabinet over which Godolphin presided, under the Queen, between 1704 and 1708 contained far too many passengers. On the Tory side it had to carry Buckingham and Wright, at least in the early stages. It also included two Court Whig magnates, Somerset and Newcastle, neither of whom had any pretensions to administrative ability or even qualities of general statesmanship, and the Whig Archbishop of Canterbury, whose health was poor and whose attendance was infrequent.* Pembroke, the Lord President of the Council, was an experienced but not a particularly gifted public servant. Many of the ablest men in the ministry, St. John, Boyle and Harcourt, for instance, were not in offices of Cabinet rank. Nowhere was the lack of ability, and particularly of specialised talents, at the Court's disposal more cruelly exposed than in the gross mismanagement of the Admiralty. From the beginning of the war naval administration had presented a tempting target to the parliamentary snipers of both parties. "Your brethren of the Admiralty", Godolphin told Richard Hill in March 1704, "have not escaped this sessions of Parliament without some of the usual complaints against that office".[81] The Admiralty Council was partly remodelled in 1704–5; but even the presence thereafter of such bright young prospects as Robert Walpole could not make up for the dead weight being carried at the top in the persons of the Queen's husband (Lord High Admiral) and his *alter ego*, George Churchill.

The disastrous winter of 1707–8 brutally demonstrated the extremities to which a coalition ministry of the centre could be brought when all three of the conditions necessary for its survival ceased to exist. In this session the

* Buckingham and Wright were removed in the spring and autumn of 1705, respectively. Somerset and the archbishop had both been in the Cabinet since 1702, and Newcastle entered it in March 1705.

parliamentary balance of forces between Whig and Tory was conclusively upset; acutely controversial issues like that of the Scottish Privy Council came to the fore; and the government was publicly accused of a number of grievous administrative deficiencies (justly so, in the case of its inability to protect British merchant shipping from the ravages of French privateers, far less justly in the case of its failure to maintain the strength of the army in the Peninsula, though this failure had been partly responsible for the recent disaster at Almanza[82]). In these circumstances Godolphin expected "to see the whole Government torn in pieces, with no friends to support it but some few in place"[83] — and his expectation was amply fulfilled. The Court was left exposed to the fury of both sets of party chiefs and had no alternative in the end but to capitulate, partially at least, to the Junto. Had the men of the centre in the Cabinet, the Court Whigs and the moderate Tories, been able to compensate for their lack of capacity by furnishing the Managers with numerous and organised parliamentary followings, it is just conceivable that the ministry of 1705–8 might still have survived, though it is very doubtful whether by 1708 it could have done so. But in this field, too, the moderates (Harley apart) were consistently outgunned by the heavy artillery on the extreme wings of their respective parties, by the Whartons and the Orfords, the Nottinghams and the Rochesters of early-eighteenth-century politics. Faced with these insurmountable obstacles the whole approach to the management of the Commons based on an alliance between the Court and a middle-of-the-road, "mixed" group of party politicians broke down.

There was, however, an alternative solution to the problem of management. It was the solution favoured particularly by Robert Harley, urged by him on Godolphin without success throughout 1706 and 1707, made the basis of his blueprint for a new administration in the crisis of January–February 1708, and adopted by him when he replaced Godolphin as the chief intermediary between the Crown and the parties in 1710. It involved giving the bulk of posts in the government (not all offices by any means, but a clear majority) to one party — the party which seemed most likely to prove the more amenable, at any given time, to the policies of the Crown — and so creating a tacit, if not a formal, partnership between this party and the Court. But it was a partnership to be made on three conditions. The first was that the leaders of the favoured party must be content to remain as far as possible in the position of junior partners, supporting policy but not dictating it, and that only on these terms were they to be employed. The second was that the rank and file of the opposing party must not be made "desperate", to use Harley's own word, by seeing the door to the Queen's service slammed uncompromisingly in their faces. There must always be a minority of the unfavoured, those who "serve without reproach", kept in office *pour encourager les autres.* The third condition was that an important sector of public administration, embracing particularly the many revenue offices no longer compatible with a seat in Parliament, should be removed from the field of party competition altogether, so that no civil servant of proved competence would need to fear for his post every time the ministry changed its character.

Harley's whole approach to the management of the Commons hinged on the crucially important place held by the country members, "the independents", in his political thinking. The Queen apart, there was no more important element in the successful working of the constitution, in Harley's view, than the great *bloc* of 250 to 300 country members; for these were "unlisted men",[84] in the sense that they owed no specific obligation either to the party leaders or to the ministry of the day. They, he felt, and not the more organised groups, were the real key to the control of the House of Commons. The first thing every Manager had to avoid at all costs was the consolidation of this inchoate mass of backbenchers into a united Country interest, broadly opposed to the Court on a succession of major policy questions. "The embodying of gentlemen (country gentlemen I mean) against the Queen's service is what is to be avoided", Harley once warned Godolphin.[85] For when this happened, as he himself had demonstrated as the leader of such a combined interest in William's reign, no government could stand for long against it. The point was emphasised periodically after 1702 by the various campaigns for Place bills and above all by the great struggle in 1706 over the "whimsical clause", which at its height led a harassed Godolphin to compare the lot of the Queen's Managers with "the life of galley slaves".[86] "By keeping firmly & closely united", that archetypal independent Sir Arthur Kaye realised after the 1710 Election, the country gentlemen in the Commons had a fair chance of holding any ministry to ransom.[87]

Harley believed that there were two ways in which the Court could capture their allegiance. One, to which we have already made some reference,* was to preserve the proper constitutional status of the Queen and enhance her position as the natural mediator between the parties: in this way, Harley seems genuinely to have believed, the true independent member, whether Whig or Tory, would find a new and healthy focus for his loyalty, one which would make it far easier to overcome his inbred suspicion of Courts and courtiers and, in the end, to wean him from other and more

* See p. 206 above.

destructive associations. But even in his more idealistic moments Harley never imagined that this transformation could take place overnight. And in the meantime another, and more hard-headed, approach was needed to the seminal problem presented by the average backbencher. This was to recognise the unpalatable but undeniable fact that, whatever may have been the case in the 1690's, by Anne's reign the first and most instinctive loyalty of nine out of every ten "gentlemen" in the House of Commons was to their party; so that the leading party figures, whether Whig or Tory, inevitably exercised considerable influence over them. These independent members may not have been bound by any direct ties of kinship or friendship or clientage to their respective party leaders, but every Manager had to acknowledge the susceptibility of Country Whigs and Country Tories alike to the pressure of these leaders once a parliamentary session was under way. Shrewsbury clearly did so, for instance, when he wrote in 1709: "I do not doubt but the generality of the nation long for a peace, and the majority of those who represent it, *when discoursed singly in the country*, agree in that opinion. But how they may change their minds *when they come to London and submit to their leaders*, I will not take upon me to determine".[88]

It was this decisive hold which the party leaders were able to exercise on the rank-and-file members of the House of Commons, especially at times of political crisis, which forced Harley to concede the necessity of driving a bargain with them. He made the concession reluctantly, for to him the great Whig and Tory chieftains, "the designing grandees on both sides", embodied the two features of party he most disliked — extremism and selfish ambition.[89] And in the years from 1704 to 1706 he still hoped it would prove possible for the Court to hold the support of the independents, once "the Queen hath chosen rightly which party she will take in",[90] by imparting the appropriate party complexion to the government without making any serious concessions to the leaders of that party. An indeterminate coalition of the centre, he knew, would never hold the country members in thrall; but as long as the ministry had a recognisable party stamp, without excluding opponents of the favoured party entirely, he believed it would still be viable. For six months before the 1705 Election and for several months after it, he clung to the belief that an administration that remained predominantly Tory in its image and composition could still command a majority in the Commons, despite the excesses of the Tackers in the winter of 1704–5 and the alienation from the Court of virtually all the old guard of the High Tory leadership. He and the duumvirs, it is clear, took a very different view of the significance of the dramatic events of 28 November 1704. To Marlborough and Godolphin the fact that 134 Tories could vote for a motion to consolidate the Occasional Conformity bill with the Land Tax bill was the final proof that the Court's alliance with the Tory party had failed. To Harley the fact that over 100 Tories had parted company with their leaders in this crucial division[91] held out hope of a new and more stable alliance, with the Queen and the Court able to offer to every sane and patriotic Tory the responsible leadership which they had failed to find elsewhere. ". . . if our friends will not be stark mad", he told one of his Tory correspondents as late as August 1705, "it is easy to place things in the hands of the Gentlemen of England without giving themselves up into the hands of that Party which may be fear'd by some, tho' I think without reason, unless those Gent^men who clamour most force people into it".[92]

By the end of 1705, however, with the vast majority of High Tories showing themselves clearly resolved to fight virtually every issue, as they had fought the Speakership in October, on party lines, Harley was already modifying his views; and for the next year at least he was prepared, though without enthusiasm, to see a Whiggish stamp put on the ministry. But if the Court was to retain its independence as well as its majority in the House of Commons he insisted that amenable Tories must not be blackballed on principle, and that above all the five lords of the Junto, with their insatiable appetites, must be resolutely denied the sweets of the high table — for "the more they have, the more they crave".[93] In the autumn of 1706 he was still defining his position in these terms;[94] but by 1707 he had reluctantly come to appreciate that unless the Court was prepared to take at least *some* of the leaders of the favoured party into business the system of management would break down. This explains why in the critical situation which developed during the winter of 1707–8 Harley came out so strongly, and in opposition to Marlborough and Godolphin, in favour of a new partnership with the Tories; since the Tory leadership, he believed, was much more divisible and much more likely to be kept in subordination to the Managers than was the Whig Junto.[95]

Yet to Harley's way of thinking the most essential point was not the identity of the partners selected by the Court but the nature of the partnership forged with them. He drew a clear distinction in his own mind between non-party government and government without party. He was satisfied, by 1706 if not before, that the latter was impossible. The former, he remained convinced, was attainable, but only if two provisions were observed. There must be no question whatever of party leaders exploiting their parliamentary strength in order to force themselves on an unwilling sovereign: "the foundation is, persons or parties are to come in to the Queen, and not the Queen to them".[96] At the same time they must not be allowed to monopolise a decisive *bloc* of policy-making posts, and so be in a position to dictate policy to the Crown and insist on "unreasonable things". Such was the essence of Harley's concept of a working partnership between the Managers and the party leaders, or at least a section of them, in which the former would remain unquestionably the senior partners in the deal and the latter the junior; the former, independent of parties, representing the views and interests of the Queen; the latter, "without expecting terms, [coming] voluntarily into the promoting of her service".[97]

It has to be remembered that when he first put forward this solution to the problem of parliamentary management in concrete, as opposed to general terms in January 1708 Harley was not advancing an entirely untried theory. He had seen his solution up to a point attempted by the Court in alliance with the High Tories between the summer of 1702 and the spring of 1704. In the formation of the Queen's first ministry at least some of the conditions of partnership on which he laid such stress had been fulfilled. Anne, following her own inclinations to begin with but subsequently acting on the advice of Godolphin and Marlborough, had made a *free choice* of the Tories as partners. Assurance had been given to the Whigs that there were still opportunities under the new order for non-Tories who were prepared to "serve without reproach"; partly through the retention of three of their representatives in the Cabinet, and partly through Marlborough's clear determination to keep those departments most concerned with the execution of war policy out of the control of the High Church zealots,[98] the Court had demonstrated its intention not to alienate the Whigs completely. On this footing Harley had whole-heartedly supported the new ministry as Speaker. He had approved of what he saw initially as a worth-while attempt, in circumstances which necessitated the admission of many leading Tories to high office, to realise the ideal of non-party government: "[the] Queen began her reign", he was later to remind Godolphin, "upon that foot of no partys".[99] There was one condition of partnership, however, which had not been clearly established in 1702, or at least had not been accepted by the High Tory chiefs when they entered the Cabinet: and this was the vital condition of who was to dictate the terms. A sharp struggle over the framing of the Queen's Speech for the opening of Parliament in October 1702[100] was an early indication that the Managers' determination to assert their own control over policy would be challenged by their powerful and ambitious new colleagues. Thereafter the tensions in the Cabinet progressively built up, and when first Rochester (in

1703) and then Nottingham and Seymour (in 1704) revolted against their second-class status, and either resigned or were dismissed, the end of the partnership was in sight.

The way was now clear for the Marlborough-Godolphin experiment of a centre coalition to be given its trial. However, the final disastrous breakdown of this experiment early in 1708 only convinced Harley the more firmly of the advantages of his own solution to the problem of managing the House of Commons. And when he became "prime manager" himself two years later it was this solution which he adopted in the summer of 1710, again in partnership with the Tories. In a bid to ensure control over a new Parliament, the Lower House of which he knew was bound to have a Tory majority, Harley accepted (though belatedly and unenthusiastically) that Rochester must be readmitted to the Queen's ministry, but on the Court's terms and not on Rochester's. He also tried to capture the influential Sir Thomas Hanmer,[101] and when this attempt failed, saw to it that Bromley, the leading High Churchman in the Commons since Seymour's death in 1708, was closely associated with the Court as Speaker of the House. Yet at the same time, Nottingham was passed over without even being approached,[102] in deference to the Queen's right of "free choice", and enough Whigs were kept in office to satisfy Harley's firm belief that the useful, the deserving or the compliant should never "be turned out for not being of a party".[103]

Harley was unquestionably right in assuming that a solution of this kind was the only feasible one when the stock of administrative talent and political influence on the "Court" flanks of the two parties was inadequate, and above all when one party or the other had a clear majority in Parliament. It gave the Court at least a chance of getting its business smoothly through the Commons without abandoning its control over the essentials of policy. The great danger was, of course, that if the favoured party enjoyed too large a majority in the Commons its leaders would seize the opportunity to use political blackmail on the Managers in order to wrest control of policy from them. Marlborough's and Godolphin's partnership with the Tories suffered irreparable damage in 1704, when Nottingham, undeterred by the failure of a similar attempt by Rochester the previous year, tried to do just this: "I have had a very long conversation with Lord Nottingham", Godolphin told Sarah on 18 April 1704, ". . . there was very plain dealing on both sides, and of his side *many threatnings from the Tory's*, intermingled with professions to mee. His aim seem'd to bee to gett the Duke of Somersett and the Archbishop out of the Cabinet Councill, and Lord Carlisle out of the Lieutenancy. He was very positive that the Queen could not govern but by one party or the other . . .". If Marlborough's information was correct, Nottingham's plan had been to threaten the Managers with a "Tack" both of the Occasional Conformity bill and the bill for renewing the Commission of Public Accounts, and at the same time to offer the Queen a choice between making "such alterations . . . in the Cabinet Councell as he thinks absolutely necessary for the safety of the Church" and accepting his resignation.[104] The result of this blatant challenge was that Nottingham's bluff was called, his resignation accepted, and his friends Seymour and Jersey dismissed from office; but the outcome was far from being preordained, and if Nottingham had been rather more skilful in playing a hand in which his House of Commons' suit was very strong but his Court cards weaker the issue could well have been different.

The next attempt of Marlborough and Godolphin at a partnership with the leaders of a party was their alliance with the Junto, finally concluded after months of manoeuvring and negotiation at the beginning of November 1708. It was a partnership in which the Managers were at a grave disadvantage from the start. The main terms of the alliance — the Junto's acceptance of the Court nominee for the chair of the House of Commons in return for the admission of Somers and Wharton to the Cabinet and the transfer of Pembroke* to the Admiralty — were too one-sided ("so great in themselves", wrote Sunderland in triumph, "towards putting things on a thorough right foot"[105]). What was more serious, far from entering into the partnership freely the Managers were forced into it by a whole sequence of adverse political circumstances. Hard on the memory of their torrid experiences in the final session of the previous Parliament came a clear Whig victory at the polls in May 1708, in which the Junto brigade of M.P.s gained valuable new ground. Then, in the autumn, the Lord Treasurer found himself faced with a serious decline in government credit and the possibility that adequate parliamentary funds would not be forthcoming to meet the following year's military commitments; and this was a prospect which, in the words of Erasmus Lewis, "frightned him out of his wits"[106] and made him quite desperate to dissuade the Whigs from renewing their harassing tactics in the Commons when the new Parliament met in mid-November.

Thus when the two chief ministers finally came to their understanding with the Whig leaders it was one negotiated under the very kind of duress which Harley had always dreaded: one which "gave the Junto such an advantage over the ministers, that they have since led them as in a cleft

---

* Hitherto Lord President of the Council and Lord Lieutenant of Ireland, the two posts now filled by Somers and Wharton.

stick".[107] Most deplorable of all in Harley's eyes was the fact that the Queen, far from accepting the bargain willingly, had bitterly opposed it ever since the spring of 1708, when she had told Marlborough theatrically that she could only regard it as "utter destruction" to bring Lord Somers into her ministry.[108] Though deprived at this juncture of the active support of her mentor,* Anne had been so carefully schooled by Harley in the past that she instinctively interpreted the struggle for power between the Court and the Whigs in terms which were essentially Harleian. Whatever the problems posed by the House of Commons, she could not believe it to be worth the Court's while to *buy* peace there at the cost of capitulating to any set of party chiefs, least of all to a group which she was still convinced was determined "to tear that little prerogative the crown has to pieces". To the Queen, as to Harley, the crux of the situation in 1708 was simply this: "whether I shall submit to the five tyrannising lords, or they to me".[109] In the end it was only when she was broken in spirit by the death of her husband at the end of October that, in sheer despair, she did submit. And it was not long before her diagnosis of the situation was proved correct, and that of Godolphin (who had continued at least to profess his confidence that judicious concessions by the Managers to the Junto need not entail surrender to them[110]) was proved mistaken. Confronted with Tory determination to oppose and obstruct the Court at every turn, with the sullen detachment of the Queen, but above all with the stern facts of life in the House of Commons, where Whig supremacy was unchallengeable, the duumvirs could only have preserved their new partnership as a going concern from November 1708 to the prorogation of Parliament in April 1710 by tacitly accepting what was in the fullest sense, 'government by party' in the years 1709–10. Even before the end of 1708 it was plain to Robert Molesworth that Godolphin was already being "teased to death by the Junto for every employment, and [that] they are now the Lords Paramount", and James Brydges was prophesying a bleak future for "those in the Queen's service who either had not the good fortune to be born Whigs, or the grace to preserve their first purity".[111] In November 1709 the last remaining nominal Tory in the Cabinet, Pembroke, was pensioned off to make way for Orford's appointment as First Lord of the Admiralty, and by this time conspicuously few Tories of any importance, apart from notorious courtiers, had managed to survive even in junior office.[112]

Harley's experience of the problems of management during the four years of his administration is equally revealing. Political exigencies, and in parti-

* See p. 207 above.

cular the refusal of a number of leading Whig ministers like Boyle and Cowper to co-operate with him, meant that the initial complexion of the ministry which he constructed between August and October 1710 was more favourable to the Tories than he would ideally have preferred. The enforced trimming of the ministry's sails to the strong winds blowing from the High Tory quarter, involving the reluctant admission of Rochester and Ormonde to high office, contrasts noticeably with the less obvious concessions made to these same forces in the 'shadow-Cabinet' which Harley was widely believed to have envisaged at the time of the ministerial crisis of January–February 1708.[113] Nevertheless the new administration was one which in October 1710 still bore a recognisably Harleian stamp. It was based on a partnership with the predominant party, but a partnership in which the Court rather than the Tory partisans yet remained in control. The partnership was also one to which the Queen had in the end freely assented, even though it did take almost four months of coaxing before Anne — still wedded to the notion of a "mixed ministry" — was fully ready to accept the logic of the advice Harley had given her in May 1710: that she must "Govern by one party or the other but not by both".*

The position changed dramatically, however, as a result of the Tory electoral landslide in October 1710. The unprecedented size of the party's majority in the new House of Commons made Harley's continued control over the situation exceptionally difficult almost from the start, and there were few who gave him much chance of success in the early weeks of the new Parliament.[114] By February 1711 he was under the severest pressure from the extreme Tories in the Commons either to identify the Court fully with the policies and personnel of "the Church party" or to abdicate in favour of someone who would do so. The pressure was all the more difficult for the prime minister to resist since it came as much from "the gentlemen of England", now organised as never before in the October Club, as from recognised High Tory leaders like Nottingham, Hanmer and Bromley. Yet resist it he did. He did so by performing an extraordinarily skilful political balancing-act, by carefully tending his unrivalled influence with the Queen, which he rightly saw as the one sure way of making himself indispensable to the Tories, and by exploiting at least one piece of timely good fortune.† Thus

---

* B.M. Loan 29/10/20: memoranda for an interview with Anne, 20, 21 May. This whole interpretation of the controversial revolution of 1710 will be developed and fully documented in the author's forthcoming study of the Queen's last ministry.

† Viz. the Guiscard assassination attempt which led to a marked emotional reaction in his favour in March-April 1711, even in some of the most hard-bitten Tory circles. See

he was able to thwart extremist measures, carry through a difficult financial programme, and even contrive to practise his old precept that the minority party in the Commons must not be made "desperate" through the total withdrawal of official favour from it. He managed, for instance, to preserve well over 30 Whig M.P.s in their offices right through the session of 1710–11 — a more-than-token attempt to realise his aim of the previous summer, to "Graft the Whiggs on the bulk of the Church Party".[115] Even in the following session some two dozen Whig placemen with seats in the Lower House still survived.

By the summer of 1712, however, even Robert Harley, Earl of Oxford, the most consummate political artist to place his skills at the service of the Court since the Revolution, was forced to abandon theory in face of reality. The loyal support given by the October Club Tories to the government's central policy of "Peace without Spain" in the session of 1711–12, and the uncompromising opposition of the vast majority of Whigs to this same policy, had made it essential by then to concede to the Tories a near-complete monopoly of civil office, except in those departments which Oxford looked on as the preserve of the civil servants rather than the politicians. It is true that he still managed for almost two more years to retain for the Court at least a negative control over major policy decisions; and he continued to block, or at least to palliate, Tory measures which offended against his ideal of domestic "moderation". Yet even here he was lucky. His problems were eased by the sudden death of Rochester and the wholly unexpected defection of Nottingham to the opposition in 1711, by the unwavering loyalty of Bromley to the Court and to Harley personally after the spring of that year, and above all by the long-drawn-out negotiations for peace and commercial privileges which acted as a brake on Tory extremism for more than two years after the autumn of 1711. Without such a fortunate combination of circumstances in his favour, it may be doubted whether even Oxford, strengthened though he was by his own great influence with the Queen, could have kept control of government policy out of the hands of the real partisans and the crypto-Jacobites in the Tory party for quite so long. As it was he contrived to do so until the last few months of his ministry, when the Bolingbroke faction was able to push through Parliament such measures as the Schism bill with the formal blessing of the Court. Only in 1714 was Bolingbroke himself able to prognosticate "that unless we are, as Tories, wanting to ourselves, unless we abandon the rules of common prudence, the

H. T. Dickinson, 'The Attempt to Assassinate Harley in 1711', *History Today*, Nov. 1965.

Church interest and the Court interest will, for the future during her Majesty's reign, be synonymous terms".[116]

Taking Anne's reign as a whole, however, the lesson which future generations of politicians could learn from it was quite simply this. Whenever politics was conducted within the framework of two genuine political parties, as it so clearly was in the years 1702–14, and whenever either party had a decisive majority of its own zealots in the House of Commons, the odds were always heavily against the formation, and even more against the survival, of any genuine coalition ministry. By imparting in such circumstances a recognisable party stamp to the administration the Court managers might hope to retain control of policy and keep the party leaders at bay for a while, but not indefinitely. And in the end something approaching our modern concept of 'government by party' was likely to prove the only feasible way of getting the Queen's business done in the Lower House of Parliament.

CHAPTER TWELVE

The Court and the Parties
in the House of Lords

THE House of Lords has been strangely neglected by modern historians of the eighteenth century.* Any politically-minded Englishman from the 1720's to the 1790's would have been justifiably puzzled by this neglect, but the Englishman of the age of Anne would have been utterly incredulous. To him the House of Lords seemed to be gaining rather than declining in importance. Apart from Walpole and Stanhope, who were just growing to full stature in the last session of the reign, there were only three politicians of the very front rank in the years 1702–14 — Seymour, Bromley and Hanmer — who did not sit in the Lords at some time in that period. Four out of every five ministers appointed to the Queen's Cabinet Council came either from the peers' benches or the Woolsack. The five members of the Junto had all left the Commons before the end of 1702; Rochester, Nottingham and Godolphin had done so well before the Revolution; Marlborough and Shrewsbury knew nothing whatever of the Commons at first hand, except the view from its galleries. It was equally apparent to contemporaries that to most of the rising men of the day, to Harley and St. John, Cowper and

* A general study, making use of all the new evidence on debates which has come to light since the appearance of A. S. Turberville's *House of Lords in the Eighteenth Century* (1927), has long been overdue. The success with which traditional interpretations in this field can be challenged has been admirably demonstrated by David Large ('The Decline of "the Party of the Crown" and the Rise of Parties in the House of Lords, 1783–1837', *E.H.R.* lxxviii, 1963); but generally speaking the priorities laid down by Sir Lewis Namier have been too faithfully followed. They are reflected most strikingly in the fact that a 3-volume *History of Parliament* for the years 1754–90, the product of years of massive and concerted endeavour, should be devoted unashamedly to only one half of Parliament, the House of Commons. The backwash of the tidal wave which Sir Lewis released in 1929 reached the reign of Anne in 1956. Dr. Walcott, in the analytical part of his study of *English Politics in the Early Eighteenth Century* and in the extensive appendices to the same work, virtually ignores the House of Lords, except as a collection of individual magnates whose real political importance (he implies) lay in their ability to command followings of varying sizes in the Commons.

Harcourt, a peerage represented political as well as social promotion. Members of the House of Commons did not turn down peerages because they were politically ambitious, but rather because, like Sir Michael Warton, they were entirely free from such ambitions. In the spring of 1712 Henry St. John, that born House of Commons' man, had St. Stephen's Chapel at his feet; yet so anxious was he to leave it that he agreed in the summer to accept a viscountcy, even though (with his aspirations to the earldom of Bolingbroke) he regarded the award as a deadly insult from Lord Oxford.

With such a wealth of talent to enrich its debates, the House of Lords was unquestionably supreme as a political forum throughout Anne's reign. Its prestige was already high in 1702, and it was higher still in 1714.[1] But it was far more than a superior debating-shop. There were periods in every one of Anne's Parliaments when the Upper House manifestly rivalled the Lower in real political importance; and in the Queen's last three years the House of Lords consistently attracted more attention and certainly absorbed more of the time and energies of the government than did the Commons. Significantly it also made increasingly heavy demands in these years on the time of its own members. When the Earl of Denbigh's rural peace at Newnham Padox was disturbed by an urgent summons to Town from Bromley in November 1711, he responded gallantly, but not without a nostalgic backward glance towards more leisurely days earlier in the reign.

I must own [he confessed to Oxford] I did not think of coming up to town so soon, knowing that our house used to have little to do at the first setting till the Commons had cutt us up some work, but I find now the case is altered. Its wee that are doing that and indeed fine work ... I shall not faile (God willing) being in town at the time to serve my Queen & countrey to the best of my poor power.[2]

Yet even in Anne's first Parliament — though not all its members may have realised it at the time — it was the House of Lords which had decided the outcome of the first phase of the party war in the new reign; by reducing the Tory leaders to frustration and eventually to desperation it had played a crucial part in bringing about the first major change of ministry since 1702. In 1702–4 the Whig peers, by masterly management, had withstood the furious assaults on Occasional Conformity and on the reputation of King William's Whig administrations that were launched from the Commons; and they had finally made such a spirited counter-attack from the Lords over the Scotch Plot and the case of the Aylesbury men that Parliament had to be prorogued in April 1704 in an atmosphere of constitutional crisis.[3]

The importance of the Upper House to the Whigs during the dark days of 1702–4, great as it was, was surpassed during the still more critical years between 1710 and 1714. So utterly powerless was the Whig party in the House of Commons after the 1710 Election that its morale must have been broken, and its whole organisation throughout the country threatened with disintegration, but for the torch of hope which so frequently blazed from the Lords' chamber in Westminster Palace, held aloft by the great champions of post-Revolution Whiggery — by Somers and Halifax, by Cowper and Sunderland and, most defiantly of all, by "Honest Tom" Wharton. Whether, but for their strength in the Lords, the Whigs would ever have survived to reap the rich harvest of George I's accession, is at least arguable.[4] There were times, too, when the House of Lords proved a blessing to the Court as well as to the Whigs. On no fewer than six occasions it delivered the Court from the incalculable embarrassments which the passing of Place bills into law would surely have entailed. Again, both in the opening years of the reign and after 1710 the Managers deliberately and successfully used the Lords to check many of the wilder acts of party extremism initiated by the Commons.[5] In this way first Godolphin (in 1703–4) and later Harley (in 1710–11) were helped to maintain their control over the administration, a control which but for the House of Lords might well have been wrested from them. To proliferate further instances of the importance of the second chamber would be to labour the point unnecessarily. It must be abundantly clear that any attempt to describe the working of politics in the age of Anne which fails to take due account of the House of Lords must be ludicrously inadequate. It was certainly the case that the complex relationship between the Court and the parties, our particular concern in these final chapters, was governed in no small measure by the special opportunities and the special problems which the Lords presented to the ministers of the Crown.

* * *

By and large the problems were less taxing than those presented by the Commons. This may seem to be belied by the experience of Lord Oxford's ministry, which in the last two and a half years of its existence was called on to survive at least three periods of major crisis in the House of Lords, the first from 7 December to 2 January 1711–12, the second from 1 to 8 June 1713 and the third from 19 March to 13 April 1714, any one of which could well have destroyed it. Yet except in one unusually stormy session, there had been little in the previous nine years to prepare the Court for the situation which arose in December 1711, when as one Cabinet minister put it, "the House of Lords prevaile[d] over the Queens management with us and the strongest House of Commons that ever meet".[6] There had been a few occasions, admittedly, between 1702 and 1710 when the Marlborough-Godolphin duumvirate was sorely harassed by the Upper House: in 1703 over the first Occasional Conformity bill, the only one of the three promoted early in the reign of which the Court approved;* in December 1704 over the endorsement of the Scottish Act of Security; and again in 1704–5 over the Aylesbury case. But only in the winter of 1707–8, when for several weeks the two Managers contrived to alienate the leaders of both parties simultaneously, was there a danger that a succession of defeats in the Lords might destroy their hold on the Queen's government. On the other hand, from the beginning of the reign up to the time of Oxford's pact with the October Club in December 1711 loss of control in the Commons was a spectre which haunted the chief ministers of the Crown in no fewer than six sessions out of nine.† Taking the reign as a whole, one can only conclude that the management of the Commons was the more daunting proposition for the Court.

In at least one basic respect, however, the problem of managing the two Houses was much the same. The political atmosphere of the Lords may have been superficially more decorous than that of the Lower House but it was scarcely less steeped in the raw spirit of party. Only the merest handful of English peers defied classification in party terms. One who clearly did so was the indigent eighth Lord Hunsdon, who voted Dr. Sacheverell guilty side by side with the warmest Junto lords in March 1710, yet whose backing Harley never doubted from the very start of his ministry.[7] Characteristically, Hunsdon saw the peace crisis of 7–8 December 1711, in which both party and personal convictions were as intensely engaged as at any time in Anne's reign, mainly as an opportunity for trying to screw an increased pension out of the government;[8] and what evidence we have of his political record thereafter suggests a conscience singularly untroubled by qualms of principle as he trod the courtier's path of virtue. He even supported the Schism bill in 1714 with the same aplomb with which he had condemned the arch-enemy of the schismatics in 1710.[9] Another peer to whom neither party could have laid claim with any confidence was Lord Delawarr, who once described the holding of office in the royal household as "a blessing farr more valewable then life it self".[10] Such blessings as came his way — the post of Groom of the Stole and First Gentleman to Prince George from 1697 to 1708, a Civil List pension from 1708 to 1713, and the office of Treasurer of the Chamber from 1713 to 1714 — did not find him ungrateful. In unguarded moments

---

* See p. 102 above, and cf. Add. MSS. 22221, f. 21.

† The exceptions were the sessions of 1706–7, 1708–9 and 1709–10.

he may have confessed to Tory sympathies, but his first loyalty was never in doubt. "I can truly say for myself", he wrote in 1712, "that to support the Queen's interest in Parliament from the Revolution to this day has been always my study and my greatest ambition."[11] It would have been equally hard and quite irrelevant to attach a party tag to Thomas Wentworth, Lord Raby, the most persistent and shameless go-getter of his day: a man of modest talents — "a very coxcomb", Marlborough once called him[12] — who by a unique combination of treachery to old friends and cultivation of new, by either flattering, hectoring or complaining almost unceasingly, and by soliciting unhesitatingly for every vacancy to which, in his unbounded self-consequence, he thought himself entitled,[13] contrived to acquire for himself between 1710 and 1714 an embassy at The Hague, the earldom of Strafford, joint charge over the Utrecht peace negotiations, the Order of the Garter, the post of First Lord of the Admiralty (with an extra £2000 bonus on his salary), and a seat in the Cabinet. The Hunsdons, Delawarrs and Straffords, however, were very much the exceptions that proved the rule. The over-whelming majority of members of the House of Lords in Anne's reign had been touched by the Whig or Tory brush — some only lightly, but most of them boldly and indelibly.

This was the fundamental characteristic which the two Houses had in common; and there were times, as we shall later see, when it proved as decisive in the final reckoning as any or all of the differences between them. But differences there undoubtedly were, and they were of real relevance to the day-to-day working of the political system. In normal circumstances the Court Managers undoubtedly possessed assets in the House of Lords which they did not enjoy in the Commons: these assets were numerous, and in most cases valuable. One obvious advantage was that the Upper House was a much smaller body numerically than the Lower, and as such easier to mani-pulate. In November 1703 its total membership, excluding Catholics, exiled peers and minors, was 161.[14] By the time Anne's last Parliament met in February 1714, such had been the toll of deaths that not even 24 new creations in the meantime and an influx of Scottish representative peers had been able to increase that number by as much as a score.* What is more, the really active membership of the House (applying the word 'active' in the most generous sense to peers who were normally ready to attend and vote when matters of the first political importance were under consideration) was rarely more than two-thirds of the total. In the first parliamentary session held during the Oxford ministry, for example, the number of peers present

* *Parl. Hist.* vi, 1243–6. The total membership in Feb. 1714 was 179.

at the time of an important division only once exceeded 110.[15] In the occasional periods of high tension between December 1711 and the prorogation of Anne's last Parliament a ceiling of between 120 and 124 voters and tellers was reached on just five days; but the average attendance when a crucial vote was in prospect in the last two and a half years of the reign was around 110.[16]

What was so important to any government in this period was not so much that the number of peers personally involved on such occasions was relatively small; it was the fact that, in sharp contrast with the Commons, the "Queen's Servants" (in the fullest sense) would quite often account for 40 per cent, and occasionally for 50 per cent or more, of the whole. The 1714 session is not perhaps entirely typical in this respect, for by this time the Oxford ministry, after suffering two years of acute pressure in the Lords, had taken steps to increase the number of aristocratic place-holders. Valuable sinecures and other posts normally reserved for commoners, such as Tellerships in the Exchequer and the office of Master of the Buckhounds, had been given instead to peers; and mainly by reviving old offices or creating new ones, over half the representative peers of Scotland had been accommodated in official employment. Nevertheless there are a few statistics for the session of 1714 which are worth recording, if only because they so clearly reveal an entirely different distribution of forces from that we have observed in the Lower House. At the end of February 1714 the number of members of the House of Lords holding places of profit under the Crown, civil, military or judicial, was 50. This number, moreover, excluded all the bishops except for one special case: this was the Bishop of London, who succeeded the recently-deceased Archbishop of York as Lord Almoner to the Queen and who still retained the seat in the Cabinet which he had held from 1711 to 1713 as Lord Privy Seal. In addition there were a further 19 peers who held unpaid offices of trust, Lord Lieutenant and Privy Councillors, a number of whom were handsomely recompensed for their honorary status by means of government pensions or royal bounties.*

With a 'party of the Crown' which, on paper at least, was some 70 strong by 1714, the Court could face the prospect of defections with a good deal more equanimity than it could afford in the House of Commons. A further source of confidence was the reflection that office was not its only direct medium of influence in the House of Lords. At least 17 peers who held no employment, paid or unpaid, had some pecuniary attachment to the Court

---

* Full details will be found in Appendix B: 'The Queen's Servants in the House of Lords, February 1714'.

at the time the Queen's last Parliament met.[17] In however loose a sense, they could be described as 'pensioners', although not all the pensions or bounties involved were official and fewer still were regularly paid. Indeed 12 of these peers were Whigs; and since Oxford was never one to dispense public money when the expectation of return was small, he had quite deliberately allowed the payments on most of their pensions to fall heavily into arrear. Unrepentant Whigs like Lincoln, Westmorland, Colepeper and Bridgewater, in company with one errant Tory, Lord Byron, had not received a penny since the end of 1710. Even the more amenable Whigs, for example Schomberg and Grantham, had been unrequited since December 1711.[18] On the other hand there were a number of lords — Cleveland, Kinnoull, Hunsdon, Stawell, Sussex and Warrington are all cases in point — who had profited substantially and quite recently from the Court's largesse,* and who therefore owed a more obvious obligation to the administration.

The proportion of the active members of the House of Lords whom Queen Anne's chief ministers were able in some way to "oblige" was always, therefore, high. By the end of the reign it was remarkably high. But in addition to this, it was bound to be of some advantage to the government of the day, under normal conditions, that many of the places allocated to peers were either working offices or positions in the royal Court and Household, for these generally tied their incumbents to London or its near vicinity as long as Parliament was sitting and the Queen was in residence at St. James's or at Kensington. Two precise illustrations, again from the 1714 session, will emphasise how valuable an asset this could be. On 2 March, the day of the Queen's Speech at the opening of Parliament, when the government was prepared for an attack from the Whigs on the newly-ratified peace treaties with Spain, 117 peers were present in the palace of Westminster. 55 of them enjoyed some official mark of royal favour — this quite apart from the group of pensioners who attended. On 19 March the Court faced a serious opposition attack on its treatment of the Catalans, and also the prospect of a hard struggle to persuade the House to agree to a long Easter adjournment

---

* The Whig Duke of Cleveland, presumably because he was of the blood royal, and Kinnoull because he was the father-in-law of one of Oxford's daughters, had their pensions regularly paid. For Hunsdon see p. 385 and no. 8 above. Stawell had received a bounty of £1000 in November 1712, probably through the intercession of his brother-in-law, Bromley, to enable him to attend Parliament (Ch.[H] 53, f. 3/3). Warrington had received a windfall of £1000 in very unusual circumstances in June 1713 (see his letters to Oxford, 18 Apr. 1713–10 Apr. 1714, in B.M. Loan 29/127), and Sussex had been paid some instalments (one as late as the end of 1713) on a pension of £2400 p.a. promised him back in 1711 (B.M. Loan 29/155: Sussex to Oxford, 17 June 1711–25 Dec. 1713).

which would give the ministry a welcome breathing-space. The attendance on that day was 112; the number of "Queen's Servants", 54. On each occasion, in fact, virtually half the House consisted of men who were technically courtiers. It was not pure coincidence that the first Whig attack was never launched and that the second could only be partially pressed home.

The capacity of the Managers to keep control of proceedings in the House of Lords, and to do so independently, if need be, of the party leaders, was clearly contingent in large measure on the behaviour of this impressive corps of placemen, local dignitaries and pensioners — a corps which by the end of the reign had absorbed nearly half the entire strength of the chamber. What mattered in the last resort was not ensuring their attendance but holding their allegiance. In the Commons, as we know, "the Queen's Servants" were notoriously unreliable. But fortunately for the Court their counterparts in the Lords, taking the reign as a whole, were more compliant. The difference was a matter of degree; but it was enough to have a marked effect on the working of politics. In the Lords, no less than in the Commons, the Managers had frequently to struggle against the powerful cross-currents of party principle and party loyalty which were always threatening to disturb the tranquil flow of gratitude to the Crown. Quite often, as in the Commons, they struggled in vain. Lord Dartmouth, though by no means a zealous Tory, freely admitted that he "commonly voted against the Court" during the years of Whig dominion from 1706 to 1710, when the Queen's favour kept him in his place at the Board of Trade.[19] If such conduct was irksome to Lord Treasurer Godolphin it must have been no less so later to Lord Oxford to find that the Whig Earl of Dorset, whom he preserved as Lord Warden of the Cinque Ports until June 1713, "oppos'd the court in everything", apart from the briefest interludes of remorse and reorientation.[20] Yet although such individual acts of rebellion were far from uncommon it is more significant to find that Marlborough, viewing the political scene apprehensively from The Hague in March 1710, was plainly shocked by the number of Court Tories who cast a party vote in the main division on the conviction of Dr. Sacheverell, against the declared inclination of the ministry: "how were these lords influenced to be for Sacheverell", he asked his wife: "duke of Northumberland, duke of Hamilton, earl of Pembroke, earl of Suffolk, bishop of Chichester, Lord Berkeley, earl of Northesk, earl of Wemyss, Lord Lexington? I should have thought all these would have been on the other side".[21]

There was good reason for Marlborough's astonishment. For in normal circumstances, at least, the pull of the Court was appreciably stronger in the

Lords than it was in the Commons, and the politicians of the day took this fact for granted. The English aristocracy had for so long stood in a unique relationship to the English monarchy that even strong partisans in Queen Anne's House of Lords could be made to feel uneasy at times about opposing ministerial policies which the sovereign had openly and unmistakably endorsed. The less committed brethren were correspondingly more susceptible. Thus not the least of the Godolphin ministry's difficulties in disciplining the Lords in March 1710 was that Anne's attitude to Sacheverell's cause was generally believed to have changed to one of open sympathy by the time the peers came to vote on his guilt and on his punishment. Indeed office-holders who applied to her directly for guidance, like the Lord Chamberlain, Kent, were told that "she thought the Commons had reason to be sattisfied that they had made their allegations good, and the mildest punishment inflicted upon the Doctor she thought the best".[22] The Oxford ministry was to face a comparable dilemma in December 1711 when it was defeated in the Upper House on the question of "No Peace without Spain". A most important factor in this defeat was the success of the Duke of Somerset in deceiving a whole squadron of Court Whig office-holders and pensioners into believing that the Queen's real inclinations were hostile to the preliminary settlement which her ministers had negotiated with France.[23] Yet two weeks later the positive influence of the Crown was clearly demonstrated in the Hamilton case, when many of these same Whig peers, who had just deserted the Court over the peace, declined to back their party leaders on an issue where the Queen had made her wishes plainly known, and after a debate which she chose to attend in person.[24]

Queen Anne's personal presence at Lords' debates on many occasions during her reign is itself a further clue to the difference between the political character of the two Houses of Parliament. To arrange for the Queen to listen to a debate "incognita" (which meant not that she donned some elaborate disguise or lurked in the galleries, but simply that she sat on the Throne unrobed and without her regalia*) was an accepted Court ploy on

---

* There was a curious convention that on such occasions the House should take no official cognizance of the Queen's presence. Writing up his account of part of the Lords' proceedings on the Scottish Act of Security the Bishop of Carlisle noted: "In the House, as soon as the Queen was come (Incognito, and without her robes) and handed to the Throne by the D. of Somerset . . . E. of Stamford mov'd that the House might consider the matter sitting; because then the debates would be more regular & solemn, wch was understood as an intended respect to Her Majesty. But the order was observ'd, & (Ld. Keeper quitting the wool sack) the E. of Sunderland was put into the Chair . . ." Tullie House, Nicolson's MS. Diary, 29 Nov. 1704.

occasions when the ministers anticipated a close issue in the Lords. It was a device used frequently in the early years of the reign, especially when the royal interest was genuinely aroused. Anne was present in December 1704, for example, when the House threw out the third Occasional Conformity bill with her manifest approval by a majority of 18; and only three days later, James Lowther of the Ordnance Office — not yet in the House of Commons but already a keen political student — observed that "the Queen comes constantly to the House of Lds every time they proceed upon the Scotch affairs".[25] In February 1705 she and her wheezing consort were induced to attend the Second Reading of Peter King's Place bill, another piece of the Commons' handiwork which Godolphin and his colleagues were particularly anxious to demolish.[26] The following winter the Queen was just as active in support of her Managers. The Tories were forced to argue their case for the motion to invite over the Dowager Electress under her sternly disapproving eye, with depressing results; and later in November Anne spent three more afternoons in the House, lending her countenance to the Court's counter-proposal of a Regency bill.[27] After 1710 this particular method of reminding "the Queen's servants" of their duty was employed more sparingly, not because Harley had any objection to it, but because Anne's health would only rarely permit its use. But that it could still be a highly effective device, especially when the party issues involved were not clear-cut, was proved very early in the life of the new ministry, when Anne was persuaded to come to the House of Lords on 9 January 1711 to lend her blessing to the government's attack on its predecessor's conduct of the war in Spain. Her presence undoubtedly helped to capture a number of wavering votes which decided the day.[28]

An advantage of a very different kind which the Court enjoyed in trying to maintain a majority favourable to its policies in the Upper House was its hold over the so-called "poor lords". To support a peerage in early-eighteenth-century Britain could be an expensive business, especially when estates were poor or heavily mortgaged, or when already-depleted incomes were further drained away by heavy war taxation and frequent election expenses. To live in London on their own resources for the duration of a parliamentary session which might last as long as six or seven months was for many noblemen frankly impossible, and for others highly injudicious. At the end of the 1713 session the Earl of Denbigh was so low in funds that he could not pay for his own journey from Westminster back to Newnham Padox and was forced to borrow from a friend; for the next few months he lived precariously on credit.[29] His Tory neighbour, Lord Stawell, pressed by

Weymouth to take his seat in the Lords after the Christmas recess at the end of 1710, at first excused himself on the ground of "extreame weakeness" following influenza. But it soon became clear that his frailties were more financial than physical. "I thanke God I am perfectly well recovered of the goute", he reported in March, "but my feet being very weeke and tender I stand in greater need of a white staffe than ever to support me. If it does not fall to my lott I readely submitt, but it shall always be a maxim for me for the future never to wage war att my own expense. . . ." This maxim sustained him most effectively during the crisis facing both his party and the ministry over the peace preliminaries in the following autumn and winter, when he at first declined to forsake his "farming affairs" in the hour of need. "I shall wish well to the Peace", he told his old comrade with disarming frankness, "but am resolved to spend no money about it".[30] It seems likely that it was only the promise of a handsome bounty[31] which eventually brought him to London for two months in December 1711 and January 1712.

Other "poor lords" were less prudent than Stawell. Party zeal, ambition or sheer pride spurred them into an active parliamentary life which they could ill afford, and the chances were that sooner or later they would be compelled to seek official charity. Denbigh had already done so in July 1711 and had been paid £500 for his services during the previous session. Lord Saye and Sele received a dole of £250 at the same time, and Lord Sussex one of £200 out of Oxford's own pocket in September 1713.[32] By 1713 Denbigh was again cap in hand, reduced (as he piteously told the Treasurer in a postscript to his begging letter) to "drinking your health in poor Irish claret".* Sheer financial necessity could leave the staunchest of party stalwarts no alternative at times but to put solvency before ideals. Nothing but the direst straits would have forced the High Tory Earl of Winchilsea, Nottingham's cousin, into Godolphin's camp in 1709–10, as his more compassionate friends recognised: "though Lord Winchilsea's unhappy circumstances forced him with reluctance to make a false step", Weymouth reminded Robert Harley in July 1710, "yet no man is more beloved and pitied there [in Kent], or capable of doing more service; and greater sinners must be restored, if they did not offend out of malicious wickedness".[33] Winchilsea was able to retrieve his honour in the county election that October "by appearing at the head of above a thousand freeholders for Sir Cholmondly Dering and Mr Hart", the Tory candidates;[34] yet after attending the next parliamentary session for a mere six weeks, during which time he strenuously supported the

---

* B.M. Loan 29/29/14: 11 Dec. [1713]. He had recently been made a Teller of the Exchequer but had yet to reap the benefit.

Court, he was once again in the position of having to warn Harley that without the Queen's generous support he would be compelled to retire forthwith to the country.[35]

Even the astonishingly loyal following of the Whig Junto was occasionally eroded by the embarrassments of its more necessitous members. Sheer desperation forced Cornwallis to succumb for a while to the Court in 1712, and compelled Lord Herbert — an unhappy victim of his family's costly electoral battles in Worcestershire — temporarily to abandon "the honest interest" in 1713 and 1714.[36] The wretchedness of Herbert's situation is stamped on every line of his letters. After receiving gratuities totalling £500 between March and May 1714[37] he made the first decent excuse to slink off into the country, professing himself "ready to come to town upon the least summons" to earn his hire in the House of Lords, but desperately hoping for some way out of his present dilemma. He was prepared to take the Governorship of Barbados, if it were offered him, or indeed any other respectable employment that would take him out of England, "no matter where, the farther the better", away from the reproaches of his friends and the dunning of his creditors.[38] His one consolation was that he was not alone in his misery. Before the 1714 session opened, indeed, the Whigs were being forced to calculate on at least half a dozen more of their supporters in the Lords being forced to accept 'expenses', in some form or other, from the Court, which would tie up their votes; or, at best, having to stay away from Westminster altogether to escape such a humiliating fate.[39]

Some of the hardest cases, however, were to be found among the Scots. Among the papers of Archbishop Wake in Christ Church library is a contemporary estimate of the landed incomes of the sixteen peers elected to represent the Scottish nobility in November 1710. Only one of the sixteen could have been considered in any way affluent by contemporary English standards, and this was the Duke of Hamilton, whose estate after his mother's death had an estimated value of £9000 a year. This may have been £2000–3000 above the average income of an English peer in 1710;[40] but it was £6000 less than the income credited to Sir Michael Warton, M.P. for Beverley, "the richest man for to be a gentleman only that was in all England", and it was mere pin-money compared with the income of some of the great English magnates of Anne's day — Newcastle, for instance, with his rent-roll of £40,000 per annum, Bedford, with perhaps £35,000, or Beaufort, with roughly £30,000. Apart from Hamilton, only Eglinton of the Scottish representative peers in the Parliament of 1710–13 was credited with an income of more than £4000, which was the level of a well-to-do country gentleman in England.* At the other end of the scale were some pitiful cases: the Earl of Loudoun and Earl Marischal with estates of under £2000, and both "heavily encumbered"; Viscount Kilsyth with £1500 a year, and Balmerino with a beggarly £1000.[41] Most penurious of all was Alexander, 7th Earl of Home. Sir James Erskine wrote to Lord Mar in November 1711: "The Earl of Home is at length persuaded to go up for London, and takes journey on Saturday next. How he has got credit I do not yet know, but he has borrowed 100 l. sterling for his journey." A few days later Lord Kinnoull reported that "Lord Home says, the devil take him, if it were not his circumstances that he has an old family to preserve he would serve the Queen without asking a farthing, he has so good will to the work. [But] he spent a great deal last time, and I believe some taken on upon tick ... wherefore I pray you by all means take care that he be supplied, and that timely."[42] All things considered, the Duke of Montrose was not unjustified in reminding Lord Sunderland, as he did in 1708, that "London jornys don't verie well agree with Scots estaits". Indeed in the early years of the Union the Marquess of Annandale had the reputation of being the one peer from north of the border capable of maintaining himself in London without a subsidy.[43]

After the first meeting of the Union Parliament in 1707–8, when the Squadrone peers joined with the Junto in attacking the Godolphin ministry in the House of Lords, especially on the issue of the Edinburgh Privy Council,[44] the Scottish contingent in the House acquired a growing reputation among the English peers for subservience to the ministry. Although in the election of Scottish peers held in 1708 the Godolphin-Queensberry alliance secured only ten of the sixteen places for men on the Court's own list of nominees, two of the six successful Squadrone candidates[45] were thought to be amenable to government influence from the start, and except for a while in the winter of 1708–9 even the rest gave the Court relatively little cause for anxiety. Indeed George Lockhart, reviewing the record of the Scottish peers in the Parliament of 1708–10 as a whole, was later to claim that, except during the passage of the Treasons bill (which Scots in both Houses opposed as a piece of anti-national legislation), it was not until the Sacheverell votes

* A Hampshire gentleman, Richard Norton, thought £4000 p.a. adequate to support a peerage in 1712, at least for one who had "been married about twelve years and [had] no child" (H.M.C. *Portland MSS.* v, 136). 11 years earlier Viscount Longueville had proposed in the House of Lords that this should be made the minimum qualification by law for all newly-created viscounts, but that a baron might be qualified with a landed estate of £3000 p.a. Add. MSS. 30000E, f. 211.

of March 1710 that the first substantial Scottish desertions from the ministry took place.[46] After the 1710 Edinburgh election, when for the first time the whole "Queen's List" of sixteen peers was returned to Westminster (a political farce which was duly repeated in 1713), the docility as well as the venality of the Scots became proverbial. The reluctance of most of them to participate in any debates save those on specifically Scottish issues (Viscount Kilsyth, for instance, never opened his mouth in the House of Lords between November 1710, when he took his seat, and June 1713, when he uttered some forty words on the subject of the malt tax)[47] did nothing to disturb the popular image of sixteen yes-men in the pay of the Court. We can see this now as a caricature rather than as a picture accurate in every detail. Individual Scots did occasionally assert their independence to the embarrassment of the Oxford ministry: some held out for long periods — Hamilton and Balmerino in 1712, Annandale in 1712 and 1713, Loudoun in 1714 — and others on specific issues, as when Islay, Orkney and Blantyre opposed the Land Grants bill in May 1712.[48] Yet apart from the two brief general revolts of February 1712 and June 1713, when the whole contingent was temporarily alienated by supposed infractions of the Treaty of Union,* the Court never had any real cause to fear an alliance between the Scottish peers and the Whig opposition in the House of Lords.

In addition to all the other assets available to them for maintaining the influence of the Crown in the House of Lords, the Queen's Managers always held one trump card, though it was one which, in the nature of things, could only be played in the direst emergencies. If a majority could not be guaranteed in any other way they could try to persuade the sovereign to create new peers who could be absolutely relied on, in the immediate future at least, to support the policies of the Court. Twice only between 1702 and 1714 did Anne's ministers resort to this controversial expedient. The first time was in 1703, when it was thought necessary to correct the very slight pro-Whig bias in the Upper House inherited from William III by promoting four Tories and one pro-Marlborough Whig.† These creations provoked some criticism, for no one doubted that their purpose was political, coming as they did after a session which had revealed "so near a balance in the house of peers that every little accident turn[ed] a question".[49] But their reception was nothing compared with the outcry against Oxford's unprecedented "dozen", created in the space of three days in the winter of

---

* See pp. 338–9 above.

† Baronies were awarded to John Granville, Sir John Leveson Gower, Francis Seymour Conway, and Heneage Finch — all Tories — and to the Whig John Hervey of Ickworth.

1711–12. Conscientious Tories lived in some trepidation thereafter of "another inundation of peers". As temperate a Whig as Lord Hervey, himself one of the beneficiaries in 1703, deeply regretted "those mortal wounds which have been given to the bleeding constitution of this country".[50] Even the Queen's personal physician was so scandalised by this flagrant abuse of the prerogative that he felt bound to remonstrate to his royal patient that it "was like to be a packing of Jurys to take away life":

... to all wch her M——y answered that King William made more; to wch I replyd, that is was sd, that was not done at one time, & therefore it was plain that this was not to reward merit, but to make votes.[51]

Sir David Hamilton's analogy of a packed jury was inappropriate in at least one sense: for Oxford's twelve peers, no fewer than seven of whom had some degree of personal dependence on the Treasurer, were designed to save life — the life of his administration — rather than to take it away. "I own 'tis not a thing to be often put in practice — soe great a promotion", observed the exiled Lord Ailesbury, "but se defendendo is allowed in Court when well proved for the prisoner".[52] Struggling to survive the crisis precipitated by his defeat in the Lords on "No Peace without Spain", Oxford could fairly have pleaded self-defence. Indeed there is every reason to suppose that without the application of this most extreme of remedies his ministry would have fallen in January 1712, notwithstanding its decisive majority at this time in the House of Commons.

This startling fact at once confronts us with the great paradox of the House of Lords in the age of Anne, and at the same time with one of the most intriguing problems to which the working of politics in this period gives rise. How can one explain how the Court party in the Lords, potentially so formidable, and with so many and such varied resources at its command, could on occasion crumble so alarmingly? How could the Managers lose control of the Lords as completely as Godolphin and Marlborough did between December 1707 and February 1708, or as Oxford did in December 1711 and came so very near to doing in June 1713 and in April 1714? How was it that even the consideration of revenue bills by the Lords, normally the purest formality, a social rather than a political occasion unless there was any suspicion of a "tack" by the Commons of matter foreign to supply, was capable at least twice in Anne's reign of throwing the ministry into panic? On Tuesday, 22 December 1702, the Bishop of Carlisle wrote in his diary:

The Money-Bill read a second time, and committed to a Committee of the whole House; wherein 'twas read again (paragraph by paragraph) and piece meal assented to. The Chairman (Lord Longvil) putting the question, and I onely answering; for no other Ld. in the House regarded what was doeing, this being onely (pro formâ) to preserve a seeming right to dissent from, or amend, any part of a Money-Bill as well as others.[53]

At a slack period of another session, in May 1711, another peer told a friend: "We have nothing (beside money matters, wch go for nothing) to do. . . ."[54] So much for the norm. Yet on 5 June 1713 Oxford's ministry only saved the Malt Tax bill from defeat in the Lords on the Second Reading by the parlous majority of two votes, and the Treasurer was reduced to such desperation by the prospect of losing the bill that to secure one of these two votes he promised what was virtually a bribe of £1000 to an incredulous Whig peer, the Earl of Warrington.[55] This particular shock Oxford was half prepared for, for it came at a time when the Scots were in one of their rare moods of disaffection, and the malt duty was a notoriously sore point in Scotland. Yet even the following May, when "the sixteen" were restored to their customary dependence on the Court, the Malt bill was again only narrowly salvaged when the Whig peers sprang a surprise attack on it in a thinly-attended House.[56]

Rare though these near-disasters were in the House of Lords, they and the handful of others not specifically connected with finance* have something of great importance to tell us about the relations of Crown and Parliament, and especially about the relationship between the Court and the two great parties, which has not so far emerged from our study of either House. A close analysis of all the main phases of crisis which affected the Upper House in Queen Anne's Parliaments leads to four principal conclusions. In the first place, we are given a salutary reminder that if the forces of the Court were undoubtedly better endowed there than in the Commons, so were the forces of opposition. The Lords, as we know, housed nearly all the great party chieftains and cornered much of the nation's political talent in the years from 1702 to 1714. There the Whig and Tory leaders were able to exercise a personal control over their followers that was often more effective than their lieutenants could achieve in the Commons. Able as were some of the Junto leaders in the Lower House, men like Lechmere, Jekyll, Powlet and Montagu were not of the calibre, nor could they carry the authority, of such seasoned campaigners as Somers, Halifax and Wharton. The vigour and cohesion of the party forces that were deployed in the Lords, especially those

---

* Particularly those of Feb. 1708 (the Scottish Privy Council and the Admiralty), Dec. 1711 (the Peace) and Apr. 1714 (the Protestant Succession); and one might add the setback of Jan. 1703, over the defeat of the 1st Occasional Conformity bill.

on the Whig side, did not depend wholly, however, on the individual brilliance of their leaders. They also owed a good deal to organisation of the highest quality. And here there is one additional factor that is vital to bear in mind. The enforced presence in the neighbourhood of Westminster of a large number of Queen's Servants, together with the enforced absence of some of the more indigent opposition peers, might give the Court a big advantage in normal circumstances, when attendances averaged between 80 and 100. Yet at times of special crisis this advantage could always be reduced if not negatived completely by the proxy-system. To this there was, of course, no parallel in the Commons; and in the hands of the Junto, especially, its manipulation was reduced during Anne's reign to a fine art.*

The second highly significant fact which emerges from a study of the main crises in the House of Lords between 1702 and 1714 is that a crucial contribution to the government's discomfiture on every occasion was the opposition of the bishops. There were 26 bishops in all but the first of Anne's Parliaments, and most of them were remarkably regular in their attendance, far more reliable in this respect, for instance, than the Scots. It was entirely typical of the conscientiousness of the lords spiritual that on a Saturday afternoon in April 1709, only five days before the end of a session, and after he had already booked a seat in the York coach for his journey north, the Bishop of Carlisle was still to be found "in the House till after three, attending on private (and money) bills; in pure duty".[57] Had the bishops formed in the years before 1715 the kind of solid, non-party, pro-Court *bloc* which they were to constitute later in the eighteenth century under the Walpole-Newcastle régime, then it is safe to say that the Court's hold on the House of Lords could never have been shaken, let alone destroyed. But despite some High Church creations by Anne in the early and middle years of her reign, notably when Hooper was elevated to St. Asaph and to Bath and Wells, Dawes to Chester and Blackall to Exeter, and more marks of favour to Tory divines during the life of Oxford's ministry,† it was the moderate and Low Church bishops who, at least up to 1713, continued to dominate the episcopal bench in the Lords in the Whig interest. The Queen's hopes at the start of her reign that these men would "vote right" (as she put it), with judicious prodding from Archbishop Sharp,[58] were quickly dis-

---

* The part played by proxy votes in party organisation is discussed on pp. 307–9. The one important limitation as it was operated in Anne's reign was the fact that proxies could not be called for at the committee stage of bills.

† Robinson, Bisse, Ottley, Atterbury and Smalridge — all Tories — received bishoprics between October 1710 and the spring of 1714.

appointed. For a year or two they showed some willingness to oblige the Court and disoblige the Whig leaders over questions which did not involve their principles. Only the incorrigible Gilbert Burnet, for instance, supported the Junto in its attempt to secure a vote of censure against the Tory admiral, Sir George Rooke, in February 1703.[59] But for the most part their loyalty to the Whig cause in general, and to the Junto leadership in particular, was undeviating. The voting of the bishops against the reprieve of the Scottish Privy Council on 5 February 1708 is a spectacular example of this. Here was a purely secular matter, and a matter, moreover, not of party principle but rather of straight party advantage, designed by the Junto lords to enable them to seize control of the Godolphin ministry. Yet of all the bishops present in the House only two, Trelawney and Talbot, voted with the Court for the extension of the life of the Council to 1 October (the extension which would have enabled it to sway the 1708 Scottish elections in the government's favour and to the disadvantage of the Whigs' Squadrone allies).[60]

When the Whigs were in opposition after 1710 the acceptance by the Low Church prelates of the lead given by the Junto was generally so unquestioning that St. John was once goaded into swearing that "if a vote shoud be proposd to un-Bishop them" by their leaders, "he believd they would concurr in it".[61] Their performance in the debate on the adjournment on 2 January 1712 was typical rather than remarkable; but it happens to be an occasion about which the evidence is unusually precise, and serves admirably to illustrate the totality of their party commitment. The debate followed immediately after the creation of the twelve new Tory peers, when Oxford was seeking an early opportunity to demonstrate the Court's reassertion of control over the Lords. The method he chose was tactically shrewd. He decided to put before the House a simple adjournment motion, carefully divorced from any of the violently controversial issues which had destroyed the solidarity of the Court party during December 1711, and prefaced by a special message from the Queen desiring the Lords' agreement to a further fortnight's recess, at the end of which time she promised to lay a number of new proposals before them. On this motion at least, it was felt, the spiritual peers could hardly fail to show some measure of deference towards the Supreme Governor of the Church. The Bishop of London's chaplain recalled how the members of the bench were known to "have paid always the most slavish subjection to the Crown upon such messages to them in convocation & here in Parliamt". Yet during the debate several bishops followed the Whig line in denouncing both the message and the motion as an infringement of the rights and privileges of the House, and in the eventual division eleven out of the fifteen bishops present voted with the Junto against the adjournment.[62] Right to the end of the reign the Whig prelates maintained this defiant front against the ministry, benevolently but firmly disciplined by Tenison, the Archbishop of Canterbury, who was too much of an invalid to come to the House himself but insistent in the demands he made on the attendance of his brethren. "The Bps in Town on our side are Ely, Lichfield, Peterburrow, St. Asaph, Llandaff, Norwich", noted Tenison's chaplain in November 1713, when the Whigs were taking their precautions against the unlikely event of an early meeting of the new Parliament; "Bangor has proposed to be dispensed with this winter, but the excuse is not admitted".[63]

The extraordinary dominance which the Whig leadership exerted over its followers in the House of Lords, both lay and clerical, especially during its long years in opposition at the beginning and end of Anne's reign, points to the third conclusion which emerges from an analysis of the main political crises in the Lords between 1702 and 1714. This is that any government which was prepared to co-operate closely with the Whigs, or even to bid for their support by promoting "Whiggish" policies like the vigorous pursuit of the land war, the Union with Scotland and the preservation and strengthening of the Toleration, had little to fear from the Upper House; and that, conversely, any government which consistently flouted Whig ideals and aroused Whig fears could expect a rough passage there.

Between November 1704 and June 1711 the Court, first under Godolphin's management and then under Harley's, embraced Whig measures, if not always Whig men, fairly consistently; and in seven sessions its hold over the Lords was only seriously threatened once. This was during the winter of 1707–8, when the Whig Junto decided that it was not enough simply to see its policies accepted by the ministry without itself occupying a commanding share of the policy-making posts in it. It therefore set out deliberately to use its parliamentary strength in the Lords, as well as the party majority in the Commons, to bludgeon its way into power. By the end of 1708, with Sunderland, Somers and Wharton already in the Cabinet and the way prepared for the introduction of Orford in the following year, it had succeeded in its object; and significantly the Court never had an easier passage in the House of Lords in the whole of Anne's reign than in the Parliament of 1708–10. Shocked as the Managers were in March 1710 by the biggest Court desertions for two sessions, Dr. Sacheverell was still found guilty by the Lords in March 1710 by a majority of 17 votes.

Even during the session of 1710–11, after Godolphin had fallen and all the leading Whig peers except Newcastle and Somerset had been forced out of the ministry, Harley was still able to manage the House of Lords comfortably by methods not dissimilar from those which the duumvirs had employed, with more modest success, in the years 1702–4. He was able to do so by grafting on to a basically Tory ministry a substantial body of Court Whig peers, of whom there were always over a score in every Parliament of Anne's reign and around thirty by 1710: men holding government and Household offices or lord lieutenancies, and also "those Lords who by the narrowness of their fortunes have depended on the Court",[64] pensioners and the recipients of temporary subsidies. Whenever the Queen's Managers found it necessary to take the Tories into partnership these Court Whig peers, forming a 'centre group' in the House of Lords, were always a key factor in the working of politics. They proved so most of all after 1710. For one session Harley contrived to hold at least a majority of them within the ministerial orbit. He did this partly by preserving them in their offices and dignities and by meeting the arrears on their pensions, but mainly by appeasing their party instincts: by continuing to support Marlborough and the war in Flanders, for instance; and by blocking at every turn the progress of partisan Tory measures like the repeal of the General Naturalization and the resumption of land grants which would have strained the loyalty of these Whiggish "Queen's Servants" too far. Not every Court Whig peer was prepared to co-operate even on these terms. "That glorious honest youth Ld Lincoln, who [as his Whig friends acknowledged] has nothing but a pension to depend on"[65] was a notable rebel, and there were a few others like him. But by and large, Lord Cowper noted, in this session "The scheme lords,* the necessitous lds, & the Scots lds vote[d] according to the Ministry"; only "the wise and independant vote[d] according to judgmt."[66]

Once, however, the peace and the succession issues had begun to bedevil the political situation from the winter of 1711–12 onwards, Oxford's hopes of continuing to control the House of Lords by a managerial policy which involved a partnership with the Tory party but not a surrender to it† began to seem increasingly unrealistic. As the resistance of the Court Whig peers to his ministry's policies stiffened, so the prime minister found himself with no alternative but to remove the more recalcitrant of them one by one from their offices and their local positions of influence, or to suspend payment of their pensions. Before the autumn of 1713 it was evident that virtually all the props which had earlier helped to support the Court from the political

* I.e. those employed in Harley's "scheme" of government.
† See p. 376 above.

centre of the House of Lords had given way under the strain which government policy imposed on Whig loyalty. It was a strain too heavy even for the
stoutest and most seasoned timbers. The Earl of Cholmondeley's removal
from his post as Treasurer of the Household in the spring of 1713; Russell
Robartes's rueful confession to Oxford some months later that "my brother
Radnor has not answer'd what I think in honor he ought to have done both to
the Queene and yr Ldship";[67] above all the astonishing news that the most
beggarly of all the "poor lords", the fourteenth Lord Willoughby of Parham,
had preferred the patronage of Wharton and Sunderland to dancing servile
attendance on the Queen's ministers:[68] these were unmistakable signs that
the management of the House of Lords could no longer be successfully
conducted on the premise that the Court could command there a substantial
body of support in its own right, without a thorough commitment to one
party or the other.

Fortunately the Court had adjusted itself to this situation before it was
called on to face its last great crisis of the reign in the Lords in the spring of
1714 (the last, that is, before its coherence was destroyed for good in June
by the struggle for mastery between Oxford and Bolingbroke). When
Parliament met in February only 13 Whig peers survived among the 69
Queen's Servants in the Upper House. Moreover one of the 13, Argyll, was
dismissed quite early in the session; two more, the Marquess of Lindsey and
the Duke of Montagu, enjoyed hereditary posts;[69] a fourth, Halifax of the
Junto, had a place for life of Auditor of the Receipt; while four of the remainder merely held lord lieutenancies, some of them in counties where
no feasible Tory alternative existed.[70] Because the Tory party was much the
more prone of the two parties to be divided on fundamentals (and never more
so, as it proved, than in 1714), an alliance with it was always a more hazardous
means of restoring or maintaining control over the House of Lords than an
alliance with the Whigs. Yet at least in March-April 1714 a Tory alliance
saw Oxford through his immediate troubles, if not without some moments
of acute anxiety.

The real significance of this final crisis, however, was that in confronting
it Oxford pursued what was literally the only sane course left open to him.
The Whig peers could no longer be tempted to support a government in
which even the mildest of them had lost all confidence. To keep twenty or
thirty of them in place or favour for the sake of preserving the theoretical
independence of the Court from party control would therefore do nothing to
strengthen, and a great deal to weaken, that government's hand in the House
of Lords. Nothing but Tory votes could now sustain Lord Oxford's minis-

try, and the only logical way to deploy the patronage of the Crown in this situation was to use it to cement as many of these votes as possible to the Court. Any other policy for managing the Upper House at this juncture — anything smacking of the various "moderating schemes" of 1704–8 or even of the qualified partnership with the High Tories attempted in 1702–4 and in 1710–11 — must have led to complete disaster. The fourth and final conclusion to be drawn, therefore, from the relations between the Court and the parties in the House of Lords at times of particular stress is simply this: not merely the Commons, where the influence of the Crown was relatively weak, but also the Lords, where intrinsically that influence was incomparably stronger, was capable of forcing the Queen and her Managers to abandon their ideal of non-party government. In driving Godolphin and Marlborough into the arms of the Junto in 1708 the situation in the Lords had played a conspicuous part; in determining Oxford's change of attitude between 1712 and 1714 it was probably the decisive factor.

We thus find ourselves back at the same point where we ended the previous chapter. As long as politics in Britain was carried on within the framework of two great parties, something not far removed from a two-party 'system' was bound, at some stage, to take possession of the Queen's government. It did so because there inevitably arose from time to time political issues so acute, and so inseparable from the real heart of the struggle between Whig and Tory in Parliament and in the country, that only a one-party ministry could command sufficient support to deal with them adequately and keep the Queen's administration viable. In these circumstances only such a ministry could prevent the House of Commons from making the government's business impracticable and the House of Lords from making the government's life intolerable.

Conclusion

THE last two decades of Stuart rule were a period of political apprenticeship for Britain. One recent school of historical opinion would have us believe that the art which the post-Revolution generation was trying to perfect was essentially that of eighteenth-century politics, that distinctive Georgian art whose subtleties Sir Lewis Namier and his pupils have so devotedly explored. One of the purposes of the present work has been to demonstrate that this was not so. In fact, to the next three generations the political lessons of the two decades up to 1714, and above all the experience of the age of Anne, were to be of only limited value; for within a few years of Anne's death the conditions in which this experience had been acquired were already beginning to disappear.

The conditions which helped to fashion the political habits and techniques of mid-Hanoverian Britain, in the comfortable years before economic revolution at home and political revolution abroad unleashed the restless forces of radicalism, were in many respects the very antithesis of those in which the politicians of William III's reign and Anne's had to develop and practise their skills. By the 1740's and the 1750's an integrated governing class, in a stable social order, had forgotten the fears and the jealousies to which a hard-pressed "landed interest" had been a prey half a century before. By that time also, religious torpor, as yet only fitfully disturbed by the Evangelical Revival, had long since settled on Anglican and dissenter alike, stifling the animosities which to the early-eighteenth-century eye had seemed irrepressible. The cries of "No Fanatic", "No Conventicle", "No Tub-Preacher", which rang round countless hustings in 1705 or in 1710, had almost passed out of the popular vocabulary forty years later; and (what would have astonished the Augustan Englishman still more) even the cry of "No Popery" was fast becoming an empty shibboleth. South of the Highland line there were few in 1740 who could still appreciate the anxieties and passions which the insecurity of the Protestant royal line had aroused in 1713–14;

and not even the brief fantasy of the '45 rebellion was capable of resurrecting the dynastic problem as a major political issue. The Britain of George II had grown accustomed to a stable dynasty. Equally it had grown accustomed to filling the rôle of a major European power, indeed a major world power, and had learnt to accept the resulting commitments which to many of King William's subjects and Queen Anne's had seemed dangerous and novel. Most significant of all, perhaps, it had come to accept as the normal foundation of its political system a largely docile and venal electorate, rarely exercised more than once in seven years and still more rarely stimulated by really great political issues: a very different foundation from that provided by the volatile, intimately-involved political nation which elected ten new Parliaments in twenty years between 1695 and 1715. In these changes lie many of the clues to the basic differences between politics in the age of Anne and politics in the age of Newcastle. The politics of oligarchy and connexion, so appropriate to the temperate air of mid-Georgian Britain, could never have flourished in the hot and highly-charged atmosphere of the early eighteenth century. These were the conditions for the politics of party.

The age of party in later Stuart Britain reached its climax in the reign of Anne. But it was inaugurated before March 1702 and it did not come to an abrupt end in August 1714. For a decade and a half after their birth in the later years of Charles II the lives of the first Whig and Tory parties followed an erratic course. The collapse of the Exclusion campaign in 1681 had the effect of stunting for seven years the earlier premature growth of the Whigs. A national reaction against the misrule of a Catholic sovereign in 1688 restored their bodily health; but the bipartisan revolution which followed, and the parliamentary settlement of the crown on a foreign King resolved to bestow his favours impartially, were the prelude to five years of uneasy existence for the Tories and to a period of confused identity for both parties in the Parliament elected in 1690. Between 1694 and 1697, however, an important change came over the character of politics. Despite the emergence of anomalous centre groups, the most notable of which were the "Old Whigs" led by Paul Foley and Robert Harley, the loyalties of most politicians polarised markedly in the last three years of the Augsburg war. Whig and Tory became again a more important basic division in the House of Commons than Court and Country. Various factors brought about this change: the death of Queen Mary;* the first great break-through into office

---

* While she lived Mary had done something to preserve the tenuous bonds between William III and the Tories, and a good deal, since 1689, to keep the Church — potentially one of the most divisive factors in politics — temporarily out of the party arena. See G. V.

of a new generation of party men, represented by the Whig Junto; the passing of the Triennial Act, which for two decades made the unreformed electoral constituencies of England an ideal forcing-ground for the luxuriant growth of party; and the establishment of the Bank of England, which quickly became for the Tory squire the most hated symbol of an unholy alliance, forged between the City and the Whig power-politicians for the perpetuation of the war. The war itself, however, was possibly the most significant factor. The longer it lasted, the more the Francophobia of the Whigs and their sense of community with foreign Protestants identified them with William's balance-of-power foreign policy and his Continental strategy; and this in turn helped to mask the uneasiness which many of them had felt, and still felt, about his conduct of domestic affairs. The effect on the Tories, however, was very different. On top of the lack of sympathy or the downright hostility which many of them felt for the King, their dislike of the Dutch and of a costly land war fought in support of the Dutch bred in them a deep suspicion of foreign entanglements and influences, and convinced them that if wars had to be fought at all they should be strictly limited in scope and maritime in character. The important contribution made by the war to the redefinition of party divisions in the mid-1690's is underlined by the reaction which set in during the three years which followed the Peace of Ryswick in 1697; for as European issues receded temporarily into the background, Country issues like the standing army and William's land grants came to the fore to weaken the hold which the Junto ministers in office had established over independent Whigs, and the pattern of parliamentary politics again became confused.

Not until 1701–2 was this confusion finally resolved. The two Speaker's elections of February and December 1701 were a measure of the change that was then in progress, the change that was to ensure that politics in the age of Anne would be pre-eminently the politics of party. In the first election Robert Harley triumphed over Sir Richard Onslow by a large majority, with the help of "a great party of Whigs" who still regarded him as a symbol of country independence;[1] but much of that support had significantly evaporated by the end of 1701 when he scraped home against Sir Thomas Littleton by a mere four votes.[2] During 1701 three developments — two parliamentary and one external — had fused together the main elements in the Whig party more effectively than at any time since the Revolution, convincing even the Country Whigs that Tory ministers were no longer fit

Bennett, 'King William III and the Episcopate', *Essays in Modern English Church History in Memory of Norman Sykes* (1966), pp. 122–3.

to be entrusted with the government of the country. The first was the impeachment of three of the Junto lords on charges blatantly trumped up out of party malice. The second was the crisis over the Spanish succession, and the evident unwillingness of the Tories to recognise the reality of the threat from France and the inevitability of a new war. The third was the passage of the Act of Settlement, which produced relatively little tension on the surface but enough below the surface to suggest that many Tories had not really cut themselves free from the bonds of divine hereditary right (an impression reinforced by the wrangling which marked the debates on the Abjuration bill in February 1702). Outside Parliament in 1701 the deliberate attempt of the Highflying Tories, prompted by Rochester, to use the Lower House of Convocation as a political weapon against the Whigs forced moderate as well as Low Church divines into the welcoming arms of the Junto and finally shattered William III's already-crumbling policy of religious pacification. Thereafter it only needed the accession of a High Anglican Queen the following March, the provocative words of Sacheverell's Oxford sermon in June and the Wilton election scandal shortly afterwards to inflame relations between Church and dissent to such a degree that the old problem of toleration once again became a dominating consideration of the politicians: and this was a problem on which Whig and Tory could never see eye to eye.

By the end of 1702 nearly all the major issues which were to divide the political world in the next fourteen years, before the Jacobite rebellion and the Septennial Act destroyed the Tories as a serious competitive force, had thus been brought on to the stage. Few men asked themselves by then whether they were for "Court" or "Country". Indeed it was only a widespread and genuine anxiety over the steady increase of placemen in the House of Commons and the spasmodic excitement caused by evidence or rumour of maladministration which made possible the survival of the old country tradition into Anne's reign, and ensured that the basic two-way division of both Houses of Parliament would very occasionally be broken up. However, the real substance of politics between 1702 and 1714 was composed overwhelmingly of the diverse issues of principle, policy, interest or plain party advantage which sustained the conflict between Tories and Whigs.

In this conflict social and economic divisions and differences over ideology and policy were often hard to disentangle. For instance, "the scandalous poverty of the clergy", against which Charles Davenant inveighed in 1704,[3] must have sharpened the hostility of hundreds of Tory parsons towards the Low Church bishops (not least those occupying wealthy sees like Salisbury,

Ely, Worcester and Lincoln), the men who consistently opposed their religious ideals in Convocation and their political ideals in Parliament and the constituencies. In a similar way the religious antipathy between High Anglican Tory and dissenting Whig had its social as well as its political background. It was not just that the votes of occasionally-conforming councillors sent Whig members to Westminster. There was also the fact that dissenters patently flourished among the thrusting middle-class businessmen and traders of London and the provinces, permeating that very monied interest whose rise the Church-of-England squirearchy regarded with as much trepidation as they did the war which had made that interest so formidable. The Spanish Succession war itself, of course, was not just a political issue between the parties. Peace and isolationism were attractive to the Tory country gentleman because he hated the Dutch and also because after 1707 he had little faith even in the genius of a Marlborough to inflict a final and decisive defeat on the French on land. But he would not have regarded them with quite the same craving had they not promised an end to a punitive system of taxation, which took four shillings in the pound from his own largely static rents but which scarcely touched the fat dividends of the Bank and East India Company shareholders, among whom the City Whigs predominated. Not even the vital succession issue at home could be dissociated from the clash of material interests. To the Whigs the prospect of a successful Jacobite *coup* after Anne's death carried the threat not merely of an arbitrary and Popish government but also of a government that would repudiate its debts, destroy the whole basis of a credit economy, and so encompass the ruin of the moneyed interest and the whole rentier class.

With so much at stake the conflict of Whig and Tory was no charade to be indulged in for diversion or excitement or self-advertisement or even for mere profit. It was at all times in Anne's reign an earnest and often a deadly business, in which men could go to the wall and frequently did. The victory of their political enemies was a daunting prospect for even the humbler partisans. An eminently moderate Whig country gentleman like Awnsham Churchill could write in all sincerity before the 1705 Election: "I cannot but tremble at the thought of a Tory H of Co[mmons] . . . I shall not think it very comfortable living in Dorsets when the T[ories] have got the possession of the country, & can let loose the C[our]t or Ch[urch] on those they please at pleasure."[4] A War Office clerk of Walpole's could not conceal his desperation in 1710 as the great Tory tide rolled inexorably in. "God deliver us", he prayed, "from such men and such principles."[5] At the real crises of the reign, when basic values were threatened, genuine and disinterested party zeal drove men to remarkable acts of self-sacrifice. The gallant but pleasure-loving Earl of Huntingdon made a special journey from Holland in 1704 to join with his Whig friends in throwing out the bill against Occasional Conformity.[6] Edward Fowler, the Whig Bishop of Gloucester, old and pathetically decrepit, struggled up from the west country in the winter of 1711 to take his seat in the Lords for the first time in years; for he knew well enough that one vote might save his country from a treacherous Tory peace. He collapsed in the chamber at the very moment when the votes were being counted on the fateful 7 December.[7]

Nor should we imagine that the principles on which the ordinary Whig and Tory normally stood so firm represented no more than useful camouflage for the ambitions of their leaders. The charge laid by the author of *Faults on Both Sides* in 1710, that "the Heads and Leaders on both Sides have always impos'd upon the Credulity of their respective Parties, in order to compass their own selfish designs at the expence of the Peace and Tranquility of the Nation", was monstrously unjust. Because they had more to lose as well as more to gain from politics than most of their followers; because of what Bolingbroke called "those mortifications which fall to the lot of such as serve the publick in our enchanted island";[8] because, in short, their steps could lead them to the gates of the Tower as well as to the corridors of power, the great Whig and Tory chieftains sometimes sacrificed principle to expediency. But it was not to promote "their own selfish designs" that Rochester resigned the Lord Lieutenancy of Ireland in 1703 or Nottingham gave up the Secretary's seals after two years in office in 1704; nor was it self-interest that made Wharton spurn a private bargain with the Court in 1708 or prompted Cowper to resist the joint pressure of Harley and the Queen and go out of office along with five of his Cabinet colleagues in 1710. Because they recognised that kid-glove methods would not always be enough to urge their claims for consideration on a Queen and Court instinctively chary of a close commitment to either party, we need not suppose that the Junto lords and their High Tory counterparts were out to pursue, capture and hang on to office *at any cost*. Notwithstanding its material rewards, office was of little value to any of them without the accompaniment of power. Only the possession of real power — the capacity to dominate the Cabinet Council sufficiently to dictate major decisions on policy — could enable them to promote the measures and defend the ideals which their friends and followers looked to them to promote and defend.

In the final reckoning, therefore, the conflict of party in the age of Anne was a conflict over policy and principles. It is true that the rival policies which

Whigs and Tories advocated were sometimes rooted as much in class-interest as in a distinctive party ideology. It is equally true that the image of Whig and Tory principles, as it appeared to the electorate, was frequently distorted by hostile propaganda ("surely there never was such a lying age", a Whig candidate in Cumberland feelingly exclaimed, ". . . & such malitious inventions to misrepresent people are hardly to be parellel'd").[9] Yet most men engaged in the heart of the battle understood well enough both what they were fighting for and what they were fighting against; whether they reduced their basic platform to the beautiful simplicity of the banners carried before the Tory candidate in Worcestershire in 1705 — "For the Queen and the Church, Pakington"* — or whether they defined their position as elaborately and articulately as did George Granville in his circular letter to the gentlemen of Cornwall in 1710.[10] That prolific pamphleteer John Toland came as near as anyone to the root of the matter when he wrote three years after Anne's death:

As for the subdivisions, or particular species of Whigs and Tories, . . . though in themselves significant enough, yet they are become very equivocal, as men are apt to apply them: whereas Whig and Tory, as here determin'd, cannot be mistaken; for men may change, and words may change, but principles never.[11]

* * *

If, however, "the subdivisions, or particular species" of the party men did not substantially affect the essence of politics in the age of Anne they did affect its working. The presence in each party of a "Court" wing and a "Country" wing introduced some flexibility into the political system: far less than would have been possible in a system based on the interplay of Court, connexion and the independent backbencher rather than on party, but enough to create certain opportunities for the Crown and, above all, undoubted problems for the Whig and Tory leaders. The nature of these problems depended on which type of party politician posed them. From a leader's point of view the Court Whigs and the Court Tories had the advantage of being more susceptible to organisation, and the disadvantage of being more susceptible to self-interest, than their Country brethren. As long as it proved possible to reconcile their loyalty to party with their obligations (whatever these might be) to the Crown and the ministry, they were biddable

---

* Similarly the supporters of Sir William Blackett and William Wrightson at the Newcastle upon Tyne election of 1710 "had red & blew favours in their hats wth this motto in letters of gold, viz. For the Queen & Church B:W". B.M. Loan 29/321: Dyer's Newsletter, 7 Nov. 1710.

enough. But when loyalties clashed there was no certainty that the claims of
party would take preference; and for the Whig Junto, struggling to impose
its authority on a large body of Court Whigs, especially in the House of
Lords, this was a particular source of frustration. The Country members and
peers on each side were much the more difficult to discipline, and they never
quite lost their inbred suspicion of the power politicians in their own party.
Yet in time of real need they were less likely to fail their leaders than men on
the opposite wing. The Country Whigs demonstrated this when those
leaders were under attack in the Commons in 1701, in 1703-4 and again in
1712; the Country Tories did so when the October Club agreed in December 1711 to give to the support of Oxford's peace policy, on which the Tory
ministry's fate depended, a clear priority over their own factious, fire-raising
aims.

In the perpetual struggle to gain or keep the favour of the Crown between
1702 and 1714 the maintenance of cohesion among those who professed the
same party faith as themselves was utterly vital to men like Somers and
Wharton, Nottingham and Rochester. At times of special crisis the cementing power of principle was sometimes enough in itself to maintain this
cohesion through every section of the party. But success in meeting the day-
to-day demands of parliamentary conflict, like success in the constituencies
which was so important a prerequisite, depended a good deal on effective
organisation. To the historian the solutions which the party chiefs and their
lieutenants evolved to solve the problems of organisation, varying from the
crude and improvised to the ingenious and sophisticated, are in some ways the
most intriguing of all aspects of this age of political apprenticeship. The problems themselves could scarcely have been more taxing. The obstacles in the
way of successful organisation were many and formidable. There were those
which arose out of the very novelty of political parties in England: the
absence on both sides of any formal party machine or central office, of a
regular party income, or of an established system of professional parliamentary
whips. There were the purely physical obstacles to be overcome: the problems of distance, of poor communications and inadequate transport, of a slow
and vulnerable postal service, and not least of bad weather (the months from
November to March, we must bear in mind, were the heart of almost every
parliamentary session of the reign before 1713). There were also the
psychological barriers to be broken down: the independence of mind of so
many country gentlemen and backwoods peers and the pride in that independence (sustained in many cases by independence of fortune) which made
them normally intolerant of restraint and discipline. Finally there was the

fact that, for all his party zeal, the average member of both Houses regarded politics as a part-time occupation. Unless very great pains were taken to persuade him of the necessity, he was reluctant to arrive promptly at the start of a session and even more reluctant to stay to the end. He found London life unhealthy and expensive; and even when the prospect of debating and deciding "party matters" did keep him in town there was much to deter him from regular attendance at Westminster: the unintelligible complexity of most public business and the ineffable boredom of all private business* seemed a poor alternative to the comforts and companionship of the tavern, the coffee-house and the club.

Yet, as we have seen, the Whig and Tory hierarchs of the early eighteenth century surmounted many of these obstacles in a quite remarkable way. Consistent success, in the nature of things, was unattainable; but effective organisation for the key parliamentary occasion was normally within their capacity. By careful planning and ingenious execution, by persistence, by persuasion and occasionally by threats, both sides could usually muster up a "good appearance" of members and peers when it really mattered, though the advantage normally lay with the party whose morale and expectations at the time were the higher. It could not be claimed that the record of the Whig Junto in the years 1702–14 exemplifies *typical* methods of party organisation, for in the art of electoral and parliamentary management they had no serious rivals apart from Robert Harley; but their record does demonstrate what could be achieved, at times in the most unfavourable circumstances, by selfless enthusiasm, meticulous attention to detail, and a high degree of political skill. In both Houses the Junto lords succeeded to a greater extent than any of their contemporaries in solving the two main problems facing party organisers in the reign of Anne, namely, getting their supporters to attend Parliament in the first place, and persuading them to vote for measures of the leaders' choice once they were there. In the House of Lords, Wharton, Sunderland and Halifax reduced the manipulation of the proxy system to a fine art. They and their friends were also adept at combining business with pleasure, a dinner party with a discussion on parliamentary tactics, a race-meeting with a top-level conference on general strategy, though business always appeared to benefit rather than suffer from the combination. Even the Junto found (in common with all political leaders at this period) that it was easier to impose unity and discipline on their party when in opposition than when in power. There were brief periods in Anne's reign when its hold over

---

* It is worth remembering that even in an age of great party issues, the private bill was still the staple diet of the normal parliamentary day.

Court and Country Whigs slackened perceptibly. It did so in the winter of 1705–6 and again in the winter of 1707–8. But in the years of Tory supremacy from 1702 to 1705 it was rarely shaken, and after the summer of 1710 it was virtually absolute: "for to be sure", Sir John Cropley acknowledged, "if they are not supported we are gone indeed".[12]

Of course, the success of the five lords as party organisers also owed much to the fact that they could command their own connexion in both the Commons and the Lords. The real importance of connexions in the age of Anne, it has been stressed, was the contribution they made to the parliamentary cohesion and electoral organisation of both Whigs and Tories. To the Junto, to friends like Walpole and Newcastle, and to enemies like Rochester and Harley, they offered in Parliament a solid nucleus of support on which they could almost invariably rely. Yet there are two things one should not forget. The first is that these nuclei were usually very small (the Junto lords, who by repute commanded the largest personal following of all in the House of Commons in the middle years of Anne's reign, could depend on a hard core of no more than 40 after the successful Election of 1705).[13] The second is that while family ties, ties between patron and client, and even ties of personal friendship were of recognised political importance at this period, they were normally put, and were expected to be put, at the service of party; they were not expected to bind men to a course of action alien to their own inclinations and incompatible with general party policy — and indeed this was something which in ordinary circumstances they were powerless to do.

Whig and Tory bulk so large in the working of the Augustan political system that there is a danger of forgetting that there was always a third side to the triangle of forces. At its centre was the Queen; she was flanked by her most trusted servants, the Managers, those few great statesmen of the day whose first allegiance was always to the sovereign and to "the public" rather than to either party; and they in their turn were flanked by a small number of politicians — mostly Household officials, administrators, minor placemen and officers of the armed forces — whom it is appropriate and accurate to label collectively "the Court". In Queen Anne's reign, in contrast to William's, the Managers were always the key figures in the working of politics. Without their guidance, and without the supervision by her two "prime managers" at the Treasury of the day-by-day work of her administration, Anne would have drifted helplessly on the turbulent political waters of the years from 1702 to 1714. Yet their relations with her are, for all that, a striking reflection of the reserves of power which still remained vested in the Crown after the Revolution. After March 1702 there was much to militate against the effective exercise of power by the sovereign — her sex, her dismal state of health, her inferior abilities; yet none of her Managers could ever take the Queen's support for granted, and none was ever in any doubt that the permanent loss of that support must spell the death, sooner or later, of his own political ambitions. Even the weakest of the Stuarts had no intention of being a figurehead. Not just for her principal servants but for every individual politician, from the most distinguished to the most commonplace, her affections, her gratitude and her aversions could be of crucial importance. Schooled by Robert Harley in the years 1705–7 to play what he considered to be her proper part in politics, that of "arbitress", Anne learned a lesson she never subsequently forgot: that it was her duty to God and her subjects to exercise her remaining prerogatives to the best of her judgement, in order to maintain the precarious balance of the Revolution constitution and to keep within bounds the virulent animosities of party, which she so detested and feared.

But these animosities were by 1702 so strong that the monarch had no alternative but to learn to live with them, and it was one of the functions of the Queen's Managers to make her relationship with the parties as smooth or at least as tolerable as possible. Another and more vital task was to try and ensure that the policies sanctioned by the Queen's ministers in the Cabinet Council received the support — financial and where necessary legislative — of both Houses of Parliament. There was never the remotest chance of their securing this support by building up an independent group of "Queen's friends", a group that would be strong enough to form — like the Court party of Danby or, a century later, of North — a semi-permanent basis for a system of parliamentary management. Placemen, as such, could certainly not fulfil this function; for most placemen in Anne's reign, like the overwhelming majority of all parliamentary politicians, were party men. There were barely three score members, in or out of office, in the average House of Commons of 1702–14 whose obligations to the Crown and the Managers could generally be relied on to override their party loyalties. In a House of 513 (later of 558) members they were powerless as a wholly independent unit, except in the rare event of a General Election producing a near dead-heat between Whigs and Tories. In the House of Lords the Court was relatively stronger, but even here it could not hope permanently to stand, in the contemporary phrase, "on its own bottom".

The Court, then, could not defy the parties: at least it never dared to defy both parties at once. Completely unchecked on both sides, the flood of party feeling could have submerged any ministry within a matter of weeks and reduced its policies to a shambles (of this the 1707–8 session left no subsequent government in any doubt). Yet properly controlled and harnessed, as Sunderland and Shrewsbury had briefly demonstrated in the middle years of William's reign, it had the power to provide the Crown with the most effectual means of managing Parliament which it had possessed since 1603. The line of least resistance for the monarch would have been to adopt the twentieth-century solution to the problem: to entrust the formation of her ministry and the conduct of her policies entirely to the leader or leaders of the party which commanded a clear majority in the House of Commons. It was, needless to say, a solution which the leaders themselves would have welcomed and there is no evidence that it would have been regarded with horror by the bulk of their supporters.[14] But it would have involved surrendering control to the parties, and not exercising control over them; and such a course was anathema to Queen Anne, as it had been to her predecessor. The only alternative in the conditions of the early eighteenth century seemed to be to place the chief responsibility for the management of her affairs in the hands of one or more of the great non-party statesmen of the day — in those of Godolphin and Marlborough to begin with, later in those of Harley and, more temporarily, of Shrewsbury — and leave them to make the best bargain they could with the parties, as each new situation arose.

The bargains struck by the Managers in Anne's reign were likely to take two forms. They could be attempts at coalition, which excluded most of the main party figures altogether but aimed to pacify both sides by employing the more moderate and least factious representatives of each. Alternatively, they could be attempts at qualified partnership, which entailed giving a clear preference to one party, and admitting some if not all of its leaders to office on the understanding that they would support the general policy of the Managers, but at the same time allocating a block of junior posts and if possible a few senior posts as well to the minority party. The conviction that coalition government was unworkable as well as undesirable, at best an unhappy temporary expedient, was common to every party leader of the day. Lord Nottingham's views on this did not change at all between April 1704, when he resigned from office over the continued presence of Whigs in the Cabinet, and early in 1711, when he wrote in a memorandum:

There are some propositions so plain & evident that I need onely mention them.
1. that a Coalition-scheme is impracticable.
2. that the attempt of it cannot be wth a good designe because wt ever tends to the interest of our Constitution in Ch. & State will be more faithfully pursued by friends than enemies . . .[15]

Henry St. John put the point more picturesquely but equally explicitly. "A coach may as well be driven with unequal wheels, as our Government carried on with such a mixture of hands."[16] But the first experience of Godolphin and Marlborough with the alternative, in their alliance with the High Tory leaders in 1702–4, was not a reassuring one, and it needed the calamitous breakdown in February 1708 of the "mixed ministry" over which the duumvirs had presided after 1705 finally to convince the Managers that partnership with one party or the other was indeed a more feasible solution than coalition to the problem of parliamentary management. Yet it was not an ideal solution. For the Whig or Tory leaders concerned in it, it was no more than a half-way house on the road to their true goal. With a large majority of their own zealots behind them in the House of Commons, urging them on and eager to engross the whole favour of the Crown, they were not likely to accept for long the position of junior partners, the inferior status which the Queen and her advisers were determined to thrust upon them. The time would come, as it did in 1704, in 1708–10 and in 1712–14, when a party would no longer be content to serve the Queen's administration, and would seek instead to command it. If that party's bargaining-power or its power of political blackmail was strong enough, the Managers were then left with no alternative but to concede, however unwillingly, the necessity for one-party government.

Whatever the choice which the Queen's Managers had to make, however, whether it was a choice between a broadly-based or a more narrowly-based administration, or between a Whig or a Tory 'partnership', or even the less palatable but sometimes inevitable choice between a Whig or Tory ministry, it was dictated in the main by the parliamentary situation in the Commons. Since this House controlled the purse-strings of the Crown, and could therefore, as Harley once wrote, "by one sullen fit the begining of a session ruine any ministry",[17] every major change in the distribution of forces there had to be followed (or, as in 1702 and 1710, anticipated)* by a change in the composition of the ministry. Yet it could not always be assumed (as Harley himself found out to his cost after November 1711) that the Lower House "can certainly draw the Lords after them, wch the Lords can not do

---

* In 1702 and 1710 the Court's decision to enter into partnership with the Tory leaders was dictated not by the situation in the existing House of Commons, but by the completely different situation predicted there as the result of a General Election which was plainly unavoidable. The coalition of 1705 to some extent, and the alliance with the Junto in the autumn of 1708 to a greater extent, were the fruits of Elections which had already taken place.

the others".[18] The choice of ministry which the Managers made on the basis of the situation in the House of Commons did not always provide the ideal solution to the management of the Lords, where the party situation was much more stable and, over the course of the reign as a whole, much more favourable to the Whigs. This was not the least of the problems which beset Anne's ministers in trying to govern the nation through two Houses of Parliament of comparable prestige and influence, whose favours were rarely if ever taken for granted.

That the Oxford ministry had worked out an answer to this problem by the spring of 1714, and this in the most difficult circumstances, may be taken as a clear indication that the post-Revolution generation had finally served its political apprenticeship. Since 1694 statesmen had learnt, slowly and at times very painfully, how to live and work in a divided society with two great nation-wide parties, whose rivalry increasingly permeated the life, the work and even the leisure of the politically-conscious classes. At the centre of public life they had come to terms with two parties which, since 1701, had made overriding demands on the allegiance of the vast majority of politicians and had dwarfed all other political groups and associations. Between 1712 and 1717* they showed that they were even reconciled to something like a two-party *system* as well as to a two-party legislature: to a system of government that was logically adapted to the existence of the two competing, irreconcileable forces of Whig and Tory, "like a door which turns both ways upon its hinges to let in each party as it grows triumphant".[19] It was the irony of the age of Anne that these lessons were to be largely wasted on the eighteenth century, and that by the early nineteenth century, when they once again became relevant to political life, they had to be laboriously relearned.

* |In the first edition I chose the date 1716, for reasons now not entirely clear to me. 1717, the year of the Whig schism (see above, p. xiv and n. 15), is a much more logical date for the *terminus ad quem* of two-party government.

APPENDICES

Appendix A

PARTY ALLEGIANCE IN THE
HOUSE OF LORDS, 1701–14

IN the case of seven important questions which came before the Upper House of Parliament in the years 1701–14 we have a reliable record *either* of how every peer voted *or* of how every peer was expected to vote. These questions were

1. the impeachment of Lord Somers: division on the motion for his acquittal.   17 June 1701

2. the 1st Occasional Conformity bill: division on the "penalties amendment".   16 January 1703

3. the 2nd Occasional Conformity bill: division on the motion for a Second Reading.   14 December 1703

4. the impeachment of Sacheverell: the final judgement of the Lords.   20 March 1710.

5. the Duke of Hamilton's case: division on the motion disabling Hamilton from sitting as a hereditary British peer.   20 December 1711

6. the French Commerce bill: Lord Oxford's estimate of how the peers would divide if the bill passed the House of Commons.   [13] June 1713

7. the Schism bill: Lord Nottingham's estimate of the peers who would vote for and against the bill.   June 1714

With the help of five division-lists and two detailed estimates by leading politicians it is possible to make some assessment of the consistency of party allegiance in the House of Lords in the age of Anne; and this despite the fact that in one of the questions involved (the Hamilton case) many peers, both

Whig and Tory, considered themselves absolved from their normal party obligations, and that on a second issue (the French Commerce bill) Tory opinion was genuinely divided. The general conclusions drawn from this assessment were indicated in Chapter 1 (pp. 37–8). The evidence on which these conclusions were based is presented below in tabular form.

The location of the seven lists here used is given on pp. 463–4, notes 103–6 below; but the identification of the last two lists with the Commons bill and Schism bill, respectively, requires some explanation.

List 6 (B.M. Loan 29/10/3) has no heading and no date. It contains the names of 154 members of the House, and they are placed by Lord Oxford into two categories, "Pro" and "Con", with some names queried under each head and three peers considered so doubtful that they are listed under both heads. The Scottish representative peers included in the list are those who were elected to the Parliament of 1710–13, and the presence of Viscount Bolingbroke among the prospective supporters of the ministry narrows down the field of search to the 1713 session of this Parliament, since Henry St. John received this title after the end of the previous session. Neither the "pros" nor the "cons" correspond in number with the votes recorded for and against the ministry in any division which took place in 1713; and this fact, together with the querying of names, leaves no room for doubt that this was an estimate by Oxford of how the House would divide on some particularly controversial issue, the outcome of which was uncertain. Only three such issues arose in the 1713 session of which the ministry had prior notice: the attack on the Union, the Malt Tax, and the bill giving effect to the 8th and 9th articles of the Treaty of Commerce with France. On the first two questions it is certain that Oxford would have expected all 17 Scottish peers to vote with the Whigs. The Union and the Malt Tax are almost automatically ruled out, therefore, by the fact that in this estimate only 3 Scots (Argyll, Islay and Balmerino) were thought likely to desert the Court. A still more decisive piece of evidence is the existence in B.M. Loan 29/10/13 of another paper in Oxford's hand, endorsed "June 13: 1713". This contains (1) a list of 13 peers — 12 of them being Tories or Court peers whose support is considered unlikely or doubtful in List 6, and (2) at the foot of the page, six numbers: viz. 25 29 23; 33 20 24. With the exception of the first, these numbers tally exactly with the totals appended by Oxford at the foot of each of the six columns of names (3 "Pro", 3 "Con") which appear in List 6. We must conclude, then, that List 6 was drawn up on or about 13 June, by which time the attack on the Union had failed and the Malt bill had passed the Lords, but the Commerce bill had still to receive its Third Reading in the

Commons (due on 18 June). At this stage it was expected that the bill would pass the Commons by a small majority but would encounter great opposition in the Lords, where the Earls of Abingdon and Anglesey had already threatened to desert the Court and several other Tories seemed likely to follow their lead. It was the outcome of this clash (a clash which never in fact materialised because of the defeat of the bill in the Commons) which Oxford was trying to forecast when he compiled List 6.

List 7 (Leics. R.O. Finch MSS. P.P. 161 [ii]), which is in the Earl of Nottingham's hand, is also unheaded and undated. It places the peers in three categories, "For" (85), "Against" (68), and "Doubtfull" (4). The names of the Scottish representative peers in the first category definitely relate this paper to the 1714 session. But the totals 85 and 68, even with 4 extra votes distributed between them, correspond with no known division in that session, so that again we must assume that this was an estimate made before, rather than a division-list compiled after, the event. There were a number of closely-fought divisions in the House of Lords in 1714. The most important were those of 5 April, on the safety of the Protestant succession (won by the government by 77–63); 12 April, on the Third Reading of the Place bill (69–69); 13 April, on the Queen's answer to the address on the Pretender (72–70); 16 April, on the Treaties of Peace and Commerce (82–62); 15 June, on the Third Reading of the Schism bill (77–72); and 8 July, on the Assiento contract (55–43). The last question can hardly have been Nottingham's concern when he drew up his list, for it was not debated until the very end of the session, in a House much thinner than Nottingham clearly anticipated: a House which included the Duke of Shrewsbury, recently returned from Ireland, whose name is significantly missing from Nottingham's list. This list was clearly compiled between April and June 1714. Of all the major issues which arose in that period, however, only one — the Schism bill — could conceivably have been expected to lead the Lord Treasurer's cousin and follower, Lord Foley, a man of strong dissenting sympathies, to divide against the Tories; and likewise only the Schism bill could have induced uncertainty in another of Oxford's moderate, undogmatic Tory friends, Lord Paget. Two of the most striking features of List 7 are that Foley's name appears among the Whigs and Paget's among the 'doubtfuls'. Equally significant is the location of the Hanoverian Tories. The education of Protestant dissenters, the issue at stake in the Schism bill, was a question in which the Anglican loyalties of all High Tories were inevitably involved. On any other big issue of the 1714 session Lord Nottingham would almost certainly have anticipated, or hoped for, the support of some 7 or 8 "Whimsical" Tory peers who generally voted with the Whigs in this session; above all he would have looked for Anglesey, Abingdon, Carteret and Archbishop Dawes of York to oppose the ministry. Yet the only Tory peers he expected to be against the measure in question, apart from himself and his brother Guernsey, were Foley, the Presbyterian Earl of Loudoun, and the Earl of Pembroke, a consistent opponent of the Court since 1711. We happen to know that in the event Anglesey, Abingdon, Carteret and Dawes did support the Schism bill in June 1714, and that Nottingham, Guernsey and Foley opposed it. There can be little doubt that this is the bill to which List 7 refers, even though the final vote was more favourable to the bill's opponents than Nottingham had feared.

The 209 lay peers and bishops whose voting records are tabulated below are those whose names appear in two or more of the seven lists analysed. They are identified by the titles they held at the time of Anne's death. On six of the seven questions concerned there was a recognised Whig or Tory position to which the majority of each party in the Lords conformed; the symbols W and T are used to indicate a vote, or an expected vote, in accordance with that position. The symbols w and t are used in the case of the Hamilton division (List 5), where there was no accepted 'party line', to indicate a vote cast on the same side as the Whig or Tory leadership [see p. 37 above]. Peers whose votes were considered to some extent uncertain in the two estimates of 1713–14 (Lists 6 and 7) are distinguished thus: W?, T?, or D (doubtful). SR signifies a representative peer of Scotland.

Note to revised edition: A new division-list for the period 1701-14 which has come to light since this Appendix was compiled is that for 21 January 1709, a list of those lords voting for and against allowing Scottish peers with titles in the new peerage of Great Britain the right to vote in the election of the representative peers of Scotland. See C. Jones, 'Godolphin, the Whig Junto and the Scots: a New Lords' Division List from 1709', *Scottish Historical Review*, lviii (1979), 172–4. Note also P.R.O., C. 113/37 for the division on the East India Company Bill, 23 February 1700; and British Library, Egerton MSS. 2543, ff. 398–9 (and elsewhere) for the division on the earl of Oxford's impeachment, 24 June 1717 (see C. Jones, 'The Impeachment of the Earl of Oxford . . .', *Bull.I.H.R.* lv [1982], 80–7).

On new lists in general, including forecasts of divisions in the House of Lords, see above, p. xi and n. 7.

	June 1701 (1)	Jan. 1703 (2)	Dec. 1703 (3)	Mar. 1710 (4)	Dec. 1711 (5)	June 1713 (6)	June 1714 (7)	COMMENTS
Abergavenny, baron	T	T	W		w	W?	T	Hanoverian Tory
Abingdon, earl		T	T					d. 1710
Anglesey, John 4th earl		T	T			W	T	Hanoverian Tory
Arthur 5th earl								d. Jan. 1710
Ashburnham, John 1st baron		T	T					
John 3rd baron						T	T	succ. June 1710. Whig (Court Whig 1712–14)
Atholl, duke						T	T	SR
Balmerino, baron		T	T		t	W	T	SR
Barnard, baron				T		T	T	
Bathurst, baron				W	t	T	T	
Beaufort, duke		T	T					Temporary convert to Toryism. Returned to Whig allegiance 1708.
Bedford, duke		T	T	W	t			d. Sept. 1710
Berkeley, Charles 2nd earl	W	W	W	W	w	W	W	
James 3rd earl		W	W	T	went out	T	T	Court Tory
Berkeley of Stratton, baron	W	W	W	T	t	T	T	
Berkshire, earl				T	t	D	T	
Blantyre, baron					t	T	T	
Bolingbroke, viscount				W		T	T	SR
Bolton, duke	W	W	W	W	w	W	W	

Name	June 1701 (1)	Jan. 1703 (2)	Dec. 1703 (3)	Mar. 1710 (4)	Dec. 1711 (5)	June 1713 (6)	June 1714 (7)	COMMENTS
Boyle, baron							W	Earl of Orrery (I). Court Whig, supporting Harley 1710–13. d. 1708
Bradford, Francis 1st earl		W	W					
Richard 2nd earl				W	w	W	W	
Bridgewater, earl		delib. abs.	T	W		W	W	Court Whig (pension)
Brooke, baron	T	T	T	T		T	T	
Bruce, baron	W	W	W					
Buckinghamshire, duke	W	W	W					
Burlington, earl	W	T	T	W	t	W	T	
Byron, baron					t	W	T	Court Tory (pension) but very "Whimsical"
Cardigan, earl					went out	T	T	ex-Roman Catholic
Carlisle, earl	W	W	W	W	w	W	W	
Carnarvon, earl	T	T	T	W		W		Hanoverian Tory
Carteret, baron		T	T	T	w	W	T	
Chandos, baron		T		W	t	T	W	
Cholmondeley, earl			W		t	W	W	Court Whig
Clarendon, earl					t	T	T	
Cleveland, duke		W?	W	W	went out	W	W	
Colepeper, baron	W	W	W	W		W	W	Court Whig (pension)
Compton, baron		W	W	W		T	T	

Name								Notes
Conway, baron	W				T	w	W?	T	Hanoverian Tory
Cornwallis, baron	W	W			W	w	W	W	
Coventry, Thomas 2nd earl		W	W		W				d. 1710
Gilbert 4th earl					T	t	T	W	succ. 1712
Cowper, baron	T	T	T		W		T	W	
Craven, baron	T	T	T		T	w	T		
Dartmouth, earl	T	T	T		W	t	T	T	Court ('Tory)
Delawarr, baron	T	T	T		T	t	T	W	Tory "poor lord"
Denbigh, earl	T	T	T		W	t	T	W	
Derby, earl		[went out]	W	W	W	w	W	W	
Devonshire, William 1st duke	W	W	W		W	w	W		Court Whig. d. 1707
William 2nd duke	W	W	W*		W	w	W	W	
Dorchester, marquess	W	W	W		W				Earl of Kingston to Dec. 1706
Dorset, Charles 6th earl	W	W	W		W	t	W	W	d. 1706
Lionel 7th earl							W	W	Court Whig
Eglinton, earl	W	W	W		W		T	T	SR
Essex, earl	W	W	W		W				
Eure, baron		W	W		T		T	T	
Exeter, earl	W	W	W		W		T	T	
Ferrers, earl		W	W		T				
Feversham, earl	T went out		W		T	w	T	T	Court Tory
Findlater, earl					W		T		SR

* Not in the division-list as printed in *Parliamentary History*; but as Earl of Kingston appears in a manuscript version in Cambridge University Library (MSS. Mm/vi/42) along with Lord Hervey. These two names bring the number of voters against the 2nd Occasional Conformity bill from 69 (as in *Parl. Hist.*) up to the correct total of 71.

	June 1701 (1)	Jan. 1703 (2)	Dec. 1703 (3)	Mar. 1710 (4)	Dec. 1711 (5)	June 1713 (6)	June 1714 (7)	COMMENTS
Fitzwalter, baron	W	W	W	W	went out	W	W	Whig "poor lord"
Foley, baron	T		T	W	went out	T	W	Harleyite Tory d. 1712
Godolphin, Sidney 1st earl								
Francis 2nd earl		W	W	W	w	W	W	
Grafton, duke			T	W	t	W	W	Court Whig (pension)
Grantham, earl			T	W	t	W	W	Court Whig (pension)
Greenwich, earl				W		W	W	Duke of Argyll (S)
Grey of Wark, baron		W	W	T	w	W	W	
Guernsey, baron	T	T	T	T	t	T	T	Hanoverian Tory
Guilford, baron		T	T	T		T	T	
Halifax, baron		W	W	W	w	W	W	
Harcourt, baron				T		T	T	Hanoverian Tory
Hatton, viscount			W	T	w	D	T	
Haversham, John 1st baron	W	W	W	T				Hanoverian Tory Whig convert to Toryism. d. Nov. 1710.
Maurice 2nd baron					w	W	W	
Hay, baron						W	T	Son of Earl of Kinnoull (S). Called to the Lords in his father's barony, Dec. 1711.
Herbert, Henry 1st baron	W	W	W					d. 1709
Henry 2nd baron	W	W	W	W	w	T?	D	Junto Whig "poor lord" (Court, 1713–14)

							Remarks
Hereford, viscount	T				T		
Hervey, baron		W		w	W	W	
Holderness, earl	T?		W	w	W	W	
Home, earl				t	T	W	Court Whig
Howard of Effingham, baron		W*	T	t	W	W	SR
Howard of Escrick, baron	T		W	t	T	T	Court Whig "poor lord"
Hunsdon, baron	W				W		Court
Hungtindon, earl				t	W	T	
Islay, earl		W	W	t	W	W	SR. Argyllite Whig (Court 1710–12)
Jermyn, baron	T	T			T	T	
Jersey, Edward 1st earl	T	T	T	t	T	W	d. Aug. 1711
William 2nd earl				t	W	T	
Kent, duke	T?	T	W	t	W	T	Court Whig
Kilsyth, viscount				t	T	T	SR
Kingston, earl (see Dorchester)							
Kinnoull, earl					T	T	SR
Lansdowne, baron	T	T	T		T	T	
Leeds, Thomas 1st duke	T	T	W	t	T	T	d. 1712
Peregrine 2nd duke	W	W	W	w	W	W	Baron Osborne until 1712
Leicester, earl	[went out]				T	T	
Leigh, Thomas 2nd baron	T	T	T	w	T	T	
Edward 3rd baron					T		d. Nov. 1710
Leominster, baron	T	T	W	t	T	T	
Lexington, baron	T	T	W		W	W	Tory
Lincoln, earl			W	w	W	W	Court Whig (pension)

* *Parl. Hist.* has "Howard of Escrick"; C.U.L. MSS. Mm/vi/42 "Howard of Effingham". The latter is almost certainly correct.

Name	June 1701 (1)	Jan. 1703 (2)	Dec. 1703 (3)	Mar. 1710 (4)	Dec. 1711 (5)	June 1713 (6)	June 1714 (7)	COMMENTS
Lindsey, marquess	T				w	W	W	Tory convert to mild Whiggery d. 1704
Longueville, Henry 1st viscount		T	T					
Talbot 2nd viscount				W	t	W?	W	SR. Hanoverian Tory
Loudoun, earl						T		
Lovelace, baron	W	W	W					
Lucas, baron	W	W?	W					
Manchester, earl		W	W	W	t	W	W	Court Whig (pension)
Mansel, baron				T	t	T	T	SR
Mar, earl	T	T	T		went out			
Marlborough, duke				W		T	T	
Masham, baron						T	T	
Maynard, baron	W				w	T	T	
Mohun, baron	W	W	W					Junto Whig "poor lord" d. 1709
Montagu, Ralph 1st duke	W	W	W		w	W?	W	
John 2nd duke							T	Viscount Windsor (I)
Mountjoy, baron								Hanoverian Tory
Newcastle, duke		W	W	W	w	T	T	Court Whig
North and Grey, baron		T	T	T	w	T	T	army Tory
Northampton, earl		T	T	T		T	T	
Northesk, earl	T	T	T	T	t	W	T	SR
Northumberland, duke	T	T	T		w	W	W	Court Tory (pension)
Nottingham, earl						W	W	Hanoverian Tory

Name							Notes
Orford, earl	W	W		W	W	W	
Orkney, earl		T				T	SR. Court
Ormonde, duke	T	T	t	T	T	T	
Osborne, Peregrine, baron (see Leeds, 2nd duke)							
Peregrine, baron	T	T		W	W	W	
Ossulston, baron	W	W	t	W	W	T	cr. Jan. 1713
Oxford, earl (Aubrey de Vere)							
Oxford, earl (Robert Harley)	T	T	t	W	W		
Paget, William 7th baron	T			W	W	T	
Henry 8th baron					T		d. Feb. 1713
Pembroke, earl	D	T	w	T	T	T	Harleyite Tory
Peterborough, earl	W	W		W	W	W	Court Tory. Hanoverian Tory 1711–14
Plymouth, earl	T	T	w	T	T	T	Whig, but went over to Harley in 1710
Portland, Hans 1st earl	T	T		T	W	T	
Henry 2nd earl	W	W	went out	W	W	W	d. 1709
Poulet, earl	T	T	t	T	T	T?	Harleyite Tory
Radnor, earl	W	W		W	W	W	Court Whig
Richmond, duke	T	T	w	W	T	T	Court Whig
Rivers, earl	W		t	W	W	W	Whig, but went over to Harley in 1710
Rochester, Laurence 1st earl	T	T	t	T	T	T	
Henry 2nd earl	W	W	w	W	W	W	d. May 1711
Rockingham, baron		W		W	W	W	
Romney, earl	W	W		W	W	W	

	June 1701 (1)	Jan. 1703 (2)	Dec. 1703 (3)	Mar. 1710 (4)	Dec. 1711 (5)	June 1713 (6)	June 1714 (7)	COMMENTS
Rosebery, earl								SR
Rutland, John 2nd duke							W	succ. 1711: formerly Marquess of Granby
St. Albans, duke	W	delib. abs.	W	W	w	W	W	Court Whig (pension)
Salisbury, earl		T				T	T	
Sandwich, earl		W	W					
Saye and Sele, Nathaniel 4th viscount	W	W	W	T				d. Jan. 1710
Lawrence 5th viscount				T	t	T	T	
Scarborough, earl	W	W	W	T	w	W	W	
Scarsdale, Robert 3rd earl	T	T	T					
Nicholas 4th earl				T	w	T	T	d. 1707
Schomberg, duke	W	T	T	W	went out	T	T	Court Whig (pension)
Seafield, earl (see Findlater)								
Shaftesbury, earl	W	W						absent through ill health 1704–12 (d.)
Shrewsbury, duke				T		W		
Somers, baron		W	W	W	t	W	W	
Somerset, duke	T	W	W	[delib. abs.]	w	W	W	Court Whig
Southampton, duke (see Cleveland)								
Stamford, earl	W	W	W	W		W	W	
Stawell, baron		T	T	T	w	T	T	

Name								Notes
Strafford, earl					W		T	Court. Baron Raby to 1711
Suffolk, Henry 5th earl								d. 1709
Henry 6th earl		W	W			W?	W	
Sunderland, earl		W	W	W	w	W	W	
Sussex, earl	T	T	T	T	t	T	T	
Thanet, earl		T	T	T			D	
Torrington, earl		W	W	W	w	T?	T?	Court Whig
Townshend, viscount		W	W	W	w	W	D?	
Trevor, baron						T	T	
Vaughan, baron		W	W	W	w	T?	W	d. 1713
Warrington, earl	T	T	W	W	w	T?	T?	
Westmorland, earl		T	T	T	t	W	W	Court Whig (pension)
Weston, baron	T	T	T	T		T	T	
Weymouth, viscount	W	W	W	W	w	D	D	
Wharton, earl		T	T	T		T	W	
Willoughby de Broke, Richard 11th baron								d. July 1711
George 12th baron								
Winchilsea, earl		T	W	W	t	T	T	Tory "poor lord"
Yarmouth, earl			T	T	t	T	T	

BISHOPS		June 1701 (1)	Jan. 1703 (2)	Dec. 1703 (3)	Mar. 1710 (4)	Dec. 1711 (5)	June 1713 (6)	June 1714 (7)	COMMENTS
Bangor	John Evans								
Bath and Wells	George Hooper	W	W	T	T	w	T	T	St. Asaph 1703–4
Bristol	see London (Robinson)								
Canterbury	Thomas Tenison		W	W			W	W	convert to Whiggery after 1705
Carlisle	William Nicolson	W	T		T	w	W	W	
Chester	see York (Dawes)								
Chichester	Thomas Manningham	W	W	W		w	T	T	apptd. 1709
Coventry	John Hough		T	T	T		W	W	
Durham	Nathaniel, Lord Crewe	W	W	W	T	w	T	T	
Ely	Symon Patrick	W	W	W					d. 1707
	John Moore	W	W	W	W	w	W	W	Norwich until 1707
Exeter	see Winchester (Trelawney)								
	Offspring Blackall			W		t		T	
Gloucester	Edward Fowler		W	W	W	w	T	T	
Hereford	Philip Bisse						T	T	St. David's 1710–13
Lichfield and Coventry	see Coventry (Hough)								
Lincoln	William Wake				W	w	W	W	apptd. 1705
Llandaff	John Tyler				T		W	W	apptd. 1706
London	Henry Compton	T	T	T	T		T	T	
	John Robinson					t	T	T	Bristol 1710–13
Norwich	see Ely (Moore)								
	Charles Trimnel		W	W	W	w	W	W	
Oxford	William Talbot		W	W	W	w	W	W	

See	Incumbent							Notes
Peterborough	Richard Cumberland			W	W	W	W	
Rochester	Thomas Sprat	T	T	T	T	t	W	
St. Asaph	see Bath and Wells (Hooper)	T				t	W	
	William Fleetwood		W	W	W		W	
St. David's	see Hereford (Bisse)			W				
	Adam Ottley		T		T		T	
Salisbury	Gilbert Burnet	W	W	W	W	went out	W	
Winchester	Sir Jonathan Trelawney	T	T	T	T	w	D	Exeter until 1707
Worcester	William Lloyd		W	W	W		W	
York	John Sharp	T	T	T	T		T	
	Sir William Dawes				W	t	W	Hanoverian Tory. Chester 1708–Feb. 1714

Appendix B

THE QUEEN'S SERVANTS IN THE
HOUSE OF LORDS, FEBRUARY 1714

Note : (C) indicates a member of the Cabinet; P.C. a Privy Councillor. The names of Whig peers in opposition to the ministry are given in italics. No bishops are included in this list, except for Bishop Robinson of London (Lord Almoner and a member of the Cabinet) and Lord Crewe, Bishop of Durham (Lord Lieutenant of Northumberland and Durham).

I. PEERS IN OFFICES OF PROFIT

Earl of Oxford	Lord High Treasurer (C)
Lord Harcourt	Lord Chancellor (C)
Duke of Buckingham	Lord President of the Council (C); Lord Lieut. of Middlesex and the North Riding
Earl of Dartmouth	Lord Privy Seal (C)
Duke of Shrewsbury	Lord Chamberlain and Lord Lieutenant of Ireland (C); Lord Lieut. of Shropshire and Worcestershire (overseas)
Earl Poulet	Lord Steward (C); Lord Lieut. of Devon
Viscount Bolingbroke	Secretary of State for the South (C); Lord Lieut. of Essex
Duke of Ormonde	Captain General of the Land Forces (C); Lord Warden of the Cinque Ports; Colonel of the 1st Regiment of Foot Guards; Lord Lieut. of Norfolk and Somerset; Pension of £5000 p.a. (Irish Civil List)
Lord Trevor	Lord Chief Justice of the Common Pleas (C)
Earl of Mar	Secretary of State [Scotland] (C); Pension of £3000 p.a.
Bishop of London	Lord Almoner (C); ex-Lord Privy Seal and

	Joint Plenipotentiary at Utrecht and a member of the Cabinet since 1711
Earl of Strafford	1st Lord of the Admiralty (C); Ambassador Extraordinary to the States General (overseas)
Earl of Findlater	Lord Chancellor and Keeper of the Great Seal in Scotland; P.C.; Pension of £3000 p.a.
Duke of Atholl	Lord Privy Seal in Scotland; P.C.
Lord Guilford	1st Commissioner of Trade; P.C.
Lord Lansdowne	Treasurer of the Household; P.C.; Governor of Pendennis Castle
Marquess of Lindsey	Hereditary Lord Great Chamberlain; Lord Lieut. of Lincolnshire
Duke of Montagu	Hereditary Master of the Great Wardrobe
Lord Delawarr	Treasurer of the Chamber
Lord Masham	Cofferer of the Household
Duke of Beaufort	Captain of the Band of Gentlemen Pensioners; P.C.; Lord Lieut. of Gloucestershire and Hampshire; Warden of the New Forest
Duke of Argyll	Commander-in-Chief of the Forces in North Britain; P.C.; Colonel of the 4th Troop of Horse Guards; Governor of Port Mahon; Pension of £3000 p.a.
Lord Paget	Captain of the Yeomen of the Guard; P.C.
Lord Berkeley of Stratton	Chancellor of the Duchy of Lancaster; P.C.
Earl of Anglesey	Joint Vice-Treasurer of Ireland; P.C.
Earl of Rochester	Joint Vice-Treasurer of Ireland; P.C.; Lord Lieut. of Cornwall
Lord Mansel	Teller of the Exchequer; P.C.; Governor of Cardiff Castle
Earl of Denbigh	Teller of the Exchequer; Lord Lieut. of Leicestershire
Earl of Abingdon	Lord Chief Justice in Eyre South of Trent; P.C.; Lord Lieut. of Oxfordshire; Pension of £1200 p.a.
Earl of Northampton	Constable of the Tower of London; P.C.
Earl of Cardigan	Master of the Buckhounds
Duke of St. Albans	Master Falconer; Master of the Register Office; Annuity of £1000 p.a.

Earl of Suffolk	Deputy Earl Marshal; P.C.
Lord Halifax	Auditor of the Receipt (office for life)
Lord Weston	Master of the Ordnance (Ireland); Colonel of the 3rd Troop of Horse Guards.
Earl of Orkney	General of the Foot; P.C.; Colonel of the Royal Scots; Absentee Governor-General of Virginia
Duke of Northumberland	Governor of Windsor Castle; P.C.; Colonel of the 2nd Troop of Horse Guards; Lord Lieut. of Berkshire; Pension of £3000 p.a. (Excise Office)
Lord North and Grey	Governor of Portsmouth; P.C.; Lord Lieut. of Cambridgeshire
Earl of Portmore	Governor of Gibraltar; P.C.
Viscount Weymouth	Governor of St. Briavel's Castle; P.C.; Governor of the Mine Adventure; Warden of the Forest of Dean
Earl of Carlisle	Governor of Carlisle
Earl of Peterborough	Ambassador Extraordinary to Sicily and the Italian Princes; P.C.; Lord Lieut. of Northants. (overseas)
Earl of Berkeley	Vice-Admiral of the Red
Lord Ashburnham	Colonel of the 1st Troop of Horse Guards
Lord Willoughby de Broke	Dean of St. George's Chapel, Windsor (took oaths 2 Mar. 1714)
Earl of Dunmore	Colonel of the 3rd Regiment of Foot Guards
Earl of Eglinton	Commissioner of Trade (Scotland)
Earl of Northesk	Commissioner of Trade (Scotland)
Viscount Kilsyth	Commissioner of Trade (Scotland)
Lord Balmerino	Commissioner of Trade (Scotland)
(TOTAL 50)	

II. PEERS IN OFFICES OF HONOUR AND TRUST

(these include Tory Privy Councillors, other than those listed above)

Earl of Scarsdale	Lord Lieut. of Derbyshire; recently Envoy Extraordinary to Vienna; P.C.
Earl of Thanet	Lord Lieut. of Cumberland and Westmorland; P.C.

Lord Crewe, Bp. of Durham Lord Lieut. of Northumberland and Durham
Earl of Plymouth   Lord Lieut. of Cheshire and N. Wales
Earl of Pembroke   Lord Lieut. of Wiltshire, Monmouthshire and S. Wales; Pension of £3000 p.a.
Duke of Grafton   Lord Lieut. of Suffolk; Ranger of Whittlewood Forest; Pension of £2000 p.a. (Excise Office)
Duke of Kent   Lord Lieut. of Bedfordshire and Herefordshire
Duke of Bolton   Lord Lieut. of Dorset
Earl of Salisbury   Lord Lieut. of Hertfordshire
Earl of Exeter   Lord Lieut. of Rutland
Earl of Manchester   Lord Lieut. of Huntingdonshire
Lord Rockingham   Lord Lieut. of Kent
Lord Osborne   Lord Lieut. of the East Riding
Lord Bingley   P.C.; recently Ambassador Extraordinary to Madrid
Earl of Clarendon   P.C.; Pension of £2000 p.a. (Irish establishment)
Earl of Loudoun   P.C.; Pension of £1000 p.a.
Earl Ferrers   P.C.
Lord Lexington   P.C.
Lord Boyle   P.C.
(TOTAL 19)

Appendix C

ROBERT HARLEY, EARL OF OXFORD, AS "PRIME MINISTER"

ALTHOUGH we are assured by Defoe that Harley (like Walpole after him) rejected this appellation, and indeed preferred to think of himself, in succeeding Godolphin, as "delivering the Government from the grievance of a Prime Minister",* the term "prime minister" (and others of a comparable nature) were so freely applied to him at the time that its use in this book really needs no apology. When Harley became Chancellor of the Exchequer and second Commissioner of the Treasury in August 1710 James Brydges, the Paymaster, judged that he was "now premier Minister", and Joseph Addison, after giving himself a week or so to size up the new situation on his return from his spell of office in Ireland, came out with the unequivocal statement that "Mr. H—ly is first Minister of State".† A contemporary historian later recorded that this was the time that Harley "in reality, became Prime Minister"; and a more distinguished chronicler, the Bishop of Salisbury, agreed entirely (though in different words) that despite the Chancellor's apparent position of subordination at the Treasury "it was visible, he was the chief minister".‡ Others preferred to suspend judgement for some weeks. Swift felt pretty sure by 9 September that "Mr. Harley is looked upon as first Minister, and not my Lord Shrewsbury" and James Craggs wrote on 23 September that "Mr. Harley seems to be the primeir". But White Kennett, with less authentic information at his disposal, thought it still an open question at this time "who is or who is to be the prime Min. — the E. of R[ochester] or Mr. H.".§

* *An Account of the Conduct of Robert, Earl of Oxford* (1715), p. 42.

† *H.L.Q.* iii (1939–40), 236: Brydges to Drummond, 24 Aug.; *Addison Letters*, p. 236: Addison to Joshua Dawson, 1 Sept.

‡ Roger Coke, *A Detection of the Court and State of England*, iii (4th edn., 1719), 387; Burnet, vi, 11.

§ *Swift Corr.* i, 195; Charborough Park MSS.: Craggs to T. Erle; B. M. Lansdowne MSS. 1013, f. 134: Kennett to S. Blackwell, 22 Sept.

Subsequently when Harley's dominance at Court and in the ministry was universally acknowledged, and especially after it had been confirmed by his promotion to the office of Lord Treasurer in 1711, terms of this kind were used to distinguish him from his colleagues by all manner of people in all manner of circumstances. They were used by his associates in the Cabinet. The Lord Privy Seal (Newcastle) assured Harley's brother, Edward, in April 1711, "that nothing in the present posture of affairs could establish . . . the tranquillity of England, but Mr. Harley's taking the White Staff, and thereby becoming the Primere Minister".* They were used by M.P.s outside the House. The member for Midlothian, for example, while maintaining in his "Commentarys" that it was only when Harley was made Lord Treasurer in 1711 that he became undisputed "first Minister and cheif favourite" and "stood in awe of none", acknowledged that thereafter there was no question but that he was "chief minister of state".† More startlingly they figured at times in parliamentary debates, as when certain leaders of the October Club in 1712 "opend with great freedom against the prime minister as enslaving the House, and one was openly checkd from the Chair and called to order".‡ Such expressions were also used with equal facility by foreign representatives in London, even by the small fry like the Elector Palatine's minister, who assured Schulenberg in the spring of 1712 that "the Premier here is very convinced" both of the necessity of the Protestant succession and of the need to regard France still as England's natural enemy.§

Finally, it should be made clear that Godolphin's primacy was occasionally recognised by a similar terminology before 1710; but as we would expect in view of Marlborough's special position in the ministry after 1702, the examples are fewer than in Harley's case. One of the most interesting samples of usage from the early part of Anne's reign occurs in a letter of intelligence from Stanley West, not himself an active politician, written to Harley from Tunbridge Wells in August 1704. "I have heard of people's talk [he wrote], that you fall in with this Ministry, not for any particular value or esteem for the persons but as what the Court has resolved upon to be the Ministry; if the Court had appointed my Lord Rochester, or any other person to be the

---

* H.M.C. *Portland MSS.* v, 655: Auditor Harley's 'Memoir'.

† *Lockhart Papers*, i, 341, 370.

‡ Bodl. MS. Add. A.269, p. 10: Edmund Gibson to Bishop Nicolson, 8 May 1712.

§ *State Papers and Correspondence, 1688–1714*, ed. J. M. Kemble (1857), p. 487: de Steinghens, 16/27 Mar. (transl.). Schütz wrote to Robethon on 30 Oct. 1713 about "le plan du premier ministre". B.M. Stowe MSS. 225, f. 264.

Prime Minister, it would have been the same thing to you, and that your aim is in time to be the Prime Minister yourself".*

* H.M.C. *Portland MSS.* iv, 119. In *The Growth of Responsible Government in Stuart England* (Cambridge, 1966), p. 402, Clayton Roberts, after comparing Oxford's position with Walpole's, concludes that 'it is not fanciful to maintain, as Walpole himself did, that Oxford in the years 1711 and 1712 was a Prime Minister'.

List of Manuscript Sources

MEMBERS of both Houses of Parliament, 1702–14, whose letters and papers are contained in the collections listed here are noted in italics. For printed primary sources and all secondary work on the period utilised by the author, including articles and unpublished theses and dissertations, the reader is referred to the notes below.

BRITISH MUSEUM (now BRITISH LIBRARY)

Loan 29   *Harley family*
    29/237–8   *Duke of Newcastle*

Additional MSS.
  4291, 4743   Charles Davenant
  6116   *William Wake, Bishop of Lincoln* (transcripts)
  7059, 7063, 7074, 7078   George Stepney
  17677   l'Hermitage to the States-General
                             (transcripts)
  22202, 22211, 22220–2,
    22226, 22231   *Earl of Strafford*
  22851–2   *Thomas Pitt*
  27440   Rev. Charles Allestree
  28055   *Earl of Godolphin*
  28889, 28893   *John Ellis*
  29576, 29579   *Viscount Hatton*
  29588–9   *Earl of Nottingham*
  29599   *Nicholas Carewe*
  30000   Bonet to Frederick III (transcripts)
  31135–9, 31143–4   *Earl of Strafford*
  33273   *Henry Watkins*
  38507   *Viscount Townshend*

Additional MSS. (*cont.*)

40621	*Thomas Harley, Robert Harley, William Bromley*
40775–6	*James Vernon, sen^r.*
42176	*Henry Watkins, Adam de Cardonnel*
47025–7, 47087	*Sir John Percival*

Egerton MSS.

2540	*Edward Nicholas*

Lansdowne MSS.

773	Charles Davenant
885	*Viscount Coningsby:* "Historie of Parties" (1716)
	Edward Harley: "An Account of the Earl of Oxford by his Brother"
1013, 1024	White Kennett's letters to Samuel Blackwell; Kennett's journal
1236	*Duke of Newcastle, 3rd Earl of Sunderland*

Stowe MSS.

225–7	Bothmar, Gatke and Schütz to Hanover

MS. Add.

A.191	*Gilbert Burnet, Bishop of Salisbury*
A.269	*William Nicholson, Bishop of Carlisle,* Edmund Gibson (copies)

MS. Ballard	Dr. Arthur Charlett
10	*Lord Cheyne, George Clarke*
15	Rev. John Johnson
20	*George Clarke*
38	*William Bromley, Thomas Rowney*

MS. Eng. Misc. e. 180	*Henry St. John, Lord Boyle* (Earl of Orrery [I])

MS. North	*Lord North and Grey*

MS. Rawlinson D.174	*Anthony Hammond*

MS. Top. Oxon. b.82   *George Clarke, Thomas Rowney*

MS. Top. Wilt. c.7   Thomas Naish: autobiography and diary

PUBLIC RECORD OFFICE

30/24/20–2   *3rd Earl of Shaftesbury, Sir John Cropley*

Lowndes MSS.   *William Lowndes*

CAMBRIDGE UNIVERSITY LIBRARY

Cholmondeley (Houghton)
   MSS.   *Robert Walpole*

Add. MS. 7093   anon. parliamentary diary, 1705–6.

STAATSARCHIV HANNOVER

Cal. Br. 24 England
   99, 107a, 113a   Kreienberg to Hanover

OTHER COLLECTIONS [R.O. signifies Record Office]

Alnwick Castle MSS.   Duke of Northumberland (*Duke of Somerset, Viscount Weymouth*)

Auchmar MSS.   Duke of Montrose (*Duke of Montrose, Duke of Roxburgh, George Baillie, Mungo Graham*)*

Baron Hill MSS.   Univ. College of N. Wales Library (*Viscount Bulkeley*)

Bettisfield MSS.   National Library of Wales (*Sir Thomas Hanmer*)

Blackett MSS.   Northumberland R.O. (Sir Edward Blackett)

Blenheim MSS.   Duke of Marlborough (*Duke of Marlborough, Earl of Godolphin, 3rd Earl of Sunderland, Arthur Mainwaring*)†

* These papers are now deposited in Register House, Edinburgh.
† The bulk of these papers are now in the British Library, Add. MSS. 61101–61710.

Boughton MSS.	Duke of Buccleuch (*Duke of Shrewsbury, James Vernon, sen*.)*
Carew Pole MSS.	Sir J. G. Carew Pole (*James Buller*)
Charborough Park MSS.	Admiral Drax (*Thomas Erle*)†
Chatsworth MSS.	Duke of Devonshire (*2nd Duke of Devonshire, Henry Boyle*)
Chatsworth MSS (Finch-Halifax Papers)	Duke of Devonshire (*Heneage Finch, 1st Baron Guernsey*)
Chetwynd (Diplomatic) MSS.	Staffordshire R.O. (John Chetwynd)
Chevening MSS.	Earl Stanhope (*James Stanhope, Sir John Cropley*)‡
Chirk Castle MSS.	National Library of Wales (*Sir Richard Myddleton*)
Clavering Letters	Durham Univ. Library (Ann Clavering)
Claydon MSS.	Buckinghamshire R.O.: micro. (*Viscount Fermanagh, Sir Thomas Cave*)
Cockermouth Castle MSS.	Lord Egremont (*Duke of Somerset*)
Corsham Court MSS.	Lord Methuen (*Paul Methuen*)
Cottrell-Dormer MSS.	Thomas Cottrell-Dormer (*Charles Caesar*)
Dalhousie MSS.	Scottish R.O., Register House (*Lord Balmerino*)
Dartmouth MSS.	William Salt Library, Stafford (*Earl of Dartmouth*)
Drake/King MSS.	Devon R.O. (*Sir Peter King*)
Dyrham Park MSS.	Gloucestershire R.O. (*William Blathwayt*)
Finch MSS.	Leicestershire R.O. (*Earl of Nottingham, William Bromley*)
Finch-Hatton MSS.	Northamptonshire R.O. (*Earl of Nottingham*)
Galway MSS.	Nottingham Univ. Library (*Robert Monckton*)

* These papers are now deposited in the Northamptonshire R.O.
† Now in Churchill College, Cambridge (Erle MSS.).
‡ Now in Kent Archives Office (Stanhope MSS.).

Gower MSS.	Staffordshire R.O. (*Sir John Leveson Gower, 1st Baron Gower*)
Haigh MSS.	Earl of Crawford and Balcarres: John Rylands Library (*Sir Roger Bradshaigh*)
Isham MSS.	Northamptonshire R.O. (*Sir Justinian Isham*)
Kaye MS. diary	William Salt Library, Stafford (*Sir Arthur Kaye*)
Kenyon MSS.	Lancashire R.O. (*George Kenyon*)
Legh of Lyme MSS.	John Rylands Library (Peter Legh)
Levens MSS.	Mrs. O. R. Bagot (*James Grahme, William Bromley*)*
Lloyd-Baker MSS.	Borthwick Institute, York: micro. (*John Sharp, Archbishop of York*)†
Longleat MSS.	
Portland Papers	Marquess of Bath (*Robert Harley*)
Portland Miscellaneous	Marquess of Bath (*Robert Harley, Earl of Godolphin*)
Thynne Papers	Marquess of Bath (*Viscount Weymouth*)
Lonsdale MSS.	Cumbria R.O. Carlisle Office. (*James Lowther, Earl of Wharton, Nicholas Lechmere*)
Lucas MSS.	Bedfordshire R.O. (*Duke of Kent*)
Massingberd MSS.	Lincolnshire R.O. (Sir William Massingberd)
Monson MSS.	Lincolnshire R.O. (Sir John Newton, *Robert Monckton*)
Neville MSS.	Berkshire R.O. (*Duke of Northumberland, Charles Aldworth*)
Newdigate newsletters	Folger Shakespeare Library: micro. in Bodleian Library.
Nicolson MS. Diary	
1702–8, 1710–14	Tullie House, Carlisle (*William Nicolson, Bishop of Carlisle*)
1709–10	Professor P. N. S. Mansergh (*William Nicolson, Bishop of Carlisle*)

* The Levens MSS. can now be consulted in the Cumbria R.O. Kendal Office.
† Originals in Gloucestershire R.O.

Norris MSS.	Liverpool Public Library (*Richard Norris, Sir Thomas Johnson*)
Pakington MSS.	Lord Hampton (*Sir John Pakington*)*
Panshanger MSS.	Hertfordshire R.O. (*Lord Cowper*, Sir David Hamilton's diary, Duchess of Marlborough)
Papillon Letter Books	Kent R.O. (*Philip Papillon*)
Penrice & Margam MSS.	National Library of Wales (*Sir Thomas Mansel, 1st Baron Mansel*)
Plas Newydd MSS.	Marquess of Anglesey (*Henry Paget, 1st Baron Paget and Burton*)
Portland (Bentinck) MSS.	Nottingham Univ. Library (*1st Earl of Portland*)
Portland (Holles) MSS.	Nottingham Univ. Library (*Duke of Newcastle*)
Somers MSS.	Surrey R.O. (*Lord Somers*)
Stowe MSS., 57, 58	Huntington Library, California (*James Brydges*)
Temple Newsam MSS.	Leeds Public Library (Viscount Irwin)
Tredegar MSS.	National Library of Wales (*John Morgan*)
Trumbull MSS.	Berkshire R.O. (Sir William Trumbull)
Trumbull Add. MSS. 133	Berkshire R.O. (*Henry St. John*)
Wake MSS.	Christ Church Library, Oxford (*William Wake, Bishop of Lincoln*)
Walton MSS.	Sir Richard Hamilton (*Sir John Mordaunt*)†
Weston Park MSS.	Earl of Bradford (Sir John Bridgeman)
Winterton Letters	West Sussex R.O. (*Sir Edward Turner*)
Witley Beaumont MSS.	Huddersfield Public Library (Richard Beaumont, *Sir Arthur Kaye*)
Worsley MSS.	Lincolnshire R.O.

* These papers are now deposited in the Worcestershire R.O.
† Microfilm deposited in the Warwickshire R.O.

A Guide to Political Chronology, 1702-14

Note : For the sake of brevity (W) is sometimes used to indicate Whig and (T) to indicate Tory, men and measures. Principal ministerial changes are given in italics.

1702

January	William III's last Parliament began its business: parties evenly balanced in the Commons.
February	Abjuration bill passed (enforcing on all members of Parliament and office-holders an oath repudiating the Pretender).
March (8th)	Death of William III : accession of Anne.
April–May	*Anne's first ministry formed under Godolphin (Lord Treasurer) and Marlborough (Captain-General); Cabinet containing 9 Tories, including the 3 main High Tory leaders (Rochester, Nottingham, Seymour), and only 3 moderate Whigs.*
May	Declaration of war on France and Spain.
	William III's last Parliament prorogued.
June	Sacheverell's Oxford sermon against the occasionally-conforming dissenters.
July	General Election: decisive Tory victory.
October	1st session of Anne's 1st Parliament opened: Harley re-elected Speaker.
November	1st Occasional Conformity bill (T) passed the Commons.
	English and Scottish Union commissioners met in London.
December	Debates in the Commons on the Queen's proposed

grant to Marlborough: High Tory opposition led by Seymour.

1703

January — 1st Occasional Conformity bill amended (W) in the Lords and dropped.

February — Union Commission broke up without agreement.

Halifax (W) cleared by the Lords of charges brought by the Commons' Commission of Public Accounts (T).

Rochester resigned as Lord Lieut. of Ireland: replaced by Ormonde (T).

1st session of Anne's 1st Parliament ended.

May — Methuen Treaty with Portugal signed: Anne's government committed to policy of "No Peace without Spain".

November — 2nd session of Anne's 1st Parliament opened.

December — 2nd Occasional Conformity bill (T) defeated in the Lords.

1704

February–March — Enquiry by both Houses into the "Scotch Plot": attempt (W) in the Lords to implicate Secretary Nottingham.

April — 2nd session of Anne's 1st Parliament ended in deadlock between Lords and Commons.

Fall of the High Tory ministers, Nottingham, Seymour and Jersey.   •

April–May — *Harleyites given office: Harley entered the Cabinet as Secretary of State (North); St. John Secretary-at-War.*

August — Scottish Act of Security (empowering the Scottish Parliament to choose its own successor to the throne after Anne's death) received royal assent.

Battle of Blenheim.

October — 3rd session of Anne's 1st Parliament opened.

November — Attempted "tack" of 3rd Occasional Conformity bill to Land Tax bill defeated in the Commons by the ministry and the Whigs.

December	Lords' debate on the ministry's Scottish policy: Godolphin saved from censure by Whig peers.
	3rd Occasional Conformity bill defeated in the Lords.

1705

March	Aliens Act (W), exerting economic pressure on Scotland to negotiate for a parliamentary union, became law.
	Culmination of conflict (1703–5) between the Lords and the Tory majority in the Commons over the case of the Aylesbury men.
	3rd session of Anne's 1st Parliament ended.
April	*Newcastle (W) appointed Lord Privy Seal vice Buckingham (T).*
May–June	General Election: heavy Whig gains left the parties roughly equal in the Commons.
October	*Cowper (W) appointed Lord Keeper vice Wright (T).*
	1st session of Anne's 2nd Parliament opened: Smith (W) elected Speaker in contest with Bromley (T).
November	"Hanover motion" (T), for inviting to England the Dowager Electress Sophia, failed in the Lords.
	Regency bill (W), providing for an interim administration after the death of Anne, introduced into the Lords.
December	Regency bill debates began in the Commons.

1706

January–February	Struggle between Court and Country over the "Whimsical" (Place) clause of the Regency bill.
March	Regency Act received royal assent.
	1st session of Anne's 2nd Parliament ended.
April	English commissioners for negotiating Union with Scotland appointed, including all 5 lords of the Whig Junto.
May	Battle of Ramillies.

July	Treaty of Union concluded.
December	*Sunderland (W) appointed Secretary of State vice Hedges (T): first Junto lord to sit in the Cabinet since 1700.*
	2nd session of Anne's 2nd Parliament opened.

1707

February ✗	Tory opposition to Treaty of Union overwhelmed in both Houses.
March	Act of Union passed.
April	Disastrous defeat of the allied army in Spain (Almanza).
	2nd session of Anne's 2nd Parliament ended.
	Pembroke (T), Lord President, replaced Ormonde (T) as Lord Lieut. of Ireland.
May–October	Growing rift between the Junto and the ministry over rewards due to the Whigs for their support.
October	3rd session of Anne's 2nd Parliament opened: Scottish members and representative peers attended for first time.
November	Enquiry into Admiralty mismanagement (W) opened in both Houses, with Tory backing in the Lords.
November–December	Whig/'Squadrone' attack in the Commons on the Scottish Privy Council.
December	Tory attack in the Lords on the conduct of the war in Spain: Somers's (W) motion on "No Peace without Spain" carried (19 Dec.).

1708

January	Greg (Harley's clerk) charged with treason.
	Tory attack in the Commons on the conduct of the war in Spain, backed by Country Whigs (1st Almanza debate, 29 Jan.).
February	Ministry defeated in the Lords on the Scottish Privy Council bill.
	Resignation of the Harleyites: Boyle (W) appointed Secretary of State vice Harley; Walpole Secretary-at-War vice St. John.

	Ministry rescued by the Whigs in the Commons from final censure of its Spanish policy (3rd Almanza debate, 24 Feb.).
March	Franco-Jacobite attempt to invade Scotland failed.
April	3rd session of Anne's 2nd Parliament ended.
May	General Election: clear majority secured by the Whigs.
November	*Triumph of the Junto: Somers and Wharton entered the Cabinet.* ✗
	1st session of Anne's 3rd Parliament opened.

1709

February–March	Bill for the Naturalization of Foreign Protestants (W) passed both Houses.
April	1st session of Anne's 3rd Parliament ended.
May	Peace negotiations at The Hague broke down.
August	Battle of Malplaquet.
November	Sacheverell preached against the Revolution at St. Paul's.
	Last surviving Tory in the Cabinet (Pembroke) resigned: Orford of the Junto appointed 1st Lord of the Admiralty.
	2nd session of Anne's 3rd Parliament opened.
December	Whigs voted to impeach Sacheverell for high crimes and misdemeanours.

1710

January	Crisis at Court over the Essex regiment: Marlborough threatened to resign, in protest against the influence of Anne's Tory favourite, Mrs. Masham.
March	Trial of Sacheverell: found guilty by the Lords but escaped the heavy punishment intended by the Whigs. ✗
April	2nd session of Anne's 3rd Parliament ended.
	Shrewsbury appointed Lord Chamberlain vice Kent (W): the first step in Harley's overthrow of the Godolphin ministry.
June	*Dartmouth (T) appointed Secretary of State vice Sunderland.*

	Bank directors advised the Queen against a change of ministry.
August	*Lord Treasurer Godolphin dismissed and replaced by a Harleyite Treasury Board: Harley, Poulet (T) and Anglesey (T) entered the Cabinet.*
	Harley and Shrewsbury initiated tentative peace negotiations secretly with France.
September	*Fall of the Whigs: Boyle, Somers, Devonshire, Orford, Cowper and Wharton dismissed or resigned; Rochester (Lord President), St. John (Secretary for the North) and Buckingham received Cabinet office.*
	Dissolution of Parliament.
October	General Election: crushing victory for the Tories.
	Harley's new Cabinet completed by appointment of Harcourt (T) as Lord Keeper and Ormonde (T) as Lord Lieutenant of Ireland.
November	1st session of Anne's 4th Parliament opened: Bromley chosen Speaker.
December	Battle of Brihuega: final blow to the allied cause in Spain.
1711	
January	Whig conduct of the war in Spain censured by the Lords.
February	October Club (T) launched its campaign in the Commons against the moderation of the Harley ministry.
	Bill (T) to repeal the Naturalization Act thrown out by Whig and Court peers.
	Bill imposing landed qualification on M.P.s passed both Houses.
March	Guiscard's attempt to assassinate Harley.
	Ways and Means obstructed by the October Tories: crisis over the Leather Duty.
April	October Club bill to resume William III's land grants defeated in the Lords.
May	Harley's South Sea bill passed both Houses.
	Harley created Earl of Oxford and Lord Treasurer.

June	1st session of Anne's 4th Parliament ended.
	Cabinet reshuffle necessitated by death of Rochester (2 May): many Tories appointed to junior office.
September	Peace preliminaries signed between Britain and France.
	Bishop Robinson of Bristol (T) succeeded Newcastle (d. July) as Lord Privy Seal: no genuine Whig remained in the Cabinet.
November	Nottingham, last survivor of the old High Tory leaders, broke with the ministry over the peace.
December	2nd session of Anne's 4th Parliament opened.
	Major government crisis following defeat by the Whigs in the Lords on its policy of "Peace without Spain" (7 Dec.): resolved by creation of 12 Tory peers and *dismissal of Marlborough, Captain-General* (31 Dec.).
1712	
January	Utrecht peace conference opened.
	Marlborough and Walpole censured by the Tory Commons for alleged peculation.
	Bill (T) repealing the Naturalization Act passed both Houses.
February	Attacks in the Commons (T) on the conduct of the allies.
	Ministry narrowly escaped defeat in the Lords on the Place bill.
April–May	Struggle over a new Land Grants bill (T): failed by 1 vote in the Lords.
May	Whig protests against the "Restraining Orders" sent to the British army in Flanders rejected by Parliament.
June	Oxford's peace policy decisively endorsed by both Houses.
	2nd session of Anne's 4th Parliament ended.
June–July	*Most Whig M.P.s remaining in civil office weeded out.*
October	Serious Cabinet clash between Oxford and St. John (now Bolingbroke).

1713

March	Treaties of Peace and Commerce between Britain and France signed.
April	3rd session of Anne's 4th Parliament opened.
May–June	Crisis over the Malt Tax and the Union: ministry narrowly survived attack in the Lords from the Whigs and Scots (1–8 June).
June	Government's French Commerce bill defeated in the Commons by the Whigs and 80 rebel Tories led by Hanmer.
	"Lorraine motion" against the Pretender (W) carried in the Lords.
July	3rd session of Anne's 4th Parliament ended.
August–September	*Oxford defeated Bolingbroke in a struggle for control over the ministry: Bolingbroke's authority reduced by appointment of Bromley and Mar as Secretaries of State.*
	General Election: Whigs again heavily defeated in England, but gained ground in Scotland and exposed Tory divisions on the Succession question.
September	Oxford's quarrel with Anne over the Newcastle title.
December	Serious illness of the Queen.

1714

February	1st session of Anne's last Parliament opened: Hanoverian Tory leader, Hanmer, chosen Speaker with both Whig and Court backing.
March	Richard Steele (W) expelled the Commons for writings accusing the ministry of Jacobite sympathies.
March–April	Critical debates in the Lords on the State of the Nation: ministry under attack from Whigs and Hanoverian Tories.
April	Both Houses by narrow majorities voted the Protestant Succession not in danger under the present administration

	Split between Oxford and Bolingbroke factions in the Cabinet became irreconcileable.
May	Schism bill (T), aimed at dissenting academies, introduced into the Commons by Bolingbroke's supporters — "A mine to blow up the White Staff".
June	Schism bill narrowly passed the Lords after heated debate.
July	Whig attack in the Lords, with Oxford's connivance, on the illicit profits of Bolingbroke and his friends from Spanish trade.
	Parliament prorogued, cutting short enquiry into trade with Spain.
	Dismissal of Oxford (27th): Shrewsbury succeeded as Lord Treasurer after Bolingbroke's failure to construct a Treasury commission before the Queen's last illness.
August (1st)	Death of Queen Anne. Elector of Hanover peacefully proclaimed as George I.
August–September	Government by Regency: dismissal of Bolingbroke.
September	Arrival of George I in England.
	His first administration formed: the triumph of the Whigs.

Notes

CHAPTER ONE: TORY AND WHIG

1. R. Walcott, *English Politics in the Early Eighteenth Century*, p. 160.
2. H.M.C. *Portland MSS.* iv, 572: to [Harley], 21 Aug. 1710.
3. Add. MSS. 47087 (unfoliated): to Daniel Dering (copy), 25 May 1714.
4. Worsley MSS. 1, f. 55. The identity of the writer is unknown.
5. B.M. Loan 29/198: [Harcourt] to Oxford, 12 Nov. 1711; Blenheim MSS. B. 1–23: James Craggs to Marlborough, 20 May 1709; Chevening MSS.: G. Markham to James Stanhope, 26 Mar. 1706.
6. P.R.O. 30/24/21/146: [Sir John Cropley] to Shaftesbury, [11 Feb. 1708], wrongly endorsed "7 Feb. 1707/8".
7. *Addison Letters*, p. 89; cf. H.M.C. *Portland MSS.* iv, 684, and for "Ld. Rochesters Squadron", P.R.O. 30/24/20/141 (ii).
8. Add. MSS. 7063, f. 38: Adam de Cardonnel to George Stepney, 19 Nov. 1703.
9. *Bolingbroke Corr.* ii, 49: Oxford to Strafford, [8 Dec. 1711]; cf. the reference in the Archbishop of York's diary, 9 Dec. 1706, to his friends "my Lord Nottingham and that party" (*Life of Archbishop Sharp* [1825], i, 300).
10. Swift, *Some Considerations . . . upon the Death of the Queen* (*Prose Works*, ed. Davis and Ehrenpreis, viii, 102).
11. W.S.L. Dartmouth MSS. D.1778/I/ii/162: Jersey to Dartmouth, 28 Sept. [1710].
12. Add. MSS. 47087 (unfoliated): Sir John to [P. Percival] (copy), 17 Apr. 1714; cf. the reference to Anglesey's "implicit Followers" in *A Letter from a Member of the House of Commons . . . relating to the Bill of Commerce* (1713).
13. H.M.C. *Portland MSS.* v, 425: [Bolingbroke] to Oxford, [21 Apr. 1714].
14. Coxe, i, 234: Mrs. Burnet to Duchess of Marlborough, 5 Aug. 1704; Add. MSS. 40776, f. 28: Shrewsbury to Vernon, 18 Jan. 1707; *Vernon Corr.* iii, 288: Vernon to Shrewsbury, 9 Dec. 1707; *Cowper Diary*, p. 46, 22 Sept. 1710.
15. Blenheim MSS. F. 2–16: to Marlborough, 18 July 1704.
16. B.M. Loan 29/238, f. 382: 26 Sept. 1710.
17. So it was to the Nottinghamites, Peter Shakerley and Sir Roger Mostyn, when they wrote to inform Sir Richard Myddleton, an independent Tory, of measures to rally "our friends of the house of commons" after their party's electoral defeat in 1708. Chirk Castle MSS. E994(ii), E995: 27 and 24 Oct. 1708.

18. Longleat MSS. Portland Papers, vii, f. 95: to Godolphin (copy), 4 Sept. 1705; H.M.C. *Bath MSS*. i, 111: to the same (copy), 15 Oct. 1706.

19. Blenheim MSS. A. 1–14: Haneft, [20]/31 May 1703; cf. Coxe, i, 132: same to the same, Haneft, 3/14 June 1703.

20. Add. MSS. 28070, f. 12: to Godolphin, 11 July [1705]; Coxe, ii, 3: to the same, 30 Aug. 1706.

21. It is rather remarkable how Swift, while making free enough use of "Whig" and "Tory" in his informal writings (e.g. in the *Journal to Stella*) made something of a fetish of avoiding "those fantastical words" in most of his major tracts, at least after 1712.

22. For the latter see H.M.C. *Portland MSS*. iv, 575; Bodl. MS. Carte 244, f. 127.

23. Burnet, v, 70–1.

24. E.g. H.M.C. *Fortescue MSS*. i, 19 (but cf. N.U.L. Portland [Holles] MSS. Pw2/291: G. Whichcot to Newcastle, 17 Oct. 1710). A Tory canvasser could occasionally expect to be told by Whig electors he "was come to the wrong place, for they were all Low Church men thereabouts" (see Add. MSS. 24612, f. 15: canvassing-book of Sir Arthur Kaye's agent in the North Riding, 1710).

25. H.M.C. *Portland MSS*. iv, 640: J. Durden to Harley, 5 Dec. 1710.

26. This expression, and its twin "the honest party" became common currency among the Whigs of Anne's reign. Drafting a letter to Somers in August 1710 the Duke of Newcastle wrote: "Tis a mellancholly thing to see in these parts how dispirited the generallity of the Whigs are, and how very active they are of the contrary party". Then, as an afterthought he struck out the word "Whigs" and wrote over it "honest interest". See B.M. Loan 29/238, ff. 356–7.

27. Claydon MSS.: Lady Gardiner to Sir John Verney, 30 July 1702; *ibid*: Sir Thomas Cave to Lord Fermanagh, 21 Aug. 1710; H.M.C. *Rutland MSS*. ii, 167; *Verney Letters*, i, 166; B.M. Loan 29/11/14: unsigned letter to Harley, London, 25 Sept. 1710.

28. *The Flying-Post*, No. 2280, 19–21 Oct. 1710. "Les rigides" was l'Hermitage's standard term for the Tories. See Add. MSS. 17677, *passim*, for the years 1702–14; also H.M.C. *Portland MSS*. iv, 571.

29. Auchmar MSS: Alexander Cunningham to Montrose, 20 May; Chevening MSS.: James Craggs to Stanhope, 1 June.

30. The calculations are to be found among Sunderland's papers in Blenheim MSS. C. 1–44.

31. H. L. Stowe MSS. 57, iv, 187: James Brydges to Tim Geers, 20 Oct.

32. Walton MSS. iii, 66: 9 Dec. 1701.

33. Wake MSS. Arch. W. Epist. 17, f. 259: to Wm. Wake, Bishop of Lincoln, 7 Aug.

34. Dartmouth's n. to Burnet, vi, 9; *Wentworth Papers*, p. 133; H.M.C. *Portland MSS*. iv, 684.

35. Onslow's n. to Burnet, v, 355; Lawson-Tancred, *Records of a Yorkshire Manor* (1937), p. 255: Wm. Jessop to C. Wilkinson, 18 June 1713; John Macky's 'Characters of the Court of Queen Anne'.

36. H.M.C. *Portland MSS*. iv, 510: [Erasmus Lewis] to Harley, 2 Nov. When the Tories returned to favour two years later it was the High Tory Bromley's turn to "hope ... that all Thoroughers shall be taken care of". Levens MSS: to James Grahme, 1 Sept. 1710.

37. E.g. H.M.C. *Portland MSS*. iv, 490, 684.

38. H.M.C. *Dartmouth MSS*. i, 319.

39. *Addison Letters*, pp. 94–5: 27 Feb. 1708. See also N.U.L. Portland (Bentinck) MSS. PwA. 945: Halifax to Portland, 19 Feb.

40. *Bolingbroke Corr.* i, 7: to Wm. Cadogan, 24 Oct.

41. Nicolson was slightly less discriminating in this respect than his friend, Wake; in Feb. 1711, for instance, he records having dined with the Highflying Bishops of Chester and Exeter. But even he moved mainly in Low Church circles when in London after 1710.

42. H.M.C. *7th Report*, pt. i (1879), p. 508.

43. See, e.g., Blenheim MSS. D. 1–32: Newcastle to Sunderland, 29 May 1708; B.M. Loan 29/238, ff. 255, 458.

44. H.M.C. *Rutland MSS.* ii, 177.

45. *Bolingbroke Corr.* i, 247: 12 June 1711.

46. Add. MSS. 49360: minutes, 16 Dec. 1709, 1 Dec. 1710.

47. B. Lillywhite, *London Coffee Houses* (1963), pp. 761–823.

48. *The Spectator*, No. 457, 14 Aug. 1712.

49. See, e.g., *ibid.* No. 1, 1 Mar. 1711.

50. *Wentworth Papers*, p. 211: to Strafford, 25 Nov. 1711; Pakington MSS.: G. Bradshaw to Pakington, 1 May 1705.

51. Lillywhite, *op. cit.* pp. 432, 534; J. Ashton, *Social Life in the Reign of Queen Anne* (1882), i, 221. Transport to convey Tory voters to Guildford for the Surrey election in 1710 was organised from the Rainbow Coffee House at Temple Gate. *The Post Boy*, No. 2404, 7–10 Oct. 1710.

52. W.S.L. Dartmouth MSS. D. 1778/I/ii/181: Mohun to Lady Charlotte Orby, "Thursday" [Oct. 1710]; *Wentworth Papers*, p. 135.

53. Bodl. MS. Carte 125, f. 100.

54. *The Flying-Post*, No. 3294, 6–8 Nov. 1712; see also Add. MSS. 47026, p. 10.

55. See H.M.C. *Portland MSS.* iv, 508; Lillywhite, *op. cit.* p. 452.

56. B.M. Loan 29/11/12: anon. to Lord Oxford, 10 Dec. [1713?].

57. See John Loftis, *The Politics of Drama in Augustan England* (1963), chaps. II and III. This paragraph is based partly on Professor Loftis's valuable work.

58. H.M.C. *7th Report*, pt. i (1879), p. 246: Lord Castlecomer to Sir John Percival, 28 Apr. 1713. See also G. M. Trevelyan, *England under Queen Anne*, iii, 250–3.

59. *Tamerlane* was not performed at all from 1710–1714, and the first performance of Rowe's *Jane Shore* was only licensed in Feb. 1714 after Bolingbroke had insisted on cutting out a passage which ultra-sensitive Tories took to be an oblique attack on the Pretender's legitimacy.

60. H.M.C. *Various Collections*, viii (*Clements MSS.*), p. 251: [Arabella Pulteney?] to John Molesworth, N.D. [May 1711].

61. Swift, *Journal to Stella*, 11 Sept. 1710; Defoe, "An Abstract of my Journey", H.M.C. *Portland MSS.* iv, 272; *Swift Corr.* i, 62.

62. B.M. Loan 29/131/7: Bishop Compton of London to Harley, "Aug." [1710].

63. H.M.C. *Portland MSS.* iv, 134. These drastic changes were due very largely to Sir Edward Seymour's influence with Lord Keeper Sir Nathan Wright.

64. Add. MSS. 29579, f. 400.

65. See *Memoirs of the Family of Guise of Elmore* (ed. G. Davies, Camden Soc., 1917), pp. 144–5; *C.J.* xv, 178–9, xvi, 14; B.M. Loan 29/29: Charles Coxe to Lord — ? —, Lippiate, 13 Oct. 1712; Chatsworth MSS. Finch-Halifax Papers, box 5, bundle 7: Nottingham to Guernsey, 17 June 1710.

66. Because he had no prearranged code, "the hazard of the Post" prevented Harley giving his close friend Sir Thomas Mansel prior notice of Godolphin's impending dismissal and Mansel's own appointment as a Treasury Commissioner in 1710. Penrice and Margam MSS. L. 689: [Harley] to Mansel, 1 Aug. 1710.

67. See H.M.C. *Portland MSS.* v, 306–7, 325; cf. Add. MSS. 47027, p. 49.

68. E.g. *Verney Letters*, p. 243.

69. *Ibid.* p. 242: Cave to Fermanagh, 10 Oct.

70. To Sir James Bateman and Thomas Pitt, for example. See H.M.C. *Portland MSS.* iv, 583; *Fortescue MSS.* i, intro. p. ix, p. 40.

71. *An Account of the Conduct of the Duchess of Marlborough* (1742), pp. 227–36; Coxe, iii, 9–10.

72. Peterborough left Spain in 1707; Galway, who was put in command of the army in Portugal in 1704, to the delight of the Whig Junto (see *Hervey L.B.* i, 207), was recalled in 1710; Stanhope was commander-in-chief in Spain from 1708 until his capture in Dec. 1710.

73. C.U.L. Cholmondeley (Houghton) MSS. Corresp. 615: Stanhope to Walpole, 11/22 June 1710.

74. Churchill, *Marlborough*, ii, 772–3. (references are to the two-vol. edn., 1947).

75. A. Boyer, *The Political State of Great Britain*, i, 8 (1711).

76. B.M. Loan 29/131/5: Portmore to Oxford, 20/31 May 1712. Portmore's Toryism was sufficiently marked to earn him nomination by Oxford's ministry as a Scottish representative peer in 1713.

77. Blenheim MSS. E. 27: Arthur Mainwaring to Duchess of Marlborough, "Friday morning" [11 May 1711]; *ibid.* B. 2–20: Ross to Marlborough, 11 May.

78. The committee's minutes are in Blenheim MSS. B. 2–15; and a letter from Marlborough to General Erle, 5/16 Apr. (Charborough Park MSS.), indicates how much its activities touched him on the raw. For a valuable account of these activities and a controversial view of St. John's attitude to them, see I. F. Burton, 'The Committee of Council at the War-Office', *Hist. Journal*, iv (1961).

79. Add. MSS. 38507, ff. 98–9; Add. MSS. 17677 HHH, ff. 159–60, 198; Panshanger MSS.: Diary of Lady Cowper, 28 Apr. 1714; *Verney Letters*, i, 274. Long before this Bolingbroke had looked forward eagerly to such a purge (see *Bolingbroke Corr.* ii, 482: to Ormonde, 23 July 1712).

80. Without such Whig-Low Church support, mobilised by Lord Halifax and the Bishop of Salisbury, the Kirk would never have secured the amendments it sought in the House of Lords to the Toleration bill in Jan.–Feb. 1712, a bill which was designed to give the Scottish Episcopalians full freedom of worship and the right to use the Prayer Book with the protection of the civil power.

81. *Wentworth Papers*, p. 261.

82. Wake MSS. Arch. W. Epist. 23, f. 203: Maurice Wheeler to Wake, 6 Mar.

83. Add. MSS. 29579, f. 401: Sir C. Lyttleton to Hatton, 15 July 1702.

84. *C.J.* xiv, 39.

85. Tullie House, Nicolson's MS. Diary, 5 Jan.–20 Mar. 1708; *Vernon Corr.* iii, 357–8; *Addison Letters*, pp. 92, 96–7; Wake MSS. Arch. W. Epist. 17. misc. i, letter 186. The irony about Dean Atterbury's defiance of the bishop's authority is that it was as much responsible as anything for Nicolson's conversion to Whiggery. As late as 1705 he was still favouring Tory candidates in Cumberland. Lloyd-Baker MSS. Box 4, bundle V.6: Nicolson to Archbishop Sharp, 19 May 1705 (microfilm in the Borthwick Institute, York).

86. The story of this struggle, or at least one side of it, is told in Naish's autobiography and diary, Bodl. MS. Top. Wilts. c. 7. In its small way it illuminates the essence of early-eighteenth-century politics as effectively as many a better-known or more spectacular incident.

87. See J. M. Price, 'A Note on the Circulation of the London Press 1704–14', *Bull. I.H.R.* xxxi (1958), for the sales of the *Post Boy* in 1712. cf. J. R. Sutherland, 'The circulation of newspapers and literary periodicals, 1700–30', *The Library*, 4th series, xv (June 1934), for an estimate of 10–20 readers per copy for the popular papers.

88. Oldmixon, p. 478; S.H. Cal. Br. 24 England 107, f. 44: Kreienberg, 7/18 Dec. 1711; *ibid.* 113a, f. 266: 5/16 Mar. 1714.

89. *Wentworth Papers*, p. 310. Similarly when Ridpath's printer, Hurst, was pilloried at the Royal Exchange in 1713 he had "a guard of Whiggs . . . with clubs to drive off those that went to pelt him." *The Worcester Post-Man*, No. 212, 10–17 July.

90. No. 42, 12–19 May.

91. No. 1398, 26–28 Apr.

92. E.g., cf. the instructions to Middlesex freeholders in the Whig interest in 1710 (*Post Man*, No. 1923) with the Tory plans for countering this effort (announced in the *Supplement*, No. 427).

93. Add. MSS. 4743, f. 32: E. Lewis to H. Davenant, 16 Mar. 1705.

94. *Swift Corr.* i, 199: 26 Sept. 1710.

95. Roger Coke, *A Detection of the Court and State of England* (4th edn. 1719), iii, 382. The pamphlet war of 1710 has been well analysed by Mary Ransome, 'The Press in the General Election of 1710', *C.H.J.*, vi (1939).

96. Lonsdale MSS: [Hy. Newman] to James Lowther, 6–8 Aug. 1713; John Oldmixon, *The Life and Posthumous Works of Arthur Maynwaring* (1712), p. 171.

97. Bodl. MS. Ballard 20, ff. 75–6; H.M.C. *Bath MSS.* i, 105.

98. Though the rewards were reduced and the hazards increased by the imposition of the new stamp duty in 1712 (see J. M. Price, *loc. cit.*, for the reduced circulation of newspapers thereafter). For an interesting brief commentary on the Augustan press and its contribution to politics see the chapter on "Grub Street" in Michael Foot, *The Pen and the Sword* (1957), pp. 73–91.

99. *English Politics*, p. 34: the italics are mine.

100. Speck, *loc. cit.*, pp. 93–4.

101. Apart from Raymond the only renegades were Charles Godfrey, Russell Robartes, John Borlace, Sir Roger Bradshaigh and Sir Edward Goodere (both of whom can be classed as Whigs only with the strongest reservations), John Ward (the Bank director), Robert Monckton, Craven Peyton, and Peregrine Bertie, Lord Willoughby. The names are so few as to be worth recording.

102. This was true of Richard Hampden, Sir George Byng, William Cotesworth, Richard Harnage and Henry Mordaunt. The other three were John Hedworth, Thomas Onslow and Thomas Wynne. These 8 are not the only members classified in Worsley MSS. 1 as Whigs "qui votera souvent avec les Torys"; but the remainder of those so distinguished can all be clearly identified as Hanoverian Tories.

103. *Parl. Hist.* vi, 170–1, 886–7. Both were current within a few weeks of the votes concerned and their authenticity is not in doubt.

104. Blenheim MSS. D. 2–10 (in the Earl of Sunderland's hand, N.D., but clearly attributable from internal evidence to 16 Jan. 1703); B.M. Loan 29/163/10. I am very

much indebted to Dr. H. L. Snyder for bringing both these lists to my notice. I have since found another MS. list of the Hamilton division among the Montrose Papers at Auchmar which corresponds exactly with that in the Portland Papers. For the circumstances of the first division see p. 102 and n. * above. For the issues in the Hamilton vote see my article on 'The Hamilton Affair of 1711–12: A Crisis in Anglo-Scottish Relations', *E.H.R.* lxxvii (1962).

105. See 'The several Proceedings and Resolutions of the House of Peers in relation to the Lords impeached or charged' (London, 1701), pp. 89, 99; B.M. Loan 29/160/1: "Anno 1701. A List of all the Lords Spiritual & Temporall; distinguishing wch of them were absent from the tryall of the Lord Sommers, & Earle of Orford; and wch of them were not content, and wch of them were content for the acquittal of those Lords". The division-list on Orford's acquittal (23 June 1701) is not of much value for our purposes since the issue was a foregone conclusion and the Tory peers preferred a mass-abstention to a vote.

106. B.M. Loan 29/10/3; Finch MSS. P.P. 161 (ii). The identification of both these lists is discussed in Appendix A.

107. *Wentworth Papers*, p. 225.

108. See *E.H.R.* lxxvii (1962), pp. 260–3, 267.

109. 'The Idea of Party in the Writing of Later Stuart History'. *Journal of British Studies*, No. 2, May 1962.

110. H.M.C. *Mar and Kellie MSS.* p. 495.

111. Viz. the *Exact List of all who voted for and against engrossing [the Bill of Commerce]* appended to *A Letter from a Member of the House of Commons relating to the Bill of Commerce* (printed by J. Baker, 1713).

112. The *Letter from a Member*, p. 25 and appx., takes special pains to distinguish from the "Whimsical Tories" those who were "very far from lost Sheep, which were hardly ever known to straggle from us but this once, and I hope never will again".

113. There were 22 Tories among the 154 voting in favour of Steele; there were 27 among the 248 voting for the Whig candidate as Speaker in 1705, most of them office-holders under strong pressure from the Court.

114. See *Bull. I.H.R.* xxxiii (1960), 227–8.

115. Viz. Nathaniel and Frederick Herne, John Hungerford and Sir Francis Child.

116. See his arguments against the South Sea scheme in Finch MSS. P.P. 141.

117. Excluding Lord Rivers, who had finally deserted the Whigs in 1709.

118. There was a mild eleventh-hour alarm in 1714, but few took the prospects of a contest on this occasion at all seriously. See Add. MSS. 17677HHH, f. 46; Trumbull MSS. Alphab[etical Series], vol. lii: Thos. Bateman to Sir Wm. Trumbull, 12 Feb.

119. Bateman to Trumbull, 12 Feb. 1714, *loc. cit.*

120. W. Coxe, *Memoirs of Sir Robert Walpole* (1798), ii, 4–5: Spencer Compton to Walpole, 12 Oct. 1704. In the event Harley remained Speaker, unchallenged by the High Tories.

121. The fact that under 30 Tories in the end voted against Bromley was a bitter disappointment to Godolphin and Harley, who had hoped for many more defections to the Court side. See Blenheim MSS. A. 1–25: Harley to Marlborough, 26 July 1705; B.M. Loan 29/192, f. 256: Harley to Baron Price, 14 Aug. 1705.

122. *Epistolary Correspondence of Atterbury*, iii (1784), 140.

123. Charborough Park MSS.: James Craggs to Thos. Erle, 26 July 1705; cf. H.M.C. *Bath MSS.* i, 75.

124. Coxe, ii, 292.

125. Blenheim MSS. E. 15: Sunderland to Duchess of Marlborough, 8 Aug. 1708; *ibid.* E. 25: Arthur Mainwaring to the same, "Tuesday one o'clock" [?28 June 1708]; B.M. Lansdowne MSS. 1236, ff. 247–8, 250: Sunderland to Newcastle, 19, 26 Oct. 1708 (printed Trevelyan, *England under Queen Anne*, ii [hereafter cited as *Ramillies*], 414–16).

126. The Whigs had a clear majority of 50 in this division. Luttrell, vi, 377; H.L. Stowe MSS. 57, ii, 121–2: Brydges to Cardonnel and Drummond, 30 Nov. 1708. Cf. B.M. Loan 29/64/3: [Godolphin] to Harley, "Thursday" [8 Nov. 1705]; Add. MSS. 4743, f. 47.

127. H.M.C. *Portland MSS.* iv, 278: [Godolphin] to Harley, "Friday" [9 Nov. 1705].

128. *Swift Corr.* i, 221: Swift to Archbp. King, 28 Nov. 1710.

129. Arthur Onslow's note to Burnet, v, 196.

130. B.M. Loan 29/194: [Godolphin] to Harley, "Fryday night at 8" [8 Feb. 1706] (cf. misdated letter printed in H.M.C. *Portland MSS.* iv, 464); Add. MSS. 4291, f. 54; Blenheim MSS. Box viii, 23 — a paper listing 21 defaulters, including absentees, when the Bewdley case was heard in committee.

131. See l'Hermitage, 9/20 Mar. 1714 (Add. MSS. 17677HHH, f. 106), for a comment on the attractions of Bar procedure for the party in the ascendant.

132. After a titanic struggle, which began on the afternoon of 20 Jan. 1709 and continued without adjournment until 3 a.m. on the morning of the 21st (B.M. Loan 29/320: Dyer's Newsletters, 20, 22 Jan.).

133. Finch MSS. G.S., bundle 23: Bromley to Nottingham, 7 Dec. 1708; *Guise Memoirs*, p. 144; H.M.C. *Portland MSS.* iv, 519, 521.

134. Legh of Lyme MSS. Box 49: Bunbury to Peter Legh, 1 Feb. 1708 [–9].

135. Auchmar MSS.: Mungo Graham to Montrose, 30 Nov. 1710.

136. See also Bodl. MS. Ballard 10, f. 124; Add. MSS. 17677DDD, f. 665.

137. Auchmar MSS.: Graham to Montrose, 19 Dec.

138. *C.J.* xvi, 452–3; MS. Ballard 38, f. 191; *ibid.* 20, f. 69. See Cockermouth Castle MSS. Box 169: S. M. Gale to Joseph Relf, 1 May 1711, for the attempt of the Tories, out of "a spirit of contradiction", to prevent Stanhope's re-election at Cockermouth by denying a writ.

139. B.M. Stowe MSS. 225, f. 208: Schütz to Robethon, 29 Sept. 1713, quoting the view of l'Hermitage; Ducie MSS. D. 340a/C22. 9: Edmund Bray to M. D. Moreton, 2 May 1714. The Ducie MSS. are in Gloucestershire R.O.

140. Auchmar MSS.: Graham to Montrose, 10, 13 Feb. 1711.

141. Lawson-Tancred, *Records of a Yorkshire Manor* (1937), p. 249: Lord Pelham to Charles Wilkinson, 4 June 1713; Temple Newsam MSS. Corr. Box 9, f. 71: Thos. Pulleine to Lord Irwin, 28 Aug. 1701; Surrey Record Office, Somers MSS. 01/1: Mrs. Burnet to Lady Jekyll, N.D. [1702] (papers formerly in the possession of Reigate corporation).

142. House of Lords R.O. The book records proxies held in 5 parliamentary sessions of Anne's reign, those of 1704–5, 1705–6, 1706–7, 1710–11 and 1711–12.

143. See, e.g., the divisions on 26 May and 3 June 1712 in *C.J.* xvii, 242, 252.

144. This point is well developed by E. L. Ellis, 'The Whig Junto' (Oxford D.Phil. thesis, 1962).

145. Add. MSS. 9092, f. 2: Hare to Robert Walpole, 1 Apr. (my italics).

146. *C.J.* xiv, 391; xv, 7; xvii, 1, 278, 474.

147. *Parl. Hist.* vi, 812.

148. *Lockhart Papers* (ed. A. Aufrere, 1817), i, 320.

149. W.S.L. Dartmouth MSS. D. 1778/I/ii/169: Jersey to Dartmouth, 6 Oct. [1710].

150. *C.J.* xvi, 685. For the inspiration behind much of this address see the memorandum in Lord Nottingham's hand, N.D. [early 1711] in Finch MSS. P.P. 150 (xii).

151. See "The October Club's Opinion of Mr. H——y" in Defoe's *Eleven Opinions about Mr. H——y* (1711), p. 56.

152. Trumbull MSS. Alphab. li: Thos. Bateman to Trumbull, 4 Oct. 1710. "I ... can't but have many fears from the mixture there seems to be in the scheme [of government]", he added. His fears were shared by the Harleyite Canon Stratford in Oxford. See H.M.C. *Portland MSS.* vii, 16.

153. B.M. Loan 29/198: Bromley to Oxford, 25 Nov. 1711.

154. H.M.C. *Portland MSS.* iv, 693: 19 May 1711.

155. Longleat MSS. Thynne Papers, xxvi, f. 143: Lord Stawell to Weymouth, 3 May.

156. Add. MSS. 22221, f. 23: 29 Apr. 1714. It is interesting to find Queen Anne applying this identical expression to the Junto Whigs in a letter to Marlborough in July 1708. See Churchill, *Marlborough*, ii, 413.

157. Bodl. MS. Ballard 10, f. 124: Simon Harcourt to Dr. Charlett, 14 Dec. 1710.

158. [John Oldmixon], *The History of Addresses with Remarks Serious and Comical* (2nd edn. London, 1711), Preface to Part II.

159. *Cowper Diary*, pp. 11–12: 6 Nov. 1705.

160. *Wentworth Papers*, p. 310: Peter Wentworth to Strafford, 26 Dec. 1712; Chirk Castle MSS. E. 4204: Brereton to Sir Richard Myddleton, 3 Mar. 1704[-5].

161. See Coke's correspondence in H.M.C. *Cowper MSS.* ii, iii, *passim*; H. L. Stowe MSS. 57, iv, 133: Brydges to Humphrey Walcot, 2 Sept. 1710; *H.L.Q.* iii (1939–40), 238: the same to John Drummond, 24 Aug. 1710.

162. Add. MSS. 31143, f. 568: Peter Wentworth to Raby, 26 Sept. 1710. For similar instances among the more small-time professional placemen note the cases of George Kenyon, M.P. for Wigan, and Anthony Morgan, M.P. for Yarmouth (I.O.W.). H.M.C. *Kenyon MSS.* p. 445; Sir F. Black, *Parliamentary History of the Isle of Wight* (1929), p. 19.

163. Add. MSS. 31135, f. 278: London, 9 Jan. 1711.

CHAPTER TWO:
THE SUBSTANCE OF CONFLICT: OLD ISSUES AND NEW

1. 'An Impartial History of Parties'. See John, Lord Campbell, *The Lives of the Lord Chancellors*, iv (1846), p. 427.

2. Later Dean of St. Paul's and successively Bishop of St. Asaph and Chichester.

3. *Priv. Corr.* i, 402: to Duchess of Marlborough, St. André, [19]/30 Oct. 1710.

4. Add. MSS. 47026, pp. 23–4: London, 20 Apr. 1710.

5. Wake MSS. Arch. W. Epist. 23, f. 207: 26 July.

6. *A Letter to Sir William Wyndham* (written 1717, published posthumously 1753), p. 19.

7. *The Works of . . . Henry St. John, Lord Viscount Bolingbroke*, ii (1754), 102–3.

8. *Ibid.* ii, 109, 111.

9. 'An Impartial History of Parties' *loc. cit.*

10. Add. MSS. 47025, p. 110. Percival had been up at Magdalen College, Oxford, from November 1699 to 1701 and had remained in England until Sept. 1703. Thereafter, however, he seems to have spent every winter except that of 1707-8, when political

conditions in England were quite uncharacteristic of those of Anne's reign as a whole, either in Ireland or abroad on the Grand Tour. See *ibid. passim.*

11. Add. MSS. 47087, (unfoliated): Percival's diary [March 1714]; Percival to Daniel Dering (copies), 25 May, 14 June.

12. *Bolingbroke Corr.* iv, 550: to Phipps, 20 May 1714; cf. *ibid.* p. 509: to Prior, 20 Apr.

13. G. F. Gent, *The History of the First and Second Session of the Last Parliament* (1714), p. 65.

14. Bodl. MS. Add. A. 269, p. 15: to Bishop Nicolson, 10 June 1712 (copy).

15. *The Memoirs of John Ker of Kersland* (3rd edn. 1721), Pt. iii, 134, 136.

16. *Bolingbroke Corr.* i, 148–9: to Drummond, 10 Apr.

17. Massingberd MSS.: Burrell Massingberd to Sir William Massingberd, 28 Feb. 1710 (draft); Add. MSS. 22851, f. 183: Lord Delawarr to Thomas Pitt, 4 July 1701; *The Post Boy*, No. 2415, 2–4 Nov. 1710; *The Rehearsal*, No. 42, 12–19 May 1705.

18. Cockermouth Castle MSS. Box 110: "Phill Ecclesiasto" to [the electors of Cockermouth], 25 Sept. 1710.

19. 'Impartial History', *loc. cit.* p. 421.

20. *Priv. Corr.* i, 402: to Duchess of Marlborough, [19]/30 Oct. 1710.

21. B.M. Loan 29/147: 12 Aug. 1710.

22. The support given by this minority, notably by Daniel Finch, the future Earl of Nottingham, to the abortive Toleration and Comprehension bills of 1680–1 is emphasised by H. Horwitz, 'Protestant Reconciliation in the Exclusion Crisis', *Journal of Ecclesiastical History*, xv (1964).

23. See J. R. Jones, *The First Whigs* (Oxford, 1961), pp. 213–16.

24. *Faults on Both Sides* (2nd edn. London, 1710), pp. 17, 25.

25. No one, in view of Anne's previous unhappy experience of maternity, would have cared to prophesy at the time the Bill of Rights became law in Dec. 1689 that her young son William, Duke of Gloucester, born less than 5 months before, would survive infancy.

26. The oath of allegiance was conveniently phrased to allow for a *de facto* recognition of William III's regal authority.

27. For an important reassessment of the struggle for the control of Church preferment in the 1690's, and of the King's attitude towards it, see G. V. Bennett, 'King William III and the Episcopate', *Essays in Modern English Church History in Memory of Norman Sykes* (ed. G. V. Bennett and J.D. Walsh, 1966), pp. 104–31.

28. It is hard to justify a more charitable description of the position of many Whig leaders in the 90's on such questions as Place bills, royal land grants and the standing army.

29. Anonymous pamphleteer, c. 1692, quoted by E. L. Ellis, 'The Whig Junto' (Oxford D.Phil. thesis, 1962), p. 3. See also John Toland, *The Art of Governing by Partys* (1701), pp. 42, 47–8.

30. Add. MSS. 22851, f. 131: 20 Dec. 1701. Cf. Chatsworth MSS. Finch-Halifax Papers, box 5, bundle 7: Nottingham to Heneage Finch, 17 June 1701; H.M.C. *Downshire MSS.* I, ii, pp. 803–4: St. John to Sir William Trumbull, 22 June 1701.

31. By these treaties William had hoped to ensure a peaceful disposal of the Spanish empire among the chief claimants to the inheritance of Carlos II: maintaining a reasonable balance between the dynastic forces of Hapsburg and Bourbon and at the same time keeping the Spanish Americas out of the control of French commercial interests.

32. H.M.C. *Various Collections*, viii (*Clements MSS.*), p. 224: to his wife, 12 May. The

Duke of Newcastle agreed with Molesworth (Chevening MSS.: Newcastle to Stanhope, 31 Mar.).

33. E.g., Sir Richard Sandford's speech to the electors of Westmorland at Orton in Nov. 1701. H.M.C. *Bagot MSS*. p. 336. The Tories recognised subsequently that such charges had done their cause a great deal of damage. See Walton MSS. iii, 53: Andrew Archer to Sir John Mordaunt, 5 Jan. 1701[–2] (printed in Elizabeth Hamilton, *The Mordaunts* [1965], p. 47).

34. Queen's Speech to Parliament, 16 July 1713.

35. *Letter to Wyndham*, p. 20.

36. *Ibid.* pp. 28–9.

37. Chetwynd Diplomatic MSS. D. 649/8: George Tilson [Bolingbroke's Under-Secretary in the Northern Dept. 1710–13] to John Chetwynd, 24 Aug. 1711. The wounds were still rankling long after the war was over. "19 millions we have paid since the war more than our quota", Sir Edward Knatchbull wrote in his diary on 19 Apr. 1714 (A. N. Newman, 'Proceedings in the House of Commons, March–June 1714', *Bull. I.H.R.* [1961], 215).

38. For the attitude of the October Club Tories see Marlborough's evidence, retailed by Robethon to Bernstorff, 21 Mar. 1711: Klopp, *Der Fall des Hauses Stuart*, xiv, 673.

39. B.M. Loan 29/7/6: draft in Oxford's hand dated "Feb: 19: 1713/14". Cf. *C.J.* xvii, 474.

40. *The Freeholder*, No. 22, 5 Mar. 1716.

41. Quoted in John Toland, *A State Anatomy of Great Britain* (London, 1717), p. 15.

42. Nicolson's MS. Diary, 9 Jan. 1703.

43. For the desperate unwillingness of the Dutch to imperil their economy by placing an embargo on trade with the enemy in the Spanish Succession War see [Sir] G. N. Clark, 'War Trade and Trade War, 1701–13', *Econ. H.R.* i (1927–8), pp. 262–80.

44. *C.J.* xiv, 103, 105: 5-7 Jan. 1703. For this incident, and for the whole question of party attitudes to the Dutch during the Spanish Succession War see Douglas Coombs, *The Conduct of the Dutch* (Hague, 1958), pp. 44–5 and *passim*.

45. H.M.C. *Portland MSS*. iv, 110: [Dyer's] Newsletter, 19 Aug. 1704.

46. Blenheim MSS. F. 2–16: 10 Nov. 1704.

47. Chevening MSS: Harley to Stanhope, 5 Dec. 1704; Add. MSS. 4291, f. 64.

48. Finch MSS. G.S., bundle 23: Sir Roger Mostyn to Nottingham, 16 Dec. 1708. Cf. the satisfaction of the Whig Joseph Addison, just elected for Lostwithiel. *Addison Letters*, p. 124.

49. Of Dawny, Sussex, and Cambwell Priory, Kent: one of the most prominent of the young Tories who had entered Parliament for the first time in 1708. M.P. East Grinstead 1708–10, Bossiney 1710–13, Sussex 1713–14.

50. *Parl. Hist.* vi, 780. See *ibid.* pp. 437–8 for the abortive bill of 1704–5 for naturalising French refugees, into which the Tories significantly inserted a clause precluding the latter from the franchise.

51. *Ibid.* p. 780; Add. MSS. 17677 DDD, f. 65.

52. Chatsworth MSS. 107–2: John Charlton to [Duchess of Devonshire], 20 Sept. 1709; H.M.C. *Portland MSS*. ii, 207.

53. *The Supplement*, No. 427, 6–9 Oct. 1710; Auchmar MSS.: Mungo Graham to Montrose, 6 Feb. 1711.

54. *The Supplement*, *loc. cit.*

55. *Bolingbroke Corr.* ii, 52: to Strafford, 8 Dec. 1711.

56. *Journal to Stella,* 20 Feb. 1712.

57. *C.J.* xvii, 69–70, 92, 119–23; Add. MSS. 17677FFF, ff. 54–5, 91; W.S.L. MS. diary of Sir Arthur Kaye, p. 8.

58. See Kaye MS. Diary, p. 8.

59. E.g. 217–54 in Committee on 4 Feb.; 217–43 when the Whigs tried to recommit the Hanmer Representation on 1 March.

60. *Norris Papers,* p. 80: Thomas Johnson to Richard Norris, 17 Mar. 1701[–2]; *Original Letters of Locke, Sidney and Shaftesbury* (1830), p. 217: Shaftesbury to Furley, 4 Sept. 1705.

61. Blenheim MSS. B. 2–5: Somers to Marlborough, 6 June 1710. For Lord Cowper's demand in Dec. 1711 that the allies should "enlarge their charge to the lessening of ours" see Panshanger MSS.: Sir David Hamilton's diary, 14 Dec.

62. A good example is Wharton's motion in the Lords on 22 Nov. 1705 in response to some very defeatist speeches from Nottingham and Rochester. Add. MSS. 17677AAA, ff. 536–7: l'Hermitage, 23 Nov./4 Dec.; Nicolson's MS. Diary, 22 Nov.

63. Add. MSS. 34521, f. 43: Somers to the Elector of Hanover, April 1706 (transcript).

64. *Wentworth Papers,* p. 269: Peter Wentworth to Strafford, 19 Feb.; see also Add. MSS. 17677FFF, f. 54; Burnet, vi, 111.

65. Rochester's preface to Clarendon's *History of the Great Rebellion,* i (1702), pp. viii–ix.

66. B. M. Loan 29/160/10: to Harley, 3 Oct. 1702.

67. There is a choice example in Sir Chas. Lyttleton's letter to Sir John Pakington, Hagley, 4 Dec. 1703 in Pakington MSS. vol. ii, f. 11.

68. Add. MSS. 29589, ff. 121–2, 143.

69. Bodl. MS. Ballard 38, f. 137: Bromley to Charlett, 22 Oct. 1702; H.M.C. *Portland MSS.* iv, 50, 55: [Godolphin] to Harley, 4 Nov., 24 Dec. [1702].

70. Finch-Hatton MSS. 277, p. 1: Nottingham to Heinsius, 30 April 1703. For a fuller exposition see H. Horwitz, 'The Political Career of Daniel Finch, Second Earl of Nottingham', (Oxford, D.Phil., 1963), pp. 383–5.

71. Blenheim MSS. B. 2–33: Harley to Godolphin, 20 Sept. 1703.

72. Later Duke of Buckingham, Lord Privy Seal in Anne's first ministry.

73. *Diplomatic Correspondence of . . . Richard Hill* (ed. W. Blackley, 1845), i, 45–6: Nottingham to Hill, 19 Oct. 1703; Nottingham to Normanby, 29 Sept. 1701, cited Horwitz, *loc. cit.* p. 383.

74. Finch MSS. G.S., bundle 23: to Bromley (copy), 15 Nov. 1708.

75. *Vernon Corr.* iii, 300–1; cf. H.M.C. *Egmont MSS.* ii, 220.

76. Auchmar MSS: Mungo Graham to Montrose, 2 Jan. 1711.

77. Add. MSS. 17677DDD, f. 685; S.H. Cal. Br. 24 England 99, f. 23: Kreienberg, 15/26 Dec. The speech was made by George Pitt, the wealthy knight of the shire for Hampshire, who according to Kreienberg "ne fut pas seulement écouté".

78. Blenheim MSS. E. 27: Arthur Mainwaring to Duchess of Marlborough, "Tuesday past six a clock" [15 May 1711].

79. See Trevelyan, *England under Queen Anne,* iii, 118–19, 129, 143–6.

80. Only Sunderland of the previous ministry seems to have shown much enthusiasm for it. W. T. Morgan, 'Queen Anne's Canadian Expedition of 1711', *Bulletin of the*

Departments of History and Political and Economic Science in Queen's University, Ontario, No. 56 (1928).

81. *C.J.* xvii, 474: 2 Mar. 1714.

82. Coxe, ii, 221: Marlborough to the Queen, 28 Apr./9 May 1708. Cf. *Swift Corr.* i, 62, 71, for public opinion and the war during the previous winter.

83. E.g. Finch MSS. G.S., bundle 23: [Bromley] to Nottingham, 7 Dec. 1708.

84. *Ibid.*: to Bromley (copy), 20 Dec. 1708. Nottingham's realistic attitude at this juncture is worth recording in view of his subsequent desertion of the Tories on the peace issue, 1711–12.

85. *Wentworth Papers*, pp. 88, 90; *Priv. Corr.* i, 182.

86. H.M.C. *Various Collections*, viii (*Clements MSS.*), 244 illustrates the determination even of a non-Junto Whig (Molesworth) to "humble the proud monarch who disturbs all the world". See also Walpole's draft for a pamphlet [1710], Add. MSS. 35335, f. 7.

87. *Priv. Corr.* ii, 359; Monson MSS. 7/12/136: Bertie to Sir John Newton, 28 Aug.

88. H.M.C. *Portland MSS.* iv, 497: J. Cranstoun to Cunningham, 25 July 1709 O.S. (misdated by the editor 1708). See also H.M.C. *Frankland-Russell-Astley MSS.* p. 199: Col. Rivett to D. Polhill, 21 July O.S.

89. See H.M.C. *Bath MSS.* i, 197: Shrewsbury to Harley, 3 Nov. 1709.

90. Add. MSS. 31136, f. 6: St. John to Strafford, 23 Oct. 1711.

91. See, e.g., W. Coxe, *Correspondence of Charles Talbot, Duke of Shrewsbury* (1821), pp. 643–4: Somers to Shrewsbury, 21 July 1704; Add. MSS. 40776, ff. 11–12: Shrewsbury to Vernon, 28 Oct. 1706.

92. H.M.C. *Egmont MSS.* ii, 221; *Vernon Corr.* iii, 301; *Addison Letters*, pp. 84–6.

93. H.M.C. *Bath MSS.* i, 194. For one Tory who agreed with him, however, see John Wyndham's letter to Thos. Pitt, 18 Dec. 1707, H.M.C. *Fortescue MSS.* i, 33.

94. Gaultier to Torcy, 12/23 Dec. 1710, printed *E.H.R.* xlix (1934), 103.

95. *Bolingbroke Corr.* i, 54–5; S.H. Cal. Br. 24 England 99, f. 35: Kreienberg, 26 Dec./ 6 Jan.; see also the view of a Tory backbencher, Sir Henry Johnson, after the end of the Spanish campaign of 1710–11: Add. MSS. 31136, ff. 135–6.

96. *Priv. Corr.* ii, 392.

97. *Bolingbroke Corr.* ii, 73: to Strafford, 15 Dec. 1711.

98. *Cowper Diary*, p. 41 n.; Burnet, vi, 19, 82 (Dartmouth's notes); *The Conduct of the Allies* (see Swift, *Complete Works* ed. Roscoe, i, 421).

99. *Swift Corr.* i, 310: Swift to King, 29 Dec. 1711.

100. Lawson-Tancred, *Records of a Yorkshire Manor*, p. 235: Jessop to C. Wilkinson, Dec. 1711.

101. B.M. Loan 29/12/4: Oxford to the Queen (draft), 16 Aug. 1711.

102. S.H. Cal. Br. 24 England 107, f. 47: Kreienberg, 11/22 Dec.; Pittis, *Second Session*, p. 11.

103. Speaker Bromley was recommending it to the attention of his Warwickshire friends at the end of November. Bodl. MS. Carte 230: John to Samuel Carte, 3 Dec.

104. *Journal to Stella*, 5 Dec. 1711, 28 Jan. 1712; [R. Walpole], *A Short History of the Parliament* (London, 1713), p. 10.

105. Boyer, pp. 571–2; *C.J.* xvii, 246.

106. Boyer, p. 577: 7 June 1712.

107. *Bolingbroke Corr.* iv, 19: Bolingbroke to Shrewsbury, 29 Mar. 1713.

108. Add. MSS. 35584, f. 141: Philip Yorke to Samuel Palmer (draft), [London], 31 Dec. 1711.

109. *Ibid.* ff. 141–2.

CHAPTER THREE:
THE SUBSTANCE OF CONFLICT: PRINCIPLES AND POWER

1. *Parl. Hist.* vi, 831: 16 Mar. 1710.

2. H.M.C. *House of Lords MSS.* N.S. vi, 322: MS. minute taken by the Clerk of the House.

3. Burnet, v, 234; Nicolson's MS. diary, 19 Nov. 1705; H.M.C. *House of Lords MSS.* N.S. vi, 322–3, which has a summary of Wharton's speech on 19 Nov. in a Committee of the whole House. See also B.M. Loan 29/237, ff. 115–16: Godolphin to Newcastle, 13 Nov., for the suggested meeting at the house of the Junto's faithful lieutenant, Bolton, at which the idea was probably hatched.

4. 'An Impartial History of Parties', Campbell, *op. cit.* iv, 426.

5. See divisions in H.M.C. *House of Lords MSS.* N.S. vi, 323–7.

6. The initial Hanoverian reaction to the Regency Act had not been as favourable as the Whigs had hoped. Chevening MSS.: Sir John Cropley to Stanhope, 26 Mar. [1706]. Cf. Dr. John Hutton to Archbishop Sharp, Hanover, 16/27 Oct. 1705 (printed *Life of Sharp*, i, 270–2).

7. Add. MSS. 34521, f. 43.

8. Trevelyan, *Ramillies*, pp. 230–1. The Tory commissioners for the Union on the English side (18 out of a total of 23 were Tories, although the bill authorising the Commission had been Whig-sponsored) "treated it as a jest or impossibility [Cowper later alleged], by absenting from all meetings appointed, and so letting it drop". 'Impartial History', *loc. cit.* p. 426; Boyer, pp. 13, 25.

9. See Dartmouth's n. to Burnet, v, 182–3, for the opening gambits in this game. The Aliens bill duly became law in April 1705.

10. Chevening MSS.: 13 May.

11. See *The Acts of the Parliaments of Scotland*, xi (1824), 163–91, for full list of commissioners and records of attendance.

12. H.M.C. *Portland MSS.* ii, 193: to Newcastle, 15 June 1706. Harley had almost certainly tried, without success, in April to get more moderate Tories added to the English commission. Longleat MSS. Portland Papers, vii, f. 49: [Godolphin to Harley], 8 Apr. [1706].

13. Somers MSS. 01/15: Sir J. Jekyll to Somers, 4 Apr. [1707].

14. Add. MSS. 17677GGG, ff. 249–50; S.H. Cal. Br. 24 England 113a, ff. 153–4; B.M. Lansdowne MSS. 1024, f. 420.

15. *Letters of Thomas Burnet, 1712–22*, p. 62: Burnet to George Duckett [13–17 Apr. 1714]; Macpherson, ii, 590–2: Schütz to Robethon and Bothmar, 13/24 Apr.; Boyer, p. 686; Add. MSS. 40621, f. 22.

16. Add. MSS. 40621, ff. 197, 205: Bromley and Lewis to Thos. Harley, 16, 23 Apr. For this whole incident see W. Michael, *England under George I* (English transl., 1936), i, 29–33.

17. Add. MSS. 47087 (unfoliated): Sir John to Philip Percival, 8 Apr.

18. Add. MSS. 40621, f. 178: Robert to Thomas Harley, 14/25 Mar.; Add. MSS. 17677HHH, f. 128; B.M. Stowe MSS. 226, f. 313: Schütz to Robethon, 19/30 Mar.; S.H. Cal. Br. 24 England 113a, ff. 282–3: Kreienberg, do.

19. Papillon Letter Book, 1713–14: Philip Papillon to E. Wivell, 22 Apr.

20. Whig M.P. for Northumberland and son and heir of the Duke of Somerset.

21. Boyer, pp. 708–9; *C.J.* xvii, 700.

22. According to the Prussian Resident in London, Colonel John Granville (later Lord Granville) was the only Tory to oppose the settlement openly. Add. MSS. 30,000E$_2$, f. 63: Bonet to Frederick III of Brandenburg, 4/15 Mar. 1701; cf. Add. MSS. 17677WW, ff. 179–80, 183, 189.

23. Norris MSS. 920 NOR. 1/137: Henry to Richard Norris, 20 Sept. 1701.

24. W. Coxe, *Memoirs of Sir Robert Walpole* (1798), ii, 3: Horace to Robert, 28 Feb. See also Norris MSS. 920 NOR. 2/244: Thos. Johnson to Norris, 31 Jan.; Add. MSS. 7074, f. 168; H.M.C. *Rutland MSS.* ii, 169.

25. Walton MSS., iii, 59: Sir Charles Holt to Sir John Mordaunt, 16 Feb. 1702.

26. Longleat MSS. Thynne Papers, xiii, f. 287: Weymouth to James Thynne, Chilton, 27 Mar. 1702. See also Add. MSS. 7074, f. 109: J. Ellis to G. Stepney, 27 Mar.

27. Blenheim MSS. D. 1–32: Charles Cox to John Gellibrand, Southwark, 24 Feb. 1705 (reporting a conversation with Lade some years before).

28. Finch MSS. *loc. cit.*

29. 'Impartial History of Parties', *loc. cit.* iv, 425.

30. For contemporary confirmation of Cowper's view see Add. MSS. 17677WW, f. 185: l'Hermitage, 7/18 Mar.; Add. MSS. 30,000E, ff. 205–6: Bonet, 20/31 May.

31. Bodl. MS. Carte 180, f. 292.

32. Longleat MSS. Thynne Papers, xiii, f. 283: Weymouth to James Thynne, 13 Mar. 1702.

33. The rumour was mentioned in a letter (unfortunately unsigned) sent to Harley at Brampton, possibly in September 1702. See B.M. Loan 29/11/10. On the other hand we do know for certain that during the Lords' debates on the Bill of Settlement in 1701 the Marquess of Normanby had urged that the Prince be given preference over the Hanoverians if he should survive his wife. Add. MSS. 30,000E, f. 211: Bonet, 23 May/3 June.

34. *C.J.* xiv, 193–4: the voting was 118–117.

35. See, e.g., *A Test offered to the Consideration of the Electors of Great Britain* (1710); *A Collection of White and Black Lists* (1715). The Whigs always maintained that had their opponents succeeded in the trial of strength on the first clause they would have directly challenged the treason clause as well. See Burnet, v, 57–8; Boyer, *Annals*, i (1702–3), 208–10; H.M.C. *House of Lords MSS.* N.S. v, pp. xviii–xix, 199–200.

36. *Cowper Diary*, p. 22.

37. For the Commons' debates on the Regency bill in January 1706 see C.U.L. Add. MS. 7093: anon. parliamentary diary, *passim*, and especially pp. 33, 35–7, 59, 65, 68–9, 72–4, 94–5, 105.

38. Norris MSS. 920/NOR. 2/446: Johnson to Norris, 4 Feb. 1707.

39. Chevening MSS.: enclosure in Addison's letter to Stanhope, 18 Feb. 1707; Nicolson's MS. diary, 3 Feb. 1707. Nottingham had changed his tune since 1702 when, unlike some of his friends, he had supported the Union negotiations. *Ibid.* 30 Nov. 1702.

40. Bodl. MS. Ballard 10, f. 65.

41. "In my opinion", Haversham said, "the best title her majesty has is her hereditary

title; though I deny not but that the act of parliament is a strengthening and confirmation of that title".

42. *Parl. Hist.* vi, 836, 846–7.

43. *Priv. Corr.* i, 401.

44. Lord Somers marked this as early as the middle of April. Blenheim MSS. B. 2–5: to Marlborough, 14 Apr.

45. Add. MSS. 33273, f. 29: James Taylor to Henry Watkins, 9 May.

46. Klopp, *Der Fall des Hauses Stuart*, xiv, 673.

47. Bodl. MS. Carte 210, ff. 168, 253; Penrice and Margam MSS. L. 695, quoted in P. D. G. Thomas, 'Jacobitism in Wales', *Welsh Hist. Rev.* (1962), p. 284.

48. Add. MSS. 17677EEE, ff. 367–8.

49. *Letters of the Sitwells and Sacheverells* (ed. Sir George Sitwell, 1901), ii, 111; S.H. Cal. Br. 24 England 113a, ff. 266, 270.

50. See my article on 'The Commons' Division on "No Peace without Spain", 7 December 1711', *Bull. I.H.R.* xxxiii (1960); Lonsdale MSS.: James Lowther to W. Gilpin, 15 Dec. 1711; also *March and October* (London, 1712) for the strongly Hanoverian sympathies of the Tory members of the March Club, founded in March 1712.

51. See *Letters of Thomas Burnet, 1712–22*, p. 41: Burnet to George Duckett, [10–18 June 1713].

52. *Lockhart Papers*, i, 475–6. Cf. Cowper, 'Impartial History', *loc. cit.* p. 422, for the revival on both sides of theoretical arguments of Exclusionist vintage.

53. To a degree which plainly bewildered Bolingbroke: see *Bolingbroke Corr.* iv, 550: to Sir Constantine Phipps, 20 May 1714.

54. Bodl. MS. Ballard 34, f. 140: Gilfred Lawson to Mr. Thwaites, 6 Mar. 1700[–1].

55. B.M. Loan 29/152/5: Leeds to Oxford, 31 Dec. 1711.

56. Boyer, p. 527; Burnet, vi, 82; Add. MSS. 17677EEE, f. 392; cf. Baron Hill MSS. 6766 for the draft of a Tory address (? by Lord Bulkeley), 1712, expressing similar sentiments. See, in general, M.A. Thomson, 'Parliament and Foreign Policy, 1689–1714', *History*, N.S. 38 (1953).

57. One instance of their inconsistency is Rochester's speech in the Lords, 22 Nov. 1705: Add. MSS. 17677AAA, f. 537.

58. Shaftesbury to John Molesworth, Naples, 29 Mar. 1712: *Life of Shaftesbury*, ed. B. Rand (1900), p. 481.

59. *The Post Boy*, No. 2407, 14–17 Oct.

60. For Harcourt's speech see *A Compleat History of the Proceedings ... against Dr. Henry Sacheverell* (London, 1710), pp. 158–176. Cf. the speeches of Constantine Phipps, another of Sacheverell's defending counsel (*ibid.* pp. 186–201), and of Anglesey, Haversham, Leeds and Bishop Hooper in the House of Lords (*Parl. Hist.* vi, 846–7).

61. See *H.L.Q.* xv (1951–2), 43: James Brydges to Cadogan, 7 Apr. 1710.

62. Blenheim MSS. B. 2–8: Godolphin to Marlborough, 2 June 1710.

63. H.M.C. *Portland MSS.* iv, 507.

64. *A Compleat History*, pp. 69, 71.

65. Blenheim MSS. B. 2–33: Robert Molesworth to Godolphin, 8 Mar. 1710.

66. Basil Williams, *Stanhope*, pp. 143–4 and Appx. F; *Lockhart Papers*, i, 462–3; B.M. Stowe MSS. 226, ff. 244–5; B.M. Loan 29/133/9: [Duchess of Hamilton] to Oxford, "Fryday night" [? Apr. 1714] for the plans and military preparations of the Scottish Whigs in Edinburgh.

67. Burnet, iv, 519. See G. V. Bennett, *White Kennett*, pp. 37–8.

68. Bodl. MS. Ballard 38, f. 187: T. Rowney to Charlett, 24 Oct. 1702.

69. *Ibid.* f. 190: same to the same, 26 Nov.

70. Walton MSS., ii, 83: Humphrey Whyle to Sir J. Mordaunt, 27 Nov. 1703.

71. P.R.O. 30/24/22/7/20: to Cropley, 24 July 1710.

72. B.M. Lansdowne MSS. 1038, f. 35: R. Reynolds to White Kennett, 13 Dec. 1709.

73. H.M.C. *Cowper MSS.* iii, 15: Scarsdale to Coke, 22 Aug. 1702.

74. Passed in 1661 and 1673.

75. P. M. Scholes, 'Parliament and the Protestant Dissenters, 1702–19' (London M.A. thesis, 1962), p. 22; Burnet, v, 49 n.; Add. MSS. 30,000E, f. 202.

76. *The Political Union, A Discourse shewing the Dependance of Government on Religion* (Oxford, 1702).

77. B.M. Loan 29/190, f. 213: Thomas Foley to Harley, 1 Sept. 1702.

78. *C.J.* xiv, 49. The poll in 1702 was: Sir John Hawles (W) 37, George Bodington (W) 37, John Gauntlet (T) 24, Sir Henry Ashurst (W) 24. (John Rylands Lib. Eng. MSS. 331, p. 81).

79. Add. MSS. 27440, f. 136: Memoirs of Charles Allestree. Hints that a bill was already under consideration were given by Seymour and Howe in the debate on the Queen's Speech in October. Finch MSS. G.S., bundle 22: Duke of Leeds to his daughter, 23 Oct.; Bodl. MS. Ballard 38, f. 187.

80. Burnet, v, 49: Dartmouth's n.; Horwitz, *loc. cit.* p. 418 and n. 102.

81. *Norris Papers*, p. 108: Thomas Johnson to Norris, 17 Dec. 1702.

82. E.g. those of the Lords' proceedings of 2–9 Dec. 1702 in Nicolson's MS. diary; that of the Commons' debate of 26 Nov. 1703 in *Epistolary Corr. of Atterbury*, iii (1784), 140–1.

83. *Epistolary Corr. of Atterbury*, iii, 136.

84. Though she was still hopeful that the Lords would accept the new and more moderate bill: see Anne to Duchess of Marlborough, "Friday morning" [Dec. 1703], printed *The Conduct of the Dowager Duchess of Marlborough* (1742), pp. 154–6.

85. For the details of the division, in which there was a majority of 71–59 against a 2nd Reading, see Boyer, *Annals*, ii, appx. See also Appendix A, above.

86. See B.M. Loan 29/138/5: Harcourt to Harley, "Saturday night" [Nov. 1704]; Patricia Ansell, 'Harley's Parliamentary Management', *Bull. I.H.R.* xxxiv (1961); *Life of Archbishop Sharp* (1825), i, 304–6; Lonsdale MSS.: J[ames] L[owther] to [Sir John Lowther], 28 Nov.

87. H.M.C. *Ormonde MSS.* N.S. viii, 120: Cholmondeley to Ormonde, 28 Nov.

88. Nicolson's MS. diary, 15 Dec. 1704.

89. I follow the figures given in the Clerk of the House's MS. minutes. Some reports of the debate put the Whig majority variously at 20 or 21, including the usually-reliable Bishop Nicolson, who gives both the personal and proxy votes in detail.

90. See also Add. MSS. 29568, f. 102: John Verney, M.P. to Lord Hatton, 10 Nov. 1702.

91. The drafting of it, however, was believed to have been mainly the work of Atterbury, by then Bolingbroke's close ally, and the measure had first been mooted in principle as far back as 1702. B.M. Stowe MSS. 227, f. 162; Nicolson's MS. diary, 6 Dec. 1702.

92. *Journal to Stella*, 25 Nov.

93. *Letter to Wyndham*, pp. 22–3.

94. These fears were cogently expressed in *The Humble Supplication of Certain of Her Majesty's faithful and peaceful Subjects called Protestant Dissenters . . . in relation to the Bill to prevent Schism* (London, 1714).

95. Burnet, vi, 16.

96. Lonsdale MSS.: James Lowther to W. Gilpin, 8 June 1710.

97. *Parl. Hist.* vi, 816–19; *Bolingbroke Corr.* i, 43–4: to Drummond, 20 Dec. 1710.

98. Notable exceptions were Edward Harley in the Commons and Nottingham in the Lords. Nottingham's nephew, Heneage Finch, who voted with the Whigs on almost every issue in the Commons this session, deserted them on the Schism bill; and the offence was held against him by dissenting voters in Surrey when he stood for re-election there in 1715. Chatsworth MSS. Finch-Halifax Papers, box 3, item 128: G. Whitehead to Nottingham, 22 Nov. 1714.

99. Papillon Letter Book, 1713–14: Philip Papillon to Rev. G. Hughes, 11 June 1714.

100. For Stanhope's appeal on behalf of the Papists during the debate on the 3rd Reading of the Schism bill see Gent, *History of the . . . Last Parliament* (1714), p. 63. Cf. Add. MSS. 17677HHH, ff. 207–8, for hostile Whig reaction in the Lords on 1 May 1714 to the relaxation of the land inheritance laws in favour of Catholics.

101. Finch MSS. G.S., bundle 23: [Bromley] to Nottingham, 7, 31 Dec. 1708; Longleat MSS. Thynne Papers, xii, f. 301: Bishop of Bath and Wells to Weymouth, 31 Dec.

102. Bath and Wells to Weymouth, 17 Jan. [1709], *loc. cit.* f. 303; Charles Davenant to the same, 12 Jan., *ibid.* xxv, f. 466; *Swift Corr.* i, 129 n., 131; *Addison Letters*, pp. 103, 134–5; Add. MSS. 47025, p. 236.

103. Gent, *History of the . . . Last Parliament* (1714), p. 63 (the indirect speech of the original has been modified). Cf. *Wentworth Papers*, p. 389.

104. A few Whigs may have voted for Campion's amendment, to judge from the relatively narrow margin by which it was defeated in committee. Add. MSS. 17677DDD, f. 92.

105. Burnet, v, 411.

106. Alexander Cunningham, *The History of Great Britain from the Revolution in 1688 to the Accession of George the First* (1787), ii, 276.

107. For a moderate view see the memoirs of James Vernon, junior, Whig M.P. for Cricklade: Add. MSS. 40794, f. 3.

108. Clavering Letters: Ann to James Clavering, 18 Mar. 1710.

109. *Parl. Hist.* vi, 846; *Compleat History of the Proceedings of the House of Commons against Dr. Henry Sacheverell*, p. 69.

110. See, e.g., the speeches of Burnet and Talbot of Oxford during the Lords' debates on Sacheverell (*Parl. Hist.* vi, 846, 859–60); H.M.C. *Portland MSS.* iv, 565.

111. Bodl. MS. Ballard 15, f. 96: John Johnson to Charlett, 15 Sept. 1710.

112. Weston Park MSS. Box 18/15: Bridgeman to J. Aubrey of New College, Oxford, 12 Mar. 1711[–12] (endorsed "not sent").

113. W. R. Williams, *Parliamentary History of the County of Gloucester* (Hereford, 1898), p. 62.

114. Bodl. MS. Ballard 9, f. 69: Trelawney to [the clergy of Surrey], (copy), endorsed "1710". Cf. Bromley's sceptical comments in *ibid.* 38, f. 153.

115. Nicolson's MS. diary, 10 Feb. 1707.

116. 'An Impartial History of Parties', *loc. cit.* p. 427.

117. *Faults on Both Sides* (2nd edn. London, 1710), p. 17.

118. See, e.g., Nicolson's MS. diary, 18 Jan. 1703.

119. N.U.L. Portland (Bentinck) MSS. PwA. 942: Halifax to Portland, Aug. 1704.

120. The Lord Lieut. of Ireland was told on 28 Nov.: "Tomorrow the Lords' House sit upon the Scotch Act of Security, and whoever hath been an adviser in it may expect to be sorely wip'd". H.M.C. *Ormonde MSS*. N.S. viii, 120.

121. With two possible exceptions his list of 90 doubtfuls consists entirely of Tories. See B.M. Loan 29/138/5, printed P. M. Ansell, *loc. cit.*

122. See Burnet, v, 182–3 n.; Nicolson's MS. diary, 29 Nov., 6, 11 Dec.; *Correspondence of George Baillie of Jerviswood* (Edinburgh, 1842), pp. 12, 14–15, 16, 18.

123. *Jerviswood Correspondence*, p. 23: Secretary Johnston to Baillie, 12 Dec. 1704.

124. P.R.O. 30/24/20/137: 18 Dec. 1707.

125. *Vernon Corr.* iii, 298–300: Vernon to Shrewsbury, 18, 20 Dec. Addison wrote on the 16th: "Every Body is wonderfully pleas'd that amidst all these little disputes the public Business never went on better". *Addison Letters*, p. 84.

126. See Holmes and Speck, 'The Fall of Harley in 1708 Reconsidered', *E.H.R.* lxxx 1965); *Priv. Corr.* ii, 11–12.

127. Chevening MSS.: Cropley to Stanhope, 20 May [1707]; *Original Letters of Locke, Sidney and Shaftesbury*, p. 247.

128. See B.M. Lansdowne MSS. 1236, f. 247: Sunderland to Newcastle, 19 Oct. 1708.

129. Pembroke seems to have accepted the post in Nov. 1708 with grave misgivings. Charborough Park MSS.: James Craggs to Thomas Erle, 15 Nov.; *Swift Corr.* i, 125, 127.

130. Blenheim MSS. E. 25: Mainwaring to Duchess of Marlborough, "Monday evening" [1709].

131. Clavering Letters: Ann to James Clavering, London, 29 Oct. 1709. As Lady Cowper's sister, Ann had access to reliable sources of information close to the Whig leaders.

132. Lonsdale MSS.: Lowther to W. Gilpin, 19 Sept. 1710.

133. Panshanger MSS.: Newcastle to Cowper, 2 Sept., and Cowper's endorsement.

134. Auchmar MSS.: to Montrose, 25 May.

135. Add. MSS. 35335, f. 7.

136. *Addison Letters*, p. 240: Addison to Joshua Dawson, 23 Sept.

137. Bodl. MS. Eng. Misc. e. 180, f. 9: to Orrery, 22 Aug. 1710.

138. The phrase is Grey Nevil's (Auchmar MSS.: to Montrose, 11 July 1708). He was a Whig M.P. with Junto connexions.

139. Auchmar MSS.: George Baillie to Montrose, 13 Dec. 1711.

140. Burnet, vi, 85, Dartmouth's n.; Add. MSS. 17677FFF, f. 3. Even so purblind a Whig partisan as John Oldmixon felt bound to condemn Wharton's part in the affair as "a sad instance of the infirmity of human minds, even of the greatest." *History of England* (1735), p. 481.

141. C.U.L. Add. MS. 7093, p. 5; Blenheim MSS. A. 1–26: Brydges to Marlborough, 4 Dec. The motions were made in the Lords on 15 Nov. and in the Commons on 4 Dec.

142. Oldmixon, p. 480.

143. *Letters of Thomas Burnet, 1712–22*, p. 41: to George Duckett [10–18 June].

144. For Wharton see *Wentworth Papers*, p. 161; B.M. Loan 29/307: Anglesey to Oxford, 12 July 1711; Add. MSS. 47026, p. 69; *Bolingbroke Corr.* i, 59. For Stanhope, Chevening MSS.: James Craggs to Stanhope, Hague, 29 Aug. [O.S.] 1710. For Sunderland, Burnet, vi, 39, 41 n.

145. B.M. Loan 29/45/I/22: [W. Thomas] to [Edward Harley], 30 Mar. 1708; *ibid.* 29/70/9: Robert to Edward Harley, 15 Feb. 1708; H.M.C. *Portland MSS.* v, 648.
146. C.U.L. Cholmondeley (Houghton) MSS. Corresp. 655: to Dolly Walpole [Feb. 1712].

CHAPTER FOUR: THE "COUNTRY" TRADITION

1. P.R.O. 30/24/21/148: to Shaftesbury, 20 Feb. 1708.
2. *Bolingbroke Corr.* i, 245.
3. See 'On the state of affairs when the King entered', MS. fragment by Edward Wortley Montagu, printed in *Correspondence of Lady Mary Wortley Montagu* (Bohn, 1887), i, 21.
4. Isham MSS. Corr. 2215–16, 3766: John to Sir J. Isham, 26 May, 12 June 1711, Sir Thomas Mansel to same, 26 May; B.M. Loan 29/133: Davers to Oxford, 2 Sept. 1712, 10 July 1713 (recd.).
5. See, e.g., H.M.C. *Bagot MSS.* p. 335.
6. Witley Beaumont MSS. DD/WBC/96: Sir Arthur Kaye to Richard Beaumont, 30 Dec.
7. *Correspondence of Lady Mary Wortley Montagu* (Bohn, 1887), i, 16.
8. There is fairly strong evidence that Harley planned to make him Treasurer of the Navy, or at least Joint-Treasurer, after Walpole's dismissal in Jan. 1711 (the post went eventually to Charles Caesar). B.M. Loan 29/10/18: memo. in Oxford's hand, 4 June 1711. See also Worsley MSS. 1, f. 12.
9. Chatsworth MSS. Finch-Halifax Papers, Box 5, bundle 11: Sir C. Musgrave to Guernsey, 19 Oct. 1714.
10. H.M.C. *Fortescue MSS.* i, 18: 16 Jan. 1705–6.
11. *Ibid.*
12. Norris MSS. 920 NOR. 1/149: to Richard Norris, 8 Jan. 1702.
13. See Elizabeth Hamilton, *The Mordaunts* (1965), pp. 40, 42.
14. P.R.O. 30/24/20/113–14: Cropley and Stanhope to Shaftesbury, N.D. [Feb. 1706], 24 Feb.
15. H.M.C. *Frankland-Russell-Astley MSS.* p. 176: J. C[utts] to Col. Revett, 13 Mar. 1704[–5].
16. Wortley Montagu, 'On the state of affairs when the King entered', *loc. cit.* i, 21.
17. Prominent examples of the latter were Sir Richard Onslow and Sir Robert Davers.
18. *The Supplement*, No. 427, 6–9 Oct. 1710.
19. *An Impartial View of the two Late Parliaments* by P—— H—— (London, 1711), p. 48.
20. *Verney Letters*, p. 223: Visct. Fermanagh to Sir Thomas Cave, 4 Feb. 1705.
21. *Loc. cit.* i, 21. At the time he wrote Edward Wortley was palpably disillusioned with the behaviour of Whig placemen in the early months of George I's reign.
22. C.U.L. Add. MS. 7093, p. 76; *Parl. Hist.* vi, 891.
23. *Norris Papers*, p. 124: Thomas Johnson to Norris, 16 Jan. 1702[–3].
24. P.R.O. 30/24/20/112: [James Stanhope] to [Sir John Cropley], 17 Feb. 1706.
25. *Parl. Hist.* vi, 891.
26. Witley Beaumont MSS. DD/WBC/93: to Beaumont, 9 Dec. 1710.

27. *Ibid.* DD/WBC/95: 21 Dec. [1710].

28. *Ibid.* DD/WBC/96: 30 Dec. 1710.

29. Kaye MS. Diary, 29 Jan. 1711.

30. The Court Tories objected that as Cope had not been petitioned against the House could take no official cognizance of his misdemeanours. *Ibid.*, 3 Feb. 1711.

31. Witley Beaumont MSS. DD/WBC/98: 3 Mar. 1710[–11].

32. Claydon MSS.: Lord Cheyne to Sir John Verney, 2 Apr. 1702.

33. *Parl. Hist.* vi, 57.

34. *Norris Papers*, pp. 103, 105: 10, 12 Dec. 1702.

35. *Ibid.* p. 78: to Norris, 16 Feb. 1701[–2].

36. Lonsdale MSS.: to W. Gilpin, London, 12 Feb. 1707[–8]. Thomas Johnson, however, was a little more heartened on this occasion when he contemplated the likely replacements for the Harleyites — men like Henry Boyle, Sir James Montagu and Robert Eyres: "in short . . . the staunch Whigs come in, for you know these were often against the Court in K. Wm's time". (*Norris Papers*, p. 167: to Norris, 12 Feb.).

37. *Parl. Hist.* vi, 889.

38. *Ibid.* For the identification of the speaker, not given in *Parl. Hist.*, see *Bull. I.H.R.* xxxix (1966), 59, n. 7.

39. *C.J.* xiv, 496.

40. And also in 1701–2. He was nominated by the Earl of Carlisle and backed by Wharton.

41. Lonsdale MSS.: to Gilpin, 3 Feb. 1707[–8].

42. Claydon MSS.: to Cave, 4 Feb. 1704[–5].

43. *Ibid.*: Cave to Fermanagh, 6 Feb. 1704[–5].

44. After the Tories returned to office in 1710 some attempt was made to meet these complaints by administrative action. At a Cabinet meeting on 22 Apr. 1711 one of the Secretaries of State was directed to "propose to the Committee tomorrow at the War Office the apointing a day for the officers that belong to the army in Flanders to goe to their posts". W.S.L. Dartmouth's Cabinet minutes.

45. Lonsdale MSS.: Lowther to Gilpin, 7, 12 Feb. 1707[–8].

46. *Ibid.*: to Gilpin, 8 June 1710.

47. *Ibid.*: Lowther to Gilpin, 2 Feb. 1709[–10].

48. The speech of Robert Eyres in the Commons' debate of 21 Jan. 1706 appears to have pursued this theme. C.U.L. Add. MS. 7093, p. 127.

49. *Faults on Both Sides* (2nd edn. 1710), p. 16.

50. See, e.g., Add. MSS. 30000E, ff. 63, 78; Add. MSS. 17677WW, ff. 179–180, 183, 185, 189.

51. *C.J.* xiv, 95, 480; Claydon MSS.: Cave to Fermanagh, 30 Jan. 1704[–5].

52. C.U.L. Add. MS. 7093, p. 84.

53. For a list of the officials selected for reprieve see *Bull. I.H.R.* xxxix (1966), 55, n. 4.

54. B.M. Loan 29/64/3: to [Harley], "Friday at 12" [15 Feb.].

55. *Ibid.* 64/16: "Fryday noon" [25 Jan. ?].

56. *C.J.* xv, 123.

57. Chevening MSS.: Cropley to Stanhope, 19 Feb. [1706].

58. *Ibid*

59. P.R.O. 30/24/20/114: [19 Feb. 1706].

60. In Feb. 1709 the Commons had appointed a Committee to consider methods of making existing laws against placemen and pensioners effective. They had also addressed the Queen for details of pensions paid out of the Secret Service money to be laid before the House. See *Parl. Hist.* vi, 779–80; Add. MSS. 17677DDD, f. 87.

61. His speech is printed in *Parl. Hist.* vi, 888–92.

62. 197 votes against 175. *C.J.* xvi, 294.

63. Add. MSS. 17677FFF, f. 85: l'Hermitage, 29 Feb./11 Mar. 1712.

64. Viz. on 7 Feb. 1705, when Wharton "& others of that side" had spoken in support of Peter King's bill in the Lords. B.M. Loan 29/192, f. 34: Dyer's Newsletter, 8 Feb.

65. H.M.C. *House of Lords MSS.* N.S. ix, 202–3; Add. MSS. 17677FFF, ff. 91–2; Swift, *Journal to Stella*, 29 Feb.; Burnet, vi, 114.

66. *C.J.* xvii, 308, 352, 354; Trumbull MSS. Alphab. li: T. Bateman to Trumbull, 15 May 1713. For the attitude of a backbench Tory to the attempted "tack" see Charles Aldworth to Northumberland, [19] May, Neville MSS. D/EN. F23/2.

67. *C.J.* xvii, 493.

68. *Wentworth Papers*, pp. 371–2: Newsletter to Strafford, 20 Apr. 1714.

69. *C.J.* xiv, 79. The tellers for the majority, Sir Wm. Strickland and Thomas Wylde, were both stout Junto adherents.

70. *C.J.* xiv, 87. It was January 1707, after the triumphs of Blenheim and Ramillies, before Anne and Godolphin at last got their way.

71. Add. MSS. 31144, ff. 371–2. The troublemakers were Nicholas Lechmere and Lord Castlecomer.

72. Blenheim MSS. F. 2–16: to Marlborough, 7/18 Nov.

73. Normally £500 p.a. For an interesting "country" justification for paying such salaries to these and other commissioners (e.g. Land Grants Commissioners) charged with detailed parliamentary enquiries see *Faults on Both Sides* (2nd edn. 1710), pp. 22–3.

74. Nicolson's MS. diary, 27 Nov. 1702.

75. *C.J.* xiv, 70. It is notable, however, that one of the tellers on the other side was the Country Whig lawyer Robert Eyres.

76. For Rochester's friendship with Ranelagh, to whom he was distantly related, see B.M. Loan 29/147/7: Rochester to Speaker Harley, Cockpit, 28 Aug. [? 1702]. Ranelagh's later associations seem to have been with the Whigs. See *H.L.Q.* xv (1951–2), 37.

77. Nicolson's MS. diary, 2 Feb. 1703.

78. *C.J.* xiv, 143.

79. The case was not actually heard until June 1704, a year after Atterbury had written disgustedly to Trelawney that "the prosecution . . . goes on very slowly". See Luttrell, v, 438; *Epistolary Corr. of Atterbury*, iv (1787), 420.

80. H.M.C. *House of Lords MSS.* N.S. v, 192–4; *L.J.* xvii, 271.

81. Add. MSS. 34521, f. 16: Hon. Charles to Joseph Yorke, 29 Aug. 1742, citing Lord Somers's correspondence *temp.* Anne.

82. *C.J.* xiv, 374–5: 11 Mar. 1704; *L.J.* xvii, 512 *et seq.*

83. B.M. Lansdowne MSS. 773, f. 24.

84. Blenheim MSS. A. 1–14: Marlborough to [Godolphin], 8 Apr. 1704; Add. MSS. 27440, f. 92.

85. *A Short History of the Parliament* (1713), p. 19.

86. *Lockhart Papers*, i, 375; Boyer, p. 530; *C.J.* xvii, 15–18, 30, 37–8, 95–7.

87. *Lockhart Papers*, i, 351.

88. Edward Wortley Montagu, 'On the state of affairs when the King entered', *loc. cit.* p. 21.

89. *Loc. cit.*, i, 352.

90. See the divisions and the names of the tellers on 30 June and 7 July 1714 in H.M.C. *House of Lords MSS.* N.S. x, 474; also the draft speech of one of the Court peers, North and Grey, in Bodl. MS. North, b. 2, f. 32.

91. *Vernon Corr.* iii, 283–4, 286, 293 (for the Tory attitude to the Admiralty see *ibid.* 286–7, *Addison Letters*, pp. 83–4); Luttrell, vi, 262; *Court and Society from Elizabeth to Anne* (1864), ii, 272: Addison to Manchester, 3 Feb. 1708; *Faults on Both Sides* (1710), p. 30.

92. See I. F. Burton, 'The Supply of Infantry for the War in the Peninsula, 1703–1707', *Bull. I.H.R.* xxviii (1955).

93. *Addison Letters*, p. 94.

94. See pp. 120–1 above.

95. W. R. Ward, *The English Land Tax in the Eighteenth Century* (1953), pp. 26–7.

96. 3 Jan.–15 Feb. 1711. See Boyer, pp. 487–8; Burnet, vi, 30–1; *C.J.* xvi, 448–9, 451, 502.

97. *C.J.* xvi, 611–13, 619; *Journal to Stella*, 27 Apr.; Blenheim MSS. E. 25: Arthur Mainwaring to Duchess of Marlborough, "Tuesday evening" [24 Apr.]; Auchmar MSS.: (G. Baillie] to Montrose, 1 May.

98. *C.J.* xvi, 598 (14 Apr.); Burnet, vi, 39.

99. *C.J.* xvii, 86–92; Pittis, *Second Session*, pp. 40–1; Kaye MS. Diary, p. 8; *Journal to Stella*, 14 Feb.

100. Wortley Montagu later testified that "it was they [the Country Whigs] that made a division among the Whigs . . . in the first session of Oxford's ministry when Sir Thomas Hanmer spoke against Lord Bo[lingbroke]". *Loc. cit.* p. 20.

101. Claydon MSS.: R. Palmer to R. Verney, 26 Jan. 1712.

102. *C.J.* xvii, 38; Boyer, p. 540; Baldwin, *History and Defence of the Last Parliament* (1713), p. 158; B.M. Loan 29/10/3: canvassing list in Oxford's hand relating to this division, which reveals that the Court expected support from only one leading Country Whig, John Morgan of Tredegar.

103. He was one of the tellers for the duke's supporters in the main division of 24 Jan. 1712. For Onslow and King see Boyer, p. 540.

104. An exception was the abortive attempt to disfranchise the notoriously corrupt borough of Hindon (Wilts.) in 1702.

105. Dyer's Newsletter, 29 May 1705.

106. 3 of its 5 sponsors, Sir Thomas Powys, Nicholas Lechmere, and John Ward, were prominent practising lawyers. A fourth, Edward Harley, was also a lawyer. Only Sir Roger Mostyn represented the "country interest" in the framing of this particular bill. *C.J.* xvi, 432.

107. The Post Office bill of 1711 (9 Anne, c. 11) actually contained a clause forbidding employees of the Office to bring their influence to bear on voters, on penalty of a heavy fine. Similar prohibitions had been imposed without conspicuous success on Customs and Excise officers in 1694 and 1701.

108. See, e.g., *C.J.* xv, 579; *ibid.* p. 555.

109. Kaye MS. Diary, p. 4.

110. For these early Recruiting bills of 1704–7 see I. F. Burton, 'The Supply of

Infantry for the War in the Peninsula, 1703–1707', *loc. cit.*, pp. 42–6. James Grahme reported to Weymouth in June 1704 the hostile reaction of the northern counties of England to the first of these acts. Longleat MSS. Thynne Papers, xxv, f. 135, 6 June.

111. Add. MSS. 40776, f. 49: to James Vernon, 22 Mar.

112. B.M. Loan 29/145/5: Thomas to Robert Harley, 27 June [1707].

113. Blenheim MSS. B. 1–2: Walpole to Marlborough, 30 Mar. 1708; *ibid.* A. 2–38: Godolphin to same, 30 Mar.; Add. MSS. 9109, f. 9: same to same, 31 Mar.

114. Blenheim MSS. B. 1–1: Boyle to Marlborough, 10 Dec. 1708; *ibid.* B. 1–22a: same to same, 7, 21 Jan. 1709; *ibid.* B. 1–23: Coningsby to same, 26 Jan.; Add. MSS. 33225, ff. 15, 17: Francis Hare to Henry Watkins, 24 Dec., 28 Jan.

115. *Wentworth Papers*, pp. 312–13: Berkeley of Stratton to Strafford, 9 Jan.

116. *Addison Letters*, p. 93; *Vernon Corr.* iii, 351–2: Vernon to Shrewsbury, 19 Feb. 1708.

117. *Addison Letters*, p. 93: Addison to Manchester, 20 Feb.

118. *Vernon Corr.* iii, 353–4: Vernon to Shrewsbury, 21 Feb.

119. *Ibid.* 356–7: 26 Feb. (my italics). "It was found very tedious", he added, "and people would rather know who and who is together".

120. The "freeholders of Buckinghamshire" (carefully coached, no doubt, my Lord Wharton) were an exception. They gave their representatives "instructions" to oppose "the method of ballotting, by which means the electors were depriv'd of knowing in what manner their representatives discharg'd their trust". P—— H——, *An Impartial View of the two Late Parliaments* (1711), pp. 121–2.

121. *Addison Letters*, p. 123: to Henry Newton, 31 Dec. 1708; *C.J.* xvi, 7.

122. *C.J.* xvi, 429; S.H. Cal. Br. 24 England 99, f. 20: Kreienberg, 12/23 Dec. 1710.

123. On the last occasion on which the matter was put to a vote (4 Dec. 1710) the House divided very much along straight party lines. B.M. Loan 29/321: Dyer's Newsletter, 5 Dec.

CHAPTER FIVE: THE CLASH OF INTERESTS

1. Speech in the Bewdley election debate, 1709.

2. Mary Ransome, 'The General Election of 1710' (London M.A. thesis, 1938), appx. p. 181.

3. *Parl. Hist.* vi, 744: speech in support of Sir Richard Onslow's nomination as Speaker.

4. Specific references to secondary authorities in the following paragraphs have been kept to a minimum. But the author's views have been influenced particularly by the basic work of W. R. Scott (*English, Scottish and Irish Joint-Stock Companies to 1720*, 3 vols. 1911–12) and by the studies of Sir John Clapham (*The Bank of England*, i, 1944), John Carswell (*The South Sea Bubble*, 1960), K. G. Davies ('Joint Stock Investment in the later Seventeenth Century', *Econ. H.R.* 2nd series, iv, 1951–2), H. J. Habbakuk ('English Landownership, 1680–1740', *Econ. H.R.* x, 1939–40, and 'The Long-term Rate of Interest and the Price of Land in the Seventeenth Century', *ibid.* 2nd series, v, 1952–3), G. E. Mingay (*English Landed Society in the Eighteenth Century*, 1963), W. Kennedy (*English Taxation, 1640–1799*, 1913), W. R. Ward (*The English Land Tax in the Eighteenth Century*, 1953), T. S. Ashton (*Economic Fluctuations in England, 1700–1800*, 1959) and R. A. C. Parker ('Direct Taxation on the Coke Estates', *E.H.R.* lxxi, 1956).

5. The contemporary term "man of business" commonly implied a professional agent who transacted legal and sometimes financial business on another's behalf. When, however, Steele wrote in the *Spectator* in 1712: "I am a Man of Business, and obliged to be much abroad", his readers would clearly take the reference to be to one engaged in commerce on his own behalf.

6. For Crowley, see p. 157 above and Michael Flinn, 'The Industrialists' (*Silver Renaissance: Essays in Eighteenth Century English History*, ed. A. Natan, 1961, pp. 58–77 *passim*). Buckingham was said to employ regularly 700 to 800 workmen in the manufacture of canvas and sail cloth at Reading. John Chamberlayne, *Magnae Britanniae Notitia* (1710), p. 5.

7. *The Examiner*, No. 14, 26 Oct.–2 Nov. 1710.

8. Lonsdale MSS.: Lowther to Gilpin, 12, 24 Aug. 1710; Charborough Park MSS.: Craggs to Erle, 14 Oct.; cf. Bodl. MS. Eng. Misc. e. 180, f. 5: St. John to Orrery (copy), 9 July 1709.

9. This brought in almost £900,000 of a projected loan of one million through the purchase of annuities, the interest being guaranteed by the imposition of new excise duties for 99 years.

10. Including Scottish companies the total was 137.

11. See J. G. Sperling, 'The International Payments Mechanism in the Seventeenth and Eighteenth Centuries', *Econ. H.R.* 2nd series, xiv (1961–2).

12. Scott, *op. cit.* i, 360. Subsequently, finding themselves ostracised by the 'upper crust' of the mercantile world at the Royal Exchange, stockbrokers began to congregate mainly, if not exclusively, at Jonathan's. See B. Lillywhite, *London Coffee Houses* (1963), p. 306.

13. *H.L.Q.* iii (1939–40), 232: Brydges to Stair, 3 July 1710.

14. Bodl. MS. Carte 117, f. 177: "The Speech of an Honourable Member of the House of Commons upon the Debate of the Malt Tax, Feb. 19, 1701–2".

15. 13 Anne c. 15, the preamble to which asserted that "the foreign trade of this nation hath of late years been much neglected".

16. See G. N. Clark, 'War Trade and Trade War, 1701–13', *Econ. H.R.* i (1927–8).

17. For the latter see A. H. John, 'War and the English Economy, 1700–1763', *ibid.*, 2nd series, vii (1955).

18. Blenheim MSS.: Sunderland to Marlborough, 22 Feb. 1709 (quoted Churchill, *Marlborough*, ii, 507). Luttrell (vi, 410) believed that almost a further million could have been subscribed that same day had it been required.

19. John Hopkins, M.P. St. Ives, 1710–14. He later sat for Ilchester.

20. E.g. much of the vast estate of Sir Charles Duncombe (M.P. Downton, 1702–d. 1711), estimated in 1697 at £400,000, had probably been accumulated prior to 1690. In 1691 two London merchants, Sir Josiah Child and Sir Thomas Cooke, held between them no less than £92,000 of East India stock.

21. Scott took this view. *Op. cit.* i, 358.

22. K. G. Davies, 'Joint Stock Investment in the later Seventeenth Century', *Econ. H.R.* 2nd series, iv (1951–2), 292. Equally suggestive is the fact that the equivalent of the whole East India Company stock was believed to have changed hands within two years in the early 90's (*ibid.*).

23. Scott, *op. cit.* iii, 216.

24. Carswell, *The South Sea Bubble*, p. 275 and *passim*; *The Spectator*, No. 299, 12 Feb. 1712.

25. Bodl. MS. Carte 117, ff. 177–8: "The Speech of an Honourable Member of the House of Commons upon the Debate of the Malt Tax".

26. C. E. Vulliamy, *The Onslow Family* (1953), pp. 34, 51 ff.; Trumbull MSS. Alphab. liv: Ralph Bridges to Trumbull, 13 Oct. 1710. At the 1710 Election Sir Richard was accused by Surrey Tories of having "manifestly put his whole dependance on his Citty freinds, and despised the interest of the country gentlemen". Chatsworth MSS. Finch-Halifax Papers, box 5, bundle 13: H. Weston to [Guernsey], 29 July 1710.

27. Lonsdale MSS.: Nicholas Lechmere to [Lowther], 7 July 1711.

28. G. E. Mingay, *op. cit.* p. 72.

29. Levens MSS.: Bromley to James Grahme, 11 Oct. 1707.

30. *H.L.B.* ix (1936), 125: Brydges to St. John, 8 July 1709.

31. *Swift Corr.* i, 62: Swift to Archbp. King, 6 Dec.; Add. MSS. 40776, f. 67: Shrewsbury to Vernon, 5 May.

32. See Lady Mordaunt to Sir John, [autumn] 1701, printed by Elizabeth Hamilton, *The Mordaunts* (1965), p. 30. Lady Mordaunt feared her husband would "come to be a great loser" as a result.

33. H.M.C. *Cowper MSS.* iii, 18, 52: J. Fitzherbert and E. Repington to Coke, 11 Nov. 1702, 1 Dec. 1704. Cf. Chevening MSS.: Lord Stanhope to James Stanhope, 10 Mar. 1702; B.M. Loan 29/145/5: Thomas to [Robert] Harley, 27 June [1707].

34. The tables printed in W. R. Ward, *The English Land Tax in the Eighteenth Century*, p. 57, illustrate how some of the counties in the north, west and south-west of England, whose quotas had been fixed unduly low from the start, were also among the worst defaulters when it came to making their quarterly payments. Cornwall had a particularly scandalous record after 1710.

35. Detailed examination both of specific counties and of individual estates has suggested that during the war of 1702–13 proprietors in Northants, Bedfordshire, Norfolk and Kent genuinely paid out 20%, or very little less, of their gross rental in tax; and contemporary comment indicates that this pattern was fairly general over the whole area. See Mingay, *op. cit.* pp. 81–2 and articles by H. J. Habbakuk and R. A. C. Parker cited above, p. 481 n. 4.

36. See Ward, *op. cit.* pp. 27–8, 39, for the methods of evasion practised by placemen, and for the unwillingness of the tax commissioners to levy on personal incomes, including income from investments, or on stock in trade.

37. The land purchaser could generally expect to recover his capital outlay from rents within 20 years.

38. Viz. from Sept. 1708 to March 1710. The United East India Company paid a dividend of 9% in the year 1709–10.

39. Add. MSS. 29568, f. 268: Francis Kirkham to [Mr. Streethay], 6 Jan. 1711.

40. For the example of Lord Nottingham see Mingay, *op. cit.* p. 62 and cf. H. J. Habbakuk, 'Daniel Finch, 2nd Earl of Nottingham: his House and Estate' (*Studies in Social History*, ed. J. H. Plumb, 1955).

41. Lonsdale MSS.: Lowther to Gilpin, 10 Apr. 1711.

42. For the norm see H. J. Habbakuk, 'The Long-term Rate of Interest and the Price of Land in the Seventeenth Century', *Econ. H.R.*, 2nd series, v (1952–3). The author hopes to discuss elsewhere contemporary comments on the state of the land market in Anne's reign, and in particular evidence bearing on the price of estates of high electoral value.

43. Add. MSS. 40776, f. 24: to Vernon, 21 Dec. 1706.

44. Lawson-Tancred, *Records of a Yorkshire Manor*, p. 218: Robert Byerley (M.P. Knaresborough 1697–1714) to Andrew Wilkinson, 18 Dec. 1697.

45. Ashburnham MSS. 843, pp. 383–4, 387: Ashburnham to John Pulteney and John Rowe, 21 Nov., 5 Dec. 1701.

46. Massingberd MSS. 20/93: Sir William to Burrell Massingberd, 1 Apr. 1711.

47. This figure does not include country gentlemen with industrial or commercial interests. See *English Politics*, p. 26 and App. I, pt. i.

48. The words are those of Hugh Chamberlain, promoter of the abortive Bank of Credit on Land Rents, the first of the experiments.

49. Luttrell, iv, 559: 12 Sept. 1699.

50. Edgecumbe sat for Plympton in this Parliament and Fortescue for Lostwithiel.

51. Folger Library, L.C. 3460: Newsletter to Sir R. Newdigate, 1 May 1712; Lawson-Tancred, *op. cit.* p. 255.

52. His wife, the daughter and heiress of James Cooke of London, was said to be worth £20,000 when he married her in 1706. See Luttrell, vi, 76. Grimston received an Irish viscountcy in 1719.

53. H.M.C. *Portland MSS.* iv, 134; Bodl. MS. Ballard 15, f. 107: Johnson to Charlett, 5 Sept. 1713.

54. For Drake, who had previously served the Whigs in the Commons until his retirement in 1700, see Lady Eliott-Drake, *The Family and Heirs of Sir Francis Drake*, ii (1911) and the Drake/King MSS. in Devon R.O. For Craven, Isham MSS. Corr. 2737A: Sir Robert Clerke to Isham, 11 Feb. 1705.

55. *Hervey L.B.* i, 172.

56. Add. MSS. 5853, f. 90: to Rev. John Strype, Leeds, 6 Dec. 1710.

57. Mary Ransome, *loc. cit.*, appx. p. 117.

58. *A Letter to Sir William Wyndham*, p. 25.

59. The eight "gentlemen of the Bank", for example, with whom the new Commissioners of the Treasury negotiated immediately after Godolphin's fall included two Tories, William Gore and Sir Theodore Janssen. B.M. Loan 29/10/2: Treasury minute in Harley's hand, 17 Aug. 1710. For Janssen, however, see above, p. lii and n. 173.

60. Though admittedly it included politicians as well as merchants and financiers.

61. H.M.C. *Portland MSS.* iv, 546. Buckingham had been the only member of the House of Lords in 1701 who still held enough Bank stock (£4000-worth) to qualify for the Governorship. Clapham, *The Bank of England*, i, 274.

62. *Addison Letters*, p. 229: to Joseph Keally, 5 Aug. 1710.

63. Folger Library, L.C. 3456: Newsletter to Sir Richard Newdigate.

64. *Letter to Wyndham*, p. 26.

65. George Yeaman, a Dundee merchant, and Provost of the burgh in 1710, represented Perth Burghs (including Dundee) in the Tory interest in the last two Parliaments of Anne's reign.

66. McHattie, *loc. cit.* p. 226.

67. See especially Finch-Hatton MSS. 275, pp. 33–4, 194–6: Nottingham to Marlborough, 26 June, 27 Oct. 1702 (drafts).

68. See Carswell, *The South Sea Bubble*, pp. 40–59. Initially he relied partly on the advice of John Drummond, the financial agent at The Hague. See H.M.C. *Portland MSS.* iv, 559, 572, 577–8, 582–3, 594: Drummond to Harley, 8 Aug.–12 Sept. 1710.

69. In his *Letter to Wyndham* (pp. 27–8) he inveighed especially bitterly against the

mere "lender of money, who added nothing to the common stock, throve by the public calamity, and contributed not a mite to the public charge".

70. H.M.C. *Portland MSS.* viii, 96: anon. to [Harley?], 10 Mar.

71. Bodl. MS. Rawlinson, Letters 92, f. 562: Richard Goulston to T. Turner, 11 June 1713.

72. Tory election manifesto, printed in *The Supplement*, No. 427, 6–9 Oct. They carefully added that they had "not entertain'd such vast hopes of profit from the continuation of the War, as to remain wholly unconcern'd for a general Peace".

73. Wake MSS. Arch. Epist. 17 misc. i, 243: W. Wotton to Wake, 21 Mar.

74. H.M.C. *Carlisle MSS.* p. 12; *Portland MSS.* iv, 578; W.S.L. Dartmouth MSS. D. 1778/V/779: Heneage Finch to Dartmouth, N.D. [1710], *re* the Surrey J.P.s.

75. H.M.C. *Portland MSS.* v, 643; Lonsdale MSS.: Lowther to Gilpin, 20 June, 31 Aug., 2 Sept. 1710, 8 Jan. 1713.

76. For the Whig problem in N. Wales, see e.g. Chirk Castle MSS. E. 6121. For Weobley, H.M.C. *Portland MSS.* v, 326.

77. It was a matter for special remark when they did arise. See B.M. Loan 29/191, f. 235: Richard Duke to Harley, Otterton (Devon), [Sept. 1704]; *Priv. Corr.* i, 397: Lady Cowper to Duchess of Marlborough, 23 Oct. 1710.

78. Oldmixon, p. 517.

79. For Halifax see p. 239 above. For Newcastle, W.S.L. Dartmouth MSS. D. 1778/I/ii/123.

80. H.M.C. *Portland MSS.* iv, 508: 8 Oct. 1708. Lille, invested on 2 Aug. 1708, finally capitulated on 11 Oct.

81. Viz. Sir William Scawen, Sir Henry Furnese, Sir Gilbert Heathcote, John Ward, Sir William Ashurst, Robert Bristow, Peter Gott, John Rudge, Josiah Diston, Sir John Cope and John Dolben. William Paterson, one of the original directors, also sat in this Parliament as a Court member for Dumfries Burghs.

82. Chevening MSS.: Robert to Horatio Walpole, 12 Feb. 1707. See also Carswell, *op. cit.* pp. 36–8.

83. *The Examiner*, No. 38, 12–19 Apr. 1711.

84. Blenheim MSS. E. 26: to Duchess of Marlborough, N.D. [? Nov. 1710].

85. For the Bank elections of 1711 see Add. MSS. 17677EEE, ff. 151, 166, 172.

86. *State Papers and Correspondence, 1688–1714* (ed. J. M. Kemble, 1857), p. 488: de Steinghens to Schulenberg, 16/27 Mar. 1714 (transl.).

87. *Eleven Opinions about Mr. H——y* (1711), p. 39.

88. The first hint of a limited working agreement with the Bank was given by St. John to Drummond on 12 Jan. 1711 (*Bolingbroke Corr.* i, 69). B. W. Hill, 'The Career of Robert Harley, Earl of Oxford, from 1702 to 1714' (Cambridge, Ph.D., 1961) provides the best account of Harley's relations with the Bank of England culminating in the *modus vivendi* of 1712–14. See also Lucy Sutherland, 'The City of London in Eighteenth Century Politics' (*Essays presented to Sir Lewis Namier*, ed. R. Pares and A. J. P. Taylor, 1956).

89. The other 3 were Sir William Scawen, Francis Eyles and Nathaniel Gould.

90. *Letter to Wyndham*, pp. 26–7.

91. H.M.C. *Portland MSS.* iv, 545–6: Harley to Arthur Moore (draft), 19 June 1710; Harcourt to Harley, 21 June; *ibid.* vii, 1: W. Stratford to Edward Harley, Oxford, 24 June; Levens MSS.: Bromley to Grahme, 28 June.

92. Some of these men (e.g. John Blunt, George Caswall and Sir Ambrose Crowley) had been largely responsible for sowing the seeds of the scheme in Harley's mind. See J. G. Sperling, 'The Division of 25 May 1711', *Hist. Journal*, iv (1961), 192.

93. Sperling, *loc. cit.* pp. 192, 194–5; B.M. Loan 29/70/1: Bromley to Edward Harley, 11 Aug. 1712; *ibid.* 45/C/6, item 18/181: T. Pindar to Oxford, 3 Nov. 1712; *ibid.* 45/C/5, item 18/135: list of votes cast for candidates in the South Sea Company election [Aug. 1712].

94. H. L. Stowe MSS. 57, v, 121: to William Benson, 7 July 1711.

95. *The Evening Post*, No. 182, 10–12 Oct. 1710; H.M.C. *Portland MSS.* vii, 21; Cornish had failed in a bid for a seat at Shaftesbury in 1708 (P.R.O. 30/24/21/158).

96. Add. MSS. 33573, f. 272.

97. *Hervey L. B.* i, 234; *Prideaux Letters* (Camden Soc. 1875), p. 200.

98. See R. Walcott, 'The East India Interest in the General Election of 1700–1701', *E.H.R.* lxxi (1956).

99. *Vernon Corr.* iii, 332: Vernon to Shrewsbury, 31 Jan. 1708.

100. H.M.C. *Bath MSS.* i, 192: 11 Oct. (my italics).

101. *Ibid.* p. 194: 6 Nov. 1708.

102. Bodl. MS. Eng. misc. e. 180, ff. 4–5.

103. Trumbull MSS. Alphab. liv: Ralph Bridges to Trumbull, 4 Sept. 1710.

104. *Ibid.* li: T. Bateman to Trumbull, 17 Apr. 1713; *Wentworth Papers*, p. 327: Berkeley of Stratton to Strafford, [3] Apr.

105. George Pitt, M.P. for Hampshire.

106. It would, hoped Sir William Massingberd, exclude "great numbers of Rt. Honourable & Commission Gentlemen". Massingberd MSS. 20/93: to Burrell Massingberd, 1 Apr. 1711. The grievance against the sons of peers seems to have been unusually strong in Lincolnshire. In 1705 Burrell had complained that both Whig candidates for the shire "want estates sufficient to keep them out of temptation, it being confidently reported that Albermal Bertie has nothing butt an annuity for life under 200 l." *Ibid.* 20/51: 1 Feb.

107. It was first promoted by How, the Joint Paymaster, in Dec. 1702, with the support of Leveson Gower, the Chancellor of the Duchy, and Hartington, another junior minister.

108. *C.J.* xiv, 95, 101–2.

109. H.M.C. *House of Lords MSS.* N.S. v, 200–1.

110. *Ibid.* p. 201. Cf. *L.J.* xvii, 300; Nicolson's MS. diary, 16 Feb. 1703.

111. The text of the bill, with the amendments made to it before it passed into law, is printed in W. C. Costin and J. Steven Watson, *The Law and Working of the Constitution* (1952), i, 117.

112. Add. MSS. 17677EEE, f. 103: 2/13 Mar. 1711.

113. W. Pittis, *History of the First Session of the Present Parliament* (1711), p. 99.

114. A. Baldwin, *History and Defence of the Last Parliament* (1713), pp. 74–5.

115. Add. MSS. 17677EEE, f. 104; Bodl. MS. Ballard 31, f. 104.

116. B.M. Stowe MSS. 225, f. 218: Schütz, 6/17 Oct.

117. *Lyme Letters, 1660–1760* (ed. Lady Newton, 1925), p. 232; Add. MSS. 31138, ff. 270–1; 31139, f. 299: Burchett to Strafford, 20 Aug. 1713, 3 Aug. 1714.

118. *C.J.* xvii, 143–5.

119. Francis Chamberlaine.

120. *C.J.* xvii, 485.

121. See Mary Ransome, *loc. cit.* App., p. 210; Monson MSS. 28B/9/114: Robert Monckton to W. Archer, 8 Aug. 1713.

122. B.M. Loan 29/156/4: 5 Apr. 1714.

123. Lawson-Tancred, *Records of a Yorkshire Manor*, p. 259: Jessop to C. Wilkinson, 27 July 1713. In this case Foley's elder brother may have come to the rescue with a temporary conveyance (*ibid.* p. 262).

124. *C.J.* xvii, 481; B.M. Loan 29/127: Bradshaigh to Oxford, 9 July, 8 Sept. 1712; same to same, recd. 26 May 1714.

125. Boyer, p. 703.

126. Legh of Lyme MSS. Box 62: to Peter Legh, 3 Feb. 1715.

CHAPTER SIX: THE MANAGERS, THE QUEEN, AND THE ROYAL CLOSET

1. This immunity from dismissal did not apply to Welsh judges, unless (like Sir Joseph Jekyll) they were fortunate enough to enjoy life appointments. For Jekyll's case see Luttrell, v, 185, 187.

2. See B.M. Loan 29/321: Dyer's Newsletter, 3 Oct. 1710; H.M.C. *Portland MSS.* v, 264, 278, 283–4; Swift, *The History of the Four Last Years of Queen Anne (Prose Works*, ed. Davis, vii [1951], 19).

3. Finch MSS. G.S., bundle 22: Sharp to Nottingham, 31 Mar. 1702. See p. 88 above.

4. *Parl. Hist.* vi, 831; Clavering Letters: Ann to James Clavering, 18 Mar. 1710. The occasion was the debate on the first article of impeachment against Sacheverell.

5. She told the Bishop of Salisbury this in Jan. 1710. Burnet, v, 446.

6. H.M.C. *Bath MSS.* i, 199: to Harley, 20 Oct. 1710.

7. E. L. Ellis, 'The Whig Junto' (Oxford D.Phil. thesis, 1962), p. 2.

8. [Wharton] to William III, 25 Dec. 1689, printed in Sir John Dalrymple, *Memoirs of Great Britain and Ireland* (London, 1773), ii, Appx., 86, 94. See also John Carswell, *The Old Cause* (1954), p. 368.

9. See J. P. Kenyon, 'The Earl of Sunderland and the King's Administration, 1693–1695' (*E.H.R.* lxxi, 1956); *Robert Spencer, Earl of Sunderland* (1958), p. 256 *et seq.*

10. *A History of the Tory Party*, pp. 282–4.

11. Cf. also Sunderland to Portland, 14 Aug. 1694, quoted by Kenyon in *E.H.R., loc. cit.*, p. 593.

12. *Calendar of State Papers, Domestic: 1694–95*, p. 185: Godolphin to William III, 15 June 1694.

13. Diary, 26 Oct. 1705, printed in *Life of Archbishop Sharp* (1825), i, 366.

14. Their correspondence in the Blenheim archives from 1703 to 1708, reinforced by the duke's letters to his wife, provides some convincing evidence to support this generalisation.

15. See P.R.O. 30/24/21/150 and the evidence cited by Holmes and Speck, *E.H.R., loc. cit.*

16. Churchill nominee for the borough of New Woodstock, 1705–16.

17. M.P. Midhurst, Mar. 1709 (on petition) — 1710. One of the 3 Whig generals suspended by the Harley ministry in Dec. 1710 (see p. 28 above).

18. M.P. Clitheroe, Dec. 1706–8; Dunwich Feb. 1709–1710; Weymouth 1713–June 1714: connected with the Churchills by marriage.

19. M.P. West Looe, Jan. 1707–9; one of the Whig generals entrusted by the Junto with organising military defence against a prospective Jacobite *coup* in 1714.

20. In Anne's reign sat for Preston, 1706–10, and West Looe, 1710–d. 1712.

21. For whom see *D.N.B.* He was Secretary to the Ordnance Office for most of the time that Marlborough was Master-General of the Ordnance.

22. Boscawen sat for various Cornish seats and Fitzharding for New Windsor in Anne's reign.

23. For one small but significant example, the case of James Vernon junr., see Add. MSS. 40794, f. 3.

24. *Bolingbroke Corr.* i, 216–17.

25. B.M. Lansdowne MSS. 885, ff. 80–83 *passim.*

26. *Ibid.* f. 82; H.M.C. *Portland MSS.* iv, 551: 24 July 1710.

27. S.H., Cal. Br. 24 England 113a, ff. 178–9: Kreienberg, 15/26 Sept.

28. See especially G. M. Trevelyan, *Blenheim*, pp. 163–77 *passim*; K. Feiling, *Tory Party*, pp. 360–3.

29. See J. H. Plumb, 'The Organisation of the Cabinet in the Reign of Queen Anne', *T.R.H.S.*, 5th series, vii (1957).

30. Nicolson's MS. diary, 20 Nov. 1702.

31. P.R.O. 30/24/21/150: Cropley to Shaftesbury, N.D. [19 Feb. 1708].

32. *Wentworth Papers*, pp. 131, 138; cf. *Addison Letters*, p. 233: Addison to Wharton, 25(?) Aug.

33. B.M. Lansdowne MSS. 885, f. 85.

34. Levens MSS.: to Grahme, 16 July 1710; cf. *H.L.Q.* iii, 230–1: Brydges to Stair, 3 July. See also W.S.L. Dartmouth MSS.: Cabinet minute, 2 July, and B.M. Egerton MSS. 894, f. 72, for the tart reply which Secretary Boyle was instructed to give the States, warning them off the Queen's domestic preserves.

35. S.H. Cal. Br. 24 England 99, ff. 166–7: Kreienberg, 13/24 Mar. 1711.

36. H.M.C. *Bath MSS.* i, 215–16: Queen to Oxford, 3, 9, 15 Nov. 1711.

37. *Ibid.* i, 223: 13 Nov. 1712.

38. *Ibid.* i, 223: 27 Nov. 1712.

39. *Ibid.* i, 237: 21 Aug. 1713.

40. *Hervey L.B.* i, 176.

41. H.M.C. *Rutland MSS.* ii, 173: Leveson Gower to Rutland, 26 Dec. 1702.

42. For the whole incident, which was one of the real turning-points in the politics of Anne's reign, see Coxe, i, 133: Marlborough to the duchess, Haneft, 3/14 June 1703; Blenheim MSS. A. 1–14: same to [Godolphin], 31 May/11 June 1703, 8 Apr. 1704; Blenheim MSS. F. 2–16: Hedges to Marlborough, 21 Apr. 1704; H.M.C. *Cowper MSS.* iii, 35: Brydges to Coke, 22 Apr.; B.M. Loan 29/70/9: Robert to Edward Harley, 22 Apr.

43. *Cowper Diary*, p. 2: 11 Oct. 1705.

44. *Faults on Both Sides* (2nd edn. 1710), p. 44; Swift, *An Enquiry into the Behaviour of the Queen's Last Ministry* (*Prose Works*, ed. Davis and Ehrenpreis, viii, 143–4).

45. *Bolingbroke Corr.* iv, 573.

46. Boyer, p. 14; Klopp, *Der Fall des Hauses Stuart*, x, 40 (citing Wratislaw to Vienna, 22 Apr. 1702, quotation transposed into direct speech).

47. Blenheim MSS. B. 2–8: Godolphin to Marlborough, 2 June 1710; *Ibid.* E. 25:

Mainwaring to the duchess, [May 1710] (undated fragment); H.M.C. *Portland MSS.* iv, 543; Burnet, vi, 9: Dartmouth's n.

48. The phrase was Somerset's, used in conversation with Wharton in 1708. Blenheim MSS. E. 25: Mainwaring to the duchess, "Thursday, one o'clock [? 28 June 1708].

49. W.S.L. Dartmouth MSS. D. 1778/I/ii/133, 158, 162, 169: Jersey to Darmouth, N.D., 26, 28 Sept., 6 Oct. 1710; H.M.C. *Portland MSS.* v, 69–70: same to Oxford, 4 Aug. 1711.

50. B. M. Loan 29/10/19: Harley's memoranda, endorsed "Navy. Sept 4: 1710" and "Sept: 12: 1710"; H.M.C. *Bath MSS.* i, 200: Shrewsbury to [Harley], 10 Nov. 1710; W.S.L. Dartmouth MSS. D. 1778/I/ii/169: Jersey to Dartmouth, 6 Oct.

51. W.S.L. Dartmouth MSS. D. 1778/V/147: Jersey to Dartmouth, "Sunday morning" [July/Aug. 1711]; H.M.C. *Portland MSS.* v, 74.

52. B.M. Loan 29/10/17: draft, endorsed 21 Aug. 1711. Cf. *ibid.* 10/4 for the draft of an earlier letter to Anne of 16 Aug. emphasising Jersey's "very great service" in forwarding the peace talks.

53. *Ibid.* 10/17.

54. Blenheim MSS. B. 2–8: Godolphin to Marlborough, 10 Sept. 1710; H.M.C. *Bath MSS.* i, 199.

55. B.M. Loan 29/151: Peterborough to Oxford, Augsburg, [9]/20 Dec. 1711; B.M. Lansdowne MSS. 1236, f. 261: Queen to same, 16 Nov.

56. H.M.C. *Portland MSS.* vii, 39; *Journal to Stella*, 24 Aug. 1711. Stories about St. John's lechery and his low taste in women were still buzzing round London in June 1714. *Wentworth Papers*, p. 395.

57. Blenheim MSS. E. 27: Mainwaring to the duchess, N.D. [March 1708]. A fairly accurate transcription of this letter is printed in *Priv. Corr.*, i, 98–9.

58. For the approach to Trevor see B.M. Loan 29/237, ff. 97–8: Harley to [Newcastle], 16, 23 Mar. 1705.

59. Add. MSS. 28070, f. 12: 11 July [1705]. Godolphin had been pressing for a change since March, and in October was still insistent that Cowper was "generally thought the most proper for it". H.M.C. *Bath MSS.* i, 67: 24 Mar.; Longleat MSS. Portland Papers, vii, f. 23: to Harley, 1 Oct.

60. See p. 199 above; B.M. Loan 29/237, f. 165; Coxe, ii, 1–24 *passim*; *The Conduct of the Dowager Duchess of Marlborough* (1742), pp. 160–173.

61. Blenheim MSS. B. 1–7: Halifax to Marlborough, 10 June 1708.

62. *Ibid.* A. 2–38: to Marlborough, 31 May 1708.

63. For instances in 1709 and in Dec. 1711 see Dartmouth's n. to Burnet, v, 359; vi, 89. See also H.M.C. *Bath MSS.* i, 222: Queen to Oxford, 21 Oct. 1712; B.M. Loan 29/38/1: Lady Masham to same, "Thursday the 6th" [Nov. 1712].

64. *Letter to Wyndham*, p. 18.

65. Panshanger MSS.: diary of Sir David Hamilton, 15, 16 May 1710; B.M. Lansdowne MSS. 885, f. 25: "An Account of the Earl of Oxford by his Brother".

66. Coxe, iii, 124: Queen to Godolphin, 7 Aug. 1710.

67. B.M. Loan 29/70/9: Oxford to Edward Harley, 13 Aug. 1713; H.M.C. *Portland MSS.* v, 466: "A very brief account of the state of her Majesty's affairs", 6 June 1714.

68. B.M. Loan 29/9/38: draft, "Sept: 25: 1706".

69. H.M.C. *Bath MSS.* i, 75: to Godolphin, 4 Sept. 1705.

70. B.M. Loan 29/10/22: paper in Harley's hand dated "Ap: 3: 1708".

71. H.M.C. *Bath MSS.* i, 191: to Harley, 11 Oct. 1708.

72. B.M. Loan 29/10/20: 20 May.

73. Add. MSS. 31143, f. 580; H.M.C. *Frankland-Russell-Astley MSS.* p. 202.

74. For one example, concerning the preparation of the writs for the summoning of a new Parliament in 1713, see *Bolingbroke Corr.* iv, 207–8.

75. B.M. Loan 29/10/7: 14 June 1714.

76. Add. MSS. 22222, f. 189: to Strafford, 20 Dec. (italics mine).

77. *Some Considerations upon the Consequences hoped and feared from the Death of the Queen* (9 Aug. 1714). See *Prose Works*, viii, 103–4.

78. See *inter alia*, Add. MSS. 22222, f. 188; *Journal to Stella*, 17, 19 Dec.; *Swift Corr.* i, 310, 313.

79. For the Queen's reluctance in 1710 to accept the view, best expressed at the time by Sir Thomas Hanmer, that "a new ministry with an old Parliament will be worse than the Gospel absurdity of . . . new wine in old bottles" (H.M.C. *Bath MSS.* iii, 437), see Blenheim MSS. E. 27: Mainwaring to Duchess of Marlborough, "Wednesday night"; and *ibid.* B. 2–8: Godolphin to Marlborough, 13, 16 June; H.M.C. *Portland MSS.* ii, 219, where Harley refers with evident relief to the eventual decision to dissolve on 14 Sept. being "resolved in her own breast".

80. Finch MSS. G.S., bundle 23: unsigned letter, 28 Jan. 1709[–10].

81. On the Masham address and the whole crisis arising out of the disposal of the Essex regiment the indispensable source is the series of letters from Mainwaring to the Duchess of Marlborough, [15–23 Jan.], Blenheim MSS. E. 25, E. 27 and E. 28.

82. P.R.O. 30/24/21/146: Cropley to Shaftesbury, [11 Feb. 1708].

83. Blenheim MSS. F. 2–16: 12/23 Sept.

84. 24 Nov. 1705, during discussion of the St. Albans election in which Sarah had actively campaigned. Burnet, v, 224; *C.J.* xv, 37–9.

85. Panshanger MSS. Cowper Family Books, I: 31 Aug. 1710.

86. *Priv. Corr.* ii, 111: N.D. [1711].

87. *The Conduct of the Dowager Duchess of Marlborough* (1742), pp. 127, 298–300; Blenheim MSS. E. 36: Halifax to the duchess, 22 May 1705 (endorsement); *Priv. Corr.* ii, 149–50.

88. *Priv. Corr.* i, 12: Sunderland to the duchess, Vienna, 8/19 Sept. 1705.

89. Blenheim MSS. E. 27: N.D. [Apr. 1708], printed *Priv. Corr.* i, 112–13.

90. To the duchess, 6/17 Apr. 1708, 14, 27 Apr. 1710, printed Coxe, ii, 210; *Priv. Corr.* i, 307–9.

91. Blenheim MSS. E. 28: Mainwaring to the duchess, "Wednesday morning" [? 12 Nov. 1709].

92. H.M.C. *Portland MSS.* iv, 647; Swift, *Memoirs relating to [the] Change . . . in the Queen's Ministry* (*Prose Works*, viii, 113).

93. Coxe, ii, 218; *Priv. Corr.* ii, 288.

94. Coxe, ii, 383: Marlborough to the duchess, 17/28 Nov. 1708, 27 Dec./7 Jan. 1708–9.

95. *Ibid.* iii, 12: the duchess to Mainwaring [19 Jan. 1710]; Blenheim MSS. E. 28: Mainwaring to the duchess, "Friday 12 a clock" [20 Jan. 1710].

96. See note 81 above; Coxe, iii, 14–15, 18: Sarah to Mainwaring, 19 Jan., Marlborough to Somers, 21 Jan.; B.M. Lansdowne MSS. 885, ff. 79–80; *Conduct*, pp. 227–35; *Wentworth Papers*, pp. 102–5.

97. See H.M.C. *Portland MSS.* iv, 495–536 *passim*.

98. *Ibid.* pp. 496, 525, 536: 21 July 1708, 4 Sept. 1709, 10 Mar. 1710.

99. *Wentworth Papers*, p. 147; Coxe, iii, 143: Marlborough to the duchess, 23 Sept./ 4 Oct. 1710.

100. *Letters of Thomas Burnet, 1712–22*, p. 44: Burnet to Duckett, 9 Aug. 1713; Add. MSS. 31144, f. 299: Wentworth to Strafford, 16 Sept. 1712.

101. E.g. in Dec. 1711. See *Journal to Stella*, 11 Dec.

102. For his renewed attentions to her at the time of the ministerial upheaval of July– Aug. 1713 see H.M.C. *Portland MSS.* v, 315, 467.

103. B.M. Loan 29/10/20. Although undated, this memo. was probably written soon after Samuel Masham had replaced Godolphin's son, Lord Ryalton, as Cofferer of the Household in May 1711. It consists of 3 entries, the first and third in Harley's hand, the second in the hand of one of his colleagues, apparently Dartmouth:

"Mr Masham wil I beleive have a Peerage now".

"I mentioned him to the Qu: but she desired me not to put it into his head, for she was sure Mrs Mas: did not desire it".

"She took me up very short last night only for mentioning it".

104. B.M. Loan 29/10/16: paper dated 27 Dec. 1711. Cf. H.M.C. *Dartmouth MSS.* i, 308–9: Warton to Dartmouth, 28, 29 Dec.

105. Burnet, vi, 36–7: Dartmouth's n. After Mrs. Masham became a peeress Anne was not slow to depress what she thought to be improper pretensions in her. See H.M.C. *Bath MSS.* i, 225.

106. *Journal to Stella*, 8 Dec. 1711.

107. *Wentworth Papers*, p. 233; Panshanger MSS.: Somerset to Cowper, "Saterday afternoone" [Jan. 1712] and Cowper's endorsement; *ibid.* Hamilton's Diary, 24 Jan.

108. Add. MSS. 22226, f. 171.

109. Burnet, vi, 34–5: Dartmouth's and Onslow's n.

110. Oldmixon, p. 509.

111. H.M.C. *Portland MSS.* v, 661.

112. B.M. Stowe MSS. 227, ff. 178, 220.

113. B.M. Loan 29/10/6: "Memdm. July 4: 1714".

114. B.M. Loan 29/10/8: 14 May. This paper contains a series of notes for an interview which, from internal evidence, can only have been with Abigail.

CHAPTER SEVEN: PARLIAMENT AND THE PARTIES: THE STRUCTURE OF THE WHIG PARTY

1. H.M.C. *Portland MSS.* iv, 81: to [Harley], 10 Feb. 1704.

2. 7 & 8 Will. III, c. 15 (the Continuance of Parliament Act).

3. H.M.C. *Portland MSS.* iv, 480: W. Thomas to E. Harley, 9 Mar. 1708; B.M. Loan 29/149/10: T. Lewis to R. Harley, 7 Mar.

4. Add. MSS. 17677GGG, f. 41: l'Hermitage, 16/27 Jan. 1713.

5. B.M. Loan 29/153/7: Poulet to Oxford, 5 Oct. [1713].

6. Chevening MSS.: Cropley to Stanhope, 28 Jan. [1707]; H.M.C. *Portland MSS.* iv, 422: [Harley] to [Godolphin], 19 June 1707. See also Angus McInnes, 'The Political Ideas of Robert Harley', *History*, N.S. l (1965), p. 320.

7. *Hervey L.B.* i, 262–3; cf. *ibid.* 265–6.

8. *Faults on Both Sides* (2nd edn., 1710), p. 25.

9. Blenheim MSS. B. 1–23: to Marlborough, 20 May 1709; *Priv. Corr.* ii, 10: to Duchess of Marlborough, "Friday night" [Dec. 1710].

10. B. Rand, *Life . . . of Shaftesbury* (1900), p. 512: to John Molesworth, 30 Aug. 1712.

11. See *Correspondence of Lady Mary Wortley Montagu* (Bohn, 1887) i, 20–1: e.g. he appropriated to the Country Whigs the sole credit for the defeat of the government's Commerce bill in 1713; but while it is true that Wortley Montagu himself, as William Jessop attested, played an important part in that campaign (Lawson-Tancred, *Records of a Yorkshire Manor*, p. 257), Junto stalwarts like Lechmere and Castlecomer were equally conspicuous.

12. For Thornhagh (M.P. for East Retford, 1689–1702, Nottinghamshire, 1704–10) see p. 225, note † above. Biddulph was M.P. for Lichfield in 6 Parliaments, 1689–1710. Gott (Sussex 1708–10, Lewes 1710–12) was something of a hybrid; for although he had a large enough estate in Sussex (at Stanmer) to represent the county he had big city interests as well.

13. There is only one recorded vote against Bowes's name in 7 years as a knight of the shire, but this fact may be a little misleading. See Add. MSS. 28893, f. 137: Bowes to Ellis, 18 May, 1705.

14. *Ibid.* f. 394: Knightley Chetwood to Ellis, 10 Oct. 1710; H.M.C. *Portland MSS.* iv, 578; Drake/King MSS. 346 M/F. 55: Drake to Peter King, 9 July 1708.

15. *Cowper Diary*, p. 37; C.U.L. Add. MS. 7093, *passim*, for the part played by both men in the struggle for "the clause"; Boyer, p. 447. Hawles took an independent "Country" line on other questions, too, e.g. on the Treasons bill in 1709, when he supported the Scots against the government Whigs. Bishop Nicolson's diary (1709–10), 5 Apr. 1709.

16. Lonsdale MSS.: to W. Gilpin, 7 Oct. 1710.

17. Add. MSS. 31143, f. 565: Wentworth to Raby, [22] Sept. 1710; Lawson-Tancred, *Records of a Yorkshire Manor*, pp. 230–1: Monckton to C. Wilkinson, 5 Oct.

18. Wentworth to Raby, 22 Sept. *loc. cit.*

19. Note to Burnet, v, 355.

20. Coxe, iii, 30.

21. Coxe, iii, 131: Sunderland to Marlborough, 24 Aug. 1710; *ibid.* i, 237: Marlborough to Godolphin, [23 Oct.]/3 Nov. 1704.

22. *Priv. Corr.* i, 300: Godolphin to Duchess of Marlborough, 8 Apr. 1710; Panshanger MSS.: the duchess to Cowper, 22 Sept. 1710.

23. Blenheim MSS. A. 1–14: Marlborough to [Godolphin], Val nostre dame, 16 Aug. 1703; Penrice and Margam MSS. L. 1435: [E. Lewis] to Mansel, N.D. [1703]; Add. MSS. 34521, ff. 51–2: Somers to Halifax (transcript), "sent 12 o'clock", N.D. [1703].

24. Blenheim MSS. E. 28: to Duchess of Marlborough, "Saturday night near nine" [? Oct. 1708].

25. *Wentworth Papers*, p. 134.

26. Blenheim MSS. E. 27: Mainwaring to the duchess, "Saturday morn" [autumn 1708].

27. H.M.C. *Bath MSS.* iii, 438–9: to Prior, 26 July 1710.

28. Panshanger MSS. Cowper Family Books, I: Duchess of Marlborough to Lady Cowper, 23 June; Add. MSS. 22226, f. 45; *Wentworth Papers*, pp. 224, 240–1.

29. *Parl. Hist.* vi, 1170; *Wentworth Papers*, p. 330.

30. *Wentworth Papers*, p. 130.

31. B.M. Lansdowne MSS. 885, f. 76; *H.L.Q.* xv (1951–2), 38: Brydges to Cadogan, 24 Dec. 1707. R. Walcott (*English Politics*, pp. 149–52) was the first historian to recognise the significance and indeed the existence of the "Treasurer's Whigs".

32. Add. MSS. 31143, f. 509: to Raby, [*c.* 12] July 1710.

33. B.M. Loan 29/237, f. 187; H.M.C. *Various Collections*, viii (*Clements MSS.*), 236; B.M. Loan 29/195, f. 112; N.U.L. Portland (Holles) MSS. Pw2/290.

34. Chevening MSS.: Cropley to Stanhope, 22 Nov.

35. P.R.O. 30/24/21/180: Molesworth to Shaftesbury, 12 Nov. 1709. For Molesworth's earlier graduation from the Country Whigs to the "Treasurer's Whigs" see H.M.C. *Various Collections*, viii, 236.

36. Blenheim MSS. E. 29: Mainwaring to the duchess, [18 Apr. 1710]; *Priv. Corr.* i, 337.

37. *Op. cit.*, pp. 205–6.

38. See J. H. Plumb's review, *E.H.R.* lxxii (1957).

39. H.M.C. *Portland MSS.* v, 224; cf. *Prideaux Letters* (1875), p. 200.

40. B.M. Loan 29/321: Dyer's Newsletter, 14 Oct. 1710.

41. B.M. Loan 29/160: Horatio Walpole to Lord — ? —, N.D. [Dec. 1710]. Only 2 of the 12 Norfolk representatives in the House of Commons before the dissolution of Parliament in 1710 had been Tories.

42. Hartington had previously held office as Captain of the Yeomen of the Guard, 1702–7.

43. Chevening MSS.: Cropley to Stanhope, 26 Mar. [1706]. For the slightly cooler note in their relations in 1707 see W. Coxe, *Memoirs of Sir Robert Walpole* (1798), ii, 7.

44. Pulteney also wrote the preface to Walpole's brilliant pamphlet 'A Short History of the Parliament' in 1713.

45. Their relationship, which began as a mainly professional one, can be traced in a series of letters, 10 May 1708 — 16 Sept. 1710, among the papers of Thomas Erle at Charborough Park, Dorset.

46. Charborough Park MSS.: Walpole to Erle, 16 Sept. 1710.

47. See Coxe's account of their correspondence during 1710 in *Memoirs of Sir Robert Walpole*, i, 31.

48. *Ibid.* ii, 4–5: Compton to Walpole, 12 Oct. 1704. A year earlier Lord Cornwallis, Compton's electoral patron, had promised the Whigs "to use his interest" with Walpole to bring him up to town at the start of the session (*ibid.* ii, 4).

49. J. H. Plumb, *Sir Robert Walpole: The Making of a Statesman* (1956), p. 116; C.U.L. Cholmondeley (Houghton) MSS. Corr. 581: Horatio to Robert Walpole, 26 Oct. 1707; *ibid.* Corr. 681: undated letter to Robert begging him to use his influence with Smith to stand for re-election in 1713.

50. Blenheim MSS. B. 2–20: Walpole to Marlborough, 22 Feb. 1711. Johnstone was M.P. Edinburgh, 1709–13.

51. Add. MSS. 9092, f. 2: 1 Apr. 1702.

52. H.M.C. *Rutland MSS.* ii, 183; W. A. Speck, 'The Choice of a Speaker in 1705' (*loc. cit.*, p. 28).

53. Cf. the number of letters from Somers, Halifax, Devonshire, Cowper and from his own clients. There is evidence that Newcastle was well disposed towards Townshend at the time of his own appointment as Lord Privy Seal (H.M.C. *Portland MSS.* iv, 199:

Townshend to Newcastle, 29 June 1705; B.M. Loan 29/147/1: Newcastle to Harley, 9 July, enclosing the above), but that is virtually all.

54. *Memoirs of Sir Robert Walpole*, ii, 4.

55. Plumb, *op. cit.* pp. 118, 115.

56. The phrase is Marlborough's. Blenheim MSS. E. 26: to George Churchill (copy), N.D. [Aug./Sept. 1708].

57. H.M.C. *Portland MSS.* iv, 493: [E. Lewis] to Harley, 17 June 1708. Walpole's sin was clearly regarded as expiable, for Lewis adds that for his intemperance "poor Jacob was severely bastinadoed".

58. See their correspondence in Coxe, *Memoirs of Sir Robert Walpole*, ii, 11–26, 30–35 *passim*.

59. The term "Junto" was not applied to them until 1696. Before that, and for some time afterwards, they were more often referred to as "Court Whigs" or "Modern Whigs", occasionally as "the prerogative Whigs" (see, e.g., *Priv. Corr.* ii, 11; *Faults on Both Sides* (2nd. edn., 1710), p. 23; also J. P. Kenyon, *Sunderland*, pp. 271–2, 278).

60. In 1697.

61. Add. MSS. 40775, f. 116: James Vernon to William III (draft), 2 Sept. 1701.

62. *Epistolary Correspondence of Atterbury*, iv (1787), 390: 6 Mar. 1703.

63. *Memoirs of Thomas, Marquess of Wharton* (1715), p. 38.

64. Macaulay pictured "the great body of the Whigs . . . arraying itself [under the Junto] in order resembling that of a regular army". *History of England* (1855), iv, 460. Trevelyan wrote as late as 1930 that "under the orders of the Junto, the Whig body moved and wheeled like a well-drilled battalion . . ." (*Blenheim*, p. 194).

65. *Loc. cit.*

66. Chevening MSS.: to Stanhope, 23 Apr. [1710].

67. B.M. Lansdowne MSS. 885, f. 75.

68. E. L. Ellis, 'The Whig Junto' (Oxford, D.Phil., 1962), pp. 799–802, and *passim*.

69. Add. MSS. 34521, f. 16 (cf. pp. 139–40 above); Bishop Nicolson's diary (1709–10), 2 Apr. 1709; Finch MSS. G.S., bundle 23: [Bromley] to Nottingham, 7 Dec. 1708.

70. Blenheim MSS. B. 2–8: [Godolphin] to Marlborough, 10 Sept.

71. Blenheim MSS. E. 25: Mainwaring to the duchess, "Tuesday one o'clock" [(?) 28 June 1708], reporting in detail on a conversation he had had with Wharton that morning. A corrupt version of this letter is printed in *Priv. Corr.* i, 139-144.

72. See H.M.C. *Portland MSS.* iv, 148.

73. This is Professor Kenyon's view (*Sunderland*, p. 270), and Dr. E. L. Ellis shares it.

74. Blenheim MSS. B. 2–8: to Marlborough, 7 July 1710; cf. Add. MSS. 34521, ff. 39–40: Halifax to Somers (transcripts of 2 letters), N.D. [1709].

75. *Priv. Corr.* ii, 156; Dalhousie MSS. 14/352: Balmerino to [? Lady Balmerino], 2 June [1711].

76. Add. MSS. 34521, f. 63: transcript, N.D. [c. Sept. 1705].

77. Lord Edward Russell (M.P. Bedfordshire 1702–13) was his first cousin, as was Lord Robert Russell who represented Tavistock early in the reign. The Marquess of Granby, who sat for Derbyshire, Leicestershire or Grantham in every Parliament but one from 1701–11, and who married a Russell was brought into the Junto orbit by Orford. For William Cavendish, Marquess of Hartington, who like Granby married a sister of Wriothesley Russell, Duke of Bedford, see pp. 242, 328 above.

78. *Wentworth Papers*, p. 118; cf. Blenheim MSS. E. 20: Godolphin to Duchess of Marlborough, "Sat. at 10" [Sept. 1710].

79. *English Politics*, pp. 46–7; *Essays in Honor of W. C. Abbott*, (1941) p. 118.

80. See the scurrilous satire in Bodl. MS. Eng. Poet. e. 87, pp. 164–6: "Toland's Invitation to Dismal to dine with the Calves Head Club".

81. A choice example is his letter to Cowper, written on 6 July 1710 from Hackwood, in Panshanger MSS.

82. *Wentworth Papers*, p. 353: Berkeley to Strafford, 8 Sept. 1713. It was Carlisle, for example, who was deputed to propose the maximum sentence for Dr. Sacheverell in Mar. 1710. Trumbull MSS. Alphab. liv: Ralph Bridges to Trumbull, 28 Mar.

83. P.R.O. 30/24/20/141 (i) and /235: Cropley to Shaftesbury, 30 Dec. 1707 and N.D.; *Addison Letters*, p. 90.

84. See, e.g., B.M. Lansdowne MSS. 1236, ff. 246–9: Sunderland to Newcastle, 19 Oct. 1708; Coxe, iii, 9; Blenheim MSS. E. 25, E. 28: Mainwaring to the duchess, [19, 20 Jan. 1710].

85. See, e.g., Coxe, iii, 131, 144, for Cowper; Add. MSS. 4223, ff. 221 *et seq.*, for frequent correspondence between Townshend and Somers, Mar.-Aug. 1710.

86. Lonsdale MSS.: Lowther to [Sir J. Lowther], 11 Oct. 1705; Panshanger MSS.: Bolingbroke to Cowper, 4, 11 Sept. 1714.

87. Montrose had not been one of the original *Squadrone Volante*, formed in Scotland in 1704; but once he did associate with the group he soon surpassed in importance men like Rothes, Marchmont, Haddington and Tweeddale.

88. Viz. Roxburgh, Rothes and Montrose; though 3 more peers, Crawford, Orkney and Hamilton were elected in 1708 on the so-called Squadrone "list".

89. See P. W. J. Riley, *The English Ministers and Scotland, 1707–27* (1964), p. 33; the contemporary estimate of 18 June 1709 in Add. MSS. 28055, f. 426.

90. B.M. Loan 29/133/3: Dalrymple to Oxford, 10 Oct. 1710. Sir David was the distinguished Lord Advocate dismissed by the Tories in 1711.

91. See the letters of Patrick, Earl of Marchmont to Somers and Wharton, 12 Dec. 1704–11 Mar. 1707, in *Marchmont Papers* (ed. G. H. Rose, 1831), iii, 282–326 *passim*.

92. *Correspondence of George Baillie of Jerviswood* (1842), p. 37: to Baillie, 16 Jan. 1705.

93. *Marchmont Papers*, iii, 378.

94. For the Treasons bill of 1709 and the Squadrone attitude to it see P. W. J. Riley, *op. cit.* pp. 119–20. For the piqued reaction of Montrose and Roxburgh to the setback over the Secretaryship, Blenheim MSS. B. 1–22a: Henry Boyle to Marlborough, 4 Feb. 1709.

95. Auchmar MSS.: Roxburgh to Montrose, 30 July 1709; Montrose to Baillie, 31 July; cf. *Marchmont Papers*, iii, 342.

96. Auchmar MSS.: to Baillie, 31 July 1709.

97. For the 1710–11 session, e.g., there is convincing evidence of this in *ibid.*: [Baillie] to Montrose, 1 May 1711.

98. B.M. Loan 29/129/3: to Oxford, 8 Oct. 1711.

99. Auchmar MSS.: 4 Dec. 1711.

100. *Ibid.*: to Montrose, 29 May 1712.

101. *Ibid.*, [Baillie] to Montrose, 7 June 1712.

102. Add. MSS. 47087: Egmont diary (unfoliated).

CHAPTER EIGHT: THE STRUCTURE OF THE TORY PARTY

1. *Bolingbroke Corr.* i, 16–17: to Drummond, 10 Nov. 1710.
2. *Priv. Corr.* i, 399–400: to Duchess of Marlborough, [19]/30 Oct. 1710.
3. H.M.C. *Bath MSS.* i, 111: to Godolphin, 15 Oct. 1706; B.M. Loan 29/10/21: paper in Harley's hand endorsed "Mds. Ma—— 3, 1708".
4. B.M. Loan 29/128/3: (copy), 20 Aug. 1708.
5. *Ibid.* (my italics).
6. B.M. Loan 29/237, f. 85: Harley to Newcastle, 21 Oct. 1704 (postscript); Pakington MSS.: [Sir John] to [Lady Pakington ?], London, 27 Oct. [1704].
7. Winterton Letters, 879: to Sir Edward Turner, Gillingham, 29 Jan. [1705 ?].
8. Alnwick Castle MSS. vol. 22, pt. i, f. 60: Weymouth to Hon. Mrs. Thynne, 29 May 1713 (I owe this reference to Dr. W. A. Speck and am grateful to the Duke of Northumberland for permission to make the quotation).
9. Stanford Hall was Cave's beloved country seat in Leicestershire. For the above see *Verney Letters*, i, 216, 245–50: Cave to Fermanagh, 14 May 1704, 17 Mar., 13, 27 Apr., 11 May, 7 June 1714; Cave to Ralph Verney, 26 June 1714.
10. Even a run-of-the-mill squire who had no reputation whatever for oratory, like William Cage, M.P. for Rochester, could soon acquire the reputation of being "a violent man". Blenheim MSS. E. 36. Halifax to Duchess of Marlborough, N.D. [*c.* 10 May 1705].
11. E.g. H.M.C. *Bath MSS.* i, 74: 4 Sept. 1705.
12. Add. MSS. 47087 (unfoliated): Percival to Dering, 23 Mar.; also Percival's general description, *ibid.*, of the state of politics in March 1714.
13. Boyer, appx. p. 55.
14. Add. MSS. 28070, f. 12: 11 July [1705].
15. Rapin de Thoyras, in his curious 'Dissertation on Whigs and Tories', shows a discrimination rather unusual in a foreign observer of the post-Revolution scene in singling out Pembroke as the kind of 'neutral' politician to whom it was prudent for the Court to give high office. "If there were in England twelve such Lords, advanced to great offices", he believed, "it would be an infallible means to humble both parties at once". N. Tindal, Continuation of Rapin's *History of England*, 2nd edn., ii (1733), 802.
16. Claydon MSS.: Lady Gardiner to Sir John Verney, 16 July 1702.
17. Burnet, v, 392.
18. *English Politics*, pp. 54, 60.
19. H.M.C. *Rutland MSS.* ii, 190; Burnet, vi, 9n. Nottingham's letter to Dartmouth congratulating him on his promotion is couched in words of reasonably friendly formality, but nothing more can be read into it. W.S.L. Dartmouth MSS. D. 1778/Iii/110: 17 June 1710.
20. Burnet, vi, 41–2: Dartmouth's n.
21. Add. MSS. 31143, f. 557; W.S.L. Dartmouth MSS. D. 1778/V/1090: Berkeley to Dartmouth, "Wednesday morning" [6 Sept. 1710].
22. Haigh MSS.: Berkeley to Sir R. Bradshaigh, 28, 30 Sept. 1710 (I am grateful to Dr. W. A. Speck for communicating these references and to the Earl of Crawford for his permission to make the quotation).

23. Their correspondence is in Neville MSS. D/EN. F 23/2. It was Northumberland who brought Aldworth into the Commons at a by-election at Windsor in 1711, although not, significantly, until he had offered the first refusal of the seat to Brigadier Masham, a Court nominee. *Wentworth Papers*, p. 198.

24. Swift, *Some Considerations upon . . . the Death of the Queen* (1714).

25. *Epistolary Corr. of Atterbury*, iii, 141; cf. *Conduct*, p. 168.

26. Although his name is to be found in Boyer's list of the October Club's members (see p. 34, n. † above), it is likely that Nicholas was one of the Harleians 'planted' there in the latter part of the session of 1710–11, along with Lord Dupplin and others. He was a bosom friend of the Harleyite Sir Thomas Mansel, at this time a Lord of the Treasury.

27. B.M. Stowe MSS. 354, ff. 161–2.

28. B.M. Egerton MSS. 2540, f. 136: 10 Oct.

29. P.R.O. 30/24/20/141(i): Cropley to Shaftesbury, N.D. [1708], Shaftesbury's annotation.

30. As Joint Commissioner for the Privy Seal to 1713 and Treasurer of the Pensions, 1713–15.

31. This memorandum, every line of which bears witness to Cowper's clarity of judgement and remarkable lack of bias and vindictiveness, is printed in Campbell, *Lives of the Lord Chancellors*, iv, 349–50.

32. W. Coxe, *Correspondence of Charles Talbot, Duke of Shrewsbury* (1821), p. 647: Somers to Shrewsbury, 23 Feb. 1705.

33. For George Churchill (d. 1710) see p. 212 above; for Charles, Add. MSS. 31143, f. 556.

34. The first was M.P. Plymouth, 1701–13; the second (who deserted the Managers at the time of Sacheverell's trial) was M.P. East Looe, 1708–10; the third represented West Looe, 1695–1701 and 1705–7.

35. *Original Letters of Locke, Algernon Sidney and Anthony, Lord Shaftesbury* (ed. T. Forster, 1830), p. 192: 30 Jan. 1703.

36. Longleat MSS. Portland Papers, x, f. 47: (draft), 11 Aug. 170 [2].

37. See, e.g., H.M.C. *Cowper MSS.* ii, 428: [Anthony Hammond] to Coke, 7 June 1701.

38. Somers MSS. B/20: William Walsh to Somers, 26 Oct. 1701; N.U.L. Portland (Bentinck) MSS. PwA. 71: Lord Woodstock to Portland, Vienna, 17/28 Jan. 1702.

39. Longleat MSS. Portland Papers, vii, f. 113: [Harley] to [Godolphin], draft, N.D. [1704–7]. On this question cf. Angus McInnes, 'The Political Ideas of Robert Harley', *History*, N.S. 50 (1965). Mr. McInnes skilfully argues that behind the outward change of direction lay a fundamental consistency of objective.

40. The earliest letter between them to survive dates from 1677. It is in B.M. Loan 29/138/5.

41. *Ibid.*/190, f. 188: [Harcourt to Harley], 3 June 1702 (passage not printed in H.M.C. *Portland MSS.* iv, 40).

42. *Ibid.*/313/7: Francis Gwyn to Harley, 14 Aug. 1695; *ibid.*/151: Mansel to Harley, 7 June 1703.

43. Sir Edward Mansel, whom he succeeded in 1706 as 5th bart. and as proprietor of an estate said to be worth £10,000 p.a. Luttrell, vi, 110.

44. Plas Newydd MSS. Box 16C: Newcastle to Paget, 4 Aug. 1705; H.M.C. *Cowper MSS.* ii, 442.

45. H.M.C. *Portland MSS.* iv, 59, 63; cf. B.M. Loan 29/153/1: Paget to Harley, 19 Apr. 1704.

46. For their relations 1705–9 see, *inter alia*, B.M. Loan 29/64/4: [Godolphin] to Harley, "Wednesday morning" [1705–6]; Plas Newydd MSS. Box 16C: Harley to Paget "in Jarmin Street", "Saturday two a clock [1707?]"; Gower MSS. D. 593. P/16/1/2a: Henry Vernon to Gower, 13 Aug. 1709.

47. B.M. Loan 29/153/7: to Oxford, 24 Aug. [1713].

48. B.M. Loan 29/195, f. 128 (Johnson was Poulet's nominee for the borough of Ilchester). For Poulet and his friendship with Harley in general see their correspondence in B.M. Loan 29/153/7 and H.M.C. *Portland MSS.* iii–v, beginning in Apr. 1700, and *Wentworth Papers*, p. 132.

49. Walcott (*English Politics*, p. 214) assumes that the intimate connection between the two men began in 1701, St. John's first year in the House of Commons, and he is not alone in perpetuating this particular myth.

50. H.M.C. *Downshire MSS.* I, ii, 803: St. John to Trumbull, 22 June 1701.

51. H.M.C. *Bath MSS.* i, 54: St. John to [Harley], 26 Dec. 1701; H.M.C. *Portland MSS.* iv, 47: [Henry Guy] to Harley, 17 Sept. [1702]. St. John had been meeting Harley socially since Oct. 1701. H.M.C. *Downshire MSS.* I, ii, 810.

52. B.M. Loan 29/156/1: St. John to Harley, "fryday morning" [1705?].

53. *Epistolary Corr. of Atterbury*, iii (1784), 140: Atterbury to Trelawney, 26 Nov. 1703; B.M. Lansdowne MSS. 773, f. 6: Charles to Henry Davenant, 1 Feb. 1703[–4].

54. As Comptroller of Army Accounts. He was M.P. for Grimsby.

55. For Webb see Add. MSS. 17677DDD, ff. 577–8; Add. MSS. 22202, f. 28.

56. H.M.C. *Portland MSS.* iv, 104. According to Elizabeth Handasyde, Granville's acquaintance with St. John went back to 1697. *Granville the Polite* (1933), p. 86.

57. Handasyde, *op. cit.* pp. 82–4.

58. H.M.C. *Bath MSS.* i, 193; B.M. Loan 29/311/1: Granville to Oxford, 3 June 1711; *ibid.*/137/4: Lansdowne to the same, 18 July.

59. S.H. Cal. Br. 24 England 99, f. 96: Kreienberg, 30 Jan./10 Feb. 1711.

60. S.H. Cal. Br. 24 England 113a, f. 148: Kreienberg, 23 June/4 July 1713.

61. Penrice and Margam MSS. L. 648: [Harley] to Mansel, 30 Sept. 1709; B.M. Loan 29/151: Mansel to Oxford, 1 Sept. 1712, 3 Sept. 1713.

62. For Harley's efforts back in 1705 to secure the Receivership of Somerset for Palmer, see Longleat MSS. Portland Papers, vii, f. 46. Bateman, Harley's chief ally in the City of London, was brought in for Ilchester at a by-election in June 1711 when Masham transferred to Windsor.

63. For Blanch see his letters to Harley in B.M. Loan 29/126/6; for Coxe, H.M.C. *Portland MSS.* iv, 74; *Court and Society*, ii, 234; B.M. Loan 29/29: Coxe to Lord — ? —, "Lippiate", 13 Oct. 1712.

64. B.M. Loan 29/130/1: Chapman to Oxford, 22 Dec. 1711, 10 Aug. 1714.

65. See their correspondence with him in H.M.C. *Portland MSS.* iv, v and B.M. Loan 29.

66. For Harley's correspondence and relations with these Whig relatives, for whose benefit he was careful to sign himself "your most faithful & most humble servant, & *kinsman*", see B.M. Loan 29/138 (Hampden), 29/125 (Ashurst and the Ashes), 29/155 (the Robarteses); H.M.C. *Portland MSS.* iv, 77 (the Newports); Corsham Court MSS. Box 3: Harley to Methuen, 27, 29 Oct. 1710; Methuen to Harley, 28 Oct.

67. *Bolingbroke Corr.* i, 245: St. John to Orrery, 12 June 1711.

68. There is at least a suspicion, however, that at times his worst obscurities and

gaucheries of style were deliberately cultivated in political correspondence. Contrast the warmth and wit of some of his purely private letters, e.g. that written to Henry Boyle in September 1706. Chatsworth MSS. 102.1.

69. See, e.g., Dalhousie MSS. 14/352: Balmerino to [Maule], 28 May [1713]; *Wentworth Papers*, p. 374: Bathurst to Strafford, 20 Apr. 1714.

70. *The Diplomatic Correspondence of Richard Hill* (ed. W. Blackley, 1845), p. 112: Harley to Hill, 6 June 1704. For further evidence that he accepted this office reluctantly see Longleat MSS. Thynne Papers, xii, f. 129: Harley to Weymouth, 25 May 1704.

71. See B.M. Loan 29/68/1: Abigail Harley to her aunt Abigail, 15 July 1704, for the long hours her father worked at his desk in the Cockpit; B.M. Lansdowne MSS. 773, ff. 42, 58, for the contrast with Hedges.

72. Angus McInnes, in his unpublished M.A. thesis, 'Robert Harley, Secretary of State' (University College of Wales, Aberystwyth, 1961, chapter 4), has produced an admirable study of this aspect of his work.

73. E.g. from W. A. Shaw, *Calendar of Treasury Books*, vol. xxv, pt. i (1711), pp. xxvii–ix, xxxiii–iv. For a recent corrective see B. W. Hill, 'The Career of Robert Harley, Earl of Oxford, from 1702 to 1714' (Cambridge Ph.D. thesis, 1961).

74. B. Rand, *Life . . . of Shaftesbury* (1900), p. 512: Shaftesbury to John Molesworth, Naples, [19]/30 Aug. 1712.

75. *Journal to Stella*, 9 Mar., 8 Apr. 1713.

76. *A History of the Tory Party*, p. 315.

77. Panshanger MSS. Cowper Family Books, I, 161: Duchess of Marlborough to Lady Cowper, [18]/29 June [1713].

78. Walton MSS. iii, 53: Archer to Sir John Mordaunt, 5 Jan. 1701[–2].

79. *Wentworth Papers*, p. 133: Raby's *Caractères*.

80. See B.M. Lansdowne MSS. 885, f. 80.

81. Trumbull Add. MSS. 133: St. John to Trumbull, 16 May 1704; Longleat MSS. Portland Misc. f. 199: [Godolphin to Harley], "Sunday [19 Nov. 1704], at 2".

82. H.M.C. *Bath MSS.* i, 191–2, 193–4.

83. H.M.C. *Portland MSS.* iv, 527: George Granville to Harley, 22 Sept.; cf. Penrice and Margam MSS. L. 648: [Harley] to Mansel, 30 Sept.

84. *Priv. Corr.* ii, 387–8: St. John to Marlborough, 8 Sept. 1709; Add. MSS. 31143, ff. 586–7.

85. H.M.C. *Portland MSS.* iv, 536: St. John to Harley, 8 Mar. 1710; Trumbull Add. MSS. 133: St. John to Trumbull, 31 Aug.; Macpherson, *Original Papers* (1775), ii, 531. See also Panshanger MSS.: Hamilton diary, 21 Sept.

86. H.M.C. *Portland MSS.* v, 464–5; *ibid.* pp. 194, 198: St. John to Oxford, [28 June], 3 July 1712; *Bolingbroke Corr.* ii, 484–5; Swift, *Memoirs* (*Prose Works*, viii, 128); Bolingbroke, *Letter to Wyndham*, p. 31.

87. See G. S. Holmes, 'The Influence of the Peerage in English Parliamentary Elections, 1702–1713' (Oxford B.Litt. thesis, 1952), p. 165 and n. 2.

88. H.M.C. *Cowper MSS.* iii, 63; *Portland MSS.* iv, 180.

89. H.M.C. *Portland MSS.* iv, 684.

90. Buckingham's rather isolated position is stressed by Poulet (*ibid.*: to [Harley], 5 May 1711), and Jersey's independence is underlined by the fact that Harley could use him to initiate peace negotiations in 1710 without fear of a leakage to either Rochester or Nottingham. Ormonde, easily the most temperate of the three, bore "the character

of a generous good natured fine Gentleman", but "not one that wou'd set up for a Polit[ic]ian"; and although the Hyde faction claimed the credit when he was brought into the Cabinet in Feb. 1703, it is significant that not even Atterbury believed them. *Wentworth Papers*, p. 150; H.M.C. *Ormonde MSS*. N.S. viii, 48, 212, 263; *Epistolary Corr. of Atterbury*, iv, 368.

91. "the great Bromley", Lord Stanhope had called him as early as 1703. Chevening MSS.: to James Stanhope, 30 May.

92. Longleat MSS. Portland Misc. f. 59: [Godolphin] to Speaker Harley, 24 Nov. [1702]; Bettisfield MSS. doc. 81: Sir John Conway to [Hanmer], endorsed March 1707–8.

93. *H.L.Q.* iii (1939–40), 240: to Drummond, 21 Sept. See also *Letters of the Sitwells and Sacheverells* (ed. Sir G. Sitwell, 1901), ii, 47; Boyer, *Political State*, i, 5; Dalhousie MSS. 14/352: Balmerino to Maule, 16 Jan. [1711].

94. Cf. *English Politics*, pp. 53–66.

95. Through Thanet Nottingham acquired an indirect interest in the representation of Appleby Borough. Finch MSS. G.S., bundle 23: Joseph Blackwell to Nottingham, 10 Sept. 1710. For William North, Lord North and Grey, see *ibid.*: North to the same, 9 Oct. 1710, and Nicolson's MS. diary, 5 Feb. 1711, for his support of Nottingham and Guernsey in the House of Lords. For Nottingham's influence on Sharp's parliamentary behaviour as late as 1711, see B.M. Lansdowne MSS. 1024, f. 252.

96. Longleat MSS. Thynne Papers, xii, f. 140: N.D. [Dec. 1703]. Weymouth held Scarsdale's proxy in 1702, and Stawell's was held by Scarsdale during the session of 1705–6 (House of Lords R.O. Proxy Book, 1685–1733).

97. Thynne Papers, xii, f. 136: Abingdon to Weymouth, London, 1 Feb. [N.Y.].

98. Thomas Hearne, *Remarks and Collections*, ii, 2.

99. Finch MSS. G.S., bundle 23: Anglesey to [Nottingham], 15 July 1710; *The Correspondence of Sir Thomas Hanmer* (ed. Sir Henry Bunbury, 1838), pp. 125–6: the same to Hanmer, 27 July.

100. H. L. Stowe MSS. 57: Brydges to Drummond, 21 Sept. 1710.

101. Heneage Finch, junior, for Surrey (he had previously sat for Maidstone, 1704–5) and Daniel, Lord Finch, for Rutland.

102. E.g. those of Sir Bryan Stapylton and Sir John Kaye. *Life of Archbishop Sharp* (1825), i, 306.

103. These connections can be traced not only in Nottingham's own papers but in the Chirk Castle and Bettisfield MSS. in the National Library of Wales and in the Legh of Lyme MSS., deposited by Lord Newton in John Ryland's Library.

104. Blenheim MSS. E. 36: Halifax to Duchess of Marlborough, N.D. [*c.* 10 May 1705].

105. Walcott, *English Politics*, pp. 63, 66, 104–5 and *passim*.

106. H.M.C. *Portland MSS*. iv, 134, 222.

107. E.g. they were at variance during the 1702 Election over the nomination of Ranelagh at West Looe. Add. MSS. 29588, f. 79: Seymour to Nottingham, 4 July.

108. A surviving letter from Seymour to Heneage Finch, written in Nov. 1695, makes it clear that in William's reign they had been on intimate terms. Chatsworth MSS. Finch-Halifax Papers, box 4, bundle 11.

109. H.M.C. *Portland MSS*. iv, 134: Richard Duke to Harley, 20 Sept. 1704.

110. *Cowper Diary*, p. 15: 15 Nov. 1705; *Bolingbroke Corr*. i, 28, 197.

111. Coxe, i, 133: to the duchess, 3/14 June 1703.

112. House of Lords R.O. Proxy Book, session 1706–7.

113. See pp. 68, 73–4 above; *Norris Papers*, pp. 106, 123; H.M.C. *Portland MSS.* iv, 50, 55, 57.

114. Walton MSS. iii, 11, 14: Bromley to Sir J. Mordaunt, 31 July, 10 Sept. 1710; *ibid.* iii, 92: Northampton to Bromley (copy), 26 Aug. 1710; B.M. Loan 29/128: Bromley to Oxford, 15 Nov. 1711; Blenheim MSS. D. 1–32: Geo. Lucy to Sunderland, 21 Feb. 1705 (for Willoughby's disagreement with other friends of Bromley over "the Tack").

115. Add. MSS. 22202, f. 6.

116. B.M. Loan 29/128: Harley to Bromley (copy), 12 Oct. 1708; Bodl. MS. Ballard 35, f. 132.

117. H.M.C. *Portland MSS.* vii, 144: to Lord Harley, 21 June.

118. See the "Character of the Primate and Earl of Anglesea" in Sir John Percival's Diary, *c.* Jan. 1714, Add. MSS. 47087.

119. For Anglesey's character see *ibid.*, *loc. cit.* and entry for 14 Mar. 1714.

120. H.M.C. *Portland MSS.* vii, 192.

121. Macpherson, *Original Papers* (1775), ii, 618: anon. to Robethon, 14/25 May 1714; *Lockhart Papers* (1817), i, 439.

122. *Lockhart Papers*, i, 472–3; *C.J.* xvii, 683, 685 for instances of the effectiveness of the Jacobites in opposition.

123. For Campion's Jacobite sympathies see Add. MSS. 22202, f. 160.

124. Tredegar MSS. 53/107: Beaufort to John Morgan, 11 July 1713. Kemys was M.P. for Monmouthshire in 1714.

125. B.M. Loan 29/143/8: [Edward Harley] to Oxford, "Saturday" [19 Apr. 1712].

126. For the original nucleus of this group in the Commons see G. S. Holmes, "The Commons' Division on 'No Peace without Spain', 7 December 1711", *Bull I.H.R.* xxxiii (1960).

127. The author of *A Letter from a Member of the House of Commons relating to the Bill of Commerce*, printed by J. Baker in 1713, whose information is exceptionally accurate as far as it can be cross-checked, classifies as many as 36 such members among the opposition to that bill on 18 June. But since he counts 3 Hanoverian Tories (Lord Finch, "Diamond" Pitt, and Pitt's son Robert) as Whigs — presumably because their opposition to the Court since 1711 had been so constant — and since a number of other well-known Hanoverian rebels, like Sir George Downing, George England and Sir Charles Hedges, were absent from this particular division, a total of 40 is certainly a conservative estimate.

128. Monson MSS. 28B/9/111: Monckton to Archer, 20 June 1713; B.M. Stowe MSS. 226, f. 36: Schütz, 15/26 Jan. 1714.

129. Since 1711 Lord Mountjoy in the peerage of Great Britain, but still referred to more commonly by his Irish title of Viscount Windsor.

130. See Feiling, *Tory Party*, p. 466.

131. Bodl. MS. Ballard 31, f. 104.

132. Edward Duncombe, M.P. for Appleby, is a case in point. This "friend of Sr. Thos. Hanmore's" did not stand for re-election in Aug. 1713. *Ibid.* f. 121.

133. H.M.C. *Portland MSS.* v, 425.

134. For Shakerley see his correspondence in H.M.C. *8th Report*, pt. i (1881) [*Corporation of Chester MSS.*], pp. 393–5; Edward Hughes, *Studies in Administration and Finance, 1558–1825* (1934), pp. 228–61.

135. Add. MSS. 47087: Sir John to Philip Percival, 17 Apr.

136. Viz. Henry Bertie (Beaumaris) and James (Middlesex).

137. One explanation of this is that he apparently included some Argyllite Whigs, former supporters of the Court, among his "four score and odd".

138. See p. 34, notes *, † above.

139. Those occasions on which the succession issue was most clearly involved were the Steele debates in March, the great debate of 15 Apr. already mentioned, the debates on the payment of the Hanoverian troops' arrears in May, and the debate on the question of a reward for the Pretender's capture on 24 June.

140. Percival's letter of 17 Apr., *loc. cit.*

141. Add. MSS. 22220, f. 107.

CHAPTER NINE: THE PARTIES IN ACTION: DIRECTION AND ORGANISATION

1. H.M.C. *Cowper MSS.* iii, 22: to Thomas Coke, 13 Mar. 1703.

2. Add. MSS. 34521, f. 14: 29 Aug. 1742.

3. Nicolson's MS. diary: 10 Nov. 1704.

4. H.M.C. *Fortescue MSS.* i, 38: Robert to Thomas Pitt, 15 Nov. 1708.

5. *Priv. Corr.* ii, 308: 7 Feb.

6. H.M.C. *Portland MSS.* iv, 505; Panshanger MSS. Cowper Family Books, I: Duchess of Marlborough to Lady Cowper, 25 Oct. [1710]; B.M. Stowe MSS. 225, f. 214.

7. For Somers see, e.g., B.M. Loan 29/237, f. 107: Somers to Newcastle, 18 Aug. [1705]; H.M.C. *Portland MSS.* ii, 196: to the same, 24 Aug. 1706; B.M. Loan 29/238, ff. 255, 263: to the same, 31 July, 28 Oct. 1708.

8. Panshanger MSS.: Somers and Godolphin to Cowper, [8 Aug.], 12 Aug. 1710; Sunderland to Cowper, 19 Oct. 1710; Halifax to Cowper, 24 Jan. 1713[–14].

9. Auchmar MSS.: Halifax to Montrose, 26 Oct. 1708; Add. MSS. 4163, f. 263; Chatsworth MSS. 98.2: Orford to Lady Russell, 2 Sept. 1708.

10. Auchmar MSS.: to Montrose, 18 Apr. 1710.

11. H.M.C. *Portland MSS.* v, 106. This conference, like so many others held by the Junto in Anne's reign, was conveniently timed to coincide with the Newmarket autumn race-meeting. Cf. Blenheim MSS. B. 2–9: Marlborough to Godolphin, 10 Nov. [N.S.?] 1711.

12. H.L. Stowe MSS. 58, v, 125: Coke to Brydges, 15 Feb. A corrected draft of this motion in Sunderland's hand is preserved among the earl's Cabinet minutes in Blenheim MSS. C. 1–16.

13. *Verney Letters*, i, 311; cf. John Bridges's comment on 28 May: "it was a concerted thing amongst the whole party". Trumbull MSS. Alphab. liv.

14. Wake MSS. Arch. W. Epist. 17. misc. i, letter 174: Gibson to [Wake], 29 Aug.

15. Sir Robert Davers assured the Lord Treasurer that, on his information, those who attended were "almost all Lords". H.M.C. *Portland MSS.* v, 106: 1 Nov. 1711.

16. H.M.C. *Portland MSS.* iv, 590: to Harley, 5 Sept. 1710.

17. Coxe, i, 133: Marlborough to the duchess, 3/14 June 1703; Longleat MSS. Thynne Papers, xxv, f. 135: James Grahme to Weymouth, 6 June [1703]; Blenheim MSS. F. 2–16: Harley to Marlborough, 16/27 June 1704; *Hanmer Correspondence*, p. 123. We also know that Rochester was very active in the summer of 1705 converting his friends to the astonish-

ing change of party policy involved in the infamous 'Hanover motion' (Nov. 1705); but whether by correspondence or by personal contact we can only speculate. Nicolson's MS. diary: 13 Nov. 1705.

18. Finch MSS. G.S., bundle 23: Bromley to Nottingham, 2 Oct., 23 Oct., 11 Nov., 7 Dec., 31 Dec.; Nottingham to Bromley (drafts), 15 Nov., 20 Dec.

19. Levens MSS.: Bromley to Grahme, 13 Aug. 1710. See also *ibid.*, letters of 28 June, 16, 28 July, 1, 11 Sept., and cf. Walton MSS. iii, 13: Bromley to Sir John Mordaunt, 8 Sept.

20. *Wentworth Papers*, p. 337: to Strafford, 19 June 1713.

21. Printed lists were subsequently circulated of the large number of Tories who assembled at the Vine Tavern in Long Acre on 11 Nov. 1701.

22. Levens MSS.: Ward to Grahme, 3 Oct.

23. H.M.C. *Bath MSS.* i, 64.

24. Thomas Hearne, *Remarks and Collections* (1885), i, 58.

25. B.M. Loan 29/237, f. 115: 13 Nov. 1705.

26. W.S.L. Dartmouth MSS. D. 1778/V/151: [Oxford] to Dartmouth, St. James's, "Fryday night" [? 29 Feb. 1712].

27. Trumbull Add. MSS. 136/1: Ralph Bridges to Trumbull, 9 June 1713.

28. H.M.C. *Portland MSS.* iv, 51; v, 652; Nicolson's MS. diary: 5, 7 Jan. 1706.

29. Add. MSS. 49360 (unfoliated).

30. *Ibid.*

31. Oldmixon, p. 479. Another member of the Kit-Cat Club in 1711 was Sunderland's protégé, Edward Hopkins, who had represented Coventry up to 1710 and was to sit again for Eye in 1713–14.

32. Defections by some members were noticed in the big debate in the Lords on the Queen's Speech at the end of the 1711–12 session. Trumbull Add. MSS. 136/3: Ralph Bridges to Trumbull, 9 June 1712.

33. H.L. Stowe MSS. 57, iii, 204: Brydges to Cadogan, 7 Apr. It seems clear from Oldmixon's 1711 list that "the Sovereign" was subsequently readmitted.

34. Clavering Letters: Ann to James Clavering, London, 1 Apr.; Blenheim MSS. E. 26: Mainwaring to Duchess of Marlborough, "Thursday afternoon" [Mar. 1710].

35. Boyer, pp. 524, 680–1; *The Post Boy*, 22 Nov. 1711; H.M.C. *Dartmouth MSS.* i, 307–8; Trumbull MSS. Alphab. li: T. Bateman to Trumbull, 19 Nov. 1711.

36. H.M.C. *Downshire MSS.* I, ii, 885–6: John Bridges to Trumbull, 20 Dec. 1709. "The fate and impeachment of the poor Doctor was some time since fully concluded upon at the Kit-Cat Club, where my Lord Marlborough himself, they say, was present, assented to it, and has actually entered himself a member of that detestable society". Robert Monckton, in an unsigned letter to Newcastle of 10 Dec. (B.M. Loan 29/238, f. 310), confirms Marlborough's admission to membership at this time; and A. Cunningham's near-contemporary *History of Great Britain*, ii (1787), 279–80, gives a curiously circumstantial account of the debate between Marlborough, Somers, Sunderland, Cowper and Halifax.

37. [Steele], *Memoirs of Thomas, Marquess of Wharton* (1715), pp. 38–9.

38. *Ibid.* p. 38.

39. B.M. Stowe MSS. 227, f. 114: Gatke to [Robethon], 1/12 June 1714.

40. See Wake MSS. 1770 and Nicolson's MS. diary: entries for 21 Dec. 1710 to 27 Feb. 1711, *passim*, for these and many other examples.

41. B. Rand, *Life . . . of Shaftesbury* (1900), p. 475: to Cropley, 1 Mar. 1712.

42. It would be too lengthy and tedious here to document these relationships in detail. They can be traced in Harley's papers at Longleat and in the British Museum (Loan 29); and in the Isham, Claydon and Chirk Castle MSS. Myddleton was the least reliable of the group, and he fell down on his job badly in 1708 (Chirk Castle MSS. E. 991).

43. Levens MSS.: Weymouth to Grahme, 27 Sept. 1703.

44. There is a reference to this club in Winterton Letters, 879: Sir Edmund Bacon to Sir Edward Turner, 29 Jan. [1705].

45. Bodl. MS. Ballard 17, f. 69.

46. *The Diary of John Evelyn* (ed. E. S. de Beer, 1955), v, 614. See also W. A. Speck, 'The Choice of a Speaker in 1705', *Bull. I.H.R.* xxxvii (1964).

47. B.M. Loan 29/171/2: Harley to William Stratford (copy), 10 Oct. 1708.

48. Finch MSS. G.S., bundle 23: Bromley to Nottingham, 2 Oct.; H.M.C. *Bath MSS.* i, 193: Harley to Harcourt, 16 Oct. Harley's letter, along with another he wrote apparently on the same day to Mansel (Longleat MSS. Portland Papers, x, f. 54 *verso*), set in motion the regional machinery in South Wales and the south-west of England.

49. N.U.L. Portland (Holles) MSS. Pw2/95: Harley to Newcastle (copy), 22 Oct. Cf. Longleat MSS. Portland Papers, x, f. 57: Harley to R. Monckton, 22 Oct.

50. Levens MSS.: John Ward to Grahme, 2 Oct.; Chirk Castle MSS. E. 994 (i): Hanmer to Shakerley, 21 Oct.; *ibid*. E. 995: Sir Roger Mostyn to Myddleton, 24 Oct.

51. Longleat MSS. Thynne Papers: Dyer's Newsletter, 16 Nov. 1708.

52. Bodl. MS. Top. Oxon. b. 82: Thomas Rowney to Geo. Clarke, 19 Nov. 1708.

53. Penrice and Margam MSS. L. 1446: C. Williams to Mansel, 29 Nov. [1709].

54. *Letters of Thomas Burnet*, p. 41.

55. *Lockhart Papers*, i, 351.

56. Nicolson's MS. diary: 21 Dec. 1702.

57. *Norris Papers*, p. 35: William to Thomas Norris, 6 Oct. 1696.

58. H.M.C. *Portland MSS.* iv, 523: 19 Apr.

59. *Wentworth Papers*, p. 189: 27 Mar. 1711.

60. Add. MSS. 27440, f. 92: Charles Allestree to Sir J. Isham (copy), 4 Feb. 1705 (quoting a letter from the injured party, one Mr. Parkhurst of Daventry).

61. H.M.C. *Dartmouth MSS.* i, 309.

62. Add. MSS. 33225, f. 13.

63. *Addison Letters*, p. 124: to Henry Newton, 31 Dec. 1708; Add. MSS. 22202, ff. 2–3; Luttrell, vi, 386; cf. *Lockhart Papers*, i, 297.

64. Add. MSS. 40776, f. 23: to Vernon, 7 Dec. 1706.

65. Onslow MSS., Clandon Park: Somerset to Onslow, 20 June, 30 June 1713 (printed C. E. Vulliamy, *The Onslow Family* [1953], pp. 31–2).

66. Bodl. MS. Ballard 15, ff. 112–13.

67. E.g. in May 1714. B.M. Stowe MSS. 227, f. 63.

68. Isham MSS. Corr. 2791: Sir Gilbert Dolben to [Isham], 2 June 1713; Corr. 2787: Beaumont to [Isham], 31 May [1711]; *Verney Letters*, i, 246, 248: Cave to Fermanagh, 13 Apr., 7 June 1714.

69. *Verney Letters*, i, 248, 250.

70. H.M.C. *Dartmouth MSS.* i, 309–10; W.S.L. Dartmouth MSS. D. 1778/V/194: Poulet to Dartmouth, "fryday morning" [29 Feb. 1712].

71. Longleat MSS. Portland Misc. f. 151: [Godolphin] to [Harley], 8 Dec.; *Epistolary Corr. of Atterbury*, iii, 147; Add. MSS. 29576, f. 150: C. Hatton to Lord Hatton, 9 Dec.

72. Add. MSS. 17677FFF, f. 176: l'Hermitage, 29 Apr./10 May.

73. Chatsworth MSS. 121. 2: [Thursday], 1 May [1712].

74. Longleat MSS. Portland Misc. f. 209: [Godolphin] to Harley, 9 Nov. [1703].

75. *Ibid.*; cf. *Epistolary Corr. of Atterbury*, iii, 138.

76. Longleat MSS. Portland Misc. ff. 196, 134: [Godolphin] to Harley, [25, 27 Nov. 1704].

77. See P. M. Ansell, *Bull. I.H.R.* xxxiv (1961), for the printed version of the first. For the second see the list in Oxford's hand in B.M. Loan 29/10/3, which is undated but can be attributed with reasonable certainty, both from internal and external evidence (see e.g. H.M.C. *Portland MSS.* iv, 139), to the period 21–23 Jan. 1712.

78. Even in the fragments of the 1712 lists which are complete and intelligible, Lowndes and Harley are allocated 23 members between them to canvass. These included not only placemen and businessmen, but also a few of the Welsh border members, for whom "the Govern^r"(Edward Harley) had a joint responsibility along with his cousin Thomas, M.P. Radnorshire.

79. B.M. Loan 29/143/8: to Oxford, "Saturday" [? 19 Apr. 1712].

80. *Wentworth Papers*, p. 83.

81. Longleat MSS. Portland Misc. f. 133: "Fryday night at 8" [? 1 Dec. 1704].

82. H.M.C. *Leyborne-Popham MSS.* p. 283; H.M.C. *Bath MSS.* i, 79; Speck. *loc. cit.* p. 30.

83. B.M. Lansdowne MSS. 1236, f. 255: Sunderland to Newcastle, 31 Aug.; Panshanger MSS.: Cowper to same, 2 Sept. For Peyton's flirting with the Tories in 1709 see his letter to Lord Gower, 18 June, in Gower MSS. D. 593: P/13/8.

84. Lawson-Tancred, *Records of a Yorkshire Manor*, pp. 249–50, 254: Pelham to Charles Wilkinson, 4, 18 June 1713; Add. MSS. 22238, f. 121.

85. Add. MSS. 33573, f. 272: W. Plummer to Bernard Hale, Paris, 28 Aug. 1713.

86. H.M.C. *Portland MSS.* iv, 531.

87. Burnet, vi, 224.

88. There is an excellent account of this struggle and its background in Philip Styles, 'The Corporation of Bewdley under the Later Stuarts', *Birmingham Hist. Journal*, i (1947). In 1713 Salwey Winnington's judicial expenses alone were put at "upwards of 2500 l." (Legh of Lyme MSS. Box 50: J. V. to Peter Legh, 5 July). Lord Herbert, in a letter to an unknown peer, written after 1714 (Rebecca Warner, *Epistolary Curiosities* [1818], p. 39), claimed that the Bewdley struggle alone had cost him at least £6000, and it is clear that much of this expense was incurred after his succession to the title in 1709, when he was already heavily in debt as a result of various electoral activities.

89. B.M. Loan 29/321: Dyer's Newsletter, 21 Sept. 1710, for the activities of Bolton and of Orford's two clients, Byng and Jennings.

90. B.M. Loan 29/133/5: Davers to Oxford, 4 Mar. 1713[-14]; *ibid.* /160: Winnington to Harley, 13 Oct. 1710; *ibid.* /152: North and Grey to Oxford, 22 July 1713.

91. See *The Case of the Borough of Buckingham* [1714]; cf. *C.J.* xvii, 600–1.

92. H.M.C. *Portland MSS.* iv, 27; *C.J.* xv, 52; xvii, 616–17.

93. National Library of Wales, Llanfair and Brynodol MS. 96.

94. *C.J.* xvi, 419. For Plympton see *C.J.* xiv, 149–50.

95. *Ibid.* xvi, 300–4.

96. H.M.C. *Portland MSS.* v, 221, 229, 234; *Ailesbury MSS.* pp. 204–9; *Kenyon MSS.* p. 448.

97. See, e.g., Luttrell, vi, 375. There is an interesting account of the party manoeuvring accompanying a London mayoral election in Bodl. MS. Carte 244, f. 123.

98. Luttrell, vi, 295: 22 Apr.

99. Add. MSS. 17677GGG, f. 354.

100. H.M.C. *Portland MSS.* iv, 153–4; Penrice and Margam MSS. L. 678.

101. Add. MSS. 21507, f. 76: Hon. Heneage Finch to — ? —, 27 Jan. 1713; *The Worcester Post-Man*, No. 189, 30 Jan.–6 Feb. 1713.

102. Add. MSS. 29579, f. 400.

103. Weston Park MSS. Box 18/15: John to Sir John Bridgeman, 29 Nov. 1701; H.M.C. *Portland MSS.* iv, 437.

104. John Harvey's nomination for Bedfordshire in 1710 was a typical example. Add. MSS. 28893, f. 394.

105. Add. MSS. 5853, f. 87; B.M. Egerton MSS. 2651, f. 206; H.M.C. *Rutland MSS.* ii, 190–1.

106. Isham MSS. Corr. 2944: to Sir J. Isham, 31 Aug. 1706.

107. Somers MSS. L/29: 18 Aug. 1707. See H.M.C. *Portland MSS.* iv, 125 for hasty improvisation by the Westmorland Tories after Sir Christopher Musgrave's death in 1704.

108. H.M.C. *Cowper MSS.* iii, 3, 78.

109. *Verney Letters*, i, 323–4: Cave to Fermanagh, 11, 22 Feb. 1711; Isham MSS. Corr. 2413: to J. Isham, junr., 17 Feb.

110. Walton MSS. iii, 98.

111. Willoughby de Broke, Leigh, Guilford and Digby.

112. Tredegar MSS. 53/94–108: Beaufort's correspondence with John Morgan, 1705–13

113. H.M.C. *Portland MSS.* vii, 18–19; *Verney Letters*, i, 323; Add. MSS. 29599, f. 117.

114. N.U.L. Portland (Holles) MSS. Pw2/138: W. Jessop to Newcastle, 4 July 1710.

115. Add. MSS. 29599, f. 121.

116. B.M. Loan 29/201: James Grahme to [Lord Harley], 18 Aug. 1713.

117. [Steele], *Memoirs of Wharton*, p. 86 (cf. the report of the Bucks election in *The Flying-Post*, No. 2276, 10–12 Oct. 1710). Wharton did not arrive back in London in 1710 after his second viceregal term in Ireland until 9 Sept., less than a fortnight before the long-expected dissolution of Parliament.

118. As he had in 1701. Seymour nominated him in 1702 for Totnes in Devon.

119. Add. MSS. 28055, ff. 3–4.

120. Blenheim MSS. B. 2–4: Sir Humphrey Mackworth to Marlborough, 19 Jan. 1709[–10].

121. *Ibid.* A. 1–20: Howe to [Marlborough], 23 May 1705.

122. Levens MSS.: 18 July.

123. Viz. Westbury, Cricklade, Devizes, Reading, Weymouth and Cardigan. See, e.g., H.M.C. *Bath MSS.* i, 190; *Portland MSS.* iv, 176 (misdated by ed.); B.M. Loan 29/154/1: Harley to Robert Price, 29 May 1708 [P.S.]; *ibid.* /138/5: Harcourt to Harley, N.D.; Penrice and Margam MSS. L. 612: — ? — to Mansel, 12 June 1708.

124. Bodl. MS. Ballard 38, ff. 133–4: Bromley to Charlett, 9 Nov. 1710.

125. Corsham Court MSS. Box 3: Somerset to Methuen, 7, 9 Jan. 1712; Methuen to Somerset (copies), 8, 11 Jan.

126. Bodl. MS. Carte 211, f. 138.

127. Ducie MSS. D. 340a/C22.2: petition from 75 citizens of Stroud to Moreton, N.D. [? Oct. 1713]; *ibid.* C22. 6–7: Wharton to Moreton, 24, 29 Apr. 1714.

128. Chevening MSS.: Robert Monro, M.P. to Walpole, 29 Oct. 1713. Much of the Stanhope saga is documented in this archive; but see also Folger Lib. L.C. 3642: Newsletter to Sir R. Newdigate, 18 July 1713; Lonsdale MSS.: Newman to Lowther, 8 Oct. 1713; B.M. Stowe MSS. 225, f. 240; Charborough Park MSS.: Craggs to Erle, 21 Sept. 1713.

129. Lonsdale MSS.: Lechmere to Lowther, 29 Aug. 1713; Cockermouth Castle MSS. Box 107: (copies of polls at elections for the borough of Cockermouth).

130. Lady Elliott-Drake: *The Family and Heirs of Sir Francis Drake* (1911), ii, 176–81; Panshanger MSS.: Sir Francis Drake to Cowper, 2 May 1710 (and endorsement).

CHAPTER TEN: THE PARTIES IN ACTION: POWER-GROUPS AND PRESSURE-GROUPS

1. H.M.C. *Portland MSS.* iv, 28: [Godolphin] to Harley, 4 Dec.

2. Add. MSS. 29584, f. 95: to Nottingham, 17 Aug. 1702.

3. B.M. Loan 29/237, f. 108: to Newcastle, Belbar, Saturday, 18 Aug. [1705] (my italics).

4. B.M. Lansdowne MSS. 1236, ff. 250, 253: to Newcastle, 26 Oct., 4 Nov. 1708. See also p. 225, n. † above, for Newcastle's connexion in 1708.

5. *Hervey L.B.* i, 273: Hervey to Porter, 25 Aug. 1710. Porter's absence is confirmed by the fact that his name is not on any of the Sacheverell lists.

6. See H.M.C. *Portland MSS.* v, 331.

7. *Priv. Corr.* i, 194: to Duchess of Marlborough, N.D. [1709].

8. H.M.C. *Portland MSS.* iv, 579.

9. *Cowper Diary*, p. 33.

10. *Life of Archbishop Sharp* (1825), i, 269, 308–10 (quoting Sharp's diary).

11. B.M. Loan 29/138/5: [Harcourt] to Harley, "Saturday night" [23 Nov. 1704], and *verso*.

12. Clarke's autobiography: H.M.C. *Leyborne-Popham MSS.*

13. Harry Mordaunt, Edmund Dunch, Albemarle Bertie and Charles Godfrey.

14. Blenheim MSS. E. 26: N.D.

15. See, e.g., *English Politics*, p. 33. Out of a group of almost a hundred members of the 1701 House of Commons who had aristocratic connections Walcott found firm evidence of only 7 who belonged to a political group opposed to that of their titled relative, and believed that 'possibly' another 15 'owed little or nothing to their connexion with a peer'. The political associations of the remaining 75, however, are identified neatly with those of their noble kinsmen, though in many cases (see *ibid.* appx. 1 part v, *passim*) the link is established by pure assumption.

16. *Ibid.* p. 215, pp. 200–15 *passim*.

17. *Ibid.* pp. 56–7, 212; Burnet, iii, 89. See H. G. Horwitz, 'The Political Career of Daniel Finch, 2nd Earl of Nottingham' (Oxford D.Phil. thesis, 1963), pp. x–xi.

18. Bodl. MS. Add. A. 269, p. 25: Edmund Gibson to Bishop Nicolson (copy), Chichester, 1 Sept. 1713; Worsley MSS. 1, f. 30.

19. For Lindsey see, *inter alia*, H.M.C. *Rutland MSS.* ii, 182: Granby to Rutland,

15 Feb. 1705; Massingberd MSS. 20/51: Burrell to Sir Wm. Massingberd, 1 Feb. 1705, referring to Lindsey having "of late taken up the profession of a Whig".

20. Oxford made him an Irish Revenue Commissioner in 1712.

21. Legh of Lyme MSS. Box 62: Ward to Peter Legh, N.D. [? Dec. 1714]; cf. H.M.C. *Fortescue MSS.* i, 39, 48.

22. Clavering Letters: Ann to James Clavering, 8 Aug. 1710.

23. *Lockhart Papers*, i, 463.

24. *Ibid.* i, 294–5. Cf. Lonsdale MSS.: Lockhart to [Wharton], 26 July, 24 Oct. 1706.

25. Tredegar MSS. 53/107: Beaufort to John Morgan, 11 July 1713.

26. Weston Park MSS. 10/4A: Bridgeman's commonplace book, ff. 3–6; *ibid.* 18/15: Bridgeman to [Samuel] Pytts and Richard Corbet, [Mar.] 1702, 10 Feb. 1707[–8]; *Verney Letters*, i, 309.

27. B.M. Loan 29/160/2: to Oxford, 19 July 1712.

28. H.M.C. *Rutland MSS.* ii, 182; *Hervey L.B.* i, *passim*; H.M.C. *Portland MSS.* iv, 591.

29. *Op. cit.* pp. 219, 222.

30. For the Finch connexion, e.g., see H. G. Horwitz, *loc. cit.* vii–xii.

31. Add. MSS. 28052, f. 130: to [Charles] Godolphin, 18 [Mar.] 1708–9. Leave had been given on 9 Mar. to bring in a bill "for the more effectual prohibiting the importation of French wines . . .". *C.J.* xvi, 147.

32. A. Cunningham, *History of Great Britain* (1787), ii, 210, 212.

33. *Bull. I.H.R.* xxxiii (1960), 227.

34. See Add. MSS. 31144, f. 381. Guernsey, after prevaricating in 1712, was fairly firmly committed to Nottingham once more by the beginning of the 1713 session. Trumbull MSS. Alphab. li: Bateman to Trumbull, 10 Apr. 1713.

35. Blenheim MSS. F. 2–16: Harley to Marlborough, 28 Nov.; Longleat MSS. Portland Misc. f. 134: Godolphin to [Harley], "Monday at 2" [27 Nov.].

36. Bodl. MS. Ballard 7, f. 5: George Smalridge to Charlett, 24 Dec. 1704.

37. B.M. Loan 29/191, ff. 349–50: Godolphin to Harley, "Sat. night at 11" [Nov. 1705]. Cf. misdated letter in H.M.C. *Portland MSS.* iv, 154.

38. *Lockhart Papers*, i, 441.

39. Macpherson, *Original Papers*, i, 618.

40. *Lockhart Papers*, i, 473, 476–8.

41. Dalhousie MSS. 14/352: to Harry Maule, 16 Jan. [1711].

42. *Lockhart Papers*, i, 338.

43. *Ibid.* i, 345–8. For Greenshields's case see also Trevelyan, *England under Queen Anne*, iii, 236–8; W. L. Mathieson, *Scotland and the Union* (1905), pp. 195–9.

44. Nevertheless, in Greenshields's case at least its leaders had good cause to be satisfied with their efforts. *Lockhart Papers*, i, 348.

45. H.M.C. *Mar and Kellie MSS.* p. 492; Auchmar MSS.: [G. Baillie] to Montrose, 1 Jan. 1711[–12].

46. H.M.C. *Mar and Kellie MSS.* pp. 493–4: Mar to Erskine, 17 Jan.; Dalhousie MSS. 14/352: Balmerino to Lady Balmerino, 26 Jan.

47. *E.H.R.* lxxvii (1962), 278–9; Auchmar MSS.: [Baillie] to Montrose, 15 Mar.

48. Dalhousie MSS. 14/352: Balmerino to Maule, 12 May–9 June (8 letters); *Bolingbroke Corr.* iv, 140, 164–5; *Wentworth Papers*, p. 337; H.M.C. *Polwarth MSS.* i, 7, 13; *Lockhart Papers*, i, 416–36.

49. H.M.C. *Frankland-Russell-Astley MSS.* p. 176: J. C[utts] to Col. Revett, 13 Mar. 1705; B.M. Loan 29/64/8: [Godolphin] to Harley, "Tuesday at 2" [6 Nov. 1705]; *Cowper Diary,* pp. 10–11: 4–5 Nov. 1705.

50. P.R.O. 30/24/20/114: to Shaftesbury, end. "Feb 1705–6".

51. *Vernon Corr.* iii, 284, 291–2, 293: Vernon to Shrewsbury, 4 Dec. (misdated 2 Dec. by ed.), 11, 13 Dec. 1707. *Addison Letters,* pp. 87–8: Addison to Manchester, 24 Jan. 1708.

52. *Addison Letters,* p. 94: Addison to Manchester, 24 Feb. 1708; Boughton MSS. vol. iv, letter 194: Vernon to Shrewsbury, 24 Feb. (I owe this reference to Dr. W. A. Speck).

53. *Bull. I.H.R.* xxxix (1966), 58.

54. Blenheim MSS. E. 28: to Duchess of Marlborough, 9 Apr. (the letter is printed very corruptly in *Priv. Corr.* i, 104–6).

55. Wake MSS. Arch. W. Epist. 17: Bishop Trimnell to Wake, 5 Apr. 1712; *Wentworth Papers,* p. 283; Add. MSS. 17677FFF, f. 187; *Lockhart Papers,* i, 366.

56. 184 new members had been elected to the House of Commons in October 1710, many of them without any previous term of parliamentary service to their account. Add. MSS. 17677DDD, f. 645.

57. Auchmar MSS.: Mungo Graham to Montrose, 6 Feb. 1711.

58. *Journal to Stella,* 18 Feb. 1711; Boyer, p. 531.

59. Nicolson's MS. diary: 6 Feb. 1711; cf. *Stella,* 13 Apr.

60. Sir Thomas Hanmer, Sir George Beaumont and Sir John Pakington were three leading High Tory backbenchers who at length became disillusioned with some of the club's excesses.

61. B.M. Loan 29/143/8: Edward Harley to Oxford, "Saturday", N.D. [? 19 Apr. 1712]; *Lockhart Papers,* i, 366 for the identification of the October Club with the attempted tack of 1712.

62. E.g. in opposing the government's plan to conciliate the Scots over the malt tax. Trumbull Add. MSS. 136/3: Ralph Bridges to Trumbull, 1 June 1713.

63. Cf. also H.M.C. *Various Collections,* viii *(Clements MSS.),* 250–1.

CHAPTER ELEVEN: THE COURT AND THE PARTIES IN THE HOUSE OF COMMONS

1. See, *inter alia,* H.M.C. *Bath MSS.* i, 191–4: St. John to Harley, 11 Oct., 6 Nov. 1708; H.M.C. *Portland MSS.* iv, 546: Harcourt to Harley, 21 June 1710; *ibid.* v, 404: Bolingbroke to [Oxford], 27 Mar. 1714.

2. B.M. Loan 29/191, f. 4: 14 Jan. 1703 (cf. corrupt printed version in H.M.C. *Portland MSS.* iv, 57).

3. W.S.L. Dartmouth MSS. D. 1778/V/194: Poulet [Lord Steward] to Dartmouth, "Thursday morning" [? Dec. 1711].

4. H.M.C. *Portland MSS.* iv, 53; Longleat MSS. Portland Misc. ff. 63–4: [Godolphin] to Harley, "Tuesday morning" [15 Dec.]; Add. MSS. 42176, f. 11; *Norris Papers,* pp. 102–3; 106–7. For Seymour's opposition in the previous month to an adequate provision for the land forces in the Low Countries see p. 73 above.

5. H. G. Horwitz, *loc. cit.,* p. 437; Blenheim MSS. E. 20: Godolphin to Duchess of Marlborough, 18 Apr. 1704.

6. *Court and Society*, ii, 276: S. Edwin to Manchester, 6 Feb. 1708.

7. Add. MSS. 29576, f. 111: C. Hatton to Lord Hatton, 12 Nov. 1702.

8. Longleat MSS. Thynne Papers, xiii, f. 348: Weymouth to James Thynne, 9 Oct. 1705.

9. *Wentworth Papers*, p. 180; S.H. Cal. Br. 24 England 99, f. 126: Kreienberg, 16/27 Feb. 1711. In 1704 few of the High Tory troublemakers of the previous session would have been surprised if the threats to dissolve Parliament had been carried out, and Atterbury had it from "a sure hand" that the question was actually debated in the Cabinet at the end of June. Pakington MSS. ii, ff. 20, 16: T. Gibson and C. Stephens to Pakington, 17 Dec. 1703, 5 Jan. 1704; *Epistolary Corr. of Atterbury*, iii (1784), 183, 214–15, 217.

10. Lonsdale MSS.: James Lowther to Gilpin, 2 Sept. 1710.

11. 'An Impartial History of Parties' (Campbell, *Lives of the Lord Chancellors*, iv, 429).

12. Burnet, v, 45.

13. For the conflicting views of Townshend and Marlborough on this question in 1711, Klopp, *Der Fall des Hauses Stuart*, xiv (1888), 675.

14. P.R.O. 30/24/20/65: to Furley, 10 Aug. 1702.

15. Add. MSS. 29588, ff. 47, 93: Weymouth and Winchilsea to Nottingham, 5 June, 12 July.

16. H.M.C. *Cowper MSS.* iii, 13–14: 20 July. It would seem from Secretary Nottingham's correspondence that much of the official initiative in this particular election emanated from him rather than from the Treasury.

17. Burnet, v, 223.

18. P.R.O. 30/24/21/144: to Shaftesbury, 15 Jan. 1708.

19. Those of Derbyshire and Middlesex, for example. Panshanger MSS.: Dartmouth to Cowper, 29 June, 1 July 1710.

20. See, e.g., *Lockhart Papers*, i, 139–20; Add. MSS. 17677DDD, f. 620.

21. P.R.O. 30/24/21/141: to Shaftesbury, recd. 30 Dec. 1707.

22. *Addison Letters*, p. 244: 17 Oct.

23. H.M.C. *Bath MSS.* iii, 439: to Prior, 11 Aug. 1710.

24. H.M.C. *Portland MSS.* iv, 291.

25. W. A. Speck, 'The Choice of a Speaker in 1705', *Bull. I.H.R.* xxxvii (1964), 23–4, 29–31. Dr. Speck's identification of 98 "Queen's servants" among the voters on 25 Oct. 1705 is striking proof, if proof were needed, that Anne's political managers knew their business when it came to counting heads and making computations.

26. The phrase is taken from the title of a pamphlet published at Cambridge in 1705, listing these "gentlemen".

27. H.M.C. *Bath MSS.* i, 64–5; *Faults on Both Sides* (2nd edn. 1710), p. 27. The motion for leave to bring in the bill was carried by only 26 votes.

28. Speck, *loc. cit.* 17 voted for Smith's Tory opponent and 3 abstained.

29. See G. S. Holmes, "The Commons' Division on 'No Peace without Spain', 7 December 1711", *Bull. I.H.R.* xxxiii (1960), 231–2. To the 17 names there listed should be added those of 2 pensioners (Sir James Montagu and William Palmes) and 2 Scottish placemen (George Baillie and Sir Patrick Johnston). Another Scottish Whig who voted against the Court (Robert Monro) was a serving army officer.

30. *H.L.Q.* i (1937–8), 468: to Oxford, 3 Feb. 1713.

31. Bodl. MS. Rawlinson D. 174: "A Character Given by a Gentleman of Himself".

32. Poulet had estimated in June 1710 (H.M.C. *Portland MSS.* iv, 543) that Harley would be able to count on the support of at least this number of Whig auxiliaries for the new 'government interest', and events proved his estimate remarkably accurate.

33. Brydges was M.P. Hereford, 1698–1714.

34. Thomas Coke, M.P. Grampound: Teller of the Exchequer, 1704–6; Vice-Chamberlain of the Household, 1706–27.

35. He sat for Bodmin 1710–13. For his smart change of allegiance after Godolphin's fall see his letters to Harley, 13 Aug., 28 Oct. 1710. H.M.C. *Portland MSS.* iv, 565; B.M. Loan 29/155/3.

36. For Edisbury's subservience to the new order after 1710 after previously serving Godolphin and the Whigs, see B.M. Loan 29/311/1. Worsley was employed on missions to Spain in 1708, Hanover in 1711, and was ambassador to Portugal, 1714–22. His cousin, James Worsley, with whom he sat for Newtown (Isle of Wight) from 1705 to 1714, with the blessing of successive Governors of the Island, was also a genuine Court member.

37. M.P. Rochester, Leake was appointed an Admiralty commissioner by Godolphin in 1709 and held his seat on the board until 1715, when he was pensioned off. See p. 50 above.

38. Despite his cultivation of Marlborough (Blenheim MSS. B. 2–3: 17 Apr. 1710), Goring had to wait until the advent of the Tories for a regiment, the 31st Foot, which he acquired in 1711. His voting record reflects his gratitude. Sutton had been a client of Newcastle's up to 1710 and had voted accordingly (Chap. 7, p. 225, n. †). Subsequently he switched his allegiance to the Tory ministry, was made Governor of Hull in 1711 and later Governor of the garrison at Bruges (Add. MSS. 33273, ff. 127, 212–15). It was assumed that after 1714 he would support the Whigs once more in the Commons (Worsley MSS. 1).

39. See *Marchmont Papers,* iii, 332 and cf. *Lockhart Papers,* i, 301.

40. P. W. J. Riley, *The English Ministers and Scotland, 1707–1727,* pp. 161–2.

41. H. L. Stowe MSS. 58, vi, 186: to Brydges, 20 Aug.

42. 9 of these members can be identified from an "Abstract of the contracts made by the principal Officers & Commissioners of Her Majesties Navy between Michaelmas 1711 and ... [1714]", dated 8 Dec. 1714, in P.R.O. T. 64/199; the tenth (Thomas Ridge) from *C.J.* xvi, 500–2. Their parliamentary behaviour 1710–14 has been gauged from the 3 surviving division lists of the period, from Worsley MSS. 1, and from any additional information that could be culled from the *Journals* and from reports of parliamentary debates.

43. The evidence on Ward of Hackney (not to be confused with Alderman Ward) is thin and rather confusing. But he apparently spoke both for and against the ministry in the important Commons' debates in Apr. 1714. See Boyer, p. 696; Claydon MSS.: Will Vickers to Fermanagh, 17 Apr., *verso*: List of Speakers on the "Church side".

44. Walcott, *English Politics,* appx. i, pp. 174–7.

45. The accuracy of this list where pensioners are concerned cannot be absolutely guaranteed, but the list is in most respects remarkably exhaustive and reliable.

46. E.g. B.M. Stowe MSS. 225, f. 317; *Letters of Sarah, Duchess of Marlborough ... from ... Madresfield Court* (1875), p. 95.

47. Add. MSS. 31143, f. 556: Peter Wentworth to Raby, 5 Sept. 1710.

48. B.M. Loan 29/45A/4/31: List of Pensions and Annuities payable out of the Civil List Revenues; *Wentworth Papers,* p. 140.

49. Luttrell, v, 187; H.M.C. *Portland MSS*. iv, 506; Mary Ransome, 'The General Election of 1710' (London M.A. thesis, 1938), appx. p. 198.

50. Cotesworth's pension seems to have been regularly paid (P.R.O. T. 48/15. Lowndes MSS.). Hedges had two years' payments on his Civil List pension of £1200 p.a. withheld, clearly on political grounds (B.M. Loan 29/45A/4/31; cf. C.U.L. Cholmondeley [Houghton] MSS. 53, f. 11 [4]). Dunch is said to have been granted £1000 p.a. on the Post Office revenue "during the Queen's life and his own" in 1708 (H.M.C. *Portland MSS*. iv, 505), though there is some doubt as to whether this grant was ever finally confirmed.

51. Blenheim MSS. B. 2–1: Sunderland to Marlborough, 1 Aug. 1710. Henley died in 1711, Bridges in 1714.

52. P.R.O. T. 48/91 (Lowndes MSS.); Pakington MSS.: unsigned letter, Dublin, 5 Mar. 1716.

53. These concern grants made to "Edward Conway" (£1200) and "Henry St. Pierre" (£500).

54. B.M. Loan 29/153: 25 June 1712.

55. Walcott, *English Politics*, pp. 36–9; appx. ii, pp. 182–97.

56. Viz. Lord Lumley, the Earl of Thomond, Sir Nathaniel Gould, Francis Chamberlayne, Philipps Gibbon and Sir John Norris.

57. H.M.C. *Ormonde MSS*. N.S. viii, 147: Fairborne to Ormonde, 15 Mar. 1705. Cf. the quite erroneous statement about the representation of Rochester in Walcott, *op. cit.*, p. 36. At Plymouth in 1705 the electors and the local gentry were significantly "*affraid* next occasion they shall have two Flags [i.e. two government-nominated admirals] to represent them". Bodl. MS. Ballard 21, f. 222.

58. For both see B.M. Loan 29/29: 'List, Dec 7, 1711'.

59. Aylmer came very near to equalling this feat at Dover. He held on to his seat in 1710, after the change of ministry, and lost it by only 20 votes in 1713. Bodl. MS. Willis 18, f. 5.

60. Viz. Thomas King (Queenborough), Sir James Wishart and Sir Thomas Mackworth (Portsmouth), General Webb (Newport, I.O.W.), Sir Gilbert Dolben (Yarmouth, I.O.W.), Sir Joseph Martin (Hastings), Edward Southwell (Preston), Christopher Wren, jun. (Windsor), Carew Mildmay (Harwich), Sir Thomas Hardy and Reginald Marriott (Weymouth and Melcombe). Thomas Medlicott (Westminster) might possibly be added to the number, making 12 in all.

61. Archibald Hutchinson (Hastings) and Sir John Rogers (Plymouth).

62. Memo. in Robethon's hand, dated 1 Oct. 1705 N.S., quoted by R. Pauli, *Zeitschrift des historischen Vereins für Niedersachsen* (1885).

63. B.M. Loan 29/10/10: reverse side of paper endorsed "Memdm. Marc: 19: 1713/14". This seems the most feasible interpretation of the cryptic way in which Oxford presented his calculations.

64. Auchmar MSS.: 11 July 1708.

65. B.M. Loan 29/64/4: "Wednesday night at ten" [? 10 Dec. 1707].

66. B.M. Loan 29/143/4: [E. Harley] to Oxford, 9 Feb. 1712[–13]; H.M.C. *Portland MSS*. v, 405, 467; Knatchbull diary, 4 Apr. 1714.

67. H.M.C. *Portland MSS*. iv, 684.

68. H.L. Stowe MSS. 58, viii, 226: to Brydges, 24 July.

69. *Marchmont Papers*, iii, 332: Pringle to Marchmont, 20 July 1708, reporting a conversation with Somers.

70. N.U.L. Portland (Bentinck) MSS. PwA. 561: Heinsius to Portland, Hague, 7/18 Apr. 1702 (transl.).

71. Rijksarchief, Hague. Heinsius MSS. (printed Trevelyan, *Blenheim*, p. 426).

72. Longleat MSS. Portland Misc. f. 217: [Godolphin] to Harley, 30 Apr. [1702]. The year of this letter has to be deduced, but since it is written to Harley as "Speaker" and not "Secretary" it must have been written in 1702, for by April 1704, the only time in Harley's term as Speaker in Anne's reign when such a project could logically have been discussed, Godolphin could never have deluded himself that a prolongation of Parliament's life would "avoyd heats".

73. This pressure was the more difficult for Godolphin to resist because for much of the time Marlborough was abroad and unable to play an active part in support of the Treasurer.

74. *Original Letters of Locke, Sidney and Shaftesbury* (1830), p. 182: to Furley, 10 Aug. 1702.

75. Add. MSS. 9096, f. 131: Godolphin to Marlborough, 22 July 1706.

76. B.M. Loan 29/12/1; cf. p. 365, n. † above.

77. Longleat MSS. Portland Papers, vii, f. 160: to [Harley], 10 Oct. 1706.

78. "I take it for granted", Harley wrote, "that no one party in the House can carry it for themselves without the Queen's servants joyne with them." *Ibid.* f. 95: to Godolphin, 4 Sept. 1705.

79. Godolphin saw "a thousand difficulties" ahead, and Marlborough was only a little more sanguine. *Ibid.* f. 80: 30 Sept. [1705]; Blenheim MSS.: Marlborough to Godolphin, 25 June/6 July (printed Churchill, *Marlborough*, ii, 28–9).

80. On 26 Nov. 1705, 1 Dec. 1705. 2 Jan. 1706, 27 Dec. 1706, and 1 Jan. 1707 respectively. Henry Fleetwood, the Lancashire Tory who unsuccessfully contested Preston, confessed that even if he won the seat he would be "but strieving against the current". Gower MSS. D. 593: P/13/10: 18 May 1706.

81. *Diplomatic Correspondence of Richard Hill*, p. 86: 3 Mar. 1704. See *ibid.* p. 183 for the more protracted enquiries conducted by a Lords' committee under Bolton the following winter.

82. Dr. Ivor Burton, in 'The Supply of Infantry for the War in the Peninsula 1703–1707' (*Bull. I.H.R.* xxviii [1955]), defends the Godolphin administration convincingly against the opposition charges of a spectacular scandal in connection with the absent troops at Almanza.

83. B.M. Loan 29/191, f. 61: to [Harley], "Saturday at 8", 25 Oct. [1707].

84. Blenheim MSS. A. 1–25: Harley to Marlborough, 29 June 1705; see also Coxe, i, 346.

85. H.M.C. *Bath MSS.* i, 74: 4 Sept. 1705.

86. B.M. Loan 29/64/3: to Harley, "Fryday at 12", [15 Jan. 1706].

87. Witley Beaumont MSS. DD/WBC/96: Kaye to Richard Beaumont, 30 Dec. 1710.

88. H.M.C. *Bath MSS.* i, 197: to Harley, 3 Nov. 1709. The italics are mine.

89. See the sentiments expressed in *Faults on Both Sides*, the famous pamphlet written at Harley's dictation by Simon Clement in 1710, and also in Harley's draft for another intended pamphlet, titled 'Plaine English' and dated 24 Aug. 1708 (B.M. Loan 29/10/1).

90. H.M.C. *Bath MSS.* i, 74.

91. A. Boyer, *Annals*, iii (1705), 157.

92. B.M. Loan 29/192/256v.: continuation of letter to Baron Price, 14 Aug. 1705 (copy), not printed in H.M.C. *Portland MSS.* iv, 223.

93. B.M. Loan 29/153/7: to Poulet (copy), 21 Sept. 1706.

94. B.M. Loan 29/10/19: draft in Harley's hand [of a letter to Godolphin, _c._ Oct. 1706]; cf. H.M.C. _Bath MSS._ i, 110–11.

95. See Holmes and Speck, 'The Fall of Harley in 1708 Reconsidered', _E.H.R._ lxxx (1965), for further elaboration of his ideas at this juncture.

96. H.M.C. _Bath MSS._ i, 74: 4 Sept. 1705.

97. _H.L.Q._ xv (1951–2), 39: Brydges to Cadogan, 24 Dec. 1707, reporting the principles of a "new scheme" which Harley had just enunciated publicly at Anne's request.

98. Blenheim MSS. A. 1–4: Marlborough to Godolphin, 18 May 1702.

99. B.M. Loan 29/9/38: draft, "Sept. 25, 1706".

100. H.M.C. _Portland MSS._ iv, 47: B.M. Loan 29/64/1: draft of speech in Godolphin's hand, annotated by Nottingham.

101. _The Correspondence of Sir Thomas Hanmer_, pp. 126–8: Harley and Shrewsbury to Hanmer, 1, 2 Aug. 1710.

102. Isham MSS. Corr. 2214: John to Sir J. Isham, 9 Sept. 1710.

103. H.M.C. _Bath MSS._ i, 75: to Godophin, 4 Sept. 1705.

104. Blenheim MSS. E. 20, A. 1–14: Godolphin to the duchess, 18 Apr.; Marlborough to Godolphin, 8 Apr.

105. B.M. Lansdowne MSS. 1236, ff. 252–3: to Newcastle, 4 Nov. 1708.

106. B.M. Loan 29/195, f. 118: [to Harley], 7 Oct. 1708; cf. _ibid._ /153/7: Harley to Poulet (copy), 16 Oct.

107. _Faults on Both Sides_ (2nd edn. 1710), p. 28.

108. Coxe, ii, 220: 22 Apr. See also _ibid._ pp. 218–84 _passim_, and Harley's memo. of 3 Apr. 1708 (B.M. Loan 29/10/22) beginning cryptically, "After Ld Somrs no quarter".

109. Coxe, ii, 292: to Marlborough, end. 27 Aug. 1708.

110. _Ibid._ p. 293.

111. H.M.C. _Various Collections_, viii (_Clements MSS._), 240: 30 Dec. 1708; H.L. Stowe MSS. 57, ii, 69: Brydges to Coningsby, 3 Sept. 1708.

112. Dartmouth at the Board of Trade was one of the few notable exceptions.

113. _Addison Letters_, pp. 91, 95.

114. Mungo Graham's letter to Montrose, 23 Nov. 1710 (Auchmar MSS.), is a typical assessment of Harley's prospects at this stage.

115. B.M. Loan 29/10/19: Memorandum, 20 May 1710.

116. _Bolingbroke Corr._ iv, 441: to Anglesey, 25 Jan. 1714.

CHAPTER TWELVE: THE COURT AND THE PARTIES IN THE HOUSE OF LORDS

1. Burnet, vi, 220.

2. B.M. Loan 29/307: [N]ov. 3[0], [1711]. MS. torn.

3. B.M. Lansdowne MSS. 773, ff. 18, 21, 23; _Diplomatic Correspondence of Richard Hill_ (ed. W. Blackley, 1845), p. 94: J. Tucker to Hill, 4 Apr.

4. It is worth remembering that in Aug. 1713 the Tory official organ, _The Examiner_, confidently predicted the total annihilation of the opposition after one more parliamentary campaign.

5. In this connection see W. Coxe, *Correspondence of Charles Talbot, Duke of Shrewsbury* (1821), p. 647: Somers to Shrewsbury, 23 Feb. 1705.

6. Add. MSS. 22222, f. 188: Poulet to Strafford, 20 Dec.

7. Boyer, p. 444; B.M. Loan 29/10/18: paper endorsed 'Peers, Octo: 3: 1710', List No. 3.

8. Panshanger MSS.: Hamilton diary, 10 Dec. 1711. What he actually acquired was a bounty of £1000 — this in addition to a bonus of £200 paid him by the Lord Treasurer at the end of the previous session of Parliament. B.M. Loan 29/45/A/10, items 75 and 95.

9. Finch MSS. Parliamentary and Political Papers, P.P. 161.

10. Add. MSS. 22221, f. 289: 3 Sept. 1713.

11. B.M. Loan 29/307: to Oxford, 19 Dec. 1712. Delawarr's dislike of dissenters may have made him a more congenial colleague for the Tories than the Whigs (see p. 56 and n. 17 above), but under any administration he would have been admirably qualified to hold Lord Hunsdon's proxy, as he did for a while in 1712.

12. *Priv. Corr.* ii, 323: to Godolphin, [20]/31 May 1709.

13. The solicitation he left, more often than not, to his unfortunate brother Peter, whose consequent trials, cheerfully borne, can be traced in *The Wentworth Papers* and in the Strafford papers in the British Museum.

14. *Parl. Hist.* vi, 146.

15. On 24 Jan. 1711.

16. These statistics are based on an analysis of the numbers attending and voting in person (not by proxy) on over 40 key political issues which came before the Lords between Jan. 1711 and July 1714. The highest number present at a single division was 124 on 13 Apr. 1714, following the debate on the Queen's answer to the Lords' address concerning the Pretender.

17. Viz. Schomberg, Cleveland, Bridgewater, Lincoln, Westmorland, Grantham, Kinnoull, Cornwallis, Howard of Effingham, Fitzwalter, Colepeper, Byron, Radnor, Sussex, Warrington, Hunsdon and Stawell.

18. Evidence will be found in the *Calendar of Treasury Books*, and in the information supplied to Walpole after 1714 about the recipients of pensions and bounties (C.U.L. Cholmondeley [Houghton] MSS. 53).

19. See his note to Burnet, v, 359; also Boyer, p. 444, for his party vote at the time of Sacheverell's impeachment.

20. *Wentworth Papers*, p. 338: Berkeley of Stratton to Strafford, 19 June 1713.

21. Coxe, iii, 27: 24 Mar./4 Apr. 1710.

22. *Wentworth Papers*, p. 146: Peter Wentworth to Raby, [23–25 Sept. 1710].

23. *Swift Corr.* i, 313.

24. See B.M. Loan 29/163/10 and Appendix A. for Whig voting on 20 Dec. 1711.

25. H.M.C. *Ormonde MSS.* N.S. viii, 125: Coningsby to Ormonde, 16 Dec. 1704; Lonsdale MSS.: [Lowther] to [Sir John Lowther of Whitehaven], 16, 19 Dec.

26. Lonsdale MSS.: [James to Sir John Lowther], 8 Feb. 1704[-5].

27. Nicolson's MS. diary, 15 Nov. 1705; *Cowper Diary*, pp. 16, 22.

28. *Parl. Hist.* vi, 939; Burnet, vi, 29–30.

29. B.M. Loan 29/307, 29/29/14: Denbigh to Oxford, 9 Sept., 11 Dec. [1713].

30. Longleat MSS. Thynne Papers, xxvi, ff. 93, 209, 203, 196: Stawell to Weymouth, 2 Jan., 13 Mar., 20 [May], 24 Oct. 1711.

31. Paid in November 1712. See p. 388, n. * above.

32. B.M. Loan 29/45/A/10, item 76: Denbigh to Oxford, 3 July [1711]; *ibid.* item 75: memo. in Oxford's hand with details of payments made, 3 July 1711; B.M. Loan 29/204: "Account of mony laid out of my owne for the Queen at several times" [July 1714] (in Oxford's hand; cf. H.M.C. *Portland MSS.* v, 480–1).

33. H.M.C. *Portland MSS.* iv, 551: Weymouth to Harley, 24 July; Boyer, p. 444 records Winchilsea's vote against Sacheverell in March 1710.

34. *The Post-Boy*, No. 2409, 19–21 Oct. 1710.

35. H.M.C. *Portland MSS.* iv, 654; B.M. Loan 29/135: Winchilsea to Harley, 15, 17 Jan. 1711. Even his subsequent appointment to the Board of Trade had not been enough by 1712 (or so he claimed) to have "mended [his] circumstances". B.M. Loan 29/313/13.

36. B.M. Loan 29/307: Cornwallis to Lord — ? —, 13 Apr. 1712; 29/308/4/5: Herbert of Cherbury to Oxford, 15 Aug., 21 Oct., 28 Nov. 1713, 5 May 1714.

37. B.M. Loan 29/204: Oxford's "Account of mony laid out of my owne".

38. B.M. Loan 29/308/5, 29/146/6: Herbert to Oxford, 3, 10 May 1714.

39. B.M. Stowe MSS. 225, ff. 264–5: Schütz to Robethon, 30 Oct./10 Nov. 1713.

40. What this average was we can only guess, but G. E. Mingay (*English Landed Society in the Eighteenth Century* [1963], pp. 20–1) rightly points out that Gregory King's estimate of the average income of the 160 lay peers in 1690 as £2800 was hopelessly inaccurate, and should probably have been doubled.

41. Wake MSS. Arch. W. Epist. 17: list appended to a letter of Richard Dongworth to Bishop Wake, Edinburgh, 11 Nov. 1710.

42. H.M.C. *Portland MSS.* x, 406–7: Erskine to Mar, 29 Nov.; *ibid.* v, 121: Kinnoull to Dupplin, 3 Dec.

43. Auchmar MSS.: Montrose to Sunderland, 2 July 1708; *Cowper Diary*, p. 51.

44. *Addison Letters*, p. 90; H.M.C. *Mar and Kellie MSS.*, pp. 426–7. See also in general the chapter on "The Squadrone's Attack on the Ministry" in P. W. J. Riley, *The English Ministers and Scotland, 1707–27* (1964), pp. 87–102.

45. Viz. the Earls of Crawford and Orkney. See Riley, *op. cit.* p. 109.

46. *Lockhart Papers*, i, 314–15. In the Sacheverell divisions 4 Scottish peers (Mar, Northesk, Wemyss and Hamilton) opposed the Court on the main vote, and 4 more, Islay, Loudoun, Rosebery and Argyll (the latter not one of "the sixteen") joined them in voting for a light sentence. Cf. Coxe, iii, 27; Bodl. MS. Carte 129, f. 445.

47. Dalhousie MSS. 14/352: Balmerino to [Harry Maule], 9 June [1713].

48. Auchmar MSS.: [G. Baillie] to Montrose, 20 May 1712.

49. Add. MSS. 29568, f. 117: John Verney to Lord Hatton, 29 Jan. 1702[–3]. Even Rutland, promoted from an earldom to a dukedom at the same time, was expected by Godolphin to pay for his new honour by "taking [his] place this next session in the House". H.M.C. *Rutland MSS.* ii, 175: Gower to Rutland, 11 Mar. 1703.

50. *Wentworth Papers*, p. 322: Berkeley of Stratton to Strafford, 27 Feb. 1713; *Hanmer Correspondence*, p. 148: Hervey to Hanmer, 27 Aug. 1713.

51. Panshanger MSS.: Hamilton's diary, 2 Jan. 1712.

52. Add. MSS. 22221, f. 23: to Strafford, [18]/29 Apr. 1714.

53. Tullie House, Nicolson's MS. diary.

54. Dalhousie MSS. 14/352: Balmerino to [Maule], 1 May.

55. Trumbull MSS. Alphab. li: T. Bateman to Trumbull, 5 June 1713; B.M. Loan 29/127/1: Warrington to Oxford, 10 and 24 Apr. 1714.

56. Add. MSS. 17677 HHH, f. 242; Knatchbull Diary, 27 May 1714; Add. MSS. 47087 (unfoliated): Percival to Dering, 14 June.

57. Nicolson's MS. diary (1709–10): 16 Apr. 1709.

58. *Life of Archbishop Sharp* (1825), i, 299. The archbishop himself, it should be said, was not prepared to try to constrain them.

59. *Epistolary Corr. of Atterbury*, iv (1787), 373.

60. *Vernon Corr.* iii, 342; Tullie House, Nicolson's MS. diary, 5 Feb.

61. Trumbull Add. MSS. 136/3: Ralph Bridges to Trumbull, 18 Jan. 1712.

62. *Ibid.*: Ralph Bridges, 18 Jan. Since on this occasion it is possible to deduce exactly, from the proxy books, the *Journals* and other sources, exactly which bishops voted for and against the Court, the division of their votes is worth recording. *Whigs*: 11 voted in person (viz. Winchester, Salisbury, Lichfield, Ely, Peterborough, Oxford, Bangor, Carlisle, Lincoln, Norwich and St. Asaph) and 3 voted by proxy (Archbishop of Canterbury, Bishops of Llandaff and Gloucester). *Tories*: 4 voted in person (Rochester, Chester, Chichester and St. David's) and 4 by proxy (Archbishop of York, Bishops of Durham, Exeter and Bristol).

63. Bodl. MS. Add. A. 269, p. 26: Edmund Gibson to Bishop Nicolson, 3 Nov.

64. *Swift. Corr.* i, 313: Swift to King, 8 Jan. 1712.

65. Clavering Letters: Ann to James Clavering, 16 Jan. 1711.

66. Panshanger MSS. Hamilton diary: Sir David Hamilton's account of a conversation with Cowper, 20 Jan. 1711.

67. B.M. Loan 29/201: [15]/26 Sept. 1713. For Radnor's earlier support of Oxford and his financial obligations to the Court see p. 49 above and his letters to Oxford, 12 Oct. 1710–2 Feb. 1712, B.M. Loan 29/155.

68. B.M. Loan 29/127: Sir Roger Bradshaigh to Oxford, 20 Sept. 1713.

69. As Lord Great Chamberlain and Master of the Great Wardrobe respectively. The latter office had been purchased by Montagu's father, Ralph, 1st duke.

70. E.g. Bolton in Dorset and the Duke of Manchester in Huntingdonshire.

CONCLUSION

1. Add. MSS. 17677 WW, f. 152: l'Hermitage, 11 Feb.

2. Though Littleton, it should be said, had the somewhat equivocal backing of the Court.

3. Add. MSS. 773, f. 17.

4. P.R.O. 30/24/20/90: to Shaftesbury, 1 Feb. 1705.

5. Add. MSS. 33273, f. 37.

6. Chevening MSS.: Dayrolles to Stanhope, Hague, 9 Dec. 1704.

7. W. Pittis, *History of the . . . Second Session of this Present Parliament* (London, 1712), p. 7.

8. Panshanger MSS.: to Cowper, 11 Sept. 1714.

9. Lonsdale MSS.: James Lowther to W. Gilpin, 1 July 1710.

10. Carew Pole MSS. BO/29/63: 29 Sept. 1710.

11. *A State Anatomy of Great Britain* (1717), p. 18.

12. Chevening MSS.: to Stanhope, 23 Apr. [1710].

13. This is on the authoritative evidence of Arthur Mainwaring. Blenheim MSS. E. 26: to Duchess of Marlborough, N.D. [1708].

14. I can find no foundation for the recently-expressed view of Clayton Roberts that '*most Englishmen* abominated political parties and believed it wrong to base governments upon them'. *The Growth of Responsible Government in Stuart England* (Cambridge, 1966), p. 329: my italics.

15. Finch MSS. P.P. 150 (xii): undated paper in Nottingham's hand [*c*. Feb. 1711].

16. H.M.C. *Downshire MSS.* I, ii, 807: to Sir William Trumbull, 14 Sept. 1701.

17. B.M. Loan 29/9/13: paper headed "Feb: 24: 1704/5".

18. Paper of 24 Feb. 1705, *loc. cit.*

19. H.M.C. *Bath MSS.* i, 181: Harley to Godolphin, 10 Sept. 1707.

Index

Principal references are given in bold-face figures.

Printed and bound in Great Britain by
WBC Bristol and Maesteg